IS THAT IT?

—BOB—
GELDOF

WITH PAUL VALLELY

IS THAT IT?

Out of Ireland have we come.
Great hatred, little room,
Maimed us at the start.
I carry from my mother's womb
A fanatic heart.

W.B. YEATS

'I don't mind being reverenced
and greeted and honoured,' said
Vespaluus; 'I don't even mind being
sainted in moderation, as long as I'm
not expected to be saintly as well.'

THE STORY OF ST VESPALUUS, SAKI

Weidenfeld & Nicolson
New York

Published by Weidenfeld & Nicolson, New York
A Division of Wheatland Corporation
10 East 53rd Street
New York, NY 10022

Originally published in Great Britain in 1986 by
Sidgwick & Jackson Limited and Penguin Books Limited

Library of Congress Cataloging-in-Publication Data

Geldof, Bob, 1952–
  Is that it?

  Includes index.
    1. Geldof, Bob, 1952– .   2. Rock musicians——
England——Biography.   I. Vallely, Paul.   II. Title.
ML420.G328A3   1987   784.5'4'00924   [B]   86–26697
ISBN 1–55584–115–5

Picture credits
t: top, b: bottom, c: centre, l: left, r: right
Mohamed Amin/Camerapix 215; David Appleby 189l,r; Brian Aris vit, 197t,b, 211, 301r; Associated Press 349tcl,bcl;
Band Aid Trust 331; Band Aid Trust/Brian Aris 229, 231; Band Aid Trust/Andrew Catlin 309t; Band Aid Trust/David
Hogan 311; Band Aid Trust/Steve Rapport viit, 8; Band Aid Trust/Syndication International 309b; George Bodnor 159;
Adrian Boot 115; John Farragher 27l, 51b; Bob Geldof Collection i, iit,b, iiitr, ivtl (photo Annie Liebowitz/Contact/
Colorific), ivtr,b, vt,b, vib, viib, 13t,b, 17, 27r, 33, 69, 75l,r, 85t,b, 91, 103tl,tr,b, 107, 127, 133l,r, 175tl,tr, 224, 301l, 304,
349tl,tcr, Bob Geldof photographs 65, 175b, 194, 247t,b, 259; Irish Times 349br; Lafayette, Dublin 49l,r, 51t; Cary
Leonard 155; London Features International/Simon Fowler 121; Daily Express/Jon Rogers 241; Daily Mirror/Peter Stone
151, 153t,b, 161t,b, 165; London Express News & Features/Evening Standard/Maurice Conroy 296; Rex Features iiibr,
viiit, 279, 349tr; Frank Spooner Pictures/John Hoffman 283r; Sunday Times/Frank Herrman viiib, 349bcr; Sunday
Times/Jeremy Nichol 2; UPI/Bettman News Photos 349bl.
    The quotation from W.B. Yeats' *Remorse for Intemperate Speech* that appears on the title page is reproduced by kind
permission of Michael B. Yeats and Macmillan, London Ltd.
    The lyrics by Sting on page 215 are reprinted by kind permission of Virgin Music (Publishers) Ltd. Words and music:
Gordon Sumner © 1980.

Produced by Shuckburgh Reynolds Limited, London

Designed by Laurence Bradbury and Roy Williams
Assisted by Sarah Collins
Photo research: Jenny de Gex
Manufactured in Great Britain

First American Edition, 1987

10 9 8 7 6 5 4 3 2 1

To Paula and Fiji

More than words can say....

ACKNOWLEDGEMENTS

I would like to thank all those who worked hard and fast on this book:
Paul Vallely for the awful task of putting it all in context so well.
Susan Hill for her editing and having to fight me over every word.
Rowena Webb for being able to read my writing.
Bee Ford and Lesley Gilbert for being able to understand my voice on
   the tapes.
Nigel Newton for his appallingly consistent West Coast enthusiasm.
David Reynolds for being unfailingly and calmly practical.
Laurence Bradbury and Roy Williams for endless work in the face of a
   difficult Irishman.
Ed Victor for letting me use his knowledge, tips and advice.
David Landsman for arguing.
Ina Meibach for arguing in an American accent.
Ossie Kilkenny for settling my messy old accounts.
Father Farragher C.S.S.P. for his camera and archivist's enthusiasm.
My sister Cleo McFarland for lending me her memories and pictures.
Likewise my Uncle Sonny and Auntie Peggy and Auntie Fifi.
Mick Foley and Sean Finnegan for being aware of how preposterous we
   still are.
Daphne Maxwell for old times' sake.
Kieran Fitzgerald for foreseeing it all and keeping everything.
Johnnie Fingers, Pete Briquette, Gary Roberts, Simon Crowe for all these
   years.
Fachtna O'Kelly, B.P. Fallon, Robbie McGrath, John Martin, Phay Taylor
   and the Mick for years past.
Penny and Kevin Jenden, Val Blondeau, Ken Martin, Judy Anderson,
   Wayne Lintott, Lionel Rotcage, and all at the Band Aid office for
   making dreams work.
John Kennedy, Phil Rusted, Maurice Oberstein, Chris Morrison, Harvey
   Goldsmith, Midge Ure, Bernard Doherty and Michael Grade for
   overseeing the dream.
All at Phonogram for humouring me.
Marsha Hunt who organizes me.
And, most importantly, to my Dad 'cos I now understand – I hope he
   does too.

CONTENTS

12.46 13 July 1985

In *Waiting for Godot* Samuel Beckett wrote: 'Let us not waste our time in idle discourse! Let us do something, while we have the chance! It is not every day that we are needed. Not indeed that we personally are needed. Others would meet the case equally well, if not better. To all mankind they were addressed, those cries for help still ringing in our ears! But at this place, at this moment of time, all mankind is us, whether we like it or not . . . What are we doing here, *that* is the question. And we are blessed in this, that we happen to know the answer. Yes, in this immense confusion one thing alone is clear. We are waiting for Godot to come . . . or for night to fall. We have kept our appointment and that's an end to that. We are not saints, but we have kept our appointment. How many people can boast as much?' 'Billions.'

And the lesson today is how to die.
The words hung in the air. I stood stock still, my hand raised above my head, my fist clenched in unconscious salute. In front of me stood 80,000 people.

Somewhere, invisible, behind them, another billion people all over the world had joined us. Together we held our breath. There are expressions we use all the time. When we are hungry we say, without thinking, that we are starving. When we are happy we declare, because the words come easily to us, that this must be the greatest moment of our lives. But there are times when the clichés are made flesh. Throughout Africa on this day people were starving. And, for me, at this particular moment, the threads of a lifetime were uniquely gathered, all there in that one uplifted hand.

Above me the sky was blue. The sun seemed at its zenith and it filled the stadium before me with the brilliant untainted light of an English summer's day. In the crowd before me sat Paula and our child. Nearby was my father, reconciled long ago to what I am. Behind me were the group of people for whom I had developed that mixture of affection and impatience and loyalty which characterizes a family though the outside world saw us merely as a pop group. And before me, in the largest audience the world had ever known, I was being watched by every living person who was dear to me.

This was the 13th of July 1985. It was Live Aid.

There must have been an element of triumph in such a moment but that was not how it felt that day.

I stopped 'I Don't Like Mondays' in its tracks. It was an old song invested with new meaning. Something special was happening today; it seemed epitomized in this moment. I stood and looked, tracking my gaze from one side of the auditorium to the other as if to fix each individual with my eyes. I wanted to make contact with them all, and draw them in. Think about this thing today. Think about this thing we are doing for it may never happen in this way again.

My hand was still held in the air, stiff with purpose. There was no element of personal power. Another banal truism had been made real: at that moment there was no difference between the man on the stage and the audience, none at all. We were all part of some greater purpose, all attempting an understanding of one another and all part of something completely outside ourselves.

As I recall it I did not think very graphically about Ethiopia. I did not conjure in my brain the images which had become fixed in memory. That one child squatting in slow death on the damp earth. Or the wall in the refugee camp which separated the chosen from the abandoned, those who were to live from those who were to die. Or the storecupboard with fifteen tiny bags of flour which was all that was left to feed a camp of 27,000 starving people. These were the things I had seen in Africa and today was not about a single continent. Today was about a single world.

I tried to look into something deeper than images. I tried to draw from the depths of my being the emotion I had encountered. The deep sense of wrong I had felt made me want to project the certain knowledge of the rightness of what we were doing now. I hoped the feeling would communicate itself to all those who had not seen what I had seen. I was trying to reach all those who, however reluctantly and unwittingly, I had come to represent.

I knew that nothing in my life had been worth anything until now. Yet I felt no sadness that this moment could not be prolonged to last a lifetime. It was enough; this clear moment of absolute certainty. All this was good and was rooted in no reasons but good reasons. No dark cloud could blot out this sun, as it always had at times of pleasure or triumph before.

All of my life I felt like I had been waiting. For what I was unsure. Things felt good or bad, but never complete. There was always something else – something unspecific. Not today. Had all the waiting been for this? Was this it?

'I think this must be the greatest day of my life,' was all I could find to say.

One journalist, writing in *Life* magazine, captured the unlikeliness of the whole affair with a vivid image. God had come down from heaven to find someone to undertake the task of alerting the world to the holocaust which was sweeping the continent of Africa. But this god, like the deities of old, bore the strength of fallibility and knocked at the wrong door. It was answered by Bob Geldof. 'Who the hell is he?' thought God. 'Oh, never mind, he'll do.'

It seemed an unlikely business to me too. Nothing in my life, I would have thought, could have led me to this. I was a distinctly unsavoury and decidedly unsuitable person for such a vocation. Yet looking back it is clear to me how in one respect everything conspired to bring me here. Plaid rugs, picnics and sequins are some of the jumbled clues I have to a mother who died before I was out of short trousers, and my father returning home only at weekends makes me now appreciate that in those rootless days alone I acquired that self-reliance which I was much later to be thankful for.

The freefall I slipped into upon leaving school in an endless round of useless jobs and self-abuse finally closed when I fell into a situation where it was I who was in control and I who could determine the way that things should be done. A rock band gave me a creative outlet, a platform and also nurtured my ego and proved that the desperate, almost neurotic and unspecific ambition which drove me could be harnessed. The Boomtown Rats became enormously successful and were then eclipsed. If the Rats had still been a success I might never have managed to start out on the enterprise which culminated for me in that moment of utter clarity of purpose, that peerless day in July 1985.

★   ★   ★

The sun burned my knuckles. I opened my hand and the crowd quietened. I will remember this forever, I thought. The crowd was quite still now, the light breeze ruffled the stage. I had to move on. The moment had passed.

CHAPTER I

An Hour Lasts A Lifetime

Frank Lahiffe loved Mary O'Dwyer as well. It was an intolerable triangle. She probably loathed both of us, but, at the age of four, I was not in the least interested in her feelings. The nuns compounded my heartache by placing Mary in a desk between Lahiffe and me. Learning my letters, I would trace the 'D' with my finger. It was cut from sandpaper and stuck on light blue card-board. We would close our eyes and feel the shape of the 'D' while mouthing its sound. 'Duh,' I muttered with the others, but my eyes were slits of guile, partly open to facilitate my observation of the nun. When she looked away, I darted to the next desk and planted a kiss on Mary's knee. She sat there, eyes clamped tight, now muttering, 'Fuh'.

Lahiffe, more absorbed by his rival than his alphabet, then repeated my manoeuvre, kissing la O'Dwyer's other knee. She burst into tears. 'Mary O'Dwyer, stop being a cissy,' said the nun, not bothering to enquire into the reasons for Mary's distress. 'Guh,' said Lahiffe and I.

Probably I was Robin Hood that day. I could have been Davy Crockett. I had both the outfits made for me by my mother or Auntie Fifi, the dressmaker. However no one could see beneath the brown smocks I and the other boys wore. The girls wore light blue. When it was sunny we had our lessons under the tree in the playground. Lahiffe and I bunked out and went to the shop across the road for sweets. This was forbidden. It was a main road and danger-ous for 4-year-olds. We were caught sometimes and subjected to a peculiarly cruel and Kafkaesque form of punishment. We had to stand at the corner till the No. 5 bus had gone before we could walk home. The No. 5 seemed to have no fixed timetable, it appeared wholly at random if it appeared at all. At four or five one was besieged with the psychological terror, not of delayed teatime, but of the possibility that you would have to wait 'all night, if that's how long it takes', or even an hour. I can remember when an hour was a lifetime.

My sisters Cleo and Lynn brought me to Sion Hill every day, where they went to school and I to kindergarten. We lived in part of a house at the bottom of Mount Merrion Avenue, near Blackrock Park. It was a ten-minute walk to the school. We had a big garden. My father was away in the week, travelling in carpeting and glassware, but at the weekend he'd garden. There was a thin stream at the bottom of the garden behind a wall. We called it 'the river'. There were bamboos there and a dead tortoise. I had a passion: I cut the heads off all the yellow flowers and placed them inside a hollow hedge. My father, who had tended his tulips with love, was incensed to find them all neatly guillotined. I was called for and immediately denied any knowledge, despite the fistful of wilted tulip heads my father had retrieved from the hedge and now waved in front of me. Not only did I deny it, I also added by way of mitigating evidence, 'Once a boy in my class picked his daddy's yellow tulips and *his* daddy didn't mind.'

Blackrock is a suburb of Dublin, but I remember the Ūachtair man, delivering cream with his horse and cart. 'Ūachtair', he'd say, 'thick or thin?'

'Thick, please.'

'Give us the jug, then.'

And he'd ladle out of his urns a stream of pure yellow cream which would go on top of the strawberries or gooseberries my father grew.

My early childhood was sweet, like anyone else's. I was frightened when I was in trouble for something, but my memory is sunny, and seems more so to me because of later events. My sister tells me I would tricycle round the table singing, 'You know what you are, but you don't know what you're doing,' which sounds precocious to me, but it's a good story. I learnt to read quickly and remember reading the children's Classics Illustrated *Ivanhoe*.

'Sisters are a mistake, Clarence, you should have set your face against them at the outset,' someone said in a Wodehouse story. My two sisters were both much older. I liked playing circuses. They would allow me to be a performing dog: I would jump through a hoop with a piece of paper on it. When they got bored, they simply removed the cushions that had been placed on the other side of the hoop and I would crash to the floor, wailing.

When I was six, Cleo, the eldest, had a lot of parties. I would lie awake in my bed and listen to the noises above. Sometimes people would stumble down into my room looking for the toilet. I directed them to the coal cellar at the end of the hall, telling them, 'I think the light's broken.' They would emerge face, hands, and possibly other parts of their bodies blackened with coal dust and with wet stains down their fronts.

We listened to the radio a lot and were allowed to stay up late on Sundays for Michael Miles' *Take Your Pick*. I had a friend who was better off than us and had a television. At five in the afternoon we would sit with the curtains closed in Stygian darkness and watch *Union Pacific*, a western railway saga, faintly flickering its way across to us from England. The reception was terrible, but I never minded.

We were Catholic. Not reverently, more automatically so. Mass on Sunday, ashes on Ash Wednesday, Communion at Easter and Christmas and fasting at Lent.

'What are you giving up for Lent?' my father said.

'Grapes', I replied.

Mum and Da, hotel manageress and manager: before I was born.

Lynn, me and friend.

'Grapes?' asked my father. 'We never *have* grapes,' he said. They were too expensive – if you could get them.

'Well, that's what I'm giving up,' I said with an expression of insufferable martyrdom. After mass that day my father stopped at the fruit shop in Blackrock and bought a pound of grapes. My family sat in the car, each one licking their grapes, peeling them, exclaiming over them, chewing them, slowly allowing the juice to pour down their chins. Licking their fingers, they ate them all. They crammed their cheeks with them, I didn't get one.

'You've given them up,' my father gloated.

I made my first communion. I told the priest my non-sins in a smart beige suit with a white rosette with a medal of the Holy Ghost on it pinned to my chest. Mary O'Dwyer was there, shimmering in her bridal veils and lace. Afterwards I was taken on the traditional rounds of relatives and friends to pick up their gifts of cash. We began next door with the two old ladies, who slipped me a coin. It felt like a shilling. My mother was saying, 'Oh you shouldn't have, oh really no, he can't . . .' when she noticed me staring in horror at the halfpenny that lay in my palm. 'It's only a hal . . .' I managed before a maternal hand clamped my mouth. 'Oh no, no, don't mention it, Mrs Geldof, he's a lovely little chap.'

It was a bad start but I ended up with about seventeen shillings, easily enough to buy the pink and white plastic four-string guitar I'd seen in the window of the toy shop. I never learned how to play it but I wore it on my back with a piece of string around my lincoln green Robin Hood shirt, my brown leatherette Davy Crockett hat and my cracked brown leatherette quiver for my Robin Hood arrows slung on my hip. I was eclectic if nothing else.

But things began to change. That time of Laurie Lee-dom when everything has a soft and golden glow about it was passing. The time of real memory was about to begin. Michael Johnson, my friend and the son of my mother's best friend, died of leukaemia. I got his trousers. Kindergarten was over. I was moving to junior school. We were leaving Blackrock for Dun Laoghaire three miles down the road, where my father had bought a house. The fifties were dying. One night we all stood out on the steps and looked up at the clear October night. The radio was on loud so we could hear the lonely hesitant little beep. Then the sputnik flew over us, tracking across the sky, a tiny little star of shining steel. Mankind was in space and all we had to say was, 'Beep Beep'.

CHAPTER II

Walking Back To Happiness

The new house was dark, covered in dark purple wallpaper with a grape design. My father and his friends scraped and hacked, re-painted and re-modelled. It was still dark to me and it will remain so to this day. The gloomy Edwardian kitchen with its servants' bells was replaced by a kitchen fashioned from the miracle new material, formica, in bright red, yellow, green, and blue bisected by chrome and black plastic lines. It was like washing dishes inside a Mondrian painting.

Ma was a tall woman who will forever for me wear long black gloves up to her elbows. On the night of the commercial travellers' ball she and my father would come into my room and cuddle me. Even now as I write this there's a sense of unbearable loss. They would have party hats on and the next morning we would wear them. Long black gloves wrapped round me, sequins from her dress sticking sideways into my cheeks. I curled her hair round and round my fingers. It was springy and my finger would go through the empty hollow of the curl. In my other hand, pressed to my nose, would be a ragged piece of cardigan that lulled me to sleep. I imagine the perfume but I remember the lipstick on her teeth. I remember her applying the lipstick and moving close to the mirror. She would press her lips together, sucking them back behind her teeth and rolling them sideways to get an even distribution of the rouge. There would be lipstick on the tea cups. Lipstick, gloves and sequins: not a bad memory of your mother. Later, visiting her grave, we would kneel on the ground and the tiny pieces of stone cut into my knee leaving the same mark as the sequins had on my cheek.

The night she died I went to bed early. We had been to Brittas Bay for a picnic. The water, as usual, was too cold for swimming. Uncle Sonny and Auntie Peg were there and the cousins too. Dad prepared dressed crabs and we stopped at Newton Mount for choc ices and Taylor Keith raspberry-lemonade, as we called it. We sang a song called 'Newtown Mount Kennedy' whose lyrics consisted of those three words. My father sang 'Susannah's a Funny Old Man' and 'The Whistling Gypsy', and I pulled my mum down a sand dune on a red plaid rug.

We returned before dark and my parents had friends around. The last time I saw my mother I sat on her knee for a while before going to bed. This too I recall with pain. It was going to be a good night. My sister Lynn, five years older than me, had her friend Olivia Neville to stay. I would fondle Olivia's hair too, as I did my mother's, and as I would do my own. They were to have a midnight feast and had promised to wake me. I shared Lynn's room that night, the same room which, later, I would share with my father – he snoring loudly and I watching the sweep of lighthouse beams across the ceiling. Sometime later I woke and asked why they were crying. They said I was mistaken and should go back to sleep, they were laughing, they said. I fell asleep.

In the morning my father came to me and sat down by the side of the bed. He said, 'I want you to say a prayer with me for your mammy, because she's gone up to see God and she might not be coming home for a while.' He tried not to cry but he did. So did I. Not because I felt very much or understood finality, but because he did, and maybe because I felt it was expected.

I'm not sure if this was when my ability to become detached from myself began, but it is an unsettling and dubious talent. Years later in Belfast I asked an 18-year-old boy from Hackney to put the barrel of his cocked machine gun into my mouth till it touched the back of my throat. I knelt down with my hands behind my back and closed my eyes. I wanted to know how it felt to be a hair's breadth from oblivion. It was in some respects an act of moral cowardice, but his temptation to pull that trigger must have been overwhelming, rather like the awful impulse to jump one feels when an incoming train rushes into the tube station. The effect, however, was strangely calming. To remove yourself from decision, choice or responsibility seemed seductively reasonable and peaceful and it was the second time that imminent death seemed almost inviting. I knelt there, a part of me begging this young man to pull the trigger, and the other part saying, how extraordinary, and examining my feelings in fine detail. One part perfectly removed from the other. I had absolutely no reason for desiring death, but its proximity was intoxicating.

My mother had woken in the night and said to my father, 'Oh God, Bob, something's happening in my head,' and then she died. She was forty-four and she had had a brain haemorrhage. My father wears her wedding ring on his little finger and constantly touches it. He would talk to her for years afterwards and went to mass every day, the better to concentrate on her and communicate with her.

On the morning of Ma's dying I took out my Nazi helmet. Someone had painted it white to exorcise the ghost of whichever storm trooper's head had occupied it. My helmet, like Ireland, was neutral. I went across to the Archers to play. Later I went to the Nevilles to stay. I was spared the funeral. On the day they buried her I was taken to see the Kings of Comedy in the Stella cinema. It was what they call in Ireland a good funeral – a lot of people went. She was very funny, my mother, and people liked her. I sat and watched Charlie Chaplin and Buster Keaton. I loved them. My mother, who had been a cinema manageress, would have loved them too.

Things changed after that. The house, dark before, was now empty. My

Mum.

father by virtue of his work was away all week and returned only at weekends. My elder sister Cleo was in charge. Lynn was at school as was I. There were various attempts to have live-in housekeepers but we hounded them out. There were frantic attempts to maintain a semblance of family life. We went on a caravan holiday that summer, the first holiday we'd had, I think. There seems in memory to have been a terrible forced jollity about the whole affair, hardly surprising given my father's desperation. Cleo complained of feeling tired constantly. My father assumed she was suffering the shock of my mother's death.

It was Cleo who had assumed the parental role. She was eighteen and on the day of my mother's funeral she had sat her Leaving Certificate, the Irish equivalent of 'A' Levels. My mother's death had a more profound effect on Cleo than on me, for at eighteen she was burdened with the young family. I still bear the marks of her attempts to discipline me: each evening as I objected to my nine o'clock bedtime she would grip my upper arm in her fingers and pinch hard, and the bruises have stayed to this day. A strange system existed in the house. We were on our word of honour not to be bad. Often we kept things from our father so as not to burden him further with worry. We were broke, but what we didn't know, and what was driving him half-crazed with grief, was the fact that Cleo's tiredness had been diagnosed as leukaemia and at the end of the year, the same year in which my mother died, she was given three months to live.

They told her simply that it was pernicious anaemia. They had to say something. At certain times her skin looked as cold and as mottled as a slab of marble. The doctors told my father there was no hope of recovery. On one visit to the hospital a Protestant doctor, strangely enough, asked if he'd consider going to Lourdes. In a rational situation one would have dismissed the notion. This was no time for rationality. Lourdes is a town where the Virgin Mary is said to have appeared to the young girl Bernadette in a small grotto. Pilgrimages to this holy site by the incurables and the cripples of our planet have resulted in a number of inexplicable cures and healings.

My father was prepared to clutch at any straw. Later, when I was eleven, I went to Lourdes, on a school trip. I can still remember the palpable atmosphere of desperation and its close relative, hope. I can still sense the tangible, overwhelming goodness. I can still smell the reek of sickening disease and I am still confused by the unquestioning belief. In Lourdes I realised for the first time something that would be confirmed to me in my teens and later as an adult in Africa. Mankind at its most desperate is often at its best. When the physical is reduced to an ugly irrelevance the possibilities of blinding human beauty emerge.

When my father and Cleo returned the word 'miracle' was never spoken but the three months she had been given to live extended itself into years. She is still alive. The cancer had utterly disappeared but my father later told me that for years afterwards when he heard there was a telephone call for him in one of the hotels or boarding houses he used on his traveller's round, he assumed the worst. None of this was known to me then. I continued to give Cleo as hard a time as she was giving me.

At around this time I began walking backwards. I would arch my back and, placing my hands by my feet, I would scuttle like some demented crab about the house. I did this for about a year. I did it at home mainly, but I did it in public too, occasionally even going up and down the stairs of the bus this way. I probably did it to get noticed, but mainly I did it to irritate people. I could walk very fast this way. It was also very useful in that it prevented me from doing a lot of chores I would otherwise have had to do. My father and sisters thought the best way of dealing with it was to ignore it. Eventually I just decided not to walk backwards any more.

At Christmas we all went away together. There were few Geldofs in Ireland and we were very clannish. There was my father, his brother, two sisters and their families. I liked the hotels and their smell of kitchens, warmth and comfort. It felt, well, rich I suppose, but we weren't. One day I saw my Uncle Sonny slipping my Dad money to pay the bill. It was fun to be with my cousins and to have TV. I was ashamed of not having a TV, it seemed such a terrible and obvious badge of poverty. I always asked for things that were expensive; a racing bike, a Scalextric. I was always told they were too expensive, but I got them. The bike was blue and yellow and had four gears but it was second hand. I was tired of second hand. I was tired of 'I know a man who can get that wholesale'. I was tired of the bike because it became the means of getting to school and saving the bus fare. The Scalextric was constructed in the hotel room where my father and uncle played with it all morning and then broke it. But I liked the hotel, I liked the frosty walks and Christmas mornings. I liked the sense of well-being, illusory as it was. Most of all I liked being away from the house. I liked the fancy dress parties that the adults took seriously and we thought were stupid. I liked them getting upset and saying every year, 'If you don't appreciate what we do for you, how much it costs your poor father, we won't bother coming next year, that's all. We do it for you, you know, not us,' which of course was a lie. 'Now you will dress up, and that's that.' I threw a towel over my shoulder and went as a Mexican bandit.

Two weeks after my mother's death I had returned to school. It would have been an unlooked for and pleasant break had it not been for the incomprehensibly long faces of all the adults who for some reason were invariably especially gentle with me during this period. This continued when I returned to Willow Park, the junior school at Blackrock College. Again, inexplicably, the Dean, Father Stanley, told me to take my time and get into things gradually. 'Fine by me,' I thought. At Willow Park most of the teachers were priests, Holy Ghost Fathers. I was a day boy but there were boarders too. After school they had a study period and I would be the only day boy to stay for it. The others had gone home, but my home was empty. So I ate my tea in the refectory with the boarders, but because I was a day boy, I had to sit by myself at a separate table. I didn't care. Who wanted to sit with the boarders, anyway?

After tea, between early and late study, there would occasionally be singing. The Dean rang a bell and shouted 'sing-song' and pointed to a few different boys. He invariably included me, probably in a misguided attempt to make me feel involved. My song was 'Fine Girl You Are,' or 'The Holy Ground'. I would stand on the seat and sing loudly. But the boarders would laugh and take the mickey because I was a day boy. I hated it. I hated not going home with the others. In study the only noise was the sound of the prefect's leather-soled shoes on the wooden floor as he patrolled the lines of ancient desks.

I was OK at school. Good results, the odd prize, but my main claim to fame was the fact that I knew the lyrics of every song Cliff Richard ever recorded –

the result of my sisters' crazed following of the English singer. Once on a school trip to Belfast I had sung over the train PA an appalling version of one of Cliff's songs, 'Have You Heard the News'. The priest who was in control of the PA, who incidentally was a Roman Catholic exorcist and a drunk to boot, commented on just how appalling I actually was by seizing the microphone half-way through the last verse. 'That's enough of that rubbish, Geldof,' he said, over the squawking system.

Belfast had a sort of foreignness about it. A kind of mythology was wrapped up in the two words 'The Border'. It was a peaceful border then, with just the odd explosion and a lot of agricultural smuggling. Mainly we knew the north as a place where you bought flat chewing gum, spangles and fireworks. All delights unobtainable in the south. The older boys knew it for its contraceptives and girlie magazines. Fireworks could, however, sometimes be obtained illegally in the fruit markets of Moore Street in Dublin where one heard the chant 'Last two bananas, the last two now, a shilling now the last two, one and six the half dozen', and then the aside, 'You want any bangers, son?' Sometimes I'd take the bangers to Kevin Cully's house when I bunked out of study. He had model bombers and fighter planes hanging by strings from his ceiling. We would put the bangers in the planes and light the fuse and blow them all to bits.

I was in study when I heard that Kennedy was dead. The prefects were not senior boys but seminarians half-way through their training for the priesthood. They were men in their early twenties who wore proper soutanes like the priests did. The study prefect was pacing between the lines when the door opened. It was behind me but I guessed it was another prefect entering.

I heard the low whispers and then, louder, the oath. But there was to be no more work. Minutes later the prefect was up on his dais. We stood, and a blessing was said. Then he told us President Kennedy had been shot in Dallas that day; we would pray for the repose of his soul and for his family. There was absolute silence. In Ireland Kennedy was a national hero. Every house had three pictures: JFK, the Pope and RFK arranged as a triumvirate. The Blessed Trinity. One or two blasphemous souls had just the JFK portrait. Most of us had been down and waved at him as his cavalcade had driven in glory through Dublin. I had, and still have, the little paper stars and stripes I waved that day. People had gone crazy. Kennedy was Ireland triumphant. He was for us the ultimate Irish success story. An Irishman, or as good as, who had got to be President of the USA.

His death was a terrible shock. We prayed for him there in study and then we filed down to the school chapel and prayed some more. I had seen my father listen with deep anxiety to the radio and had heard words like 'nuclear' and 'world war three' bandied about in conversation with his cronies. There had been the palpable air of fear and uncertainty and then overwhelming relief apparently brought about by Kennedy himself. But it was the fear I remembered when three years later I joined the anti-nuclear campaign.

Sometimes I would bunk out of study and go down to see Cully. He had a big tree in front of his house where you could play Tarzan and Boy, or Plarzan and Lad, as we called it. But Cully always got to be Plarzan because he was stronger. When it was time for tea Cully would never ask me in. I don't know why. I'd have to wait outside on the steps and then it would grow dark but I couldn't go home because study didn't finish till eight and therefore I couldn't appear in the house till eight-thirty for fear of my skiving being discovered. If I had any money, I would go down to the fish shop in Blackrock and get smoked cod and chips. It cost two shillings.

Two shillings was a lot, but I had the cash from my school fees. Every week before he went on his travels around Ireland my father would give me my school fees money in an envelope. It was nice to have some money so I opened the envelope myself instead of handing it in to the school office. It was a few pounds. You could buy cream buns from The Nook or use it to go to the pictures on Saturday afternoon at the Adelphi. No one seemed to mind. But then, at the end of that term, a bill came. He rang the school without telling me.

'Good morning, Father Stanley,' said the boys in chorus. He did not enter the class during lessons except for some serious reason.

'Robert Geldof. Will you please leave the classroom.'

Everyone looked at me. I moved my books to the corner of my desk and straightened my pencil – half wanting to impress the Dean with my neatness, half wanting to put off, even if only for a few seconds, the awful moment when I would discover why he wanted me. I had no idea. But I felt in my stomach that it must be bad.

I stood in the corridor in silence as the story of my wrong-doing was recounted. Somehow from his lips the whole thing sounded far worse than it had ever seemed to me. '. . . It is not simply the amount, though that is grave of itself; your father is by no means a wealthy man, he makes sacrifices to send you here. He will now have to find the amount which you owe to the school. But it is more than that. It is the deceit and dishonesty it embodied. Such behaviour is sinful. Your father and I have talked about the whole matter. He is going to beat you and so am I.'

Father Stanley had what the boys called a 'biffer'. The word was a joke, but the implement was not. A thick, flexible rubber strap, it hurt unbearably. I was outraged and shamed by this terrible injustice. But what happened at home was much worse. There was no one to plead for me. I was utterly alone. On the bus home, in panic, I prayed to my mother. I was in pain from the beating at school and in terror of what lay ahead.

First there was the silence and the sobbing.

'Why did you do it?' Lynn asked me. Lynn was supposed to be my friend.

'I don't know. It didn't seem that important. I'm sorry.'

'Don't you know that since Mammy died the house has had to run on trust while Daddy is away all week? We are all on our honour to behave ourselves,' said Cleo. Cleo was a grown-up, more than twenty now, but she was only my sister. Why should she be allowed to speak to me like this? 'I'm on my honour to be in by ten o'clock every night and I don't break the trust. Lynn is on her honour to do her schoolwork for her Intermediates and she doesn't break the trust. But you, you can't even be trusted to take in your dinner money. Why did you do it?'

'I don't know. I'm sorry, I'll pay it back.'

'Go upstairs, Robert,' said my father.

There was a sofa in the room where he hit me. He spoke to me first. 'This will hurt me more than it hurts you.' He actually said that. It did not seem real, it was like some schoolboy novel. What was most horrible was that he had got a bamboo cane to hit me with. Had he gone out and bought it? The cold-blooded calculation of that simple act is the thing that still bothers me. He had decided to inflict as much pain as he could. He had thought about that as he chose it: 'No, that one won't be as painful as this cane.'

'I am going to hit you six times.' His voice was cold. 'You are never going to do this again. Hold onto the back of the sofa and bend over.'

'No, Da. Please don't hit me. I'll be good now.' I still didn't really grasp what had been so bad. I ran around the sofa.

'Come back.'

I went to the sofa and held fast to it. My knuckles were white with the gripping, but they did not seem like my own. I felt as though I was watching someone else's hands. The cane swished and a hot line of pain cut across my buttocks. It burned like the pain you got when your hand brushed by accident against the kitchen stove. I howled, but I did not move. The second would be easier, I told myself. But it wasn't, it was a hurt on top of the hurt. My whole body was now entirely concentrated in those few inches of flesh. The third set my entire being into a contortion of agony. I screamed and ran away.

'Come back.'

'No.'

'Come back.'

'Please, Da. Please, no more, please.'

He chased me around the room, grabbed me and hit out again and again. I could not believe he would do this. Then, at the end, the bastard tried to hug me. How dare he salve his own pathetic conscience with that act of hypocrisy? If you're going to hurt someone, hurt them, but don't pretend it's love. That's perversion. I was filled with disgust and I hated him. The hurt, the rage, the shame and the bewilderment were too deep. From that day on, my father and I were at loggerheads. He would pay.

CHAPTER III

Diphthongs And Monothongs

The liver trembled. It was bright red and it twitched like it was hooked to the mains. It was not the sluggish grey-brown of your average cooked lunch café liver, more a wet slidy thing that jerked and jived on the shining railway tracks as the train disappeared. It looked like the liver from a butcher's shop, cold and self-contained. This one had come out of a man. It was warm and still shimmering.

Behind me the bay stank. Still and flat and grey, the sea lay out beyond the now abandoned swimming pool and occasionally it slurped around the stinking end of the sewer pipe where the blasé seagulls bobbed. But it was a good place to have your lunch, down by the decrepit old buildings of Booterstown station. It was away from the school and yet within sight of it. I had paused, sandwich midway to gob, while the strolling man had crossed the tracks, following his dog who now waited on the opposite platform. Half-way across the track he stopped and his head went back. He slumped across the rails and lay still. He was about twenty-five yards away. I scrambled up onto the sea wall and ran along it still holding the sandwich. I didn't see the train coming. There's a bend in the track there where it curves to follow the line of the coast along to Dublin. It tore him apart before I could even jump down from the wall. There was no squeal of brakes. There was no time for the train to stop. The driver probably didn't see him anyway, and the train just thundered on through the station. I must have closed my eyes when it hit him because I don't remember the wheels cutting through his body or tossing parts of it in the air. I don't know what happened to his head and legs and things, just his liver. I had no horror. I watched the liver wobbling.

The dog seemed bemused, he sniffed the air. Maybe he thought it was a new game. He smelt the blood and began to lick distractedly at the small pools of the stuff about him. Soon he began to nose about the smaller gobbets of flesh that had burst upon the platform. He chewed, tentatively at first, and then enthusiastically he began to eat his master.

I looked down and saw my legs had been spattered with gore. My grey socks with the blue and white tops were wet. I walked onto the damp sand and very methodically I washed it off in a pool. Later I returned to school.

In the days that followed I returned to the sea wall. At lunchtime I would leave the school grounds and walk down the little lane to the station. Most of the day boys would go home for lunch so I would go down to the sea to eat the sandwiches I had prepared for myself that morning. Usually they were lettuce. I liked tomato sandwiches but was useless at making them. The bread would go soggy and I could never work out why. Sometimes I just put sugar in the bread: it was quick and neat. The old man was away all week as usual. Cleo was busy rushing off to the hairdressers where she worked. Lynn was busy studying for her Leaving Certificate and couldn't be distracted.

Sitting on the sea wall that summer at the age of eleven I first formed the idea of being imprisoned. The wall was long and seemed to stretch like an encircling arm from the gigantic concrete towers of the electricity generating complex at the northern end to the old church spires of Dun Laoghaire which stood in weak silhouette at the other. These were the frontiers of my existence. Sometimes I would sit looking out into the bay, a gaping maw whose wide jaws seemed to swallow everything and belch out nothing in return. On foggy days Hoath Head looked like a huge ship looming out of the murk and on clear days I would pretend I could see as far as England.

I had been born within sight of the sea and brought up within earshot of its wilder waves. The purposeless movement of the seaweed in the water's ebb and flow held no special interest for me. The sea was simply a fact of life. We barely noticed it and we rarely went to it. Sometimes I faced away from the bay, staring up at the Dublin mountains which rose like an insurmountable wall in the distance, way back beyond the school. It did not require any great leap of the imagination to see the mountains and the sea as being prison bars but this physical illusion of barriers was echoed by my psyche. Things happened that year which have stayed with me more than memories of any other period. After the school money incident and the beating I was not to be trusted. Indeed I remember my sisters actually saying, 'He's not to be trusted, he tells lies,' to people who were strangers to me. I developed a sort of prison mentality as a form of self-defence. I would remain detached and objective no matter what was being done to me. There would always be a coolly deductive part of my mind observing and questioning the part that was under stress. It was like a civil war inside my head. Even today everything I do or say is questioned by another part of me. Even now as I write it says, 'are you absolutely sure about that or is it just for effect?' Sometimes it gets so overwhelming you want to stop this constant internal argument. Your head throbs and you want to sit in a dark room and bring yourself under control. The trick is to be unbearably honest about yourself. It was a solution to the dilemma I found myself in. If no one was to trust me I would only trust myself.

The priests at school changed towards me and became harder. If something went missing at school I was blamed or at least suspected. I simply gave up. My schoolwork became disastrous. Overnight I ceased to care about grades and learning. That year, one year after winning academic prizes for excellence, I failed utterly in my primary exam, the Irish equivalent of the eleven-plus.

The pressure came down harder after that. I loathed the priests and my father and their systems of authority. I refused to co-operate in any way. This was not a conscious decision, more an unconscious understanding. There was no one I could talk to, no one to go home to, so forced in on myself I became self-sustaining and self-reliant. But then, almost exactly when the money incident occurred I developed asthma. I've read, and it must be a psychological cliché to state it, that psychosomatic asthma is a direct result of the mind crying out for the mother, and at the first time since my mother's death that I consciously needed her I became breathless and turned purple with panic. I got asthma.

From the age of eleven until today I have had only superficial contact with my family. Essentially I grew up on my own, which makes it a strain when I'm with my sisters now for we don't understand each other. We've nothing in common except our parents. They grew up in different circumstances with a different set of precepts. Of necessity I made my own. Their memories of me before I was eleven are very clear but after that what they think happened and what actually did take place are worlds apart. They couldn't know because they weren't there. Often we would not see each other from one end of the week to the other. Cleo was now ensconced in her own home with her husband Noel. He was a motorbike cop and he was a good bloke. The local yobs called him Babyface and when he came to pick up my sister I would play the Little Richard track of the same name on the record player and turn it up very loud. He took me out dirt track racing and he kept an eye on me throughout my teens. When I stole some food from a shop later on he warned me gently that everyone knew about it. When I was caught driving without brakes, lights, licence, insurance or tax, he fixed it up and told me that would be the first and last time. Occasionally he would even try to spur me into academic achievement. Once he neatly dissected an apple in a valiant attempt to stimulate my interest in the arithmetic of fractions. I stared blankly at the fruit throughout.

'Any questions?' he said at the end.

'Just one.'

'What is it?'

'Can I eat the apple now?'

One day, in 1983, Cleo, now with two children, called up to Noel to come down for his breakfast. There was no reply, and she found him dead from a heart attack at the age of forty. Fate had repeated itself. Cleo is a very strong person. She has had to be.

Lynn, on the other hand, was thriving at university. She wouldn't come home till late, if at all, and she would leave later than me in the mornings. This meant that we never saw each other. Once I had been sick at the top of the house for three days before Lynn discovered me. Most days the alarm rang, I got up, threw on clothes, made my breakfast and cycled to school.

Blackrock College was a grey and imposing building with many wings. It stood at the top of the playing fields which rose from the road which separated the school from the marshy foreshore and the Dublin to Dun Laoghaire railway line. As younger boys in the prep school at Willow Park next door we had been taught to regard the place with some awe. Eamon De Valera, the great Irish President, had gone there we were told. I saw the revered old hero only once. It was sports day and the boys were lined up neatly on the front field facing the balcony over the school kitchens. The priests emerged first, followed by De Valera, a tall, frail and almost blind man then in his eighties, helped by his ADC. The band struck up the national anthem and De Valera, unsure of his bearings and tottering slightly behind the upright priests, turned around and faced the wall, standing to attention. No one noticed that he was facing the wrong way except the assembled boys, who were stifling their hysterics. There he stood, inches from the white wall, his back to the band as the national anthem played on. Could be that he did it on purpose.

I had been considered bright and compliant enough until my final year in the junior school but at Blackrock itself I was never a great success. Those playing fields, which years later I was to gouge and tear up happily some late Saturday night, drunkenly spinning a beaten up VW in circles on the pious turf, were too much at the centre of life there. My asthma however provided a ready excuse for opting out of games. It was like opting out of school itself in a place where the rugby field was considered the crucible in which young Irish gentlemen should be tempered and where the country 'culchies' played Gaelic football. We Dublin boys called the country pupils 'culchies', which they hated. To us they were thick-limbed creatures with hair like straw and great boils on the back of their red necks. The masters called them Scholastics because they came to the college on free scholarships before going on to seminary to train for the priesthood. In their hands lay the future of the Catholic Church in Ireland. Many of the sharper ones were just there for the free education and had no intention of becoming priests. Lessons were a never-ending catalogue of chalk-dry facts, dates, formulae and conjugations. It was a disembodied world enlivened only by the antics of the more eccentric masters or the baiting of those who refused to be otherwise amusing.

The Latin master, Father Lodge, was paranoid about germs. He never went anywhere without a plastic bag and a box of Kleenex. He strode into the classroom like a man with urgent news and threw open every single window. Then began the ritual. With the exactness of a celebrant placing the water and wine on the altar he laid out his equipment. Then he inflated the plastic bag with a brisk shake of his hand and, with the other extracted a paper tissue from the box. With a practised flourish he blew his nose and then tossed the hankie into the bag and, with a twirl of the fingers, twisted it closed.

Ramsay coughed. Ramsay could spit further than anybody else in the class.

Third spear carrier in Gilbert and Sullivan school operetta.

Da, Cleo, Lynn and me in my Shadows jumper.

'Ramsay, you butt-sucking puke . . .'

'Yes, Father?'

'Stop that coughing.'

'Sorry, Father.' Ramsay pretended to stifle another bout.

An epidemic of coughs would then convulse the class.

The priest who taught us French had malaria. Sometimes he'd shake badly and leave the class to shoot some quinine into his system in the toilet. He was an indifferent French master, but he was passionate about cricket. The school was not geared towards soccer or cricket, it was probably 'too English', but this man had assembled a team even so. Lovingly he tended his crease and sometimes late on spring evenings, I would see him bent double pulling the heavy roller up and down behind him on his hand-mown grass. He would abstractedly conjugate some irregular verbs whilst gazing out of the long windows towards his crease. He would be startled abruptly from his reverie by the sight of some boy wandering across the field toward the gymnasium. As soon as his sole touched crease, the verbs would be thrown aside and the window slammed upwards. Gathering his long-skirted soutane, this malarial man of sixty would jump through the window shouting 'Get off my crease, you bastard!' He would drop down into the bushes, vault the fence, scramble across the field and rugby tackle the unfortunate and sacrilegious lad to the ground. 'You think you can laugh at me,' he would scream, 'you think cricket's a joke.' He would boot the boy in the backside and haul him by his hair off to the Dean who, by now familiar with this, would pacify both priest and boy advising the former to calm himself and the latter to respect school property. 'Did you see that?' he would demand on returning to class. 'Yes, Father.' 'I'll show them,' he'd mutter picking up his book of verbs. 'McCormack, why are you wearing a scarf?' 'I'm a bit cold, Father.' 'Get out.' 'Ah, Father, why?' 'Out, out, out!'

As for the rest, I gradually switched off. Arithmetic, algebra and geometry I did so well at that my total mark in three exams one year was three per cent. French could be made tolerable only by boring holes in the master's chalk with the point of a compass, then packing the hole with the heads of matches and filling the end with chalkdust so that the chalk would explode like a firework as he wrote his lists of irregular verbs on the blackboard. German was memorable only for the odd little master who cycled to work and parked his bike outside the classroom window. During the time it took him to walk along the outside of the building to the entrance and then back along the corridor to the classroom the trick was to haul his bike through the window, take it to pieces and then lay the bits on his desk. We did it once too often and he stormed out of the classroom to fetch the Dean, but by the time the two masters returned it had been reassembled and put back through the window in its original parking place. History I could have enjoyed but they never told you the interesting stuff: that Napoleon was in agony from his piles the night before Waterloo and got no sleep because he had to lie on his stomach; or that Wellington had a little tail growing at the base of his spine and liked nobbing endless lines of women. Instead it was all: Battle of Austerlitz 1805, Battle of Waterloo 1815, Congress of Aix-la-Chapelle 1818. I packed my schoolbag at night but it would never be opened until it returned to the classroom the next day.

Ours was not an easy house to go home to, particularly when winter came and the evenings grew dark. It was in a tall, Edwardian terrace, high ceilinged, full of black corners and lurking shadows with the chill of emptiness upon it. On gloomy winter evenings I would stop by the trefoil-topped iron railings and look up at the windows in the front door. Sometimes on those foggy November nights as I walked slowly up the cracked pathway and mounted the steps I was seized with terror that the pale figure of my mother would be standing at the top of the stairs smiling down at me. She would be wearing a flimsy nightgown which would blow about her in a wind which did not even ruffle her hair. I put the key in the lock of the front door. Sometimes I imagined she would smile in a crazed leering way, her eyes black and staring. Other times they would be gentle and kind, and still other times she had the vacant, lifeless smile of death. I had no memory of her face in animation to correct this fixed obsession. I knew what she looked like only from photographs. I could not remember her and it is a shock now to see old home movies of this woman. Turning the key in the door, I would keep my head down for fear of her wan, hanging face at the top of the stairs. I'd grope for the light and then steel myself to look up. She wasn't there. Each day I would berate myself for my stupidity, but sometimes I was in such panic I dared not look up at all.

The house was cold and I would fetch the yellow plastic basin, which had melted on one side from being placed too near the fire, and climb down the deep stairs to the cellar. I'd fill the bucket with coal, return and set the fire. Still wearing my coat, I rolled up old copies of the *Irish Times*. It was not very good paper for lighting fires, but the *Sunday Independent* had been used up by Wednesday. Sticks were broken across my knees which sometimes bruised; later, when I could, I would steal firelighters from the corner shop to start it up. For the first hour I sat with my coat on until the room heated and the flickering fire became warm. Often I couldn't face the drudgery of cleaning out the ashes from the previous night and simply lit the gas stove in the large kitchen. But it was not a comfortable place to be. Always, whichever way I faced, my body was divided into hot and cold parts; the side next to the fire would bake and the skin on my face would tingle with the dry heat while the back of my body was chilled by the draught. I would pass the time reading or listening to the radio. But the kitchen too was a place of psychic terror. Often on those evenings I would feel a face at the window – not my mother's this time but something so malevolent that to confront it would mean instant insanity. This too was the chimera of imagination.

I was not consciously aware of my mother's absence or jealous of other people's complete families. It would perhaps have been more noticeable to me had my father been at home. Being virtually parentless seemed normal. Far from missing him or my mother I resented his homecoming at weekends for then the house was no longer exclusively mine. I would maintain a shallow pretence of a life of academic application and domestic pride. He would impose a parental discipline for those two days, probably exaggerated because of his absence for the remainder of the week; for one who had been free of such restraints for the other five days it seemed excessively restrictive and severe.

On Friday evenings I would begin the journey home in a state of abject fear. Often on the 7A bus I would pray to the Virgin Mary or to my own mother to intercede for me. On really bad days I would say decades of the Rosary but mostly the prayers were made up and consisted of one word repeated over and over in desperation: 'Please, please, please'. Later in the evening my heart would thump as I heard his car approach and he announced his arrival with a blast of the horn. One of his first requests would be for the Judger.

Blackrock College had a weekly system of assessment. Each subject was marked out of nine. Six was considered average and there was a blacklist for everyone who got three fives or under and an honours list for anyone whose marks in every subject were seven or over. Most boys managed to keep themselves off both lists. I was always on the blacklist; once I even managed to get a three which was said to be unprecedented. Being, even then, a scruffy boy, I often got only six or five for deportment where everyone else got nine. The results were sent out each week in Judgement Books. You had to get your Judger signed by your parents and take it back so the school knew that it

29

had been seen at home. They were handed out on Fridays. I came to dread the moment. Most weeks the results in my Judger were poor and often they were bad. My father devised a system whereby he beat me once for every six, twice for every five and so on in an ascending scale of punishment.

He was not, in retrospect, a heartless man. He merely carried with him the values of his age. But they were not values which I shared. He may have felt guilty about his absence and possibly like a stranger in his own home. To me his presence was simply an intrusion on my life. After Cleo married Noel and moved away parts of the rambling old house were converted into bedsits to supplement the family income. That meant my father and I had to share a bedroom. During the week the place was my territory; at weekends he would move in and complain that the room was not tidy. I was furious but I always bit back the suggestion that he should get his own room. He did make attempts to spend time with me to compensate for his absence. But I did not want to be with him. I would rather have been with my friends down at Murray's record shop. His insistence only antagonized me further. Most weekends he would take me sailing on a friend's boat. I would wait with trepidation on Saturday mornings to see whether this week I might be spared his hearty request.

I hated sailing. The tossing and heaving of the little boat in the choppy waters of the Irish sea scared me for I couldn't swim. In fact I hated the water. Today I can only swim on my back with my face turned upwards. The feeling of water on my face induces panic. Da had insisted I take lessons in Blackrock baths where I would jump with the other kids out to the beckoning pole. They got there, I simply sank. Once we were lifting the punt which took us out to the yacht down the slipway of the harbour. As we got near the edge to drop the boat in the water I either fell in or was nudged. I sank the ten or twelve feet to the bottom. I think it was an attempt in the 'if he has to he'll do it' school of swimming. I didn't. I sank and rose three times. It was on the third occasion that my father grabbed my outstretched hand and pulled me out.

Occasionally I would enjoy these expeditions. Once we sailed to Wicklow and threw lines overboard for the mackerel which were in season. The sea was glinting silver with them and we could just pull them in on bare hooks with no bait. I remember him frying them on the boat. They were delicious. But most of the trips were a tedious imposition. Throughout the journey I would huddle into the side of the boat and withdraw into my thoughts as the adult chatter of my father and his friends was whipped in the wind all around my ears. Overhead the seagulls screamed.

Every Sunday after lunch came the harsh injunction that I should get down to my studies to repair some of the academic damage of the previous week. My father would say that and then fall asleep in the big armchair with the *Sunday Independent* over his face. I deeply resented having to work while he slept. The snores which reverberated through the newsprint filled me with disgust and contempt. Sometimes I would sneak another newspaper to my side and read it, turning the pages with exaggerated care in order not to disturb his slumber. Otherwise I gazed blankly out of the window, my pen elaborating an ever-wilder doodle on the exercise book before me as the rooks made their slow and heavy landings in the trees over the road.

Sometimes we would go for walks down the mile-long east pier at the harbour. We would go on Friday evening or sometimes on a Sunday night. Those were the times we would talk. He would sometimes walk behind me and then insert his thumbs between my shoulder blades and say, 'Stand up straight lad, don't slouch, be proud.' It irritated me and I'd mumble something. He'd say, 'Don't mumble, no one ever understands what you're saying, you know. Those bloody adenoids, you should have elocution lessons.'

'Diphthongs and monothongs,' I mumbled.

'What's that?'

'Elocution.'

'Really?'

'Yeah'.

I liked him then, without his worries. He'd hide on me. Simply disappear. I would be talking away and then I would look beside me and he'd have gone. Usually he'd just drop behind and then jump over the wall and walk along parallel with me but out of sight. Other times he'd simply sit on one of the green wooden benches and hide behind his newspaper. I would be frightened, then I'd feign indifference, then he'd pop up. He'd point out boats. He had endless friends. Quite literally it would take sometimes an hour to walk down the street as people he knew from his travels or town accosted him. People like my father, he's a funny and gregarious man but they didn't have to grow up with him. It would take a half hour to reach the end of the pier and then we'd stand on the lighthouse tower and watch the fishermen. I think he gave me his wanderlust. One day he put his arms around my shoulders and we both stared out to sea beyond the Kish lightship. We stood there awhile and then he lifted his other arm and pointed into the distance.

'Eastward Ho,' he said.

My father felt so strongly about my academic performance at Blackrock because he had been to the same school himself and had been a complete failure there. He didn't want me to go the same way and end up like he had, unqualified, and tied to a job which forced him to be away from home all week, leaving his kids to fend for themselves. My grandfather was a Belgian chef who had moved to Ireland in search of work just before the Easter Uprising and the Troubles of 1917 began. He set up a catering business with a sideline in import/export and he very much wanted my father to follow him in it. The old man was sent to Blackrock which was, and remains, quite a chichi school, socially, if not academically. Grandfather's name was Zenon Geldof and he founded a number of up-market establishments in the twenties and thirties beginning with the Patisserie Belge and then the Café Belge. It became part of high society Dublin life and was frequented by the members of Yeats' Irish Renaissance circle, Countess Markovitz, Maud Gonne and Sean McBride. His plan was that my father, Robert Albert Zenon Geldof, should take over the Café Belge and that his elder brother, christened Herbert Alphonsus Zenon Geldof, but known as Sonny, would take over the import business.

The pair of them had not done well at Blackrock and when my father was thirteen they had been taken out of school and sent to a lycée just outside Paris for two years to learn the French they would need in the catering and import trades. But the old man had subsequently not enjoyed life as a chef and hotel manager, finding the hours too demanding for someone with a young family. When Zenon Geldof died in a car accident in 1939, the business was sold and after World War Two, my father was employed by Uncle Sonny as a commercial traveller in the import firm Z. Geldof & Son. He had qualifications, he told me, for nothing else. So the subject of my own 'qualifications' became a preoccupation for him. Every Friday for a year there would be beatings, and there would be the same in school on a daily basis. It was stupid. It was one sure way of increasing my resistance to their will. I dreaded the handing out of the Judgers. I was not interested in improving my work perhaps because I felt that would have been a victory for them. I had to find another way.

One morning I went to buy an ice cream from Brother Gaul in the stationery storeroom cum tuckshop. The door was ajar. I entered, but there was no one there. All around the shelves were stacked with the paraphernalia of inscription: copy books, exercise books, graph books, notepads plain, notepads narrow feint, notepads broad feint, notepads broad feint with margin. It smelt of pencil shavings and chocolate. Then, in the corner, by the monk's desk, I saw a pile of virgin Judgement Books in their dark red covers. I turned and looked down the broad oak-panelled corridor. For a few seconds I stood and waited, breath held, listening for the sound of any footstep on the tiled floor. It was silent. On impulse, I ran across to where the Judgers were piled. I grabbed one and stuffed it under my blazer, pulling the stationery room door closed behind me. It locked itself with a click and I returned to my classroom with the intelligence that Brother Gaul was not about and that his room was locked.

The forger's art is a slow and painstaking one. That evening I sat at home at the table where I should have been hard at study and applied myself to my homework with an assiduity which would have surprised my father. On a sheet of rough paper and with a variety of different pens I practised the handwriting of my several schoolmasters, my tongue stuck out in concentration. English: 7. Good. French: 6. Satisfactory. Geography: 7. Good work. German: 6. Some progress. History: 8. Excellent work.

With practice came fluency. Satisfied, I went to the fire and threw on the

My grandfather with my father, left, and my Uncle Sonny.

rough sheet and watched the flames. Now I was confident enough to write straight into my new Judger. I disciplined myself, however, rationing the number of good marks and restricting myself in the main to 'satisfactory'.

That Friday the old man was pleased. 'This is a pleasant surprise, Robert.' He gave me two bob. He signed my new Judger which I immediately hid beneath the mattress in my bedroom and counterfeited his signature in the proper Judger which I handed in at school on the Monday. From then on the reported quality of my schoolwork gradually improved by the week until eventually I was regularly on the honours list.

The system held together for the best part of a year. The beatings at home, at least, finally ceased. Then one Saturday morning the phone rang. I was in the room at the time. It did not take long to work out it was the Dean of Studies at the other end and it did not take much imagination, from listening to my father, to fill in the other side of the conversation.

'Good morning, Father. How are you?'

'Good morning, Mr Geldof. I'm well, thank you. I hope you are, too. I am telephoning about Robert's schoolwork. What do you think about the present state of affairs, Mr Geldof?'

'Well, I'm very pleased with him, Father. He seems to be doing very well, he's really pulled his socks up in recent months . . .'

The old man's face darkened as the conversation continued. It did not last long. As he put the phone down, he marched straight across the room and hit me across the face. 'You're still lying. I'll teach you never to lie to me again.'

I was incensed. I had not wanted this. I had been forced into this position by them. I felt entirely justified in what I had done to get out of the intolerable situation they had created for me. 'Don't you ever hit me like that again,' I said. He was surprised, but he never did.

CHAPTER IV

The Upturned Cockroach

Mrs Armstrong from down the road was my first fuck. I was thirteen and not looking for it. I was looking for lemonade. It was a hot summer's day during the school holidays. I was alone in the house. I had lain in bed all morning and wanked until it became boring. It was well into the afternoon when I got up. Idly I wandered around the house, rummaging through the kitchen for something interesting to eat, switching the radio on and then off again, picking up Lynn's latest Cliff Richard LP and throwing it back onto the settee. I could work up an interest in nothing. I picked up the phone to ring Foley. It was engaged. Foley's dad worked for the *Irish Times* and their phone was often engaged. Perhaps he was working from home. I tried again. Still engaged. Not that I had anything to say to Foley, but ringing him might spark off an idea for something to do. Foley had been brought up in England when his old man worked in Fleet Street. We saw in him a certain sophistication. It was Foley I'd rung with the news of my first ejaculation. I had been told at school by Kiersey about wanking: you just pulled at your dick till it happened.

'Hey, Foley. It's Geldof. Have you ever wanked?'

'What do you mean? Course I have.'

'It's great, isn't it?'

'It's alright. What are you on about Geldof?'

'Er . . . nothing really . . . I mean, I was just ringing to find out if you were going down to Murray's later on.'

Foley had obviously been wanking a long time. I didn't want to blow my cool. Still, I managed to upstage him in a later call.

'Foley, it's Geldof. Have you ever looked at spunk under a microscope?'

'What?'

'Have you ever wanked and then put the stuff on a slide and looked at it under a microscope? It's great. I thought you'd be able to see some tadpoley thing or something kind of wriggling around.'

'Geldof, that's fucking disgusting.'

In the early days sex was interesting, but then it became a compulsion. Once down by the sea wall I had seen a woman masturbating. I had not known what she was doing. The wall was about eighteen inches wide and you could walk for long distances along the top of it. From the station I could see the woman lying in the sun on the side nearest the sea. I did not deliberately walk towards her. She was just there, in the way I was going.

The woman was in her late twenties. She was lying inside the concave curve of the wall, hidden from view with her legs spread apart and her long skirt bunched up around her waist. Had she not been so absorbed she might have seen me. I sensed that this was a private act, and I walked carefully along the last few yards of the wall. From behind her I could see that the skirt was pleated and flowery. She had pulled it up so that her white pants showed and her hand was inside them. I could not see her face because of the curve of the wall but she must have had her eyes closed or else she would have seen me. I stood for about five minutes and watched as she basked in the strong summer sun with the waves breaking at the bottom of the wall not far from her spreadeagled feet. I watched, feeling intrigued and somehow sad. It's something I still don't understand.

Now masturbation had become part of my daily life. And not just daily. It was a mortal sin, of course. At school during retreats one of the priests would go on about it. Your body was the temple of the Holy Ghost and if you abused it you abused God because the Holy Ghost was in God. It was throwing your seed on fallow ground. You would tell it in confession to get rid of the sin but when they told you to stop you knew you couldn't. I did feel guilty, though, because I was doing it so often. I felt tired all the time. I thought it was sapping my strength. I worried, like Hemingway, that I only had a certain amount and that once it was all used up that was it. That day I lost my virginity I had probably used up my quota already.

I tried Foley again. Still engaged. It was hot in the living room as the strong afternoon sunshine glared through the window. I decided to go out to the corner shop for some lemonade. There were two ways to the shop, along one side of the square with its grand Victorian façade or along the muddy back lane which ran behind the terrace. I rambled slowly down the lane and into the little store which sold everything from shovels and soap to bone-meal and biscuits. The shopkeeper was serving the woman from down the road, Mrs Armstrong. I lounged sullenly, picking up bars of chocolate and cans of cat food with equal lack of interest while her order was completed. She turned to leave.

'Hello. Robert, isn't it?'

'Hello, Mrs Armstrong.'

The little bell tinkled at the top of the door as she left. 'Goodbye,' she said, and set off down the square.

Taylor Keith lemonade came in pints and quarts. I asked for a big bottle. Holding it by the neck and swinging it I set off down the lane. At the end of the terrace, where the lane curved and rejoined the road, I bumped into her.

'We meet again,' she said.

'Yes,' I replied. I felt gangly and awkward.

We walked together towards my home. 'What a hot afternoon,' she said. 'Perhaps you'd like to come for a glass of lemonade?'

She looked at me. The Taylor Keith was in my hand and we would have to walk past my house to get to hers. I looked at her. She was thirty, perhaps, quite tall, her hair tied up at the top of her head. She had on a cotton frock.

'Well?' she asked unselfconsciously. She had an oval shaped face with dark hair and deep brown eyes. Her lipstick was bright.

'Yes, please,' I said, my throat dry from the heat of the day. The fireplace in her front room was just like ours.

'Sit down, Robert,' she said, pointing to a sofa. 'I'll get the drink.'

The solid wooden screen which separated the front room from the back had been removed and I watched her move into the kitchen. From my place on the settee I looked around. At one end of the room was a small dining table with its front leaf folded down and three chairs with leather seats. In the bay window was a new stereogram with the lid open. I wondered what was on the turntable but didn't like to go and see.

'Here we are,' she said, coming back with a single glass. Mrs Armstrong sat down next to me so that her leg rested next to mine.

I could feel the warmth of her thigh through the thin cotton. She smelt faintly of dust. I drank the lemonade in one gulp.

'Do you go out with girls now, Robert?' she asked.

'Sometimes.' My brief encounters with girls at the junior dance at Stella House might, by stretching the terminology, be described in that way.

'Have you ever kissed them?'

'Sometimes.'

'Was it like this?'

She leaned across and, putting her arm around me, drew my body to her. Her lipstick tasted like a boiled sweet on top of the lemonade. Then I felt her tongue push between my lips and toy with the tip of my own. I could feel her breasts squash against my weedy little chest. Then she pulled away.

'Have you ever seen a girl naked?'

I shook my head.

'Would you like to see me naked?'

I nodded dumbly.

She stood up. Her light summer dress had buttons down the front. She undid them from the neck downwards. The dress sprang open at the top. She unbuttoned it completely and stood before me with the frock just open. My eyes went down from the edges of her breasts to the dark triangle of hair between her legs. In Catholic Ireland there was no *Playboy* or *Men Only*. The only such magazine was *Health and Efficiency* and that had all the tits and pubes airbrushed out. It had not been long since I discovered that girls had nipples, I'd assumed that their breasts were smooth skin all over. As for what else there was, I had no idea. A girl had once said to me, 'Girls are different because their bottoms go all the way round.' Whatever that meant.

Mrs Armstrong lifted her hands to her shoulders like a Charleston dancer and flicked the dress off them. It fell onto the patterned green carpet behind her. Her hips were wide and her breasts were very full, they hung like strange fruit. She leaned over. With one hand she gripped the waist of my jeans and with the other she pulled down the zip. I wriggled in my seat. Her hand went inside the top of my underpants. I could not believe what was happening. I was trembling. She pulled me to my feet and pushed my jeans down to my ankles, then she fell back onto the sofa.

'Kiss me here,' she said, pointing to her tits. I did. 'Good boy. Rub me here,' she said, indicating between her legs. She held my bottom and with her other hand she pulled my head to hers and kissed me again, her tongue forcing itself roughly round my mouth. Then she guided me inside her and then, realizing that I did not even know it was necessary for me to move, she started to slide me up and down. It lasted all of three seconds. She kissed my neck. She stroked my head and whispered: 'Ssssh, ssssh.' She said: 'You're a very good boy. Did you like that?'

'Yes.' I was strangely ashamed but proud and utterly confused.

'Good, so did I,' she said, though she probably didn't.

★　★　★

Back at school they would not have believed me, so I didn't tell anyone. At break the boys would congregate in the lavatories to smoke out of sight of the masters. There the talk, invariably, turned to sex.

'Got off with Maureen Whatsits at Stella on Saturday.'

'Goer, isn't she?' (Said as if you knew from experience.)

'Too right.' (Defensively, in case he got something you didn't.)

'What did you get? Did you feel her tits? How far did she let you go?'

'Got me finger up.'

'What, with Maureen? No chance!'

'I did. I fucking did. I fucking finger fucked her.'

You could get a 'wear', a kiss with open mouth; a 'feel'; a 'dry ride', a crunching of pubic bones; or 'a ride'. Sex was a competitive event in those days and the only thing that you could take as a certainty was that everyone else was lying, just as you were. Most of us had our single rubber johnny which had been smuggled in across the border from Belfast because condoms were and remain illegal in Ireland. We carried them everywhere like good luck talismans. The only wear they ever got was from the lining of your pocket.

Stella House dance hall was the proving ground in which all these fantasies were put to the test. In this weekly trial by ordeal my triumph with Mrs Armstrong faded away as though it were nothing more than a figment of my inflamed adolescent imagination. Stella House was a ballroom in a huge prefabricated building on the Stillorgan housing estate. At the weekends, in the afternoons, they had dances for the under-eighteens. Existing as we did in single-sex schools the whole business of meeting girls was nerve-wracking. We would arrive in groups; the boys from Blackrock, the girls from Sion Hill. We would come from the pub. In Ireland they would serve you in a bar from when you were about thirteen as long as you weren't misbehaving. I aided this procedure when, at the appearance of my first facial hair, I pencilled more in with my sister's eye-liner and for the remainder of the holiday sported this ridiculous wisp. On the first day back at the end of the summer holidays, the teacher approached me and said, 'Geldof, what is that preposterous item beneath your nose?' I feigned ignorance. 'Wash it off by tomorrow, Geldof.'

It was a question of fine judgement: you had to drink as much as you could in order to win the approval of your peers but not so much that the bouncers on the door would be able to smell it on you. Inside there were two acceptable places to stand; either at the bar along the side where you could buy soft drinks – you'd stand there trying to look mean, drinking your Coke – or else around one of the pillars, hovering in a group and passing comment on the talent and on the various boy/girl exchanges that were taking place.

As you were making your cool, well-practised remarks, inside you would be jellied with nerves at the prospect of everybody looking on when you made your move, as you had to sooner or later. It was like my life generally. Like a swan it would be all serenity on top but paddling like fuck underneath. Fear was the over-riding emotion. You had to walk up to a girl and ask her to dance under this public scrutiny. It was like a TV game show in which how you performed before the audience was more important than what happened with the girl. Likely as not when you got there she'd say: 'Ask me sister. I'm sweating.' Then you'd have to take the long walk back to the lads and try to laugh off the rebuff. The shame was crippling. I was never rejected, because I never asked unless I was sure. I was ugly: a big gangly youth, with a huge mouth and scruffy hair. They called me Liverlips and White Nigger. Later Mick Jagger came along and redefined standards of acceptable male appearance but then I was still extremely uncomfortable with girls. I preferred not to approach them than make a fool of myself. I would stand at the bar, catch their eye and then look away. I'd catch it again, to make sure they were really interested. That would have been enough for most of the blokes, but not me. I'd go through the business ten or twelve times and then in the end still do nothing. Now girls I meet from those days tell me they thought I was trying to be cool by ignoring them. Even now I don't like dancing. I'll only do it on stage.

At this age everything was a proving ground. And being distinctly unsuccessful in most spheres I would turn in uncomprehending desperation to any new endeavour. In school, having rejected academic work and the sports field, I had already tried forming extramural clubs as a way of asserting myself. In Junior school I had had the Stamp Club. It was exactly the sort of thing approved of by the school. Schoolmasters are always taken with collections in general and stamps in particular. I wasn't interested in stamps at all but I thought it would be a good way to get out of one study period. With a few shillings and a visit to the stamp shop I put together a superficially impressive collection full of triangular exhibits and Olympic issues, marshalled a few key phrases about perforation marks and first day covers and took it along to the Dean. Fooled by the jargon he agreed to let me form the club and I began recruiting members. The gameplan was simple. People paid a shilling to join, which sum was for the purchase of stamps which would then be auctioned or swapped within the club. But the unofficial corollary was that the profits from the auction would then be used for club feasts and other irregular purposes. I got away with this for about a year until I over-reached myself by calling too many ad hoc meetings in one week and the Dean rumbled us. Later, at the age of fifteen, I made a short-lived attempt to take over the music society. I spent two meetings listening to Handel and Mozart and then introduced Muddy Waters, Tamla Motown and King Crimson. The Dean of Scholastics, Father Flood, who fancied himself as a music buff, put a swift end to that when during an hour of lyric discussion, I put on Big Mama Thornton's twenties song 'Shave Me Dry': *I got nipples on my titties as big as my thumb, I got a thing between my legs make a dead man come.*

The Scouts were more promising. The school had its own troop which I joined when I was ten or eleven, the 77th CBSI, the Catholic Boy Scouts of Ireland, as opposed to the Prods, the BPs, the Baden-Powells. I enjoyed aspects of it; hiking in the rain and the camping. I got to be an assistant patrol leader. But at the weekly inspections I was humiliated every time about the state of my uniform. It was clean, Lynn went to the laundrette every week, but no one ironed it for me and I didn't care enough to iron it myself at home. People still go on about me being dirty, untidy and unkempt. It always staggers me that it bothers them so much and me not at all. I still never iron anything; I simply don't think about it and even if I did I wouldn't be bothered with what seems to me to be an unnecessary task. I was reported to the chaplain for telling dirty jokes soon after my taking school money, and the scout master had been told about it. He, too, was aware that I was not to be trusted.

Curiously, the boy who showed me how to masturbate, saw God while on drugs and then became a monk, was a scouts' officer when I was up on a charge of 'lying'. I was hauled before a court of honour, the scouting equivalent of a court martial. Half a dozen adult men making stern accusations stood in judgement of a frightened 11-year-old boy. I was not found guilty or innocent. I was told I was a bad example and they'd be better off without me. 'Fine by me,' I thought defiantly, behind the tears. But I was afraid of being expelled. My father, I thought, would go crazy. I had run away to see my sister during the scout trip in Spain. I'd been caught telling dirty jokes on summer camp.

They'd gone crazy, they went crazy every Sunday at Dress Parade. In the end the Scouts were just another establishment I couldn't co-operate with. I never got to be a patrol leader because I wanted to do things my own way, so I came into conflict with their system. They only saw a scruffy uniform. Christ, I even looked like I couldn't be trusted. But they never threw me out; they forced me out.

I really wanted to go to the Scouts' world jamboree in Seattle. America, wow. To be eligible you had to be a first class Scout. I did my tests and finally passed them all. I begged my father to pay for it. It was expensive, but every week he paid a little bit and finally he paid it all. I got out the *National Geographic* atlas at home and looked up Seattle. I read about it and I lived for it. Three weeks before we were to go the scout master, a small man, puffed with self-importance and faintly ridiculous with his exposed, hairy legs, thick glasses, and pigeon chest, called me over.

'Geldof, you have to have passed all your tests to go to Seattle, you know.'

'Yes I know, I've passed them all.'

'Who passed you?'

'Different officers', I said, and named some.

'Right, let's check them then,' he said, seizing a pair of semaphore flags. We went outside where he re-examined me on every one of the thirteen tests. I forgot some things. 'I don't think you've passed at all, Geldof. I think you've failed. In fact, I know you have. You won't be coming to Seattle with us.'

I left the Scouts. Every Sunday morning for about five weeks afterwards I dressed in my uniform and went for a walk somewhere, returning at lunchtime pretending I'd been at Scouts. Eventually I told my father. To my surprise, he understood and was sympathetic.

★　★　★

At fourteen nothing interested me. Occasionally I'd not go to school and visit a biscuit or beer factory to pass the time. On the pretence of being on some class project I would collect my free box of biscuits in the former and get drunk in the latter. Sometimes I'd watch the gang wars in the bowling alley near school: Mods wearing chic clothes with sharpened, finely-honed umbrellas fencing and jabbing another group from the aptly named Donnybrook area who attempted to crush the bowling balls down on their opponents' heads. I thought the bowling alley was clean and very American. I drank Coke there, though I hated it.

In the long holidays I'd wake late and masturbate, finally rising at about 1 or 2 p.m., exhausted. I liked clothes, I liked the Rolling Stones, The Who and the Small Faces. I wore shirts that came in a curious coffin-shaped box: they had different coloured collars with a tab button. I wore denim shirts with a false polo neck beneath the open shirt collar. The polo neck ended in a flap either side of your neck below the shirt's opened first button. I had a pair of flared hipsters with a huge check pattern, and a brown plastic belt with an enormous gold-coloured tin buckle. The trouser material was cheap and after the first day the knees stretched and bagged. I wore zoot shoes, square toed. For school I had a knitted navy blue wool tie like the Beatles wore. Later I had a Parka with The Who written on it. I wore ex-army, navy and police. I had badges from Carnaby Street, I thought I was hip.

I got dressed and read for a bit. All I liked doing was reading. I read anything. I'd masturbate again. If I didn't have any money, I'd steal some out of the electricity meters in the bedsits that now honeycombed the house. Before, I had sold jam jars to the grocery stores for a halfpenny each or returned old lemonade bottles to get the deposit back. I was too old for that now. One summer I went to the pictures every day for three months. I'd ring Foley; 803747.

'Foley?'

'Yeah.'

'What are you doing?'

'Um, don't know.'

'Anything happening?'

'Don't think so. What are you doing?'

'I don't know.'

'Yeah, OK, I'll see you. Ring me later.'

'Right, OK, see ya.'

Sometimes I'd hang out at the local record store and listen to whatever was new. Maybe at night there'd be a barbecue at White Rock. We'd climb down the steep steps cut into the rock face, light a fire and drink Cidona. It wasn't alcoholic, but we pretended it was cider and we ended up drunk anyway. People would play guitars, they'd play blues and they were good, but I didn't like it. It was as pointless as anything else. You couldn't pull girls there and you only pretended to be pissed. On Saturdays you'd get drunk quickly on barley wine and Pernod. Then you'd get sick, then you'd drive around and get a hamburger and greasy chips and that would swill around your stomach with the Pernod, the barley wine, the Guinness and the cigarette smoke and then you'd get sick again. Then you'd go home to bed, but you weren't tired and the room began to swim and you'd masturbate again and you'd get sick again. I spent all the time waiting, I was waiting for something. Anything.

At night I would lie in the room at the top of the house, with my father snoring in his bed by the other wall. The lights were out for fear of waking him. I wasn't tired. I masturbated, I lay there, eyes open, looking at the white ceiling, listening to the boom and moan of the lighthouse foghorns up and down the coast, getting nearer. Two more to go, I thought. There goes Bray Head and, closer still, Dalkey Island, and then the familiar dull explosion of the Kish light way out beyond the bay. Then suddenly, there'd be a blinding burst of light followed by two more in fast succession speeding across the bedroom ceiling and then they'd be gone. The lonely moans continued on up around the fog-bound coast until the sequence began again seconds later. Sometimes it went on all night.

The foghorns, too, seemed part of my imprisonment: searchlights on the prison walls. The sound of lighthouses was to me what the sound of train whistles was to all those American songwriters: the unbearable wailing in the night that represented places faraway and escape from their own circumstances. For me the foghorns simply confirmed my predicament.

All night the lights came and went with maddening irregularity. They lit up the political posters dotted around my side of the room. For a split second I would see the lurid atomic cloud with the word NO stamped on it. I imagined that's what the bomb would probably be like: a split second of light, enough time to gasp NO and then oblivion. I almost welcomed the idea, I had been reading Sartre. There were anti-apartheid posters, one smeared with blood from when I had been battered by an over-zealous uniform at some rally against the South African rugby team and had wiped my head with the poster. I hung it up like a battle honour. I was a political romantic and quite silly.

Sometimes the foghorns woke the dachshunds in the house next door and they would begin barking, joining in the chaos of the night. I would fall asleep around four. If my father was at home, he would wake early and tell me to get up. I'd pretend not to hear, and he would begin his morning ritual of clearing his throat and spitting in the basin. I gritted my teeth. Then would begin the scraping of razor against bristle and the hawking in between. Sometimes I wanted to scream. One day, the fog still down, the foghorn blowing and the dachshunds barking, my father paused mid-shave and picked up the airgun I kept beneath my bed.

'Clear out the filth under your bed this morning, Robert, it's a bloody mess.' He put a pellet in the gun, leant out the window, took aim at a dog and shot. 'Feck it,' he muttered, 'feckin fog's too thick.' Later on I tried. There was a quick whine and a respite for five minutes before the barking resumed.

My father wanted me to help him with chores. I had to clean out the yard: a mess of discarded junk and rain-soaked moss. I had to help with painting. My father was irritated by my reluctance. 'That's not how to do it,' he'd bark in agitation, grabbing the paintbrush. 'Like this – up, sideways, down, sideways.'

'Who fucking cares?' I thought. 'Any cunt can paint. Once it's on, it's on.'

'Look, if you don't want to help, bugger off,' he'd say.

But I couldn't, because then he'd be in a worse mood for the remainder of the weekend and I felt sorry for his loneliness, though by my churlishness, I was probably making it worse. All afternoon in the tool shed, he'd say, 'Pass me the screwdriver. Pass me the hammer. Hold that piece of wood.' Numb with indifference I watched another wasted afternoon grow dark. As he sawed and hammered, planed and painted something or another, he'd say, 'That was a good afternoon's work, Rob, eh? You're a great help.' The afternoon would be another failed attempt at the two of us being together.

The simple fact was I didn't want to be with him, I wanted to be with my friends. There's nothing more embarrassing than parental attempts to understand their offspring. The generation gap should be enshrined and enforced by legal statute. There is no point in a 40-year-old trying to come to terms with someone who is fifteen. There is a quarter of a century between them. Can a 25-year-old understand a 5-year-old? Why should they even attempt to?

One of the more embarrassing moments of my life, still blindingly clear, to me was one of my father's and his friends' attempts to 'join in'. My sister, Lynn, had a new pink Twist dress. It was long and tight and had the customary lace flare below the knee. Lynn was a tall, gangly teenager who got embarrassed easily. My father's friends were in the sitting room when Lynn was summoned and they asked her how she was doing.

'Oh, it's all the twist now, of course,' said my father knowledgeably.

'Is that right? How in God's name can you manage it? It looks bloody awful,' said one of them.

'How does it go?' said another.

'Go on then, show us,' said my father.

'I don't really want to,' Lynn said.

'Go on, put on your dress and stop being so bloody stupid,' he said.

Lynn appeared ten minutes later and stood hesitantly by the window in her new frock. There was no music, but she softly hummed a Chubby Checker song to herself and began to twist. Everyone clapped, she was bright red.

'Show us again, how does it go?' my father said, and joined in in a grotesque shamble of arms and legs.

Lynn had a small fixed smile on her face as she danced in the bay window on that Sunday afternoon. Let's twist again like we did last year. I died for her.

Lynn had disapproved of the Beatles. She was a Cliff Richard fanatic. Cliff and the Shadows covered the entire room she had shared with Cleo. Every concert was attended, every record bought, every picture cherished. In the kitchen her job was to wash up, mine to dry. We would sing duets during the entire process to pass the time. The Beatles destroyed Cliff and they would never be forgiven. I only learnt to love the Beatles when I was seventeen and only came to be in awe of them when I could play music. But first the Rolling Stones burst into my life. Jagger fascinated me. Suddenly my big mouth was acceptable. Suddenly my scruffiness became something to be emulated rather than sneered at. The Rolling Stones looked and sounded like they were saying 'fuck you' to everything. They were my boys.

'They're so ugly,' my father said. I loved their beautiful ugliness. 'They can't sing; at least the Beatles can sing.' I loved Jagger smearing words like soft

43

butter across my brain. 'They're so bloody dirty, look at the state of them. At least the Beatles are clean.' FUCK OFF. 'What a bloody racket!'

That racket was the first thing I'd ever heard that felt like someone knew what *it* felt like. They were indecipherable to parents, there was no mutual point of contact, but my father made the mistake of trying to appreciate the music. Appreciate! The whole point was that he couldn't ever, not even if he tried. Parents should never try to understand. I wanted something of my own. Something *so* totally *mine*, and incomprehensible to the older people, they could never take it from me, because they didn't know what it was. They only knew that it irritated them, but they weren't sure why. It wasn't just the music, it was because they couldn't get to me. When I listened to it, I was lost to them. Like Elvis said, 'Let's get real gone, fellers.' I went.

In school my hair hung down in an unruly fringe. I tried to grow it long, but was forced to have it cut. I tried everything, parting it neatly before class, brushing back my sidelocks which hung down in lank streaks of hair behind my ears, so that after school I could pull it forward; in a pathetic gesture to show we had some control over our own lives. But the ruse usually failed. A biro would be inserted behind the ear and the hair flicked forward. 'Get it cut, Geldof. Go home and don't return until it *is* cut.'

I was sent home for a hair cut so often, the barber eventually told me he'd cut it for nothing if I cut the old men's hair on Wednesday afternoons. I agreed.

I began wearing my tie like the Kinks did. The knot would never be pulled tight, but hung over the fold like a cravat, obscuring it. This too was forbidden. 'Wear a proper tie, Geldof.'

To irritate them I would buy remnants of material from the local draper's and run up a new lurid tie each evening. I would sport a different one every single day of the week. They went berserk. I found them preposterous. At one point, there was a hair-cut committee, composed of adult lay-teachers who sat in judgement of a boy's hair style.

Later, when the role models changed to Pete Townshend of The Who and Steve Marriott of the Small Faces, myself and Foley would steal lime green Dippity-Do styling gel from Woolworth's to straighten our wavy hair and make our own partings and side locks perfectly flat, straight and even, in imitation of our idols. The result was grotesque. We would plaster the gel on our hair at my place on a Saturday evening. It would dry quickly, gluing the hair at the front and the side of our heads in place. Throughout the evening the gel gradually flaked off in scabs onto our shirts and shoulders. When we arrived under the new ultra-violet lights of the dance hall, it would glow like terminal dandruff on the shoulders of our remodelled ex-police greatcoats.

Reading continued to be my passion. Our history teacher was prepared to talk to me about Camus, Sartre, Kafka and the others I was reading. I was brain-flexing. I found them difficult, but exciting. I felt like an upturned cockroach myself most of the time. I gave him a book called *Macbird*, a political satire of Lyndon Johnson and the Vietnam War.

I'd become involved earlier with protest politics. Foley and I had begun the ponderously named 'South Dublin Youth Campaign for Nuclear Disarmament'. He was chairman and I was secretary. We wrote to CND headquarters in Gray's Inn Road in London and received the badges and *Sanity*, the movement's newspaper. We were too lazy to actively campaign, but we became a sort of conduit for those people who wished to obtain badges and the other ephemera still considered fashionable. I was convinced then in the clear, dogmatic view of the passionate, that the cause was just and that this was the right way to fight for it. I believe now that disarmament is desirable, but nuclear weapons cannot be disinvented and at a moment's notice, such as the outbreak of war, they will be produced again instantly.

I believe disarmament impractical, like peace. We have never had peace since mankind appeared on this planet. I am prepared to accept that there is some deep liking for combat and war within us which ideally should be eliminated, but will not be. I believe we are impelled towards conflict, although peace is the ideal we should constantly strive for. It is the great failing and at the same time the greatest attribute of humanity that we constantly reach for things that exceed our grasp. Peace isn't possible, but we should never stop trying for it.

I believed at fourteen exactly what I believe now about apartheid: that it is a system so evil it putrefies the morality of the world. I could not accept, then or now, that any man is less because of accent, colour, religion or class. Curiously, when I was first confronted by racism in England, I was not in the least offended. 'No dogs, no Irish,' said the bedsit sign. Fine. It didn't even depress me. But I didn't have to live with the constant grind of it.

Certainly I dislike whole countries for their national characteristics. I dislike certain religions for being reactionary and preposterous, but I feel in no way superior because I am not burdened with that specific characteristic and don't share that belief. To use that assumption of superiority as an instrument of suppression and a denial of a person's rights, a much misused word, is a consummate evil. Those who perpetrate it, like in South Africa, deny their own intelligence and act purely on an instinctive and emotional level. We have a word for that behaviour, 'animal'.

The summer was over. The long nightmare of school and winter and inactivity loomed. The things I was interested in were passive – reading, listening to music, talking politics – and yet I wanted to be active. I wanted to play music not listen to it, to be involved in politics not talk about it. I wanted to write. In a notebook of that year, I either wrote or copied: *A million things to say, some extraordinary, welled up inside him. Daily they died.*

CHAPTER V

Acting the Maggot

My father's obsession with qualifications continued to grip, and he could see, now that the summer exam results were in, that my progress at school was continuing downhill.

One Friday evening, he returned late from the country. 'Robert, I've been to see the president of the college. From next term you will become a boarder. Perhaps that will remove you from some of the distractions which seem to prevent you from working while I'm away. Next year you have your intermediate exams and two years after that your Leaving Cert. Father O'Driscoll said that this would be the best for you.' My father was emphatic.

The corridors of Blackrock, oppressive to me as a day boy, were positively claustrophobic as a boarder. I noticed then, for the first time, just how cold the place was. The cold began in the dormitory, a long spartan room with metal pillars, high ceilings and eight-foot-tall windows which were always kept open. At first light the prefect, who slept in a little panelled room partitioned from the rest of the dorm, would walk between the rows of beds clapping his hands and shouting for the twenty-six boys to rise. Then under the life-size crucifix hung on one wall which dominated the room he would say morning prayers as the inmates stood by their beds in shivering oblation. Then there was a rush to the washroom where at a huge marble trough more than twenty feet long we would splash ourselves with icy water from its twenty-five taps. It was a perfunctory operation which was more than could be said of the weekly shower, for which we would have to troop down to the games block. We were required to shower in our shorts to preserve us from the impure sight of an alien scrotum. It was so cold there that we would take the blankets from our beds to wrap ourselves in after we were dried and dressed. On the way to morning mass I would sometimes see fog creeping up the main corridor outside the chapel, obscuring the stained glass window at the end of the corridor. For the rest of the school day, in which we were joined for lessons by the day boys, you would never really warm through.

After the day boys had gone at 4 p.m. there would be a break and then an afternoon tea of bread and butter and tinned fruit. The bread was ancient, its ends curled up from where it had been dipped in water to soften and the tea sometimes had a golden scum floating on the top of it because the serving youths, whom we called 'skivs', would occasionally put an old dishcloth in the teapot as a form of revenge.

46

A boarding school is designed to distort its pupils' perspective. There are no outside concerns or demands to dilute the intensity of the school experience so everything which happens in it assumes an exaggerated importance. At tea there would be fierce fights over who would get the extra peach from the can.

Though I still saw all my old day boy friends like Foley and Cully I found that, increasingly, I had less in common with them. Their interests were focused entirely outside Blackrock and I could no longer go with them down to Murray's, to Stella House or simply round to their homes to drink tea and watch TV. But I also carried with me a residual antipathy to the boarder's claustral world with its bathroom gropings and dormitory faggotry. I began to feel as if I belonged in neither world. If I looked out of the window I could see my home. It was only a few minutes away. But there was no respite in my monthly visits home. I felt like a stranger there too.

At school the ideology of the church became more dominant too. Every day there was mass before breakfast in the school chapel, its gaudy baroque splendour made sinister by the misty morning half-light. To me it had always been an empty ritual, lacking even the theatre of Benediction, with its rich sensual scent of incense and its dark magical music. Besides, Benediction only lasted ten minutes. Mass bored me. I wasn't sure what I believed, but it wasn't this. I had nothing against religion, in fact I like to see people praying. I felt about the mass like the men who you can see attend every Irish Church every Sunday. They hover about the entrance and stub out their cigarettes before the consecration, then they hitch up their trousers and drop to one knee in reverential habit. Then the 'stabber' is re-ignited and the dash to the pub begins.

I actively disliked the church and its institutionalized morality, which I felt bedevilled Ireland. The bishops were the doddering old creeps who imposed it and the priests the ones who implemented it. They were not the same as the men I met later in Africa and elsewhere who were giants in comparison: great, pragmatic men driven by a sense of responsibility towards others. I felt humbled by them; they had given up everything and saw God in the suffering of others. This is something I cannot see. I see there a negation of God.

It is one of those unctuous Irish Catholic assumptions that 'pain is cleansing'. It is probably the reason they resorted to so much pain as punishment at Blackrock.

'Why did the Church use a fish as a symbol, Father?'

'Because Peter was a fisherman.'

'What sort of fish is it?'

'What do you mean?'

'Is it cod or mullet or gurnet, or what?'

'Sit down, Geldof.'

'Father, is God in everything or *is* he everything?'

'That's a good question, Geldof.'
'Thank you, Father.'
'God is *in* everything, because he *is* everything.'
'So, um, God is an ant.'
'No, God is all ants.'
'Then you could have an ant as a symbol, Father.'
'That's enough, Geldof.'
'If God is in everything, Father, then I'm God.'
'Yes, God is even in you, Geldof,' he said wearily.
'But you said he's *in* me, Father, because he *is* me. So I must be God.'
'That's blasphemy, Geldof. Perhaps God passed you by,' he smirked.
'Surely *that's* blasphemy, Father.'
'Right, Geldof, get out.'

Pain is cleansing – I got beaten. The priests could also be tormented by the Church's less than fabulous political history. The Spanish bishops' support of the fascist state was always a good one to get them floundering. So, too, was their hesitant denunciation of violence in the North, less than a hundred miles away. I also felt them responsible for many of the horrendous social evils of our country. They were insular, self-protective, powerful, omnipresent and faceless. They were almost my natural enemies. But as I, to use a very apt expression in this case, kicked against the pricks, I could not shirk off my fifteen years of training. Intellectually I resisted, but though logic stripped away the cant and ceremony I still could not rid myself of the voodoo.

Guilt is the heritage of all Catholics. You are never without it. It is one of the more disgusting notions of the Catholic Church, that you are born in sin. Even to use it as a symbol is a perversion of something so entirely unblemished, so utterly innocent as a new-born infant. But from the day of birth on, one castigates oneself for being 'sinful' or 'bad'. Psychologically, the Church seeks to own you from the day you are born; it becomes the sole means of your redemption and if you reject it, well, fine, there's always screaming agony for eternity. It is a system of control and, of course, I hated it.

But the voodoo still worked its magic. My guilt was about masturbation, which I felt had become an addiction that would eventually consume me. It had gone beyond a self-indulgence, like the occasional enjoyment of a sweetmeat. It had gone beyond a comfort, a way of putting myself to sleep at night. It had gone beyond a habit done without thinking like the smoking of a cigarette. My fantasies had become lurid and extreme: the vivid montage of naked, pouting, inviting women which sped through my imagination had been overtaken by fantasies of increasingly complex perversity.

There was little succour in the confessional. 'Bless me, Father, for I have sinned. It is one week since my last confession and these are my sins: telling lies, Father, I was disobedient, I said some bad words, I had some bad thoughts.'

Wearing one of my self-made ties in lurid pinks, greens and yellows.

Foley.

But the priest would see through the cloak. 'And did you follow these thoughts, my son?'

'Sometimes.'

'Did you abuse your body?'

'Sometimes.'

'How many times?'

'Twice.' *Tell him about the leather.*

'. . . temple of the Holy Ghost . . .'

'Twice a day.' *Tell him about the orgies.*

'. . . doing to your health . . .'

I wrote in my notebook, in an almost indecipherable scrawl punched with holes from my pen, 'The devil is chasing me, forcing me to think these things. Please god, stop him. I cannot help it. I'm very frightened.'

The tension between reason, emotion and guilt, was magnified in the school's cloistered atmosphere, which was doing nothing for my academic work. I didn't study, I had no concern with passing exams. Torpor filled my days. I would gladly seize on anything which broke the monotony and which got me out of study. The Debating Society was one activity which did that, though I was not a great success there: when I spoke against the American involvement in Vietnam I lost by 142 votes to one. The other great artifice was getting involved in the school operettas. Not that I liked Gilbert and

49

Sullivan, but they got you off more academic work than anything else did. I played the female lead in *The Pirates of Penzance*, or something. My voice had already broken so I must have been an unconvincing soubrette. I was also the lead in the chorus in a Black and White Minstrel Show.

But it was not long before I was resorting to more illicit methods of relieving the boredom. Some were provocative, like refusing to wear a blazer during school debates. Others were strictly practical, like reading my own books instead of the prescribed ones during study periods. You could be beaten if you were caught, especially with something subversive like Chairman Mao's *Little Red Book*, which I would ostentatiously read during Religious Instruction. 'It makes a change from your little green one,' I would say, alluding to the Catechism, a question and answers textbook on simple Catholic theology.

On half-days, like Wednesday afternoons when everybody else was playing rugby, boredom would reach a peak. I couldn't even go to my own dormitory to lie on my own bed and read a book, because on Wednesdays even the dormitories were out of bounds and were locked. So for want of something better to do, I would borrow Justin Fawcett's guitar and sneak off to the stage in the school hall. Fawcett didn't mind lending me his guitar, but he wouldn't let me change the strings around to suit my left-handed style. I had to learn to play upside-down, which I still do. I learnt by making up chords. I found the chord of A and then I simply played that where the D and E shapes are meant to be. It sounded like The Who; I was amazed. I learnt to play all of their singles.

The school hall was out of bounds. It was there the honours lists and black lists were read out every week and here they held the school operettas. It also doubled as a gymnasium and a cinema where we would sit in the cold, wrapped in blankets, some boys fumbling one another underneath them while the projector broke down every half hour. Alone, while the others ran up and down the playing fields, I sat side-stage and played the guitar. Once I got carried away and was standing on the stage in front of the curtain, pretending I was Pete Townshend, jumping around and singing very loudly to the empty hall. I was on my knees, playing to an imaginary devotee in the front row, when a voice said, 'What in God's name do you think you're up to, Geldof? See me in my room at 6 o'clock.' I got beaten.

In the end, I began to play truant on Wednesdays. The problem was where to go. The Bamboo Coffee Bar where I would go and drink hot Fanta lemons on rainy afternoons was out of the question. The school barber, who came in twice a week and to whom I was constantly being sent, with ballpoint marks on my cheek and neck to indicate the length my hair should be adjusted to, had shorn my hair to the point where it would have been a serious embarrassment in front of the girls in the coffee bar.

Often I would just go for walks by the sea. Once I was caught. I had been with Quintin Hogan, who like me had been a day boy and was now a boarder.

The Debating Society, 1967.

Black and White Minstrels at Blackrock College. Note Fred Astaire at extreme right.

He, too, lived quite near the school. Usually he played rugby, but a couple of times we had been down to the bookmakers to bet on the horses and then gone back to his house to watch the races on television. We were hauled up to the study of the Dean of Boarders, Father O'Boyle. We had developed a very combative relationship: he thought I was a cheeky bastard and I thought he was a stupid cunt. At the end of the disciplinary lecture, he said something which astonished me even then. 'All right, you may go, Hogan. Though you are in the wrong on this occasion, you are a boy who contributes something to the life of the school. But you, Mr Geldof, contribute nothing and you will be caned.'

Hogan became a doctor and then one day, a few years ago, he booked himself into a room in a Dun Laoghaire hotel and killed himself.

It was shortly after that beating that I was caned for the last time. I had been thrown out of Spanish class, which was not difficult to organize. The Spanish teacher, who was small and fat, was fond of telling his pupils of his holiday in Seville where the oranges had been, in his unfortunate and memorable phrase, as big as footballs. The ludicrous nature of the simile had often been brought home to him. The minute he came through the door we stood.

'Sit down, boys.'

'Sir?'

'Geldof?'

'Sir, how big were the oranges . . .'

'Right, Geldof. Out.'

Rooney giggled.

'All right, Rooney. You get out, too.'

We wandered up and down the corridor looking at the photographs of previous generations of Blackrock students. One group dated forty years earlier included a small fat boy with protruding ears. In the caption beneath I discovered the name of the present Dean.

'Christ, Rooney, have a look at this,' I said, and burst into a raucous laugh. Rooney was surprisingly unamused. 'Look at the fucking lugs on it!'

Rooney looked uncomfortably into the near distance behind my shoulder. I turned to see the Dean standing behind me, cane, as always, in hand.

'I am going to treat you like a dog, Mr Geldof. Bend over.'

He hit me twice. As he lifted his arm for the third blow a realization struck me with sudden clarity. I did not have to put up with this. I stood up, faced him and said: 'That is the last time you will ever hit me.' I walked off down the hall.

'Geldof. Come back', he shouted.

I took no notice. I thought I would be expelled, but I wasn't and I was only half glad.

★　★　★

52

The beatings, and the rest of it, were becoming intolerable, but I avoided being publicly or overtly glum. The despair and panic were kept strictly for the notebooks, splashed over random pages and then tucked away. They always began, 'Maybe if I write this down it will help.' To everyone else I was always 'acting the maggot', i.e. acting the fool. 'They're laughing at you, Geldof, not with you,' I was told constantly. I was loud, gregarious and always arguing. But they misunderstood. I wanted to distract myself – not them.

The holidays came as a blessed relief. My hair grew longer and soon I went down to Murray's Record Centre, where Foley and I had hung out before I was a boarder. Murray's sold all types of music, but the strength of the section dealing with grass roots American blues revealed the particular taste of owners, Jimmy and John Murray.

Some older guitar players and blues aficionados and us would spend afternoons in there listening to the music. The Murray brothers never seemed to mind, though when the crowd in the shop grew so big that it was bad for business they converted their basement into a small coffee bar. It was wonderful – a sort of shrine to the new times, and it did its best to pretend that it could have been found in any of the great centres of the new culture: Hamburg, Liverpool or London. The walls and ceiling were painted black and a large mirror flickered the reflection of the pink and green lights from the centrepiece of the whole place, the jukebox. The furniture was sparse with seats around the walls, and a few tables and game machines. In the corner a small bar sold coffee, sweets and soft drinks. It was more of a club than a coffee bar and the place became the new focus of my life.

Foley and I would go there afternoons to join the handful of Murray stalwarts who gathered to listen to music, talk, and smoke. The girls were there from the Dominican Convent in Dun Laoghaire and the schools in Monkstown. Cigarettes were an essential prop, it was impossible to look stylish without them. I'd begun smoking, but I'd originally stuck to menthol cigarettes, Solent. In a place like Murray's or afterwards in the Bamboo Coffee Bar opposite, where the windows were always misty with the condensation of conversation, menthol was decidedly uncool, so I got into Black Russians – I loved the smell of them. Or Gitanes, but they were expensive and they also aggravated my asthma.

There was an élite who ran the place. I knew one of them, he was a year or two ahead of me in school. He studied music as an additional course. He was addicted to some cough medicine and would spend the mornings on a bus, going from chemist to chemist buying two bottles at each, drinking them and arriving at school late. Sometimes I'd see him in the toilets knocking it back.

The others were a mixture of blues buffs and players who tolerated Foley's and my insistent questions and used us as a willing audience. Foley and I bought harmonicas and practised endlessly getting that 'waah waah' sound just right. I listened for hours to Sonny Terry's harmonica imitations of train whistles. I wanted to sound like a fog horn. The talk was of people whose very names said something: Muddy Waters, Howlin' Wolf, Blind Lemon Jefferson, Mississippi John Hurt, Son House, and Robert Johnson. It was not long before indigenous acoustic blues became a point of snobbery with us. If a singer wasn't black and at least ninety, you could forget it. We joined the pompously named 'Irish Blues Appreciation Society', a duffle-coated organization which met in Slattery's Bar in Dublin to swap records and listen to guest singers.

Foley and I had done bad Sonny Terry and Brownie McGhee impersonations into my cousin's tape recorder one day, me playing my atrocious guitar and him playing his appalling harmonica. My guitar-playing never improved, but, my harmonica-playing got better; it was the first instrument I really mastered. I played with Champion Jack Dupree and then with Mississippi Fred MacDowell when they came over to do gigs at Slattery's. I was not up to much, but I enjoyed it. For the first time I understood that music could provide something more than enjoyment, it could offer something much more satisfying.

One afternoon I sat and watched a Murray's regular playing. He played a Mississippi John Hurt folk blues style and he was very good. He was older than me and affected a Cliff Richard type of English accent. I was the only one watching and in the middle of some number he stopped playing and turned to me and said, 'Have you ever seen any dope, Geldof?'

'No,' I said.

He unwrapped a tiny piece of silver paper and showed me the small brown sticky square of hashish.

'Is that it?' I said.

'What do you mean, is that it? It's not the size that counts, you know.'

'Well, how much was that?' I asked.

'Three quid.'

'Three quid! For that! What a rip-off.'

He snorted in disgust and rapidly put it away. Some weeks later we bought some hashish for ten shillings and went back to my place.

I ate mine, Foley smoked his.

'Do you feel anything?'

'Yeah, I think so.'

'Are you sure?'

'Well, yeah, I think so.'

'I don't think I do.'

'Yeah I know, I don't think I do either, really.'

During the week Foley and I would steal exotic foods from the local supermarkets. We stole some Yalacta, Bulgarian natural yoghurt. It was the first time I'd ever seen yoghurt. We took jars of mussels, cottage cheese, things like that. We went back to my place and ate them, but on Saturdays my sister Lynn would make tea. Foley and Pat Moylett or Brian Devon would be there too. We'd make tea with marijuana or hash. Then we'd go to the pub and then to a party or a dance. Sometimes my father would be back early from sailing. We had to be careful he got the right cup. He'd be chatting to us and we'd be doing our best to maintain our demeanour and make sense. He must have thought we were very happy young people.

Soon there seemed to be quite a lot of dope around. Sometimes we'd buy some for ten shillings, keep half and sell the other half for the amount we paid for the whole lot. But we preferred being drunk and we couldn't afford both. Some years later, I got some LSD and went up the top of Killiney Hill where the old Victorian monument is. They sometimes have black masses up there and it's a bit strange, but it was a lovely summer's day and I looked down over Killiney and Dublin bays. It was my first acid trip; it was nice.

Murray's wasn't a nest of dope fiends, however. It was just part of the scene, like the jukebox, the pinball, the steaming coffee machine, and the music and talk. I talked a lot. Foley says my house wasn't like other people's. There was more freedom, you could do things there you couldn't in your own, because of your parents. But when my dad was there, he says, you couldn't talk for all the shouting. My father would provoke this, not for the conversation value or because of deeply-held political convictions, but simply to tease and irritate.

'Bloody South Africa. They should lock all the niggers up, put an end to it.' Uproar. 'Drop the bloody bomb on the Russians now I say.' Uproar. 'Long haired layabouts, should be forced to bathe.' He didn't actually believe this, but we didn't know because he would argue so vehemently for the point of view he'd adopted. One evening I remember crying out of sheer frustration and rage because I couldn't articulate what I wanted to say. Everyone was very passionate. Most of that time my father was opposed to the things I held true and argued for. Most of the time we all spoke at once. But I was getting tired of sterile argument and protest politics. I wanted to understand more and get involved.

I began going to the Simon Community, a group of people who looked after the drunks and homeless in Dublin. They had a room on the Quays and I would go there and help them prepare the soup for the night. We would fill flasks and collect fresh bread from several bakeries who liked to help. I got to know several of the people who were suffering what seemed to me intolerable privations, unnecessary in a wealthy society. Mary was a woman of indeterminate age, but easily in her late fifties. She was a tattered and kind woman. She wore a torn knitted woolly hat, a couple of dresses, woollen socks and a dirty beige raincoat. She lived in a doorway. I talked to Mary for a long time every night. I would sit on the doorstep while she huddled up inside the porch. I found it repellent that the owner of the house could step over this woman every night and shut the door. 'Ah, he's a lovely man,' said Mary, 'lovely.' I couldn't stomach it, full as I was then of juvenile Marxist rhetoric and passion. But he *wasn't* bad. As the others pointed out, he let her live there, at least. I hadn't asked her back to my house to live. Who the hell was I to judge?

'How are things tonight, Mary?' I'd ask, as she wrapped a newspaper and a cardboard box around herself. 'Ah, could be worse, you know.' No. I didn't know. How could things possibly be worse? I brought her a blanket one day and she put it over the paper and boxes. She wasn't ashamed to take the soup but in the depths of winter I was ashamed to leave her there in the freezing tiled porch with the lights on inside the house.

There was a big fire in Smithfield where we made soup. The winos would come and they'd sing but it wasn't romantic or friendly. It just seemed we shouldn't have to do this. But even if the Government took responsibility it wouldn't negate our own. Old people still die of cold every winter in houses beside us. Children still get abused. People still go hungry. It must be our responsibility. We can't simply blame governments. These are our own neighbours. We must rediscover a sense of individual responsibility for each other. That's why I liked the Simons. They never tried to preach, lecture, or rehabilitate. They simply did what they could to help, unconditionally.

One night in the room on the Quays I was talking to some hookers who had come in out of the street. We were making the soup on the stove and they had a bottle of orange squash. They were very ugly, young and sickly. Suddenly they became very frightened when they heard some voices on the stairs.

'Shut the bleedin' door, quick,' one of them said. We did. They scrambled about looking for an exit. We were three floors above the street. 'Jesus, he'll kill us,' they screamed.

There was a pounding on the door. 'I know you're bleedin' in there and when I get in I'm going to kick your fuckin' heads in, so come out now,' said the man behind the door.

The guy in charge said, 'Whoever you are you can go away. These girls are on our property and you've no right here.'

'Open the fucking door, now!' he screamed.

The girls began screaming: 'He'll kill us, he'll kill us.'

An axe began breaking down the door. We pulled some chairs against it but there wasn't much furniture in the room. Eventually the door gave way and a very small, squat man with a greasy black haircut like Mo from the three Stooges came in. 'You's keep out of this,' he said, pointing at the four Simon people there including myself. He grabbed one of the girls by the hair. 'You got my money, I think,' he said.

'I only kept a bit of it for the orange squash, I swear.' She screamed, as he twisted her head around. The others cowered in the corner. 'It's my money,' he roared. 'I'll buy the orange squash if I want to.'

He punched her four times in the face while he held her hair, then he let her drop to the floor where he kicked her. We tried to stop him. We were shouting and the two girls with us had put their heads out the windows and were screaming for the police.

He hit one of the guys I was with. His nose was bleeding and I was scared. He then picked up a piece of wood and waved it at me. 'Stay away from me, kid,' he said, and began to hit the other girl with it. He kicked them both down the stairs and I watched him beat them and kick them up the quays beside the Liffey. I felt ashamed and inadequate and I wanted to kill the man.

All this seemed more real and important to me than anything else I'd done. I wanted to do more but school loomed. I had to find a solution. I couldn't tolerate being a boarder any longer. I couldn't return to the cloistered and petty world of school. I decided I did not want to be expelled from the school entirely. All my friends would be going into the sixth form and I could not think of anything else to do myself. What I needed was to do something that was considered sufficiently serious to get me expelled as a boarder but would allow me to continue as a day boy, where I could spend some nights each week with the Simon Community. Chairman Mao offered the solution.

The history master, in a last ditch attempt to convert my own obvious interest in an academic subject into some sort of scholastic achievement, had asked me to produce a project on the Chinese Cultural Revolution, a subject which he hoped might suit my rebellious inclinations. It had not been an enormous success but I had got a wealth of material from the government in Peking. I now wrote again, and also to the government in North Vietnam, asking for a hundred copies of Chairman Mao's *Little Red Book*. They arrived and were duly distributed to my classmates during study. It was only one of the later batches that was intercepted by the police. The Special Branch visited Blackrock one morning. I was summoned before them in the presence of the Dean.

'Let's start by saying that we take a very serious view of this,' began the Special Branch Officer.

I knew he was Special Branch because of his sheepskin coat. Oh shit, I thought, I've gone too far.

'Why are these books being sent to you from communist China?'

'I asked for them.'

'You asked for them.'

'You *asked* for them?' interrupted Father O'Boyle.

The policeman ignored him and continued. 'Do you have any connection with the Internationalists?' The Internationalists were an extreme Maoist group which was very active in Dublin at this period. It was 1968 and the year of student revolution in Europe.

'No.'

'Have you ever been to their meetings?'

'No. I don't know anything about them at all. I don't belong to anything.'

'Why have you been distributing these books in the school?'

'I thought it was interesting, that's all.'

'That's all? Listen, boy, from now on you're going to be a marked man. We'll be keeping a file on you.'

It was 8 a.m. the next morning that the Dean telephoned my father and asked him to visit the school as soon as was possible. Later my father told me that in the car on the way to Blackrock he'd decided that I had probably been stealing books from the school library. His second guess, when the Dean threw a brown paper package on the desk with the words 'Robert has been distributing this', was that the parcel must contain pornography. When he saw it was nothing more than Mao's political aphorisms in English, Vietnamese and Chinese, relief swept over him. His response surprised me.

'Is that all he's done?'

'I have to tell you that we take a most serious view of it,' said the priest, parroting the policeman.

'Father, Robert has had this book at home for over a year. He has read it, as have I, and he has formed clear views of his own about where Mao is right, where he is wrong and where the internal contradictions lie.'

The Dean was taken aback by my father's relief which now began to manifest itself as aggression. 'But he has been distributing it to others,' he said.

'Father, you have had these boys since they were eight. In two years' time they will be going out into the world. If you do not have the confidence that the education you have given them equips them to deal intelligently with views contrary to your own then that is a poor reflection on the quality of your teaching.'

The schoolmaster blustered and then fell back on his authority. 'I have to say, I'm afraid, that we think here it would be better if, from next term, Robert was no longer a boarder at the school.'

I had pulled it off. For the remaining one and a half years I was a day boy in the fifth and sixth. I spent two nights every week with the Simon Community, getting to bed at five in the morning and then going to school. I was no more distinguished academically than I had been before. In my Leaving Cert on some papers I actually did no more than take the blank sheet of foolscap, write my name at the top and then put down my pen.

CHAPTER VI

Deep In The Heart of Nowhere

When I left school, I ran out of the front gates, and didn't look back once. I embraced whatever lay ahead with trepidation, but an overwhelming feeling of release. I tried to return once for a TV show and then I could only go twenty yards inside the gate before I was filled with loathing and anxiety and retreated. But in order to remember and be accurate here, I returned recently and felt an unbelievable sadness for the ghost of the boy in the fog-filled corridors. It was not self-pity, it was more as if I had held hands with someone else, someone who lived a long time ago and who had no connection to the man who stood in the high-windowed dormitories and the fresh-painted chapel. It was hard then to accept that every moment of the past makes its contribution to the present.

I had no hopes when I left, no ambitions, no clue as to what I should do. Even if I'd got my exams, I would have refused to contemplate university. I'd had my fill of academia. Besides, students to me were pretentious wankers who wore Kenneth More-type scarves, dabbled in silly politics and joined earnest clubs. I could see no value in having a degree: it didn't seem to brighten the prospects of anyone I knew. Despite my father's insistent chanting of the benefits of a further three years in school, I was off.

Off meant England. England had given me my first sense of real liberty when I was fifteen and I had gone to Lincolnshire and worked there in a factory. We stayed in houses owned by Italian or Pakistani families who slept three or four to a room in order to make some extra money from these rowdy Irish kids who came over every summer and worked long night shifts, six days a week. The factory produced tinned peas – sweet, stinking peas in numberless profusion and they put £32 a week into our hands, which was OK money in those days. Now I was back again for the third year running. I had lied about my age originally to enable me to work nights and thus double my income. Now I was seventeen, and I had to be consistent and pretend to be twenty-one. This took a lot of sorting out later when I collected dole and the social services had me registered as four years older. It was a boring job, sorting peas on the conveyor belt. You would fall into a trance, occasionally flicking a blackened pea off the line. Chlorine stung your eyes and dried your mouth and nose. Your ears were assaulted by the constant clatter of empty cans rattling down the runners onto the hoppers, then onto loading racks to be boiled. When we got bored, we turned a can sideways on the runners and the line would stack up behind the overturned tin until it ran back and jammed the machines. We'd hang around until the fitter came to fix it.

It was mind-numbing. I had jeans with two holes on the cheeks of my arse. I was very thin, my jeans were tight, and I wore red underpants. I don't know if this was why I nearly got raped. I was threatened with a crowbar and pushed against a can feed-line behind the hoppers. I was shouting and fighting, but the noise obscured my terror. He was a big man and I was ineffectual against his swinging crowbar. He grabbed my crotch. I tried to kick him. He put the crowbar against my throat. I scratched his face and put my fingers in his nose and my thumbs in his eye. One of his mates came looking for him, called some other people and pulled him off. They began to beat the hell out of him. I got in one really good kick.

We'd buy trendy clothes at Harry Fenton's and wear them at the weekend in Peterborough. We thought we were cool. In fact, we were green. The green dye never washed off your face and hands and your hair stunk of brine, sugar, dye, mint and chlorine. We were usually drunk on scrumpy at sixpence a pint. We would lurch, puking, up the road carrying Doyle, or Cully, or myself. Once we got locked out. Doyle climbed up on the spiked metal fence and began scaling the drainpipe. Somehow he reached the top and was forcing open the window when he fell back, missing the spikes by inches. He picked himself up and we pressed the doorbell continuously. The Italian landlord yelled, 'Fuck off, Irish peegs.' We began to insult his fat son Bruno at which he opened the door, charging at us. We ran past him, shut the door and ran upstairs to the room. He never threw us out. In fact, he never mentioned it again.

I was caught in bed with a girl by her Polish parents. Her father was a flight sergeant in the RAF. He was a big man. It is a funny thing being caught – the girl is always called a slut and a whore by the mother and you can just hear as you disappear out the front door the strangled sob, 'How could you do this to us?' The father is usually speechless and slightly confused and a little embarrassed. I was a coward and it was a cliché. I grabbed my trousers and shoes and shirt as soon as the mother came into the room and screamed. The father was just behind her. It was a ground floor room with a window to the garden which was open in the summer night. I went through it. The following day, to my horror, I received an invitation to tea. Maybe they thought I was going to marry her. I went. Mother and father were very polite and not too inquisitive. No one brought up the night before and as I left her mother gave me a parcel. I opened it when I returned to my digs. Inside were my socks, underpants and jumper, freshly laundered and pressed.

This year I was surprised to get the job again. The year before, when a vast consignment of peas arrived to be canned as 'petits pois' for a famous up-market store, we had been prominent in organising a strike. The peas were in fact the same as the ones that went into the factory's ordinary cans, but it was a prestige order and who was going to tell the difference? The strike was timed for when there was a danger of the entire batch rotting and was an attempt to gain equal pay for the casual workers – us – and the permanent staff. We worked the same hours, did the same jobs, we wanted the same money. Foley rang up some papers and filed a story. We negotiated, and the peas began to rot. Within two days we'd won. It was thrilling, we were beholden to no one. I thought we were justified and therefore any risk was acceptable.

Now it was July 1969. I wasn't going back to school. Whatever money I was going to get was going to have to last a while. Still, as I stood out on the loading bay in the early hours of the morning and looked up at the moon huge in the sky, the factory quiet behind and the transistor loud on the packing cases beside me, I listened to the disembodied voice another planet away and I thought of the time ten years earlier when I'd stood open-mouthed with my family, staring wide-eyed on our steps at the sky, trying hard to find the sputnik. The intervening years had been spent in a state of panic and confusion. My mother was dead, my schooldays had finished but at least now I had some freedom. No longer would I have to go back to that house, no longer endure the ennui, the pretence, the emptiness. I had hated being a teenager, I longed to be twenty. Now life could begin. The sixties were dying and I was delighted. I listened with genuine wonderment to the awkward platitudes of the man on the moon. I considered I hadn't come very far, but then neither had mankind. Neil Armstrong was saying, 'beep, beep' up there.

★   ★   ★

It came as something of a shock when the voice on the phone said, 'I'm sorry, Geldof, you've failed'. We were ringing home for exam results. I don't know why I was surprised. Sometimes I'd just filled my name in and sat in the exam hall until I could go. I didn't even understand the French questions. But hearing it: 'You've failed,' I composed myself. Doyle had been first in the phone booth. Somehow he'd passed. All of us had been joking, saying, 'Come on, let's get it over with,' and, 'what are you going to tell your folks?' Cully, out of all of us, was the only one expected to pass. I came out. 'I fucked up.' I said it casually. Doyle was going crazy, still not believing his luck. Foley went in and stood, serious-faced, listening. Then I saw him grinning and then he banged the phone. Out of them all, I was the only one to fail the Leaving Certificate. I was shattered with humiliation, and then anger, and then betrayal. What the fuck was going on? Weren't we all in this together? Now they were talking about university all of a sudden, having to rush home and apply for entrance. What is this? Everyone said they'd never go. What am I going to do? I'll be on my own? So, what's new? All of this rushed through my head. 'Congratulations,' I said, lamely, fighting back the tears. They'd calmed down and felt embarrassed. They wanted to go off and celebrate but didn't know what to say, or whether to ask me, or what. 'I'm going to get a drink with Grealy', I said, in a rough equivalent of Captain Oates. Grealy was an old friend who now lived in America and therefore had nothing to celebrate or cry over. 'See you later.' Foley says he remembers me as being utterly crushed. He's right. They left for home immediately, the prodigal sons returning to a herd of slaughtered fatted calves. I lingered on my own in London for a bit, dreading the inevitable.

'Well, what are you going to do now?' said my father.

'I don't know.' He said nothing. 'I'm going to leave home.'

'Quite frankly, I don't care where you live, so long as you get a job.' But he did care, and I felt deeply sorry for him. Galling though it was to admit it, I knew he was profoundly disappointed in me. In an odd way, which I could not define, so was I. In an attempt to defuse the situation and as a pathetic gesture of reconciliation, I spent the last money I had on an expensive pair of binoculars for him. 'I'm sorry,' I said and handed them over. 'Thank you,' he said, and put them aside without opening the case.

For a while I worked in Murray's coffee bar in the afternoons. It was OK; I got ten bob an afternoon and I didn't have to spend money on food because I could eat the chocolate biscuits and crisps there, and drink the coffee. People gave me dope so I didn't have to spend anything on that either. In fact I'd sell most of it to supplement my income. Weekends were OK, I'd still see the lads, but now our lives began to alter. They talked about lectures and I talked of nothing. There was still music, of course. I hung out more with Pat Moylett, who wasn't in our school but used to come around with us. He was slightly older and had a car and worked. He was fun and energetic and always had a million schemes; a bit of a wide boy who wasn't great looking, but pulled some gorgeous girls. His endless optimism was the antidote to my increasing despair. Sometimes Gary Roberts, who lived down the road, would take me into Trinity College on his motorbike and we'd play snooker in the common rooms. Then I'd wander round town looking at shops and then I'd come home.

My sister got me a job in a photo-processing plant. I had half-baked ideas about being a photographer, and bought a second-hand camera. But I kept opening the doors to the dark room without thinking and ruining entire rolls of photo-sensitive paper. There were two girls there I liked. We'd sit in the dark room and smoke a joint. The pictures came out blurred with orange specks where the paper had picked up the lighted joint ends. I got made a messenger boy. I got a Honda and drove round town all day picking up rolls of film. But soon it was summer again and definitely time to go. Just the very act of leaving was important. The eternal argument inevitably began. Where are you going now? Don't know. What are you going to do? Doesn't matter. What's the point? Leaving here. What's the point when you arrive? Not being here. But you're there instead. Yes, but I'm not here; not being here is the victory, being there is irrelevant.

There was a time on the mail boat to England when I would look back at the gaping mouth of Dun Laoghaire harbour and my eyes would mist and I would wonder what happens next. Not any more. As the boat slipped away, I broke into the linen cupboard I'd discovered several trips before and made a bed for myself on the top shelf. It was comfortable and kept you out of the flow of vomit that slushed up and down the lino floors.

All of my life the mail boat had been an object of almost mystic power. It was the instrument of my release – England was irrelevant. If China had been next door to Ireland, I'd have gone there. England was convenient and, not surprisingly, they spoke English. I would sit on the east pier and watch the boats come and go. Eastward ho! One day I saw Robert Mitchum, making a film, jump into the harbour off the boat. It gave the ferry a sort of glamour. The Nazis had bombed it, it being English, so there was some excitement to it. The mail boat had to stop when the sailing boats were coming through the mouth of the harbour at the same time. My father would stand up ostentatiously in the bow of the Bonita, the boat we sailed in and shout 'Steam must make way for sail, steam must make way!' And then run right across its path. The mail boat never stopped. We would buck and wallow in its wake. 'Bastards!' my father would say. I was delighted.

That year they were working on the construction of a new motorway, the M25, an orbital road to ring London. There were plenty of jobs for Irish labourers. The people who worked on the road were a wild collection of men and for some reason they took me into their midst, like some sort of mascot. On my first stint they gave me the job of operating the makeshift traffic lights where the heavy digging equipment crossed the public highway.

It was a nice way to spend the summer, with a book, listening to Slade on Radio 1 and watching the cars go by. Most seemed to be driven by women. Fiona Richmond used to go by every day in a yellow E-type Jag with the number plate FU2. She would wave. I had read in one of the girlie magazines the accounts of her sexual odyssey around Britain. She probably waved at everybody, but I could imagine her inviting me into the car for a quick blow-job. When I saw her coming, I'd quickly change the lights to red and grin idiotically.

Because they lived a self-contained life, removed from society, the guys who worked on the roads behaved like genuine outlaws. They worked, ate and slept on the vast site. I loved it. They were great-bellied men who drank, whored and fought like comic book characters. The vehicles they drove were monstrous too: T23s with ten-foot-high tyres and a sixty-ton payload. On Saturday nights they would dress up in their best clothes, drink gallons of beer and then hurl chairs through bar room windows. They would pick up the most horrendous-looking prostitutes and take them back to the boomtown of huts and the quagmire of mud which were the sites where they lived.

'You aren't going to fuck that, are you?' I asked Dan in disbelief one night, passing his room. Dan, like the others, was from the West Country. That night he lay naked on top of his bed with a balding woman of fifty inside it. Her hair was lacquered stiff and high on her head. I could see her scalp through it. Her smudged make-up was on thick enough to measure. Her lips were sunk somewhere back inside her mouth. One breast lay exposed and stretched over the blanket – there were no sheets. 'Fuck it. You must be joking, Dublin,' he said. No one ever asked me my name, just where I was from. Dublin became my name. 'Haven't you seen her false teeth?' he added, reaching over the bed and rattling the loose dentures in the glass of water on the table. The woman giggled as he pushed her head down past his beer gut. 'It's gobble gobble time, Dublin,' he said. 'Gobble, gobble, that right, darlin'?'

Their sexual behaviour was as monstrous and funny and heroic as everything else about them. On a Saturday afternoon when heavy rain stopped the delicate work of levelling the road base, I came back to the hut to see if there was anyone who would join me at the nearby transport café. I walked along the muddy corridor between the bare rooms. I looked into one to see a naked woman, again in her fifties, lying on Alan's bed with her legs apart and a vibrator inserted inside her. Alan, fully clothed, was sitting on the bed squelching her flabby chest in his hands. 'Hello, Dublin,' he shouted with a cheery smile.

'Oh, sorry, excuse me, I'm er . . .' I backed hurriedly out of the room.

'No, hang on, Dublin,' he shouted, coming to the door to detain me. 'What was you after?'

'Er . . . nothing. I was just looking to see if anyone fancied the café, but I see you're otherwise . . .'

'That's OK, lad, just a min, I'm quite peckish, I'll come along with you.'

'No, no, it's all right. I'm OK,' I said, gesticulating back towards his bed.

'Oh, right,' he said, and turning to look over his shoulder he shouted to the recumbent figure, 'I'll be back in a minute. Stay there, dear, don't go away.'

He had double sausage, egg, beans, tomatoes, fried bread and chips and went back. When we returned, his conquest was exactly where we had left her, vibrator still buzzing soothingly, and a copy of *Men Only* raised above her head while she read.

On my second stint on the roads, I was made a ganger's assistant. That involved going ahead of the massive T23s with a yardstick estimating the amount that needed to be scraped from the road base before the surface was laid and then lining up the huge machines to perform the task.

'How many times did you wank last night, Dublin?' said Dan in his broad West Country accent.

'Six or seven, Dan.' I answered the ritual question with the ritual answer. 'You horny bastard,' came the ritual riposte.

Some of the lads building the M25, 1971. Bert, the gangerman, at left.

'Never mind that,' said Bert, the ganger, 'two inches off the top.'

Bert was in charge of all the drivers and was responsible to the foreman. For some reason he liked me and one day when a driver was fired, he shouted across from the T23 in which he sat, 'Come here, Dublin! Can you drive?' I couldn't. 'Well, you might as well learn by starting on one of these. Hop up and I'll show you.' On a road gang this was like an initiation into manhood. The machines were gargantuan. Driving one was like sitting on top of the world. On the move between sites you felt you were part of a convoy of tanks. They did about forty-five miles per hour when they got their speed up and even unloaded they must have weighed around forty ton. They were unstoppable and quite frightening. Doing the edging work on steep sliproads, they would sometimes topple over. It was because of the brute power of the T23s that ordinary cars were barred from the motorway while it was under construction. I found out why one day as I came slowly around a corner and there in the middle of the main haul road was a little Renault 4 with a local corporation site inspector sitting in the front seat. I slammed on the brakes, but there wasn't sufficient air in them. Normally on a haul road that wouldn't have mattered, you would simply have let the machine drift to a halt. I waved madly at the driver to get out of the way. In slow motion I saw the front of the little car disappear between my gigantic wheels. I heard the crunch beneath me. I was screaming at the man to get out. I was sure I had killed him. The T23 ground to a halt. The front wheel had crushed his engine flat. The car had gone under the T23 itself. I backed off and jumped down. There inside the car sat the man, trapped in his driving seat, his face the colour of cold ash. It was him that got the sack, not me. He shouldn't have been there, and the report on my vehicle showed that it was the brakes which were faulty, not my driving.

The other drivers thought the whole incident hilarious. After the accident, they would constantly get on their radios and broadcast mock warnings that all traffic should beware because Dublin was within a two-mile radius.

Teasingly, they called me the hard man, but in reality I was out of my league alongside characters like Tommo, a great hulk with a prodigious stomach who in the summer used to work naked except for his huge, filthy underpants. He would stop his T23 so that it blocked the public highway. He would then lecherously display his awful nakedness to any woman motorist forced to stop behind him. Or Stan who used to carry his shotgun in his cab and shoot at pheasants in the nearby woods and who had perfected the technique of scooping up the birds between the jaws of his machine in full sight of the lines of toffs from the local pheasant shoot. Or Dan who, when he was told that he could not take the top off his cab in hot weather, simply got a sledgehammer and bashed out all the windows. 'Oh you're a hard man, Dublin,' said Tommo. 'He is that,' said Bert. 'A hard man,' winked Dan.

There was an unmistakable warmth in the clannishness of their life. They were cowboys. However grotesque it all was, here were a group of people who had come to terms with a kind of living. But despite its humour and its rewards and the fact that I was making a lot of money, ultimately I found it brutish and boring. I didn't want to live outside the constraints of society, I wanted to live within society, ignoring the constraints that bothered me or perhaps changing them.

As the winter set in, I left the roads and headed for London. In a derelict old terraced house in Tufnell Park a group of ex-Blackrock pupils and some friends had formed a squat. It was an option and I didn't have many so I joined them. It was a depressing place that stank of rotting carpets and damp. It had once been a fine building, but the owner was allowing it to fall into severe disrepair, giving him the excuse to redevelop its prime site. The hall was dark, cracked linoleum of an uncertain age partially covered the staircase and the wind blew through the broken windows. The place was filthy. It was furnished with old beds, settees and chairs found in rubbish dumps or in the streets. The heavy smell of leaking gas lingered in the stairwell, but the toilet was clean.

I was attracted immediately to Daphne, a tall striking girl with long legs and a beautiful figure. The day I arrived at the squat she was wearing a paisley mini-skirt and long cardinal-red boots. She sat on the bed with her legs tucked up beside her. I could see her knickers and I thought her very sexy. Her boyfriend was a former classmate of mine, David Kiersey. He was the one who had told me how to masturbate and was my tormentor in the scouts. At this time he was using a lot of LSD but when I first arrived he wasn't around. A few weeks before, he had seen God in a vision when on acid and had gone off to visit a monastery. When he returned, his wide-set eyes were even more deeply sunken into his queer angular face than I remembered. He slept with

Daphne as before but he put a board in the bed between them to bar the source of diabolical temptation. He acted extremely strangely to everyone but especially to her. Daphne had been going out with him for years and his behaviour made her distracted. He would carry on with the acid in order to see God and eventually he went off and entered the monastery permanently to take preliminary vows.

Little by little, almost of necessity, given the close proximity in which we lived, Daphne and I were drawn together, she finding a focus for the emotions which Kiersey had refused to accept and I still searching for something which was missing and had always been missing from my life. We began to sleep together, which at least got me out of my original quarters, in the kitchen, but it was an odd relationship. Sometimes she would be loving and kind, other times it was as if she couldn't care less. The truth was I had fallen for her with the passion of desperation, whilst to her I was probably just a convenient body at a time when she needed a shoulder to cry on. She was on the rebound and I was lonely. We were always much more two-thirds of a threesome with another girl, called Penny, than we were a couple.

Daphne earned a fair wage typing as a temp and Penny had what we regarded as a proper job working with an organisation that cared for stray dogs. She kept one of them. It kept pissing on the floors so we washed them with disinfectant. Gas and disinfectant were the stinks of that house; gas, disinfectant and dried yellow paper sticking to the cracked lino on the kitchen floor. I was the only one who was out of work. I would stay in bed until the early afternoon, then just hang around making cups of tea, listening to the transistor, catching some mice. I had a brief spell as a photographer's assistant in Oxford Street, but it didn't last. The photographer used to wear his trousers tucked inside his boots, which marked him out as a wanker for a start. But what I really couldn't stand about him was that he expected his assistants to do all the work, while he went off, nobbed the models and then took credit for the pictures. I lost some rolls of film the photographer had shot in Greece for some big fashion spread. Not cool. I got the DCMs: Don't Come Monday. I didn't need much money; there was no rent and the girls had money for the food. I got some dole money and I had odd jobs. I began to pretend I was a photographer myself. I had bought a Pentax S18 when I was in Dublin. I wanted to go to concerts so I rang ahead saying I was coming to take photos. I got in free, I got to take pics and I got to sell the results. But I also took along a couple of empty camera cases to make me appear more professional. Daphne and Penny were my assistants; I don't suppose anyone believed them, but they smiled sweetly at the doorman which was what really counted. We got in to see the Stones at the Round House, and The Who and Rod Stewart at the Oval. I bought a little Bolex Super 8 movie camera from a pawn shop for a few quid and filmed the Stones and The Who and then took stills from a blow up. I got one good picture of Townshend. He was whirling his arm and when I blew it up from Super 8 it was so grainy it looked as though his hand was exploding through the guitar. I sold it and the picture of Jagger to Big O Posters, and got thirty quid. I still see those pictures around.

Basically I did any job that was going. Once I gave out leaflets, but the pay was bad, and so the procedure was to just pick them up in the morning, then dump them in a rubbish bin and go back to the flat to read or look for another job. In the evening I would go back and get paid and when they asked where I was when the inspector came round I would say that the police were hassling me and I had given the leaflets out elsewhere. They must have been impressed with this dedication for they made me an inspector eventually which opened the way for even greater enterprise. I went around all the people I was supposed to be inspecting and said, 'Look, I don't want to go around all day checking on you so why don't you just bin the leaflets and we can all piss off home.'

We did quite a lot of dope in Tufnell Park. It was recreational rather than vital. It was a distraction, something to do. We would go to the pictures or out for a cheap meal and then come back and do the dope, or sometimes acid. I'd no bad trips with the acid, just that quiet, floating detachment where everything is intense: colours, the feel of things, the sensations. In the end I got bored with it.

Late at night when the others, who had to get up early for work the next morning, had gone to bed, I would stay up. I tried to read, but couldn't concentrate. I wasn't tired. I would catch mice: there were mice everywhere. It was a cold winter and they'd come in from outside to nest. They were so fearless they would come out and sit on top of the television while we were watching it. It was a warm place, I suppose, but one night six mice sat up there chewing and eating things. I remembered what the gougers did. Gougers were corner boys, gurriers, yobs, hooligans, streetwise kids who used to lay trails of seeds for the pigeons outside the Pavilion Cinema in Dun Laoghaire. The seed would lead to a box which was propped up by a twig. When the pigeon was under it, they would pull the string they had fastened to it and the bird was caught. They would wring their necks and try to sell them to house-wives for pigeon pie. In the languid hours of the morning I propped an old shoe box up on its side with a biro. I threaded white cotton thread back carefully to the table where I sat beside the gas oven, lit to keep me warm. I sprinkled sugar from the TV set to underneath the shoe box and I sat there waiting perfectly still for an hour until the mice came down from the TV and began to eat their way along the trail of sugar. I sat with bated breath while one of them peered inside the box and then quickly I pulled the biro away, the box fell down and I jumped on it. I rattled the box violently from side to side until the mouse inside was stunned. Then I lifted the box, pulled out the unconscious rodent and hurled it outside the kitchen window where it fell

Deep in the heart of nowhere at the Tufnell Park squat, 1972.

four storeys down into the overgrown garden below. I stayed up till five that morning catching mice. I caught twenty-six, and at 5.30, finally overcome with a futile and dispiriting tiredness, I went to sleep.

Downstairs was a guy from Scotland. He was full of love and peace, but he was very violent when stoned and would rush around the squat hacking doors down with an axe. We would stay barricaded upstairs.

A guy I'd known in junior school came to the house one day while the girls were at work. He had just got out of prison for possession of heroin. He had nowhere to stay. I told him he could stay a week, but if he jacked himself up in the house, I'd kick him out. Heroin horrified me. It still does, and I have no sympathy for those who use it, or their whining self-pity. It disgusted me to see life negated so totally, so violently. To see the syringe fill up with blood made me want to snap it off in the user's arm and jam the needle into the vein. I wasn't afraid of him stealing anything; although junkies always steal, for there was nothing worth taking in the house. Daphne and Penny smoked Players No. 6 and I collected the coupons and kept them in an empty cornflakes box. We were saving up for an iron or a carpet sweeper. One day I went to the toilet and found blood marks on the bowl. I kicked him out. The next day he returned, while I was out, and took the No. 6 coupons and a letter from the Social Services giving me a new day to collect assistance on.

'It's funny, out of the people in that house one became a monk, another became an alcoholic and junkie, Paddy Stanley died and I became a pop singer, and the guy I've just written about is in jail.

It was only a question of time before we got busted. The police seemed somehow to become a more intrusive presence in my life. One week I got a job selling hot dogs, but it only lasted a few days. There were problems on two fronts. First there was a hot dog war on between rival operators. The opposition would send out heavies to harass you. Then there were the police. It was in the West End where the main purpose of their job appeared to me to be giving street traders a hard time. My pitch was Dean Street. It was a good spot, with a lot of tourists. French people would give you a fiver for a disgusting hot dog, saying, 'Eez enough?' and you said, 'One more, please.' You had to move on if the police came. They didn't mind you coming back after you'd shifted, just as long as you weren't there when they passed by. One night they put me in a cell overnight for causing an obstruction.

We lived in trepidation of the police arriving at the squat and they eventually came in the middle of one night. About six of the others had all chipped in and bought 300 tabs of acid which they were going to bring to the forthcoming Isle of Wight Festival. They had bought the tabs at three bob each and they were hoping to sell them for twenty-one shillings after they had taken whatever they needed for themselves. The tabs were hidden in a plastic bag up the chimney. At 2 a.m. we heard a thumping on the front door and then a banging down below stairs. I went into a blind panic. The chimney was too obvious, I thought, and seized the bag from it and stuck it outside the window behind a plant pot. Just as I closed the window they kicked in the bedroom door. There were a dozen policemen. They kept pounding up and down the stairs, but they found nothing. They weren't even looking for drugs, as it turned out. The owner of the building who wanted us out had reported that we had an air rifle and were shooting at people in the dark out of the window, so they were looking for the gun. Shortly afterwards we had a leaflet slipped under the front door saying that if we had any trouble with landlords we should telephone the Irish Community Protection Group in London. I suspected that that might mean the IRA. I didn't want to put myself in a position where they could later call in a favour. I didn't phone.

In the event the police collared us without us having to provide any provocation. There were three of them in uniform and one in plain clothes. 'We have a warrant here . . .'

'OK, fine, come in. Do you want a cup of tea?' It was morning, about ten thirty. There was nothing illegal in the place, so I was fairly relaxed.

Then I heard the voice come from the bedroom, which was now occupied by Jean, a young black girl, and Penny. Daphne and me were sleeping in the kitchen. 'Sarge, come and have a look at this.'

'What is it?'

'It's joss sticks, incense, have a look down inside the tube, and what's this at the bottom?' He shook out a minuscule amount of marijuana.

'I have to warn you that anything you say . . .' It definitely wasn't ours. The coppers had planted it, though I suppose in view of the amount of dope they thought was normally there they felt there was a rough justice involved. 'You'll have to come with us.'

They were quite amiable. When we got into the squad car, they asked me if I'd ever been in one before, and then, as if I were a child, asked whether I would like them to put the siren and lights on. We sped the short distance round the corner to the police station as if in hot pursuit. 'If you plead guilty, we'll say you were very co-operative and helped in every way possible and we'll recommend the minimum sentence on the grounds that we don't believe it will happen again. If you plead not guilty, we will tell the court that you lived in a squat, you're unemployed and that your neighbours complain regularly about your anti-social behaviour.'

The civil rights organization, Release, said that we should fight the charge, which was against all four of us, but that would have meant the whole business dragging on over Christmas, so we decided to plead guilty. The resulting scene in Clerkenwell Magistrates' Court was something of a surprise. We must have looked pretty pathetic, evidently frightened, the scruffy youth trying to look neat and three young girls lined up mumbling, 'guilty,' because when the prosecution began to give evidence the magistrate interrupted, 'Were these four young people each individually holding a corner of this 0.94 grams as you entered the room?'

'No, Sir, but the law states . . .'

'Young man, don't you ever presume to tell me the law. If it was left to me, I'd dismiss this case. As the defendants have pleaded guilty, that isn't possible. However, I am going to adjourn this case until the New Year and suggest they use the time to think about their pleas.' The policeman was receiving an unofficial reprimand from a senior colleague as we left.

That Christmas I had no money, as usual. I had been ringing home and saying I was working, London was wonderful, life was great. London actually frightened me. It was huge, it was lonely and I clung to Daphne for consolation. She was indifferent. I felt empty. My life was a meaningless jumble of no-hope jobs and days. 'I'll be a millionaire by the time I'm thirty,' I said to Daphne once. I said it with such intensity she said, 'I believe you.' I was surrounded by ugliness. There seemed to be no future of any kind. I wanted to be surrounded by beautiful things. Sometimes I thought so hard, I'd feel my head going hot as if my brain were boiling, as if I had a raging temperature, then I'd wash my face with cold water and pace around the tiny kitchen. Any other room was too cold. Sometimes tramps and drunks slept in the base-ment. They'd kick in the front door and I'd reach for my pickaxe handle, but they never came up. Sometimes the girls left me on my own and sneaked out to concerts to get away from me and my gloomy depression. Panic again. Sometimes I couldn't get up, sometimes I couldn't go to bed. We'd hear people walking around at night, but we were the only people living in the house now. Days were an appalling ritual of job-searching, looking for money to get the tube, or listlessness. One Saturday, not being able to sleep, we went to the all night horror movies in Baker Street. You got your ticket, an apple, a packet of crisps and a Mars bar for a quid. There was a movie, then a cartoon, then a movie. The cinema was full of old tramps sleeping. It was funny coming out on a fresh Sunday morning, the sky clear and the air brisk and the streets empty after the stinking smoke of the cinema. I was shabby in body and soul. Life was squalid. I could see myself in those old tramps in that cinema trying desperately to find somewhere to sleep that had a bit of warmth. When I listened to Loudon Wainwright III I would cry. Nothing was working. Rites of passages, yes, but only if the passage led to the road.

Now I had to go home for Christmas and pretend everything was fine. I was broke. I had to get presents to maintain the pretence. I pawned my camera and bought gifts from the Oxford Street traders. Six fake Chanel No. 5s for £3 for my aunts and sisters and something else for the boys. They were sure I was flush. Christmas was horrible. I was going back to a nightmare: court, and no work. What if we were found guilty of possession of 0.94 grams of marijuana? Enough just to fit onto the blunt end of a pin.

When the case came up again, we all pleaded not guilty, except for Jean, the girl in whose room it had been planted, because as she was under eighteen, there was no question of her risking the danger of acquiring a criminal record. The three of us were acquitted and we all helped to pay her fine.

In the end, it wasn't the police who put an end to my association with marijuana, it was the experience of the night I tried to kill myself.

★   ★   ★

It was a Saturday evening. Rooney had arrived and had eaten with us. We had put dope in with the spaghetti and after the meal had eaten a quarter of an ounce between us. Everyone had done something: dope or pills or acid. Rooney and I were playing draughts. All the lights had gone because no one had paid the electricity bill and the room was lit by candles. I was edgy. All at once it struck me with a flash of panic that everybody in the room was stoned on something. I shrieked without warning, 'There should be someone who's together!' Two of the girls giggled. Suddenly two big tears came rolling out of the corners of Rooney's eyes. He reached out to move a piece. He was white and I was black. Slowly he toppled over and lay on his side. A look of horror filled his face. 'Oh my god, I'm paralysed, I can't move, oh my god.' Fear washed through my stomach and surged up through my chest and my mouth. 'Don't worry, you'll be OK. Don't worry, you're OK.' The panic spread through my limbs into my head. I began to lose control of my body. 'OK, keep it together,' I heard myself say. 'Jesus, what's happening to me?' I screamed and ran down the four flights of stairs to the front door. 'OK, let's keep it together,' the voice inside was saying, 'run around the block, get it out of your system. It's a sedative, remember? Run, run.' I ran around the block, it was 1 a.m. Lights sped by me, headlights, neon signs, dull yellow streetlamps. I ran faster. I ran around six times. I can remember the number because I saw myself do it. My conscious self was in the air above my body, watching it run. 'What a wanker,' I thought dispassionately. I had no horror, only the mesmerised numbness. 'Christ, please stop,' said my body. I stopped. The world had ceased moving round me, but now that I could see it better I was sure that something malevolent was lurking in the shadows. It was hot, I needed to find coolness. I was in a little yard, the wall there would be cool. The bricks would be calm and solid, I felt them with the palms of my hands. They were cool and comforting, like the fingers of my mother had been on my brow when I was in a childish fever. I spread my arms against the dark wall, I spread my entire body, but I was hot, so hot that I soon warmed the bricks. Slowly I edged my way along, inch by inch like a man on a high ledge, finding cool, fresher bricks. Then my hand felt something cold. A nail stuck out of the wall, old, rusty and pointed, but cold, cold as burning ice. I centred my forehead against the nail. It was firm and inviting against my throbbing brow. I pushed my head into it so that the coldness would enter me and suffuse me entirely. It worked. That was good, I pushed, I pushed, I was about to push it all the way in.

'Christ, Geldof, what the fuck are you doing?' It was Brian Carroll, I don't know where he had come from. He dragged me away from the wall. 'Christ, where's that blood coming from? What's that mark?' He tugged me back upstairs to my room and away from the seduction of self-destruction. The people had gone. I lay down on my bed. Then huge tears came to me too and poured down my cheeks. I reached out and grabbed the transistor. It had to be switched on. Switched on, it would drive everything away.

'Oh please let me go to sleep.' I clutched the radio to my ear and turned up the volume. There was no music. There was no human word spoken. It was tuned, mid-station, to nothing. That was what I needed to sleep, white noise to drive away the demons of silence. I turned it on full and fell asleep with decibels of nothingness shrieking in my ear.

The next morning I awoke trembling. I was jerky and paranoid. 'Oh god, never again,' I thought. 'What have I done?' I knew that I had opened a Pandora's box inside myself which should have remained tight-closed. I was due at Herne Hill for lunch. Another schoolfriend, Sean Finnegan, lived there with his family. My inclination was not to go out at all but there was another voice which said that this was something which had to be fought and I had to go. At the tube station I could not bring myself to go down into the subterranean darkness. I stood at the entrance for about twenty minutes and then, like a swimmer about to dive, I took a deep breath and plunged into the underground. As the train came moaning and wheezing into the station I felt a barely controllable impulse to jump in front of it. I held myself in check and boarded the train. As soon as the swaying motion began the panic swelled in my stomach like vomit. At the first station I got out and rushed up the escalator into the light and air. I rested and then steeled myself to continue. I got out at every station. There were nearly twenty of them.

Finnegan's house was slightly unnerving at the best of times. His sister was a pale and gaunt figure with a weird demeanour. His father had been badly affected by his war experiences. His mother seemed obsessive: if someone stubbed out a cigarette, she would jump up with an ashtray, take it to the kitchen, wipe it clean, then wash it and dry it before bringing it back. With the next cigarette she would do it again. Finnegan's house was not what I needed that day. At lunch I sat there and gazed at the chicken, the brussel sprouts and potatoes. 'You can't eat this, you'll throw up. You can't stare at it, eat it. I'll get sick. I don't want anything. Don't be stupid, eat it, it'll put you right.' I sat and listened to the voices in my head and stared at the plate.

'I don't think Geldof feels well, Mum.'

'I have to go, I have to leave,' I said, and rushed from the house.

Finnegan at the entrance to the Tufnell Park squat
before leaving for Spain.

Cully in Dun Laoghaire harbour, 1972.

The paranoia did not leave me for weeks. The cold shivers which coursed through my body at the smell of marijuana did not leave me for years. I was nervous, I could not sleep, I would cry for no reason. The doctor put me on Librium and Valium to slow me down. I was still taking amphetamines for my asthma. It became a roundabout of uppers at night and downers in the morning.

'I have to get out, Finnegan. My health is in pieces. I am living in a shithole. I'm sleeping with a woman who doesn't love me. I have nothing to do all day. I have no real home to go back to. There is no point to my life. I have to get out.'

'I'm going to Spain,' said Finnegan. 'I fancy being a bullfighter. Come with me.' I looked at Finnegan. He was serious. He was five foot two with a chirpy red face and a shock of flaming orange hair. He was going to be a bullfighter. 'Why not?' I said. So we went.

★ ★ ★

There had been tears at the station; Daphne had come to see me off at Victoria, but they weren't tears of sorrow so much as of frustration for the wasted time. Finnegan and I had done a lot of busking in Leicester Square in the tube station with my guitar. We were pathetic, doing a mixture of folk, blues and standards, but we made enough to raise the fare for the train to Southampton and then the ferry to Bilbao. We hitch-hiked to Madrid and made our way to my sister's flat. After university, Lynn had gone to teach in Spain and the possibility of teaching English in Madrid for a while had crossed my mind. But there were no jobs and, in any case, I found it hard to cope with the attitudes of the English-speaking expatriate community in the capital. They were by and large just a bunch of ordinary teachers, but living in Spain they had developed a self-image that was tinged with little touches of Hemingway and Scott Fitzgerald which made them faintly preposterous. Lynn suggested a language school which had two jobs on offer in Murcia, in the south-east, well inland from the holiday resorts of the Costa del Sol. But after the pace and squalor of metropolitan London that was a recommendation rather than a discouragement. Lynn gave us the money for the train fare, supplied us with food and wine for the journey and waved us off.

It was a rickety, rural train though it went by the name of an express. We looked through the window with half-interest as the dusty plains of La Mancha gave way to citrus groves and the railway meandered down to the valley floor and the little provincial capital of Murcia. The Tutelingue School was in a solid-looking three-storey building which had seen better days. We checked into a cheap hotel near the bull ring, which Finnegan lost no time in locating, and then set off to find the language school's director. We climbed the flights of marble stairs and knocked on the big oak door and went in. We were an odd looking couple, me tall and rangy with long unkempt hair, a beard and wearing an old jacket and flared jeans with holes in them, and Finnegan, small, red-haired and spruce in a suit left over from his days as a London mod. He used to be an apprentice hairdresser, now he was going to be a bullfighter by way of teaching English, but we didn't seem to disconcert the occupant of the director's desk. She was a shrivelled woman in her late forties and wore a shapeless cardigan and a long, pleated woollen skirt.

'Now, tutlingue metodo any one thing, ni!' she said. Finnegan and I looked nonplussed at one another. As an opening gambit of conversation it was something of a show-stopper. Señora Monaga spoke Catalan, German and English – all of them badly, all of them without discrimination and all of them continually muddled one with another. This personalized Esperanto was often completely unintelligible. Even her own staff couldn't make her out, which was hardly surprising since many of them could barely speak the language they were supposed to be teaching. She took us on a tour of the building. In the first classroom a German was taking an English class. From the moment we entered he began winking at us.

'Zo, let us speak again the alphabit,' he said to the class. 'Ah, beh, say, der . . .'

'What the fuck is this?' whispered Finnegan from the corner of his mouth as the strange alphabet proceeded. 'He hasn't got a bollocks.'

'I think he knows that,' I said, 'but they don't.' It was a fair summary. The man's technique, when he was asked by a pupil for a piece of vocabulary which was beyond the bounds of his very limited knowledge, was to make words up. The sole qualification for being able to teach in the school was that you knew no Spanish, a qualification Finnegan and I were able to meet perfectly. The idea was that the pupils, who ranged from the age of seven to seventy with all levels of general education, would learn by example.

'What is this, pliss?' asked a stocky little Spaniard, pointing to the buckle on his belt.

'Zult,' replied the German, without hesitation. 'Zis is called in Inglish a zult.'

'Zult. What is the morphology of zult, pliss?' asked the student, who was clearly better educated in his native tongue than the German was.

'Ja, ja. Zat is a gut kvestion. We will not talk about it now.'

It was not hard to fit in at the Tutelingue school. My pupils varied from schoolboys wanting to supplement their schoolwork, to secretaries from the local banks who hoped it might mean a transfer to the Benidorm branch, to a retired admiral, the governor of a bank and a history professor. The work was not demanding, though with my own schooldays so recently behind me it was unsettling for me to find the tables now turned. I worked hard at the theory of English grammar which I had happily neglected to learn at school, so as not to let down my more dedicated students.

I wasn't a bad teacher, but, unlike Finnegan, my heart wasn't in it. The young kids between seven and eleven were the best. Every Friday we'd have a party with cakes and sweets. They picked up pronunciation immediately and retained information longer than their elders did. It was strange hearing these small Spanish children speaking English with a Dublin accent. The teenagers took advantage of my generally lax attitude to class discipline. They were fine at first, but gradually they assumed my slovenly appearance indicated a sloppy mind. They were mistaken. There was a game to be played. They probably didn't want to be there, especially not after a day at high school. Fine, I would relax all rules and try and make things interesting, not only for them, but also for me.

I chucked out the official school book. I let them smoke. They didn't have to stand up when I asked them something or came into the room, and in an attempt to interest them I brought in the pictures of rock stars I'd taken and we would discuss lyrics. In return they had to learn. Eventually they relaxed with me and then began messing around. Boys would throw things across the tables at girls, kicking them under the table, passing notes. All the things I'd done. I stopped it by hauling one 16-year-old out of his chair and slamming him against the wall. With my fist under his nose, I told him in perfect colloquial Spanish to get the fuck out of my class. There was a shocked silence. He tried to answer back with some bravado. I knocked his books off the table and made him kneel to pick them up. I told him to crawl out of the door, because if he stood up, I'd kick his fucking head in. I demanded his parents see me in two hours or I was going round to his place to see them myself. The class was orderly from then on. The parents came and if they thought it strange to see their son's teacher in his vest, jeans, bare feet, wine bottle, stringy hair and beard, they didn't show it. I don't think they even thought of it, they only saw Teacher. They were very respectful. I refused to have the boy back.

77

In an older class of 70-year-olds, admirals, professors and captains of industry all rose as this ragged 21-year-old shambled into class and intoned, 'Buenos días, Señor Robert.' I was probably a curiosity to them. 'Sit down, lads,' I'd say, 'sit down.' If I asked a question, a Spanish admiral would leap to his feet, medals jangling, and rattle off an answer. If he got stuck, the head of the history department at Murcia university would prompt him out of the side of his mouth. Once I caught the governor of the bank cheating in an exam I'd set; he was peeping in his book.

That no one complained about me only contributed to the feeling of recovery which was gradually building inside me. Murcia, boring old place that it was, without a doubt was doing me good. I had some self-respect. I'd found something which, if the worst came to the worst, I could do to make a decent living. There was no stress in the cheerful absurdity of the Tutelingue job and there was plenty of time away from it. There were no drugs except for a happy excess of local wine. There was no music except that which we played on borrowed guitars in the flamenco bars on Saturday evenings, there were no entanglements with women, for all the local girls were locked into the restrictions of a conservative rural society. There was no pressure to achieve anything for we existed in a community of which we were not a real part. We were the English hippies, curios of whom nothing was expected. But finally the free fall I had felt myself so hopelessly entangled in had stopped.

It was Franco's Spain. I would be stopped occasionally by the Guardia Civil in their tri-cornered patent leather hats and pushed with machine guns against a wall. I would gibber drunkenly at them, scared but functioning and they always let me go. If you brought up politics, in particular Spanish politics, then your conversation classes would seize up and people would cough embarrassedly. The social and sexual mores were backward too. The young doctor I took for individual conversation classes told me of several newly-wed couples who had come to him after several months of marriage saying they were having difficulty with their sexual lives. He would talk to them and find neither of them was experiencing much pleasure. He'd quite often found the reason when he examined the woman and discovered bruising around her navel. It's a story that indicates the Catholic and social mores of the period.

The one girl I did go to bed with in that period was the niece of an extremely famous and preposterously wealthy American. She was very ugly and she gave me the clap. I was horrified. It was the first time I'd had it and it disgusted me. In Spain also it was no joke; I was lectured by doctors and nurses and priests and I am sure they were unnecessarily painful in their smear collecting and diagnostic behaviour. I paid for my sins.

All around Murcia the desert plains wrapped us in a comforting isolation. Now at last we had time on our side. Finnegan and I would climb the mountain to the classic little Andalusian bar at the top where the local men drank and sang for hours in the dark and sweaty interior. We would journey to Fortuna to bathe in the hot geysers and afterwards eat a stew with white beans in a little low-roofed white-walled tavern nearby. We would walk out onto the feature-less desert plains and lie with a couple of bottles of wine by the smelly old river while the penetrating heat of the sun warmed the marrow of our bones. I was twenty-one; until now I had tried to cram one experience after another on to everything I had become as a result of those years in the empty house and the cold catechising school. Now I was no longer adding. I was peeling things away. It took a year for the lack of pressure to turn to a lack of purpose. We had moved to a cheaper room by the cathedral where the passing of the days was marked with deafening certainty by the adjacent belltower. The crumbling walls of my room lost a little more of their chalky plaster with every peal.

One of my pupils was a film-maker who had just been working on a promotional exercise for the local silk industry. He brought some silkworms into class one day as a conversational topic and afterwards gave them to me. I took them back to my room and put them on the edge of the washbasin, wrapped in their little cocoons of silk and watched their daily progress. Gradu-ally they began to secrete a glutinous transparent liquid to soften the outside of their silken prisons. Then one day I came back to find that one had fallen off onto the floor. A horrible looking white moth was beginning to emerge. It stumbled out of its swaddling bands, dumb and blind and sticky from its birth. Crowds of small black ants gathered about it. The moth squirmed furiously on the tiles as the ants attacked. They swarmed around the white creature, devouring it. They pulled at its still wet and flapping wings. They had it on its back, eating it alive, eating its eyes out. I got on my knees to look. Its feelers trembled back and forth, desperately searching for an understanding of what was happening to it. Some of the ants had already burrowed inside its stomach. The colours on the floor were intense, the white, the black and the red. Inexorably, the ants dragged the wretched thing towards the hole from which they were pouring. It was still alive and twitching. With revulsion I reached for a bottle of after-shave. I tipped it over the frantic insects and threw a match on the lot of them. I could not stay in that place any longer.

At the end of the term I said goodbye to Señora Monaga and asked for my back pay. Her response was to prostrate herself on the floor and with her silk scarf fasten her neck to the leg of her desk. 'I am ici, ja? I am here,' she shouted, restricting herself to a mere three languages.

'Well, I'm going,' said I, restricting myself to one and, unpaid, I set out, via Madrid, Paris and London, to Dublin.

★ ★ ★

The blood beneath my fingernails was from the dead animals. I had returned from Spain to find Dublin as it had always seemed. Even my asthma was there, where I had left it. In my bedroom at night, staring at the moulding on the ceiling, parallel lines that ran round and round doomed never to meet, the beam of the Kish lighthouse flashed periodically around the walls like a prison searchlight, as it had ever done. Then one day I was told that my old school-mate Brian Devon had got out. He had married, emigrated to Canada, and had then moved to Vancouver. What was to prevent me from doing the same? I still had in savings some of the money I had earned in England on the roads. To top it up I would need another temporary job. That was how I came to be in the abattoir.

It was not a place where, in ordinary circumstances, I would have chosen to work. But because the money was good, the overtime was plentiful and my stay was to be limited I decided to take the job. I was hired to shovel crushed bones into sacks, but it was not that simple to maintain job demarcation and soon I found myself wading in wellington boots through troughs of blood and offal. The odour of death is sweet, sickly and miasmic. It was something which, with the awful blow of recognition, would filter through to my nostrils again ten years later in parts of Africa. But then, at the age of twenty-two, the animal horror was enough.

The cattle were penned up in a yard that backed onto the Grand Canal. The floor of the pen was criss-crossed with grooves to channel away the piss and ordure, for the animals would crap themselves in fear as they scented the blood of their fellows on the air. Some made a high-pitched whining noise. Others would desperately mount one another as the stink of death produced in them a crazed sexual arousal. One by one the beasts were led to aluminium tubes and pushed down them by men with electric cattle prods. Ordinarily the cattle would be killed humanely with an electric bolt, but for months the abattoir had been on a special kosher order for America. By rabbinical law the animals had to have their throats slit and then be hung upside down to bleed to death. The tubes twisted so that the animals were turned on their backs. As they reached the end, chains were wrapped around their hind legs. A crane shot the cattle into the air one by one and snapped their back legs. Then a fork was inserted into each beast's nose as one of two Jewish butchers blessed the long knife in his hand, said a short prayer and slit the throat of the animal which was then pulled higher into the air, the blood pouring in sheets from its neck and its front legs kicking wildly. We would sometimes watch in horrified fascination from a window above the killing box as the creatures were hauled along the bleeding trough in their final throes. Once a thrashing cow hurled itself against the window where we stood, shattering the glass and spattering us with gore. You could not watch for long.

After the killing the animal was cut up into various joints and the remains were boiled. After the scum of the offal was skimmed from the top of the huge vats, the tallow was tapped and taken off for soap and candle making.

The bones were put into a lime solution which burned off any remaining flesh, and then they were milled into a fine powder. My job was to shovel the bonemeal into sacks for sale to farmers who would feed it to other cattle to fatten them up. But often I had to clean the yard, slopping around through the blood, guts and the crappings of the terrified creatures. It was after this task that I would find the blood beneath my nails. On the bus on the way home I could smell myself and the smell disgusted me. In those days the abattoir became to me like a metaphor for my existence in Dublin.

My chief workmate was a stocky little man called Paul. He carried an axe in his waistband in readiness for the fight he hoped was coming. He was totally without fear, which is a terrifying thing in its ultimate stupidity. It was Paul in Dublin whom I had in mind years later when I wrote 'Rat Trap'. 'Hope bites the dust behind all the closed doors and pus and grime ooze from its scab-crusted sores.'

One Sunday he insisted I went for a drink with him after mass. It wasn't an invitation so much as a summons which it would have been imprudent to ignore. That day he showed me a side of life in Dublin of which a boy like me from the soft south side of the city had little conception, though I had some glimmerings from working with the Simon Community all those years before. There was a stripper in the pub he took me to, but nobody was watching her. Instead he and his mates were concentrating on some heavy drinking to warm up the Guinness consumed the night before. Suddenly, Judy, his girlfriend, stood up in her seat, walked across the room, over the table-tops, smashed a glass and, screaming 'you fuckin' whoor' stuck it into another girl's face. That night we went to a club and on the way we passed a parked Mercedes. Its windows were steamed up and the car was rocking from vigorous sexual activity going on inside. As we reached it the door flew open and a girl's head fell out. She looked unconscious. But then a man's head appeared on top of her. As he lunged into her, the girl turned her head sideways and vomited. It went inside the car and it went onto the pavement. The man carried on lunging, and as he lunged, she puked. He came and collapsed onto her, then recovering himself shouted at the drunken woman's face, 'Jaysus, look at the fuckin' mess you've made of my brother's car.' This was the rat trap, this was the future, deadening and dispiriting. I saw clearly then that I would never be able to get started on anything in my life unless I got out of Ireland.

One glum November night with the fog coming in heavy from the sea and the upstairs windows of the No. 7A bus all steamed up with a mixture of dense cigarette smoke and the condensation from damp coats and body heat, I pressed my head against the glass and watched the pale yellow glow of the street lights as we passed. The conductor sang 'Delilah' loudly and continuously as he moved back and forth between the lower and upper decks.

'My, my, my Delilah,' he brayed, and then *sotto voce* added the orchestral counterpoint in words of his own lewd invention: 'Get yer knickers off, get yer knickers off.'

The passengers hunched their shoulders against the assault of his unfailing jocularity. I folded the bus ticket in two and tried to clean my nails.

'Tell you what,' he repeated yet again, as he approached a schoolgirl for her fare. 'You tell me you haven't got the money, then I'll take your name and address and, you never know, tonight could be your lucky night.'

The girl smiled fixedly. Opposite me sat a man in his mid-thirties. He wore a grubby Gannex coat with a blue muffler tied in a knot at his neck. His face was pinched and expressionless as he gazed vacantly out of the grimy window. On the seat before him were two boys, an eager-looking dark-eyed child and his ginger-haired friend. They were about eleven years old and knelt on the seat facing him, requesting his attention.

'Hey, Da, d'you know any spelling?' said the dark-eyed boy.

The man nodded without taking his eyes from the window. The boys knelt up and stared into his face. The man wiped the window distractedly.

'You tell us words to spell and if I don't know 'em Ginge will do 'em.'

Ginger smiled assent at this suggestion. It appeared that Ginger smiled all the time.

'Ballsbridge,' the father said, looking at a road sign through the window.

'B-a-l-l-s-b-r-i-d-g-e, isn't that right, Da?'

The father nodded. 'Landsdowne.'

'L-a-n-d-s-d-o-w-n-e, isn't that right, Da?'

'Yes. Northumberland.'

'N-o-r-t-h-u-m-b-i-r . . .'

The man's head shook from left to right banging against the bus window.

'N-o-r-t-h,' the boy began, watching his father's face for the faintest sign of corrective movement, '. . . u-m-b-e-r-l-a-n-d, ain't I right, Da?'

The man nodded. The bus passed the American embassy. 'Embassy,' he said.

'E-m-b-a-s-s-y,' spelled the son and Ginger was smiling.

'No,' said the father and continued gazing out into the darkness.

The bus continued its unsteady progress along the route which touched the major landmarks of my life so far: Booterstown and the train, Blackrock and the school, Mount Merrion Avenue and our first house, Murray's and the dope, Glenageary Road and the dead hand of the present. I turned from this landscape of unchanging drabness, my forehead damp from the glass. All around me were faces in sullen concentration, faces in empty conversation, faces coughing wetly into *Evening Herald* situation-vacant pages and faces set in the pragmatic resolution which was the only heroism of the times. The bus seemed full that grey evening of the hopeless and the doomed, certainly full of everything I never wanted to be. And here I was with the blood of the abattoir staining my hands. But I was getting out. Again.

CHAPTER VII

The Freefall Stops Here

The snow-covered plains of Ontario were wide and open and so flat that at the horizon they merged into the sky. From the windows of the Greyhound bus there was nothing to see in any direction except virgin snow. Beside me sat Daphne. There had been the occasional pining love letter from Spain, there had even been one in the opposite direction, but basically we'd lost touch. Then, shortly before I was due to leave for Canada, we had met again in Dublin where she was once more living. Occasionally I would walk from the abattoir to see her. It was some distance, but the night air seemed to be cleansing after a day at the meat factory. One night I slept with her and from then on things drifted back to what they'd been before.

We went shopping in Grafton Street for an outfit for the journey, just before we left. She chose a rather chic beige suit, and I made her buy a hat which she hated. I thought it was extremely stylish and insisted that she wore it. My father and her parents came to see us off at the airport.

The Greyhound stopped sporadically for no apparent reason. Later, I asked someone who said, 'Company rules.'

'Oh', I said.

'Yeah, driver gotta stop every time we cross a rail line.'

I hadn't noticed any.

'Oh yeah, he's gotta stop and check there's nothing coming'.

But it was so flat and white that he'd be able to see to both horizons.

'That don't matter. Company rules. You wanna see the guy fired?'

'No.'

'Then he gotta stop.'

So flat, so white, so fucking endless. Out of a desert into an abattoir and now another desert of ice and snow. My life was developing into a movie, one that didn't seem to have any point. Still, here I was, first time in North America. I'd been on a plane before. I'd gone to Lourdes on a school trip, and to Spain with the Boy Scouts when I was eleven. I ran away to see my sister and got on the wrong train back – the Madrid–Paris Express. I cried when we passed the French border. Someone got me back. Now Daphne and I were together and about to arrive in Montreal. The flight was cheap, I don't know how much. Daphne still says she owes me the money for the journey. We were both leaving Ireland again for the same reasons: the change, the chance, boredom, a little edge of desperation. I'd talked of jobs in the Yukon, gold-mining in Northern Ontario where I could drive the machines that I'd used in England and she would be paid almost top rate to be trained at using them. We were going to make a fortune. I was frightened, I always am when I stop one thing and start another, or leave a place finally for somewhere else. In the end, even if only to overcome the insecurity, you must always opt for the unknown, otherwise you limit the options fate can hurl at you. Besides, you can never know the value of something until you've thrown it away.

I had thought the French-Canadian thing was a joke. I thought they might say 'merci' or something every now and again, but that would be the extent of it. It is very unsettling to arrive in North America and not understand anything. I said 's'il vous plaît' a few times on my way out of the terminal into the freezing cold and found a hotel near the Greyhound station. We had to get across the continent as cheaply as possible, to Brian Devon who lived in Vancouver three thousand miles away. The Greyhound was fine by me; I was full of blues imagery, Americana, turnpikes, Highway One, Route 19, Jack Kerouac going somewhere, man this was me, I was grown up now, I was going somewhere. I was frightened too, because I had a girl to look after. I had to be seen by Daphne to know what I was doing, take control. I lied through customs. Two weeks I said, that's all.

'Have you enough money for two weeks?'

'Yes sir, three hundred dollars, return tickets and we're staying with friends.' I didn't know how long we were staying; as long as it took, I suppose, but it wasn't two weeks.

The hotel was stifling. We went out, had a coffee at a real American, well, Canadian delicatessen. Americana: 'Pastrami on rye, please.' 'Wheat, whole, rye, white, brown?' 'White, please.' 'Mustard? Mayonnaise?' 'Mustard.' 'Hash browns, fries?' 'Fries.' 'Coffee?' 'Please.' 'White, black, decaff?' 'White.' 'Salad?' 'Small one.' 'Oil & vin, mayonnaise, Roquefort, meal eel?' 'Sorry?' 'Mille isle, that's Thousand Island, sir.' 'Fine, have you any salad cream?' 'No sir, we've got oil, vin, mayonnaise, Roquefort. . . .'

I don't know if she was tired or not, or jetlagged, or something, Daphne had said nothing since we had arrived. She had snapped on the plane and now she was quiet. I suppose it was awkward. We hadn't actually lived together since we were in England two years before. Maybe she was frightened too. That night, our first night in a new town, she wouldn't make love to me. I had felt scared, yes, but exhilarated too. I'd pulled it off, here we were; now I was confused and hurt. I felt terrible. We'd all come to look for America.

Every six or eight hours the drivers would change. There was nothing to see. We'd passed down the lakes looking at people pushing their huts out onto the ice and fishing through the holes. Sometimes they waited too late in the thaw to bring the hut back in and they sank. Sometimes they drowned.

In Sault Ste Marie, where they dig copper or nickel or something, there

Daphne and I impersonate Nelson Eddy and Jeanette MacDonald, somewhere in Canada, 1973.
Inset: Daphne, Vancouver, 1974.

Held upright by Dan McLeod, publisher, left, and Nick Collier.

was a giant cent on top of a hill. The clouds were flat and grey and the bus crossed endless plains. Later, with the band, I passed through these same plains and they rolled and swayed in the heat and dust haze hovering everywhere. It was endless and boring then, too. It was cornflake country gone to sleep for the winter.

Now and again we'd stop off for coffee. Nobody used the toilet at the back of the bus – it was as if it didn't exist. People would wait for hours for these coffee stops and then rush for the 'bathrooms', as they would be called, not even wishing to acknowledge the scatalogical noun. Pissing outside was out of the question, not if you didn't want a petrified dick.

It was a little bar somewhere the other side of Medicine Hat. It stood by the side of the road in utter isolation yet outside little groups of snow mobiles were parked much as cars might be outside a hostelry in any other part of the world. There was just one long bar inside and at it were sitting a row of men with steins of lager before them. They were dressed identically in checked lumberjack shirts, quilted baggy pants and big mukluk boots. Each had slung his jacket over the little backrest at the top of their bar stools, and each smoked a fat cigar. Their eyes were all on the television above the bar. With perfect synchronization each lifted his beer to his lips and took a draught.

You could just make out through the murky glow from the red and yellow bar lights that they were watching a beauty contest, Miss Teen America, the TV announcer told us, as Miss Teen Nevada appeared on the screen.

'All right,' said one.

'She's got it,' said another.

'Woo hoo.'

They all took another gulp at their beer and lapsed into silence.

Two old ladies from the Greyhound approached the barman and announced that they wanted key lime pie and ice cream.

'You can have the key lime pie, mam, but we don't have ice cream,' he said to one of them.

'He says there ain't no ice cream, Marie.'

'No ice cream? Can't have key lime pie without ice cream.'

Miss Teen Florida appeared on the screen.

'That's her,' said one of the men again.

'That's the one,' said another.

'I like it.'

'Yup.' They pulled at their cigars.

'We have to have the ice cream.'

'Lady, do you have any idea what the temperature is out there? It's fifteen below. Nobody wants ice cream in this weather. There ain't no call for it.'

'Well, there is now.'

'OK, I'll go out back and see what I can do.'

Miss Teen Arizona appeared. 'Now you're talking.'

'I'll take that,' said another.

'Yup.' With a single action they drained their glasses and reached behind for their quilted coats and left as the unctuous TV announcer reappeared with some witticism they were content never to hear.

The bartender arrived with two slices of synthetic green pie with ice cream.

'See you tomorrow night, Charlie,' the loquacious drinker said to him. The other three grunted.

'Key lime pie, *with ice cream*, ladies.'

'You're a nice man. He's a nice man, Marie.'

'That's what they tell me,' said the barman with exasperation.

In the corner Daphne and I sat with our coffee, silent in amazement.

Oh, I loved it all. I was definitely in a film or at least a song.

Back on the bus there was no one else who'd been on since Montreal. Some got out at their city, others stayed over some place and got on the next bus the next day. Eventually we did that too. We looked for the nearest, cheapest hotel to the Greyhound station and booked in. Mainly they were flop houses for transient workers, hobos or drunks. Outside was so cold that the moisture on your body froze instantly, gluing your trousers to your legs like a suction vacuum. Your breath was caught down in your chest. We sludged our way on.

Somewhere at some rank and evil place the owner led us up the stifling hot stairs, past bare board landings. He said, 'This is your room,' and opened the door. A man sat, bent forward, on the edge of his iron bed. He wore a grey vest and a three-day beard. He had khaki pants with a piss stain down the front and no shoes. There was a striped mattress on the iron bed and a stained grey blanket. The bare bulb overhead illuminated the floor which was strewn with thousands of dried out and different sized bones. 'Oh God', I thought. 'Oh dear God, where are we now?' You couldn't see the floor there were so many. They were spread out, flat and evenly across the floor. His shoes rested on bones, they were under his bed. I didn't know if they were human or animal. The man simply stared between his feet. 'Wrong room, wrong room,' the owner said, and quickly shut the door. We were very frightened; we slept in our clothes and left early.

One shithole was a men-only place. Eventually Daphne was allowed to stay by herself downstairs in a storeroom by the boiler. I was led to the top floor dormitory where maybe twelve beds were crammed. The stink and heat were unbearable. Men gasped and breathed open-mouthed, farting as they turned in restless sleep. My mattress was rolled up on the bed with a sheet and a blanket folded on the other end. The pillow had no case and was marked with dried spittle and blood from shaving gashes. I made the bed and used my knapsack as my pillow. As discreetly as possible I removed my money and hid it under my knapsack.

As I got into bed, an intense stench rose from the mattress. I felt the stirring of a million bugs and eventually fell into a fitful sleep. Some time in the early morning I was woken by the steady squeak of bedsprings. In the bed beside me two men were fucking. The older one on top raised himself on his elbow and said, 'You lookin' at anything, kid?' I shook my head, turning away more in fear than embarrassment. 'Well, mind your own business.' The squeaking continued accelerating to its incoherent end, but I got no further sleep. I lay awake in a state of acute anxiety, nursing the fear that the man might decide at any moment on a change of partner. At 5.30 a.m. I rose. The two men lay in each other's arms. I got dressed, went downstairs and woke Daphne. We went to sit in the Greyhound station, waiting for the first bus out of town.

I have a ticket from that journey. On the back I pencilled, *I spent a week in reclining seats, They reclined the back off me. I'm inclined to think, Reclining seats, Incline too much for me.* It was uncomfortable and most of the journeys were spent in silence. It was impossible to read and the dreadful cold outside was reflected between Daphne and myself. She still had not made love to me and I had ceased suggesting it. I hated her. Outside Calgary, we drove up into the Rockies. Finally we had crossed the plains. Now as we ran down the last miles into British Columbia it was as if nature ran riot after the almost existential bleakness of the prairies; the lushness and size of everything we saw seemed preposterously exaggerated. Our spirits lifted with the beauty of the place and its lush vegetation, huge waterfalls, deep black fjords and massive dark green pine forests. Daphne changed her mood utterly. I, too, felt elated. Another milestone; the movie wasn't over, but it was getting there.

Vancouver was a beautiful city set between the Rocky Mountains and the Pacific ocean. We moved in with Devon and looked for jobs. It was not easy because we had entered on tourist visas and were not officially allowed to work. That restricted us to the kind of employers who were not too fussy about whether we had social security numbers. Daphne worked at a drive-in diner as a waitress. I did a bit of building site labouring for a week but the temperature was too cold for that sort of thing. I picked up the alternative newspaper the *Georgia Strait* to look for a job, figuring that the sort of people who advertised there wouldn't be bothered about social security cards. It contained an ad for the paper's own bookstore which needed an assistant. I looked at the paper. It was a bit hippy. I liked the fashion aspect but hippy music and the general values struck me as self-indulgent, unrealistic and com-placent. It was not a bad paper, however, so I applied for the job.

The character in charge of the bookshop was called Sharkey. He was a hugely fat guy with his hair tied in a pony tail; he looked more like a Hell's Angel than a hippy and did not quite seem to fit in with the general ethos of the shop which was full of Whole Earth Catalogues, the thoughts of Timothy Leary, books on growing your own grass, on mysticism and alternative politics.

He smiled and sent me up to see the publisher Dan McLeod.

McLeod looked like an albino with pale eyes behind the wire-framed John Lennon specs and his long, lank white hair. His office was a mess. 'You ever worked in a bookstore before?' he whined, tugging his lower lip.

'No, but I've worked freelance for the music papers in England,' I lied.

'What doing?'

'I'm a writer. I haven't got any of my stuff to show you unfortunately,' I added, thinking on my feet, 'because I only came here for a holiday, but I like it and I've decided to stay. I'd like to write for the paper.'

'Well, perhaps that can be organized but only on a freelance basis. We'd pay you for anything we printed. But what we need right now is someone for the bookstore. How much do you want to be paid?'

'As much as I can get.'

'Well that's agreed then,' said McLeod, with a smile, 'because I'm looking to pay as much as I can afford.'

I began downstairs with Sharkey. The money wasn't bad, but the *Strait* had terrible cash-flow problems and some weeks you wouldn't get paid at all, though in the end Dan paid you everything you were owed. In addition to producing the weekly tabloid paper, the *Georgia Strait* handled the distribution in Western Canada of *Rolling Stone* and the glossy drug magazine, *High Times*. It also distributed a couple of record labels. It was a congenial place.

Things seemed to be going well, so we decided to move out of Devon's place before we fell out permanently with him and his wife. We found an apartment of our own at Burnaby on the road out to Grouse Mountain. It was the basement of a detached house belonging to a little Latvian woman. We had three rooms, all furnished in local wood and quite comfortable even if the natural light was poor. I applied for a social security number, changing my middle name and date of birth in an attempt to confuse the computer. If it had checked my real name against the immigration records it would have discovered my tourist status and I'd have been thrown out of the country. I decided that utter confusion was my best bet so I filed in the name of several Robert Geldofs, all with different middle names and all with different birthdays. It worked, because eventually I got two cards. In the meantime I set about collecting as many makeshift bits of ID as I could; bank cards, blood donor cards, anything so long as it had my name on and looked official.

The offices of the *Georgia Strait* were in the old part of the city, Gastown. It was still a run-down area but the city council had recently decided that the entire district had either to be knocked down or entirely renovated. They had decided on conservation and the place was in a state of transition. Gastown was on the railhead at the end of the Canadian Pacific by the edge of the river where gigantic rafts of logs came downstream from the forests. It was being gentrified and turned into a tourist attraction but much of the old character remained.

There were the workmen's cafés, Lew's Chinese and The Only Fish Bar where that day's catch was freshly fried. There were fine old wooden waterfront buildings and there were many original bars. But there was squalor too. This was where the Indians hung out, the hopeless and the dispossessed, the kids always with their heads in plastic bags sniffing glue, the adults always drunk and often in trouble, hustling for drugs, pissing where they stood, slumped on the sidewalks. It was the red light district and in the evening it was a rough place to be. Later I wrote a song about it called 'The Neon Heart'.

Gradually at the *Georgia Strait* I began to move upstairs from the bookstore into the editorial department. The editor had agreed to have a look at anything I wanted to submit and I had started covering local bands. So I began writing. I loved it. I had nurtured secret ambitions all through school. I had never said much to anyone except my Aunt Fifi. She thought it was reasonable. Foley, Cully and myself all wanted to be journalists. I don't think we ever talked about it, but when their exam results came they began talking openly of it. I didn't have a hope with my results. Now finally I had my chance. It wasn't like work, it was a pleasure and I was writing about music. I became immersed in the local band scene and broadened out to national and international music papers when big acts came to town. I became more and more involved with the paper and its tall, stooped, almost Dickensian-featured owner. It was the time of the radical press's decline. John Lennon was working for the release of John Sinclair of the *Detroit Free Press.* The alternative papers had either gone mainstream or faded. McLeod tried a lot of options, but failed. He had tried going national, going mainstream, going populist, had tried a porn classifieds paper, a sports paper, anything to keep afloat. In the beat-up office of the paper Dan would sit in his tiny, chaotic, paper-strewn room, bewildered by the changing times and his falling circulation. The sixties were over, no one gave a shit any more. This was the 'me' decade. Possibly it was something I understood intuitively; I had been a child in the sixties, but I was not a sixties child. I'd been too young. Now I would take the chance to do something with what had been till now a sickeningly futile and chaotic life. The seventies were made for me. 'Seize the time,' the man said. I would.

The music had changed: no longer adventurous, it was self-indulgent or narcissistic or engaged in embarrassing pastiche. I'd stopped listening. Heavy Metal bored me, the Bay City Rollers were laughable. I listened to David Bowie, though I thought him twee then, and to Lou Reed. The New York Dolls were fun and Roxy Music were interesting. Attitudes hardened. With recession came a drawing in. 'I'm all right Jack, I'm looking after number one,' was the norm, and in 1976 I was to write about it in a song, the year before Tom Wolfe's polemic on the 'me' decade.

Dan was out of time. People may not have cared about politics much any more, but they still liked music. I suggested that to broaden the readership we should devote more space to the one thing people still liked. I was made Music Editor and fifty per cent of the paper became devoted to the subject. We began to get more music ads, then free circulation was adopted for the campuses, trebling the readership overnight and bringing a commensurate rise in advertising. I loved the paper. It was the first work I liked: I would stay late and be in early. The people were great, the physical surroundings of British Columbia outstanding and, as my group of friends extended, I depended less on Daphne for peace, love and understanding.

I was happy. I realised that during a picnic when Nick Collier, my best friend there, lent me his wet suit and tried to teach me to swim. I floated head back in my sponge raft on a summer's day up by Shannon Falls, the sun bursting off the water and exploding on the giant pines. That same day Rye, Brian Devon's dog, reached its head down into a roadside ditch and simply lifted out a giant salmon. Oh, land of plenty, I am happy. The thought was so startling and new my mind started racing down its list of objections. Are you sure? What about Daphne, for example?

The funny thing was, as I grew more independent and less concerned, she became the opposite. One night late at my typewriter where I'd been working for hours, she said, 'We never do things any more.' I said, 'I do things. You don't want to do them, that's all. Anyway, we never used to do things.' She was lonely. She'd made one or two friends at the drive-in, but it was transient. 'You must make a life for yourself,' I said, and went on typing.

But inevitably in accordance with the Geldof law of emotional dynamics,

Rob Geldof pans Crosby, Stills and Nash almost exactly 11 years before they play Live Aid.

GEORGIA STRAIGHT

The Big Show. CSN & Y

July 18-25, 1974

by Rob Geldof

I used to think that stars shone and twinkled and that superstars positively hummed and glowed with brilliance. The dull flickering gleam of Crosby, Stills Nash and Young last Wednesday night was more equitable to black holes than any other astral body that comes to mind. The casual anarchy and constant excuses are excusable for a band of lesser stature and experience but hardly the stuff of which rock heroes are made. One was almost fooled for a second in believing "well, maybe there is something more to it than meets the eye." I mean here is a tour organized by Bill Graham arch-deacon of rock impressarios, complete with Paul Wasserman a high-ranking Asylum Records executive plus an entourage of an unnecessary 80 and of course the ... super-tight, over-react ... Well there must be ... ind it all. Not so ... Nash and ... one of

which we endured for the better part of three hours. He played and sang adequately and did what he was there for: warmed us up for the Big Show.

The Big Show was unfortunately late in arriving. One wonders at the expediency of having a touring troupe of at least 80 persons and then forcing a capacity crowd to wait twenty minutes or more. There appeared to be more persons rushing 'round backstage with thin black leatherette briefcases than there were on the stage itself. Of poseurs there were plenty, each striving to appear as significant as the next. Finally the boys arrived. Before appearing on stage however they performed a little ritual which as it turned out did them little good at all. The boys formed a circle, extended arms, and clasped hands one on top of each other — it was a touchingly pathetic moment, rivalled only by the performance that followed this unheeded invocation to God or Gods unknown.

As soon as they touched the stage awards it became obvious that they were on home ground. he crowd positively crowed in ... and for brief seconds

the show became. "Wooden Ships." And indeed that's what they were and sounded—wooden. ... artist the point it became

a pity that this didn't happen. It ... xcuse

STILLS · CROSBY · YOUNG & R. GELDOF

that the lads had played for four hours in Seattle and their voices were damaged beyond repair — at least for tonight, and sure they ... hat the guitars were a ... ch was the check list arrived at immigration. Something would have to be done. I wanted to spend the rest of my life here. I'd become a minor celebrity. My opinion, considered vaguely outrageous in the paper, was sought after on radio and in the big provincial papers. I got into gigs free. I knew the musicians and promoters and they liked me. And I had money. With confidence came a whole flood of ideas and endless energy. Anything was possible. Look, that's my name on that article. I exist and I'm seen to do so. I'm fucking *somebody*, pal.

One night on Vancouver Island, three hours by boat from the mainland, we drove through the city of Victoria and into the country. Nick was driving and falling asleep. I stayed awake, singing loudly in his ear so we'd not crash. Eventually, though, he ran off the road. We pulled the car out, drank black coffee and we laughed and laughed. I was alive.

McLeod, because of his association with the sixties' radicals, was not welcome in the U.S. He decided we should put on a concert, promoted by the paper, and the profit would help keep the show on the road. We had to go to Los Angeles and talk to the agents. The plan was to drive down over the border by Point Roberts, a town just inside the U.S. dedicated to loose drinking laws, porn movies and peepshows. The Canadians are strangely Victorian with regard to all three. Point Roberts does wonderful business. At the border, in Dan's van, used for distributing the paper, we said we were going to Point Roberts for the day, drove straight to Seattle and then got on a plane to San Francisco. America, finally.

Seattle. Jimi Hendrix came from there. And there's the hotel where Led Zeppelin tied up a girl and did some fishing from their bedroom window, or something. It was funny three years later to go back with my own band and fish from the same windows of the Edgewater Inn. From observer to participant.

In San Francisco we stayed with Max, the owner of the *Berkeley Barb*, the legendary chronicle of the students of '68. I spent hours in the City Lights book store. One day we went to the beach, six of us in some beat-up car. I don't know who drove, but I was in the front squashed between Allen Ginsberg and the driver, listening to some country station, and Ginsberg was talking shit about country being the only true American music. The beach was warm but grew cold and foggy quickly. Somewhere I have a picture of me in shorts kneeling on the backs of Ginsberg and McLeod, who are on all fours in the sand and the fog. We look like unhealthy, bearded beach boys in the murk. My intellectual pretensions were risible, but so were theirs. I felt nauseated that I was flattered to be in their company. But the company of clever men who know it tires quickly.

Los Angeles was only remarkable for its dullness. How could a city so large be so dull? The conversational pretensions of San Francisco were one thing, but here talk was as flat as the city, and the Perrier water they constantly drank was all that fizzed. I went to look for 77 Sunset Strip. God knows, I had looked at Kookie Byrnes's picture enough in my sister's bedroom. Efrem Zimbalist Junior wasn't there, of course. It was a girlie peepshow now, and so was the rest of Hollywood.

We did some business, picked up the van and headed north. I was worried. At the border they were sure to ask me questions and I was now an illegal immigrant. I had no ID and if they wouldn't let me back into Canada, they'd throw me out of the States. I assumed a preposterously bad American accent. If they rumbled McLeod as being 'persona non grata', they were sure to question me and my accent would not hold up under questioning. I was sure they would find the records and magazines we were bringing back under the mat in the back of the van. We looked suspicious, with Dan's small nervous eyes and my incoherence. We got through, but what about next time? If I was to stay, I would need to travel up and down a lot. If I switched jobs, I would need proper papers. If I was stopped by the police in the car, indeed, if I applied for a car licence, if I went to hospital . . . Everything I could do in the future was limited by the fact that I would be discovered in two, five or ten years' time; found out, sent home and never allowed to return. And what if by then I had a great job, kids, a house, what then? I had to do something. I'd missed the Trudeau government's amnesty for illegal immigrants by only two months when I had arrived the year before. If I wanted to spend the rest of my life in Canada, if I wanted the same sense of freedom and possibility, I would need to return to Ireland and apply legally for immigrant status.

I was returning to a parochialism and a morality so stifling it literally manifested itself in me as an inability to breathe. I was returning to a place where ambition and talent were denigrated. I was returning to a place where the cardinal rule was to know your station, where to try and rise above that, to attempt anything ambitious was to invite derision and to court failure. If you succeeded, it was, 'Who do you think you are? I knew you when you were nothing.' If you failed, you met open scorn and complete contempt: 'What an idjeet, he thinks he's bloody great, that'll learn 'im, serves him bloody well right.' It was best to be anonymous, but I could never be that now I'd felt the butterfly of delight in my stomach when I read my by-line in the *Georgia Strait*. Canada had taught me that your level of effectiveness increased in direct proportion to your level of power. The more people you knew, the more you could do.

I would return to Vancouver three years later with a Canadian gold record and a sold-out tour and be presented with the keys to Vancouver City sewers. But now I was returning to the bolted doors of Dublin. With regret, Daphne and I packed and left. At Dublin airport, for the benefit of Daphne's parents, we maintained the pretence of not having slept together. It seems preposterous that after such a year we parted, her to her parents' house, I to mine. All we said was, 'See you later.' We didn't even kiss. We were back home.

CHAPTER VIII

Do the Rat!

At the time I set fire to my father's house we first formed the band. The two events were unconnected, though they did have two things in common. Both were entirely accidental and on both occasions I was actually concentrating on something else at the time.

The fire came about when Daphne and I were engaged in a bout of spontaneous nobbing on the floor of my father's bedroom and she neglected to stub out her cigarette before we set to. We went for a drink afterwards and when I returned in the small hours the back of the house downstairs was a blackened shell. Because my father had converted the large house to a series of individual bedsits the blaze was contained and so the entire place was prevented from burning down. As it was the back was gutted, even the floor boards were burned through. Daphne claims it was faulty wiring. My father, who had been on holiday in Spain, was greeted by his nervous son at the airport. 'Eh, we had a bit of a fire while you were away.'

'Much damage?'

'Well, eh, you remember your flat . . . ?'

He was delighted; he got the insurance and was able to do the whole place up like new.

The start of the band was considerably less dramatic. In the beginning there was no real thought that it would be anything more than a bit of fun for the evenings during the time I was working towards the launch of a new magazine. Indeed when things began I was not even in it, merely an interested observer.

Soon after I got back from Canada I went down to Fitzgerald's bar and met Gary Roberts. He was not a close friend but I had spent some time with him when I was unemployed after leaving school. He was drinking with Johnnie Moylett, the younger brother of my friend Pat from Murray's. They were talking about forming a band. Gary was a guitarist and Johnnie played the piano, I knew that. The discussion continued over coffee back in the large kitchen at Gary's house where the Aga stayed warm until the small hours. Johnnie's cousin, Pat Cusack, was also talking of starting a band along with a friend of his called Gerry Cott, who we knew from playing blues guitar at parties. Pat, Gerry and Johnnie were all studying architecture at Bolton Street College of Technology.

'Why don't you all get together,' I suggested. 'That would give you keyboards and three guitars, one of you could play bass.'

'They want to play blues, or something,' Johnnie said.

'Well, you could give it a try,' I said. 'The main thing is not to behave like a local band. It's essential to get your act together from the start. I know a bit about local bands because I've worked with them in Canada. You've got to have an idea of what the band is about. You need an identity, both on stage and off. It's no good just doing any old style of thing, a Doors song here, a bit of blues there. You need a clear image right from the start.'

'Yeah.'

'You need to act like stars right from the word go. Even with people who know you, you have to behave like you're special. You have to be consistent.'

'Yeah, you're right.'

A couple of days later I asked what progress had been made. The answer was none. I wasn't surprised. I was used to people in Dublin talking late at night in their kitchens.

I ought not to have been bothered. I had my hands full. Now that I was back in Dublin I was beginning to remember why I had left in the first place. I expected to be able to pick up the threads of my life in Canada when I went back there, but in Vancouver there was a local magazine called *Buy and Sell*. It had been started by a very small publisher and it had quickly burgeoned into an enormous success. It contained only small ads but its novelty was that the classified advertisers, mainly private individuals wanting to sell a washing machine or a car, did not have to pay. It survived on its cover price and on its display advertising from major companies, and it was making a very healthy profit. I reckoned that if I could not get back quickly into Canada I could do the same in Dublin and then use the profits to start my own music paper. But what was a successful and prosperous idea in North America was beginning to feel doomed and impossible in the unenterprising atmosphere of Ireland.

Things had begun well enough. Brian Devon and his wife had come back from Vancouver with us and had put up £2,000 for the new paper. That doubled my own initial capital from my Canadian savings. I had commissioned a survey from magazine distributors who were enthusiastic and said that it was the most positive report they had produced for any new paper in the previous five years. I had a deal with a printer in Bray which gave me thirty days' credit, enabling me to publish four weekly issues before I had to pay for the first one. I had persuaded three of the participants in a leading car rally which was covered live on television, to paint their vehicles in *Buy and Sell* colours. I had some pretty girls, all old friends, wearing sashes advertising the publication, canvass the response of housewives outside supermarkets with dummy issues. Armed with all this research and promotion and accompanied by the heavyweight solicitor and accountant I had engaged, I went to the bank.

I didn't open my mouth but let the professionals set out the case. The two Dublin evening papers were full of classified ads at that time. The demand for personal advertising and sales would continue to flourish. Even with a downturn in the economy there would be steady growth, as in a recession the demand for cheap second-hand goods and therefore such advertising would continue. The magazine would be distributed free in certain problematic areas and would therefore circulate outside metropolitan Dublin which would gain it national advertising as opposed to the restrictive city-only advertising which was the bane of so many publications. The several contingency plans were outlined and the accountant explained that it was on conservative estimates that he projected that I would have repaid all loans within six months and would be in a healthy profit by the end of the year.

The bank manager listened in silence. Then he sat back in his chair. He put his fingers together in a gesture of such pomposity that I knew he was going to say something ludicrous.

'Mr Geldof, how old are you?' I told him I was twenty-four. 'Then I suggest that you come back to us when you are forty and have something to show for yourself.'

I lost my temper and raged about the difference between Ireland and North America and told him that the country was in a mess precisely because of people like him. Yes, I was only twenty-four but here I was offering to take eleven people off the dole and give them jobs as typists and telephonists and here he was saying that all twelve of us should continue to live off the state rather than use our initiative to create wealth. I raged at him, doubtless in his mind proving his point about my relative youth and immaturity, but by then it was clear that there was no way I was going to get the money from him.

At this point I still had approaches to make to other banks, credit unions and finance houses, but even more pressing if the paper was to work, I had to organize the telephone lines for the new business. Devon's father-in-law had given us the use of a building near where I had worked in the meat factory. We moved into the front room and set up shop. Despite the bank's refusal to help I decided to push ahead. We needed at least six phone lines, all preferably coming in to one number. I rang the phone company.

'Forget it,' they said.

'I can't forget it, this is my job. How long will it take?'

'It'll take at least three years and then you could probably only have two.'

I couldn't believe it. In Canada if you wanted a new phone you had a choice of companies and you got it that day. 'But that's ridiculous,' I said.

'It's too bad, you mean, we're up to our neck in work. We can't meet the demand, especially in the Ballsbridge area.'

I knew it was impossible talking to this man or any other but I still could not accept the situation. I phoned the government and got the number for Conor Cruise O'Brien, then the Minister for Posts and Telegraphs. To my surprise I was given an appointment to meet him. Conor Cruise O'Brien is a journalist, editor, diplomat and intellectual. He listened to my argument, my 'What Sort of Country Is This?' schtick.

At the end he said, 'I know, I agree, but I can't do anything.'

'But you're the Minister,' I said.

'I know, but I can't dig the holes and put down the lines. The whole thing's a bloody mess.' He was very honest.

I'd been told by other people that it was possible to bribe some union guys into giving you what you wanted. I rang the unions. I went in to see some middle-ranking time-server. I told them they were stopping people working. I got nowhere. I even suggested a holiday for two in sunny Spain might be in order should anything be forthcoming. I think my approach was so subtle he never really got what I was suggesting, or else ignored it, or else it didn't matter if I bought the entire membership a holiday in Spain, they still couldn't do anything. Nothing happened.

I was unbearably frustrated. I was also disappointed in the fact that Johnnie and Gary, when I saw them soon after our meeting in the kitchen, had not taken things further. I was quite intrigued by the idea of the band and it would certainly take my mind off the problems I was having with the paper. 'Ask Pat and Gerry over on Monday, will you?' I said to Johnnie. That same day Gary saw an ad in the paper and bought an electric guitar. It was our first proper instrument. Next day I went into the city with him and he bought a Meazzi 100 watt amp. We were very excited. All afternoon we played with it in his room. It had echo and it lit off and on in synchronized time with whatever rhythm was being played. His mother told us to shut up.

I had known Gary dimly for years. He went to a Quaker school in Waterford and I would see him in the holidays screaming round corners, his knees as close to the ground as he could make it on his Honda. I thought he was insane. Now he went to Trinity College where he had done a year of psychology, a year of medicine, and now he wanted to give that up and start something else. He was very clever but easily influenced by others. He's a great guitar player but he's not very pragmatic and doesn't possess great organizational skills. Maybe in recognition of this, in between loud bursts of amplified echo, he said, 'Perhaps you'd better be our manager and get things organized.'

'Yeah, OK,' I said.

After his mother had told us to be quieter I was playing harmonica while he played acoustic guitar. We were playing 'The Prodigal Son' from the Rolling Stones' 'Beggars' Banquet' album. I was singing.

'Why don't you be the lead singer as well?' he said.

I didn't really want to, I still had high hopes for *Buy and Sell* and anyway I couldn't sing. 'Yeah, maybe, I don't know,' I said. I'd no intention of actually doing it.

Next day I went down to Johnnie's place. Johnnie had always been the baby-faced brother of Pat. He was quiet. He went to school in Limerick where he took piano lessons. He'd been a member of the Beatles' fan club. He was very different from his brother, who was constantly on the look out for some new scheme that would make him millions or at least a living. Pat made things happen. Johnnie let things happen to him. He was chronically sleepy, it seemed, in everything but his music. He was very likable, friendly, cuddly and lazy, but because of his very friendliness and laziness, people didn't mind doing things for him. I think he knows that and uses it.

Pat and Gerry said they'd give it a try. That gave us three guitars and keyboards and a singer. It was enough to start.

One Saturday afternoon Gary, Johnnie, Gerry, myself, and Pat Moylett on drums met in Pat's basement flat. Johnnie had bought a Tiger electric pianette. Things were getting serious. Pat, I think, had one or two borrowed drums but was pretty useless at keeping time, so it became apparent we'd need to get a drummer quickly. Gary blasted everyone out of it with his Meazzi as it flashed and sparked in the corner by the bed and Gerry tried to play bass on an acoustic guitar.

'OK,' I said. 'What sort of music are we going to do? We have to pick one thing and stick with it.'

'Well, I thought Doobie Brothers sort of thing,' said Gary, blasting out the introduction of 'China Grove'.

'Oh, that's crap,' I said. 'We can't do that.'

'Why not?'

'Because it's hopelessly bad.'

'What about . . .' someone suggested something else.

'That's crap too. It means nothing, that sort of music. It has no passion or excitement. It's not about anything real. You can go to any Dublin band and hear that sort of thing. It has to be something different. Something that isn't just copying. We need to get back to basics. R & B and dance music and then make out our own direction from there.'

All of us liked R & B. It was our common sixties heritage and Gerry and Gary could play it. Unbeknownst to us there were bands all over Britain and America who were thinking the same thing. People were going into pubs, because that was where these bands were playing with a feeling and conviction that was almost totally lacking in the established bands who had now got into the business of refining their technique. Pop music was saying nothing and had plenty of money to say it with.

Soon I moved out of my father's house and into a flat in Clyde Road. Daphne left her parents and we took up where we had left off in Canada. I had now decided that I would put answerphones in six friends' houses and publish their numbers as being the official *Buy and Sell* phone numbers where you could phone in your free ad. Meanwhile, there was a small shed out the back of the flat where we began to practise. Pat Cusack had shown up for rehearsals at Clyde Road and Gerry introduced him. We began imitating his country accent immediately and taking the piss out of him for being from Ballyjamesduff. I hadn't known the place actually existed, it also being a very famous song in Ireland. Pat was Johnnie's cousin, he'd grown up in County Cavan. I didn't know much about him except he'd had jazz guitar lessons and kept playing all these horrible jazz chords. He was a very fast jazz player and took it quite seriously. I was impressed with his Gibson semi-acoustic guitar but it didn't sound very good. He seemed quiet and serious at first, possibly because of our constant teasing, but as he grew more confident he became more extrovert and funny. Although he denies it I remember him wearing brown stack-heeled shoes the first time I saw him. I thought he was very unhip, and wondered how the fuck were we going to look any good with this lot.

Gerry was married and I had known him from around Dun Laoghaire. At parties he'd always played Big Bill Broonzy's railway blues and other things. He was a blues buff and always told people what he was going to play and who wrote it and where it came from. Gerry was very practical. He would listen and make up his own mind. He would go along with things if it made sense to him, but if he was unhappy he would come down when everyone had gone and say, 'Why are we doing this and what are we doing next?' He wanted it to work. I think his plans were bigger than ours at the beginning.

We rehearsed for about a month without a drummer, which is like trying to make an omelette without the eggs. Gary said, 'What about Simon Crowe? I used to play in the school band with him.' Simon had lived beside my Auntie Fifi so I knew him vaguely. 'Yeah, ask him, will you?' we said. Simon had more or less given up playing and he didn't really want to get into a band, but he showed up and played. It sounded complete. It sounded right. 'It's crap,' Simon said.

Simon was very serious, I thought. He was a big man who was intensely pragmatic. He was good with his hands and was a superb singer and drummer. He was, as they say, solid. I thought him a bit dour and removed. I didn't like him being so noncommittal and I couldn't understand his reluctance. After all, it was only fun. We weren't supposed to take it seriously. He wasn't crazy about the music. He'd done it all in school, he said. He wanted to play Little Feat style. It was more challenging to him. He was right, of course; it was a mess, but it was an exciting mess that exuded fun and a love of the music. Simon was the perfect foil for my chronic impatience. I would want to move quickly from one song to another as soon as it sounded vaguely right. He insisted on it being played over and over till we got it perfect.

I had been making some money writing articles and small pieces for the *New Musical Express* in England using my Canadian by-line, Rob Geldof. Everyone felt uncomfortable calling me Geldof now that we had left school and were older. Robert seemed too formal to them, and to the Canadians who had abbreviated it to Rob. Back in Ireland they thought Rob ludicrous and had begun calling me 'Barb' in a long-drawn-out America drawl to get over the initial shock of no longer addressing me as Geldof. Even Daphne called me Geldof.

I would accompany Fachtna O'Kelly, a journalist friend of mine, to whatever pop events were happening in Dublin and write about them. On one of these occasions – a Gary Glitter press conference – Fachtna and I had stolen the microphone. That was what I used in rehearsals, hung from a rafter in the shack, plugged into the bass guitar amplifier Pat used. Fachtna and I were now banned from any further press conferences. Fachtna was a very tall, thin, ascetic looking man. He's very handsome and intelligent. He had one of the biggest collections of records I had ever seen and a brilliant taste in music. One afternoon in his flat in Sandycove I let slip, 'Some friends of mine are in a band. I was wondering if you've got anything we should listen to?' I was too embarrassed to admit that I just happened to be in the same band myself. Fachtna revealed a treasure trove to me. He played me Doctor Feelgood. This was the very thing I wanted to do; brilliant new rhythm and blues, wonderful, wonderful lyrics. *Standing, watch the towers burning at the break of day.* What was the point in continuing? These guys had already done it. He played me Bob Marley and Max Romeo and Burning Spear. I had heard some reggae in Canada but didn't much like it. Now I heard Marley's 'Catch a Fire' and it seemed to me to burn with the same passion as the early R & B I'd heard and to have a distinct relevance. It was also great dance music.

I brought the records back and played them to the others. They were electrified. We soon learned every Doctor Feelgood track, but reggae was much harder. It took us a while to understand it and be able to play it, but we didn't care. Other songs from our own collections we just adapted. We played very fast. Much faster than the originals. I don't know why, it just seemed to fit our excitement and the mood of the times. We were still hopeless, though.

For three months we rehearsed two or three times a week. I enjoyed rehearsals and would probably have remained content for some time with just practising had not Gerry announced that it was about time we got some gigs organized. 'Sure, Gerry,' we all said. 'Out you go and get them organized.' One evening in September 1975, he announced that he had a gig lined up for us.

'It's a Halloween gig at Bolton Street Tech,' he said. We swallowed hard. That was less than a month away.

'How much do we get?' I asked.

'Thirty quid,' he said.

'Thirty quid! We're not doing it for that,' I said, pleased to have found a credible excuse for backing out. My voice was amplified during rehearsals only by the stolen second-hand bingo-announcing microphone and the old speakers. I was able to hide in this inadequacy. I did not relish the ordeal of a full public performance. 'Thirty quid! It's a fucking rip-off.'

'Well, if you're so bloody clever, you go and talk to them.'

I did, but my bluff was called. When I said that £30 was an insult and we wouldn't do it for less than double that, the college promoter said: 'All right, £60 then.' We were committed.

We were not sure what was expected of us and so we rehearsed a set which lasted two-and-a-quarter hours. We had plenty of material. What was really bothering us was what name we should choose. We could no longer continue calling ourselves Mark Skid and the Y-Fronts, as we did occasionally. It was too undergraduate and obvious.

'What about Traction?' suggested Gary.

'Crap, sounds like a heavy metal band. It has to sound dark and brooding. People have to respond to everything, even the name. It all must be exciting.'

'What about Nightlife?'

'That's not bad. But it needs something more. It needs to be a name like the Rolling Stones that can be shortened to the Stones or whatever. What about Darker Days?'

'Sounds like a Doors number. What about the Nightlife Thugs?'

Nightlife Thugs was written in neat lettering on the blackboard in the classroom at Bolton Street College of Technology. We regarded it with mixed feelings as we entered from the nearby pub where we had spent the last half hour fast-forwarding through the words of the songs and revising the order of the numbers. I was terrified. What the hell was I doing? I wanted to pull out, explain I'd only been joking, then someone said, 'We'd better go.'

There was a moment of sheer panic in those initial seconds with their faltering false starts and the sudden strangeness of the PA we had hired for the occasion. But we stumbled on into our set and noticed, with a feeling of disbelief, that people were dancing, dancing to what we were playing and apparently enjoying it. I couldn't believe it. I was in a band. It was extraordinary. When the set ended there was an explosion of applause. Suddenly Daphne and Penny were there smiling and clapping. We were obviously much better than anyone thought we were going to be. It was exhilarating.

'It's brilliant,' said Daphne.

'Really?'

'Really, it's really brilliant.'

The night before I had been reading Woody Guthrie's autobiography, *Bound for Glory*. I had reached the part where, at the age of about eleven, oil was discovered in his home town in Oklahoma. Teams of casual labourers moved in and the place became a boom town. A split had developed between the native kids and the children of the newcomers. Excluded from existing gangs, the new kids formed their own. It was called the Boomtown Rats.

Even at that tender age Woody could spot the moral discrepancy and left his old friends to join the new gang. As a result the two gangs eventually merged. Suddenly in the interval during that first gig the aptness of that gesture struck me. I went up to the promoter and said that the band had changed its name. He rubbed out Nightlife Thugs and in its place scrawled the Boomtown Rats.

The others thought that was a laugh. After that we kept the Rats, but changed our individual names every week: Mike Raphone, Max Volume, Max Headroom, the Van Rentl brothers, Hertz and Avis, even totally ludicrous things like Cup O'Tea and Ray Di Ator. Two stuck. We changed Pat Cusack's name because we thought it sounded too Irish. We made it more Irish. We changed it to Pete Briquette, which was a pun on the fuel cakes made in Ireland from compressed peat. Johnnie Fingers became a permanent nickname possibly because it was so obvious for a pianist. All this also provided a talking point for the local press who were becoming increasingly aware of the band as we began to do regular gigs each week. The line-up was Pete Briquette (Pat) on bass, Johnnie on keyboards, Gary and Gerry on guitar, Simon on drums, and me as singer.

We still looked terrible. After the first couple of gigs we did a photo session. We realised our beards and moustaches were awful. With the exception of Gary we all looked so polite. It was the first time we had been conscious of ourselves as a group. We had to look like the Boomtown Rats. We became more conscious of how we looked and what we wore, simply because we were no longer ourselves, we were the Rats. Everything had to be exciting.

Kieran Fitzpatrick, a Beatles fanatic I'd known in Murray's who was now a commercial artist, was attempting to be our sound man, a job he got simply because he had a lot of records. Now he began designing our artwork. One day I brought him a frame from a comic I'd seen. It was a man walking up a dark cobblestoned street holding a severed head by the hair. Kieran blew it up and wrote the band's name in globs of dripping blood. There were posters that showed a long shapely leg inside a rubber stocking. Feminists took great exception to these and went around inscribing the word 'sexist' in purple felt-tip markers on every one they could find. The papers said I had put up the posters and then gone around the next night and written on them. It wasn't true, but it was a nice story. They missed the best bit of all, though. The leg was mine. It seems silly now, but no one else was doing posters. Bands got up on stage, ignored the audience, spent ten minutes tuning and then took a drink between every excruciatingly boring guitar solo. The posters along with the name and the shows we did were designed to make people react.

Simon had a silk screen in his room where he would print T-shirts and posters. Johnnie's mother and sisters made up some arm bands and we printed the rat logo on them. Gary, whose father was a photographer, took pictures of montages I had assembled from various news cuttings and history books.

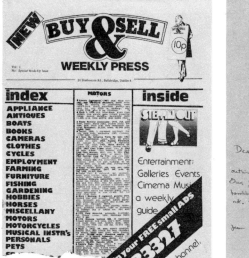

Could have worked. Lucky it didn't.

A letter never sent. A gig never played.

R&B, flares and moustaches: The Rats, 1975.

We made slides of them and projected them on a huge screen we'd made out of lining paper. As three projectors flicked the slides onto the screen, we would come onstage from behind it. Behind us would be a false brick wall also made by us from fake plastic brick façades. On top of that barbed wire was strung and sprayed on the wall was the name of the band. As the slides and electronic music built to a crescendo Gary would start playing, the screen would collapse and we'd be off. People loved it.

Sometimes we got an educational film from Rentokil. Pat Moylett pretended he was a teacher and needed it for a class project. It was wonderful. There were pictures of rats in space with a voiceover saying in a loud American voice, 'Who were the first in space?' There was a pause and then he answered, 'Rats! Who were the first to explore the deepest regions of the earth?' A pause, and the crowd shouted along with him, 'Rats!' It ended with a shot of a woman leaving a ham in a fridge. A rat gets in the back of the fridge and gnaws at the ham. As the door opens, it scurries off. The woman reaches in, takes the ham and cuts her husband a slice. As the unfortunate man is about to bite into his tasty meal the voice intones: 'Beware! One of the greatest enemies of mankind is the . . .' The crowd would scream 'Rats?' I'd tear the paper screen apart and we'd begin. I even think I told one paper we let live rats into the audience. We didn't, and they knew it, but it became a story that still haunts us today.

The other Dublin bands grew jealous and were slightly bewildered by our sudden appearance and rise. They accused us of being musically inept, but we turned that to our advantage with a poster campaign which announced 'The Boomtown Rats have learnt a fourth chord – hear it at . . .' I had seen some guitar player in a local band wear a 'Clapton is God' badge. I sprayed 'Geldof is God' on my T-shirt and at the next gig wore it ostentatiously. There was uproar from the local pop journalists. I was enjoying myself. The band were becoming notorious. We began to appear in the gossip columns of both the alternative and the established press. My friend Fachtna who wrote Dublin's leading rock column for the *Evening Press*, started to write enthusiastically. People began to ask for autographs.

Success is a self-propagating phenomenon. Within a couple of months I'd developed enormous self-confidence. Before I had been nervous, but now I was flooded with the sensation that I had found what I was born to do. Suddenly the peg fitted the hole. I didn't think about it too much, but I found the whole experience of being in a band so liberating, a total catharsis. You could lose yourself in the band and the music, but you could stay in control: you were lost but your senses were razor sharp. It was better than any high I'd known. You could scream and beat the demons out of you. You could do anything on stage and it was acceptable. It was mentally and physically exhausting, so that after a gig I slept like I had never done before. You could force the audience into exhaustion with you. Everything became irrelevant but the moment. All my nervous energy was dissipated. My nerve ends were fused and focused on one point. All my exhibitionist tendencies were catered for. My frustration had an outlet. My ego was gratified. My senses calmed. My awkwardness became an asset. And I had fun, utter fun.

The problems with raising the finance and organizing the telephones for *Buy and Sell* became peripheral. Compared with this, Canada gradually lost its attraction. I had the immigration papers, I had even filled them in, but somehow they never got despatched. All my life I'd listened to pop bands, I'd bought pop records, I'd reviewed pop bands. In Canada I'd taken pictures of pop bands, I'd written about pop bands, but now I was in one. I began to write my own songs. After that nothing else seemed quite so satisfying.

From the very first gig I had discovered just how powerful an aphrodisiac rock music could be. At Bolton Street I was sitting on the edge of the makeshift stage, winding up the microphone wire, when I heard a voice say: 'Would you like to come home with me?' I looked up. Before me was a tall girl with long brown hair. She was very pretty and I was taken aback. Never before had I known a woman be so forward. It had always been clumsy approaches by me and clumsy responses by the girl.

'You were really good,' she said, as though the other had been small talk.

'Thanks.' I wound the cable around the microphone.

'Well, would you?'

I looked around. Daphne was at the bar with someone. We were getting very bored with each other and she had been making moves towards Gary.

'What's the address? I'll follow later.'

'You won't come.'

I did. It was dirty, sweaty, totally cathartic sex like I had never experienced before. When it was over she expected nothing else. That was all she wanted from me and all I wanted from her. We understood each other completely. Always sex had been so complicated. This was sex for the fun of it. This was new. I found that this was now to be a regular occurrence. In Poulaphouca after the second gig a girl approached me and said that she had had an orgasm during the set. I was still unused to this so I mumbled inadequately, 'That's nice, thanks.'

We were not, of course, making a living from the band. Three days a week I did an early morning bread round which gave me the great advantage of being able to take the van home and thus provide the band with transport for all its gear. The rest of the time Pat Moylett and I would sell the little fisheye lenses which people installed so they could see who was knocking at their front door. We would keep an eye on the local paper and find areas in which there had been a rape or a mugging and then do a blitz on the nearby estates. 'I don't want to worry you, madam, but did you know that there is a mad rapist loose in this area? Have you ever thought about having one of these ingenious security devices installed for only £5?'

'What are they? How do they work?'

'Well you look through them and you see who's on the other side of the door.'

Slam. The door would open seconds later with the prospective purchaser pressing the viewer to her eye. 'It's a complete and utter hoax. I couldn't see the other side at all when I shut the door.'

'Eh, no madam, you have to drill a hole with this brace and bit we have here.'

'A hole! In my door! Get away the hell out of that. Go on off with you.' The door would begin to close.

'All right, fine, I hope you say that to the rapist when he comes around. He won't be as polite as us.'

The door would open. 'How much is it?'

'£5, madam.'

'All right. But I'll only have one, mind you.'

'Of course, madam, a very wise decision.'

They cost us £1.50 each, which meant a net profit of £3.50. We'd sell sometimes ten a day, which was good money. It was so good, in fact, that we wrote to the manufacturers in Japan asking for exclusive distribution rights for Ireland. I think Pat still has them. It was easy money, but more importantly it also gave me the flexibility I needed to devote my energies to the band.

We had got to the stage where we were the biggest new band in Dublin. We had to do something extra. The obvious thing was to tour Ireland. The problem was that the major venues outside Dublin were part of the showband circuit. The Irish showbands are one of the most anodyne creations in the history of pop. Their line-up is usually larger than that of a rock band and their performance is a cross between a modern variety show and a traditional music hall. The showband system has wasted an enormous number of talented young musicians who are fed into the machine for a pittance of a wage and then spat out when they are forty. The only sensible option was to establish an alternative circuit. I did not have the resources to do it but University College Dublin did, so I persuaded its Entertainment Secretary, Billy Magrath, to come in on the scheme. Using the university offices and phones I set up a tour of all the country's major towns using whatever venues were available – the local community building, arts centre or even the town hall – and wrote to the local police or Boy Scouts or parish priest promising that if they put up posters and we got a good crowd we would make a donation to their charity.

The Boomtown Rats did not have the money or the audience-pull to do it alone, however, so I approached two other Dublin bands to join us. Nightbus were a funk rock band who modelled themselves on Little Feat. Cheap Thrills

THE BOOMTOWN RATS

Phone: Fachtna O'Kelly (01) 803392

1976; a little more together.

played country rock in the style of the Eagles. They were both good bands of their type and in almost every respect better musicians than we were, but we could blow them off the stage. I invited Fachtna O'Kelly to accompany us.

It began with a preliminary gig at Moran's, a small club in the basement of Moran's Hotel which was Dublin's leading rock venue. It was packed out. By this stage the Rats would have packed it out alone. We also hired a flatbed truck and, loading a generator and all our gear on the back, arranged to play a mobile concert all along the main street of central Dublin. I alerted Irish television to the event. I wanted to try and get on the national news. It was the first time that a local rock band had ever been filmed for television news in Ireland, we were told. The plan had been that all three bands would have a turn at playing on the truck. But suspecting that the police might arrive and put a stop to the whole event I opted for the Rats playing first. The others followed behind the lorry in cars. They kept leaning out of the window shouting: 'Get off, it's our turn.' But we ignored them and kept on playing. Before they could get a turn the police arrived.

The event confirmed the others' suspicions that the Rats had set out to stitch them up. I told them we were just out to blow them off the stage and get people to like us, and they had the same opportunity to do it to us. And it was a golden opportunity to set up gigs for later. No matter what happened, they benefited. We had agreed to take it in turns topping the bill and so we did; there was a rota. It just so happened that we were top of the bill in the five main towns: Dublin, Cork, Galway, Limerick and Wexford. But because our styles of music and stage show were so different, the others ended up saying we should go on last anyway. We were more visual and musically more simple. We were more exciting. It was a good tour for all the bands. The whole thing was set up as if we were top rank professionals, which was something the others had not organized before. We pooled our PA so that we had, by local standards, an extremely powerful system. I hired a tour coach which was impressive even if it did turn out that the driver had smelly feet and was drunk all the time. We organized a press conference and a photo session for the local papers in every town. It was all pretty standard stuff so far as most English bands were concerned but in Ireland it was all new. There was a pop industry in England. There was nothing in Ireland. No studios, no pop paper, no gigs, no nothing. We were trying to create a pop sensibility in 1975 and 1976 that could make these things thrive.

What the other bands found hard to understand was that on the one hand, we were demanding as high a degree of professional organization as possible, while on the other, we seemed not to take the performances very seriously. It was a problem we were to encounter later on the post-punk scene in London. We regarded the performance as something to be enjoyed but the prevailing wisdom was that it ought to be taken in deadly earnest. On stage we would persuade the audience to crawl around on the floor and 'Do the Rat', we presented the best 'Rat' dancer with a pound of raw liver. Gary would produce a dead fish from his flies, we would launch into parody songs of the other bands on the tour. We would also come on during the other bands' sets wheeling the tea trolley, pour a cuppa and read the newspaper. We could also lower the mike volume at the sound deck just as they were about to start their first number. They in turn tried to faze us. Sometimes it worked, but we were a much more energetic band and we'd either incorporate the trick into the song or just steam on.

Some of the venues were so desperate that we could only cope with them with a mixture of hard work and good humour. We arrived at the town hall in Youghal to find that no one knew we were coming. Not one poster had been put up. We decided to bluff our way out. While a handful went inside to set the gear up the rest of us formed a queue outside, saying to each other loudly so that passers-by might overhear: 'Great gig here tonight, eh?' Killarney was the same, so we toured the pubs telling people that if they brought ten people with them then they would get in free, and we had a full house within four hours.

The tour ended at the National Stadium in Dublin. It seated 2,000 and everyone said we were mad to use it. It cost £400 to hire when most of the town halls had cost a mere tenner. But I maintained that we had to behave like stars and between the three bands we should be OK. Anyway I wanted to end on a high. We got 1,300 people there that night. At the end of the tour we each had made £16 profit on top of the £1 expenses I had allowed everyone each day. But we had proved that we could play around Ireland without the showband circuit. We proved that there was an aware pop audience out there who needed to be catered for and could give Irish rock bands a living. And we had proved something altogether different to ourselves – we were good.

There seemed to be nothing left to do in Ireland except repeat ourselves. For some reason, though, I did not feel we were quite ready for England. I went to see a guy who was interested in managing us. He was a likeable, shrewd young wide-boy with a large American car. He wore a satin jacket. 'If you do it like this,' and he chopped the edge of his hand down the table, 'ABC, straight down the line, you won't have any problem, you guys are going to make it.' He spoke in an animated staccato. He was full of nervous energy and kept jumping up and down, his jaw muscles working.

'Try Holland,' he said, chopping out several lines of cocaine onto the glass-topped table in the mews house which was the height of sixties pop art kitsch. He rolled a clean new Irish pound note into a tube and offered it to me. I'd never done cocaine. I hadn't done any drugs whatever since the time in England with the hashish and its aftermath of prescribed Librium and Valium tranquillizers. I had grown dependent on those pills and would get anxious if I didn't have any on me. Finally in Spain I had thrown them away in self disgust. But now I thought, 'What the hell? I'm in a band. This is a rich man's drug. You may never do it again'.

'There's some great venues, it's a good experience,' he continued. 'I know a DJ there, Harry DeWinter, he can give you some contacts.' The cocaine stung my nostrils and made me feel suddenly alert, enthusiastic and optimistic. Holland seemed like a good idea. He chopped out five more lines and rolled a note for the two women who were with him. 'And you need to have some demos of your own songs. Have you written any?'

'Yeah. I've got a couple. "Mary of the Fourth Form" and "Lookin' After Number One", they're called, but we've no money to record with.'

'Here's £500 to be going on with. Remember,' he said. 'ABC, straight down the fucking line.'

We played the Groningen festival. It was a total disaster. It was open air, and it was also bitterly cold and pissing with rain. The stage was huge and we seemed to be miles away from each other. Simon was above us on a drum riser and he couldn't hear us. We'd never worked with monitors before and couldn't hear ourselves as we were used to. Bravado carried us through but it was hopelessly bad. Later whenever the band had a bad gig we would say, 'Groningen,' and it would not seem so awful. Afterwards we were interviewed by Dutch television.

'What did you think of today's performance?' the reporter asked.

'Brilliant.'

'Really?'

'Yes, really. I expect you thought it was crap?'

'Well, yes, to be honest I did.'

'That's because your idea of music is outdated. Playing is supposed to make people react. We knew we were out of tune, we knew that our hands were freezing, we knew that we couldn't hear each other, but that didn't bother us. What was important was the passion of the thing. Now give me a bottle of Scotch.'

He did. I was talking crap. We had been awful. But they broadcast the interview and later I saw it transcribed everywhere, as if it were a sort of manifesto.

We drank the whisky on the way to the second gig that day at the Milky Way in Leidseplein. We were totally despondent after the fiasco in the afternoon. We wanted to give up and stop this ludicrous pretense of being professional and going places. We arrived late and had to play without a sound check. For our opening number we used to walk out one at a time and begin playing one after the other to create a build-up. Gary went out onto the stage first. He picked up his guitar, hit a single note and all the power in the entire building went out. We felt doomed. When the power came back on we were all so pissed off we just played as if we didn't care. It was a stormer and the audience loved it. We could not have had two greater extremes in one day.

The tour of Holland was a great success. We even picked up a couple of extra gigs, supporting Frankie Miller who was a big name there. We returned to Ireland determined that a recording contract had to be the next stop. News was coming across the water of the new wave of English bands, the Sex Pistols, the Damned and, the real big news of the moment, Eddie and the Hot Rods. They were practically getting colour supplements in the music press. We were intrigued and jealous. Shortly afterwards Eddie and the Hot Rods arrived in Dublin to play at Moran's. I went along to see them and got pissed before they came on. When they did I could not believe my ears.

'They're crap,' I shouted. 'They're fucking crap. We're better than them, we're a load fucking better.' It did not go down well. Already I was beginning to earn a reputation as a big mouth. I had forgotten Joyce's dictum that to succeed an Irishman needs three things: silence, cunning and exile. And the absurdities of the British pop industry were guaranteed to provoke me to further unwise comment.

By this time Fachtna O'Kelly had left his newspaper. He was a frail-looking character, thin and gaunt and very pale with that translucent glow of people who are near death, almost like the luminosity of the insane. He liked that nineteenth-century romantic consumptive look, I think. But the appearance was deceptive for he was a man of enormous energy and acumen. I had asked him to be our manager. I could no longer organize the gigs, the publicity, the money, the lights, the PA and write the songs. We had by this stage had visits from recording company representatives and had a couple of offers of contracts from Chiswick Records and from Decca, but there were trifling amounts involved. Everyone said the record companies weren't signing anybody these days. They said we wouldn't get much money. We reckoned £20–25,000 would be enough. Fachtna played us a new record by the Sex Pistols. We'd heard about them. 'They'll last six months,' said Johnnie. He was about right.

We decided to go to London and organise a contract ourselves. Phonogram was our first stop. Phil Lynott of Thin Lizzy, who was also from Dublin and liked to keep an ear out for new Irish bands, had suggested them to us. We took with us a few copies of a tape of four songs. 'Mary of the Fourth Form', 'She's Gonna Do You In', both written by me, and two cover versions, 'Riot In Cell Block No. 9' and 'Barefootin'', an old soul song. When Nigel Grange of Phonogram played the tape I could not bear to sit there and watch as he listened. I rushed out to the toilet. When I came back he was still listening so with Fachtna I diverted myself by stapling Rats posters all over the walls of his office. He said he'd like to hear it again.

We went on to Island who had signed Eddie and the Hot Rods. 'Yes, it's OK, it's not great,' said the man.

'It's a lot fucking better than Eddie and the Fucking Hot Rods.'

'Maybe you shouldn't have said that,' said Fachtna, after we were thrown out.

United Artists was next. 'Hmm,' said the man. 'We've just signed a new band, actually, the Stranglers.'

Frankly I couldn't see why they shouldn't sign us too, especially when I heard the advance they'd given the Stranglers was £60,000. 'Let's hear these Stranglers, then.'

He played the tape.

'Fuck, they're awful.'

Then Virgin offered us a million pounds.

CHAPTER IX

Bought + Sold

It was hard to turn down a million pounds. Virgin Records had offered the contract and began to send company executives across to Ireland to see the band in action. We would pick them up in our yellow transit van, which had no seats. Richard Branson, Virgin's owner and Simon Draper, its head, would huddle on the floor in the back among our equipment. The man from Phonogram, Nigel Grange, kept coming along too with a friend of his called Chris Hill, a DJ. Nigel had decided to leave Phonogram and with Chris form a new label called Ensign. They wanted us to join them. There were some other contenders, too, but we decided it was going to be between these two, simply because we liked them.

Fachtna thought we should play one off against the other. He got Ensign to fly him down to Cannes for Midem, the record industry's annual get-together, and then he got Virgin to pick up the hotel bill. He conducted the negotiations publicly, having lunch with one and then dinner with the other in the hotel restaurant. The bids kept getting higher. The Virgin offer was good, but bore scrutiny. The million would commit us to ten albums over the next five years. It is very hard to be unemployed and turn down a million pounds, but when we broke it down it was £100,000 per album. After paying the cost of making each album, we'd be left with about £30,000 between seven of us. That was less than £4,500 apiece. Not only that, we had to get new equipment and accommodation and pay the road crews, the lawyer and the accountant who had now become vital. Still, Simon, who had got bored and actually left the band, heard about the money, suddenly reappeared and asked if he could come back. Virgin's offer also meant that we would have to sign away our song publishing rights, which, innocent as we were, we knew was where the real money was to be made. Ensign, on the other hand, though they were offering only a three-album deal, were putting up proportionately more per album and were not asking for the publishing rights. Sometimes we'd throw a party for the visiting virgins and ensigns.

It was after one of these that things finally ended between Daphne and myself. I had gone to one of these parties with her, but after she had gone home I had been dancing with the girlfriend of the guitarist from another band. She was a tall girl with a wide mouth and very dreamy eyes. As we danced, I told her that I wanted to go to bed with her and she suggested we go upstairs. There was a row because her boyfriend, who was drunk, found out and came up to get us. We were hard at it when he began hammering on the door. We carried on as he kicked and railed outside, then we heard Gary walk up the staircase and pacify the bloke. Meanwhile, Pat Moylett, who had always fancied Daphne, rushed home to tell her what I was up to. It was a sad end to a sad relationship. We had had a kind of love, but it was based on a clinging desperation. We were mutually destructive. The problem was we were totally incompatible. She was introverted whilst I was loud and extrovert. She liked calm and routine, I got bored quickly. We had lived together for years, but now my life was about to change fundamentally and drastically and it was not the sort of life she wanted. I felt now I'd be able to shout out the things I wanted to say, whether people agreed with me or not, I didn't care. Fame would liberate me. I could do things, I was excited. It was the right time to split. We still slept with each other, but we hadn't made love in months. We were simply bored with each other. The Rats signed with Ensign and the first album included a song for Daphne with the lines, 'Don't trust anything, especially love,' and, more telling, 'Our eyes are dry, but we're bored to tears.' We parted not with a bang, not even with a whimper, we simply parted. I am glad the both of us are happy now.

Ultimately, we had chosen Ensign partly because Chris and Nigel seemed genuinely interested in the music we were doing and partly because we thought they would work hard for us – they were a new company and their success would depend very much on ours. We would have to pay for the production of our first album from the advances and so our accountant tied the money up in a scheme which meant that if we did all our recording outside England and kept the money, which we grandly assumed we'd make, out of the country too, our tax bill, we hoped, would be minimal. That was the theory. There was no sudden massive influx of money, nor a change of life style for us.

The others had had a much harder choice than me. I leapt at the chance of getting out of Ireland again. Johnnie, Pete and Gerry now had to choose between architecture or gambling on the Rats being successful. If we failed, they were left with nothing. Possibly they could go back to college, but they'd be that much older. Gerry had the hardest choice: he was married and had a house. I didn't think he'd leave; he had the most to lose, but he did. Gary was more or less in the same position as me and Simon had already decided.

We all moved to England, leaving behind a furore created by my announcement to the press in Ireland that the Boomtown Rats had been signed up for more than the Beatles or the Rolling Stones. This was true, but it was no great achievement. In the days when those bands signed their first deal, the sums paid in advances, were negligible. But the press still ran headlines like 'Boomtown Rats sign for more than Beatles'. The fact that no one was prepared to tell them the exact amount for fear of jeopardising the tax arrangements only fuelled the whole business further. We moved to England with Fachtna, who was like a seventh member of the band, and our roadie Phay Taylor, who I persuaded to give up his job in the Solus light bulb factory and take a chance on it. We also hired a publicist, B.P. Fallon, who had previously worked with T. Rex and Led Zeppelin, whom he constantly referred to as Zeppo. He had some association with the leading new wave independent label, Stiff Records.

B.P. had an anarchic sense of humour which proved a mixed blessing. Many of his stunts were outstandingly successful. Others were outrageous to the point of being counter-productive. Like the time he bought a hundred dead rats from a laboratory, and sealed them in plastic envelopes containing formaldehyde, planning to drop them from a balloon over the crowd at an open air pop festival on the weekend of our first single release. The plot was foiled by the fact that he couldn't get into the record company balloon he intended dropping the rats from.

Now that we had access to the centre of the British punk movement, we were able to see just how little we had in common with it, apart from the fact that we were both doing something new in reaction to the lassitude of the more established bands. We went along to places like the 100 Club. The first night we went, the Damned were playing in support of another band called Roogalator. There were not many people in the audience, hardly more than thirty, and they virtually ignored the support band, as audiences so often do, but the next week we read in the *New Musical Express*, which to us had always been the bible of the pop industry, that the place had been jammed with people there to see the Damned, who had been given a riotous reception. In fact, the Damned had been booed mercilessly. We quickly realised that much of the New Wave phenomenon was sheer hype, created and nurtured by an élite within the music press as bored as the bands were with the lack of excitement and the need to have something new to write about. Nor could we believe just how bad many of the bands were who received critical raves in the music papers. Later, people said that that was the point, but it wasn't because in the reviews they referred to brilliant players. To me, who had always heard how bad we were musically, this came as a revelation. The difference between them and us musically was that we had been allowed to develop in relative obscurity in Ireland where we had learned how to play and write songs over a period of eighteen months. Bands like the Sex Pistols, the Clash and the Damned were having to learn in the glare of media attention and in public.

At first, this greater musical knowledge was to our advantage. The pop papers were suspicious of our ability, but the radio, desperate to get in on this New Wave thing, thought most of the records awful. But in fact bands were able to disguise their inability in the studios and could produce great records. Live they were unexciting and hopeless. Of course, there was much more involved besides the music, and we understood that, but the radio stations didn't. So that, later, when our first single came along, they jumped on it because it sounded familiar to them; it had a connection with a musical past which, unlike the punk bands, we had never disavowed. The single, 'Lookin' After Number One', had a melodic hook, was fast and urgent and sounded fashionable. They loved it and they played it. We became 'the acceptable face of punk'. The alternative establishment of the new music turned the phrase on us with scathing disdain. The irony was that this 'respectable' ring of musicians and songwriters became known as 'new wave'.

Fachtna had found a big house for us out at Chessington in Surrey. It was an old mansion which had once been given by Henry VIII to one of his mistresses. Ironically it was owned by Virgin Records and one of its largest rooms had been soundproofed, so it was perfect for rehearsing in. Chris and Nigel introduced us to Mutt Lange, a brilliant record producer who was then relatively unknown, but who has gone on to become one of the most successful in the world. We played for him at Chessington. 'What do you think?' the Ensign man asked him hopefully. 'I think they're terrible,' he replied, in his clipped South African accent. 'What on earth do you expect me to do with this lot? I really would rather not get involved.'

They took him to see us perform and he changed his mind. One week into recording at Dieter Dirk's studio in Stommeln, just outside Cologne, we began to wish that Mutt had stuck to his first instinct. Robert John Lange was a martinet. He was a perfectionist who drove others as hard as he drove himself. We had made our demo tapes in a little studio owned by Eamonn

September pin-ups in the 1978 Punk Calendar.

Andrews in Dublin. The whole thing had taken a couple of hours. We just ran through the songs a few times and picked the best version. With Mutt the recording lasted eight weeks. We did seventy-eight takes alone for 'Lookin' After Number One'. We had in our brief two-hour experience in the studio played together as if it were a live performance. Now we were required to create a layered production with each instrument playing on its own away from the others. The sound had to be broken into its component parts in order to give the producer greater control in the final stages of mixing the instruments together. It caused us enormous initial difficulties. For the first time we actually heard ourselves individually, and we were embarrassed because some of us were playing completely different chords to the others. We had been playing these mistakes live for months. We lived in an apartment connected to the studio and often worked from 10 a.m. through to 2 a.m. Mutt was obsessive about detail and would spend hours going over and over the same thing until in the end we lost the feel of it. We felt inadequate, the more so, because Mutt himself was a brilliant musician and was impatient with our fumbling.

'Hit it harder, hit it harder, Johnnie,' he would call through at Fingers pounding the keyboard.

'Harder, Pete, it's not coming through.' In the end Pete's fingers were raw with playing. Mutt was a bass player himself and, unintentionally, he kept belittling Pete's ability. 'That's no good. You're not playing it properly. It goes like this.' Then he would play it and completely outclass Pete.

'Pete's a nice bloke, Bob, but he's a lousy bass player. You'll have to get rid of him.'

We laughed, years later, when critics, reviewing our records, asked, 'Why can't they get back to the spontaneity of their first recording?'

Our first single was to be 'Lookin' After Number One'. I'd written it in Ireland, like the other songs on the first album. Most of them I had written in the kitchen of 17 Seapoint Avenue, the house we had moved to after Clyde Road. Billy Magrath would be in bed above the kitchen and he'd wander down and say, 'That wasn't a bad one.' Or, 'Didn't think much of that.'

Most of the songs were about people I'd known, or about Dublin. *He said, I'm leaving, I'm getting out, I'm going to go somewhere it doesn't stink, away from the alleys, somewhere I can think. It's a strain on the brain living close to the brink. Look at that brick wall gravestone where some kid has sprayed, 'Nobody could be bothered to rule here, OK?'*

'Number One' was more general. It was a quintessential seventies song – for the 'me' decade. *I am an island, entire of myself,* and, ironically, the lines, *Don't give me love thy neighbour, don't give me charity, don't give me peace and love, or the good lord above. You only get in my way with those stupid ideals.* It was not a personal song, with the exception of the lines, *Never underestimate me,*

I'm nobody's fool, and, *I don't want to be like you, think like you, talk like you, I'm going to be like me.* It was a manifesto in one sense and it was about the pervasive selfishness of the time which was beginning to tire me.

We knew that if the record was going to get anywhere we would have to do some concerts to build up an audience in England. It was to be our first performance in that country, other than a small club gig we had done in London for the employees of Phonogram records, of which Ensign records was a subsidiary. I had hated that concert, I had felt like we were on trial, which we were in a sense. People there hung around halfway down the hall, sipping drinks and staring at us. 'It was like playing,' I said, 'to filing cabinets.' Later, they joined in. 'Any company who's got Demis Roussos is OK by us,' I told them.

Now we thought it best to avoid London. It was 1977 and there was too much competition there with the Pistols, the Damned, the Clash, the Jam and Elvis Costello all happening at the same time. We thought if we built support in the country and left London to the others, we could get a larger following. With this in mind, we went to the north and began a short tour there.

Our first concert was in Blackburn in a pub called the Lode Star. We got £70. There was an audience of about fifteen or twenty. Four months later, when we returned there, there were 500 people in the same venue which was some indication of how quickly it all took off. 'Lookin' After Number One' was named Single of the Week in the *NME* and entered the charts at Number 78 the week it was released. We were ecstatic. To be in the English charts at all was a great achievement for an Irish band. Phil Lynott had asked us to go back to Dublin to support Thin Lizzy at a big concert in Daleymount soccer ground. It was a triumph and a vindication. Now they could all eat the many words they'd written putting the Rats down. Soon the record had got to Number 11. I rang my family, I was so proud. They were staggered. All our lives we had sung songs from the charts, followed the progress of our favourites and now here I was. I felt I had finally done something to make my old man proud of me and show him that all those years I wasn't a complete no-hope.

The day after Daleymount we did our first TV show. B.P. had got us on the *Marc Bolan Show*. Marc died two weeks later in a car crash. He was making a comeback at the time and he was doing B.P. a favour by having us on. The show itself was awful. There was no opportunity for a sound check beforehand and during the performance we were surrounded by dancing girls waving numbers in front of us. But it didn't matter, we were on TV. Then came the news that we were going to be on *Top of the Pops*, the single most important pop show in the country. We knew that a *Top of the Pops* appearance could make the difference between failure and success for a record. In the New Wave gestalt, as defined by the *New Musical Express*, the fashionable view of television in general and *Top of the Pops* in particular was that it was part of the decadent old order which had to be overthrown. New Wave music was about an alternative. It had a political or quasi-political function. It was not the same as pop music, which was merely about the kids being diverted by mindless tunes and performers getting rich on their backs. By going on *Top of the Pops* we were supposedly betraying the values of the New Wave and were in danger of being smeared with that most awful of accusations, commercialism. I had no time for this sort of nonsense. I simply thought it pathetic to equate a TV pop show with a political act. Much of it was mere hypocrisy. The Sex Pistols were pretending they didn't want to go on the show; the reality was they were desperate to appear, but couldn't get on simply because of who they were. Finally, after 'holding out' for a year, the Pistols 'decided' they'd go on *Top of the Pops* as a radical gesture. In fact, they had made a video acceptable to the BBC who allowed it to be played. This was hailed as a 'revolutionary triumph' by the press: our appearance, the year before, was apparently a 'sell-out'. The Clash made it a central tenet of their stance that they would never appear – the net result being that they only had a few minor hits. They could all go and fuck themselves as far as I was concerned. I wanted to sell records, I wanted as many people to hear and see us as possible.

In any case, we did not feel ourselves to be primarily part of any new grouping. We could not help being around the same age as the people in the other bands, or that the fashions and styles of our times made us appear to be in the same camp as them. All we had in common was the conviction that something new needed to happen in music, but the Boomtown Rats never wanted to be part of a political, or pseudo-political movement. That is not to say that the songs themselves were not political, but it was for the individual to interpret and agree or disagree with us. I wrote: *The only act of revolution left in a collective world is thinking for yourself.* We were on a collision course.

Later in 1977 we released a second single from the album. It was called 'Mary of the Fourth Form'. It was the imaginary life I'd made up for a schoolgirl I'd fancied in Murray's called Mary Preece. The record went to Number 14. We decided, after a triumphant year, we'd return to Ireland as the conquering heroes. The day after we arrived in Dublin I was sitting in the promoter's office working on tour plans when this weird girl walked in. She was about seventeen and dressed in an outfit of ragged lace, which made her look like a cross between a hippy and a punk. She was small and waif-like, her hair was platinum blonde, and she was gorgeous. When she spoke, she sounded like an upper class English person.

'Hi,' she said looking straight at me.

'Hi, I'm Bob Geldof.'

'I know, we've met before.'

'Have we? Where?'

'In that restaurant in the Fulham Road, at the party for "Lookin' After Number One", remember?'

'Oh yeah, I remember.' I didn't.

'How are you?' she said.

'OK. Don't stand at the door, come in.'

'There's nowhere to sit.'

'Come over and sit on my knee.'

She did. Great, I'm going to get fucked tonight, I thought. Her name was Paula Yates. She'd just finished doing her 'A' levels at St Clare's in Oxford and was now a charlady in London.

'I have my own squeegee,' she said.

I invited her to the concert that night. The promoter hired a row of Daimler limousines to transport us. We were in Dublin, we were going to flaunt it. Halfway down Grafton Street she leaned over and unzipped my trousers. I looked up towards the driver. 'Don't do that,' I said. He wasn't looking. Outside the limousine, familiar places were passing the window. 'Stop it, will you?' I said halfheartedly. Christ, this one has been around, I thought. Afterwards she told me she thought she'd better do it, because she imagined that's what all rock stars expected.

After the concert that night, we all went to a night club. She was sitting talking to Fachtna when a shifty and embarrassed young man approached. 'Hi,' he began awkwardly. 'I'm Bono. I'm the singer in a band called U2.' 'So what?' said Paula. Bono walked away crushed. At the end of the evening I said, 'Well, are you coming back with me, or not?' It wasn't really very romantic.

I was staying with the tour promoter. We were sleeping on the floor. It was Christmas and it had been an incredible year, but there was no money coming in yet from the record and we were living pretty frugally. Other people may have been surprised: after all we'd been on telly, had two records in the charts, had limos, so we must have been bona fide 'pop stars'. My bed was three cushions and an afghan coat. 'Listen to the rain on the skylight,' I said, as we lay there. It was my attempt at a romantic pause. The next morning we found it hadn't been raining – the toilet cistern had burst. Later she told me that she thought that night I was a pervert, but at the time all she said was that I had pinched most of the coat during the night and so she'd pay for us to stay in a hotel the next night. I was very impressed; I wasn't to know that she used up all her money doing it. When I went to Dun Laoghaire to visit my father, I tried unsuccessfully to get rid of her. She kept hanging on to me and kissing me while I was trying to talk to the old man. I was quite embarrassed.

The band began to call her 'the limpet'. She went off to stay with her mother who was living in a castle in County Clare for Christmas, but the day after Boxing Day she was back. I kept trying to give her the push, but she wouldn't take the hint and even once talked her way onto the tour bus. She was very funny, she had a lot of bottle, I thought she was brilliant, but I didn't want a long-term relationship. The memory of Daphne was a bitter and painful one; I wasn't going to get into all that again. Besides, I had just become a pop star and the world – and its legs – had opened up for me. I didn't want to limit my options – it was the first time I'd had any.

On New Year's Eve at Galway Daphne turned up to see the band and I had to ask Paula to go up to the hotel room after the gig while I had a drink with Daphne. I didn't want Daphne to think I was trying to rub her face in it, coming over as the famous pop star with his blonde bit from London. Paula was piqued, but she tried to pretend that she wanted an early night anyway. I kept sending people up with sausages on sticks to keep her company.

There was some doctors' convention at the hotel and they were trying to pick a fight with us. Everyone, including the doctors, was well stewed, so to avoid it we went upstairs at about 1 a.m. Some of the others had retired earlier with their girlfriends, and the rest of us tiptoed along the corridor, then knocked quietly on their doors. 'Have you got a fag?' we'd ask. As they opened the door, we all rushed in and dumped the naked couple, blankets and all, in the bath and turned on the cold tap. If they didn't answer the door, we kicked it open and did it anyway. After about half an hour, we were exhausted and all went off to bed. My own door had been kicked down so I just propped it back into place and got into bed with Paula. Robby McGrath, the tour manager, who had been riding up and down in the lift with all his clothes off, went down the corridor making a note of all the broken doors with the intention of paying the manager in the morning.

It was not long, however, before the police arrived. Probably the manager called them, or possibly they'd been keeping an eye on us. They regarded us in Ireland then rather like a home-grown Sex Pistols. Perhaps we'd attracted attention because the day before in Cork B.P. Fallon had asked the Irish Prime Minister Jack Lynch to have his picture taken with us. He didn't know who we were and just assumed it was a gang of lads who wanted it done for personal reasons. There was a crash as the door was knocked over and in walked the cops. We sat up in bed. They grabbed hold of me and dragged me out, bollock naked.

'Now, little girl, just because he's a pop star it doesn't mean you have to sleep with him,' they said in thick west of Ireland accents to Paula, who sat with the sheet pulled up around her. They were disappointed to find that she was English, not under age and that she was quite happy to be there. They began to root through the collection of medicines I carried to keep my throat in order. 'Aha, what's this?' one said holding up a sachet of Lemsip.

'It's a Lemsip,' said Paula.

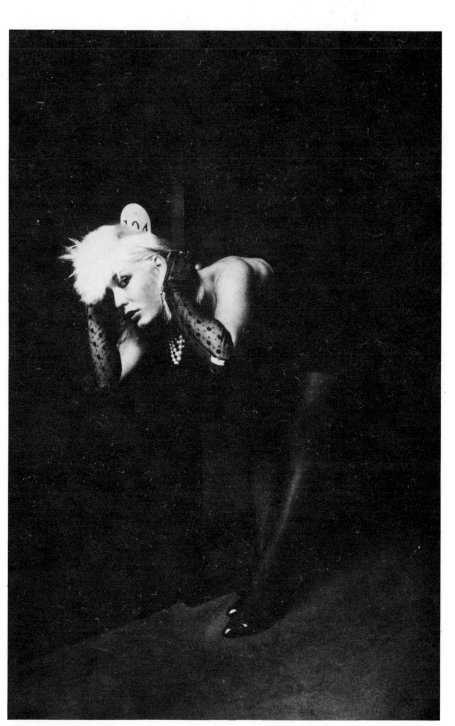

The limpet: Paula in 1978.

'And what's this?' he said, holding up a throat pastille.

'It's a throat pastille. Do you mind if I go back to sleep now?' They were not amused, but I was.

Paula had been taking the train to each concert, because, as in most bands, there is a 'no girls on the bus' rule. This is to avoid the tension created by a canoodling couple in the back seat. But now I wanted her with me and felt an idiot for my previous behaviour towards her. She made me laugh a lot and I felt more comfortable with her than I ever had with Daphne. She was also very clever. I began to miss her when she wasn't there and now resented the others teasing her and imitating her accent. In Wexford I overheard some local yob commenting on the way she was dressed. I grabbed his collar, begging him to repeat it. He didn't. I became very protective towards her, but I was becoming uneasy, because I didn't like what was happening to me. I was never going to become dependent on anything or anyone again. I had dispensed with cigarettes, getting drunk, asthma preventatives and drugs. I was not going to fall in love again.

Back in Dublin, before we left the country, the band was asked to play on *The Late, Late Show*, the biggest TV show in Ireland. Its host, Gay Byrne, was to interview me. This was the opportunity I'd been waiting for. I made no attempt to curb my views or my language. The venom and frustration which had been welling inside me for more than a decade spilled out. Ireland was a place for which I felt only complete loathing. Riddled with prejudice, stymied by the dead hand of conservatism, tainted by the false martyrdom of nationalism, in the thrall of medieval-minded clerics, despoiled by the greed of property speculators, betrayed by the mendacity of corrupt politicians, it suppurated in a sea of self-pity and hypocrisy. Cries of 'shame' greeted this.

Yet for all its smug piety, I railed, it had its price, everyone did, even those nuns in the audience had their price. *Uproar.* Their price was an easy life with no material worries in return for which they gave themselves body and soul to the Church. *Greater uproar.* I did not stop there. I vented my personal griefs. Blackrock College was a toilet. Its old boys' association was nothing more than a Mafia. My father had been insensitive and had beaten me frequently and needlessly. *Total uproar.* But I didn't care. We'd left all that behind. This time next year we'd be Number 1.

I couldn't help it. As it poured out, I could feel the burden of resentment gradually lighten. At my father's yacht club, where he and his cronies had gathered to watch the programme, there was deep embarrassment and commiseration that the boy should have turned out like this. From the pulpit the next morning I was denounced. 'Let us pray for the soul of this poor, demented boy and for his father who has been caused such anguish.'

'You were a bit hard on me, lad,' said the old man, the next day.

'Well, there you go,' was all I could reply. At least now he knew the depth

of the resentment I had harboured. Somehow, though, the whole exercise had
been necessary to me. I felt my revenge was complete and I felt purged.

★   ★   ★

We returned to England, where I was seized with a sense of panic that we
might be a two-hit flash in the pan and, as a result, sat down with Johnnie to
write a song which we hoped would be a certain hit. I'd written on a tube
train the lines, *She's so twentieth-century, she's so 1970s, she knows the right things
to say, she's got the right clothes to wear, she's a modern girl.* I wrote endless verses
about girls I knew who were considered 'hip'. Paula was in there, but I
removed that verse before recording it. The result was 'She's So Modern'
which I think is the worst of all our singles. It now sounds very Benidorm and
rather squeaky. But at the time, it did the trick. It got to Number 12 and had a
lot of airplay, but we still hadn't cracked the top ten.

The band were now, with our third hit, the first pure pop band of the new
era. This was because the BBC were keen on us. They were acutely aware of
the power and dynamism of the punk movement but they could see no way
to harness it, for by definition many of its values were anti-establishment and
anti-social. Many of its exponents deliberately produced work which was
unsuitable for the BBC. For them bands like the Rats embodied the spirit and
the sentiment of the new times but also had the virtue of being able to actually
play and write melodic songs with hooklines just like the traditional sixties
pop songs. This pat view of us was no truer than the neat pigeonhole scorn-
fully allotted to us by the increasingly malevolent papers. There was an ambivalence about the Rats at this period. On the one hand we were a new band
struggling to get our start in music, on the other we were contemptuous of
the system, but prepared to use it. 'A record company's job is to exploit our
talent,' I said. 'Our job is to exploit theirs.' As I wrote in a song, 'You scratch
my back and I'll claw yours.'

But I also loathed the alternative establishment of the music press who I perceived as no different from anyone else who tried to tell me what to think. They
seemed to me self-indulgent and trite and their politics self-concerned and
puerile. They were staffed by self-conscious exponents of the 'new journalism'.
Most of them wanted to be in bands. I found the whole thing a joke, but at
first we played the game. We had to. They were, whether we liked it or not, a
determining factor in our career.

We'd started off, like most bands, in a honeymoon period with the pop
papers. A person in a new, successful band with a good line in rhetoric is good
copy and interesting. But when the rhetoric continues and, indeed, increases
in direct proportion to the band's success, that person apparently ceases to be
interesting and becomes a loud mouth. In those days everybody took everything seriously. It was very infra dig to be seen to laugh or enjoy yourself on

stage. It was all supposed to be angst or anger or projected boredom. People seemed to think we were taking the piss out of the whole business just because we'd mess about and indeed we were.

On Good Friday in 1978 we were doing a gig at the Lyceum in London and during the sound check we found two massive pieces of wood at the side of the stage, so we decided to make a cross out of them. We began the gig that night in darkness with white light flashing across the stage like lightning and clouds of dry ice pouring over the edge of the stage while Fingers made wind noises on the synthesizer. Then I came on with the huge cross and a massive voice boomed across the PA, 'This is my beloved son in whom I'm well pissed off.' The audience loved it, but not the music press. 'Geldof's ultimate messianic complex,' they spat. They seemed incapable of understanding the concepts of humour and irony. I'm Irish and therefore have a highly defined sense of the ridiculous. Who could look back at what had happened to me over the previous ten years and not find it preposterous? Certainly, I did. I found it almost unbelievable. I projected self-assurance and confidence through bombast and bravura. The more bombastic I became, the more they hated it, but an absolute belief that what I was doing was right and enjoyable was always undermined by an undertow of insecurity.

I refused to take pop music seriously. It wasn't the be all and end all, it was important to me because it was what I did and in that regard I was serious about my writing and playing and recording, but then the ironic side of me would quietly snigger at the thought of me taking anything I did seriously. Pop music should be treated with the disrespect it deserves. If this society chooses to over-compensate some people for having the mediocre talent of being able to think up a few lines worth whistling, fine, take the money, but don't confuse the amount of money with the value of the work. Respect for *artists* I believe to be a total nonsense. It sickens me to see so many egos so carefully pampered. The only thing to respect is yourself and others.

Two things contributed to the build-up of the feud which developed between the punk establishment – as embodied by the *NME* and bands like the Clash – and us. The first was the undoubted success of the band. So far as record sales were concerned we were going from strength to strength. Our next single was 'Like Clockwork' which Pete, Simon and I wrote jointly. It got to Number 6. Then came 'Rat Trap' which was our first Number 1. The second album, 'Tonic for the Troops', made a million pounds and went gold. This was not what punk bands were supposed to do.

They were certainly not supposed to delight in it. I continually annoyed the purists by saying in interviews, as I had done ever since the early days in Dublin, that what I wanted out of pop music was to get rich, get famous and get laid. Getting rich would give me what Humphrey Bogart called Fuck You money – the ability to do exactly what you liked, and you could only do that if there was no one who had any financial leverage on you. To the Stalinist music press this was evidence of my capitalist deviancy. Getting famous seemed to be no more than an articulation of what is implicit in the very act of playing music on stage as distinct from playing it for pleasure in the bedroom at home. To the music press this was proof that I was on a gigantic ego trip from which everyone else in the pop world seemed to be exempt. Getting laid, regularly and often, as most musicians did, seemed to me to need no recommendation to someone who had been nervous about even asking a girl to dance. To the music press stating it was a form of sexist exploitation.

We had, in their terms, nil credibility. Street credibility was perhaps the most important and unquantifiable asset to possess in the music world then. Talent and ability couldn't get it for you. Record sales positively stripped you of it, unless you had already become icons like the Pistols. 'Cred' was achieved by your rhetorical stance and no one had more credibility than the Clash.

The second factor in the growing rift was my inability to keep my mouth shut. When a band like the Clash accused us of being the Bay City Rollers of punk, I laughed at them. They were total hype from beginning to end, I said. I thought a song like 'Lookin' After Number One' was much more of a political statement than 'Sten Guns in Knightsbridge'. 'Do me a favour,' I would say. 'Are they supposed to have Gucci stocks and Harrods gun-cases?' It was just cant and rhetoric. The revolutionary Joe Strummer, who is a nice bloke, lived in a beautiful house in Regent's Park which he shared with Sebastian Conran, whose brother Jasper, the clothes' designer, used to produce shirts for them. The Clash used inane tokenism like playing an entire gig with a broken string; it was supposed to be indicative of their passion and, of course, a true son of the proletariat like Joe *would* only have the one guitar and one set of strings. The fact that he had three or four spare in the wings was kept pretty quiet. It was total hype. When I retaliated like this, they would say I was jealous. They were right, but so was I.

Tokenism also extended to cars. Being seen in a limo or a large car was leaving yourself open to the most vituperative abuse, never mind that the large car probably belonged to the record company. If the Pistols were seen in a large car, it was probably because they were taking the piss. If the Rats were seen in a large car, it was probably because they 'meant it', whatever that meant. The car itself, in the middle of this ideological struggle, magically transformed itself into an anti-revolutionary symbol akin to the Bastille. I would argue that if two cars came to pick you up, it didn't matter which car you chose so long as either would get you there. If the cars in question were a Mercedes and a Volkswagen, for example, why not take the Mercedes? It was more comfortable, faster and fun. They were only cars and to make your choice of car into a political philosophy seemed to me to be utter and complete nonsense. The real world was more important.

The Sex Pistols seemed to me to be one of the few genuinely nihilistic bands around. The atmosphere in their camp seemed to be permanently poisonous. I once saw them at a university gig. They were fighting before the concert. Steve hit Sid Vicious; he was fed up being in a band with someone who hadn't a clue how to play bass. Malcolm wanted him there simply as a catalyst, so when Steve hit Sid, Sid was doing his job properly. The concert was awful. It was empty and sad, almost. As they were leaving, Sid and Nancy walked over to the bus door and Malcolm slammed it in Sid's face and told him he could fuckin' walk back for all he cared. I liked Johnny Rotten. He was an extraordinary character with a fierce intelligence. He was very Irish in his attitudes. There's an Irish joke about a man who gets off the boat in a new country and asks the nearest person, 'What sort of government do they have here?' The man tells him, and the Irishman answers, 'Well, whatever it is I'm against it'. Johnny was like that.

One day when we were both in Cork, he on holiday visiting his relatives and me picking up an Irish pop music award, we met in a pub. A man came over and put his hand on Johnny's arm and began asking him a question. Johnny interrupted him halfway, turning around with those laser eyes and said, 'Don't touch me, I'm special'. The man quickly removed his hand, mumbled an apology and disappeared. Johnny loved being famous, probably even more than I did.

There was a real mad wit about the Pistols. Once we were sharing recording studios with Queen, who were in the studio next door. It was about 2 a.m. and Freddie Mercury was tinkering on a piano in the glow of a single blue light. In lurched Sid, out of his mind on something or other, with a can of lager in his hand, and he shouted in his most uncouth tone, 'Oi! Freddie'. There was a pause as he slumped against the door. 'They tell me you're bringing ballet to the masses'. Then he lurched out to be sick. But for all the anarchy in the UK, the Pistols still signed contracts, attended rehearsals, and wrote songs; whatever the rhetoric in the end, being in a band was hard work and demanded self-discipline. But saying things like that about the Pistols in those days was like attacking Marx in a Soviet politburo meeting.

My mouth even managed to alienate people who were initially on our side. The Radio One disc jockey, John Peel, was quite keen on us right from the start in Ireland, indeed he had even offered to make an EP from one of our demos. Later he became quite scathing. I had made some pointless remarks in the press in Ireland about ageing hippies, but I doubt if this affected his judgement.

Many of the ordinary things which we did became the object of criticism. An interviewer once asked Pete Briquette what was the best thing about being famous. He thought about it and replied: 'You can get into other people's gigs for free'. In a sense it was true. One of the great pleasures of London after Dublin was seeing what other bands were doing, meeting people associated

THE
Boomtown
RATS

Clockwork

I'm not disconnected
I'm not unaware,
I'm in one place at one time,
I'm neither here nor there,
I'm locked to the mainstream,
Tied it to the world,
Plugged into my surroundings.
I'm not out on a limb,
I'm thinking in a straight line,
I'm thinking that these thoughts are mine,
I hear the minutes rushing by
I feel the hours flying ___ 'cos
my mind beats time like clockwork,
And we think in sync"

She's alone away with emotion
she sees things clearly now
she says she sees it all plainer
now everything look small from here now
It's alright, it's alright
I'm on your side for a while,
she thinks time is a concept by which
we measure our pain, she wants to
say it again but she don't have
time, 'cos
Here hearts beat time clockwork
And then blood flows by like clockwork'

Count the hours, count the months and minutes,
Born in tears and die in pain that's your limit
There is no ___ but ___ a little logic,
___ their the ticket,
Take the most of what you got,
try.

I stayed in that room for ___ long while,
We watched the seasons gliding past,
We've got ___ say... that's the matter,
___ ___ ___ time,
It's alright, it's alright,
I'm on your side for a while,
We won't fight, we won't cry,
___ be to kill there were ___ ___
Well ___ up ___ ___ ___,

'So ___ our lives beat the like
And our minds ___ ___
And our hearts beat time,
And we think in sync'

The words of *Like Clockwork*, 1978.

with the industry and talking. We would go to other people's performances, we would go to parties thrown by record companies to launch records or new acts. We were in the middle of things for the first time in our lives. Wherever there was anything of any genuine interest we would turn up. So would most other bands, yet for some reason we were singled out by the music press for derision as if we were the only freeloaders in town.

The atmosphere and the rivalries at this time were poisonous. No one seemed to speak to each other any more. The bands became factionalized and violence at gigs became commonplace, both between rival supporters in the audience and the bands themselves. I didn't enjoy it. I wanted to talk to other bands, but it was only when the post-punk people like the Police came along, that we got friendly with people in other groups. But the violent and spiteful attitude being propagated by the press was not necessarily one shared by the fans. We were friendly with the management group surrounding Johnny Thunders and the Heartbreakers, a New York band. Lee Black Childers, their manager, was a famous rock photographer who had taken on Johnny and had brought him to England where he had a chance of success. The group's first gig was to be in Birmingham and in order to get a good crowd, Lee had intended bussing up as many hip kids out of the clubs as he could find to create an impression with the press and to get some people interested in Johnny Thunders. Lee asked the Rats if they wanted to go along on the bus. Some of us said yes. That night on the way up the M1 towards Birmingham, we were surrounded by these exotic and wonderful looking people who had made their very lives a theatre; pins and needles hung out of them everywhere, their hair was spiked and coloured as if a child's paintbox had been poured over it. They were rowdy and shouting and singing and drinking cans of beer. Some of the group asked for a chance to stop and go to the toilet and get cigarettes, so we pulled into a nearby service station. Everybody piled out and ran into the sweet shop. There was a general crush and melee as the kids crowded round the counter to pay for their cigarettes, sweets, and beer.

'Queue up, queue up, form a queue there,' said the elderly woman behind the cash register. Without a murmur these extraordinary visions formed an orderly and silent queue. It took a while for the line to diminish. One young punk muttered, 'I'm bored, and when I get bored I get violent'.

'You just mind your manners and wait your turn,' said the elderly lady.

'Oh, sorry,' mumbled the punk with the anchor pin hanging out of his cheek.

On one occasion the unpleasantness did spill over into violence on the stage. We were playing at the Music Machine in London. It was at the time when the aggression of the punk era was being manifested not in posturing or in spitting, which had been one of the original marks of the movement I could not tolerate, but in actual physical violence. The people on the balcony had begun dropping beer glasses onto the people who were dancing below. Girls were crying and people were leaving with serious gashes in their legs from the flying glass. There were fights in the audience between different factions – punks, skinheads, rockers, National Front people, Clash fans, Siouxsie Sioux followers. We could hear that running battles had developed on the dance floor. The atmosphere was foul, we could sense that even from a stage seventeen feet above the dance floor. The band on before us, who were half skinhead, half punk, had been holding forth about how awful I was and what a sell-out the band were. We refused to go on until things had calmed down a bit. Eventually we went on and half-way through the set, which was coincidentally being filmed for TV promotion in the U.S., a character from one of the earlier bands walked on stage and punched me in the face. He hit me very hard, twice. I staggered to the side and fell over a cameraman who was almost knocked over the seventeen-foot drop. I got up and wiped the blood off my face. We went straight into 'Lookin' After Number One' and sang with special emphasis, with the blood pouring down my face, the refrain, 'I don't want to be like you'. They used the picture on the cover of the *NME* the next week with a holier than thou article on 'Now the Violence Has to Stop', which was ironic considering that they had played a large part in inciting the phenomenon.

There was a welcome respite for us in the time we spent out of public view. For all the imagined glamour of the lives of successful pop stars, we seemed to spend most of our time at Chessington working. All of us lived there with our wives or girlfriends and the crew. We were there for a year and never fought. Because we knew nobody in London, we drew in on ourselves and were quite self-protective and supportive. I was writing a lot of material for the next album. The confidence I'd acquired from seeing our record in the charts made me write fluently: I was very prolific. I would stay in and write while the others just tossed around. Because of the tax scheme there was still not a lot of money around. Fachtna would keep a big box of pound notes under his bed and the band would just wander in occasionally and grab some, but it was just spent on the sort of ordinary things we had always spent money on. A lot of the time was spent practising in the soundproof room. The lyrics of some of my songs, began to reflect my reaction to the dominance of this new establish-ment and its values. 'Watch Out for the Normal People' hinted that there was something more subversive in the rest of us than in the posturings of those who styled themselves as political activists. I sang as one of the normal people: 'there's more of us than there are of you'. But there was a hint in it that I was still feeling an underlying insecurity: 'you're a really lucky bugger that you haven't been discovered'.

We went to Hilvarenbeek in Holland to make the second album. Outside the studio they sprayed the fields every night with fertilizer. It was liquid shit. Plagues of flies descended on the soil. The smell and the insects seemed to find their way into us.

We had done a demo of some of the early tracks with Jimmy Miller, who had recorded 'Beggars' Banquet' and 'Exile on Main Street' with the Stones. He had seen us at the Round House, which was one of our best early gigs in London, and had come backstage. 'You people will be the next Stones,' he had said and offered to work with us. We tried to do 'She's So Modern' with him, but it never sounded quite as I felt it ought. So we tried John Punter who had worked with Roxy Music, but that didn't work out. We were avoiding going back to Mutt because he was such a tyrant. But in the end we decided there was no alternative. He saw immediately what was good and bad about each song and where we had been going wrong in the earlier attempts.

Mutt was much more relaxed this time. It transpired that when he'd worked with us he had been under a lot of strain from the break-up of his first marriage. This time, although he was just as demanding, the atmosphere was more relaxed. We even made time to do a couple of joke tracks, one a calypso about Dun Laoghaire ('Tired and weary, Drab and dreary, That is the way to spell Dun Laoghaire') and the other a grotesque heavy metal parody called 'Hanging Around'. They were made especially for visiting journalists and the bigwigs from the record company who had begun to treat us like special people now we were stars. When we played them the tracks some were literally speechless with the awfulness of it, some tried to make helpful suggestions, like, 'Maybe the middle eight needs a little work before it's just right'. Others simply and sycophantically gulped and said, 'Brilliant', presumably wondering what was going to happen to their big investment.

We were pleased with the second album. Where the first had drawn mainly on the claustrophobic experience of adolescence in Dublin, the second was more outgoing and concerned with people I knew. It also began to look at some things from an oblique angle. This was new for me. The album used all the experience we had gained from our first album and what Mutt had taught us. The band were hardly recognizable from the eager amateurs of the year before. A year of playing had changed that. Our confidence showed on the new LP. It was classic pop and was to prove our biggest selling album in a period when we sold more records than any other British group. We called it 'Tonic for the Troops' and to celebrate its completion I went on holiday with Paula to the West Indies. It was the first proper holiday I had ever had. I lay by the sea in Barbados with this beautiful girl with whom I was in love and waited for the weekly telegrams to arrive chronicling the rise in the charts of the first single from the new album. I had never been for a holiday on a beach before and I finally learned to swim. In one and a half years my life had changed utterly and totally. It seemed ridiculous but I was now a 'pop star'.

CHAPTER X

Truth And Consequence

One night watching television, *Coronation Street*, I think, I saw myself as a pin-up. The action began in a nondescript northern working class pub with the traffic of community gossip. It shifted to a nondescript northern working class living room and the tension of marital discord. From there it switched to a nondescript northern working class bedroom and the surly frictions of adolescence. And there, in the middle of the generation gap, was me, stuck to the bedroom wall.

I had got used to seeing photographs of myself in the teen magazines and the pop press. I had even come to terms with watching myself flicker across a television screen. But here I was as a factual pin-up on a fictional teenager's bedroom wall. 'I'm on *Coronation Street*,' I thought. 'Bloody awful picture.'

Things were beginning to take off with an acceleration which was bewildering and undeniably exciting. When 'Tonic for the Troops' was nominated for an award I attended the ceremony to find that Paul McCartney was one of the other guests. 'You've got cute hair,' Linda said to Fingers.

He freaked. 'I used to be a member of the Beatles Fan Club,' he gibbered in explanation.

'Hi,' said Paul.

'Hi,' I replied, casually. I had seen him, it occurred to me, in *A Hard Day's Night*.

'Liked the album.'

'Thanks.' I had seen him in *Help*. He liked the album.

'What's that song on side two, second track?'

'"Me and Howard Hughes",' I replied, without engaging my brain. I had listened to 'Sergeant Pepper' during the hippy festival we had organized, a half dozen of us in the local park that summer we had become flower people and stolen all the Dun Laoghaire Corporation daffodils.

'Yes, I was interested in that bit in the middle. What is it you use where . . .'

I had seen him over and over again in *Let It Be*. Here he was asking me about a song *I* had written one morning in my bedroom in Chessington. Two years ago I was working in a meat factory.

There was no way that 'Rat Trap' would get to Number 1. We knew that. For a start we had never intended it to. We released it because we were sick of being thought of as a singles band. 'Let's pick the most album-orientated track,' I said, 'and release it as a single so people will see we're an albums band too.' It had entered the charts at Number 22 and then leapt to Number 9. It had climbed slowly to Number 7, then to Number 3, then to Number 2. There was no way it could sustain the momentum to become Number 1. Records just never did that and the current Numbers 1 and 3 and 4 were John Travolta and Olivia Newton John with songs from the movie *Grease*. I asked the record company to clip the chart from *Music Week* which showed us at Number 2 and have it framed. It was the highest we'd ever got. That was an achievement, wasn't it?

I was in bed the morning that Fachtna came in and said, 'We're Number 1!' I leapt, quite literally, from the sheets and ran stark naked all around the house screaming with delight. I met the others in the hall behaving in a similar manner. This was not happening to another person, it was happening to us – and to me. I'd never thought those nights among the stench and steam and dirt of the meat factory would have got us to Number 1, but they had. 'Rat Trap' had been Paul's story, the bloke at the meat factory. It had been about Dublin, but everybody seemed to recognize themselves or their city in the song. *Billy doesn't like it living here in this town, he said the traps had been sprung long before he was born.*

The months which surrounded the release of 'Tonic for the Troops' were like a fast-forward flicker from some fantasy video. We needed to tour to promote the album, but before that we had to go on a short promotional tour of the States to persuade our new American company to get behind the album. Our first record had been released in America on the Mercury label. It had been critically acclaimed, but had not been a commercial success. We were convinced that this was because the label had not done enough for it. They had a promotional man named Mike Bone, who had come up with the idea of sending a dead rat preserved in formaldehyde and wrapped in a plastic bag with 'The Rats Are Coming' written on it, out to every DJ in the country, echoing B.P.'s idea of twelve months earlier. It killed the record stone dead. Years later I was still meeting DJs who said, 'You're the guys who sent that dead rat. Boy, you sure turned us off that record.'

With the exception of Mike Bone, we felt that the company didn't understand us and were not interested in the band. In America you count commitment in dollars and the company had not spent enough money pushing the record. We decided to get off that label, but they refused to release us. We had no weapon to fight with except the withdrawal of co-operation. And so, taking a leaf out of the Sex Pistols' book, Fachtna and I went to Mercury's headquarters in Chicago and invaded the president's office. We had been horrendously abusive about him in the press, but that didn't seem to work.

'Please let us go,' we said, very politely.

'No,' they said.

We started with the filing cabinets. We opened them a drawer at a time and

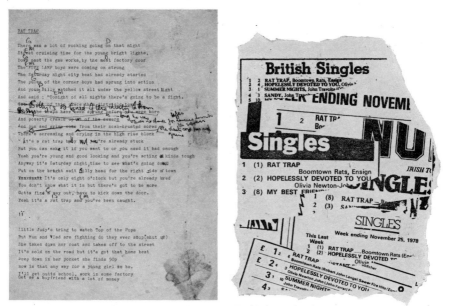

From this: trying to change 'objectionable lyrics'
for *Top of the Pops* consumption.   To this: hurray!

scooped out armfuls of documents and scattered them around the room. We turned over shelves of books. We threw things out of the windows. 'Please let us go,' we said.

'No. Now get out,' he said.

We got out aerosols of shaving foam and began to open drawers at random and squirt it inside them. We opened files and squirted in a foam filling and then sandwiched them closed. We tipped his piles of records into a heap. We pulled the tape from cassettes and flung it like ticker-tape all around the room. 'Please let us go,' we said.

'No, not after this,' he screamed.

The windows of his penthouse overlooked Lake Shore Drive. With our cans of shaving foam in letters four foot high, clearly visible from below, we wrote on the glass: 'Mercury Sucks'. We went into the next door office to continue the message. 'Please,' we said.

'Bastards,' they said. The next week we were dropped and we signed with Columbia.

Columbia was the biggest record company in America, but like everyone else at the time in that country they were confounded by the punk phenomenon, which we, living in Britain, now regarded as the norm. They were afraid that we had irreparably damaged our reputations with the dead rat stunt and were desperate to redress the balance. They wanted to forget the word 'rats' A diktat went out from 'the Black Rock', the giant black-windowed corporate headquarters on 52nd Street in Manhattan. From henceforward no Columbia employee was to refer to us as anything but 'the Boomers'. Fingers and I went over for what was called 'a short promotional tour': it took in thirty-three cities in thirty days. The aim was to prepare the ground for the release of 'Tonic for the Troops', to show that we were really nice guys and to play some videos of the band to the local DJs, sales people, record store people, distributors and journalists, each one of whom had to be talked to.

We had begun to make videos. It was a logical progression from making promotional films as we'd done for the first two singles. I suspected that video would become very important to music. In an interview I said that video would have as powerful an impact on music as the talkies had on movies. They would certainly be as crucial as the FM radio revolution in the sixties. 'Video,' I argued, 'has wrested control of TV out of the hands of the professionals and into the arms of a waiting public.' Bands were the first to exploit this because they had money. With video we could control what we looked like, we could make minimovies to express the band's attitudes and the spirit of the song. Video was easy to use for it worked on the same principle as sound tape, our stock in trade. The fact that you could play back instantly and re-shoot if you didn't like it, as opposed to hanging around for the film to be developed, made everyone instant directors.

From 'She's So Modern' on, we began to use imagery rather than performance to put across ideas. 'She's So Modern' was basically a performance video, but we dabbled with the pictures and the settings at the end, where we draped ourselves, lifeless, over forty flickering TV screens. With 'Like Clockwork', a neurotic song, we tried to emulate the classic films, *Metropolis* and *Modern Times*, not very successfully, but we were groping our way forward in a new medium. I was determined to master it. It was another creative outlet, and it was the first time we were ahead of the field in something; we could make video our own.

For 'Rat Trap' we had done a classic pop film. The Musicians' Union had forbidden me to play saxophone on the video, as obviously I hadn't done so on the record. But I saw a candelabra on the piano at the shoot and I put a mouthpiece in the central candle holder and played it. The impact of video came home when during the next few British gigs kids pulled out candelabra from nowhere and began playing them during the sax solo in 'Rat Trap'. We began to win awards for our videos.

'What's that?' said the Columbia Vice-President, looking at the plastic container suspiciously.

'It's a video,' I said.

'What's it for?'

'Well, while we're here, we can show it in the hotel rooms, or whatever, to the jocks and journalists, and you can get it on TV.'

'Why can't you appear on TV?' he said.

'Well, we will when we get here on tour, but these can be shown for the moment. Anyway, in some ways they're better than the band live, because they express the song better, as well as giving the vibe of the band.'

'Look, let me get this straight. You want me to go to the TV stations and say, "We can produce better TV than you can, use this."'

'Well, you don't have to say it, but in effect, yes.'

He picked up the video cassette and dropped it in the waste paper basket. 'You guys kill me. Bob, just stick to singing and leave the US market to us, OK?' In 1978, there were no video outlets in the US.

★　★　★

There was a guy in Columbia who had really worked hard to sign us, and we became his pet project. Nicholas was a terrible bullshitter, but the more bullshit he expended the more effective he was, unlike most of the other wankers we met on that 'short promo tour'. He was unintentionally very funny. In one interview, I overheard him say, 'So I asked Faulkner,' – as they constantly called Fachtna – '"Faulkner can you sit there, look me straight in the eye and tell me that this is the greatest rock band that you have ever seen?" There was a pause. Faulkner said, "yes," and I signed them. Then I saw them and I said, "Faulkner you were right. Bob Geldawf is not just a star, he is a megastar. Bob Geldawf is the single most dynamic person I have ever met in my entire career."'

He was not short on hyperbole. All of this was delivered in a slow, deliberate manner with much eyeball to eyeball contact. He was a very neatly dressed man with a trim beard, a tanned and balding head, and he did lots of cocaine. So did everybody else. New York seemed to run on the stuff. Everyone pretended no one else was doing it. Someone tapped your elbow, tapped their nose and swivelled their eyes towards the bathroom. As they unscrewed the inevitable little brown bottle with the spoon inside, they'd say, 'Do not mention this to a soul, especially so-and-so, Jesus, if they found out, my balls would be on the line'.

Five minutes later, so-and-so swivelled his eyes. 'Do not tell . . .' he'd say.

'We're talking cabbages and kings here, guys,' Nicholas would say enigmatically. No one knew what he meant, but it seemed to fit.

Wally Meyrowitz was our agent. He assumed I was an Irish Jew. 'With that name and that nose, come on, Geldorf, there's no need to be embarrassed. I've never met an Irish Jew before.'

'What about the President of Israel?'

'Don't be a wise guy. I've never met the President of Israel either.'

There was a lot of confusion with my name. I was used to that. In Ireland I would get letters addressed to 'Kilduff' or 'Gildoff' or 'Gilder' and in one case 'Catchpole'. In England it was 'Geldorf', 'Geldoff', 'Geldov'. As one headline in *Melody Maker* had it, 'Over Here He May Be The Mouth, But Over There He's Just Plain Old Brad Gandalf'.

I liked the people in Columbia, but I began to get irritated when the nth person told me how much they 'believed in the project'. To me it was my life. To them it was one more project. I understood that, it could not be any other way, but I began to resent it. By the end of the month I hated the idea that my life could be determined by these people who I hardly knew. If I wasn't nice to them, if I didn't leave a favourable impression, they could destroy me by their indifference. This was a red rag to a bull. I felt humiliated. All my life I had reacted against people telling me what to do or think or being in any way dependent on anyone or anything, and now I'd got myself into a situation where the control of my professional destiny was in the hands of hundreds of individuals in this vast country. In Dallas I wrote in my notebook,

> 'Tell me what it's like to have to spend
> your life crawling up the arse of
> everybody else.'

At that point our career began and ended in America.

In a deep, ponderously slow and meaningful tone, Columbia's senior executive intoned, while continuing to hold my outstretched hand, 'Bawb, I want you personally to understand that this record company believes in the Boomers one thousand per cent. We're going to get behind this project like you've never seen. When that Columbia machine starts rolling, whoo-oo, watch out boys, stand aside. Your record is great, you are fabulous. No, no, I mean that, you are fabulous, and the band, I'm told, is the hottest thing this country has seen in years. We are all very, very excited and proud to be working on this.'

'Thank you very much.' I looked around the room. Nicholas had his chin down and both his eyebrows raised in a pleased, 'there you go, what did I tell you?' expression. Fachtna nodded appreciatively, stern-faced. He had to put up with more crap than me.

Columbia had not stinted in the itinerary. New York, Buffalo, Cleveland, Detroit, Chicago, Seattle, Portland, San Francisco, St Louis, LA, Washington, Philadelphia, Pittsburgh, Denver. The month was a whirligig of airports, radio stations, hotels, record stores and TV studios. On the plane, Nicholas, in his cocaine-inspired enthusiasm, would begin the chant. 'The next city is hot. We're picking up very positive reports from the college stations. We've picked up some light rotation on WXQYZ, only light, but this is a key station in this marketplace.'

'What's light rotation, Nicholas?' Johnnie asked.

'Johnnie, let me put it this way,' much eyeball contact here, indicating honest talking, no bullshit, cabbages and kings time, etc., 'if your record gets played in light rotation, it's good. Medium rotation is better and heavy rotation it's . . .' the eyebrows would raise and the voice drop, 'we're talking hit, without the "s" on the front, either'.

We were met at the airport by the local company rep. They were usually nice guys who were instantly effusive and defensive of their position *vis-à-vis* what they had or hadn't done for you. After a month, they tended to blend into a seamless line of satin jackets, free T-shirts, sneakers, and baseball hats. They were slightly nervous in the presence of Nicholas and slightly resentful of the orders emanating from headquarters. I felt sorry for them. Their jobs depended on our performance. It was my career, but their lives were spent in the thrall of the programme directors who dictated what was to be played on their local station. If the reps couldn't get their own company's records on the air, they were dead. Their resulting sycophantic behaviour in front of the DJs and programme directors was horrible to witness. They laughed too loud at their jokes, used physical contact too much, humoured the inevitably self-important radio people. I did too, but I didn't intend making it my life.

'Hey man, I'm your local rep, Ray. These are some of my main men. Geoff here is from Q10M, Dean from Z49. You guys want to do an interview with Barb? Great.' Then, in a whispered aside, '(Barb, forget Z49, they're a pile of shit. They're on your record medium rotation, but we've got to get Q10M) Geoff, hey man, Barb would love to do an exclusive with you. He heard the station on the way in, loves it.'

'Great, bring him down, about 4 o'clock, we'll give "Mouse Trap" a spin.'
'"Rat Trap".'

'"Rat Trap", "Mouse Trap", what the hell, it's a great record, Barb, we love it down here.'

'When is the station going to go on it, Geoff?' said Ray.

'Early days, Ray. We're taking a wait-and-see policy. We find it a bit hard to programme. It doesn't really fit our format. We love it, though. Great record. Bring him down, exclusive.'

'Why can't we do it at the press conference?' I asked. 'You heard it, Barb. Exclusive. Believe me, we need this station. I need this station. Trust me.'

There were exclusives with four different stations, all on light rotation. Light rotation seemed to be that they played your record once a lunar month, so far as we could tell; no one would actually tell us. Medium rotation was once a day, heavy rotation we never found out about; we were never on it. Then on to the next place and more, 'Hi-I'm-Bob-Geldof-of-the-Boomtown-Rats-We've-got-a-Number-1-in-the-British-charts-at-the-moment-and-we'll-be-coming-over-here-soon-with-the-band-and-I-just-wanted-to-meet-you-beforehand-and . . .' It was interview after interview, meeting after meeting, smile after smile. Sometimes I would pause momentarily in mid-sentence and wonder if I had already said this once, or whether it was in the last interview. 'Hi-I'm-Bob-Geldof-of-the . . .' Then Nicholas would get out his little coke bottle and his little spoon, 'Just to help you along'.

Some mornings it was two Good Morning Columbus Ohio shows in two different cities with an airport and flight between. And a new local Columbia rep to shepherd us around: 'Barb, you gotta understand it takes eighteen plays in the States for a listener just to identify one particular sarng with a band. We're getting you medium rotation on an experimental station here. They've just changed their format. They've come off disco and are going New Wave. You need the airplay. Have you met Harvey? He owns just about the biggest record store in town'.

'Hi-I'm-Bob-Geldof-of-the-Boomtown-Rats-We've-got-a-Number-1-in the-British-charts-at . . .'

'Great, Barb, great to meet you. Love the record, love the record, "Mouse Trap".'

'"Rat Trap". We really appreciate your help here, Harvey. Are you giving the album much display space?'

'Absolutely', he chomped down on his canapé, 'up front, right up front of those Bs, BO, right in front, BO for Boom.'

The interviews, the video screenings ('Boy, Barb, you look just like Mick Jagger') continued until late at night. And yet another Holiday Inn, Ramada Inn or Howard Johnson. The prawn cocktail canapés grew a film of reddish-tinged scum along the top and the crackers beneath grew soggy. The scotch and soda went flat. My cheek muscles ached from being one of the boys. Sometimes we would stay the night in whatever town we were in, instead of moving on to be somewhere else early the next day. Sometimes we could get a couple of hours to ourselves, but there was nothing to do, so we'd do some cocaine. Sometimes the cocaine had been cut with sulphate and I would get cramps. Sometimes I would wake up after the coke feeling in such a down mood that yesterday's high now seemed counter-productive. Then it seemed less effort to just maintain my cool without taking anything at all.

St Louis. The sign at the airport said St Louis. 'Bob, this is St Louis,' said Nicholas, 'where the big rack-jobbers are. These are guys who can fill the racks in 27,000 stores; that's a lot of records. They work outta St Louis because it is central for distribution. Bob, this is your local guy in St Louis . . .'

'Hi-I'm-Bob-Geldof-of-the-Boomtown-Rats-We've-got . . .'

'Hi Brad, pleased to see you, I thought you might like to meet some of our sales people out here.'

'Hi guys, how's it going? Good luck with our record . . .'

'Sure thing Brad, we're so excited about it, I can't tell you . . . These guys are so keyed up,' said the guy. 'Let me tell you, Brad, that I have never seen this company so keyed up about a project. If the Columbia machine gets behind you . . . you just watch that thing roll . . . these guys sell records like there's no tomorrow . . . Michael Jackson, Bob Dylan, Bruce Springsteen . . . I want you to meet him, him, him and him . . .'

Four neat moustachioed men, the four sales reps, crowded round me in a circle and began to chant like an American football team psyching themselves before a game: 'Sell records, sell records, sell records . . .' they screamed at me inches from my face.

Nicholas winked at me. 'What did I tell you?'

I smiled wearily and went to the toilet with the bottle.

There was a DJ called Sky Daniels. It was Denver. Or was it Detroit. He took us to a club. There was no pressure. It was our only break. We had a great night, but when we came out of the club it was snowing badly and we heard from the airport that the flights had been cancelled. We had to get to Chicago by the next day.

'We have to get to Chicago by tomorrow,' said Nicholas.

'No problem,' said Sky, 'I'll drive you there in the limo.' The limo was the size of a room. We got there, as Sky had predicted, no problem.

'Shit, look at that snow drift,' said Fingers. The main highway was clear but the side roads were blocked. We passed a phone booth.

'Drive down into that snow drift,' I suggested. 'Then we can go back and phone to say that we're stranded. They'll have to come and rescue us. It'll get us into the Chicago papers.'

Sky took a picture of us pretending to be stuck and drove off to Detroit. It was a good story. It made not only the Chicago papers, but the English press back at home, who embroidered it with details of the rescue helicopters.

We finished in Dallas at the CBS Convention. I was handed a name tag that, quite literally, said 'Brad Gandalf'. 'Hi Brad.' 'Brad, great to meet you.'

They asked me to address the sales reps. Columbia had a new general manager, Jack Craigo, and we were his first major signing. 'I want to introduce you to a band I have a lot of faith in. I anticipate that they will be the main flag band of Columbia Records and my judgement is that they will turn out to be the next Rolling Stones. I want you all to give a big hand to Mr Bob Geldof who will say a few words to you all.'

'Hi, I'm Bob Geldof. For the past thirty days I've been here touring around with some of your people to promote the record "Tonic for the Troops" and our first US tour which begins in a few weeks. I've met DJs, journalists, record store managers and I've got a pretty good idea of how you people work out there on the ground. And I'd just like to say that in those thirty days I've discovered what a bunch of bastards you are . . .' I had meant it in a jocular 'we're all lads together here' way of speaking, but the words felt uncomfortable even as they left my mouth. I looked into the hundreds of faces. The smiles remained nailed to their lips but the eyes became glassy. I felt as if I had opened my mouth to sing with the band and then discovered that what came out was in a different key to everybody else. I steeled myself and continued with what had set out to be the English punk equivalent of a 'Sell records, sell records' chant. '. . . so you may be a bunch of bastards but you're the best bunch of bastards in the entire United States of America. So get out there and sell 'em.'

They had to cheer, but they didn't really want to. Nicholas was on his feet in a flash and at the microphone before I had a chance to draw breath. 'So you heard what the gentleman from England said . . . we're gonna go out there and sell records. Right.' There was a dull cheer. 'I said, RIGHT.' The cheer increased. But not by much.

I sat down and closed my eyes. The nightmare continued. I knew it in my stomach that they would never forgive me.

'That was great, Bob,' said Nicholas as we boarded the plane for Heathrow, 'though maybe next time you address a sales convention you might just . . . y'know . . . pitch it a little bit lower. They loved you . . . they're going to kill for you. You boys are gonna be huge . . . I'm gonna see to that. Trust me. Wanna toot?' he said, producing the little brown bottle.

'No, I think I'll try and sleep on the plane,' I said.

★   ★   ★

Chessington was like a calm awakening. Paula was there to meet me. After our tour of Ireland and Canada I had seen her on and off when we returned to England, but then she had gone back to Oxford and later stayed with friends in London and I did not see her for a few weeks. Then one night at Dingwalls, the Camden club, I'd phoned her.

'Hi, it's Bob.'

'Bob who?' she had said.

'Bob Geldof,' I'd said, exasperated. How many other Irish people did she know called Bob?

I suggested that she come back to Chessington. There was a screech of brakes and she was outside in a taxi almost as soon as I put the phone down. She had brought with her two huge suitcases, the size lady explorers used to take into the African jungle on the heads of a train of native porters. Shit, I hope she doesn't think she's been invited permanently, I thought. When we got to Chessington, I asked her to stay downstairs and make some tea, while I rushed up to my room and kicked all the dirty underwear and other un-savouries under the bed. She was not impressed. The next afternoon she returned with a new set of sheets. 'I've got rid of the old ones,' she said, with a sweet smile, 'I didn't like the bloodstains and other sundry blobs. I hope you don't mind. I got a nice set with little flowers on.'

'This is nice. It's fun to have you about,' I said one night, as we lay between the tasteful floral sheets, 'but you know that I can't get into another long-term relationship. They hurt too much, I can't bear it.'

'Of course,' she said. 'I understand.'

'That's why it's important that you don't live here but go home sometimes and have a place of your own. You have to have an independent existence.'

'Of course,' she said, snuggling down. 'I think I might buy a new eiderdown tomorrow, if that's all right.'

The band still teased her something rotten. 'Are you cooking Bob his dinner?' asked Fingers artlessly one day, as she was in the kitchen making some instant coffee.

'No . . . why?'

'Oh nothing . . . I just wondered . . .'

'Wondered what?'

'I thought you must be cooking his dinner. His other girlfriends usually did.'

'Ah, no. We're, er, going out tonight. I'm cooking his dinner tomorrow.' She had never cooked a meal for someone before in her life. She had never even been shopping for food, except for the necessaries. Usually she ate in cafés. Wishing to impress me, she took the train into London and then a taxi to Harrods and bought steaks, tomatoes, mushrooms, potatoes and a ready-made dessert. It cost her £27. She couldn't work out how people could afford to eat at those rates. Then she burned it to a cinder. I smiled grimly as I cut into the succulent carbon and told her it was delicious. It would become a regular spectacle in our house on Saturday evening. The band would gather in a cheery circle to watch their singer consume the latest burnt offering. Her culinary skills developed with painful slowness.

The turning point had come one night in Paris. The band were doing a gig there, she was having dinner with friends in London. She must have been moon-faced throughout the meal because one of them said, 'There is still a late flight to Paris. If you left here now you could get there for the end of the concert.' They drove her to the airport. It was snowing and all she was wearing was the ballgown in which she had started the evening. She borrowed money for the flight and for a taxi at the other end. She was depending on reading a poster to discover where we were playing and team up with us. The only French words she knew were 'oui' and 'courgette'. I came out of the gig that evening and there she was, standing in the snow, with the Eiffel Tower behind her, wearing a stunning pale blue ballgown, off the shoulder, sparkling with iridescent sequins. Her toes protruded out of the front of her high heeled shoes and she wore no stockings. She was beautiful.

My old friend, Pat Moylett, was in Paris, so that night we drove in his car out to Versailles and did wheelies, spinning slowly around in the snow in the moonlight in front of Louis's palace.

'If you hadn't said yes after that I'd have given up. What more can a girl do?' she said afterwards. We spent the night in a little hotel in Montmartre with pink satin furnishings and roses on the wallpaper.

The concierge said, 'With or without a shower?'

'What's the difference?' I said.

'A shower is ten francs more.'

'That's about a pound,' said Paula.

'We'll take the room without, please,' I said.

★ ★ ★

Not long after we returned from the States the band began a European tour to promote the second album. We had done a smaller tour in 1977 to put our faces about, but this was to be a long haul. We began in Scandinavia. Sweden was cold. Everything was cold – the climate, the drinking, the fucking and the fighting. They were getting the messages across from England about the extremes of punk behaviour and the Swedes were, in their organized manner, implementing them. The first night we were there someone threw a pint glass on the stage. I saw it flash in an arc through the air, but it was too fast for me to even duck. It whizzed past my ear, smashed with a terrific crash on a cymbal and shattered all over the drum kit. Simon was cut on the face by the flying shards.

I stopped the gig immediately. 'Right, close all the doors to this place. No one's getting out of here.' After what had happened at the Music Machine in London the year before, when I had been punched on stage, I was not prepared to put up with violence at our concerts. The boom of a single human voice over a PA system designed to amplify an entire rock band is staggering. To people in a silent hall it becomes awesome. 'Right, you're staying here until I get the fuckers who did that. We don't come here to have things thrown at us. Turn the spotlights on the audience. Move them from the back along each row. I want the security guards to walk up from the back and, as they pass your row, I want someone to point out whoever it was in the row in front. It isn't telling tales, it's trying to get rid of scum.'

The spotlights were trained on each row in turn. Then, about half-way down, someone pointed to a character in front. 'Right, he's over there. Are you sure that's him?' Several people attested to the fact.

The security men obediently hauled him out and up onto the stage. Our road crew surrounded him and shoved him down the stairwell at the side of the stage where the police waited. On the way down the stairs the crew managed to beat the shit out of him while we continued with the concert. The man was a member of a gang of bikers. When we left the hall to go back to the hotel, he was there with his mates, all carrying crowbars. There was a pitched battle.

There was no room in those days for ambivalence towards violence. This was certainly no time to intellectualize your response to it. I don't like violence and I don't enjoy fighting. I am not a physical person. But I will not be a sitting target for someone. In Belgium earlier we had heard the crowd baying like bloodhounds. The moment we walked onto the stage a guy threw something. I warned him. He spat at me. He'd probably read this was the correct response in the punk ethos. I jumped down and hit him. Phay, our roadie, was in after me as the guy's friends set upon me. Our new roadie followed Phay, who was lashing out at all and sundry. Unfortunately, in his thrashing he hit our new crew member, who was a timid soul, and knocked him out. Gary had joined in at this point and the others were following. They'd picked the wrong band. It was a good gig, though.

In Sweden the girls, from the age of thirteen upwards, would gather in the hotel lobbies and try to follow us up to our rooms. No one seemed to have much fun in Sweden in winter. Drink was restricted, gambling was prohibited and it was too cold to do anything except fight and fuck with clinical vigour. I'd never seen humans hibernate before.

On the ferry to Finland we had played on the boat with some Estonian gypsies. When we went to bed, I felt like I was an olive floating on the top of some cocktail – the ice tinkled against the bulkhead with jarring irregularity all night. We arrived at six o'clock in the morning. It was cold and miserable and we'd had two hours' sleep. We drove to the hotel. It was a large modern place, and the doors were locked.

'Go away,' shouted a member of staff through the glass doors.

We banged on the window.

'This is not the right time of the day to arrive. Go away,' the man shouted.

'Go away? You must be fucking joking, mate. Let us in, we're booked in here.'

'It is too early. You are not booked in until tonight. You cannot check in until midday. That is the proper time. Go away or you will wake everyone in the hotel.'

The noise which ensued threatened to wake the whole of Helsinki. Grumbling, they let us in and found us rooms where we slept for a few hours before beginning the routine of press conferences, interviews, the sound check, more interviews, and a short rest before the performance.

The concert was held in the local Communist Party headquarters, the Lenin Hall, or something, it was called. The gig had hardly begun when a policeman came on stage. 'You will please tell everyone to sit down. This is a concert room, not a dance hall. Everyone must sit down.' He went to a microphone and addressed the audience: 'Everyone will please sit down and remain seated'.

'No they will not,' I said through my microphone. 'If the people who own the hall don't want dancing then they shouldn't book rock bands. Everyone will dance if they want to. And the police will please get off the stage. Seats are not for sitting in with rock 'n' roll, they're for standing on to get a better view.' The man was a senior police officer. Someone said afterwards that he was the chief of Helsinki's police. Either way he did not take kindly to being told, in public in his own town, to sod off. His men tried to shove me off the stage. There was a scuffle and uproar from the audience. The police left hurriedly.

After the gig when we got back to the hotel, we found that the doors had been locked again. We banged on them. The staff came and shook their heads. It was well below freezing and we were still sweating from the performance. The stage crew began to thump the plate glass window which began to wobble violently in response. They opened the doors and we trooped in, swearing at them. A crowd of young girls had followed us. We got our keys and went to the lift. Two of the girls squeezed into the lift. Just as the door was about to close the manager entered.

'Papers,' he said to the girls. They produced their IDs. 'You're under-age. Out!' he said.

'Hang about. What age do you have to be to come into this hotel? Is there a minimum age for drinking coffee here?'

'You can drink coffee in the foyer.'

We did not want to drink coffee but, out of bloody-mindedness, we went to the lobby and ordered drinks. We were exhausted and, as we waited, I put my feet up on the glass-topped table in front of me.

The manager walked over and kicked my feet off the table. 'Get your feet off, pig,' he said.

I stood up and hit him. He fell down. It was a put-up job. Within two seconds my arms had been pinned back by two policemen who had come from nowhere. Robbie Magrath, our tour manager, was a big man. He approached the police. 'Excuse me, I'm the tour manager. Do you speak English?'

'Enough,' said the policeman ambiguously.

'Bob did hit the manager, but the man has been very rude and provocative all day, not letting us in, insulting us, calling us pigs . . .'

The policeman spread the fingers of his hand wide and put them over Robbie's face and pushed him back slowly. 'I said, enough, didn't I? Don't *you* understand English?'

Robbie pulled the copper's hand away aggressively, but suddenly the lobby was full of policemen and he thought better of it. They took me away. I wasn't particularly worried until I saw the police bundle the two girls, who had been in the lift with me, into the car also. 'Christ,' I thought, 'they're going to do me for statutory rape, or something.' The girls began what seemed to be a very friendly conversation with the cops. 'I'm done for,' I thought. 'They're going to get their revenge for the gig.' I was frightened.

The police made me strip naked in the front hall of the police station and then asked me a series of entirely pointless questions while I stood in full view of the policewomen and members of the public who passed. Then they threw me into a concrete cell with only one blanket. I thought, 'Someone from the band will have got a lawyer and I'll be out in an hour'. But they didn't and I wasn't. I felt like a martyr as I listened to the vomiting in the other cells – Saturday night in Helsinki. My skin was grey with the cold by 5 a.m. when they gave me back my clothes and told me to get out. I realized I did not know the name of the hotel. The police at the desk smirked and pretended they did not know either. I had to get a taxi to drive all around the city looking for big modern hotels until we found it. The band thought the incident hilarious.

The further into the rural wastes we went in Finland, the more grotesque the caricature became. I liked the Finns, though, they seemed very Irish to me. Their relationship with Sweden was like Ireland's with England and even the national characteristics seemed similar: roaring drunken mischief-making and wild humour. At Turku, near the Arctic Circle, the local record company reps had only a small annual budget for publicity, as the Finnish record market is understandably tiny, and they had clearly chosen to blow the entire amount in one go to celebrate our arrival. We were not sure whether or not to be flattered.

First they took us to their local sauna where great, red-faced, beer-gutted Finns sat naked and greasy around a roasting fire, cooking sausages and drinking beer while women in white gowns cleaned all around us. Then, already slightly heady from the heat and the strong beer, we turned up at the press conference where the rest of the record company people and the journalists were well stuck into the vodka. Many were already rolling drunk and there was a good deal more drinking before the press conference began.

'Burb, can you pliz tell me what does it mean, the name of the Boomtown Rats?' asked a reporter, who seemed to have a congenital hiccup. They spoke English very naturally, even to each other.

'Well, it . . .'

'That is a vuckink stupid kvestion,' slurred one of the rolling executives.

'Wadder you mean, a vuckink stupid kvestion?' said the journalist, not aware they were arguing in English.

'I mean it is a completely totally vuckink stupid kvestion, like all your kvestions always are.'

'Ah, vuck off, you vuckink Russian vuckpig.'

'Russian! Who you calling a Russian, you Moscow kerksucker?'

The record company man, with an eye to good public relations, then smacked the journalist in the eye. Another journalist put his arm around the

PR man's neck and pulled him to the ground. Soon the entire room was a writhing mass of media people giving vent to the traditional hostility between their respective professions. We sneaked out of the room and left them to it. We got up early to leave Turku and drove to the airport. It was closed. After half-an-hour, a cleaning lady let us in.

On the day we arrived in Berlin, two people were shot at the wall. We paid our money at Checkpoint Charlie and went into the East. It was like going to the movies. We looked at the Reichstag and the husks of bombed-out buildings. We walked round, we went to the new opera house, where I thought it odd to see people arriving in limousines, and beautiful women with furs and diamonds. Inside the opera house, a vast art complex, two men suddenly approached and removed Johnnie from our midst. They waved IDs at us and told us to stay away. They examined his passport. He had already been stopped twice that afternoon for wearing his customary pyjamas. Now they took him somewhere. We followed. We waited outside a room in a building for him to come out. We sat on a long bench and said that we weren't leaving without him. Inside Fingers tried to explain he was in a band. 'Beatles, Beatles,' he said. They only spoke German. They told him he must leave the East immediately. They opened the door and I saw a wooden table, a light bulb and chairs. It was like *The Spy Who Came in From the Cold*. As we left, someone said, 'You know, if someone wears pyjamas here in the day time, we say he's mad and send him away.'

As we left the East, the border guards between the tank traps said, 'You're a group?'

'Yes,' we said.

'Sing us a song.'

'Some day,' we said, and ran to Checkpoint Charlie.

The U-Bahn underground train runs in a circle through East and West Berlin. You are not allowed off in East Berlin if you come from the West or vice-versa. The tube circles endlessly, and it is warm. On cold nights, the drunks from the East and West get on the train and spend all night down there in comfort. It's nice to think of the fact that although above ground they're shooting people because they want to live somewhere else, below ground there's a party going on, circling endlessly with its oblivious guests. You know which one I think makes more sense.

From Munich, we went to the suburbs of Dachau. As we approached the remains of the concentration camp fear descended on me. I checked myself. It was too much of a cliché, but cliché or not, I was frightened. 'Arbeit macht frei.' I was terrified. I gazed in horror at the lists and the endless names. The whipping-block made me sick. And then we saw the photos and almost died. All the prisoners were wearing pyjama-like uniforms. We no longer thought about Johnnie's constant wearing of pyjamas. What had started out as hype and seemed to fit his sleepy style was now comfortable and normal for him to wear. But we felt ashamed. We were afraid the other pilgrims would think it was a macabre joke or, at best, that it showed a lack of respect. He covered up his clothes with a coat. It's true, no birds sing in these places. Maybe they do, maybe you're so lost in horror that you don't think about them. But I can't remember a single bird singing.

In Zurich we were taken to the ubiquitous 'Punk Club'. We were always taken to punk clubs. I was approached by a stunning blonde, whose shape, I believe, is best described as 'Junoesque'. Her hair was pulled up tight in a bunch and then fell down her back. She was dressed in leather and she said, 'Can I give you some cocaine?'

'You certainly can,' I said.

We went to the women's toilet, where neatly folded paper was unwrapped, and two lines of cocaine were laid out on her compact mirror. She came back to my table and said nothing. When I left, she said, 'Here's my address. Come there'.

'Right. Fine. Thank you. Yes I probably will.'

We left and went to a *bierkeller* where some knee-slappin', beer-swillin', sausage-eatin' group in lederhosen were doing their Teutonic thing. We got drunk on the excellent lager, roared a few token abusive gems at the good burghers, and left. We walked through some weird pedestrianized part of Zurich, reeling and singing happily. There may have been thirteen of us. We passed a carpet shop, where someone got the idea of picking up a brick and hurling it through the window – for a laugh, you understand. We ran off. Half-way down the next street, Pete got the idea (which made strange sense when he was drunk), of going back to get a carpet and bringing it home with him. Without our noticing, he wandered back and was hauling the Swiss equivalent of a three-ply Wilton from the damaged window, when a passing citizen, espying this crazed Irish midget pulling a carpet from the shattered shop front, quite rightly called 'Thief!' Pinning Briquette's arms to his side from behind, he shouted, 'Police!' No matter what language you speak, 'police' sounds the same everywhere. Briquette, now realizing his dilemma, immediately and with the intuitive logic only the drunk can bring to bear in such a situation, also started shouting, 'Help! Police! Thief!' Our citizen friend was startled, realizing it was his word against Pete's. He released the drunken bass player, who scarpered. Meanwhile, the remaining twelve good men and true arrived at the hotel, where they noticed a Rolls-Royce parked on the other side of the street. There was, for some odd reason, a Christmas tree standing in a large green wooden tub between the Rolls-Royce and the hotel. We began to lift the tub. So as not to damage the paintwork, one of the crew removed his jacket and placed it on the roof of the car. We put the pine on top of that.

I am stopped as I enter the hotel. It is the Junoesque blonde. 'Come with me.'

'What time is it?'

'Two-thirty.'

'How far is it?'

'Up the road.'

'OK, see you lads.'

At her tiny flat, I'm shocked to see her boyfriend. He puts on our first album, the slow track, 'I Can Make It If You Can'. I am drunk, but embarrassed listening to myself in this tiny flat in Zurich with the beautiful girl dancing with me to my song, pressed against me, and her boyfriend watching.

'You want to fuck her?'

'Well . . . er . . . Yes, I do, actually.'

'OK, if I can watch.'

He stays in the corner where he is sitting, and she takes her clothes off. Oh God, she was splendid. We start and we finish. It's five in the morning. 'Before you go,' he says, 'here's a signed copy of my book.' The man is a very famous artist.

Back at the hotel, I clambered into bed in the room I was sharing with Pete, who had now returned. I fell asleep, but I was awakened soon by shaking. 'Stop wanking,' I shouted to Briquette in the next bed. I was still drunk, but I was aware of the small chandelier and the picture above my head shaking.

'Oh, for Christ's sake, Bricky, give it a rest.'

Briquette woke up. He had obviously not been wanking. We staggered naked to the window. Outside, the lampposts were bending like trees in the wind. The room was throbbing with low shudders.

'Christ, it's an earthquake,' said Pete.

'Yeah, or else it's a tube train,' I replied rationally.

An old man, a street cleaner, paused in his brushing and looked up at the lamppost, bemused as if he half expected the ground to open up and he could sweep the dust he'd accumulated at the end of his broom into the hole in a neat act of divine housekeeping. The last thing I noticed after the rumbling stopped was the pine tree still sitting on top of the Rolls-Royce's roof.

'Tube trains,' I said, before I fell asleep again.

Three hours later, in the hotel lobby, the manager said, 'Tube trains? Noh, noh, don't you know tventy willages were destroyed in an earthqvake last night in South Germany?'

★   ★   ★

'Bob, this is some list you've put together here.'

'Well, America chooses to export its cultural values through television, and this is our first tour here, and we are all excited, so we thought we'd play in places that reflect the image we have of these towns through TV. Besides, it's good hype.'

'Well, I think we can get you visits to most of these places . . . but what do you mean by venues?'

'As I said, these are the places we want to play.'

'You want to *play* there . . . ? I don't think that's going to be possible. Do you know what these places are . . . ? St Patrick's Cathedral, New York . . . I mean, that is a *church*, Bob . . .'

'Yes, Nicholas, but it is also a cultural landmark. That cathedral . . . St Patrick's Day Parade . . .'

'. . . the Ford Motor Works, Detroit . . . ?' Nicholas had still not grasped the point.

'Motown, Tamla Motown, soul and cars, that's what Detroit is to me.'

'Yes, but, shit, Bob, that is a car factory, not a concert hall. And what about this? The Texas Book Depository . . .'

'That's where Kennedy was shot from . . .'

'Yes, I know that's where Kennedy was shot from . . . I mean, are you trying to commit sacrilege or something?'

'Well, that's what I think of when I think of Dallas.'

'Bob, Dallas has concert halls as well. And what about these others . . . the CocaCola plant in Atlanta, McDonald's Hamburger University in Chicago and what's this . . . Frederick's of Hollywood. What do you want to play there for? Do you know what Frederick's of Hollywood is?'

'Yes, it's a mail order firm . . .'

'It's a mail order firm that sells goddamn peephole bras and crotchless panties . . .'

'I know, I used to see small ads in magazines from it when I was a kid. I thought about a movie lot for Los Angeles but that's too obvious. Then I thought how false everything seems in LA. You know, petrol pump jockeys who are all actors, waitresses who are all actresses, houses with fake façades, and there's nothing more fake than false sexuality. So – Frederick's.'

'Well Bob, it's certainly a point of view, but I think you might just have to settle for a few more conventional venues.'

Our first gig was in San Diego. We were playing at a convention for programme directors, the people who decide what records will be played on about ninety major American radio stations.

'You could break America tonight Bob,' said Nicholas. 'These are the men who make life and death decisions for bands.'

I had had my fill of brown-nosing people who made life and death decisions for bands. I had done thirty days of it in thirty-three cities. 'OK, OK, don't push it,' I said.

'No, I'm serious Bob. Don't call them bastards . . . please. Trust me.'

I really wanted to break America. We were going to be the first of the new bands to do it. Vanity, arrogance and ambition were all caught up in this. I wanted to impress these people. I had no doubt we could, but if there was one thing which was going to incite me to do something, it was people telling me what is good for me.

Columbia were promoting two bands that day, a band called the Fabulous Poodles and us Rats, or Boomers, as Columbia insisted we be called.

'The Boomers! You cannot be serious!' said Gary.

'Just stick with us on this one Gary . . . Trust me . . .'

The programme director, who Pete was accompanying to the gig, sat in complete silence for the first half of the journey. It was uncomfortable, and in an effort to make conversation he said, 'Now let's see, you're the keyboard player from the Fabulous Rats – right?' When Pete told me this in the dressing room, I thought, 'What the fuck are we doing here? These guys don't even know who they are coming to see. We're being used as cheap entertainment'.

That evening, despite our jet-lag, we did a good gig, but the programme directors missed half of it. They left early. We did a song called 'I Don't Like Mondays' for the first time. It was coincidental that the gig was on a Monday in San Diego. It was in San Diego that the incident which inspired the song had happened, four months previously. I had been in Atlanta University doing one of those endless interviews. I was on automatic pilot, answering questions mechanically. But while the radio station was playing the record, the ticker-tape machine beside me began chattering. I glanced over to it to see what news was coming off it. As I sat there a young girl called Brenda Spencer was leaning out of her bedroom window with a gun, shooting people down in her school across the street. There seemed to me something singularly American about what happened next. A journalist telephoned her. She answered the phone, which seems a bizarre thing to do anyway in the middle of murdering strangers. He asked her why she was doing it. She paused, and then said, 'Something to do. I don't like Mondays'. I stared at the machine. She had probably replaced the phone by now and returned to shooting. Schoolchildren were dying as I sat answering another inane question. Pop music is so terribly unimportant.

On the way back to the hotel, I had started to write the song. I had a guitar in my room, and I just sat down and wrote it. It seemed in some way to be peculiarly Californian to me; the pointlessness, the lack of reason and logic. I wrote, 'What reason do you need to die?' The shooting went on as I continued writing. I tried to picture the girl. I tried to visualize the scene: the police captains, the bullhorns, the playground, the parents. The girl must be some sort of automaton. And I wrote, *The silicon chip inside her head gets switched to overload*. And of course, why was she doing it? *Tell me why*. Maybe she's right. Maybe there is absolutely no reason. But it seemed the Californian ethos didn't allow for reasons or logic for doing anything. They just did it. I'd written the song originally in a soft reggae style but we didn't have the time to

Fachtna and Fingers on the bus, America 1979.

rehearse it properly. So Fingers and I did it alone – just voice and piano. The crowd loved it that night in San Diego.

It was a good gig. I was enjoying myself. When we got to 'Rat Trap', I prefaced it with a few remarks. 'This next one got to Number One in England, but you won't have heard it. For some reason we don't get played on American radio. Which I think says more about American radio than it does about us.' And then addressing the audience, I asked disingenuously, 'What do you think about American radio?'

The crowd erupted with roars of 'it sucks man', 'rubbish' and boos.

I thought of Pete in that limo, I thought of all the arse-licking, the hype, the false politeness and the show enthusiasm, and I was tired of it. On stage, you don't think of consequences. 'I've got to tell you that tonight, for the first, and probably the only time in your lives, you'll be able to tell the people who determine what you hear exactly, *exactly* what you think of their programming. See that last quarter end section of stalls? Put the spotlight on those guys. See all those satin jackets that they get free from record companies? Well, they're the guys who decide what you hear on the radio, so tell them what you think.'

The audience started to jeer and hiss. 'Sucks,' the kids nearest to the satin jackets began to shout at them. 'Fucking sucks, man.' The programme directors stood up *en bloc* and walked out. Whatever major stations we were on took us off that night. But it gave me a feeling of liberation. I had expunged the guilt and self-loathing I had felt for allowing myself to be compromised. And I must have enjoyed it because I carried on with the abuse.

Before we arrived in the US, *Rolling Stone* magazine had taken their lead from the English music press and, noting our lack of credibility (the result of five hit singles), dubbed us the new Bay City Rollers, without even seeing or hearing us. I had a bone to pick. Later in the concert, I told the audience that I wanted them to buy our records because I wanted to be rich. They cheered in sympathy with this pedestrian ambition. They always cheered. I'd say in England, only half-joking, 'You're probably never going to be rich, so one of us may as well do it. If you go out and buy our records, at least we'll be rich – why not?' They always cheered, only half-joking too. But they understood. And now in San Diego I told them I wanted to be rich enough to buy *Rolling Stone*. They cheered. So that I could burn it. They laughed and cheered deafeningly. One senior contributor to *Rolling Stone* was there and not amused. Throughout the trip, I continued to dig my own grave. I couldn't believe they took themselves so seriously. I couldn't believe they took a pop singer so seriously. They, too, seemed never to have heard of irony or the ridiculous. 'I feel like I'm putting out the deck-chairs on the *Titanic*,' said Nicholas.

In New York, when we played 'Rat Trap', I said that this was the only song of ours the New York radio stations ever played, and that was only because the DJs thought it sounded like a Bruce Springsteen song. I put my hand on my hips and lapsed into a sort of mock-serious, slow, Columbia record executive-type American voice. 'But I want you to know that Bruce Springsteen couldn't write a song half as good as this if he tried.' It was meant to be self-deprecating, for it was quite obvious the man *could*, but there was uproar in the hall and on the radio the next day. I only made things worse by saying that I thought Springsteen had ripped off Van Morrison, the same as we did. It was nothing to be ashamed of, because Van Morrison is a bona fide rock genius. 'I don't think anybody understands your sense of humour, Bob,' Nicholas said nervously.

We played some great gigs that tour. We were selling out the halls and we travelled east to west, north to south and back again, but it got exhausting. Lawrence, Kansas had a Rat Day when we arrived with parades in the streets and people dressed as rats. We played the opera house there. I still have pictures of the entire audience down on all fours doing 'the Rat', the first song we'd written for the band. But that was Lawrence, Kansas, and not a town with a wide screen.

We played at Hamburger University where McDonald's train their employees. In LA we did get to play in Frederick's. It was only a tiny little shop on Hollywood Boulevard and when Columbia made enquiries they panicked because the insurance they would have to pay for us to play there covered $2 million worth of stock. They wanted us to play a huge heavy

Off stage. . .

On stage. America does the Rat, 1979.

metal festival called the California Jam. We said, why be one band in a massive heavy metal festival when you could do Frederick's and get coast-to-coast television? Then we offered a compromise: we would play the festival if we could play Frederick's as well. Wearily they agreed. I think they were finding us a little 'difficult' by this stage.

Frederick's themselves loved the idea and *Playboy* came down with lots of models to do some pictures of us with women sporting the Frederick's products. Fachtna even had some special Boomtown Rats knickers made for the occasion, horrible black satin things with Boomtown Rats written on the crutch. Nobody wanted them so Fachtna wore them himself for years afterwards. There was room only for an audience of 200, so we got KROQ, which was then a little New Wave station, to broadcast that there were 200 tickets available. They got 2,000 replies so I suggested they put a few video screens in the window showing what was going on inside. It was better than my wildest expectations. The whole of Hollywood Boulevard was blocked. The police had to form lines outside. That night it *was* on coast-to-coast television.

The next day we did the California Jam. Aerosmith, Cheap Trick, Ted Nugent and Van Halen were all on the bill. It was like a circus backstage. Dave Lee Roth from Van Halen was having his hair done and preening in huge mirrors around the dressing room caravans and those other heavy metal guys were practising their stage moves like body-beautiful pumpers. It was hilarious. Captain Beefheart came in out of the desert and played on stage with us. Ninety thousand people stood in front of us in the LA Olympic Coliseum. It was a Sunday. I told them, 'I hope you've all been to mass'. From there things went downhill. An audience who had come almost exclusively to see Ted Nugent did not appreciate me saying I hated 'that crap' and I thought Aerosmith were awful too. I thought it was a good gig.

Someone fucked up in Nags Head. We drove all night to get to Nags Head, North Carolina. It was a two-street town on a sandbar that stuck out into the Atlantic Ocean. The gig was a pub. We ate in the ladies' toilet and we changed in the gents'. We played on a tiny stage in a tiny room.

The check shirt and jeans crowd of fifty shouted, 'Led Zeppelin!'

I said, 'This is a Led Zeppelin song, it's called "Rat Trap".'

'Joe Cocker!' they shouted.

I said, 'This is a Joe Cocker song. It's called "She's So Modern".' They loved us. The promoter felt sorry for us when he saw us so dispirited. He filled the bath in one of our rooms full of champagne bottles and ice.

We said we'd had enough, we were going home. Four executives flew to see us the next day to explain that it was all a dreadful mess, it would never happen again. We kept going. The album was doing brilliantly in Canada, where we were now a big name. It was an odd experience to cross and re-cross the border between the two countries and go just as easily from being a hit

The California Jam, the day after Frederick's. Fachtna bored at left.

band to a bunch of unknowns. Sometimes the distance between fame and obscurity was only forty miles.

One day, on the bus, the others were asleep and we were travelling through the desert. I was tired and I looked weary. I took a self-portrait polaroid in the brown-tinted mirror and continued staring out of the window. There was nothing outside except some rocks and tumbling weeds and a few cacti. We flashed by a sign that said 'Truth or Consequences 5 miles'. What did that mean? Was I going to meet my fate five miles down the road? It might as well have said 'The Twilight Zone 5 miles'. I got very excited. I ran to the front of the bus, eagerly looking ahead. Wiggly Beard, our driver, was talking on a CB radio. He was a big, friendly man who had lost all his hair while in the U.S. Army on patrol in the Arctic Circle when he was eighteen – it simply froze, died and fell out. The sign flashed by: 'Truth or Consequences, Population 351'. I saw nothing. It was flat and empty and dead. I grabbed the map. 'Where are we?' I said.

He jabbed at a spot. Truth or Consequences is a town in the middle of the US military nuclear testing area.

'What a wonderful name,' I thought. Years later, Bruce Springsteen said he'd seen it too. They named it after a TV game show. I'd like to live there for a week.

CHAPTER XI

Divers Bends

'This may never happen to you again.' I remember thinking precisely this in Liverpool in 1979 as I stood there and felt the noise of the 4,000-strong audience hit me like a solid object. This is what I wanted, wasn't it? What else do bands do? They have hit records, hit tours, have their picture taken, get screamed at. Screaming had not been a phenomenon of pop music for some years and I was taken aback by the fact that it was me who provoked this response. I looked at the kids wearing pyjamas in imitation of Fingers and black-and-white check jackets in imitation of me. For a fleeting moment as I stood and looked at the heaving sea of hands and faces I felt a jumble of responses flood through my brain. I was satisfied I'd achieved this. Our previous tours had been more friendly, intimate even, with the audience seeming to share our ambition, willing us on: 'Go on, do it'. We'd done it, and now possibly they were screaming in acclamation. But I couldn't talk to them any more, I couldn't joke. We were stars and you don't talk with stars. Anyway, they wouldn't be able to hear me talking with the noise. There seemed to be an invisible and unbridgeable distance between us now. I wasn't one of them any more, and yet I revelled in this. It felt simultaneously comfortable and disturbing. It wasn't the old saw of 'the failure of success'. It wasn't disillusionment or musical pretension that they couldn't hear 'my art'. I couldn't care less about that but I did like them listening to the words, whatever they meant.

'This may never happen again,' I thought. 'Remember it.' I turned to look at the others. Simon stuck his chin out and elaborately winked like an Irish bogman. Gary raised his eyebrows in a 'What the fuck is this?' expression. Pete was in a panic, untangling his lead, as always. Gerry gave a small smile and Johnnie was grinning ear to ear. I took a mental polaroid. It was a moment of triumph and at the same time it wasn't. The ambivalence lasted a moment before we crashed into our first number.

1978 had been a stunning year. We had sold more records than any other band or individual in Britain. All the polls told us we were the Number One group in the country. It was weird. Of course I'd always said we would be, but you know that what a boy says and what he believes are two different things. As Johnny Rotten said, 'It depends on what lie I'm telling that day'.

We had laid the groundwork for our inevitable domination of the U.S., or so we thought. We were sure we had another hit with 'I Don't Like Mondays' though I had told Chris and Nigel at Ensign I thought it was no more than a decent B side. For the next year we would define what pop music was and looked like and sounded like in Britain. Now, in 1979, just before the beginning of the third tour with the new album, *The Fine Art of Surfacing*, we were at our peak. 'Mondays' had been a bigger hit than anybody expected. It was Number One in thirty-two countries around the world and was about to be released in the States where we felt certain it would give us the breakthrough we needed. We were about to embark on our biggest tour ever, which included places we had wanted to see all our lives: Japan, Bangkok and Australia and places behind the Iron Curtain.

In my personal life too, things had come together. I was now utterly in love with Paula, who was loving in return and clever and great fun. I could no longer understand my reluctance to fall for this girl who now made me so happy. And I felt very self-contained within the band where I achieved enormous satisfaction from writing the songs and then hearing the others, who were all better musicians than me, breathe life into them. The songs were working and doing well. I was not fooled but I was flattered when one of the music papers said of 'Mondays', '[Geldof] dipped effortlessly into the back pocket of his genius and pulled the song out of nowhere'. Yeah, sure.

My own life was sorting itself out. I had completely cut out of it everything that had been a repressive or darkening influence – my family, school, Ireland, the sterile Dun Laoghaire relationships, the seemingly endless drifting. The long desperate scramble up the ladder of ambition had been, by and large, achieved. I was once more finding time for things outside myself and the band. Although I generally believe marches and other kinds of protest politics a waste of time, I had spoken at a rally in Trafalgar Square in support of the Greenpeace campaign against whaling which I had been involved in in Canada. But I was still ambivalent about my stand. I wrote in the song 'Someone's Looking at You': *They saw me there in the square when I was shooting my mouth off about saving some fish. Now can that be construed as some radical's view or some liberal's wish.*

We had come back from that first tour of the United States undismayed and convinced in our exuberant arrogance we were going to crack it. The tour had been too long, though: next time, after 'Mondays' was a hit, we'd do a short one. Now we were supposed to have conquered the New World. We claimed we had. It had been arranged that we would top the bill at a massive open air pop festival at Loch Lomond to celebrate this feat and mark our return. We thought the festival was a disaster. Paula, who was in the audience, thought it was a great success and so did most of the press: ironically they gave us brilliant reviews. But we knew in our hearts that while we were by then sufficiently professional to turn out a creditable performance in most circumstances, too much was expected of us.

157

We had decided to start with 'Mondays' but we were nervous. No one expected us to come up with a song like that, quiet, with just piano and voice. It was a huge risk to start our first major festival as headliners with an unknown and experimental song. Maybe that's why the press liked us that night. The crowd loved it. I smiled over at Johnnie who mouthed 'thank god' at me.

We had several gimmicks organized: all went horribly wrong. Helicopters were supposed to hover over the stage as we made our entrance, shine a spotlight down on us, then swoop right across the audience, turning their lights on them. They turned up half an hour early and meandered aimlessly over the crowd. I rushed out of our changing room shouting into a radio, 'Not yet, you bastards, not yet'. Our tour manager was screaming at the sky and waving his fist impotently as they sailed miles above us. We called him 'Chopper' from then on. Still, the band before us, who had spent £10,000 on fireworks in an attempt to upstage us, had a mishap and the fireworks went off half an hour after they left the stage. We walked on five minutes later and said, 'Thank you, I hoped you liked our fireworks'. Then the Scottish pipe band which came on after the military drum roll in the middle of 'I Never Loved Eva Braun' from the *Tonic for the Troops* album wouldn't get off the stage. They were supposed to play a short wistful melody before we crashed back into 'Eva Braun'. Instead they went on to do 'Scotland the Brave'. The audience went wild and started singing football songs. I tried to join in and look as if it was all part of the act. The pipers went into a third song and I had to sidle up to the pipe master and shout in his ear because the band were making such a bloody din. 'Get off,' I said very deliberately. He stared rigidly ahead, transfixed like a rabbit in headlights by the sight of the crowd. Finally, I screamed, 'I WANT YOU TO FUCK OFF. GET OFF THE STAGE NOW.' I was furious because it had ruined the song which it was supposed to enhance.

At the end of the show, because the gig had been held near the Loch Lomond Bear Park, the promoters sent on some people dressed up as bears to dance about the stage. We kicked them up the arse and pushed them off. We came off profoundly depressed. Fachtna was in the dressing room. He'd been on the stage and knew our mood. He got everyone out. 'We blew it,' I said. I was almost crying. 'We gave them all the ammunition they needed,' I said, meaning the press. We couldn't believe the good reviews we got later.

But the success of 'Mondays' ameliorated our depression that day. We had decided to record without Mutt to see if we were capable of working with someone else or whether we were dependent on him. With the confidence of success we had begun to resent his dictatorial attitude in the studio. We were grateful, we knew he had taught us a lot. In fact I think he made 'Rat Trap' such a good song, but we thought we would see if we could manage it without him. We asked Phil Wainman if he could do it. He was a strange choice, having produced the Bay City Rollers and the Sweet, but we wanted a

How long can this go on? Loch Lomond, 1979.

classic pop producer. The song needed strings, I knew. But strings were anathema to our style of band in those days. When I walked in and saw a twenty-four-piece orchestra I freaked. 'We can't use that, it's too syrupy, it sounds like Andy Williams.' In the end we pared them down to a pair of cellos, violas and violins. We took it down to Nigel and Chris. 'It's a Number One', said Nigel. It was.

A good part of the success of 'Mondays' was the video. We had been getting more and more adventurous with our videos. Graham Greene said of *Dr Fischer of Geneva* that it was not a book about Dr Fischer but a book about greed. That was how I felt about 'Mondays'. It was not a song about Brenda Spencer, it was about psychosis. I didn't want the video to tell the story of that girl, rather I wanted it to create the mood in which such a psychosis is believable. I had seen a TV ad for butter filmed in a Welsh village with a dark over-cast sky. I wanted this atmosphere, the brooding feel of a Valley of the Damned horror film. I wanted the children to be like zombies. To get the effect Dave Mallet, who made the video, got a load of schoolkids and filmed them saying 'tell me why' over and over like an Indian mantra until they were so hypnotized by it they began to say it blankly. I did not want the girl in the song to be a heroine but a victim. I had never seen a video notice before but it was reviewed by the national press who called it a rock video classic. It started the mini-epic type of video, which I almost regret, but then it was new and different.

While we had been in America our option on the place at Chessington had run out. I telephoned Paula from the States and said that I had enough money to buy a small house in London and asked her to find one. She bought a small terraced house in Clapham in South London. It was the first place which ever seemed like home to me. I enjoyed spending time there with her and it was in Clapham that I wrote most of the songs for *The Fine Art of Surfacing*. The title was lifted from an article on psychology in *New Scientist*. It seemed apt to someone who had for most of his life felt like he was slowly sinking. It also fitted the psychological mood of the album. Most of the songs were brutally honest about myself and my preoccupations and touched on the bleaker side of life, even though I was more contented now than I had ever been. But still I don't believe that contentment is part of the plot. I don't think I can ever be content, there will always be the push and pull of an eternal, internal conflict, the tiresome civil war that screams on perpetually inside my head, the constant tedious questioning and analysis of motive.

I felt then and I still feel that the purpose of life must be more than going to work, coming home and going to bed. I don't believe in the work ethic. I don't believe in the rich man, poor man lie about the 'dignity of labour'. There's no more dignity in labour than there is in not working. I never felt ashamed to be out of work: I just felt broke. The dignity and value of a man is not in his labour or abilities, it is in his worth as a human being. The value and dignity of a man is in his humanity. The purpose of your seventy years seems to me to be about discovering what your brain and body are capable of. Seventy years is nothing so you may as well push yourself right to the very extremes of your capabilities. I find it interesting to test myself, so long as I don't hurt other people. I'm capable of doing more than some people and less than others. So is everybody else, but as you can only be capable of so much and as you will always wish to do more, and probably be dissatisfied with what you've already done, then you can never be content. It's a problem. The only real sin is wasting time.

Paula would ask why I never wrote her a romantic song. I tried. Somehow each one got taken over by its darker imagery. Still, by the time the third album was ready, I was pleased with what I had put together. The songs were intensely introspective but they were some of my best. Even now when we perform, we include quite a few numbers from that album. We tried recording a few with Phil Wainman but they just did not work out; we went back to Mutt, who was pissed off because we had done 'Mondays' without him and thus played hard to get. Eventually we recorded the third album with him at Hilversum in Holland where Phonogram had its headquarters. This time it was fun. We were good, confident musicians now. We had mastered studio technology and we played with it perfectly on the album.

When we announced the tour for *Surfacing* it sold out within hours. We

Before: with Fingers.

During: with two girls
and Mick the roadie.

After: with Gary.

began in Liverpool with those 4,000 screaming fans and went on through Britain. We ended in London where we had a gigantic model of King Kong, which we had found on a scrap-heap in Scotland, erected on the roof of the Rainbow, and dressed it in huge striped pyjamas. We went from triumph to triumph. 'Diamond Smile' was our second hit from the record. The video won more awards. While we were in Paris 'Someone's Looking At You', which was the third single from the album, was at Number Four in the British charts.

We loved Japan, it was our first taste of anything different from the West. They were interesting people. When we walked out on stage they went bananas but a security guard in the front said, 'Sit down, please,' and they obeyed. After three songs I couldn't stand it and asked them to dance. Equally obedient they jumped up as one, screaming hysterically. Later I asked them to sit down for a while. They sat. We were walking in Osaka one Saturday night when both ends of the main street were sealed off by police. It was the Bozo Kukus, explained the Japanese guy with us – Japanese street and bike gangs. By and large they were all well-to-do kids being 'rebellious'. As they streaked past the waiting line of cops they pulled down their trousers and mooned. They roared by on hot rods and Hondas waving joints and screaming abuse. The police stood there and took photos. In the morning they went and arrested the kids. It was ritualized confrontation.

Girls were not allowed in the lobby of the hotel so they queued patiently outside. They always gave us gifts of dolls, good luck charms and sake. They would throw bottles of the stuff on stage. If you wanted you could walk along the queue and pick a girl for the night. When one was picked she would touch her nose with a finger, say 'me?' and giggle. The big new thing when we were there was 'No-Panti' coffee bars. Waitresses in mini skirts that only covered half their bottoms brought you coffee. The photographer with me took a picture of one of them as she looked back over her shoulder. She ran over to see the polaroid. She said to the interpreter that she thought we might put the picture in a paper so she ran her ball-point over her eyes so her parents wouldn't recognize her. 'What happens if they recognize your bottom?' I asked.

I had food poisoning in Japan and was on an intravenous drip until ten minutes before one gig began. I knew if I could get on stage then this other person, the guy who performs, as opposed to me, would take over, and I'd be OK. It's a very funny thing, but as soon as I was on stage the adrenalin pumped and I was able to do it. I came off half-way through to be sick, went back on and then collapsed afterwards.

In Australia and New Zealand they loved the huge production set we had taken with us. It was like a high tech *Jailhouse Rock* scene with lots of scaffolding and a gigantic computerized neon noughts and crosses game flashing in pink, white and blue behind us. I liked the idea of this random game of chance going on behind us, operated by a computer. It was expensive, taking tons of equipment to Australia, but we thought if kids in Britain could see it, why shouldn't kids in Sydney?

★ ★ ★

Despite having been called the Irving Berlin of Rock on a major U.S. talk show the next United States tour was no more successful than before. By this time I had said in an interview what 'Mondays' was really about and the press had contacted Brenda Spencer's parents. They had threatened action against the record; so radio stations refused to play it. After only one week's sale Columbia panicked and withdrew the record rather than be taken to court.

The rest of the world had bought the song, not the story. Most people thought it was about waking up with a hangover, going into the office and saying despairingly, 'Oh god, I don't like Mondays'. The title had been used by a major engineering union in Britain as its slogan for its one-day stoppages each Monday. To different people it meant different things. I was incensed. I had been specifically ambiguous. I hadn't wanted to make this creep a heroine. The song didn't mention her by name, nor the city nor the school. In any case it would have brought into the open the question of the culpability of a father who had supposedly given his daughter a gun for Christmas every year since she was ten. But the parents maintained it was exploitation, and were deeply upset by what their daughter had done. As they saw it, I was making money out of the event. It was a bit like saying 'I Never Loved Eva Braun' exploited the tragedy caused by Hitler. I didn't think it would wash and was prepared to go to court. I knew this record was our best chance of making it in America and if we threw away the opportunity we might as well forget it. But Columbia didn't have the courage. After that, although we went through the motions, we had no stomach for touring the U.S. and the inevitable hype that went with it.

Ironically Brenda Spencer herself didn't share her parents' view. A fan of ours wrote to her – she was in jail doing twenty-five years – and received a reply which said that she didn't like us but was delighted about the song because she had always wanted to be famous. The record got to Number Sixty, even though it was withdrawn after one week. We fell into that limbo state from which there is no return. We became a cult band.

In retrospect, there was very little chance of us breaking through in America in 1978. Radio was playing what was euphemistically called 'hard rock', on FM. There was a constant diet of AC/DC and other heavy metal bands or disco and Top Forty on the AM stations. We were neither hard rock nor disco. America could not understand us or our contemporaries. They had not gone through the same period of musical reassessment that had underpinned New Wave. With the exception of a few musicians, mainly in New York, they didn't know what we were talking about and couldn't understand our attitude. There was no video outlet then. The only way to win people over was by playing well, but the only people who came to see you were the ones who had heard or read about you in English papers. You were preaching to the converted and they could never generate enough record sales to put you in the charts. In each town you played and with each interview you gave you were at least guaranteed a few plays, but as soon as you left town you were rarely heard of again. None of us English bands broke through then. The Pistols' notoriety sold out their one and only tour but American audiences thought them hopeless. The Jam, the Stranglers and the Damned had no success. Elvis Costello got respect and a hit album but precious little else. The Americans simply didn't know what everyone was going on about. Later in the States people said to me: 'But you did have one major hit record here, of course, "Mondays"'. I would tell them it was only Number Sixty and they would reply: 'But everybody knows it'. Everybody in the record industry knew it, but it was not the breakthrough we so desperately needed.

Even though the *Surfacing* tour had been a brilliant success in most other respects, it crippled us financially. We ended in huge debt, despite the fact that the album had sold well. The cost of transporting the huge set all around the world was enormous, as was the wage bill for the stage crew we had to take with us. We made no money in America and yet had in relative terms to do a lot of gigs there. It was Ireland, of course, where else? that things turned really sour at the very beginning of the tour.

Belfast had been a triumph. They were wonderful people and it felt like home. But in Dublin we had been refused permission to play. Someone suggested it was to do with my earlier television outbursts about Blackrock College and its old boys' association. Now, they said, it had come home to roost. Suddenly no venue in Dublin was available to us, but we were determined to play in our home city. We had heard that the giant yellow and white striped tent where the Pope had conducted mass in Ireland was available. That would be a laugh, we thought, and hired it. We also rented Leopardstown racecourse on which to erect the tent but an injunction prevented us playing. Whenever we found somewhere to play, someone, on behalf of the local residents, would protest and take out another high court injunction to stop us. We tried at least a dozen other sites, and were stopped each time. We had been regarded as an Irish Sex Pistols, which was ridiculous enough, but this campaign was out of all proportion to our importance. Yes, we were the conquering Irishmen coming home to a fatted-calf reception from the youth of the country, but this outburst of spite from what could only be, we felt, some sort of tacit coalition of establishment figures was nonsense. I was furious. To me it was obviously a deliberate campaign of vengeance. It only fuelled my determination to stay and play.

Closed Mondays. Fingers holds the cards, America 1979.

165

Fachtna spent more time in court than anywhere else but we lost every time. The longer we stayed in Ireland the more problems were caused and the more money it cost. The huge crew were being paid just for sitting round and we were even cancelling gigs in the U.S.A. to remain in Dublin, but I opened my mouth yet again and said we would not leave Ireland until we'd been allowed to play in our own country. It became a *cause célèbre*. Bishops spoke. Politicians railed, judges judged and thousands upon thousands of letters were written supporting us. Old people thought it a scandal. In the end we succeeded only by a sleight of hand.

For the sum of £10,000 Desmond Guinness, the owner of Leixlip Castle, allowed us to play in his grounds. For two weeks the Irish media had been following the course of events. It was a major news story, second in priority only to the Iranian hostage crisis. We had told ticket holders that their tickets would be valid on whatever day we were playing the concert. We had decided to play the following Sunday but we were afraid that if we announced the venue and the time there would be another injunction. The national broadcasting station, RTE, had promised to announce the venue whenever we decided to play. All Saturday and all night our crew worked to build a stage from scratch. They dug toilets, built fences, everyone joined in; our lighting people, our sound people, our tour manager, our truck drivers, our equipment people. By midnight Saturday everyone was exhausted. The stage was half-built, the fencing incomplete and the toilets partially dug. Our tour manager went to the site with what he called 'some hurry-up' – enough speed and cocaine to keep the boys going through the night and all next day. I overheard a local the following day saying, 'I thought they were knackered but, by God, they went in for a cup of tea at 12 o'clock and they came out as if they'd just woken up from a long night's sleep. Great workers those lads.' By Sunday morning there was a sixty-foot-wide stage, twelve feet off the ground with a thirty-foot backdrop.

We waited until very late on Saturday night to ensure that no one would have time to rouse a judge from his slumber and then at midnight, RTE announced that the Boomtown Rats would play their long-awaited concert. I feared that we had left it too late, that only people from Dublin would be able to come up to see us and maybe they would be only three thousand. I woke up early on Sunday morning and looked out of my hotel window, the same hotel where I had spent the last two weeks practically besieged. All down the quays people were gathering to get on the special buses with the words Leixlip written on the front. It was a great moment of triumph. We drove out to Leixlip Castle where we stood on the battlements and watched the crowds blocking the roads as they moved slowly towards the grounds.

As we walked out on stage I went to the microphone and asked one question. 'Who won?' The answering roar of, 'We did', made me glad we'd decided to stay and fight it out. We were nervous. Fingers was jumping up and down working off his adrenalin before he began when I heard a crash and looked around to see him disappear through the stage floor. His head and arms were sticking out of the hole. 'Christ, what next?' I thought. He was pulled out grinning. We began.

We had had difficulty getting good enough security to satisfy insurers. Most of the security men in Dublin were so well known and so violent that their very presence instigated trouble. Thus we had hired security from the university. They were no match for the street gangs who throughout the concert rampaged up and down in front of us, hitting and kicking each other. It was a running battle. The stage was full of bodies being ejected or chased or climbing up the lighting towers and sound systems. Punches were thrown, people wrestled to the floor. Others were dragged grinning and waving off the stage to be dumped behind it, when they would begin clambering back up again. Amidst all this, in the wildly swinging spotlights as the lighting crew desperately tried not to illuminate the onstage chaos, was us trying to be 'cool' and pretend that this was just another gig, nothing out of the ordinary at all. Pete was slightly behind me trying to fend off the attention of some drunken lout who felt he ought to be playing bass with him when from the side of the stage stepped a slight man of about fifty with a trilby pushed back on his head. He weaved his way across the stage, passing in front of me, and approached Pete with outstretched hand. 'Paddy Cusack,' he said, using Pete's real name, 'I knew your father well.' 'Oh,' said Pete, too shocked or bemused by this time to do anything else. He stopped playing and shook the man's hand. 'Good man. Good man yerself,' said our friend, and wandered off untouched amongst the chaos.

Ten feet from the stage nobody seemed to be aware of the battle. Still it was only a tiny minority of perhaps forty people causing trouble and I ignored them as much as possible and concentrated on the other twenty thousand who lay out in front of us in the field. They had come overnight from all parts of Ireland and I was not going to let them down. It was a good gig but the people in front, the street gangs, had ruined it for us.

Our moment of triumph, our great homecoming, had been soured. We were back in Dublin and Dublin hadn't changed. We drove straight for the airport in disgust after the concert, and left. The next day the press were characteristically pathetic. 'Thirty Hurt in Rat Trap Terror' was the most 'purple' of the headlines. In my rage I later wrote a song called 'Banana Republic' about Ireland. It was a big hit, strangely enough.

By the end of the tour I was knackered. A sense of shock crept over me when we got back to London and everyone began talking about the next single, the next album and the next tour and how our strategy could be improved next time. In the previous twelve months we'd had six singles, one

Ireland welcomes the Rats.

album and a world tour. Already they were asking for more. I began to acknowledge the pressure. I say *acknowledge* because I had already begun to feel it without understanding what it was. Sometimes at night in England during the *Surfacing* tour I would weep alone in bed. I couldn't stand to read one more nasty thing about myself but also, suddenly, there was a lot to live up to. We had got to the top, but now we had to stay there. It became a treadmill. You keep working to maintain the same position. A lot of people depended on me and my ability to write songs: the band, the stage crew, the people who ran the office, the people at Ensign. These people relied on me for employment and thus their homes and their families were my responsibility.

I had to write the songs, produce the videos, do the interviews, create the artwork ideas and then go out on stage and deliver every night. And then the critics invariably slated us as they had done before. Indeed it had got to the point on that tour when one writer spent his first three paragraphs apologizing for liking us before he continued with his story, and another, on her first assignment for a major music paper, was fired for writing a positive piece on the band. It all seemed too much. 'The Fine Art of Surfacing' may have been a massive worldwide hit but for the moment I had diver's bends. I needed to withdraw.

★   ★   ★

The train journey from Siberia through Mongolia and across the Gobi Desert down into China had two great advantages apart from the obvious romance and mystery of so epic a trip; it would take me to places where nobody knew me and because it was a holiday, an expedition organized by an international travel company, my only responsibility would be to relax.

I flew with Paula to Moscow to join the rest of the party of travellers. It was like stepping into an Agatha Christie novel. There was a dapper little German with a very clipped haircut who was a senior officer in the West German police force. He and his wife had fled East Germany before the end of the war leaving behind her entire family. There was a fat American lady, who informed everyone that her name was Velma and added almost immediately that she had been divorced a few times. She spoke constantly of her relationship with her psychoanalyst lover and, within half an hour, had told the entire party what her husband used to do to her and what she did to him. There was a tall middle-aged British gentleman in khaki shorts and sandals called Maurice. His hobby was train-spotting. There was a burly, crew-cut American Army colonel called Dick who had fought in the Second World War, Korea and Vietnam and who now ran a military academy; with him was his wife Lou, a war bride from Manchester. She had adapted to the U.S.A. with gusto, as her blue chiffon dresses and diary on the doings of their two poodles testified. There was a young Californian man travelling on his own in orange dungarees and a bad temper. There was an attractive brunette who was a stewardess with Air Canada. There was a very tall young Englishman named John who was a doctor and there was the feckless Paddy pop star and his gorgeous journalist girlfriend. As a travelling party we looked suspiciously like a film-maker's idea of a perfect cross section of humanity. Failing a Murder on the Trans-Mongolian Express the very least we could expect was to be stranded for weeks without food in the Gobi Desert and be forced to draw lots for who should be eaten first.

From the beginning the members of the party each exhibited national characteristics to the point of caricature. We dubbed the German Cecil after Cecil B. DeMille. There was never a moment when he was without his cameras. Once I found him filming a brick. He was punctilious, frowned heavily and always complained in a prissy high-pitched voice whenever I was late, which, playing the devil-may-care Irishman, I usually was. Maurice, the train-spotter, was always leaning out of the window and taking notes with schoolboy enthusiasm. Velma, the fat lady, had her entire trunk filled with different brands of patent medicines and nerve tonics. Dick, the colonel, was constantly taking pictures of sand dunes in the belief that there would be a radar station lurking behind one of them, while Lou fretted about the well-being of the two poodles, Esther and Julie, one of whom was due to have her glands done.

The official guide seemed to have stepped from the pages of a different type of novel altogether, far more Graham Greene, this one. His name was Oscar, he was English and taught at a small private school in London during term time. He was grubby and grossly fat, with his stomach bursting through his shirt buttons. His trousers, with the fly always left undone, were a filthy khaki with vicious yellow stains around the groin. He was balding with a couple of wisps of hair which protruded at ridiculous angles and he looked out on the world through tiny piggy eyes behind tiny piggy spectacles. He sweated a great deal and he smelt. He was gross but I disliked the others making fun of him.

He was so inefficient that he almost had us miss the very first of our departures from Warsaw. From that point onwards we took an unconscious collective decision to ignore him. We were to fly via Novosibirsk to Irkutsk in the middle of Siberia by the massive Lake Baikal. From there we travelled by train into Mongolia and on through China to Hong Kong. Before we boarded the train at Irkutsk I wanted to buy some revolutionary posters. 'You must hurry,' said Cecil.

I was fifteen minutes late. Cecil was furious. 'You really must be on time.'

'Mind your own business.'

We were not off to a good start. Later in Ulan Bator I was one minute late to go somewhere. He began to lecture me.

'You really must be on time, we will not wait for you again, we will leave you. It is your own fault,' he said. I wanted to kick him.

'He's only a minute late,' John the doctor said.

'Yes . . . he was a minute late,' Cecil reiterated. 'I will not tolerate.'

Nine o'clock in the morning is not a good time for me. It takes me about two hours to wake up. As Cecil continued screaming inches from my face I decided I'd better hit him.

Dick stepped into the affray and looked down at the stunned Cecil. 'Gee,' he said, 'I don't think you should've said that to Bob.'

Siberia was surprisingly hot and lush. Nature had gone mad; fields, forests, rivers and mountains without boundary. The waters of Lake Baikal were black, rather like the strange fish which the local fishermen pulled from its waters. The official government guide was called Tania. We had a Natasha in Moscow. Tania and Natasha, it's like John Smith or Paddy Murphy.

There were wooden houses painted in bright colours and mud streets down which cows wandered followed by babushkas in shawls. One night I went for a walk by the lake. In the distance I caught the strains of what sounded vaguely like rock music. Following the sound I came upon a little café which had its own jetty out into the black waters. At the end was a tiny bandstand where a band was playing something which I could not quite place. At last I recognized Led Zeppelin's 'Stairway to Heaven' sung in Russian. Heavy metal meets the Volga boatman. They played with home-made gear. All around

Red Army soldiers were dancing with their girls. I was in Siberia listening to a local band playing in their anoraks in the cold night air. Pop music reaching across the world, I remember thinking; I wondered what problems that band and my own had in common. No one objected to me being there. People are friendly in Siberia, not like the Muscovites who share racism and conceit with the inhabitants of most imperial capital cities.

We stayed a few days, then we set out for a place which schoolboys in my day knew as Outer Mongolia. Today it is just Mongolia and, though there is a fantasy of independence, it is to all intents and purposes part of the Union of Soviet Socialist Republics. It is impossible to fly out of Mongolia except through Moscow and even all telephone calls are routed that way. The train was primitive. It was dirty and depressing with grey and white formica walls and two spartan bunks in each compartment. The mattress reminded me of the one in the flop house in Canada so I threw it out of the window which made the guard apoplectic. 'I'm not sleeping on that. I want another one.' Everybody else began to throw theirs out, or at least hang them out of the window and beat them on the side of the carriage. Of course I didn't get another and ended up sleeping, freezing, on just a couple of blankets.

Security at the border was heavy. Russian soldiers boarded and searched the entire train. The officer, cold and sophisticated, even inspected our books. 'Do you *only* read detective novels, madam?' he asked Paula in the tones of a rather superior butler.

He discovered Lou's poodle diaries. He flicked the pages and read snatches. 'What are these?'

'They are my diaries about Esther and Julie. They're our little darlings back home in St Petersburg. That's St Petersburg, Florida,' she said artlessly. 'Esther is having trouble with her glands. Would you like to see a picture?' She produced the pictures of the poodles which she had constantly shown us throughout the trip. 'That's Esther and that's Julie, see.'

The officer scrutinized the pictures, realizing that Esther and Julie were dogs. He handed them back without a smile. He didn't find the roubles. Exporting Soviet currency was illegal, but everyone had taken a couple as souvenirs, elaborately hidden in sticks of deodorant or taped inside the toilet cisterns or to the wall where they would be obscured by the door as it slid open. Very Ian Fleming, we thought.

Ulan Bator, the capital of Mongolia, was a dump. It had two hotels, Hotel A and Hotel B. We were in B, but we were assured that they were identical. The place was full of Russian soldiers on leave from Afghanistan. The sight unnerved Dick, who'd reckoned that we could knock the fresh-faced guards in Red Square in Moscow, but was not so sure about these bastards, who were all six foot tall and mean-looking. 'Like an army of Clint Eastwoods,' Paula said admiringly.

Mongolia is the fifth biggest country in the world, but a large percentage of its two million population are nomadic. They live in 'yurts', very large canvas tents which are fitted out with the most beautiful mahogany interiors. This nomadic life makes the people, despite the oppressive atmosphere, less susceptible to the rule of the Central Committee. But in the city centre the repression is clear. One Mongolian film student from Moscow University who struck up an innocent conversation with me in a poster shop on the merits of Francis Ford Coppola, the film director, was dragged away by his hair by the squat Mongolian police and when I followed to ask why, I was smashed against a wall with a truncheon.

Out in the country it felt as though little could have changed in centuries. Mongolia is popular with Russians for their holidays. The contrast between these holidaymakers with their white, unhealthy, fleshy bodies paddling in the river at the holiday camps and the native people could not have been more dramatic. We rebelled against the official programme and made our driver take us to a nomads' encampment. We found the 'yurts' by a small stream by a copse on the great wide plain. Horses were tethered here and there, old women tended fires of animal dung which were scattered around the small encampment. The men, bare-chested and brown as nuts, stood by the stream and watched as we approached. They were exquisite people whose Mongol features were refined rather than coarsened by hard living. It was a look I was later to see on the faces of the people of Ethiopia. In the distance approached fast horsemen; young boys, shirtless, riding bareback, controlling the horse only by holding onto the mane and applying pressure to the flanks, their legs clad in baggy pants and soft riding boots. One could easily see Genghis Khan riding out of these plains carrying all before him. The headman approached, muscular and in his early forties and with a long, drooping moustache and cropped hair. He invited us into his circular home. Its fire at the centre stank, and its hardwood fittings were gleaming. He gave us foul-smelling mare's milk to drink and offered a plate which contained one sweet each. It seemed a world away from the main street of Ulan Bator with its dingy rows of embassies.

What impression the inhabitants of the Mongolian capital have of the outside world may be misleading if they take the pictures outside the embassies as a guide. Each consulate has outside it a small glass-fronted notice board of the type found by rural churches. For some reason the Hungarian embassy had chosen pictures of models in a variety of trendy outfits, as though Hungary were the centre of the world's fashion industry. The English embassy, of course, had a range of curling yellowed photographs of the Royal Family.

We did, in the end, have recourse to the British Ambassador, who was an inoffensive little man with large sunglasses and a pipe at which he puffed imperturbably. What he had done to some high-up in the Foreign Office to deserve exile here was difficult to imagine. He seemed an amiable chap. We called him out because there was an impenetrable row going on about the train. We were told there was no room for us. We would have to stay in Ulan Bator for another fortnight. 'Not much I can do, I'm afraid,' said our man in Mongolia, puffing contentedly on his pipe, when he turned up at the station the morning we were due to depart. 'But I'll go and have a word.'

We did not wait for the outcome. In a remarkable display of international co-operative action all twelve of our party, Cecil too, made a dash for the train. We installed ourselves and refused to move.

The Chinese train was an amazing contrast to the Russian one. Everyone had their own rosewood cabin fitted with armchairs with lace antimacassars on the back. The light fittings were Tiffany brass lamps with handblown glass and little brass Victorian plaques. There was a tiled shower, lace curtains and lace covers on the beds. Everything was new, everything except the design which was pure twenties; they hadn't changed it because they didn't see why they should in a country where every industry is labour-intensive.

The train was spotless, and there was a friendly attendant at the end of every carriage who came in to replenish the flask of tea every three hours. Even the vacuum flasks were wonderful, stencilled with brightly coloured emblems which mixed the ancient with the modern, a rose with a radar station, a peony with a jet in flight. At each station the attendant would get out and polish the plaque at the side of each carriage which said 'Moscow–Ulan Bator–Peking Express, and he would shine the windows of every carriage. Maurice, the English train-spotter, who was, back home, a deputy director of British Rail Southern Region, couldn't handle it. Envy was writ large on his face. I suggested he transfer. He laughed mirthlessly.

Outside the window a cloud of dust appeared on the horizon. Within a few minutes a horseman was galloping alongside the train. He wore the traditional dark high-collared skirted coat with a lime green silk sash around his waist, baggy trousers and boots. The edges of his coat flapped in the wind, revealing a garish lining of polka dot blue and white. Then, spurring his horse with his knees, he overtook the train and galloped ahead for about a mile. He stopped and whipped a yellow flag out of his belt and held it aloft as the train passed. The steam engine whistled in recognition and the linesman, his weekly task completed, rode off again into the distance.

It was terrifically romantic charging through this beautiful place in this beautiful train. It demanded some radical gesture so in a half-humorous way I threw myself on my knees and proposed to Paula. We had been together for five years. She laughed and said, 'Get up, you idiot.'

'Say yes, say yes', I begged, in mock hysteria.

'Yes,' she said. That was four years ago but we still haven't got around to getting married.

The border with China was even more heavily guarded and security-conscious than the Russian frontier had been. The Mongolians, insecure, have a more oppressive security system than either of their imposing neighbours. The Mongolians started roaring and rushing around the train, looking everywhere, even under the beds. It was dark by now and you could hear the heavy footsteps of a soldier on the roof and catch glimpses of the beam of his torch. From beneath the wheels came the sound of sniffer dogs. Then the train started slowly through the no man's land with its heavy anti-tank fortifications. Spotlights were directed on the train until, half-way, Chinese spotlights took over. But once out of Mongolia the oppressive atmosphere lifted immediately. The Chinese border station was called Erh-lien-hao-t'e and it was decked out with fairy lights. A squeaky little tannoy played 'Auld Lang Syne'. Chinese customs officials lined up on the platform, apparently in order of height, waving. 'Welcome to the People's Republic of China,' squeaked the tannoy in five languages. The train had to change gauges here.

The Chinese were relaxed and open in sharp contrast to the Russians. In Moscow I had been shocked when the bells rang out in Red Square and the police moved all pedestrians off the road and refused to let them across the street. Soon the giant gates of the Kremlin swung back and a black limousine with smoked windows sped out from behind the huge palace walls. The police snapped to attention as it rushed past in a special lane reserved for government VIPs, heading towards a guarded and reserved VIP housing area in the city. I hated the cynicism of it, it was such a blinding metaphor for how unaccountable these people are. I'd never seen power so demonstrably removed and secure and untouchable. The Russians were suspicious and reserved, their guides hysterical if you simply refused to do what they wanted and went off on your own, as Paula and I did.

We had gone for a picnic on the banks of the Moscow river among Muscovite families on a Sunday afternoon. No one spoke to us. In China, where I would go for late night walks, children would walk beside you, and adults wished you good evening. One old couple, the lady rocking side to side like a wallowing boat on her tiny bound feet, were shocked to see their first western couple. Quite literally, they fell back into a doorway as we passed, the woman reaching for her throat in shock, the old man staring. Admittedly, they had probably never seen a six-foot-two long-haired person with a big nose and a tiny platinum blonde in Chinese boy's clothes holding hands before. But then, they had probably never seen anyone who was not Chinese before.

We were shown around factories, nurseries and crèches where the children practised their limited English: 'Hurro Auntie, Hurro Uncle'. We were the subject of endless curiosity. The children would laugh at us. They called westerners Big Noses and certainly the description was accurate enough in the case of me and John, who was six foot four. The children would come up and

On the train in the Gobi Desert.

The Great Wall.

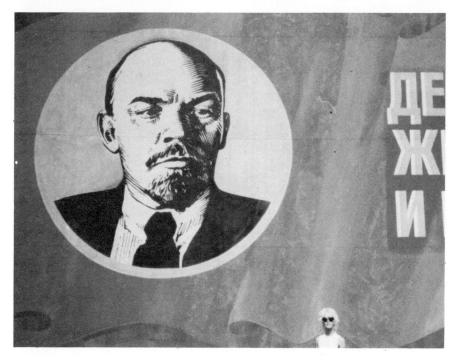

V.I. Lenin and P.E. Yates.

measure their feet against his size elevens and break up laughing. The fascination was not limited to the children. Later in the day Velma, the fat hypochondriac, was surrounded by little flat-chested Chinese women who took turns in feeling her breasts, which were objects of amazement to them. Velma laughed. In Beijing, when Paula went into a large store to buy a Mao suit, the women assistants all squeezed into the changing rooms to watch her.

Even our games were a source of amusement to them. One night in Da Tung, John and I sat in the hotel lobby and played Scrabble. Gradually the local men gathered to watch. Within half an hour we had acquired an audience of about forty. They chattered as they watched. At first they seemed to think it was a game like chess or Mah Jong. They watched our movements and then peered at the score sheets. Then John played a long word and all the people in his corner clapped. The people behind me started to point to my letters for me, pointing out the triple word score squares, just in case I hadn't seen them.

Leaving the others behind in Beijing, Paula and I took another train across China to Hong Kong. China was a country of dire poverty, but the tourist guides made no effort to hide their problems, as the Russian guides had done, going on great detours to ensure that you were driven through their horrendous model suburbs. The Chinese seemed happy to let westerners see the scale of the problems they faced and showed considerable pride in the improvements they had made. There was no restriction on where we could stop and what we could see. We stopped at one small town overnight and went to the local Chinese opera. It was difficult to work out the plot of the five-thousand-year-old story which was being enacted and I couldn't understand the music. I tried to keep time, but there didn't seem to be any. I tried to hear melody amongst the bangs and crashes and scrapings of the orchestra, clearly visible in the wings. They didn't seem to be too bothered either, as they smoked, chatted and drank tea and then, seemingly at random, bashed their instruments.

The touring company was from another province and spoke a dialect unknown to the audience so the text was projected onto sheets hung on either side of the stage, like movie subtitles. To the people in the audience the words were as well known as 'to be or not to be'. Chinese opera is highly stylized and if the actor misplaces a gesture or his intonation is wrong, it is roughly the equivalent of our own actors saying 'to be or maybe it was' or something like that. As the audience sat in the church hall-type of building in their wooden chairs and working clothes, they gave short shrift to the actors, yelling and booing and laughing openly. Sometimes they would turn to us and say something in Chinese, shaking their head in disbelief at the ineptitude of the performers. We got the meaning: 'Can you believe this? This is the worst.' They assumed, of course, that we knew this – it's five thousand years old, doesn't everybody know it?

More importantly, they just treated us as one of them. It was extraordinary, and a great night. At the end when the actors bowed, a couple of people clapped but most people ignored them. Later, twenty-two acrobats hung in a pyramid off the shoulders of one cyclist who pedalled furiously around the stage. Then they climbed up a large pole and holding on with one outstretched hand, they stuck themselves out at right angles to the pole rather like human flags, then they lowered themselves still like flags, still with one hand. They bowed extravagantly, and they got desultory and bored applause. I liked the audience's healthy disregard for the artistic ego.

Our guide was a gentle young man in a neat Mao suit with a slow, quiet smile. He talked readily about the recent history of his country. He told us how one day during the Cultural Revolution, when he was twelve, he and his younger sister had gone to school and half-way through the day had been sent home with the announcement, 'School is finished, not just for today, but forever'. They hurried home to tell their parents, who were themselves teachers in another school. But their parents never came home, and the children never saw them again. Their neighbours were too afraid to help for fear that it would be seen by the authorities as complicity. On the day the Red Guards came and before the children were sent to live for years on a farm in the country, they held a little trial for them. They were made to stand on a platform holding each other's hands while they were accused of 'bourgeois deviationism'. Their pet hamster was cited as the main evidence. They were found guilty. The hamster was brought out of its cage and beheaded in front of the terrified children. I thought of the innocent rebellion which was all that the *Little Red Book* had been to me in my schooldays. 'It was different now,' he said, with his nervy little smile.

He had seen from my passport that I was a musician. As we neared the border with Hong Kong, which he had never visited, he asked me what was the name of the orchestra in which I played.

'It's not an orchestra. It is a pop group.'

'What is a pop group?'

'You know, like the Beatles – pop music.' It seemed a far-fetched comparison but I assumed it would suffice.

'What is the Beatles – pop music?'

I had never been anywhere in my life where they hadn't heard of the Beatles. I laughed. 'It's just music, pop music. The Beatles are the name of some people who play it, I play it too. Some people in the west like to listen to it.'

CHAPTER XII

Wading Through the Swamp

'Let me just read you a bit. I'll open the script at random and read out a page. And if you can listen and keep a straight face, then I'll do the bloody thing.'

It was 1981. We were in a taxi on the way to Heathrow to fly to the recording studios in Ibiza where we would make our fourth album. On my knee in the back of the car was a film script. The cover said: 'The Wall, directed by Alan Parker, written by Roger Waters, music by Pink Floyd'. Fachtna was trying to persuade me that my next career move was to make a film.

'It's the lead part, Bob. The money isn't bad. Alan Parker is a big name – you know, *Midnight Express, Fame* and *Bugsy Malone*. You should do it. It'll be good for you. And it's a good introduction to films because there's no dialogue. The soundtrack will be entirely Pink Floyd.'

'Well, that's another reason for not doing it. Pink Floyd are crap.'

'But you don't have to sing.'

'I'm not bloody miming.'

'You don't even have to mime.'

'Look, I'm not playing second fiddle to Pink Floyd.'

'Bob, they are not even in it.'

'Look Fachtna, I've read this script. On every facing page it has the lyrics of the Pink Floyd song pertinent to the scene. They are awful. OK, I'll open this at random and read what's on the page, and if you don't laugh I'll do it.'

Fachtna creased after only half a dozen lines of my rendition.

'Right that's it, end of subject. "We don't need no education". Bloody hell! It could only be written by social-conscience-stricken millionaire pop singers. It's saloon-bar leftism.'

'You should do it, Bob.'

'It's all right for you, Fachtna, you're not the prat who'll be up on the screen with everybody breaking their arses over it. I am. So shut up will you.'

The taxi driver looked up and glanced quizzically at me in his mirror. It was only later that I found out he was a relation of Roger Waters, the writer of the script, and singer, writer and bass player with Pink Floyd.

Throughout the recording Alan Parker kept ringing me, which was a nuisance as the nearest phone to the studio in Ibiza was twelve miles away and I would have to travel into town to return his calls. 'A lot of the early plans have changed,' said Parker. He wanted me to do it because he had seen our videos and seen me interviewed on television. I possessed, apparently, a dangerous quality, a physical unpredictability which was especially needed because my character in *The Wall* had no dialogue and had to convey everything through his appearance. However, my main objection was that I didn't want to play a pop singer. I said I would see him when I returned.

★　★　★

The new album was to be different. We had changed record labels from Ensign to Phonogram, not because we had fallen out with Chris and Nigel but just because we felt we needed a bigger company with more money to promote us. We had a new producer, Tony Visconti, who had done some of David Bowie's best albums and had a name for being experimental and creative. We wanted a new approach. We had two platinum albums and one silver and seven hit singles. It was time to branch out. We had mastered studio technique and were no longer in awe of the machines, so we decided to eschew that for more spontaneity. In the past, I had always come into the studio with songs more or less complete. This time, I deliberately avoided that and went in with general ideas and tried to work the songs out.

Visconti turned out to be entirely different from Mutt. He had good ideas, but he got bored very easily and would tend to say something was right when it wasn't because he wanted to go on to something else. This was difficult for me, because I also have a low boredom threshold and want to move on to something new as quickly as possible. I dislike the whole process of rehearsing, arranging and recording. Once a song is finished on my guitar, I have very little interest in it. In the end, we used to tell Visconti to go off on his motorbike into the nearest town, twelve miles away, while we got the backing tracks right. The album was being made in a beautiful studio which provided fabulous food and a wonderful swimming pool. If you were doing nothing on a particular track for a while, you could go out to the pool or go into town. The problem was disciplining yourself to do any work. Musically we were trying a lot of things that were different, but if you are not careful, you can confuse self-indulgence with experiment, like we almost did with the track 'Mood Mambo'.

In keeping with the dance feel and spontaneity of the album which we called *Mondo Bongo* in homage to our recent world tour and in imitation of the jargon of the fifties when dance was king, Pete, Simon and I one day recorded a song from scratch. I said, 'Play anything you like, we'll take it live. I'll conduct, so if I signal, stop, it's because something's gonna happen in the gap later.' I had wanted to do a sort of beat poem. I was just going to say anything and see if it made sense. We played for about ten minutes. I spoke words – anything that came into my head, as I listened to the bass and drum. We cut it down in sections to about three-and-a-half minutes, put on some backing vocals, and that was 'Mood Mambo'. We started the *Mondo Bongo* world tour with that track. Another time, we put the drums outside in the open and a microphone in a tunnel to record them and got an eerie double-echo off the nearby mountains.

We did a cold, empty, fifties jazz track called 'The Little Death', an anti-heroin song. I felt now that every drug was predictable; I knew how it would affect me. Cocaine, which had once been stimulating and had enabled me to put up with nonsense when I was collapsing, I now found irritating. On it, you talk garbage. I heard people who had taken it gabbling furiously, their jaws snapping left and right with manic involuntary activity, their eyes shining and beads of sweat ringing their upper lips. I no longer liked the sharp burn in your nose as you sucked it up your nostrils, or the cramp you sometimes got next morning, nor the fact that ninety per cent of the cocaine anyone gave you was at least fifty per cent Italian laxative.

I had never touched marijuana or hashish after that time I almost killed myself in London. I had long ago, in Spain, thrown away my Librium and Valium downers. I had rejected my psychological dependence on my asthma inhaler and the speed pills I had been given for my asthma, and as a result, it disappeared. Acid was irrelevant, especially in the light of what I'd seen it do to my old school friends in the squat in London.

The only drawback to all this clean living (I never drank much except at weekends) was my self-imposed exclusion from 'the swamp'. The swamp was a social phenomenon of the Rats, and probably most other groups. After a concert, and after you've eaten, changed, and showered, there's never much to do in a town. It is the peak of your day. To bring yourself down and to enable yourself to go to bed and sleep at a reasonable hour, you would all gather in someone's room and smoke a few joints and chat before turning in at three or four. It was a nice convivial relaxing thing, but I couldn't stand the smell of the stuff, it still made me nervous after all those years. I also couldn't stand the same conversations that went on every night; it was like being in the pub. A pub, to me, was a place to go and get drunk if you wanted to, or meet someone, have a drink and go some place else. The idea of sitting all night in a bar drove me mad. I thought it was one of the great shames of Dublin: so many great ideas, so much talent and energy talked away during the night. Instead of doing things, people only talked about them. Maybe if there wasn't such a pub culture, they would be forced to actually enact their ideas in order to give them expression. At the same time, I preferred going to pubs to sitting in watching TV all night with people never talking to each other. At least argument, thought, discussion and conversation were kept alive. The Irish can talk – everyone knows that. But why is it that they can only translate talk to action when they leave Ireland? Where is the dynamism of the Irish immigrants in the U.S. and Britain reflected in those who stay at home? Is it that the ideas expressed in pubs, when translated into action, get sat on by the men who control the purse-strings? Or is it simply that in Ireland ideas close when the pubs do?

The swamp, like the pub, never relaxed me. I'd retire to my room, feeling the unique pressure on me: to the band I was the man expected to deliver, to the Press I was the main man, and to the fans I was the 'star'. I had also excluded myself from the camaraderie of the swamp, and my constant feeling of being uncomfortable with myself was manifested in the song 'Wind Chill Factor Minus Zero'.

It's one of those days where I don't like myself
But I get along with me OK
I'll slip beneath these sheets
And shiver here a while.
I find this happening more frequently these days.

I preferred to write songs about reality; real events or real people. I forced myself to be honest about myself. We had been touring solidly for two years, and as times not touring were spent in the studio, I had less contact with people outside the record industry than before, so when the songs weren't experimental, like 'Mood Mambo', 'The Little Death', and the first instrumental I had written, called 'Whitehall 1212' (which was the telephone number for Scotland Yard), they were snapshots of things I'd seen on our way around the world during the *Surfacing* tour. The songs were also more overtly political. Rhodesia had become Zimbabwe while we were in Auckland so there was a song about the loss of empire, 'Another Piece of Red'. *I was reading in New Zealand about Ian Smith, I was thinking they were lucky to be rid of that shit.* In America, we had seen the riots in Florida: *It's Disneyland under martial law.* I had also seen a programme about the judicial system there: *Justice isn't blind, it just looks the other way.* The song was called 'The Elephant's Graveyard'.

In Japan, I was startled by the sight of people cleaning the sea of mercury poisoning while they listened to their Walkmans.

Thunder over Tokyo
Pressure on my eyes
Hi–Fi on their heads
While they tidy the tides
Dear Auntie Fifi
You should see this place
They grow a cushion on their backs
And a flu–mask on their face.

In 'Go Man Go' I summed up my feelings about yet another tour: *I'd stay at home today. But the world said, 'Go man go'.* Then there was 'Banana Republic', which became the big hit from the album. It was the bitter song I'd written in the wake of our homecoming to Ireland. In revenge, I attacked those I thought were destroying the country. *The purple and the pin-stripe* [the Church, politicians and businessmen] *mutely shake their heads, a silence, shrieking volumes of violence worse than they condemn.* I accused them of a silent complicity with those other evil thugs who murder Irish people, the IRA and the UVF. The violence will continue, because Ireland cannot forget its history. I called history 'Ireland's whore'. *Sharing beds with history is like licking running sores.* If you pick at the scab of history, it bleeds. The IRA and the UVF and the other obscene nationalists make sure that the scab always weeps. *Banana Republic, septic isle screaming in a suffering sea, it sounds like dying.* It was a sad song and it was a massive hit. It surprised me that people interpreted the song to fit their own situation. The Germans, for example, thought it was about them; it was a bigger hit there than 'Mondays'. The Americans refused to play it because of the violence of its imagery. They didn't like the word 'whore'. After 'Mondays', in the U.S. everything I wrote was examined. In Ireland some papers said it was simply spite, others said it was puerile rubbish, still others said it was true.

Nationalism, I believe, is the single most dangerous of all political philosophies. Patriotism – a pride in your country – is understandable and healthy. I have never felt proud or ashamed of being Irish, I just am, and that's fine by me. I am proud of its literary and cultural heritage, and of the people, and certainly the thing I am most proud of is the compassion shown by the Irish when they massively responded to Live Aid, giving more money per head of population than any other country in the world. But nationalism, which seeks to turn those natural feelings into a system of control, and then transform them into a jingoistic political ideology, seems to me abhorrent, and little more than fascism. Nationalism is tribalism, and constantly prevents different parts of the world from attempting to understand one another. It's something we'd better come to terms with soon, in the age of a ubiquitous global culture perpetrated and spread by a global media network. This was the basic logic underlying Live Aid.

The experiments of *Mondo Bongo* continued. I asked Simon to sing a song I'd written one night on the *Surfacing* tour. I'd wanted to be at home with Paula, I didn't want to do another gig or read another lousy music paper. I was overwhelmed with self-pity and depression.

Not only cripples
Have a need for crutches
And if they
Ever took
You away
From me

I'd fall down
And lie still.

Simon sang it beautifully in his clear, choirboy voice.

*   *   *

However, despite my complaints on 'Wind Chill Factor Minus Zero', I liked stardom. I found it liberating and enjoyable, especially as I set the parameters to my own fame. I rode on tube trains, I took taxis, I walked. I didn't do it to show them 'hey, wow, he's really one of the people'. I did it for myself. I refused to be removed from the things I actually enjoyed. If I was asked for autographs – so what? It's an occupational hazard, and anyway, I would remember the first time I was asked, when I said, 'Are you serious?' The girl said, 'Why not? You're going to be famous.' If you didn't want to do it, you could simply say, No. If you were reading on the bus and someone wanted to talk to you, you would say, 'I'm sorry, I just want to read'. If they persisted, you simply told them to fuck off. If they then never bought another record, that was your tough luck. Come to think of it, that may explain our recent lack of sales. Perhaps I told millions of people to fuck off.

I'd use fame to talk about things that bothered me. I like to provoke argument and discussion. If people disagreed with me, fine. I'd like it. But at least, perhaps in some living room or pub where there was a TV on, someone would say, 'What a wanker,' and someone else would say, 'I don't know, I think he's right,' and begin arguing. The only way I could do this was through TV and radio. The national press, which we were now almost courting in an attempt to neutralize the constant attacks on us by the music press, was good for this, but it was edited to fit the readers' perception of what a pop star should be. I didn't want to be edited and cut to suit the reporters' preordained view. The most direct way to reach people was through live radio and TV.

This 'wooing' of the national press incensed the music press even more. As I became the 'media darling', 'this articulate young man', 'this spokesman for his generation' (which I never claimed nor wanted to be), the screeches of the music press rose to an impotent crescendo. I was beyond their reach, but they wanted their revenge. I was on everything: the Parkinson shows (both Mary's and Michael's), political shows, art shows and, on one memorable occasion, the Eamonn Andrews show.

Eamonn was a Dubliner like myself and had been primed by that first talk show we had done four years earlier in Ireland, when I purged myself of all my demons. Now we talked of the Dublin we both knew and agreed that it wasn't the people, it was the attitude of the city itself that was so wrong. I went on to say they were the attitudes by and large enforced by the Church, State and city authorities. I condemned the policy of rehousing Dubliners away from the city, destroying communities. What point was there in having the city at all without people? Oh no, he wouldn't go that far. If the city of Dublin wasn't Dubliners, it was certainly nothing else, I argued. He thought this a little extreme.

He moved to the other guests, Jilly Cooper, Patrick Campbell, the brilliant Anglo-Irish humorist, and Vidal and Beverly Sassoon. Sassoon wore a deep tan and beige casual clothes. He told us he'd made sixty million dollars, or something, the year before. He was now sixty, or something, and suggested that he looked great. 'You know, nobody should let themselves go when they get to my age. You want to get out and exercise.' He claimed he did something like four billion push-ups every day, 'and look at me!' He continued in this narcissistic Californian way for a few more minutes.

I was incensed and finally exploded. 'I've never heard such crap in all my life.'

His wife spat, 'You're obnoxious.' Vidal tried to keep things calm. 'Hey, c'mon Bob, don't you exercise?'

I told him that I got up at five in the afternoon, which wasn't true, but I wanted to provoke him further. I pointed out, after more nonsense of his about doing a few lengths of 'your pool', that not many people in England had a pool, and that when you came in from work at the office or the factory, all you wanted to do was to sit down with a beer and watch telly or go out with your mates. Whilst you might have time, when you earn sixty million dollars or whatever, to be as self-obsessed as he seemed, most people were too busy trying to stay alive to bother about eternal youth. The discussion ended when I asked Sassoon whether he didn't think he was rather overpaid for being a 'barber'.

The next day, lorry drivers leaned out of their cab windows and shouted, 'Well done, mate! You showed those wankers.' A taxi driver refused to charge me. It seemed people did agree, or at least agreed with me about pretentious and self-indulgent hairdressers. I enjoyed venting my spleen and my opinions. I was called 'arrogant' and an 'egomaniac'. It's possibly true, but I was having fun, and people often confuse being dogmatic with arrogance. I was simply saying on TV what I believed, and unlike other people I had an outlet for my opinions.

★   ★   ★

We undertook the inevitable tour to promote *Mondo Bongo*. It went well. It sold out in most places and we gave some good performances, though the music press continued to attack both in England and the States.

When the LP was released in England we had taken it to the States and played it for all the top Columbia executives – all in vain. So Fachtna played them six new songs we had recorded only in rough form. They said that there were three hits among them. 'OK,' said Fachtna. 'You tell us what they are and how you want us to do them and we'll do just as you say.' That was how desperate we had become. They sent over one of their own executives to produce the three tracks, one of which was then placed on the American version of the album. It was the same old story. The company put little or no money behind promoting us on radio and *Mondo Bongo* flopped.

We did a dozen gigs in America, with the same result as before. We stopped in Hawaii to break up the flight to Japan, and then played in Bangkok.

South-East Asia was an eye-opener. We were Number One in Thailand when we arrived. We learned later that this was no great achievement as the character who promoted the concert also controlled seventy-two hours a week of national radio and virtually declared by personal fiat what was Number One at any given time. For weeks before we arrived all the unfortunate Thais heard on their radio was the Boomtown Rats. The fact that the promoter was a senior officer in the local police force also helped.

Corruption isn't an aberration in the system in Thailand – it *is* the system, from the lowest street level to the top. Because it embraces all classes and all classes must therefore understand graft to survive, Thais seem to be very ingenious and entrepreneurial. It was an invigorating place to be and the audiences were extraordinary. I felt my western complacency and many of my attitudes knocked sideways. I remember saying in an interview, 'America is young and tired, Europe is old and tired, but Asia is just old'. I'd grown blasé about Europe and didn't care if I never saw Gottenburg or Düsseldorf again. America had become predictable and disappointing, but Asia was astonishing. Our first gig was in a Chinese graveyard in Bangkok in the scented tropical night. As we finished, I thought, I must come back here. It was the same feeling I'd had in Mongolia or China; I could lose myself in a totally alien surrounding. It was all refreshingly new and I liked the people's lack of pretension and disregard of sophistication.

Gerry, our lead guitarist, was feeling exactly the opposite. For some time now he had sensed that not only was the band beginning to slow down after the initial drive to success, but it was also not even doing the sort of music which he liked. Tension grew between him and the rest of us and we began to treat him as a kind of scapegoat. Throughout that tour he had frequently left us and wandered off on his own around the cities. It came to a head one night in Japan when we were celebrating Simon's birthday in a bar and Gerry refused to come. The band decided that he had to go. The feeling was that he wasn't playing very well, though he was a good guitarist, and probably that was just a rationalization on the part of the rest of us. As usual, I was deputed to tell him. Fortunately I was spared this task because the day before the tour ended, Gerry told Fachtna that he was quitting. I was sad to see him go in this atmosphere of bad blood. Later he made a couple of solo records which I thought were good, but they were not successful.

We never got another guitarist. The music had changed from the days of the classic two-guitar R & B line-up. As the music became more arranged, the keyboards became more predominant. Fingers bought more instruments, like string machines and synthesizers, which along with the bass largely filled out the sound and did away with the need for a rhythm guitar. Gary could now swap between lead and rhythm. Deciding who would play had once been a source of conflict between him and Gerry. The one good effect of Gerry's departure was the increase in Gary's confidence.

$$\star \quad \star \quad \star$$

When I got back home to Clapham, Alan Parker rang again. The changes he had talked about in *The Wall* over the phone in Ibiza still did not impress me. The film was originally to have been directed by the political cartoonist, Gerald Scarfe, with Parker simply involved in production and general advice-giving. But Parker had gradually become more and more involved in the direction. What he said didn't alter my conviction that the music was over-blown and old hat and that the script was corny. But he seemed a nice bloke and I had liked his earlier films. Moreover I couldn't stand the idea of having to produce another album straight away. I also wanted to learn the difference between video and film. I'd never done a film before so it was a challenge, and the money was good.

They wanted me to do a screen test. The day before I was due in Pinewood Studios in Elstree I got a phone call from Parker: 'It'll be quite straightforward. I just want you to improvise a quick scene and then do a bit of a speech – you know that bit in *Midnight Express* where the boy is in the dock? That bit. I'll send round a script.'

I was horrified when it arrived. It was one of the most dramatic moments in the film. The main character is an American boy sentenced to gaol in Turkey for drug smuggling. He has been given a ridiculously long sentence and he appeals against it. Parker wanted me to do that courtroom speech. The boy has to argue that what is right and wrong is different in each country, and when the judges are unimpressed he starts to plead and then, realizing he is still getting nowhere, feels he has shamed himself by begging and loses his temper and screams at them. It was a soliloquy. I walked around the little conservatory in Clapham reading it aloud to myself. It sounded ludicrous. I could not get over the ridiculous sound of my Irish accent in the part. I rang up Chris Hill from Ensign who had once spent three years in rep as an actor. He came and read it for me, and suddenly it came alive. He did the same piece another way, and then another. I began to read it in different ways, and thus to grasp the technique of what I was being asked to do. I learned the part by heart that night.

Early the next morning a long limousine called for me and took me to Pinewood. Stage D was like an enormous Nissen hut with a corrugated iron roof and a vast echo. Slap in the middle of its giant space was a large group of technicians around a couple of cameras and a tiny set which consisted of a chair, a small table with glasses and a telephone on it, a lamp and a television. I walked around the perimeter of the building, avoiding the people in the centre. I was nervous and deeply embarrassed. I was frightened that I would not be able to do it and would be rejected. It was like being back at a Stella House dance. I thought, 'Who are you kidding? Get out now, pal'.

'OK Bob, if you're ready . . .'

It's pathetic. How old are you? Twenty-eight? At your age you're embarrassed? You must overcome this, I thought. I crossed to the middle.

'We'll do the improvised scene first,' said Parker. 'Just sit in the chair. OK, it's this – you're in LA, it's one or two in the morning. You ring your wife, it's about six in the evening in London. She doesn't answer the phone. A man does, who you've never heard before . . . you take it from there.'

I sat for a moment and thought. What would I do? I decided I would put the phone down immediately. My anger would be cold. I would sit and work out in a black mood who it could be and how I could get even with them.

'OK, when you're ready . . . in your own time, Bob. Action!'

I sat and looked at the black screen, looked at the phone and back to the TV. Then, as if on impulse, I picked up the phone.

'Hang on,' shouted the focus puller. 'Are you going to do that?'

'What?'

'Pick up the phone like that, that way?'

'Yes, that's the way I pick up phones.'

'Hang on.' He produced a tape measure and measured the distance between the camera and my hand as I touched the receiver. 'OK. Fine. Carry on.'

I began again, picked up the phone, dialled the number, waited, said 'Hallo', then put the phone down, turned back to the TV and sat stock-still looking at it and doing my best to convey cold anger and calculation. Then I looked up.

'Is that it?' asked Alan.

I explained.

'Bob, we want you to externalize a bit more.'

Next time I swept the glasses off the table. I felt enormously hammy. I expected that they would all be thinking, 'Bloody pop singer – what a wanker'.

And so it went on, getting more and more melodramatic. 'I don't believe this, it's so corny,' I thought. I could hear myself shouting. The fourth time around I went right over the top, picking up a glass, grinding it into the mouthpiece and screaming, 'You slut! You bitch! You whore!' I could see the technicians inches from my face. I could hear my voice echoing round the empty warehouse. I felt a prick.

'Great, great, I think that's enough of that,' said Parker with delight.

'Too bloody true,' I thought.

They must have liked it because next they brought out a courtroom dock from somewhere and I did the main speech. It was weird for Parker to hear this Paddy version of a scene he knew so well, but he liked it, and the Floyds liked the screen test. They had not originally wanted me for the part. Other people were tested so I was rather pleased and relieved that I hadn't been a complete flop.

Walking out on to the set of *The Wall* was like negotiating a minefield which had been sown with exploding egos. The disagreements between Waters and Scarfe, on the one hand, and Parker and his co-producer, Alan Marshall, on the other, had by this stage grown into feuds. Parker, acting on Michael Winner's dictum that 'democracy on the set is a hundred people doing what I tell them', had asked Waters not to come to the studio and the whole thing had deteriorated to the point where the atmosphere was sour and full of childish recriminations. I tried to keep out of it and just put my trust in Parker who, I reckoned, knew what he was doing.

But there were occasions when I felt as though he didn't. In one scene the pop singer I was playing, who was going mad, had to wreck a hotel room while a horrified groupie looked on. It had already got out of hand. When I was tearing the louvred doors from the wardrobe, I ripped the nails from my fingers and I had cut my hands smashing them through windows. Then Alan said, 'When she gets to this point, I want you to pick up this trolley and throw it at her'. It was a huge room service trolley, a great metal thing, and I assumed that Alan had told her what I was going to do. When I threw it she hurled herself to one side just in time as the whole thing, laden with food, hit the wall where her head had been a few seconds earlier. She lay there, surrounded by shards of broken crockery, and had hysterics. 'Great,' said Parker. 'Cut.'

Nor was I thrilled about the scene in which I had to be covered in a mixture of flour and water and then dragged down an iron staircase. It was the point where the film moves into the realm of fantasy. My skin begins to boil and burst and develop a crust, becoming a sort of chrysalis out of which I burst to emerge as a clean, neurotic fascist figure. Personally I thought the idea of the pop star as incipient fascist was a load of bollocks. But I was even more unimpressed by being stripped naked, covered in a cold flour and water paste and then dragged on a freezing night down a metal staircase. I was hauled by the shoulders so that my feet went duk, duk, duk down the stairs. My heels began to bleed. After four takes the gunge was beginning to harden like an icy shell all over my skin.

'Right, that's it. I'm supposed to be acting, not being fucking tortured. I will not be physically abused. Fuck off!'

Parker ordered a break and then sent a bottle of whisky to warm me up.

The inner man emerges. Alan Parker talks to the wrong one.

And all this for a shot of the back of my head.

I smashed it against the wall. 'Tell that fucker I will not be bought off with a bottle of fucking Scotch.'

They implied that I was throwing a rock star's tantrum, but I wasn't. We had been doing it for two days, and so far as I could see we weren't getting anywhere new, just messing around. I agreed to do it one final time.

'Just a bit of hair out of place,' said the hairdresser coming over with his comb and spray.

'Just fuck off, Barry, will you.'

'Oh, all right, dear, don't take it out on me. I'm only the crimper.'

'Oi will nort be physically abused. Oi will nort,' mimicked the make-up men, Peter Frampton and Paul Engelen, in awful bog-Irish accents in the background.

'And you two can fuck off as well,' I yelled.

They did, too, leaving me alone in a shower in the awful building for two hours trying to get the awful muck out of my hair.

The other really trying scene was one in which I was supposed to be floating in a swimming pool in which the water suddenly turns to blood. It was only at the point where I actually entered the pool that they found I couldn't swim.

'Well, just fucking float, for god's sake.'

'I can't float without moving my arms and legs.' I knew that because I had been with Paula down to Putney Baths to practise. I could swim now, I had just about learnt during our holiday in Barbados, where the water was hot enough to entice me in, but I could only swim on my back and I had to keep moving. I had given up after one session, because I kept getting surrounded by little kids who cut through the water like Jaws saying, 'What's up, Bob, can't you swim? It's easy, look'. They darted round and under me like little fish. My cool and dignity utterly shattered, I gave up forever any hope of being the new Johnny Weissmuller.

The props people devised a transparent cylinder anchored to the bottom of the pool on which I rested just below the water level. The problem was that the clear plastic cut into my back quite seriously after a while.

'Why don't we get Superman's body mould and he could lie in that?' someone suggested. We went along to the props department to find the transparent stand in which Superman had lain to do his flying while the universe was projected at various angles onto a screen in the background. But it wouldn't fit me, I was far too thin and weedy and kept slipping around inside the shell which had been moulded exactly to fit Christopher Reeve's muscular frame.

'Why don't we try Supergirl's?' suggested some bright spark. To my humiliation, like Cinderella's slipper, it fitted. So there I was, sitting for five days in Supergirl's arse, in a freezing swimming pool, while buckets of blood were poured over me.

It wasn't real blood, of course, but it was a very eerie experience for all that. I have a phobia about blood. I can't stand the sight of it, not even in bottles, where it looks sickeningly thick. The sound of my own heart terrifies me and when I press my ear to the pillow and hear the blood bubbling and coursing through my veins it disgusts me. It takes my mind back to that dripping liver on the railway tracks.

In *The Wall* my character was a manic depressive and I found that to sink myself into the part I would edge myself into black moods which could not easily be dispelled after filming. I was churlish, snappy and desperately miserable at home with Paula in the evenings. I experienced an awful sense of slipping down, away from the reach of my conscious mind.

One day I had to film a scene where in a hotel room I stared at a television set in blank despair, looking but not seeing, totally withdrawn. In the same room a groupie was to chatter away and I was not to hear her, not to acknowledge her existence. I do not know whether Alan Parker had primed her or whether she did it instinctively, but when the cameras were rolling she knelt beside me and stroked my hand with exquisite tenderness. 'Are you all right?' she asked, in a voice totally different from the one she had been using until that moment. The voice reached out to me as a hand might reach out to a man in a pitch dark room. Two large scalding tears seeped and rolled down my cheeks like those which had welled up from somewhere deep inside me that nightmare night in the squat in Tufnell Park. Just that simple gesture, those everyday words. They kept filming it. I didn't shake or sob or anything, but whatever part of my brain I'd burrowed into, something dark and deep and hidden had been revealed. It was a bit like consciously willing myself back into that part of me I'd unlocked all those years ago with drugs. Parker realized this. He said, gently, 'OK, let's stop for lunch.' When everyone had filed out he came across and asked the same question the girl had asked. I just sat there for a while in this pit of deep black despair.

I understand suicide. People look back at others and say, 'How could he do that? He had everything going for him'. But I can understand how all these things which are 'going for you' can suddenly become meaningless. But I could never kill myself. It is the final triumph of self-pity, of ego. There is too much passion for life in me to allow an obsession with death. Suicide is the ultimate defeat. No matter how depressed you are, to succumb to that is to throw in the towel and I'm not very good at that. Too Irish, too stubborn. But the dense moods which *The Wall* brought down upon me carried with them an insight into depths which were normally buried, and I would prefer remained so.

Towards the end of filming Parker decided that he did, after all, need me to sing part of one of the songs. I was adamant I wouldn't. That had been part of the original understanding. The Floyd's producers had refused to give me even half a per cent of the film's profits in my contract. This is quite normal procedure, so if they wanted me to sing a Pink Floyd song I wanted more money or points. Eventually we agreed. I went to the sixteenth-century manor house in Henley where Dave Gilmour, the Floyd's guitar player, has a twenty-four-track studio in the outbuildings, to record. When it came to singing the six lines I had been allocated, I sang them in a highly accented Irish folk-singing manner. It was a delight to see the look of horror creep over the faces of Gilmour and James, the engineer in the control room. Dave Gilmour sank down to hide under the desk.

'Stop, stop, stop,' I shouted. 'What's the matter?'

'Er . . . it's the phrasing, Bob. You haven't quite got the phrasing how Roger sings it.'

'I'm singing it exactly as Roger phrases it . . .' There was silence. 'Shall I have another go?' I made the second attempt even worse – like a drunken farmer at a Kerry agricultural show.

'Stop, stop, stop,' they shouted.

'What is it now? What is it? It's not just the phrasing, what is it?' I asked.

'Er . . . do you always sing like that?'

'Course I do, haven't you heard any of my records?'

'Yes, well, it's very Irish, isn't it?'

'Well, I am Irish, can't fucking help that.'

'Yes, but it sounds more Irish than normal.'

I tormented them for as long as I could and then I sang it properly. At the end a voice came from the control room over the studio monitors: 'You bastard!'

★ ★ ★

The film got fifty per cent good, fifty per cent bad reviews. I was disproportionately praised. It was ironic. These reviews didn't matter to me; had
they been for the Rats' next album I would have been ecstatic. I couldn't have
cared less about the bad ones. It wasn't my film, so why should I care? Were it
my album, though, I'd have been upset.

I felt very uneasy about seeing myself on film. I refused to watch any of the
rushes. Nor did I watch the cut version. Nor did I go to the BAFTA screening
for the crew. I do not understand why, but I do not like listening to myself on
the radio (which, ironically, isn't a problem these days), or hearing any of our
records at a party or in a club. If I see myself in a video doing a song with any
passion or drama, I feel deeply embarrassed. I agreed to go to Cannes with
Parker to do the hype but tried to get up and leave when the opening credits
began. Parker, sitting next to me, grabbed my legs and made me sit down.

It is extremely weird to see yourself the size of a building. At the same time,
it was very interesting to see how all these things which you had shot out of
sequence and which you thought wouldn't work did actually fit together. It
was also an odd experience to go into a cinema unhindered by the paparazzi
and come out barely two hours later deluged by publicity. Despite everything,
I had enjoyed making the film. For a change I had no responsibility other than
to myself, to be as good as I could be. It was like a holiday. It became clear to
me how important the director is on a film and how much an actor is only a
cypher for the director. The director's job is really the only one worth having,
I thought. At one point in *The Wall* an actor who had to pretend to be
terrified of me was having problems with the scene. She was American, and a
method actor. 'But Alan,' she said, 'what is my motivation for doing this?'
Parker sighed, paused, and said, 'The money.' She got it right next time.

★   ★   ★

The Wall was a necessary break from the band and its work: record, tour,
write, record, tour . . . I still wasn't prepared to go back to the routine. I
wanted to continue in the experimental mood of the *Mondo Bongo* album, I
wanted something different and invigorating. Our agent, Ian Flukes, suggested
Asia. Not just Bangkok this time, he said, but India, Malaya, Hong Kong, and
Singapore as well. We loved the idea. It's a curious fact that as a band we think
quite similarly. The others like the idea of challenge and change as much as me.

We got an offer from an Indian maharajah called Vickram Singh. He had
never heard us and why he wanted to book us was a mystery we never quite
solved. Certainly he never made a penny out of us and indeed we only got
paid our expenses, but that was OK. We arrived just with our guitars and
Simon's snare-drum and inspected the bizarre range of local equipment he
had assembled. Some old keyboards with a distinctly unsafe collection of
wires hanging out the back were produced for Fingers. Pete raised his eye-

brows when he saw the amps. The PA system was the sort we would have turned up our noses at during the early days in Dun Laoghaire. But it worked, and we were in India, doing it for fun, and it was an adventure.

The first two concerts were in Bombay. They were sell-outs, despite the fact that few people had heard of us; the mere presence of a western pop group was sufficient. We played in the open air, in a bowl-shaped arena, and as soon as the gig began everyone who hadn't been able to afford a ticket just climbed over the walls and pushed their way in. In the best tradition of pop concerts the world over, the crowd invaded the posh seats at the front, pushed them to one side and jostled as near to the stage as possible. Curiously, the billboards that had been erected around the city advertising the concerts had heavily Indianized Boomtown Rats. We were made chubbier and darker, with black hair and almond eyes.

For us it was so different in every way to what we had been doing in recent years. There was no pressure at all, nothing was expected of us and therefore, of course, we played brilliantly because that is always the way you play when you couldn't give a bollocks. We played lots of different things, not just our own songs – David Bowie's 'Ziggy Stardust', the Stones, Bob Marley, the Beatles – it was quite clear that they had heard little or none of them before. It was marvellous. We had not enjoyed playing so much for years. We were there for the same reasons as the audience – out of curiosity and to have fun.

What stunned me was the way the audience reacted. They moved and danced, shouted and sang just like an audience in any part of the world. In Bombay perhaps they were used to pop music, but at the other concerts in India they had never heard it before, but they behaved as if it were a part of their normal lives. I realized then what later I was to articulate more consciously when I was trying to organize the Live Aid concert – that rock music is one of the great twentieth-century art forms, not least because of its internationalism, its ability to transcend the artificial barriers of language and frontiers and speak instinctively to the whole world in a way that other sorts of music have never quite done. It communicates on a much more fundamental level than any culture's classical music. Rock music has an aggression that articulates a basic emotion through rhythm. It's sexy. It beats on some primal pulse and the response of any human being to it is intuitive and emotional.

We played for three hours and we were brilliant. At the end the audience shouted for encores. They even shouted for songs by name after only one hearing. We sang Bob Marley's 'Stir It Up' and a vast swelling of Indian voices joined in. Under the huge Indian moon, with the sky full of different stars and the air heavy with the scent of jasmine I felt in touch with something wider than ever before.

After the gig a flat-bed truck pulled up and a mattress was thrown onto it. A row of amps and equipment was placed on it, then another mattress, then

Simon sound checking in Bangalore, India.

more equipment and so on, until it was all loaded. Then it wobbled off over the plains to the next gig.

Bombay was our first dip into India. It was a shock. Stepping from the bus one day I saw the ubiquitous beggar with outstretched hand shaking a long pole. Tied to the top of the ten-foot-high pole was a baby who was shaken to make it cry. I went to the infamous Bombay cages where the prostitutes worked. Down dark, stinking alleys were buildings with iron bars over the windows. From behind these bars peeped grotesquely made-up women. We went for tea and strawberries at the Bombay Cricket Club and the Taj Mahal Hotel, which was built in front of the old yacht club by an Indian, to deny the colonists the view of the harbour in an act of subtle revenge. They hadn't allowed him to join their club.

After Bombay we played in Bangalore where the stage was just four or five planks shoved together on boxes a couple of inches off the ground. As we set up, I asked Vickram if there would be any lights. 'Here they are now,' he said and pointed. Through a gap in the fence came a man on a bicycle, a coil of wire slung around the handlebars and two light bulbs hanging around his neck. He slung the wire between two trees so that the two bare bulbs hung over the stage. 'Clearly into minimalist lighting here,' I said. Vickram laughed.

India invigorated me. *The Wall* and now this tour had reaffirmed my belief that what I was doing was not only valid, but important, and that the band were superb. Earlier I had begun to believe the critics and a crippling self-doubt had set in. I now rejected this.

★   ★   ★

With regret and diarrhoea, we left the sub-continent after our last concert in Madras. We flew to Hong Kong and played a couple of gigs and visited the

Kung Fu movie studios. We played Singapore in the ballroom of a hotel because we couldn't get a gig anywhere else and we only got that because the proprietor's son had been to school in England and had heard of us. It was in Singapore that we had a strange request from the wizened old waiter in his crisp white jacket.

'You sing Three Creatures?'

'Three Creatures, don't think we know that one.'

'Three Creatures.'

'Is it a band or a song? Maybe it's a sixties band. Anyone know the Three Creatures?' We tried him with the Big Three and various permutations of groups with animal connections and trios.

Then the old fellow, exasperated, his towel across his arm, began to do a passable imitation of Cliff Richard.

'Ah, Cliff Richard!'

'Hyes, Chree Reechah.'

When we got to Bangkok where we were sufficiently well known to be playing the massive local stadium, Cliff was actually playing there on the night we arrived. We went backstage and told him of the waiter's request. 'Three Creatures. That makes a change. They usually call me Kibbly Cha.'

Really the only thing I wanted to do while in Singapore was visit Raffles. I was in search of Somerset Maugham. I wanted to find planters who had gone to seed drinking themselves into oblivion in the jungle, their wives half-crazed with boredom. The heavy sensuality of the long, wet afternoons, women who found amusement with gin slings and the locals. You know the stuff: natives watching, knowing, and sniggering in derision and contempt behind the palm fronds. We went to the hotel and ordered gin stengahs. I was with Brian Aris, the photographer, and Pete Biziou, the cameraman from *The Wall*. They had come on the trip with us. We got quietly and colonially stewed. Later we stumbled into the hot night to find our own hotel. At the door a rickshaw driver said, 'Boogie Street?' It was 1 a.m. in the morning, I'd been in Raffles drinking gin, the night was hot and youngish and a rickshaw driver asked me if I wanted to go to somewhere called Boogie Street. The only possible answer was 'yes'. It transpired it was actually called Bugis Street and is notorious, but I'd never heard of it. We sat down at the tables outside a small bar to watch the traffic. The street was full of the most beautiful hookers. It was very hot. Insects crashed ferociously around the strip lights which hung by wires from a network of poles. From nowhere appeared the most stunning of women. She slinked across in a very mannered way and sat on my knee and asked for my autograph. I was flattered. At least they've heard of us in Singapore. I scribbled and then looked up to find myself surrounded by a buzzing crowd of the women, all demanding the same.

'Go away, he is mine and I am the Queen of Bugis Street,' said the woman on my knee. Her voice was very husky, very sexual. The others scattered. She showed me her identity card, as if it carried proof of her royal status. I looked at her name. She was a man.

The ID carried the picture of a little schoolboy. 'That is me before the operation. Do you think I am beautiful?' she said, stretching herself across me and throwing her body into the pose of a twenties dancer.

'You are very beautiful,' I agreed.

'Would you like to fuck me?'

'I would. But I'm not going to.'

'Why not?'

I asked about the operation.

'You can get it done in Tokyo or in London. We all prefer London. In London they give you a nine inch one, but in Tokyo it is only six inches.' The most painful part, she said, was not the removal of the testicles and penis which is then turned inside out to form a replica of the female genitalia, but the exposing and shaving of the Adam's Apple, in which the cartilage is pared down to approximate a smooth womanly neck. Everyone in Bugis Street agreed. For in Bugis Street all the hookers were transsexuals.

'So why won't you fuck me? I am very nice down here,' she said, drawing her hand up between her legs.

'No.'

She pouted, 'What is wrong with me?'

'It's not what's wrong with you. It is what would be wrong with me. I would feel as though I was doing it with a man. I am too insecure, it would open up a whole can of worms for me.'

She began to tell me the story of her life. At one point, after she became a woman and went on the streets, she met a 'John' and he fell in love with her. They lived together as man and wife, though she was still on the game. He grew jealous and then decided to join her on the streets. He, too, decided to have the operation. After it they lived together in a lesbian relationship, but now both of them were prostitutes. In this way they each met another man. The Queen began to drift away from her original lover and spend more time with the new man. In a fit of jealous rage the original lover killed her new man and was executed for murder. Now she was unattached and still on the streets.

I asked if she had ever read Somerset Maugham. It was very late now and time to go.

'Are you sure you don't want me?'

'No, but thanks anyway.'

★   ★   ★

I was delighted to be in Bangkok again. I loved the contrasts of South-East Asia, at their most extreme in this city. The smells of traffic, orchids, open

Deep in the heart of Malaya, waiting for a haircut. Note barbers in mirrors.

The Rats at Raffles, Singapore, 1981.

sewers, frangipani, the extremes of heat on the street or cold in the buildings, the violence of the crowd, the gentleness of an individual, the snarling sounds of traffic by day and the almost soothing insect, jungle noises at night, the openness of the people's character and the closed nature of the political systems. I strolled down to the Thai equivalent of Soho or Times Square, the Patpong, named after Mr Patpong who owns the two streets that make up the area. There are a hundred bars and a hundred girls in each one. I pushed open the door of one and we sat down. To my astonishment the girls were dancing on the tables to one of my songs, 'When the Night Comes'.

They were beautiful creatures, blank-eyed and indifferent, and, almost naked, they spun on table tops like tiny humming-birds oblivious of everything but the loud beat. When the Clash came on, a man who had been drinking alone in the corner stood up to dance by himself. He was like something out of *Apocalypse Now*; bald, no eyebrows, no arm hair, like an uncracked egg on permanent R & R. He stood in front of the big video screen and danced in slow, murderous karate moves, scissoring outwards in rigid, rhythmic precision to the 4/4 beat of the strobe system. The girls danced unenthusiastically on either side of him on small platforms beside the screen. No one danced with him. The spinning lights just caught the emptiness of his eyes. He was everywhere else but here, deep in the heart of nowhere. He never looked at the girls, or the boys for that matter. No one pestered him for a drink like the girls were doing to the other customers. No one suggested he spend the night with them. No one paid him attention. They understood blankness and they knew better than to trouble it. He stayed out there for four or five songs, then stopped dead. He moved a bit sideways. Behind him Mowgli rode an elephant and two girls did the Bangkok Hustle. Then he said very loudly, 'What sort of fuckin' dump is this, eh?' Nobody could be bothered to answer. 'You know something,' he said, 'fuck you!'

I had become quietly unsober. A man said, 'You want girls?'

'No.'

'You want boys?'

'No.'

Now I was silently locked into my movie. Now I wanted to see all these things I'd read about in these places. I imagined if we went down far enough we'd find the Russian roulette scenes from *The Deerhunter*.

'You want donkey, animals?'

'No, no. Something else, show us something else.' Show me something that makes me wonder why I want to see it, something that makes me sick and sad for us all, show me something where the other side of us is made real, except we don't have to live it or die it.

He took us through varying degrees of human degradation. How far down does it go, I wondered. 'Something else,' I said.

He took us to a tiny door in the side of a white-walled building. It was hot and there was a smell of damp and dirt as we walked down a narrow passage with stone walls. It opened out into a tiny bar in a small unevenly shaped room with stained concrete walls. At the bar, beneath the neon, sat four totally emaciated opium addicts, their eyes blank.

Behind the bar stood an old woman with cold hard eyes and a face twisted with the malignity of a lifetime of exploiting the hopeless addicts whom she supplied. We were the only customers besides the junkies in the stinking room. She spoke English. 'You want drink?' she snapped. Assuming that the water would not be safe to mix with the whisky I asked for a Scotch and coke. She called to the back room and a naked girl with the same vacuous look in her eyes came out. She stood before me, put one leg up on the bar stool, stuck the Coke bottle into the lips of her vagina and opened the bottle. The old woman clapped her hands and shrieked again and from the back came another girl with the same wasted look, carrying a filthy rug which she put down on the floor. She was naked and very ugly. She lay down on it with her feet towards us and then threw her legs over her head so that her genitals stuck out towards us. She produced a packet of cigarettes and stuck two into her behind and three into her vagina. She lit them. We watched as she smoked them down to the end. I had an attack of giggling nausea. Afterwards she rose, and with the same blank expression, produced two stubby candles, lit them, and dripped the hot wax onto her breasts. When the wax had formed a solid layer she took the candles and stuck them into the wax so that each one protruded from a breast. They dripped melted wax into her stomach. With them still balanced there, she opened her legs and drew a string of razor blades out of her vagina. Tricks of violence. The magic of self-loathing. I was beginning to get afraid. I was afraid of the physical danger if we continued our journey into degradation, but I was more afraid of the mental danger.

'You want to see more?' asked the woman. 'Girl cut herself with knife.'

'I want to go,' I said. Some time later we went back to the hotel. I think we'd have found those *Deerhunter* scenes if we'd wanted. Who needs it?

★   ★   ★

After the concert at the stadium we went to stay at Pattaya Beach. Paula had joined me, but I got bored after a few days on the sand. I left her at the hotel and caught a bus into Bangkok in order to catch the train for the north. At Hualompong station, I joined the others sheltering from the quivering blister of mid-afternoon heat. Inside, people wandered about aimlessly, fanning themselves occasionally, their voices disappearing into the stained glass roof far overhead like in some cool cathedral. The clerk at the ticket desk said the overnight Bangkok/Chiang Mai Northern Express was full. I gave him some more money, he gave me a ticket. I settled down as the train pulled out, rattling through the back canals of the city with the sun, a giant orange, sinking down. It grew dark immediately. At seven I had to lower the metal blind, not just to stop the dust and insects entering, but, so the guard had told me, to prevent bandits entering the train as it slowed down in the northern highlands. There were two guards, one at either end of the carriage, with helmets and machine guns and sunglasses. My seat transformed itself into a bed later. At seven-thirty I went to the restaurant car where I was joined by two ex-patriates, both working on the oil rigs in the South China Sea. One had been in the record industry in London working for a subsidiary of my record label, we found we knew a lot of people in common. We drank beer and kept the window open and smelt the wonderful night air. Overhead the fans turned sluggishly, like in all the best movies. Scattered about the other tables were various soldiers and passengers.

'You know Pattaya,' Joe said. (I'll call him Joe.) Pattaya was a strip of hotels and VD clinics built specifically for the American soldiers on leave from Vietnam. Now they were trying to make it family-orientated. It was difficult: there isn't much call for a VD clinic on your average family holiday. At one end of the strip there is a collection of huge open air bars. The bar girls congregate there around the mainly German male customers. The Germans are usually red-faced with large white bodies. The tiny and perfect girls clustering round them reminded me of the ants crawling over and around the blind white moth on my floor in Spain. Even the after-shave I had killed them with smelt the same as the clean-faced Germans. The object for the girls was simple: to get a man for the night and hope that by their beauty and skill and subservience they will be kept the next day, and so on until he returns to Düsseldorf or wherever. The longer they can 'hold their man' the more face they gain in the eyes of their peers. The ultimate is, of course, to have one of these chaps send you a monthly cheque in return for your distant love and fidelity. It is not unknown for the girls to be sent for, and live god knows what sort of life in Europe. Bar girls are not considered the same as prostitutes, for some reason, possibly because their expectations are different.

Joe had been staying in Pattaya. He got a bar girl and subsequently moved in with her. She continued plying her trade without him becoming in the least bit jealous. He mistakenly thought this liberal attitude was a mutual understanding and began sleeping with her friends. One night, immediately after they had made love and she was still on top of him, she reached over the side of the bed, rose from him, took him out of herself and cut his penis off with a curved knife. She put it in a plastic bag full of ice and called a clinic to send an ambulance and explained what had happened. She told him, 'You've one hour,' and left.

'What happened?' I asked.

'They sewed it back on.'

'I don't believe it,' I said.

We were slightly drunk as we staggered to the toilet where he showed me a huge and ugly purple welt round the base of his dick.

'Does it work?' I asked.

'Good as new, but I don't like girls on top any more.'

Later I made my way back to my carriage. There was a curfew on the train and the lights were off. I stumbled and nearly fell over a prostrate body which jumped up and put a revolver to my temple. I waved my ticket furiously at the soldier who produced a torch and looked at it carefully. I finally got to my own bed. Before I retired, I needed to visit the bathroom. I searched down one end of the carriage and opened the door, unzipping my fly. The tiny little room belonged to the young carriage attendant who could have been no more than eighteen and was certainly bemused by this westerner barging into his room, pointing at his crotch and drunkenly muttering something about 'toilets'. He pointed up the other end, but it was dark and I couldn't see and in the sort of clear logic of the drunk I got it out and tried to urinate between the overlapping plates that connected the carriages. Between the swaying of the train and, indeed, my own unstable self with a foot unsteadily placed in either carriage, I negotiated my aim not too successfully. I gave up and lurched for the other end of the carriage and the official toilet. Finally I got to bed and was horrified to be woken at about 4 a.m. by the carriage attendant who had clearly mistaken my earlier entree to his room and my feverish gesticulation at my nether regions as some sort of invitation. He climbed into bed with me, no doubt hoping for money.

'Get out!' I roared. He fled, alarmed and bewildered. I couldn't sleep and rose early as we were crossing beautiful hills. I breakfasted on the train and got out at Chiang Mai where I rickshawed to the hotel.

After two hours' sleep I hired a motorbike, strapped petrol and provisions to the back of it and set out into the jungle alone to look for the hidden poppy fields of the heroin triangle which were controlled by the opium warlords. I travelled for half a day into the jungle, the canopy of leaves getting darker and darker. The more dense the jungle grew, the more I was seized with the conviction that this time I had got way out of my depth. I panicked and began, with ludicrous desperation, to mark trees with a biro. It was only by chance that I stumbled across a tiny village whose inhabitants guided me home on a parallel and clearly-marked path that had been about fifty yards from me, as I did my *Raiders* thing, hacking through unexplored territory. It was quite preposterous, but I had wanted to see a village that lived off opium. They were nice people, especially the yellowed and toothless ones of indeterminate age. I got the bus back from Chiang Mai to Bangkok and met Paula for cocktails at the Oriental Hotel. There is a cowardice in vicarious living.

★　★　★

Once back in London we immediately began work on a new album with a new feeling of determination and defiance. I was tired of hearing we'd had it. To hell with them. The new album was to be called *Five Deep*. The term came from a Japanese description of one style of love-making, 'Four shallow, five deep,' which I thought was cute. It was our fifth album and now that Gerry had left there were only five in the band, so it seemed appropriate.

We got Kevin Godley and Lol Creme to produce it. They were brilliant songwriters and musicians and hilarious people. But things did not work out. They were working at the time with a new band called Duran Duran who I had met at a TV show in Birmingham a year before. Their singer, a chap called Simon Le Bon, said, 'Seriously, Bob, what's it like being a pop star?' Godley and Creme were also establishing themselves as one of the world's leading rock video producers. We got on well with them, they were a good laugh, but the work was just not getting done. With their own records they can afford to spend ages in the studio because they have their own at home. They'd forgotten the discipline of tight working, essential when you are on a budget and paying for a commercial studio by the hour. In the end, and by mutual consent, we gave up on each other and went back to work with Tony Visconti in Ibiza. We were happy with the album. It set out to be a solid collection of good songs in a more traditional pop style than some of the exuberant mood experiments of *Mondo Bongo*. My attitude was very much one of, 'They say we've had it, but I'll show them'. A song I'd begun writing in India became the theme song of the record. It was called 'Never in a Million Years'. It summed up my sense of defiance. It takes the form of call and response between me and the band:

I'd tear down the sky
Don't stop now
No, never in a million years, I'd spit in their eye,
Don't stop now
But I won't be a volunteer
And now I'm always dreaming
Of dreams that lie in state
Waiting for me to wake
And make a life for them.
I know I'll never let
Those self-defeating fears
Spoil those golden years.

The dreams that lay in state would have to wait a while though.

Five of the people whose musical taste I respected most, Fachtna, Chris and Nigel from Ensign, Clive Banks, our promotion man, and Chris Briggs, who was Head of A & R at Phonogram, were convinced that it was a hit record. When it came out it was a complete and utter stiff. I could not understand it, I was very despondent. Of course, I knew that within the dynamic of pop we were yesterday's men, but this itself didn't bother me as I had always been under the illusion that in Britain if you had a good enough song, no matter who you were, no matter what your status, it would be a hit. It was illusory of course. Clive said to me, 'Don't be naive, Bob, why do you think I go for the guys with the funny haircuts?'

It had been well over a year since our last record and, even though that had been a gold record in Britain (i.e. sales in excess of one million pounds), it had not been a great success elsewhere. While I'd made *The Wall* and we'd been away in Asia, a new generation of bands had arrived: the Human League, Adam Ant, etc. We were old hat. The music press were ecstatic, it seemed they had won. Although the people who now worked on the papers were too young to remember the original reasons for the enmity, they continued it as it was now almost a tradition. I understood the reasons for the record's failure. Our success had been dependent on selling singles, but as our own singles were completely different from one another it was difficult to have a distinctive sound and therefore a fan following. Ours was the more fickle pop audience. Unless we had hit singles we had no fans. No fans, no sales.

We decided, desperately, to do a tour. Usually a band does a tour to promote a record which is already doing well. The tour then helps to sustain its performance or to lift it even higher. It was considered a waste of time to tour without a hit because no one would come to see you if you weren't in the immediate public consciousness. Record companies would refuse to give you the cash to support such a tour. We decided to go ahead anyway.

We did it on the cheap and built a big production set from columns of wood and plaster which we hired and reels of old gauze which cost next to nothing. We hired a wind machine to blow the gauze and some basic lighting to illuminate it. It looked beautiful. The performances we gave were good, but the tour was limited to England. Afterwards, we toured the Mediterranean countries. We were in Greece when we heard that 'House on Fire', a reggae track that we'd recorded in one take with me shouting the chord changes into a microphone, had entered the Top Thirty. We flew back for *Top of the Pops*. It was our only minor hit off the album. We did not even bother trying to tour the States. After the *Mondo Bongo* fiasco we had shot our bolt there and we knew it. It seemed that all we had built over all those years had been nothing but a house of cards. Depressed and despondent I'd written in a track off the album called 'Skin on Skin': *Tonight I go to sleep with the lullaby sound of buildings falling down.*

*   ★   ★   ★*

We made a few trips to keep our interest up. We played Israel on the first day of the 1982 Lebanese War. When we left Heathrow the end of the Falklands

War had just been announced. As we landed at Tel Aviv another war was beginning. At the hotel I was woken by dull, thumping sounds. I dived under my bed assuming we were under fire. It was the jets taking off. Downstairs the ballroom of our hotel had been transformed into a blood bank where lines of elderly blue-rinsed American ladies in singlets and shorts stood in bare feet with their fat, tanned, bermuda-shorted, cigar and sunglasses, golf-hatted husbands, waiting to give their plentiful blood. Up the road hundreds were dying. Israel was a strange place.

I, however, was lucky. I was going to escape despondency on my promo trip for *The Wall*. I went to Hollywood for the opening there, flown first class and driven in a limousine which seemed ten times the size of those used by the poor relations in the record industry. I liked being a film star. I arrived in LA and was taken to the Beverly Wilshire hotel. I had not even got in the door of my six-room suite when the phone rang.

'Mr Goldblat? This is Paramount Studios here. We were very impressed by your performance in *The Wall* and we have a director here who would like to see you with regard to possibly having a part in his film. Would you be interested, Mr Goldfarb?'

Paramount Studios. Fuck me. 'Well, yes I'd be interested in meeting him.'

'Fine. Well, listen, could you come and see us? About a half hour?'

'Yes, that would be fine.'

'OK, Mr Gilfat, we'll send round a limousine to pick you up.'

This one was even bigger. It carried me under the famous Paramount arch in a state which swung between excitement and disbelief. I was shown into a huge office where behind the desk was a cockney director called Adrian Lyne who turned out to be a friend of Alan Parker.

'I'm doing this film called *Flashdance*.'

'That's a bloody awful name for a film.'

'Well, it's this "*ciné noir*" thing.'

'What, you mean all that dark Orson Welles stuff, *A Touch of Evil, Body Heat*?'

'Sort of. You play a streetwise Philadelphia kid.'

'But what about the Paddy accent?'

'Doesn't matter, we'll sort something out.'

I read the script that same night. Next day I rang him. 'Adrian, it's fucking crap, it's one of the worst things I've ever read.'

'Hey, why don't you come down off the fence on this one, Bob?' he replied laughing. 'Don't be afraid to say what you think.'

'Seriously, it's crap, I don't know why you're doing it. It can only be because the studio wants you to.'

'Well, that's got something to do with it. But I think it can be good.'

'You're talking about this girl who's a welder, but all her workmates respect her and no one grabs her tits in this steel works. She wants to be a dancer, really though, and then she falls in love with the boss who pays . . . Adrian, it's crap.'

'It's a really good part, Bob, and we'd consider giving you a part of everything the film makes.'

'Adrian, forget it.' It was probably the most expensive mistake I ever made.

I flew to New York to join the band for two highly-paid club gigs we'd decided to do. I was awakened in my hotel at about 5 a.m. by a call from England.

'It's me.'

'Hullo, love.' It was Paula. What the hell was wrong? I thought. There was the sound of sniffling from the other end. Was someone dead? I wondered. 'What's the matter?' I asked.

There was a pause. 'I'm pregnant,' she howled, bursting into tears.

Good sweet jumping Jaysus on the cross, I thought. 'That's brilliant,' I said, hoping it sounded more confident than I felt.

'You don't mind?' she sobbed.

'No, no, I think it's wonderful. What are you crying for?'

'I don't know,' she blubbered. 'I'm so . . . shocked.'

She wasn't the only one. Like everyone else who gets a small surprise, I was a little taken aback. I checked the clock to make sure it wasn't a dream. We hadn't talked about a baby, really. I'd seen her mooning at other people's and we were beginning to collect cats – a worrying sign, I've always felt – but we hadn't planned anything. I'd no objections, but if she'd asked me I'd probably have found some financial excuse to put it off. She doubted if she could have them anyway, she was so irregular. Now as I looked at myself in the mirror, I was delighted. There was some uneasiness. It wasn't the best time financially, in fact it was terrible. I'd just bought a house and spent whatever money I had, the rest was being spent on keeping the band going and I didn't know what future I had. Still, Paula had a decent job. I didn't look like a father when I looked in the mirror. It felt strange. I thought, I'm not going to be like my father. Just as long as it's happy. Fuck school. I wonder if it's a boy or a girl? I hoped it was a girl.

Jesus, I was shocked. We had thought Paula was ill. She had kept being sick and crying all the time. I wondered whether she was having a nervous breakdown, and the doctor told her that it was from the strain of working too hard and that her back pain was probably from a trapped nerve. She was almost five months pregnant before she discovered the truth and phoned me. Oddly enough we both had the same way of bringing the idea home to ourselves. I went out to Bloomingdale's and bought a little baby's tracksuit, at least I thought it was small; Fifi has yet to grow into it. At the same time, Paula was sitting in London with a pair of baby shoes made to look like little fluffy ducks with maribou feathers, and crying.

Paula had just got a job presenting a new TV rock show *The Tube*. Along with Clive Banks (who had got her the job) we now had to sell the TV company the idea of an ever-ballooning Yates as an additional attraction. 'Just what a radical new youth-orientated programme needs,' we told them. They bought it. Fifi was born one week after the close of the first series of *The Tube*. There was a deluge of presents, flowers, and cards from viewers. We called the child Fifi Trixibelle, for me after Auntie Fifi, who had never discouraged me from doing anything, and for Paula because she had always fancied the idea of being a Southern Belle. With a name like that, we thought, she could do anything: 'And this year's Nobel Prize for Physics has been awarded to Dr Fifi Trixibelle Geldof'. Other people felt sorry for the child being inflicted with that name, but they didn't grow up as Robert Frederick Zenon Geldof. Most people when they heard my third name wondered why my father had named me after an inert gas.

★   ★   ★

Paula and I are in love with each other – a very corny thing to write, but it's simple and true. Every day, after all the hassles, there was always Paula to go home to. The house in Clapham was a place of rest and reassurance. I never talked to her about work, about songs, the band, the hassles or the tours. It was nice to go back there just for a relaxing supper from the local takeaway in front of the telly. She is funny and sharp, and warm and loving – the perfect antidote to the outside world. Things were more fun and more complete with her. I was proud of her.

When she first moved into Chessington with me she had not had a job. It seemed to me that she spent the first year lying in bed; I would come home to find her sprawled there like some fifties starlet whom the years had passed by untouched, a dizzy peroxide blonde languishing between the sheets surrounded by magazines, detective novels, kittens, and boxes of chocolates.

One day I had given her a lecture and made her get a job. 'Apart from the fact that it is ludicrous for a person of your talents to waste your time like this, I hate the idea of women being financially dependent on men. I'm not saying that because I'm too mean to give you any money, but financial dis-harmony is the major reason for arguments in most households, anyway. It just seems degrading for you to have to ask, and me to condescend to dole it out. Why not work as a journalist? If you write the way you talk you'll make a fortune.'

The next week she met Alf Martin of the *Record Mirror* at a party and got a job from him as a gossip columnist. 'The Natural Blonde Column,' was a brilliant success. One of her real triumphs was that she never wrote anything nasty about *anyone*. Why bother? She knew too well from what she saw at home the hurt it caused. Why be vindictive, was her rationale: most people interested in the characters she was writing about in the pop world were fans who were actually pleased to read something nice about their idols. Besides, we knew most of the people she wrote about and they were usually a lot nicer than the journalists who wrote about them.

As a result of her column, she had been asked to write for *Cosmopolitan* and other magazines, from where her career took off. Work to her is a necessary evil, she doesn't like it but she happens to be very good at being a writer, presenter, model, and humorist. She prefers being at home and will do anything to get off work. The sole rationale for work is that she likes to buy things. I bought her a T-shirt in New York which said, 'When the going gets tough, the tough go . . . shopping'.

She, too, had had a strange childhood. Her parents were separated and divorced and her father, who was Britain's most celebrated producer of popular religious TV programmes and was known throughout Britain as The Bishop, had been hounded out of his job by the tabloid press when his affair with a showgirl was disclosed. It had placed enormous stress on her and her mother. Normal life was entirely disrupted by the gutter press who camped out in their garden and peered constantly through her window. When eventually her father's news value abated, the media turned some of its attention on to the Bishop's punk daughter. The papers called her 'the Princess of Punk' and treated her as an emblem of youth culture. It was a culture she denied existed, unless you call a consensus on things fashionable a culture. She hated discos and the whole 'hey wow, we're young people' thing. Like me, she hated pubs. She has never drunk alcohol or smoked. Like me she dislikes the condescension implicit in the word 'youth' and the term 'young people'.

It was not all sweetness and light. During *The Wall* there was a bad patch because of the introspection which I would slip into after playing an evil megalomaniac all day. By day I would be filming, by night recording. I thought everybody hated me. My moods at home were poisonous and unbearable. And the extensive touring would often put our body-clocks out of synch. She was modelling and writing and had an entirely independent lifestyle during the long periods that I was away. When I came back from a tour, I was still plugged into tour hours. My peak of physical energy would come at the times I was used to performing, between 8.30 p.m. and 11 p.m. I would want to go out; she would be drowsy and want to stay at home in front of the telly. She would go to bed at 9 p.m. and I would be up at 2 a.m. waiting to get tired, wandering around the house. Often I would write my songs at that time of the day. Sometimes I would feel depressed alone in the middle of the night. Probably the best songs came when the two things coincided: all my better work seems to come out of depression, frustration and rage. It took a long time for us both to readjust after these absences. We would feel, not like strangers, but uncomfortable with one another. Still, that always passed and with the house in Clapham, she and I were able to build a home we both felt we had never had before.

The week before we discovered that Paula was pregnant we had bought a new one-bedroomed flat in Chalcot Square. It was a beautiful place, but was too small for three of us. In the months before the baby was born I went house-hunting. We had been broken into five times in one year in Clapham. I had caught the burglars the first time, but they grew increasingly brazen until at one point they were breaking the downstairs window and taking the video while I was upstairs reading. No place for a pregnant woman, no place for a baby. I had a bit of money and decided to buy a nice house somewhere just outside London. One hot day we rode down towards Canterbury on the motorbike our record company had given me after I complained that they never doled out Christmas presents to bands in the way that other companies did. I knew there was a house for sale out that way, at Faversham. I had decided that it was too far away, but thought it might be fun to have a look. It was an old priory which had fallen into private hands at the time of the dissolution of the monasteries. When we walked in I said to Paula: 'We have to buy this place'. I had never wanted any physical thing so much. It was not just the ancient character of the building, though that was evident in every room, with much of the original stonework, paintings on the ceiling and even some very old glass. It was not just the Tudor gardens with their little walls of box. It was something to do with the atmosphere of the place, with the old church attached at the side, still in use every Sunday. There was an air of calm, of peace, of being removed from the world. We bought it and moved in.

With the announcement of Paula's pregnancy the music press plunged to new depths to express its hatred of us. *Melody Maker* said, 'someone ought to tell Bob Geldof that one Geldof bastard is enough'. *Sounds* printed a picture of Paula with the unforgivable and evil caption, 'Abortion of the Year'. I'm still not sure what we could ever have done to inspire that sort of venom. Paula cried and was utterly bewildered and so saddeningly hurt that I wanted to find the bastards who had written it and hurt them in return. They truly were scum, as were the editors who printed it, no doubt thinking it was a good laugh.

We were never clear in advance how we would cope with parenthood but we were very excited. Paula carried on working until the last moment. It was odd to see her head working away at one thing while her body got on with something entirely separate. On one thing we were quite adamant. We did not want to get involved with any of the post-hippy Hampstead style of parenting with fathers being trained in the art of acting as 'coach' for the big event. I had no desire to lie on the floor, like a prat, learning how to breathe. I was going to have *a* baby, I wasn't going to have *the* baby and there was no point in pretending I was. Paula wanted me pacing up and down outside in the corridor, or running off for kebabs or pieces of coal or whatever pregnant

Top: Grandad's calling card.

Centre: My grandfather's shop, where my father learned to cook.

Bottom: Cleo, Mum, Lynn and me on Blackrock Strand, 1954.

Right: The beginning: a
school hall in Dublin, 1975.
Note Pete's and my
moustaches.

Right: Almost there:
Sweden, 1978. In the pants
that Paula fell in love with.

Left: The rise: The Marquee,
London, 1977. Very hot.

Below: The pop star: Loch
Lomond Festival, 1978.
Long hair again.

Below: Me, Iggy, Bowie, the Rest of the World vers[us] Europe soccer match, Meadowlands Stadium, New York, 1983.

Above: Coney Island, 1985.

Left: Wally in Venice.

Left: Famous people posing in my garden after Connolly opens church fete, 20 July 1985. Left to right; (back row) Jools Holland, Jasper Conran, Paula, Billy Connolly, me; (front row) Gary Kemp, Pamela Stephenson, Daisy Connolly and Missy the dog.

Below: Holidays, Ibiza, 1984.

Left: The boys in the band,
Sunday 25 November 1984.

Above: Bruce and Michael
snapped by ardent fan
B. Geldof at USA for
Africa recording session,
Los Angeles, January 1985.

Above: 9.54 p.m.,
13 July 1985.

Above: Rat Trapped?
San Francisco, 1978.

Left: Mother Theresa at Addis airport, January 198[?]

Below: Western Sudan, nea[?] Al Geneina, October 1985.

women desired. I concurred and told her I subscribed to the Evelyn Waugh school of fatherhood – the chap buggers off to Abyssinia and then sends a telegram saying, 'Have you had your child yet and what have you called it?' We simply ignored the propaganda on how men should behave, or how to give birth 'properly'. Paula never once went to a class or read a book. It seems your body knows perfectly well how to do it without being told. The night before Paula went into hospital a doctor friend of mine called round.

'What happens?' Paula asked.

'Do you really not know?' said Phil.

'No,' replied a completely unworried Paula.

Phil gave her a basic explanation of what was going on and what to expect. That was it.

In the event I was in the room at St Mary's, Paddington, when the moment came. Paula asked that the TV be left on while she had the baby. She had just watched *The Sullivans* and was on to the farming programme when it started. I was, she recalls, enormously helpful at the time, keeping her informed of what was going on.

'My God, Paula, your face has gone all black.'

'Thanks, Bob, that's very reassuring.'

'Oh God, I can see its head. It's bizarre.'

Then Fifi came out and they plonked her, covered in blood, on Paula's tummy. 'Oh look,' she said. 'Isn't it sweet?'

The baby was quiet so the doctor flicked her toe to make sure she wasn't dumb. She gave a little squawk. Paula was cuddling her and examining every square inch of her hands and face.

Then it occurred to me to ask, 'What is it?'

'Oh, yes,' said the doctor, having a look, 'it's a little girl.'

I stood and tried to imagine what she would be like as an old lady. I wasn't overwhelmed by the 'miracle of birth', just fascinated. It had seemed to me to be very animalistic, but not at all undignified. Corny as it sounds, I immediately felt very protective towards them both.

I watched as Paula gorged herself on a box of Turkish Delight and drank two bottles of fizzy apple juice which had been transferred into old champagne bottles for the occasion. Then she was sick.

★   ★   ★

I was now almost broke and a huge tax debt was looming over me. I was working in an office my record company let me use when an old friend from another record company came over with a script. It was called *Number One*. It was written and directed by G. F. Newman and Les Blair, who had reputations as brilliant TV drama-makers. It was arranged that I would do the film. It starred Mel Smith who is hilarious and a superb actor and director. He also tends to enjoy life's little pleasures. At six in the morning on the way to the set I would stop by his flat to pick him up. He'd be in bed after getting in at 5 a.m. He'd stagger down to the car after one hour's sleep, hauling his coat on and clutching a script which he'd read on the way to the shoot. In make-up he'd have breakfast, then at eight would be completely fresh, line-perfect and ready to put in a day's work. As soon as shooting was finished he was off for another debauch. Mel actually looks like the way he lives, a sort of twentieth-century Hogarthian figure. One day at my house, on the day of our annual local church fete which he'd agreed to open, he sat in my living room, two feet from the TV screen, watching the horse racing. In one hand was a portable phone left open to his bookies, in the other a full tumbler of malt whisky. A box of cigars were on the table beside him and the blinds were drawn against the eyes of the fete visitors. In between races he'd join the rest of us, tell some story, roar with laughter, impersonate somebody, knock back some wine and resume his betting. He won and lost a fortune that afternoon, and seemed to have a nice time.

Number One's leading lady was Alison Steadman, without doubt one of Britain's great actresses. I was to play the hero, a Jack the Lad brilliant snooker player, 'Flash' Harry Gordon, who falls, by dint of circumstance, into the arms of Mel Smith, who through bribery, corruption and other skills makes him world snooker champion. Harry is supposed to take a fall, thus ensuring all the 'baddies' make a fortune, but integrity triumphs just in time. It was an enjoyable film to make. The cast were the cream of British acting and I learned a lot. I also got my first cinematic lay with Alison who seemed more worried than me about it. I imagined I'd be crippled with embarrassment, grunting and gasping on top of her. I didn't know whether to worry more about getting an erection or not getting one at all; I didn't know which would be more insulting. As it was, there were so many rehearsals and takes it became academic. Lying in bed all day under hot lights just makes you sleepy, and the two of us would be semi-comatose between takes. It was Newman and Blair's first feature film and despite its interesting subject, the film teetered between playing for laughs and trying to say something serious. Falling between the two stools, it was a commercial flop, though it did fair business outside London. I watched it the other night on video. It was really the first time I had properly seen it. I liked it. It had been fun, and financially it bailed me out that year.

We had one more album to make to fulfil our contract. We were broke and we owed a fortune. We had spent half of our advance from our next album a year before we had even begun writing it. We were at our lowest ebb ever. No one was interested in the band. We were drifting, and we realized that things were in a parlous state. We started rehearsing for the next album in Acton Vale and worked for months writing new songs and perfecting them.

Two gorgeous girlies: asleep on
Christmas Day in Orlando, Florida,
aged nine months; awake, aged
eighteen months.

In all that time, no one came to see us. Not even Fachtna, who was now
involved in managing another band, Bananarama, who were having some
success in the charts. We had no gigs in the offing, no one was interested in
whether the new album would be any good or not. We were using up what
small savings we had on day-to-day living and there didn't seem to be any plans
for the future. Every afternoon up in the rehearsal room was like wading
through an ever-thickening atmosphere of despondency and dejection. We
sat there waiting for someone to tell us what we should do but no one did.
Finally we had to conclude that Fachtna was no longer interested. Where
once we had worked so well together, now I rarely saw him and there was a
terrible forced camaraderie between us when I did. I went to see him. Fachtna
had always looked unwell – he was a vegetarian who seemed to eat nothing
except sweets and ice-cream. But now he had a blank and wasted look.

It was a one-sided conversation. I told him that the band were giving
everything, twenty-four hours a day, towards the new album at the moment
and that he wasn't. The whole situation was fucked up. I itemized it, as
though he did not know the problems already. The tax scheme had fallen
through when it was discovered that it wasn't legitimate and now we were all
being stung for back taxes. We had no money and yet we were employing a
manager, a secretary, a fan club organizer, press officers, a tour manager, a

sound guy, a lights guy, the backline man for the road crew – all these were on a salary or a retainer. We owed money to our English lawyer, our American lawyer, our accountant, our agent, the pluggers, even to the road crew. This was the last album under the existing contract with Phonogram, but no work was being done in trying to set up deals for the future. The band was dispirited. Fachtna was making no attempt to galvanize them or lift morale. He was just abdicating responsibility. 'For Christ's sake, we've even spent the money from the advance which we were supposed to use to make the next record.'

He said nothing, but his sunken dark-ringed eyes filled with rage.

I was hurt. We had once been good friends. 'What the fuck is happening, Fachtna?'

'Nothing. Nothing is happening.'

'Well get something happening by tomorrow. Ring me and let me know what you've got planned. If you haven't rung by tomorrow, you're out.'

He did not ring. I hadn't expected him to, but I was sad. At that point I took over. I rationalized the office – a euphemism for sacking everybody. I went to Phonogram to try to establish some sort of direct relationship with the people there, for I had rarely dealt with them personally and I had the impression that they thought I disliked them and was deliberately uncooperative. I was anxious to cultivate them because we would soon need to renegotiate our contract. We couldn't afford to go abroad to record and would have to record in England. We needed help.

But first we needed some money. We could only get that from performing. But by this time it was over two years since we had had a real hit and we just could not get bookings at the big venues.

'Either we knock the whole thing on the head and just give up totally or we do the universities to get some readies,' I told the band. 'I know it's going down a notch to do the university circuit, but it's that or nothing. Either we fight back or we give up.'

We made enough money from the universities to make the record. It was not the sort of studio we were used to but it was all we could afford, a little reggae studio in Southwark with a single twenty-four-track machine. The equipment was ancient and would sometimes slow down without warning. We would come in some mornings and find that when we tried to overdub something on yesterday's work the whole thing would have slowed into some other key. We could not afford to pay a producer and decided to keep what extra cash we could squeeze out of Columbia to have it really well mixed in New York. We called in old favours and drew on old friendships to get assistance from some of the top engineers and producers we had worked with in the past. Some did actually come down to Southwark but left saying it was impossible to do anything decent on such machinery. Others helped out. James Guthrie, the Pink Floyd engineer, produced tracks. Mutt Lange came and gave us a hand on revamping some of the tracks for America. Bob Clearmountain, who engineered *Five Deep* and who had also worked with Bowie, Springsteen, the Stones and Roxy Music, did a brilliant mixing job.

We called the album *In The Long Grass*, an Irish expression. When you have not seen someone for a long time and you ask them where they have been they might reply, 'Oh, I've been lying in the long grass,' meaning they've been around but not visible. We were pleased with it. Everyone we respected said it had three hit tracks. We decided to release one as a single and then when it got into the charts release the album and subsequently use the other two to keep it up there. Everyone was quietly optimistic. There were even positive noises from America, though they did raise an objection to 'Dave', a song for an old friend written the day after his girlfriend was found dead in a lavatory where her body had lain for three days with an empty heroin bag next to it.

'The thing is, Bob, you see "Dave" sounds good but . . . I mean they're great lyrics but the title . . . I mean you're singing emotionally to another guy. I gotta tell you . . . faggots don't sell records.'

I changed the lyrics. No one could accuse me of not trying. To hype a record into the American charts costs about $150,000 with no guarantee of success and Columbia just weren't prepared to make the investment. Yet when I asked them to release the band to a company with more commitment, they said they would only release us if the newcomer was prepared to pay them $5 million.

'What we need from you, Bob, is another album like Mingo Bingo,' said one, mispronouncing the very album they'd rejected. 'You guys are just too ahead of your time.'

In England we released the singles one by one, and they were total stiffs. I couldn't understand it.

What's the story?
What's the score?
What did we do?
What are we guilty of?
Will you shoot us down?
Bring us to our knees?
And when we hit the ground
Kick us in the teeth?

I was desolate.

Like a ship that's going under
I run for home through rain and thunder

We even went out and tried to hype the second single, 'Drag Me Down'. I set aside a thousand pounds. We went to all the stores we knew were 'chart return' shops and bought it ourselves hoping to buy it into the charts. Gary crashed his motorbike in the Midlands on one buying trip and was in hospital for months. We did two gigs without him. I couldn't actually do any buying because people would recognize me, and if you are caught your record is banned from the charts. What option did we have? No one was playing it, so therefore no one heard it, so therefore no one bought it. We gave away a free ticket to any one of our concerts with every copy of the see-through version of 'Dave'. Nothing. In these songs I was responding to the negative feel of Britain and my own personal dilemmas. In retrospect 'A Hold of Me' seems extraordinarily prescient in the light of what happened four months later.

I'm for thinking
Between the ears
For mental process
For cogs and gears
I'm for flesh and
I'm for mind
I'm for people
I'm for life

I was writing about people again.

And Dave I see you bleed
I know you feel the squeeze

The songs were more consistent than on *Five Deep* or *Mondo Bongo*. They were also more commercial. The record company was terrific. They allowed me to work out of the press office without once quibbling or asking me to pay for the phone. They tried every legitimate promotional device they knew of. We made four superb videos very cheaply. The skill of a video is in the idea, not the money. But still nothing.

We decided to tour the album anyway and decided to go for the big venues by offering the concerts for very low guarantees – the venues were committed only to giving the band £50 each a night and we stayed in bed and breakfast places rather than chi-chi hotels. We made our own production set – Simon painted a gigantic backcloth with a woodlouse and long grass on it and we had sails that we sprayed like a Kandinsky abstract expressionist thing. The whole set cost us £40, less than we used to spend in the Dun Laoghaire days. The tour did well. We did forty-four gigs in forty-eight days and sold out in many places, including huge venues like the Dominion and the Hammersmith Palais in London and the Manchester Apollo.

But the records never took off. The third single, 'Dave', which one critic said was the best song I had ever written and which Pete Townshend of The Who said was 'one of the best songs of 1984', got no airplay at all. Ironically, it was released just before Christmas 1984 and had stiff competition from another song I had written jointly with Midge Ure.

CHAPTER XIII

Driven to Tears

A mother crying at the death of her two
children who died within 24 hours.

All day I had been on the phone trying desperately to get something happening
with the single. It was coming to the end of 1984 and I could see no prospect
for the release of *In the Long Grass*, which we'd sweated over and were proud
of. I went home in a state of blank resignation and switched on the television.
I saw something that placed my worries in a ghastly new perspective.

The news report was of famine in Ethiopia. From the first seconds it was
clear that this was a horror on a monumental scale. The pictures were of people
who were so shrunken by starvation that they looked like beings from another
planet. Their arms and legs were as thin as sticks, their bodies spindly. Swollen
veins and huge, blankly staring eyes protruded from their shrivelled heads.
The camera wandered amidst them like a mesmerized observer, occasionally

215

dwelling on one person so that he looked directly at me, sitting in my comfortable living room surrounded by the fripperies of modern living which we were pleased to regard as necessities. Their eyes looked into mine. There was an emaciated woman too weak to do anything but limply hold her dying child. There was a skeletal man holding out a bundle wrapped in sacking so that it could be counted; it looked like a tightly-wrapped package of old sticks, but it was the desiccated body of his child. And there were children, their bodies fragile and vulnerable as premature babies but with the consciousness of what was happening to them gleaming dully from their eyes. All around was the murmur of death, like a hoarse whisper, or the buzzing of flies.

Right from the first few seconds it was clear that this was a tragedy which the world had somehow contrived not to notice until it had reached a scale which constituted an international scandal. You could hear that in the tones of the reporter. It was not the usual dispassionate objectivity of the BBC. It was the voice of a man who was registering despair, grief and absolute disgust at what he was seeing. At the end the newscasters remained silent. Paula burst into tears, and then rushed upstairs to check on our baby who was sleeping peacefully in her cot.

Often at night I am unable to sleep because my brain seems to be a battleground of conflicting thoughts. Self-doubt and self-questioning turn over the certainties of the day in turmoil which accelerates until I think my brain will explode. That night I could not sleep. I returned to the old sleep-inducing formula I had employed so successfully at school. I would imagine myself spinning ever faster towards a point of pure white light in a black void. As I reached maximum velocity, I would reach the light and fall fast asleep. But this time the point of light was an image from Michael Buerk's news report. There were tens of thousands of people in the camp in Ethiopia where it had been filmed and where a handful of European aid workers were distributing a pitiful amount of food. One young nurse had the awesome task of selecting the few hundred individuals who were to be fed. They sat inside a compound enclosed by a low wall and waited for the food. Outside thousands of their fellows stood and watched. They had been condemned to death and now they stood to watch the few who had been offered a small chance of immediate survival. There was no anger in their faces, no bitterness, no clamouring. There was only the hollow dignity of waiting for death in silence.

The second image was of the man running. 'Things are out of control here,' the reporter had said as crowds of starving people rushed wildly across the dusty plains towards a lorry which they hoped against hope might be carrying food. In the foreground was a spindle-shanked figure teetering madly after the others. It seemed impossible that in his condition he could move so quickly. On his back he carried another figure, perhaps his wife, perhaps a child, the body was so distorted by malnutrition you couldn't tell. He ran, hundreds of yards behind the others. He ran without any real chance of there being anything left by the time he arrived. He ran, and he did not jettison the human being who clung to his back. I felt disgusted, enraged, and outraged, but more than all those, I felt deep shame.

The images played and replayed in my mind. What could I do? I could send some money. Of course I could send some money. But that didn't seem enough. Did not the sheer scale of the whole thing call for something more? Buerk had used the word biblical. A famine of biblical proportions. There was something terrible about the idea that 2,000 years after Christ, in a world of modern technology something like this could be allowed to happen as if the ability of mankind to influence and control the environment had not altered one jot. A horror like this could not occur today without our consent. We had allowed this to happen and now we knew that it was happening, to allow it to continue would be tantamount to murder. I would send some money, I would send more money. But that was not enough. To expiate yourself truly of any complicity in this evil meant you had to give something of yourself. I was stood against the wall. I had to withdraw my consent.

What else could I do? I was only a pop singer. And by now not a very successful pop singer. I could not help the tottering man to carry his burden. All I could do was make records that no one bought. But I would do that, I would give all the profits of the next Rats record to Oxfam. What good would that do? It would be a pitiful amount. But it would be more than I could raise by simply dipping into my shrunken bank account. Maybe some people would buy it just because the profits were for Oxfam. And I would be withdrawing my consent. Yet that was still not enough. I fell into a fitful sleep.

The next morning when I awoke Paula had already left and taken Fifi with her up to Newcastle for that week's recording of *The Tube*. On the fridge was a notice. It said: 'Ethiopia. Everyone who visits this house from today onwards will be asked to give £5 until we have raised £200 for famine relief'.

I went off to work. At the ad hoc desk I had in the Phonogram press office I tried to apply myself to the concerns of yesterday. The album was due out in the second week of December. It was almost certainly going to be a flop. None of the three singles already released from it had made any impact. What I was supposed to be doing that morning was the same as yesterday: ring around to check on sales figures for the last single, 'Dave', in different regions, so that we would know where we should concentrate our efforts for promotion. Yesterday it had seemed desperately important. Now it seemed meaningless. I tentatively suggested I was thinking of doing a record for Ethiopians to the four people in the press office.

'Yeah, you should,' said Bernadette. 'I saw it last night, it was awful,' said Mariella.

'What sort of record?' said Steve.

Linda said, 'My friend is driving a jeep down to Eritrea with supplies, but they won't let him in. Can you do anything about it?'

I had never heard of Eritrea. How the hell could I help? It seems ridiculous now that the very first time I suggested the record I was handed a transportation logistics problem. But they hadn't laughed, they liked the idea.

I telephoned Paula at the TV studio in Newcastle. 'I've been thinking about doing a record to raise some money for Ethiopia . . .'

'That's a good idea.'

'The only thing is, if the Rats do it it won't sell very well. So I thought I might ask a few other people to come in on it. Who is there this week?'

'Midge.'

Midge Ure of Ultravox was an old friend. He agreed at once. 'Have you got a song?' he asked.

'No, I've got a bit of a thing . . . but if you've got something . . .' I had a song called 'It's My World', just a couple of lines and a rough tune. But I was embarrassed to suggest it. After all, Midge was the one having the hits. I was having the flops.

'I'll try and think of something,' he said. 'I'll ring you tomorrow when I'm back in London and we'll work on something.'

I rang Sting. I knew him quite well and liked him. Again it was embarrassing. Pop stars get phone calls all the time from people asking favours. Will you do this . . . will you do that, and I didn't want to impose. My only advantage was that I was not an outside charity, but someone in another band. 'Did you see the thing about Ethiopia on the news last night?'

'Yes, it was terrible, wasn't it?'

'I think we should do something. I'm thinking of getting a few people together to get a quick record out before Christmas to raise a bit of money.'

'OK, I'll be there.'

I rang Simon Le Bon.

'We're going to Germany for a tour soon. When will the recording be?'

'I haven't got a date.'

'Well, we're up for it, if we can. Count us in.'

I didn't understand why people were so amenable. Yes, they were friends, but as John Lennon said, 'You can be benefited to death'. Maybe it was the time, and the *feel* of the times. Maybe things had been shabby and cynical and selfish for too long. Maybe people in bands wanted to do something, become involved and active again. Or maybe they'd watched TV last night. In one afternoon I had enough people to make it work. I began to compile lists of more people and telephone numbers, to ring the offices of bands that I did not know personally and left messages. On the way to the house we had moved to in Chelsea, I stopped to look in the window of an antique shop in the King's Road. Inside was Gary Kemp of Spandau Ballet.

'We've got to go to Japan,' he said when I spoke to him. 'But if you can hold the recording dates for two weeks till we get back, we'll do it.'

That, I knew, was going to be a major problem. When it came to fixing the recording date how many would not be around and have to drop out? I knew I needed more names. At a party that night talking to Martin Kemp, Gary's brother and the Spandau's bass player, the notion began to form that this could be more than a one-off money-raising exercise. It could be a massive gesture, and for that the more people we had on the record the better.

That weekend I flew to Ireland to see my Auntie Cleo who was ill. On the way to the airport my father, with whom I had long since buried old hatchets and who was now a good friend, said, 'What are you up to next?'

'I don't know,' I said. 'I'm thinking of doing a record for this Ethiopian famine.'

'That would be great,' he said, 'you should do it.'

The next day I was on my way to visit Kuka, a sculptor friend, who was also ill. In the back of the taxi I scribbled in my diary the words of the song. I wrote fluently with little crossing out. The words poured out. I wanted to evoke pity and concern and I wanted to make people think. Kuka's mother was with him when I arrived. We talked about 'Dave' and how badly it was doing. Then I told them about the Ethiopia idea. 'I wrote the words on the way over.'

'Oh, play it for us,' he said, producing a battered old Spanish guitar.

Normally I hated doing that, but I wanted to see whether the words worked. I didn't know it, but for some reason he was taping all his conversations that day and unbeknownst to me had switched on a little tape recorder. It's weird that right from the start of this thing there is an electronic record of most of the things that happened. The two of them liked the song, which boosted my confidence in the business of playing it before Midge the next day.

I carried on ringing people. I called Virgin records to get the number for Boy George. I rang ZTT for Frankie Goes To Hollywood. I got hold of numbers for Paul Young, Paul Weller of the Style Council, and Phil Oakey of the Human League. I began to make notes in my diary. 'What is the *BPI*? Get each record company to donate £20,000? Do we need a trust fund? How do we handle the publishing and the Performing Rights Society?'

It was beginning to become clear to me that all this was becoming more than a 'gesture' and would soon need to be formalized in some way. I organized a meeting with four of the top people at Phonogram: Brian Shepherd, the general manager, John Watson, the legal advisor, Tony Powell, whom I'd known since the Ensign days and is the marketing director, and John Waller, who was the product manager responsible for the vinyl, the labels, the printing, the packaging and all the rest of the sheer mechanics. They agreed to tackle it.

'What's the top priority if we're going to do this quick?'

'The artwork for the cover. That takes the longest to produce. We need that within a couple of days.'

If it was to be the best of British music, I decided to call Peter Blake, who for years has been associated with music through his now classic artwork for the pop industry. In inventing pop art with a few others he had provided the arrow and target logos for The Who in the Sixties and had done the cover of *Sergeant Pepper's Lonely Hearts Club Band* for the Beatles. Blake is one of Britain's most respected painters. I was not sure how to contact him, or whether he'd be interested in helping. I looked up galleries in the Yellow Pages and phoned one at random. It was Waddington's.

'We're Peter Blake's agent, as it happens.' That was weird, too. 'Well, can you ask him to ring me. I want to talk to him about a project.' I didn't expect him to call. Why should he? He was probably busy. Never heard of me. Within half an hour the phone rang. I began my long preamble, assuming from our lack of success no one would remember me.

'Yes, I know who you are, Bob,' Peter interrupted.

I explained what I wanted. I met him in Fortnum and Mason for tea the following day and he said he was into montages at the moment. After I'd called he'd begun a rough. He showed it to me. 'Christ, that's perfect. Can you finish it in a couple of days?'

That night I went to a reception where I knew Wham! and their manager, Simon Napier Bell, would be. I did not think they would be interested. They were too big, seemed too poppy, were probably busy. I didn't know them at all.

'How many do you think it will sell?' Simon asked.

'If we can get it out with three weeks' selling time to Christmas, but with all those names on it, it might get to Number One and sell half a million.'

'Well, if it sells half a million – and you'll be lucky to do that in three weeks – and if you get a good percentage from Phonogram and donate all your publishing rights as the composer that would be £72,000. Can't you eliminate some of the percentages? It's not much.' He was immediately practical.

'Yeah, I'll try, but you're right, it's not much. Still, Oxfam or Save the Children could do something with it. And it's a gesture. It raises the issue, which is probably more important than the money anyway. Do you think George Michael would do it?'

'I'll ask him.' I didn't believe he would.

I went back to John Watson in the legal department. 'Can't we eliminate some of the percentages?' The cover price of a record can be broken down into separate elements or percentages: the cost of both recording and physically producing the record, the band's portion, the record company's share, the distributors' and retailers' cut. We had, as artists, already forsworn our share. He spoke to the rest of Phonogram. 'We will waive our profit. Now if you can get the costs and the labour for nothing, and if you can get the distributors to do it for nothing, you're close to one hundred per cent profit, apart from VAT.'

'OK, who makes the most profit?'

'The retailers.'

I contacted them and was told that most records in England were bought from Woolworths, Smiths, HMV, Virgin, Boots and Our Price.

'Do you think they'd do it for free?'

'No. Why should they?'

I phoned them up one at a time and systematically lied to them. We had a fairly impressive collection of artists, but I read out to them not only the list of those who had agreed, but the list of all those I intended to approach. I told them that I had already approached all the other major distributors.

'And have they agreed to it?'

'Yes', I lied. 'Everyone has agreed so far. You are actually the last one I'm calling.'

'OK. If they're doing it, I think we ought to too.'

The next morning, a tape arrived from Midge. It was something he'd written on a Casio mini-keyboard over breakfast. It was the voluntary of notes which would eventually appear on the record as the backing for the end chorus. He rang.

'What do you think? I thought it sounded sort of Christmassy.'

'I think it sounds like *Z Cars*.'

'No, it's not *Z Cars*. I think it's *The Dambusters*,' said Midge. 'It'll probably sound OK with whatever you've ripped off.'

I went up to his house in Chiswick which has its own twenty-four-track studio at the back. I took my acoustic guitar with me and with deep embarrassment, croaked out the original version of 'Do They Know It's Christmas'.

'That's not bad,' he said.

'Well, it might be all right when you've got to work.'

'Let's try changing the key. Take it up from A to C.'

I did a rough tape for him and went back to the office. It was still difficult making some people believe it was going to work, but the interest was escalating. Things were starting to come together. I had been on the phone for five days now. I had been expecting resistance in the 'not that old has-been, what does he want?' style, but not once had that happened. All the people in Phonogram were working flat out. The production people were talking to sleeve manufacturers and label printers. The workers at the Phonogram factory were to donate their services free. ICI was donating the vinyl. ZTT Studios offered to donate free engineering and studio time. Recording was to be in their studios in Basing Street, Ladbroke Grove. Bob Marley had recorded there.

I was still phoning bands. I tracked down U2 to their tour hotel and spoke to Bono. It was 2 p.m. and he'd just got up. He sounded like a truck had rolled over his throat. He said he would do it. The list in my diary for that day read:

Eurythmics, Bananarama, Culture Club, Thompson Twins, Frankie Goes To Hollywood, Wham!, Sade, Paul Young, Human League and Style Council, As I was telephoning, Francis Rossi of Status Quo came into the Phonogram office. 'You can put us down, me and Parfitt.' I rang Paul Weller with some trepidation. I assumed he thought I was a prat. We had never got on. At the Bilsen Festival in Belgium, we had borrowed one of their amps. In an attempt to be friendly afterwards we had bought them three bottles of Scotch. 'We don't drink whisky,' said Weller brusquely. 'Fine, we'll have it,' I said. Later, in the hotel, Weller said to Gary, 'What's it like playing in Bob Geldof's backing band?' 'It's better than making a living out of bad Pete Townshend impersonations,' Gary had replied. There had almost been a fight between the Rats and the Jam, who were of the school that saw New Wave music as being a political phenomenon. Ever since, we had frequently been brusque about one another in public. But when I rang him I didn't even have to give him the sales pitch I'd developed.

'Yeah, we'll do it, Bob. Have you got a song?'

'Well Midge and I are working on something . . .'

'We'll be there.'

I came to discover that I didn't really have to sell the idea at all to the artists. If I got through to them direct, the response was always positive. But if I got through to the managers, their attitude was often negative, like that of Phil Oakey's manager. It is irritating when managers assume the moral guardianship of their charges. Often they are simply obstructive in the misguided notion that they are 'doing their job'. Sade's manager said she wouldn't be able to do it. The Thompson Twins were in a similar position. Later they donated the profits from one of their singles to us. I kept on phoning the Eurythmics manager, who said they'd be in Switzerland and they'd send a tape for the B side, which was to carry individual messages. I never got it. Simon Napier Bell did phone back, saying Wham! would do it. We had all the really big record-selling names. I went to see Paul McCartney, who I'd met now and again over the years, and David Bowie, who I knew socially. Both would be away, but would send tapes. Peter Blake's artwork came: it was perfect. We had eliminated the percentages, where only the VAT problem remained. We would have practically one hundred per cent of the money from the sale of each record and we had gained an extra two weeks on my estimated three-week selling period. We stood to make a million pounds.

It was time to choose a date. There was bound to be someone who couldn't make it, whichever day I picked. At random, I selected Sunday, 25 November 1984. I went to John Waller and asked how quickly we could get the record out. I thought it would take at least two weeks. 'If we pull all the stops out, we can do it in four days,' he said. This was extraordinary. But every individual concerned was now in a professional and personal fever. This fever was their contribution. Not just money, but themselves. All the record company could think of now was this record. They would not make a penny from it. It was the same with everyone else I asked to help. There was complete commitment.

I was tired with the endless calls, and now the phone began to ring at home too. I had completely forgotten about 'Dave', the Rats' single, so caught up was I in the organization. After the two years of begging and pleading for the Rats, this all seemed too easy. With the extra two weeks' selling time achieved, Midge and I rushed to finish the song. We had worked out how to join his piece with mine by writing the middle eight. I wanted something which sounded like a football chant or 'Give Peace a Chance' laid over his riff. It had to be completely direct, simple and to the point. I began singing the words 'Feed the World' and at first it sounded a bit like one of Midge's old songs, but we changed it sufficiently and knew it said everything.

I had had the idea for the band logo, a round map of the world like a plate, with an Africa in black and a knife and fork at the side. This could go on the label. All we needed now was a name for the group of stars. In the press office I suggested 'Food for Thought' or 'The Bloody Do-Gooders'. Then Linda suggested Band Aid. Everyone pooh-poohed it but I thought it was brilliant – apart from the obvious pun on the word band, there was an extra dimension. What we were doing and what we would raise would be so small in the context of the problem that it would be like putting a tiny plaster on a wound that required twelve stitches.

We needed a big launch – as spectacular as the record itself. Everything connected to the record had to be superlative. Media interest in the whole project had become enormous as it became apparent how many big names were involved. I contacted the *Daily Mirror*, which had been running a big campaign to raise money for rather melodramatic 'mercy flights' to Ethiopia. Because of their obviously established link with the famine, I offered them exclusive pictures of the recording session if they promised us the entire front page.

'Sorry Bob, we'll do the story, but it's just not front page material.'

That morning the *Mirror*'s front page had been taken up with a picture of the back of the Princess of Wales's head.

'Have you seen today's cover on your paper? How do you have the nerve to say that to me about a whole page of the back of someone's head? This isn't just about another pop record. This is the biggest record ever and it's about millions of people who are starving to death.' I got hold of Robert Maxwell's private number, and dealt direct with him.

The executive I'd been dealing with phoned back, and with feigned nonchalance said, 'OK Bob, you've got the front page.'

'I know I fucking have.' It was my first lesson in always going straight to the top. I had learned to speak to the engineer, and not be content with talking to his oily rag.

One outstanding problem concerned the Musicians Union. Under its agreement with the BBC, a fee would have to be paid to every artist every time the record was played. Obviously this was ridiculous. It would have cost the BBC a fortune every time the record was played; it would not be in their interest to play it at all. The artists wanted to waive their fee but this could have led to the union boycotting the BBC, so the MU's consent was needed. I anticipated the union to be reluctant to co-operate, so I drew up contingency plans for the formation of a new union, the Pop Musicians Union, which we could have created with the collective strength of the names on the record, to make a separate agreement with the BBC. In the non-stop continuum I was in the grip of I never once considered I couldn't do it, and would do so if I was forced. I could do *anything* to make this work because the one luxury of this particular exercise was the certainty that anything you did was morally justified. I called the head of the union and the consent to waiver came through almost immediately. They couldn't have been more helpful.

Phil Collins had said that he wanted to come and play drums. Two days before the recording Paul Weller rang and asked if we wanted him to play

The 25th I call *The Tube*, 26th I make a video, 27th and 28th I go to Ireland, 29th all hell breaks loose. The idea crystallizes with music notes at top of page, followed immediately with 'FEED' 'WORLD'.

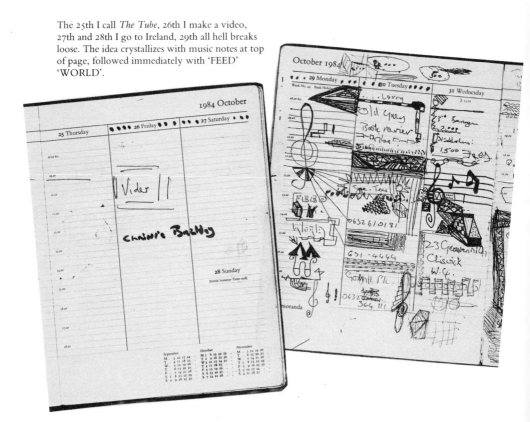

guitar on the backing track. Sting and John Taylor from Duran both asked if we wanted them to play bass. It was the biggest band of all time. I was surprised and pleased. I had thought people would just turn up under sufferance on the day. Weller came and did some nice guitar work, though in the end we couldn't use it because Midge had done the rest of the backing with electronics and they just didn't work together. Taylor was sweating with nerves at playing in front of Sting. It was a good session and we got the bass and some backing vocals done at Chiswick the day before the actual recording. It had been four weeks since I had seen the news bulletin, four weeks in which I had kept those images I had seen alive, so that when I spoke to people, I conveyed a genuine sense of conviction and urgency.

But there was more to it. I am not a great believer in notions of coincidence, serendipity, synchronicity and all the other rag, tag and bobtail of karmic law, but some things seemed too easy. It is not normal for Sting, for example, to even be in the country, but to find him at home in the afternoon when I rang was extraordinary. It happened not once but often. When I randomly picked a day for recording, the studios who had lent us their facilities were free. Also, most people would be in London on that day or nearby. Writing the song had been easy, the words had run out of my biro. Midge and I worked fast and well together. Kuka taping the conversation and the song when I first played it. Peter Blake's agents selected at random from the directory and his already working on a montage which could be altered for our cover. Hundreds of people dropping everything and concentrating on this one thing. It was not something that I thought about then, although in retrospect I think I was aware of it from the moment Linda mentioned Eritrea in the press office and when no one smirked or laughed when I suggested the whole thing. No one seemed to think it was odd that I wanted to do this, no one particularly stood in my way; on the contrary, doors impenetrable a week earlier swung open effortlessly. I thought it was something to do with the fact that I wasn't doing it for myself. People would say, 'OK, we'll help', but it went beyond that.

There was no reason for the record distributors to take a loss. They get given a hundred charity records every year and take their profit. It was the busiest time of their year where most stores, especially the smaller ones, make enough to keep them going through winter. It was obviously going to be a hit, they'd lose a lot, so why did they agree so easily?

For the record company and the individuals involved it was like the most important record they had ever worked on. John Watson, head of Phonogram's legal department, informed Phonogram International that all territories must give the same deal as the one agreed in London. Some bridled. Watson, exceeding his authority, told them that he would give the record to rival companies. The heads of Phonogram International had not initially been keen, but eventually John persuaded them. He thought this issue so crucial that he had gone against his own company. No one fired him, and if they had, it was quite possible the whole company in London would have walked out.

I was in a fever of activity. Everything I did seemed to work. I sat in the press office, not really aware of what was happening. People walked in with artwork, the phone rang non-stop.

'Check this, Bob.'

'OK.'

'What about this, Bob?'

'OK.'

'Bob, the ladies who package the sleeves are working all night for free to get them ready.'

Not once did I stop to think, 'Why am I doing this?' But I know that I often thought 'Why me?' Four weeks previously, I had sat with my head between my hands at some desk and almost cried with despair. Now as *Life* magazine wrote at the end of 1985, 'When you meet this man you wonder, "Why?" Did God knock at the wrong door by mistake and when it was opened by this scruffy Irishman, think, "Oh, what the hell – he'll do".'

★　★　★

Midge and I were first to arrive in the studio on the day of the recording. Outside, the studio was surrounded by TV and press photographers.

'How's it going, Bob?'

'Well, it isn't yet,' I said nervously, 'because we're the only ones here. We're just hoping that the rest turn up.'

I had no certainty that anyone would come. They said they would, but maybe it was just so I'd leave them alone. It was an odd sensation watching them all drift in. It was very low-key. Most people looked as if they had just got out of bed, which by and large they had. I remember seeing Sting strolling up the street half-reading his Sunday paper, Paul Weller, all nervous energy, emerging striding from the opposite direction and Marilyn flouncing round the corner like a beautiful starlet on her way to the corner shop to buy some milk. I looked around and saw that the room held most of the stars of British pop music. They looked like a bunch of yobs down the pub on a Sunday lunchtime.

Duran Duran had come back early from their tour of Germany to do it, Spandau Ballet were just back from Japan, U2 had given up one of their few free days in their world tour and flown over from Dublin, Culture Club had flown back from New York.

Except for George. 'Where's Boy George?'

'Maybe he's still in New York.'

'Which hotel was he in?' I dialled the number and asked for the room. 'George, it's Geldof, where the fuck are you?' It was 6 a.m. in George's bedroom.

'What? Er . . . I'm in New York,' he yawned.

'What the fuck are you doing in New York?'

'Er . . .'

'You're meant to be here.'

'Who's there?' the sleepy voice asked. 'Everybody. Sting is here, and Paul Young, the Spandaus, the Durans, Marilyn, Bono, Quo, Bananarama, Kool and the Gang, George Michael, Weller, Heaven 17. Everybody is here. Everybody except you. There's a Concorde leaving at 9 a.m. Get up and come.'

'I'll try.'

'Don't fucking try. It's important. Get up now and get on with it.'

George Michael was looking around the studio a bit taken aback. To put him at ease, I performed a most bizarre and unnecessary introduction. 'George, do you know Midge Ure, Phil Collins, Paul Young . . . ?'

Phil was setting up his drum kit. We had reservations. Recording drums is notoriously tricky and we already had electronic drums on the backing track. 'Nah, it'll be better if I play live', said Phil, 'I can do some fills between the electronics. Give it a bit of bottle. I'll mike it up.' He was very casual about it. 'Brilliant,' said Midge uncertainly.

We had restricted the press by having one official photographer, Brian Aris, who had been with the Rats in Asia and whom all the bands trusted. He was to release his pictures to all the papers, but the studio was full of television crews. We had to get the picture session over before beginning the song to make the news deadline on TV and to make the print deadline for the *Daily Mirror*.

We played a rough version first so the musicians could hear how the song fitted together. Everybody, I think, was pleasantly surprised. I got the impression that they were expecting it to be rather naive and obvious. But Midge had done a brilliant job on the backing track by putting a sort of empty African drum sound on the opening, which was foreboding and sad at the same time. It was radically different to what I had originally played him. Then we began recording the first line of the chorus, 'Feed the world'. We recorded it over and over again, double-tracking all the time, to give the impression of hundreds of voices. Then we did the same with the second line 'Let them know it's Christmas time'. And then we began recording the verses which we had split into individual lines so that almost everyone had a line or two to sing as a solo.

'OK, who's first?' asked Midge, who was producing it. There was a lot of shuffling. Nobody likes singing in the studio. You do it with the backing track being played to you through the headphones. All anybody else in the studio can hear is your weedy strainings. It usually sounds awful and at that moment there were still four different TV crews in there filming.

'Come on, Tony, you go first.'

'What do you want me to sing?' asked Tony Hadley of Spandau Ballet. We gave out sheets allocating the lines. He was given two lines from the middle of the song: 'There's a world outside your window and it's a world of dread and fear'. We were dying for the poor bloke as he stood in a huge empty room with no one except four TV cameras, looking straight into the control room that contained all his peers. It was early in the day for a vocal. Usually your voice warms up over the day and you can sing better at night, but here was Tony doing the first one before midday. He was very brave and very good. When he finished, everyone clapped. The solos were sung out of sequence. The first two, which I'd written hoping David Bowie might get back in time for the session, but which were taken by Paul Young came next. The rest were handed out more or less at random. There was a lot of very creative input, to use a horrible expression. George Michael improved his line beyond recognition by taking the movement of the song upward where the tune had gone down. Sting's harmonies over the part Simon Le Bon had sung were perfect. We kept two lines for George, who eventually arrived from New York on Concorde and swanned into the studio like Joan Collins. He grabbed Le Bon by the hand. 'Simon Le Bon,' he said in his highest of high camp voices, 'come on, let's start some rumours.' He dragged him up to the studio door where there were now thousands of kids who had heard all day on the radio and TV what was going on. As Simon and George went up the stairs arm in arm, the massed media outside exploded into flashbulbs and the fans screamed. Then, entering the studio, he began to sing and suggest things to Midge.

'Get on with it, you old queen,' I shouted from the back.

'Shut up, you Irish tart.'

He has such a beautiful voice. He sounded like a black female blues singer. Soul. Don't matter what you look like. You got it or you ain't.

It was the juxtaposition of styles and attitudes I found so fascinating. Here were Le Bon and Bono, George Michael and Paul Weller, Phil Collins and Bananarama, Sting and Boy George. These were simply people who played music. There was a difference between them, but not the bitter divisions so lovingly created by the jerks in the music press with their sixth-form literary pretensions. In one corner Rossi and Parfitt were doing the Status Quo equivalent of a Morecambe and Wise routine. In the other, Paul Weller was having an intense political discussion with Marilyn and John Moss, who was arguing with great knowledge and intelligence. Before the recording, Weller had been on the phone asking me to get people to volunteer for his record to raise money for striking miners. It was the winter of the great Scargill v Macgregor prize-fight. I told him that I couldn't because we had to keep Band Aid non-political if it was to work properly and that he would have a chance to ask people to make a record for the miners on the day of the Band Aid recording.

Band Aid was a moral issue: whether you were of the right or left was irrelevant. It transcended local politics because the issue was global. Before the recording I had always thought Paul Weller mouthed specious political platitudes. Now I saw he was a person of genuine conviction. Whether I agreed with his point of view or not was irrelevant. He had got a call out of the blue from a bloke he thought was an idiot, i.e. me. He had listened to what I had to say and regardless of his opinion of me he agreed with me on the issue and performed. He put his money where his mouth was. Now he was obviously recruiting hard, but, it seemed, unsuccessfully.

In the corridor some were getting the curry and chips we had been given by the studio, while others were practising their part of the song or crowding into the control room to listen or shout suggestions. Upstairs Brian Aris was splitting up well-known bands and photographing odd combinations; a bit of Duran plus a bit of Wham!; Sting with Bono and George; Midge and me.

George's lines were virtually the last thing we recorded, but most people hung around until 6 p.m., when we watched ourselves on a BBC news bulletin similar to the one which had shown the awful report which had prompted this gathering. For all the exhilaration of the day, always in the background were the cadaverous spectres whose faces we had seen from Ethiopia.

We worked through the night to mix the record so that the completed tape could be taken direct to the factory first thing in the morning. We finished side A around 2 a.m. and then began mixing side B, using the backing tracks and some of the vocals as a background on which to overlay the messages

The Band.

from McCartney, Bowie and Frankie Goes To Hollywood, whom I rang in Detroit, as well as the messages recorded in the studio from the participants. Steve Norman, the Spandau percussionist and saxophonist, had mistaken the purpose of the taped messages and, thinking it was for the kind of fan tape that bands do endlessly for radio stations, said, 'I'd like to say hi to all our fans in Ethiopia. Sorry we won't be able to make it over there this year, but we're going to try for next year'. We didn't use it.

At 3 a.m. the phone rang. It was Robert Maxwell of the *Daily Mirror*. We had had the papers brought in just after midnight. We had the whole of the front page. 'Oh, hullo Robert, thanks very much. You kept your word.'

'I always do that,' crackled the voice at the other end of the phone. 'We'd like to use the group picture to do a poster and sell it for the Mirror Ethiopia Appeal. That'll be all right, won't it?'

'No,' I said.

'Why not? We've done you a favour. Now let us use the picture.'

'No, fuck off. You know very well that the agreement was that the poster and the money would go to us.' I was indignant. We had a long argument. He had done us a favour, but we had done him one too, and now he seemed to be trying to get me to agree to turning the whole Band Aid thing into an adjunct of his newspaper. 'These people have made a special effort. You're trying to take that away from them. It should be their thing: Band Aid.'

In defending our position to Maxwell, the whole concept of Band Aid began to crystallize in my mind. But we wanted the poster and this wasn't any time to quibble. I said we would split the poster money fifty-fifty.

'OK, fifty-fifty, minus costs.'

'What do you mean, costs?' I asked.

'The cost of printing.'

'Well, you'll have to account to us for that.'

'Can we say in the paper we'll be working on future projects together?' he asked. 'After all, it is all for the same cause.'

I wasn't sure it was for the same reasons. But he was right. 'Yes, if you've got planes to transport stuff, then very possibly we'll be working together.'

As I put the phone down it dawned on me that we were now going to make a lot more than the original £72,000. Why shouldn't we be thinking about getting our own planes? Maxwell's talk of costs reminded me of one of the things that irritated me about existing charities. There was always talk of 'administration expenses'. Surely there ought to be some way of getting *all* the money out to Ethiopia? It was now 3.30 a.m. and I dismissed the thought as Midge and the engineer began to mix.

We finished at 7 a.m. We logged the time very clearly at the end of the B side. It is odd to hear that now. When I spoke I was very tired. It sounded sad. When Bono saw the lyrics he said, 'I think you've written a hymn, Bob'. Boy George

Me, Midge and Fifi, November 25, 1985.

had said being there 'was like Christmas itself'. Sting said, 'You can never send enough money. You have to give of yourself'. It was a very emotional record. At the final message, I thought of all those people, but mostly I thought of why they'd done it. I gave that final message thinking all those things.

It had been a monumental day. There was never one second of rancorous feeling. People wanted to hang around and talk to each other, suggest things. Some were in awe of each other's abilities. Inside that room had been the single greatest collection of contemporary musicians in British history. The total security had been the artists' liaison man from Phonogram records, Barry Murfitt, who had stood at the door as the people came in. I had played guitar with Paul Weller and Gary Kemp, a preposterous combination of people. Weller had called the group 'the Grinning Idiots'. For Midge it had been a day of professional triumph to produce his greatest contemporaries singing and playing on a song he'd co-written. Trevor Horn, the owner of the studio and one of Britain's greatest producers, had come in late in the evening and coached the singers through the rest of the song. Sting had gone home, thinking he was finished, and when I rang him, he travelled without complaint back across London with his girlfriend and kid. It felt good, it felt like it should. It sounds corny, but they had trusted me, now I was determined I would do my best for them.

I left the studio and went straight to the BBC to offer an exclusive play of the tape to Radio One. 'I want you to play this record. I want you to play it all the time,' I said to the producer at the BBC.

'Thanks, we'll look at it and if it's good it will get the same treatment as any record.'

'No. This is not just any record. It is a way of helping to stop people from dying. You don't play this because it is a good record. You play this because it is your way of helping. Everyone has to do what they can. We make records, that's our job: we've made this. You play records, that's your job: you play this, that's how you help. Sting said, "You have to give of yourself." That's how you do it.' He thought I was a pious, over-the-top twat.

Before Simon Bates played it I explained to the listeners, 'First you will hear Paul Young, then Boy George, then . . .' and I ended by saying, 'Virtually one hundred per cent of the money from this record, apart from the VAT, goes straight to Band Aid and I swear every penny will get to Ethiopia. I want everyone listening to buy it. We've only got three weeks. Let's make it the biggest selling record of all time. Paul McCartney's "Mull of Kintyre" sold about two and a half million and that's the biggest so far. But there's fifty-six million people in this country. So we can easily beat that. Even if you've never bought a record in your life before, get it. It's only £1.30. That's how cheap it is to give someone the ultimate Christmas gift – their life. It's pathetic, but the price of a life this year is a piece of plastic with a hole in the middle.'

I began a round of TV, radio, and newspaper interviews. The mouth that had got me into trouble so often now talked about the simple idea of personal responsibility. The thing I first groped with back in the Simon Community in Dublin now became clear, 'Everyone can do something. No matter what you do, you can do something. Use your talent, your circumstances, anything. There are millions dying in agony. How many more children will you let die in your living rooms before you act? You can do something, and please buy this record. Buy one for each of your family. If you have no money, club together and buy one. Even if you hate the song, buy it and throw it away.'

The idea caught the imagination of the public and the media too, who began to catalogue the innumerable bizarre ways in which people were responding. People were buying boxes of the record and sending them out as Christmas cards. Others walked in, bought fifty, kept one, and then gave the other forty-nine back for re-sale. A butcher in Plymouth rang me to ask if you needed special permission to sell records. When I said no, he got rid of all the meat from his window and filled it with the record. The Queen's grocer, Fortnum and Mason, phoned to ask for two boxes to sell in their restaurant; by the end they had sold thousands there.

It was impossible, during the very first few days of sale, for the record to register in that week's charts as these had already been compiled. When we tried to get the video on *Top of the Pops*, I was horrified to find that the producer, Michael Hurll, who is possibly by default the most powerful man in the British music industry, refused to include it on the grounds that the programme's policy was that only records already in the charts should be played. There were no special cases, he said. Not even for eight million people at risk of dying. Learning the lesson from Maxwell and the *Mirror* I went straight to the top. I went to the BBC reception desk and asked to be put through to the controller of BBC 1, Michael Grade. He told me to send up the video which we had had made of the recording session. It was a brilliant piece of work by Nigel Dick who had assembled the crew and equipment and filmed, processed and edited it for free. He had it ready in an unprecedented forty-eight hours. The video perfectly captured the emotion of the day.

I waited in the BBC lobby for five minutes, and then I rang Michael. 'Have you seen it yet?' 'Yes, it's brilliant. What's the problem?'

I explained about *Top of the Pops*, but suggested we had our own little five-minute programme possibly getting David Bowie to introduce the video. This would, in fact, be better than actually being on *Top of the Pops*. I waited in the lobby half an hour, then I spoke to Michael again.

'Fine,' he said. 'I've shifted the programmes here by about five minutes just before *Top of the Pops*.'

This was incredible. We would be listed in the papers as a TV programme. Millions would watch. We were slotted between the news and *Top of the Pops*

– giving us a massive captive audience. As I'd hoped everything about this record was proving superlative.

At Number One that week was a singer called Jim Diamond who had never had a hit record before. I heard him interviewed about his success and he said, 'I'm delighted to be Number One, but next week I don't want people to buy my record, I want them to buy Band Aid instead'. I couldn't believe it. As a singer who hadn't had a Number One for five years, I knew what it cost him to say that. He had just thrown away his first hit for others. It was genuinely selfless. The next week 'Do They Know It's Christmas' went straight in at Number One. That was the kind of generosity of spirit which was abroad.

The record was a phenomenon. We were printing 320,000 copies a day and still it wasn't enough. Every record factory in Britain, Ireland and Europe was pressing it. The T-shirts which we had franchised out to make even more money could not be made quickly enough, and when pirates started bringing out counterfeit merchandise we got the breakfast TV programmes to track them down. The indignation of the public and the ruthless exposure stopped that quickly.

Things began to blur. It was like the first experience of coming from Ireland to England and entering the pop world, but this time the driving force was outside rather than inside me. There seemed a different point to this, a point which was undeniable.

I flew to the States. Already the record was massive out there too. But I had had less time to concentrate on America, unsure as I was four weeks previously whether we'd even have a record in England. We only had a total of ten days' sale in the U.S. before Christmas. I went to make those ten days as productive as possible. Will there be an American Band Aid? they asked. It was not impossible, I told them, but it was up to the American bands to organize it, not me. I was willing to help and give advice.

That night I called Cyndi Lauper, the Cars, Hall and Oates, all of whom said they'd love to do a record. But my own priorities had to be the Band Aid record, and in the meantime people in the States could buy the British record. 'Do They Know It's Christmas' sold a million and a half copies in the U.S. in two weeks. Ironically it never got to Number One although it was outselling the actual Number One by 400 per cent, because the American charts are based on a ludicrous combination of factors of which sales are only a part. Moreover we did not get the same cooperation that we got in Britain. I suspected many retailers did not report record sales because it was not in their interest to have a non-profit making record at Number One during their peak period. I rang *Billboard* to accuse them of graft. How could we possibly outsell the Number One record four to one and not be Number One? 'It doesn't work like that, Bob.' 'Obviously not,' I thought.

No one had had the chance to do any accounting yet but already it was quite clear that we had raised around two or three million pounds. One night I sat at home listening to carol singers outside on the street. They were singing 'Silent Night'. Then they began to sing 'Do They Know It's Christmas'. I was by myself so I cried. On Christmas Day on *Top of the Pops* the Band Aid team got together and sang it prior to the Queen's Speech to the Commonwealth.

I had assumed that soon after Christmas it would all be over. Midge was in the middle of making an album and went back to it. The Rats had a tour lined up to promote *In the Long Grass*. I had decided against releasing the LP half-way through December as planned, fearing that people might think that the whole of Band Aid was a publicity stunt for the record. In fact, of course, it was the opposite. While people were playing 'Do They Know It's Christmas', no one thought of playing 'Dave'. I could understand this, but I was saddened to think that 'Dave' had missed its time. Our tour was a success, but the album, released in the dead period of early January, was a failure, as we knew in our hearts it would be. The music press predictably had now begun to attack the band on the grounds that Band Aid had been a Geldof gimmick.

But the national press didn't. The whole Band Aid phenomenon was manifestly too huge and too deep to be so reduced. Indeed they fanned the issue.

'When are you going to Ethiopia to see for yourself, Bob?' They kept asking. I knew why. It would be a good story: the pop star and the starving child in the same photograph. That was precisely why I had no intention of going. 'It is not necessary. I don't need to go there to see it. I've seen it already on television. There are experts to help decide how best to spend the money. They don't need a half-assed pop singer. Can't you see how distasteful that would be?' But taste never having been one of the strong points of the British popular press, this point seemed to elude them.

There was a man called Peter Searle who kept phoning me too. He said he was from a charity called World Vision.

'I don't know why you're ringing. I'm not able to distribute any money.'

'We don't want any money. We just think you should go and see the problem. We can organize a flight for you and we have a plane in Ethiopia.'

I was very suspicious. I had never heard of World Vision. Then I was told they were an excellent organization but with roots in the right-wing American evangelical revival. Later we backed several of their projects.

I was rapidly learning more about the problems of Ethiopia and its hapless peoples, caught between the millstones of natural disaster and international politics. I was finding out about the imbalance which characterizes the relationship between ourselves and the poor of the Third World. The United Nations Children's Fund, UNICEF, had sent their resident representative in Addis Ababa to give me a detailed briefing on the situation. Even Searle, who continued to call with his requests that I should visit one of his projects and thereby draw attention to it, was giving me useful information about the place.

Record sales had now put five million pounds in Band Aid's bank account. The problem now was what to do with that money. Nearly every agency I'd talked to would have had to take part of the money to cover their colossal overheads. These are necessary when organizations are permanent, and require a large staff if they are to function properly. But I had given my word that a hundred per cent of every penny would go to Africa without being side-tracked or wasted. If someone gave a pound, then a pound would go. The only way around the problem was to eliminate the middleman and go direct to the source. That meant going to Addis Ababa, the capital of Ethiopia. I also felt that as the money came from all over the world, no agency from a single nation should have access to it.

But how was I to decide who got what? Equally, if we did not simply hand over the money, how was *I* to order grain, charter planes and ships, fill out order sheets, custom forms, bills of lading, and so on. Band Aid was me, Philip Rusted, the accountant who had agreed to look after the money, and the lawyer John Kennedy, the last two recruited by Midge's manager Chris Morrison. 'I think you'd better go,' he said. 'At least find out what they want.'

I capitulated. I had no money to get there and I was determined that I was not touching one penny of what had been given. All I could do was get those who had insisted I went to pay. The *Daily Star* covered my hotel bills in Ethiopia and the breakfast television station, TV AM, paid for my flight. In the end they did not accompany me because of the small-minded and mercenary attitude of the television unions who scuppered all coverage, insisting it was a documentary story, not a news story which only required half the number of film crew. I found this unbelievable. The *Daily Express* were to pay my hotels in the Sudan.

Before we went I talked to the papers and TV stations concerned. I said there must be no pictures of me with starving children. They said I was being unreasonable. I said, 'Fine. I have to go. I have no money myself. I cannot spend Band Aid money, but I will get there and you won't be with me.' I didn't want it to be an exclusive story, because that would have been shabby, selling something so awful for the price of a ticket. Everyone had given money, everyone deserved to know where it was going, everyone was involved, there could be no exclusives on Band Aid. They finally agreed and they still paid my bills. The *Daily Star* tried to book every seat on the flight to Addis, but were told to shove it. In the event the flight out to Addis had a heavy quota of television and newspaper journalists from other organizations. We had not been in the air long when I felt a tap on my shoulder. I turned to see a large, ruddy-faced avuncular character who extended his hand and said with a smug smile, 'Bob, Peter Searle, World Vision'.

CHAPTER XIV

Sainted in Moderation

It was just before midnight and it was Christmas Eve. In the calendar of dates Ethiopia is thirteen days behind the Western world. In the calendar of centuries the figure seems even greater.

Within one day I had gone from London to Addis Ababa and then on to Lalibela, one of the most ancient centres of Christianity in the world, and probably the most changeless. In this mountain fortress, in the heart of a massive plateau which for centuries had proved as impenetrable to conquering armies as it now was to relief workers, little had altered since Christianity was first brought to the highlands a mere 400 years after the death of Christ. We were to attend a midnight mass which would last for more than twelve hours.

The moon was silver. Its light had turned the landscape of browns and ochres into a monochrome of black and pearly grey. We picked our way across the rough ground from the centre of the little town down the rocky hillside towards the churches. All around were large uneven shapes in clusters. 'Watch out for the boulders, Bob,' someone warned me. The light picked out their shapes in eerie contrast. It seemed like a scene from a Steven Spielberg movie. Almost at once the ludicrous nature of the simile struck me. Here I was in one of the most culturally ancient lands in the world yet I carried with me the alien baggage of modernity. There was no path. My feet scraped and twisted against the stones and the heel was torn from my London shoes.

Down the slope of scree we slid until we came to a large flat clearing. It was full of people. There were thousands there, mainly peasant farmers whose lands had been devastated and who had flocked to the town in the hope that they would find something there. They had heard that there were feeding centres run by the Ferenji who came to the mountains in aeroplanes or by lorry. Tonight the moonlight had silvered their poverty and distress. It was Christmas and they had come to mass in the eleven rock-hewn churches which were created here in the twelfth century. I had never seen anything quite like the church we looked down upon. It was a magnificent feat of architecture. It had not been *built*, it had been carved. On a flat part of the rock plateau a massive moat had been chiselled, hundreds of yards square and about sixty feet deep. In the centre a huge column of the original rock had been left, standing now like an island. Into this rock doorways and windows had been cut and then the rock behind them had been hollowed out, to create an enormous shell which became the vaulted spaces of a church nave. It was exactly the opposite of all building techniques developed in the West. It would have been, even with modern technology, remarkable. With the hammers and chisels of the twelfth century it was almost beyond credence.

Down through a series of tunnels and arches we twisted along a maze of passages to come out down in the pit, at the floor level of the church. Above us, all around the edge, thousands of faces looked down. The pit was covered in carpets. I bent to feel them, for collecting old carpets had become an interest during the Rats days when I had had some spare cash. But they were not the ancient rugs I had hoped for; they were modern Saudi Arabian and Belgian cotton, some were even polyester, I thought, feeling the weight of the twentieth-century luggage shift uneasily on my back. The moonlight picked out some details of the carving on the church before me. Elaborate crosses carved with the delicacy of lacework stood alongside pre-Christian symbols resembling the swastika. The ritual of the religious celebration was not formalized or linear like a western Christian service would have been. It seemed a chaos of simultaneous action, with scores of priests and acolytes carrying umbrellas over the heads of the holy men who milled around in an apparently aimless fashion. It was as if the chief celebrant had issued the order 'Pray at will'. The men were chanting, singing, and reading apparently on impulse, overlapping one another, drowning one another out, even at times breaking off to have what looked like ordinary conversations in the middle of the ceremony and paying only occasional attention to what anyone else was doing. They spoke in Ge'ez, though that is a dead language used now only for religious purposes rather as Latin once was in the Catholic Church. I sat and listened to the mesmerizing murmur for about two hours before we rose to make our way back to the little town.

At the entrance to the tunnel which led to the outside world another priest was on his way in. He was introduced to me as the Archbishop, though he did not appear to be more grandly robed than any of the other clerics. He spoke to me at length, in what was translated as a speech of thanks for Band Aid. I was astonished and touched that he had even heard of it.

We picked our way back up the slope, through the boulders. The scree was uncertain underfoot and at one point I slipped and fell against one of the rocks. It moved and then stretched itself into the gaunt figure of a man. His face was pinched by hunger. He looked into my eyes and mumbled a few words as if he were apologizing for being there. I was chastened by the realization that this landscape of dead stones was in fact a landscape of living beings, homeless, huddled into foetal shapes, covered by their thin blankets, sleeping wherever they had found themselves when the sun had gone down on those Abyssinian highlands.

★   ★   ★

We had arrived in Addis Ababa only a matter of hours before. At the airport I had been welcomed as an honoured guest. A little girl had given me a bunch of flowers and I was greeted by Berhane Deressa, the deputy commissioner of the Ethiopian government's Relief and Rehabilitation Commission, the RRC, which had been established ten years before, after the revolution which overthrew Haile Selassie during the famine of 1974. There was tea, photographs and perfunctory conversation. Then he said: 'January 7th is Christmas Day in Ethiopia so tonight is Christmas Eve. We wondered if you'd like to go up to Lalibela for the celebrations?'

I had read about Lalibela on the plane. It sounded amazing, but I had been told it was in the control of the Tigrean rebels. 'I'm not really here for that sort of thing. I'm here to meet people to find out how best to spend the money. I don't think I'll have the time.'

'Well, there are some feeding camps in that area which you could visit the day after. It would give you a grounding for your conversations with the relief workers here in the capital when you get back. We can lay on a plane this afternoon and, if you like, you could meet Mother Teresa, who will be at the airport then too.'

He was obviously keen for me to go so I agreed. We drove to the hotel. Addis Ababa surprised me. This was my first visit to Africa and I'd expected somewhere very hot and dusty rather like towns in New Mexico. But it was very open and, being more than 6,000 feet above sea level, cool and fresh with the scent of eucalyptus. The roads were broad and well-kept and there seemed an air of bustle and well-being even in the shanty town as we sped through.

Entering the city we drove beneath a massive concrete arch with gaudy trappings and the legend 'Long Live Proletarian Internationalism'. Above it was a hammer and sickle. 'What the fuck is that?' I asked.

'It is the arch of the revolution.'

'Christ, no wonder there's a famine here if you insist on putting up crap like that. In any case, it's palpably not true. If there really was any proletarian internationalism you wouldn't have millions dying here.'

Berhane shrugged his shoulders. The car drove into Revolution Square which was dominated by a gigantic poster of Marx, Engels and Lenin.

'For fuck's sake, what is an Ethiopian peasant supposed to make of that? Three nineteenth-century Europeans in high-collars and flowing locks?'

Berhane began to explain, caught a glimpse of the total disbelief on my face and then just laughed. Later, a more forthcoming official explained: 'If we agree to have a revolutionary arch built by the Koreans, then they will build us a hotel. We wanted the hotel. It's as simple as that'.

We arrived at the Hilton. There were, I later discovered, two rates. All the rooms were identical, but you paid more for a view of the swimming pool than for one of the shanty town. As the *Daily Star* was paying I got the former.

Berhane looked out of the window. 'Before the revolution we had a house there,' he said, pointing beyond the pool. He had come from a wealthy family but after the overthrow of the Emperor the new Marxist government had his house pulled down and the Hilton built in its grounds. 'I was a student during the revolution and took part in the riots which brought the Army to power. We needed the revolution. Under the Emperor things had gone too far.'

'Let's go for a walk,' I said. 'Just you and me, not with your entourage or my gang of reporters.' We walked for four miles around the city, and then came back to the hotel in time to leave for the airport. We were sitting in the departure lounge when Mother Teresa came in with several other nuns all wearing the white habits with blue borders of the Missionaries of Charity. She was astonishingly tiny. When I went to greet her I found that I towered more than two feet above her. She was a battered, wizened woman. The thing that struck me most forcibly was her feet. Her habit was clean and well-cared for but her sandals were beaten up pieces of leather from which her feet protruded, gnarled and misshapen as old tree roots.

I bent to kiss her. I do not normally kiss strangers on a first meeting but it seemed like the right thing to do. She bowed her head swiftly so that I was obliged to kiss the top of her wimple. It disturbed me. I found out later she only let lepers kiss her. The photographers crowded round. We sat down. I felt like a clumsy giant next to her. I showed her my shoes which were beginning to fall apart and asked her if she had any spare sandals. She laughed. Actually she cackled out loud. I gave her a copy of the record. I could not think what else to do. I'm sure she got rid of it as soon as she was on the plane for Calcutta. Then she began to tell me about her work in Ethiopia. Her nuns were working in the shanty towns of the capital and they also ran a feeding centre and hospital in Alomata in the famine-stricken province of Wollo where they cared for the old, the blind, the disabled and the incurably ill – the people tragically overlooked by the other agencies who concentrated on trying to save the children, the pregnant and mothers of the very young. It was the same philosophy she adopts in India. I told her that my band had played in India and that, if it seemed a good idea, next time we were there we would do a benefit concert for her mission. She said that she didn't need fund-raising activities – God would provide. She then gave a clear demonstration of the way in which God provided.

While the TV cameras were rolling she turned to Commissioner Dawit Wolde Georgis, the head of the RRC, and said that on the way to the airport she had seen a couple of old palaces which she had been told were empty and she asked him if she could have them as homes for orphans. With the cameras whirring Dawit did a bit of fancy footwork. 'Well, I'm not sure about those particular places. I don't know what they're being used for. But . . . er . . . I'm sure we can find you some suitable premises for an orphanage. . . .'

The sinner and the saint, Christmas Eve in Addis, January 1985.

'Two orphanages,' she corrected.

'Two orphanages,' he conceded.

Back home the press were starting to call me, cynically at first, then half-seriously, St Bob. At first I was pissed off, but then I found it ludicrous rather than offensive, given the sort of person I knew I was. The second I met Mother Teresa she struck me as being the living embodiment of moral good. I felt I had no business sitting beside this tiny giant. But there was nothing other-worldly or divine about her. The way she spoke to the journalists showed her to be as deft a manipulator of media as any high-powered American PR expert. She does a sort of 'oh dear, I'm just a frail little old lady' schtick.

She was outrageously brilliant. She made them laugh and she defined the terms of the questions they could ask her. She understood that the moral ground she occupied gave her the right to march up to airlines and ask for a free ticket to Washington and, once she arrived, to ask to see the President of the United States knowing he dare not refuse her. There was no false modesty about her and there was a certainty of purpose which left her little patience. But she was totally selfless; every moment her aim seemed to be, how can I use this or that situation to help others. She was never pious about this. She had given over her whole existence to a life of moral worth. That is what makes a saint, not all the Catholic Church's bollocks about performing miracles in their names after their death. She is one of the few people who have ever impressed me on sight. I was in awe of her. She held my hand as she left and said, 'Remember this. I can do something you can't do and you can do something I can't do. But we both have to do it.'

★   ★   ★

The plane for Lalibela arrived. It was an antique DC9 which looked like something out of *Casablanca*. Inside were bucket seats and hammock webbing benches down the sides. I lay on the floor and dozed a little on the journey. It was only early afternoon in Ethiopia but I had been awake for twenty-four hours now. I had not slept during the nine-hour flight from England and my walk with Berhane had tired me. I awoke from a shallow doze as the plane touched down to refuel in Kombolcha, one of the food storage centres of the northern regions. The valley was green and fertile. I was wearing a pullover and a jacket and yet it felt quite cold on the landing strip. This was not what I had expected from Africa. Across the other side of the strip I could see a couple of Soviet helicopter gunships. But Lalibela was high on the northern plateau and that was more as I had imagined.

We circled twice over the town, hoping some aid worker would see us and pick us up. We landed in a cloud of dust on a dry mud field. A few hundred yards away a small knot of children and two cows watched us from beneath a tree. There was no other sign of vegetation for miles. We were picked up by a German aid worker in a Landrover who bumped us along a tortuous route around steep slopes and down sand-filled ravines. It was my first recognition of the problems the terrain posed for the transport of food. In the winter months when the rains came in the mountains, these ravines would be full and Lalibela would be cut off. As we drove along people stopped by the side of the road or came out of their grey straw houses and watched. They wore shifts and cloaks made out of sack-like material, always a lifeless pale brown. Some stood and stared. Others waved and smiled. It felt like being in a film, so obviously did we not belong, the pop star and the press, in this desolation.

Not least of Ethiopia's problems is that it is fighting two separate civil wars with the rebels of Tigre and Eritrea. The Tigre People's Liberation Front had taken Lalibela six weeks earlier and the government forces had only just regained control. The town was full of soldiers. It was my first experience of an African army. The soldiers are often no more than kids and there is always the suspicion that they are not fully under the control of their officers as they wander around nonchalantly waving their AK47s. They had taken over the town's hotel. It took Berhane several hours to find somewhere else for us to stay. The place was basic but it was clean and it had beds, and a balcony which overlooked the town.

Dusk was growing as I stepped out onto the balcony. As the sun set, the whole land took on a crimson-orange tinge. Blue smoke rose from the fires of the town and mixed with the dust which the twilight rays showed to be hanging everywhere in the air. The evening was still. I stood there thinking what a short journey it was between two worlds, from a dull January morning car ride through the grey wet streets of London past shops with all their sales and post-Christmas bounty to the panoramic African sunset and the strange tranquillity of Christmas in a country where famine is upon the land.

Berhane came out onto the balcony carrying a tinny little cassette recorder. It was playing 'Do They Know It's Christmas'. It took me completely by surprise. All at once the two worlds married into one. That little song and now all this. He had not contrived it, he was playing it simply to show me that, from somewhere, he had got hold of the tape. He smiled. It filled me with an enormous sadness. I wished everyone who had made that record could be here. I looked out through the straw-thatched roof of the small circular Tukuls and the smoke of the fires drifting up into the orange and purple sky and out over the vast plain. 'And the Xmas bells that ring there are the clanging chimes of doom.' I looked at the people, ragged and undernourished and desolated by unnecessary miseries and I looked at the journalists about me just as Bono's voice shouted, 'Tonight, thank God it's them instead of you'.

That evening a goat was killed in my honour. The villagers led the animal up to me and before I had time to say a word they slit its throat, cut out its guts and started hacking it to pieces. I thanked them for the honour. I wasn't shocked. I'd seen worse in the meat factory. We were led into a pitch black room to wait while it cooked. Candles were produced and we sat and talked. We had had nothing much to eat all day and I was very hungry when the food was produced, the Ethiopian national dish, wat and injera, the first being a thick stew and the second a sour-tasting spongy pancake bread made from local grain. We picked at the tray of tough goat meat and drank excellent bush beer. Later we went to mass. I couldn't last past 2 a.m., and retired.

The next morning at six we revisited the churches. The mass continued, but without the silvering of the moonlight the place looked far more desolate. The priests' robes and umbrellas, which were splendidly coloured and embroidered, now looked old and crumpled and rather shoddy. The landscape was parched and sterile and the air was filled with the swirling dust which had once been topsoil. The people who had sat huddled like stones during the night sat there still or moved about in a lethargic, purposeless way. More were coming in from the desert land around, in small family groups they moved slowly and steadily towards the town. Their destination was the feeding centre. It was ours too, but before we left I called all the photographers and the TV cameramen together.

'You really do have to understand this. I do not want any pictures taken of me with starving children. We've seen them before, visiting politicians looking fat and concerned as they hold a child in their arms who is near to the point of death from malnutrition, who may well die the day after the western celebrities and their photographers have left the camp.'

'Christ, Bob, you know that's the picture we've been sent to get, you with one of the children who Band Aid is trying to help. That *is* the picture,' said Kenny Lennox of the *Daily Star*.

'I know it is. And it is the picture that I don't want. Can't you see how cheap it is. It's disgustingly sensational. It degrades the people involved. It's exploiting their misery to give you a nice shot.'

'But it's not like that. You're not here for publicity, we know that. You're here because you are trying to help. All we are doing is recording the horror which is the reality of the situation. It'll also get you more money.'

'That's not how it will appear to people at home. It will simply be construed as shameful, distasteful and patronizing. You can take pictures of me in the camp. You can take pictures of the kids. But not the two together. This is my trip and anybody who is not prepared to agree to my rules can fuck off back to the plane.'

I did not trust them. Earlier Kenny had told me that he was one of the photographers who had taken pictures of Princess Diana in her bikini when she was pregnant. In all other respects he was a nice bloke. He tried to keep certain problems off my back and you notice things like that. He spoke of his own child in relation to some of the kids we saw in a way that was sensitive and moving. But it was weird, as soon as he started to do his job he seemed to throw all sense of personal morality on one side. He told me how he had lain out in a boat for a couple of nights to get that bikini picture. He was clearly proud of himself.

'Do you call that a job?' I asked. He was clearly surprised at my response. I could imagine him telling the story in El Vino and everybody saying: 'Good man, Kenny, you got the picture.'

'The public have the right to know,' he parroted.

'Right to know what?' I asked. 'Why do you want to hurt people? Did you take pictures of your own wife when she was pregnant and show everyone in the neighbourhood? Is the woman not allowed to enjoy her pregnancy in private? I don't suppose she went to the beach in her bikini again after that!'

In trying to defend himself he revealed that he had been one of the photographers who had prevented Elizabeth Taylor from going to mourn alone at Richard Burton's grave. Sometimes, he said, one photographer would be prepared to make concessions but was unable to do so because a competitor would refuse to do the same. She had risen before dawn to be at the grave before anyone else was up. When Liz got to the cemetery gates she had been confronted by photographers and had pleaded with them to leave her alone, just that once.

'We said we were all going to leave, and then one guy said he wouldn't go. What could we do? We couldn't leave him to be the only one who got the picture. What would our editors say?'

'So what happened?'

'Well, as it happened there weren't any pictures, because when we wouldn't go she didn't go in. She just went away.'

'So she didn't get the chance to say her last goodbye. Are you proud of that?'

'No, but if I'd gone the other bloke would have taken the picture anyway. So it would have happened whatever I did.'

'So because this woman is a star she has no right to mourn privately? Is that it, Kenny? That's unacceptable. By involving yourself with that you are just adding to that horrible cheapness and nastiness. You're a nice bloke, Kenny, but spare me your self justification.'

I went to each photographer and made each swear on his honour not to do it. When people actually do that, it becomes serious. They all did, even Kenny.

'Right. You're on your honour. The minute anybody takes a picture I'll attack them, rip the camera to bits and ask the Ethiopian authorities to stop them from following me around. OK?'

They were a good crowd of blokes to travel with. Ross Benson from the *Express*, was legendary for his vanity and hairdryer. He revels in his job and when reporting a war, for example, he sports neatly pressed combat fatigues, or for an Irish horse kidnap case he wears cavalry twill and tweeds. Now in Africa he donned his casual lightweight khaki tropical gear. He was over there standing in front of the spinning propeller of the DC9 in order to preserve his coiffure. Chris Morris of the BBC and his crew showed their unflappability and humour. The *Mail* man kept missing the plane. The *Star* man, deeply serious and upset by what he saw, kept asking me some nonsensical nonsenses for the benefit of his editor.

If there was any bad feeling as a result of these exchanges it was soon forgotten when we arrived at the German Emergency Doctors' feeding camp. The Landrover pulled up at the fragile little hut of straw and poles which constituted their clinic. By a gigantic Red Cross flag lines of people were queueing. They did not look in bad shape.

'Christ, Bob, have you seen round the back here?'

A couple of journalists came back, their faces drawn.

'No, I don't think I need to see.'

'For fuck's sake, Geldof, we won't take any pictures,' said Kenny. 'Go and have a look.'

I was afraid of the photographs. I was also afraid of what I would see. There was a circle of people in the process of being fed. They were like the grotesque creatures of some distorted imagination. I stood and watched their slow, apathetic movements and fended off the awful truth that these were human beings. It was not the physical affliction which most upset me, though that was bad enough. The skin was wrinkled like crêpe paper over limbs which were no more than bone and nervy sinews, for all their body fat and even their muscles had been eaten from the inside by the starving body which had begun to feed off itself. The joints were bulbous and distended. Their bodies were lacerated with sores and festering wounds which would not heal because their systems lacked the reserves to repair themselves. In her arms one woman carried a baby which was so shrivelled with a chronic starvation disease which the doctors called marasmus that the child looked like a little monkey. But what was worse than all that was the look in their eyes. They were glazed, blank, and vacuous. They looked but did not see. They were the eyes of people who had given up.

They stared through an impenetrable window at the meaningless succession of events which flashed before them. These white men had come to make them eat. Why? They did not want to eat any more. Eating hurt the stomach. They sat on the ground with the milky high-energy porridge dribbling from the corners of the mouths while their seeping eyes were thick with flies. The eyes were looking at me. I began to cry. I was angry. Crying was useless and a waste of energy.

I looked around. There was silence from the press corps. The reporter from the *Star* had gone completely white. Kenny, the professional, could hardly take a photograph. He had taken two and then finally this scene bled through his lens and into his consciousness. I watched him. From beneath the camera a single tear trickled down his cheek. Chris Morris, the BBC reporter, was visibly shaken. I wondered what Berhane felt. These were his people. Yet he must have seen this a hundred times. He must have watched westerners encounter it before too. We drove back to the airport without speaking.

We flew on to Mekele, one of the two biggest camps in Ethiopia. It was even worse. This was a camp run by several organizations including the Red Cross. Round the edges were tens of thousands of people without any shelter. Towards the middle were rows upon rows of Army surplus-style tents sent from all over the world. In the centre were the Red Cross buildings for the worst cases: huge huts made of corrugated iron with concrete floors and

The BBC filming in the dust.

One family's ration of grain. There is no water to make porridge, but she cooks it anyway. It will pass right through her and take parts of her stomach with it.

hundreds of people packed inside. It reminded me of the films I had seen of Auschwitz. Outside, as I was passing some children, three or four held my hand. I half turned and out of the corner of my eye I saw Kenny take a shot of me with a long lens. I decided to say nothing. The row blew up later.

Everything horrified me. Rows upon rows of people had each been given a handful of seeds which they were roasting in wok-type pans over tiny fires. They did not have the water to turn them into porridge. Water supplies were rationed. Firewood was getting more and more scarce. There were 50,000 people here and more arriving every day. This place was hot too, and the tents buzzed with flies and disease. There were camp guards employed to try to prevent it, but people would just piss and shit anywhere. Many of them had such awful intestinal diseases (from contaminated water and from the hard grain which tore at the stomach) that they had no control over their bodily functions. It was in this camp that I had forced upon me one of the images which has haunted me ever since.

I came out of one of the long huts and saw a small boy squatting by a pool of his own urine and diarrhoea. He looked about four months old but malnutrition is deceptive. He was nearer two, the age of my own child in England. A tattered dusty piece of cotton hung from one shoulder across his distended stomach. His face was huge, a two-year-old face on a four-month-old body. His eyes were moons of dust and flies. He was crying and the tears rolled down to the awful swollen stomach before they dried in the heat. Only a few yards away were his family, but they were too ill to notice. The diarrhoea trickled out in a steady flow. Then, as I stood there, as I watched, the child began to shit out his own intestines. He had nothing left inside to evacuate except the torn shreds of his own stomach which had been ripped open by dry grain. I was watching a child die. There can be no doubt that the little boy is dead now. But he will not die in my imagination. There, nothing can free him from the agonizing process of death which is fixed in my mind.

Back in Addis Ababa the next day I embarked on a series of meetings to take advice on how the Band Aid money was to be spent. I realized now more than ever just how much of a novice I was. I was only certain of one thing – that my strategy must be to meet all the charities together and between them establish what their priorities were. We only had a limited amount of money, so let them tell me how best to use it.

I had learned quickly how much special pleading existed in the rivalry-ridden world of the agencies. Speaking to them alone was not always a tactful way to proceed. I had Peter Searle constantly at my heels as a reminder of that.

Brother Gus O'Keefe was an Irish monk who ran the Christian Relief and Development Association which had become the umbrella organization co-ordinating the activities of the private agencies like Oxfam, Save the Children and dozens of others. He called a meeting with representatives from most of the charities along with those from the international bodies like UNICEF. They agreed to draw up a list of the most urgently needed supplies and where they should be first distributed.

I then met the officials of the Ethiopian government's relief commission. 'It seems to me that your basic problem is one of PR,' I said to Commissioner Dawit, thinking of the enormous damage they were doing themselves by not explaining their policies, such as resettlement, to the press. 'I may not know anything about famine but I know a lot about PR and you get a lot of bad press because of simple misunderstanding. The press is the most important ally you have, because once people in the West appreciate the scale of what is going on here you won't be able to stop them from helping.'

'What do you mean?' Dawit asked.

'For a start there's the politics. You have got thousands of so-called Russian agricultural advisers here. Let's assume that for every thousand three hundred are KGB. That's OK because I'm sure there is some CIA in some of the agencies. But seven hundred! What do these "experts" do? What do they know about agriculture in this type of climate, anyway? They managed to fuck up their own system of agriculture to such an extent that they ended up importing food every year from their sworn enemy, the United States. How are they going to help you?'

Dawit laughed. 'You can say that, but I can't,' he said.

'Let's take something else. Resettlement. Every time your ministers open their mouths to the western press they manage to put their foot in it.'

'True. But I can't say that either.'

'Well, I don't care, I'll say it to them. You've got yourselves in a position where you are actually stopping people from helping.'

Dawit laughed again. 'I think you should meet the Minister for the Interior'.

I then brought up the agencies' shopping list and we discussed priorities as he saw them. In the end we agreed to set up a liaison committee, organized by Brother Gus, to bring the agencies and the relief committee together to draw up suggestions for spending the Band Aid money. Whatever they would agree upon, we'd supply.

It was with the Minister for the Interior, Berhane Biyuh, that I first realized what enormous potential there was for me in particular and Band Aid in general for saying the unsayable and confronting those in power with problems which aid workers and even diplomats dared not raise for fear of jeopardizing long-term relationships. Band Aid was not only short-term, it was also essentially a one-way traffic. I had asked aid workers what they would say if they got a chance to meet the Minister of the Interior. I brought with me a list of notes, but I had some understanding of the problems, having been surrounded by them for three solid days and having been briefed extensively.

I had no chance to think this through, in advance, I went in only with the intention of speaking plainly and was put into a slightly irritable frame of mind by the obsequious shuffling of the government flunkies as I entered. The minister stood up and began on what was quite clearly a formal address.

'On behalf of the Revolutionary Committee of . . .'

'Please, let's cut out that crap, Minister, and get down to business.' Berhane looked at the minister and said, 'I warned you.' The minister just laughed.

I asked if the television cameras which were present could stay. They had been told they would have to leave after the formalities, which were surprisingly brief. It was clearly not part of what the officials had planned, but the minister reluctantly agreed.

'You can't live all your life in fear of the western press,' I began. 'They're the ones who will help most to get you what you need. I know that you have said in the past that you don't want aid on those terms, but I've just come from a part of your country where they do want it, very badly. And every time you make some preposterous statement like that, which you know in your heart is nonsense, but which you state for ideological reasons, not only are you evading issues, you are also betraying the country and those people.'

'Yes, but there is a conspiracy in the western media . . .'

'Spare me all that. You've seen the outpouring of sympathy in the western press. Ninety per cent of the stories are very positive or sympathetic. The answer to the negative stories is not to attack the press, but to look at your policies.'

I gave him a list of areas that the agencies had told me about. I could feel the encouragement from the journalists behind me. Suddenly I saw the purpose of Band Aid. They had to listen because I had not only the money but the constituency of support which that money represented. And it was a populist, non-governmental constituency. I represented nobody but myself and the millions who wanted to help. A constituency of compassion.

The discussion grew heated. The journalists joined in. The minister argued cogently and relevantly. I think he surprised himself. He was a committed Soviet Marxist arguing his point with the hated western media. He had lost his fear in the openness of the discussion. I love a good argument. 'Your government is consistently shooting itself in the foot,' I told him, banging the table to make my point. 'Punk diplomacy', as it was later called, was born that day. I thought it was just speaking my mind.

There was nothing else I could usefully do at that time in Ethiopia so I went to the Sudan, from which we had been getting reports of a situation as potentially disastrous as that in Ethiopia. Before I left I went shopping with Berhane in the large Addis market. Many of the stalls sold gold and silver jewellery. 'Look at them,' he said. 'They're the old family jewellery and wedding bands of many peasants who had to sell them in the last resort to get food.'

On the stalls there were tens of thousands of abandoned heirlooms. I bought two silver bracelets, knowing their original owners were now probably dead.

I did not doubt their provenance. In Lalibela I had been approached in the street by a man wanting to sell a battered old bible. The sweat-stained wooden binding, the well-thumbed parchment pages, the Amharic script and the dead language it enshrined summed up the richness of the place as well as its poverty, a birthright sold for a mess of potage.

The flight to Khartoum was on Ethiopian Airlines. At one point the pilot announced that I was on board and that, on behalf of the Ethiopian people, he wanted to thank me. After all I had seen I felt a complete fraud.

It was hot and dusty when we landed in the Sudan. It was much closer to what I had expected Africa to be, except that the Arabic gave the place a slightly Middle-Eastern feel. There was no official welcoming party this time and the dingy customs hall was in a state of total turmoil. It was there, I later decided, as a kind of welcoming metaphor to introduce the newcomer to the way the entire country was run. In the foyer there was a representative of UNICEF to meet me.

I was in the Sudan to get a general impression of the scale of the problem, but also to meet someone from the private office of the Sudanese President. Shortly before I left London I had received a curious message. It came via Stewart Copeland who was the drummer with the Police. His father, who had been a CIA agent, worked for the Arab millionaire Adnan Khashoggi and had passed on the information that Khashoggi was interested in donating some planes for us to use. On the eve of my departure for Ethiopia I met up with Khashoggi's son who was passing through London. The planes would be for famine relief in the Sudan only, he said, and a meeting would be arranged between me and President Nimeiry's personal adviser, Baha Idris. It all seemed very complex, but the offer for the planes was firm, I was assured.

I checked into the Hilton and found that no telex had arrived from the *Daily Express* confirming that my bill would be paid. 'You'll have to pay cash and settle your bill every day.' They clearly did not like the look of me.

'That's OK,' I said, deciding to test the water, 'if the telex doesn't arrive Baha Idris's office will take care of it. I'm here to see him.'

'Oh, Dr Baha Idris. Well, of course, everything is in order then, sir.'

I arranged meetings with the field directors of Oxfam and Save the Children. I found it all difficult to fathom. Certainly hundreds of thousands of refugees were pouring into the Sudan from four different countries and the massive influx of those fleeing both famine and the civil wars in Ethiopia was causing enormous problems along the eastern border. But the real problem in the Sudan was that the entire country, which was engaged in its own civil war, was in a permanent state of chaos. A short taxi ride to the city outskirts proved that. In nearby Omdurman tens of thousands of native Sudanese had gathered in an ad hoc camp without any food, water or sanitary facilities. The government's solution was to periodically ship them back home, whereupon the people would make their way back to the outskirts of Khartoum once more.

I had lunch with Andrew Timpson of Save the Children in the Sudan Club. Looking around this rather seedy relic of British colonialism, with its polo trophies, its framed letter from a ninety-year-old Winston Churchill and its menu featuring steak and kidney pudding on days when the temperature was in the upper nineties, it was hard to comprehend the problems of this country which is the largest in the entire African continent and whose economy and government seemed to be held together with sticking plasters. The most pressing problems, Timpson said, were in the east with the Ethiopian refugees, but within six months there were likely to be several million Sudanese at risk in the west of the Sudan where the harvest had failed for the seventh consecutive year. His briefing was depressing, but it did contain one enlightening piece of information. Adnan Khashoggi was said to have oil interests in the Sudan and a special relationship with President Nimeiry which led to his getting a remarkably good return on his investment. It was said that if anyone could arrange a cease-fire in the civil war which was disrupting development of the oil field which was thought to be the biggest in black Africa, it was he. Curiouser and curiouser.

My shoes had given up entirely after the rough terrain in Ethiopia. By now I was wearing carpet slippers. The British ambassador was horrified when he found that I intended to wear them to the People's Palace to meet Dr Baha Idris. 'You can't wear those old things,' he said. He asked me what size I took and then gave me a pair of his own desert boots. There were three foreign ambassadors being received at the palace that day and there were military bands, looking exactly like British regimental combos, but staffed entirely by Sudanese parading in full uniform. I wandered in, looking at the plaque by the staircase which marks the spot where General Gordon was killed by the Mahdi's troops. I watched the marching bands as I waited. The Blue and the White Nile met outside the palace gates, just within my vision. It was extraordinary. What the hell was I doing in Khartoum, in the palace, waiting to see the highest official in the government? I was caught up in some political financial manoeuvring with very powerful and wealthy men, talking about a famine so horrendous the UN called it the worst disaster known to man. What is going on? I'm a pop singer, I thought somewhat hysterically, before I was summoned in.

The conversation with the good doctor which followed must rank as the most preposterous I had had with any politician during all my meetings throughout the past year. He listened as I asked a series of preliminary questions based on the briefings I had had from the agencies. I concluded by enquiring about their plans for the famine which was now knocking on the palace gates.

'Whatever do you mean by that?' asked the urbane and astonished doctor.

'Well, I've just come from Omdurman. There are tens of thousands of people out there with no food and no water. I have seen people collapse from malnutrition.'

'That's most interesting. How did you get to Omdurman?'

'In a taxi. What's that got to do with it?'

'There is no famine.'

'No famine. You must be fucking joking. I've just come from Omdurman.'

'We have the situation under control.'

'Your idea of control seems to be trucking people back out to the desert and dumping them there. But they just walk straight back.'

'The problem of food supply in the Sudan is entirely under control. Mr Geldof, my experience as a scientist tells me that because of the cold snap in Europe, you will perhaps not be aware that it is snowing everywhere. Even in Nice. Because of this the Sudan is guaranteed rain in three weeks.'

'Is that government policy?' I asked incredulously.

The man was clearly mad if he believed the crap he was telling me. The conversation continued getting progressively more ludicrous. I left in a state of total disbelief. Famine is the most destabilizing of all political factors and it came as no surprise to me that when the Nimeiry regime was finally overthrown three months later, Dr Baha Idris was the first man the new regime put on trial.

I went out to the camps in the east to see for myself what the position was. I thought I was incapable of further shock after what I had seen in Ethiopia. But this was far worse. It was not simply the state of the people which made me despair, it was the state of the organization, which was non-existent. At least in Ethiopia there was a good indigenous relief agency, even if it was underfunded and hamstrung by the ideology of its Marxist government's policies. In the Sudan there was no organization at all.

I visited a camp called Tukalabab near the town of Kassala only a few miles from the border with Eritrea, where the Ethiopian government had been fighting a civil war with Eritrean rebels for the past twenty-five years. Escalation in the fighting and the severity of the drought and famine in the region had caused around 80,000 peasants to flood across the border to Tukalabab. To call the place a camp would have been a misnomer. It was just a mass of people who had sat down in one place. Their only shelter came from ragged bits of cloth they had spread between bushes to provide some shade from the sun which burned relentlessly in the sky over these lowlands. There were two European doctors working there, in total despair. The place was a burning reflector of heat by day and freezing by night. As well as all the intestinal diseases which the relief workers had to cope with in Ethiopia, here they had a high incidence of pneumonia and malaria. They showed me into what they pitifully called the camp store. There were fifteen bags of flour for 27,000 people.

On the way back I visited the provincial governor in Kassala. He was obstructive at first, but under pressure he admitted that he was getting no help from Khartoum; there were no funds available and there was not even any official acknowledgement that a problem existed at all. Because Band Aid had stated on the record that all funds would go to drought-affected victims in Ethiopia, legally we could not help in Sudan. We would have to find some legal loophole to enable us to get supplies and equipment here rapidly. I talked further over dinner with Samir Basta of Unicef and Nick Winer of Oxfam who depressed me even further with their pessimism and the picture of disarray they laid out for me. The Sudan was only six months behind Ethiopia in the scale of its disaster.

I returned to England, my mind reeling with visions of intolerable destruction, political ineptitude and mass death. As I landed I felt I understood the impulse which sometimes prompted people to kiss the ground. It was good to be home, but I now knew that we had not yet done enough.

The shock of returning to the world which I acknowledged as my own was startling. No one who has not made that transition from the horror of the African famine to the everyday profusion of riches in our western world can fully appreciate it. Had I thought about it on the plane on the way back I would, I suppose, have said that I was returning to normality. But suddenly London did not seem normal. The things I had once taken for granted – the rich variety of food, the elaborate nature of even our most basic clothing, the sophistication of the houses we lived in with our electricity and hot and cold running water – all these now seemed like a wonderful and disproportionate blessing. But I felt no guilt. Guilt was a nonsense, we were simply lucky.

The contrasts were made more stark by the urgency with which I had been summoned home. Before I left Ethiopia there had been many telexes and messages that I should fly back from Africa on a certain date. This urgency had been reinforced by several of the journalists there who made enigmatic references to an important development which would require my attention. They had been supposed to come with me to Sudan, but suddenly they all cried off. What the hell was happening? My first thought was that something awful had happened to someone I knew. No, it was not anything like that, I was reassured. Were there unforeseen problems with the Band Aid money? No, nothing like that.

'It's really important. Just trust me, Bob,' said Kenny Lennox, who was the most persistent in his reminders of my flight time and date of departure for London.

'Trust *you*? After you sneaked that picture with the long lens when you thought I wasn't looking? You bastard.'

In Khartoum there had been several more telexes, even one from one of the reporters who was now in Nigeria, urgently reminding me of my date of departure.

Back in London, I did the rounds of the TV and radio stations to talk on the outcome of the trip and paint pictures of what I'd seen. Sometimes just evoking those memories made me cry. I didn't care. I wanted them to feel it too. I said we needed to 'give until it hurts'.

Soon I discovered the point of all the cloak and dagger. As I entered one studio Eamonn Andrews rose from a seat he had been sitting in with his back to me and clutching his red book said, 'You thought you'd come here to record an interview for the BBC World Service, but Bob Geldof . . .'

'Oh no . . .' I had always wondered. 'What do people think when that happens, I know I'd tell him to . . .' My first inclination was to reject the whole business, but it occurred to me that all my friends and family must be up there, waiting behind the *This Is Your Life* stage with all its dreadful familiarity. A few days before I had stood watching a child die, but I knew it would be unfair to expect anyone who had not held these two worlds one in each hand as I had to understand that. As I walked down the staircase to the stage I experienced great warmth in the cheers from the audience. It was the first time that I had personally felt the emotion which Band Aid had generated among people. It was not the sort of adulation or admiration or even mere enthusiasm that comes off an audience at a pop concert. It was a kind of friendliness. I thought the show was fun.

★   ★   ★

I now began a tour with the band. It was a good tour to packed houses in major venues but it did little for the Rats' record sales. Band Aid was always occupying part of my mind. The audiences had changed; there were Rats fans as always, there were those fans who had stopped coming as they grew older but now, because of Band Aid, their interest was revitalized, and there were people who came because of Band Aid. At the end of each gig we played 'Do They Know It's Christmas'. It was the first time I'd experienced the 'God syndrome'; people who came up afterwards moist-eyed, touching you and looking at you as if they expected you to ascend on a cloud. I told them to fuck off. One unctuous cretin told me if Christ was on earth he would be with me. I replied, 'If Christ was on earth I'd ask him why he wasn't in Africa'. I told the audience there were buckets for donations at the back and it would be nice if everyone gave 50p – they responded generously. We raised an additional £50,000 for Band Aid that way. Even by that simple act I was accused of using Band Aid. Forget the fact, even if it were true, that that money represented relief for thousands.

But the more money which came in the greater the problem of how best to spend it. I had realized Band Aid needed a proper organization. Until then I had been working in the Phonogram press office where the staff had grown used to coping simultaneously with calls about the new Tears for Fears tour and calls about the current market price of sorghum in Port Sudan. But the problems were getting way beyond me. I now had to obtain and ship all the items the agencies had asked for. I had no knowledge of grain or medicine. No experience of shipping. No experience of anything. Like everything else, I played it by ear. I was wondering how the hell I should start. We obviously needed a board of trustees to oversee expenditure and we needed a group of people to actually do all the practical work.

One day early in 1985 a smartly dressed and bearded young man came in and offered his help. Kevin Jenden was an architect with a successful practice in designing modish things like record studios, restaurants and shops. But Jenden had also worked in Ethiopia building warehouses for the Red Cross and he and his wife Penny, who was an anthropologist, had lived for some time in India. We hit it off at once. We were both suspicious about the expenditure and cost effectiveness of the traditional agencies. Jenden offered to work in the afternoons for nothing after spending the morning in his architectural office. But he soon found, like I had done two months earlier that it would not be enough, and abandoning his business to his partner he began working every moment. His wife, Penny, came to join him too, bringing her professional expertise to bear on the problems of development. She later set up a committee gathered from several specialist agencies to deal with expenditure on our long-term projects.

The trustees knew nothing about relief work or the Third World. I asked each of them to join the board simply because they were distinguished, or were successful businessmen who had a proven record of achievement, an obvious business acumen and a reputation worth preserving. I told the trustees that their work was to hold the money in trust for those most in need. They were to protect the financing. I went to Lord Gowrie, then Minister for the Arts, and asked him to become the figurehead sponsor. He agreed. Then I organized the board, which included Lord Harlech, the head of Harlech TV, Michael Grade, the controller of BBC 1, Chris Morrison, the manager of Ultravox, Maurice Oberstein, the chairman of the British Phonographic Institute, John Kennedy, a pop industry lawyer, and Midge Ure. I was chairman. The system was to be that agencies or individuals in Africa would suggest suitable schemes to the committee set up by Penny, which would select those which seemed workable and then pass them on to the board for approval.

Two other volunteers who had responded to my 'everyone can do something' call, were now undertaking office administration and emergency purchasing: Judy Anderson, an American labour lawyer who was taking a sabbatical in England, and Valerie Blondeau, who had slipped me a note one afternoon in a café. 'Do you need help?' she wrote on the back of a serviette. 'Yes,' I wrote on the other side. We began to get volunteers from individual industries. I told Kevin we could extend the value of what we did by setting up various 'Aids' in the industries most of our essential purchases for Africa would come from. Dee Flowers of *Motor Transport Weekly* organized Truckers for Band Aid to try and get free vehicles and parts for transport in Africa. Builders for Band Aid began to look for waste products in their industry which could be useful in Africa. The truckers collected them into our central warehouse, the office which had been given to us by the Greater London Council. Already another central tenet of the Band Aid philosophy was taking shape; whatever needed doing, there was someone in that industry you could ask to help. This helped to keep the money donated by the public free for absolutely vital things. IBM, British Telecom, Gestetner, Canon, all provided us with the office equipment we needed for free.

A shipping agent called Ken Martin phoned with a plan. I had been shocked by the huge price of shipping. 'If we pay those prices,' I said on TV, 'we'd only be able to afford one or two trips.' There was a buyers' market, he said, so why try to ship loads to Africa on an individual basis? Why not charter ships for very long periods and then, having built up a fleet, as well as despatching our own goods offer space to all the other agencies so they could send out their goods for free. It was the kind of maverick scheme which a single permanent charity could not have afforded and would not have had the loads to justify doing on their own. It was perfect. Here was another Band Aid characteristic – we were flexible and could look around to see where gaps were left by the other agencies, and then plug them. By shipping agencies' goods for nothing, we were freeing their money so they could spend it on their own projects.

I was getting requests from all over the world. Channel 9 in Australia asked me to go down to take part in a telethon against hunger. It was too far and I had too much to do. Then I got a call from Ken Kragen in Los Angeles. He was the manager of a number of top American pop artists including Lionel Richie and Kenny Rogers. He had called me before to ask about the possibility of an American Band Aid record and I had talked to him about it. He had previously managed a singer called Harry Chapin who had dedicated his life to the eradication of world hunger and had, over a period of years, contributed a large percentage of his earnings to various development projects. Chapin had died in a car crash.

Kragen saw in Band Aid the embodiment of what Harry had been trying to do to make this a truly popular issue. He had got together with Harry Belafonte who had seen me on TV when I had gone to New York to promote the Band Aid Christmas song. Belafonte had said publicly that as a black man he was 'ashamed and embarrassed at seeing a bunch of white English kids doing what black Americans ought to have been doing'. Kragen and Belafonte had got together an American version of Band Aid. He was phoning to ask if I would go over for the recording.

I had no money for the ticket. Years of the Rats being in the doldrums had done nothing for my bank account. And I couldn't touch Band Aid money which was specifically for Aid purposes. Then I realized that the recording was to be the same night as the Australian telethon. I telephoned Channel 9 and said that if they would pay for me to fly to the recording then while I was there I would do their programme from their ground station in LA.

The recording had been timed for the same night as the American Music Awards to which Paula and I had already been invited as honoured guests with front row seats. It was a clever piece of timing because it ensured that most of the American artists needed for the recording would be in town that night.

The contrast between the British and the American recordings could not have been more dramatic. Where in London everybody had just rolled up looking pretty much as they would look on most Sundays at home, here in LA the whole affair was 'show-biz'. When in Hollywood. . . . ·

In England we had had one guy on the door; in LA, the security was formidable. We were all issued with passes. Mine admitted me to the actual studio as well as the dressing rooms, make-up rooms and photography rooms, but Paula's only allowed her admittance to the friends', liggers' and free-loaders' enclosure. I went in with her past guards who checked passes at every other step. There, in front of two huge video screens which were linked by closed circuit TV to the studio, was an astounding feast in a cornucopia of Hollywood extravagance. Fish stood with the tongues protruding, carved in ice, caviar poured out of their mouths onto the silver salvers below. The tables were loaded with smoked salmon, meats, and canapés of every description. Drink was stacked in limitless quantities. The room was full of Hollywood fat cats and their wives eating and drinking effortlessly and talking smoothly about how wonderful it all was, this contribution to famine relief. I knew the food had been given free. But it was too much. The extremes between this room and what was happening in the studio across the hall was too great. In London there had been the offerings of a local take-away. I left in disgust and went off into the studio.

The producer, Quincy Jones, was there with three assistants, making last-minute arrangements. The song, which had been written by Michael Jackson and Lionel Richie, was called 'We Are the World'. Michael Jackson had already arrived and was standing in the centre of the room recording some vocals. Even without accompaniment they sounded marvellous. He sang through the melody and then improvised some harmonies.

'Try a third, Smelly,' suggested Quincy Jones, turning to look at Michael Jackson. For some reason everybody called him Smelly or Smelly Socks. Michael Jackson sang a perfect third.

Ray and Stevie fight over headphones. Smokey breaks it up. Dylan doesn't see the joke.

'Or a fifth.'

He did it again, in a voice of total purity. He was just practising, but it could have been recorded as the finished product. It was a preposterous level of professionalism and talent.

The door opened. Bob Dylan came in and sat down beside me. 'Hi,' he said. He looked terrible. His face was all puffed out and there were deep black bags under his eyes. He looked as if he had just got up. We started to talk about his last tour of Ireland. He began to laugh as I reminded him of things I'd been told about it. I was sitting there, talking to Bob Dylan. It was like talking to a man in a pub, I thought.

The door opened again. It was Diana Ross. 'Hi, Bob.' She was talking to me, not him. 'It's great what you've been doing. We're really proud of you.' We talked about children. She asked about Fifi. Then she got out the photos of her own little boy.

Every time the door opened it was like a bit of my youth walked into the room: Paul Simon, Dionne Warwick, Stevie Wonder, Tina Turner, Smokey Robinson, Ray Charles.

In walked Ken Kragen, a tall, thin, worried man with kind eyes. He is extremely clever but was, like me at Band Aid, almost in a state of disbelief at what he had wrought. 'Bruce Springsteen has just parked his car on the other side of the road and walked across – by himself – to the studio. Can you

259

believe it?' I could believe it. 'No, I mean he drove himself, no chauffeur, no limo. Then the Boss walked across himself, no bodyguards, no security.' Paul Simon looked across at me and smirked at such West Coast attitudes.

Springsteen and I were talking when Ken Kragen announced that before the recording began he wanted me to speak. I told them that I didn't really know what I could say to a group like that except that I had just come back from Africa and would tell them what I had seen in the hope that it might help them understand how important this record was, not just to raise money but as a gesture too and to raise the issue. I talked quite uncompromisingly in the hope that it would inject some passion into what they were doing.

It was odd to see these people lined up before me, some of the most famous entertainers in the world, standing in a group as if for a school photograph. Diana Ross was holding Stevie Wonder's hand. The skittish schoolboy atmosphere disappeared. I told them what I'd seen and they became sober. When I had finished Quincy said, 'If you didn't before understand what we are doing tonight, now you do.' 'OK,' said Quincy, standing on the points of his toes and gesticulating with the tips of his fingers. 'Let's run through it . . . OK, can you give us the note, Stevie?' Stevie sang with perfect pitch. They were tuning off his voice. 'OK, now let's do it again, only up a third, all the fellows with high voices please . . . Bruce, were you singing then? OK, well leave it out this time . . . again please . . .'. I felt totally outclassed, not just because of the Geldof croak, but because of the sheer professionalism of these people. I stopped singing and spent the rest of the night taking pictures with my tiny Olympus Trip. I stood beside all these great singers one by one. It was a great honour for me. Later I took the music sheets and made everyone sign them.

The next morning there was a press conference to officially announce the launch of the band which had called itself USA for Africa. Harry Belafonte spoke brilliantly, but before he did I tried again to tell the press how crucial they were to the project's success and how critical it was not just for those buying the record, but in a strange way for ourselves. 'You guys are not here just to report something. You could be here to make your contribution. I don't want you just to buy the record to send off the money. I want you to make sure that instead of two paragraphs, this story gets half a page. That's worth much more to us. Give us your skill. That can be your contribution.'

'Now before you all go,' said Ken, 'we're going to give you each a USA for Africa T-shirt.'

'No we're not. They're going to pay for them. Ten dollars each. Come on, cough up.'

'Oh, now I understand how it works,' said Ken, and laughed.

CHAPTER XV

All Day And All of The Night

'And the other thing is, I want it to be exactly the same in America. We can link the two concerts by satellite, alternating between them, live, so that people on one side of the Atlantic will be able to see people on the other at the very moment they perform. We will satellite every country, linking the whole world with this concert.'

'What?'

'Remind me,' Harvey Goldsmith, the chief promoter of Live Aid, was to say later, 'next time Bob has an idea I should go on holiday.'

I am not certain when the Live Aid idea was first planted and I could not know that it would turn out to be the biggest fund-raising event, the biggest TV event and the biggest concert in history. Had I known this from the outset I might never have had the nerve to begin. But certainly the idea was half in my mind soon after the Band Aid recording because I mentioned it to Nik Kershaw when I bumped into him at Heathrow in January. He volunteered there and then, even though there were no firm plans. At the USA for Africa recording I added a rider at the end of my speech: if I were to contact them about a concert I hoped they would respond. It had become increasingly apparent from the reports and requests that poured into the Band Aid warehouse from Ethiopia and Sudan that the £8 million which the record had made was nowhere near enough. I knew that there were 22 million people starving to death in Africa and that £8 million was enough to keep them alive for two weeks. The point of the record had been to raise money but, more important, to raise issues and make a gesture. After my trip to Africa, that issue had to be writ larger. I had already seen the outpouring of compassion in Britain that would soon be repeated around the world through other Band Aid type records – USA for Africa, Austria für Afrika, Chanteurs Sans Frontières, three German groups, Northern Lights in Canada, altogether about twenty-five. It should be possible to link them all up, I thought. Ken Kragen from USA for Africa said it should be done next Christmas. I didn't think so. We should act quickly to maintain the momentum. People needed something sooner to keep them motivated and prevent what I called 'compassion fatigue' from setting in.

During that long tour with the Rats in the early part of 1985, I began making notes. I called the Rats' agent, Ian Flukes, and asked him to talk to Wembley. Nothing very constructive came of the meeting. Chris Morrison, a Band Aid Trustee, and Midge Ure's manager tried to talk to them, but still nothing was agreed. Both, I think, thought the idea of the one concert on two continents going out to the whole world nice, but a bit of a non-starter. 'If you want to do something, act for yourself,' I thought irritably. I had to wait though. Our tour wouldn't finish till March 3. On March 4, I rang Wembley. I didn't know then, but I had 20 weeks to do it in starting from scratch.

The trigger was a letter which I received from a secretary at Wembley Stadium. If I was thinking of organizing a Band Aid concert she was sure that levers could be pulled to get Wembley for nothing. I began to mention the idea to a few bands. The response was overwhelming.

'Wherever I am in the world I will come back for it,' said Paul Young.

'We'll cancel whatever we're doing,' said Spandau Ballet.

'OK,' said Paul Weller.

'No problem,' said Mark Knopfler of Dire Straits. 'We're doing fourteen nights in Wembley Arena so maybe you can slip us in after sound check and we can walk across, do our bit, and be back in time for our gig.'

The phone rang. It was Britain's leading pop promoter, Harvey Goldsmith. 'I hear that you're talking about doing a Band Aid concert. You want to be careful or it could be the most almighty cock-up. I'll give you a hand if you like.' Harvey is as well known in the British music industry as the most famous of bands, all of whom he has promoted. He was also well known for his work with charities including concerts for the Prince of Wales' Trust and he is renowned as one of the most adventurous yet shrewd pop businessmen in Britain. This was a good start. 'I'm going to China now with Wham!. Let's meet when I get back,' he said.

Meanwhile other bands were responding. 'We're up for it. We'll start work on persuading Freddie,' said Roger Taylor and Brian May from Queen, whom I met at the Ivor Novello Music Awards. I had won one of the trophies with Midge for 'Do They Know It's Christmas'. Elton John was there too. He agreed without hesitation to do the concert. An hour later his manager, John Reid, rang. My heart sank. This would be the beginning of the problems. So often artists would agree to things and then their managers would phone and wriggle out of the commitment.

'It's John Reid here. Just ringing to say how keen we are on this concert. Is there anything else we can do to help? Do you need use of an office, phones, or anything?'

'Thanks John. There is one thing you can do. You know the managers of the other bands. When you bump into them just make sure that you tell them that Elton is doing this.'

I did not keep a diary during all this, but in a sketchy appointments book I can see that I had called a lot of people on the 15th April. Eric Clapton said he'd do anything. He was on tour in America, but he'd cancel if need be. I phoned Queen in Australia, Rod Stewart in Los Angeles, Hiroshi Koto in Japan, and Bill Curbishley, the manager of The Who, in Spain. I already had a fairly impressive list when I saw Harvey at that first meeting. I think anyone's initial scepticism had been dispelled by the success of the Band Aid record. I invited Maurice Jones, another big promoter, to the meeting with Harvey on 18th April. I thought that the major promoters should all chip in their services free just as the artists would do; in any case, it was also potentially too large for any one organization to handle. Maurice and Harvey carved up the areas of responsibility, Harvey looking after the acts and the production problems and Maurice dealing with the ticket sales, marketing and promotion. When that had been settled I told them about the transatlantic link-up. Their reaction was simultaneous.

'What?' they chorused. Then, 'Why?'

'The idea is we start at noon here, go on until 5 p.m. Then we join with America on a live two-way satellite relay. We have five hours of relay, back and forth every other act, and then at 10 p.m. we hand over to America and they run for five hours. At the same time we broadcast constant appeals and give people phone numbers pledging donations with credit cards.'

'You must be fucking mad,' said Harvey.

'It's not technically possible, surely,' said Maurice pragmatically.

'Why not?'

'I don't know why not, but it just isn't.'

'Course it is,' I said, well aware that I was coming across like Mickey Rooney's Andy Hardy: 'Hey kids! We can put on the show in the backyard!'

'Look, it's a non-political issue so access to media internationally shouldn't be difficult. The other crucial factor is, a lot of bands will be on tour in America at the time, and there'll be U.S. acts here so neither have an excuse for not appearing. They can do it in whatever country they're in.'

'No one's going to clear a network for seventeen hours just to have pop music,' said Harvey.

'It'll be the best in the world, Harvey, a global event, they won't be able not to. MTV, the American pop music cable station, will definitely take it and we'll ask Channel 4 here.'

'Who'll organize the TV end?' asked Harvey.

'I don't know. I'll find someone. Are you going to do it or not?'

'When will it be?' they said, wearily.

I'd picked July 6th, which was Independence Day weekend in the States when I thought people would be more inclined to go out to a stadium or be at home watching TV.

'Springsteen's here all that week. This is all I need on top of that,' Harvey said. He'd organized Bruce's UK tour.

'Brilliant. He can play here,' I said.

'We can also use his stage. It will be already in place,' Harvey realized.

'We should try to have the most important rock artists of the last twenty-five years on one stage.'

'This is getting worse. You're fucking mad. How are we going to do that?' This was a typical Harvey reaction. First he saw the problem. Then the beauty of the idea, then the solution. If you ever want him to do something, let him first think it can't be done. 'How many bands are you thinking of?'

'About fifty.'

'Fifty! FIFTY? There aren't fifty bands on the whole planet.'

'Look, the object is to make money. If people watch a concert on TV, they get bored, it doesn't matter who it is. We want them to give money, so the more multi-million record selling acts the better, because people will watch their favourites and contribute. Secondly, they won't get bored because bands will only have time to play their hits. And because there are so many of them, each band only gets fifteen or twenty minutes, which will suit them better than doing a whole concert. In fact, I'll specifically ask them to do that. It's like a global juke box.' I hadn't actually thought this out before, but the more I talked the more sense it seemed to make.

'That's impossible, you could never get a band and their equipment on and off stage in fifteen minutes . . . unless you divide the stage . . .' Harvey was now exasperated and excited. Maurice was making notes and sketches. Harvey said, 'They had that at the Rio rock festival. It worked brilliantly, but they didn't have bands every fifteen minutes.'

'The crucial period for that is the first five hours,' I said. 'On Stage A, a band is performing while on Stage C the previous band is coming off and on Stage B the next band is setting up.'

'It'd work,' said Maurice.

'Then when America comes in,' I saw Maurice raise his eyes to heaven, 'we have double the time to change over because it alternates between there and here.'

'Wait a minute, you said earlier people can contribute. What does that mean?' Maurice asked suspiciously.

'It's going to be a global telethon.'

The two of them looked at me. 'How?' said Harvey, looking at the floor.

I shrugged my shoulders.

'Why?' said Harvey, still looking at the floor.

'Because people are dying, Harvey.'

We had fourteen weeks.

★　★　★

I never assumed that asking the BBC to clear seventeen hours of TV programmes would create a problem. I don't know why. It just didn't seem an unusual request at the time. But first I rang Channel 4 where I knew the Head of Youth Programming, John Cummins.

'It's a wonderful idea, but I'll have to go further up to clear it,' he said.

I rang Tony Boland, a senior producer in RTE, the Irish national TV station. I'd known Tony forever. 'I'll have to clear it, Bob,' he said.

Harvey drew together his production team. Andy Zweck set to work on a strategy for working out the physical and chronological requirements for a concert schedule. He got Pete Smith to ring all the bands I had approached to tell them the date, and get details of what equipment they'd need – partly a practical measure and partly a psychological one to fix it in their minds that something was really going on and that they would be taken up on their promise. Harvey got on to Wembley Stadium.

I phoned Bill Graham, America's leading promoter in California. Bill Graham's involvement, like Harvey Goldsmith's in England, would reassure the bands that it was going to be a professional affair and not a shambles.

'I could get you Stamford Stadium free,' Bill said.

'That's no good, Bill. It's got to be East Coast otherwise it won't work with the time differences.'

'You'd make more money at Stamford. I could get you six good acts on the bill and . . .'

'This isn't just a question of making money from the gigs. It is primarily a television fund-raising event. Also worldwide TV gives it an important symbolism. Don't you see?'

He may well have seen, but he didn't sound very enthusiastic or convinced even though he said he would do what he could. I began to ring the American bands. For some reason the first person I called was Ric Ocasek of the Cars. This was coincidental as a Cars song was to play a massive role in the telethon aspect. Ric agreed at once that the Cars would perform. He said he'd tell his manager, Elliott Roberts. I was still very frightened the managers would botch things or at best impose unnecessary hindrances.

I phoned Bruce Springsteen and got through to his manager, Jon Landau.

'Bruce will be in England then, and he'll be on the way home either that night or the Monday.'

'Well, he can either do it in England, or we will put the whole thing off until the 13th and he can do it in America, if that suits him better.'

In 1985 Springsteen was rock's biggest star: we needed him. It would be easier to get everyone else if he agreed. I was nervous about calling – Springsteen gets asked to do a million benefits. But so does everyone else. Ideologically he would be inclined to do it, I knew. 'OK, I'll ask him. We'll think about it,' said Landau. I phoned a lot of people's managers in America.

Harvey came back from Wembley. 'There's a boardroom battle going on there. There are two consortiums on the board who each own forty per cent of the equity. No one is quite sure who owns the place. One guy hinted we could have it for free, but the others said the opposite.'

'Aston Villa said we could have their football ground, and Maurice reckons we could have Milton Keynes arena for nothing.'

'Let's try Wembley again. It'd be easier there. It's London and it's got four walls.'

At that time all the Band Aid office expenses were being paid for by a Malaysian oil millionaire called Ananda Krishnan. While he was in London, he came around to see me in our house in Chelsea. He was interested in turning Band Aid into a permanent institution. I told him that there was no point as we intended to wind it up after we had done the concert. I explained that we didn't really know how to orchestrate a TV event. 'You should meet a guy I know called Mike Mitchell. He part-organized the TV satellites and sponsorship for the Olympics.' Ananda set up a meeting in New York for a week later, on April 28th.

British Caledonian paid for my flight that time. Earlier, in the aftermath of the record, I had asked British Airways, Virgin and British Caledonian for some free flights. British Caledonian and Virgin responded positively. On April 28th I met Mitchell in a smart New York hotel. From the outset he was very keen. His firm was in the business of 'event management' and handling an event like Live Aid was obviously a good platform for them. He had also been involved in the End Hunger campaign. He was the perfect man for the job. That same day I met Tommy Mattola, the manager for Hall and Oates, then Gary Kurfirst who represented Talking Heads and the Eurythmics.

Back in England Bernard Doherty of the PR firm Rogers and Cowan had offered to take on the job of handling media enquiries. He was also the press agent for Paul McCartney and David Bowie. 'Try and persuade Paul, Bernard. I've already spoken to his office and they think he should. He's just a bit nervous because he hasn't played in so long. Try Bowie as well.'

I rang Sting. He was away, but I spoke to Miles Copeland, his manager. 'I'll ask him. Meantime, have you thought about Adam Ant?' I hadn't. I thought he was a bit passé. But then so were the Boomtown Rats, and each represented a certain period in pop history, so I agreed. I also thought that might entice him to encourage Sting, or perhaps all three of the Police.

Harvey came back from Wembley. 'There's no way we're going to get the place for free. They say the rent is £150,000.'

'The bastards. Everybody else is doing it for nothing. Should I have a go?'

'No, I haven't finished yet.'

That evening I spent several hours on the phone trying to track down Queen, who were on a world tour. It was 11 p.m. when eventually I got hold of their manager Jim Beech. 'Will they do it?'

'Well, the others want to.'

'Yes, but does Freddie? Will he do it?' We were talking about Freddie Mercury.

'Well his vanity wouldn't let him *not* do it, but he's a bit worried about his solo album, so leave it for a couple of days, Bob. We're working on it.'

It was midnight. The phone rang. It was Mike Mitchell in New York. 'I've put together the basic plan for the telecast. I'll get it across to you. I'm bringing in Hal Uplinger to help put up the European networks. Later I'll bring in Tony Verna, who will actually direct the whole thing on the day. He's good. I worked with him on the Olympics. How's the TV going at your end?'

'We're working on it.'

It was 1 a.m. The phone rang again. It was Elvis Costello in London. 'Sorry it's late, Bob. I got your message. I'd love to do something. I'll be in Moscow just before, but I think I'll be back in time.'

It was 4 a.m. The phone rang. It was Bill Gordon in Australia. 'Bill who?'

'Bill Gordon. Sorry it's late, Bob. Listen, I've had this idea about extending your Live Aid coverage to Australia . . .' I snatched a few hours' sleep. This was to be the pattern for the next two months.

Next day I phoned Bryan Ferry. We had mutual friends. His wife, Lucy, answered the phone.

'Has he decided?' I had put Lucy on the project, making it her special duty to persuade him. Ferry is a very shy man. He seemed nervous when I first put it to him.

'He still hasn't decided. And his band will all be over in America then. He says it will cost a lot to fly them and the gear across for a fifteen-minute appearance. It's a problem.'

I gave her what was becoming my standard spiel. 'What problems are there? There is no such thing as a problem. Whatever problems there are tell me, because we can eliminate them. If he can't get a sax player, I can get him a sax player. If he can't pay for the flights, I can get someone to pay for the flights. Whatever he wants I can organize. All he has to do is say yes.'

'I'll have another word with him.'

Harvey came back from Wembley. 'I've got them down to £100,000. I don't think we'll get anything better than that. There are the other possibilities we talked about, but Milton Keynes is not much more than a field, and Aston Villa's in Birmingham. Wembley is enclosed and has better security, it's in London, which is easier for the bands. And, of course, it's the big flagship venue. We've got the stage already set up there from the Springsteen gigs, which will save a lot. What do you think?'

'Pay them. It's got to be London, for the symbolic value if nothing else.'

IMG is Mark McCormack's international promotions firm. McCormack manages major sports personalities and other celebrities. He even managed the Pope's tour of England. Quite early on IMG had intimated that they would be prepared to organize international sponsorship and television. A week earlier we had met them and they had said that the concert would be worth about $200,000 worldwide.

'That's a joke. I could raise that without getting out of bed. You have four days to come up with a proposal. We anticipate at least three million on TV rights alone and God knows what on sponsorship.'

'You won't get it,' one of the men said. They were all in their late fifties.

'I don't think you understand what we're doing, or pop music.' They didn't and they were out.

I rang Bernard Doherty. 'How's it going with Bowie and McCartney?'

'David's office has told him and they said he was asked to do another benefit for Africa. He asked, "Is Geldof involved? I'm only doing the Geldof thing," so that's positive. However, he's filming at that time and it'll be touch and go whether he can put a band together. Paul's people all think it's a great idea. They're really trying to persuade him. Basically he is nervous. He hasn't played for eight years and you're asking him to play in front of half the world. But they're working on him.'

That night I bumped into Stewart Copeland, the drummer with the Police. Stewart was becoming more and more involved with doing things for Band Aid at that time. 'Why don't the Police play? Has the band broken up?'

'Well, it's not supposed to have, but it has in effect.'

'Well, why not get back together for it?'

'You'd better ask Sting.'

I phoned Sting. 'Did Miles tell you about Live Aid?'

'I don't remember it.'

I told him what was planned. 'Why don't you do something with Police?'

'Oh, Bob, don't ask me to do that. I'll do something by myself.'

I needed to confirm the TV companies. Channel 4 had been enthusiastic, but when I rang they told me they couldn't afford to do it. It would cost them half a million pounds in cancellation fees to clear their schedules for a whole day. Then it would cost them a similar amount to reschedule the same programmes for a future date. A million pounds. I hadn't considered this. I had thought I was giving them a day's free programming. I had thought they would be grateful. They turned it down and I was worried.

Our old promotions man, 'Spanner' Sweeney, had called the BBC and spoken to Mike Appleton, the producer of their major rock show *The Old Grey Whistle Test*. Appleton called me and asked who was on the show. I gave him the list of people playing. I lied about some, but it was only because I hadn't asked them yet, I rationalized.

It was May 13th. Eight weeks before the date and still no TV. Appleton went to Roger Laughton, Head of the Special Projects department. He told him he wanted to do the show. He had an all-night rock show going out in the autumn called Rock Around the Clock. He said he was prepared to sacrifice that for the Band Aid concert. That evening there was a meeting with BBC 2's controller, Graeme McDonald. In the minutes of that meeting, at the very bottom of the page, is item No. 16: 'Mike Appleton raised the possibility of a Band Aid rock marathon'. 'Listen,' said Appleton later, 'we're not quite sure what we're getting ourselves into but basically our response is yes. There will be problems with the telethon aspect because it may be against the BBC charter and we're going to have terrible problems if you get any sponsorship. But we like the idea of it and we're prepared to say yes in principle and then work on the details . . .'

Next week we had risen from item No. 16 to No. 1: 'We agreed Band Aid concert something the BBC *must* be involved in'. But BBC2 were already scheduled to broadcast Handel's Fireworks Music live from Hyde Park on July 13th. The Handel organizers agreed to have it filmed and put out a day later. It was also illegal to shift the Open University programming scheduled for just after midnight and this looked like becoming a major problem. Michael Grade, the Controller of BBC1, and now a Band Aid Trustee, suggested that at 10 p.m. the show transfer to BBC1 for the remaining five or six hours. This was perfect. When BBC1 came in so did Radio 1. We now had blanket national coverage for seventeen hours of pop music. It was one of several firsts.

Tony Boland, the Irish producer, had called me back and said, 'We're in. All the way. Full telethon. No problem. See you'. I don't think I heard from Tony again until he showed up at the international producers' meetings with his partner, Niall Matthews. Without doubt the Irish Telethon was the best produced, resulting in the greatest net contribution per head of population.

After that it became really serious. I had got the American music television station, MTV, to agree to turn their whole day over to Live Aid; even if we didn't get networking we had, through MTV, 40% of the American TV market. I had asked MTV for money. They hadn't any, but they gave us all the advertising revenues received that day as well as the use of their satellite and a tie-in with their independent station affiliates. Meanwhile, Mitchell had begun negotiations with the big three American TV networks.

I phoned Bowie's office in New York and asked if he was going to do the concert. They were still dithering. I needed to know about Bowie because he was one of the really big names. I took a risk. 'Look, it's not a problem if he can't do it, but just tell us because we've got to know now.' David agreed. Harvey had rung Phil Collins' manager in Japan, where Phil was touring. Phil said he'd do it, but he suggested playing in *both* concerts. Harvey agreed.

I phoned the office of Lord King, head of British Airways, to ask about getting free flights for all performers getting to the concerts. I had wanted to use an aspect of the west's technological advancement to show how ridiculous it was that we could stage something like this and still people starved. Concorde was the obvious means. I asked Lord King for Concorde to link the two venues. Phil Collins was serious about trying to play both gigs and there were others who would want to go too. It would be very practical and only possible with that plane, which can cross the Atlantic in under four hours. They said they'd let me know.

I was working from anywhere I could find a phone and anywhere I had to be for any other reason – home, Harvey's office, the Band Aid office, Phonogram. I was in the record company office one day, having another crack at getting a coherent response out of Stevie Wonder's office, when Francis Rossi came in. Status Quo had split up some time ago.

'How's it going, Bob?'

'What do you want, the good news or the bad? The successes or the problems?'

'Try me with the good.'

I gave him a list of those who had promised to play.

'That's fantastic. God, I wish Quo hadn't split up. It would be great to play on a bill like that. Maybe we should get back together for it. Would you have us?'

'Like a shot.'

'I'll talk to the others.'

U2 were in America. It took a while and a lot of toing and froing to get hold of them. I thought for a horrible minute they were going to refuse. They were one of the great new bands. They were Irish like myself. They had been so great on the record, why should they say no? They couldn't say no. They said yes.

Harvey came back from Wembley. 'They have got this catering firm, called ARA, which has the franchise to do the catering at any Wembley event . . .'

'So? They can just donate all their profit to Band Aid.'

'They could. But they won't. They said they won't forgo any of it.'

'But we can't have that. We can't have the *food* company being the only one making any profit on the day when everyone else is working free to help the starving.' I did a quick piece of arithmetic. 'I reckon they could make three-quarters of a million quid that day. I think I'd better go and see them.'

That night at the regular Thursday Band Aid trustees' meeting, the other trustees seemed less sceptical than before. It seemed like it was coming together. They had been nervous, thinking I'd over-reached myself. Now they said, 'What are you going to call it?'

'Well, it's like the record live,' I said. 'I was thinking of "Live Aid".'

'Yeah, I like it,' said Harvey.

Sade, whose manager had seemed indifferent to the record, now told Harvey she'd love to do it. Wham! were in. I reminded Spandau Ballet and Paul Young, who had said yes so long ago I wasn't sure they remembered. Alison Moyet would play. She was pregnant and therefore didn't want to make any guarantees, but said that if possible she would do a song with Paul Young. George Michael would sing with Elton. Boy George had told me that he didn't think Culture Club would necessarily be able to do the gig but that he would certainly appear and would do something with a black singer called Pauline with whom he had been working.

We went to a meeting with the European Broadcasting Union. Representatives from all the European TV stations who would be taking the BBC pictures were there, all except the French who didn't show up and consequently made a mess out of all the Live Aid fund-raising there. The Europeans came up with dozens of technical objections. 'Listen, I'm not a technician', I said. 'But it seems simple enough. There is a feed out of England and a feed from America. If you are a commercial station, as soon as you see the Live Aid logo spinning it means you have a three-minute commercial break. At any point you can opt out of the international signals and if you have a domestic band or commentator standing by, you can put them on your own national network. At specific times you will have an up-line to the satellite and that will go out on the international feed. Four shows will be coming from Philadelphia: the English signal, the international signal, the American domestic signal, and the ABC special. We will be taking the BBC signal. You must organize your own fund-raising, but again I stress it is a pre-requisite of the show. Our accountants will check with you. Any problems call us.'

That night Mitchell rang from New York to report on his progress with the three major American networks. He was playing a very risky game. Two networks had turned it down out of hand. The only one which was interested was ABC, which had slipped to second in the ratings and had least to lose and most to gain by doing something adventurous. 'They have offered half a million, which is not good, not good at all. So I have told them it is not enough because the other two have each offered a million.'

'Have they?'

'Gee, no, they haven't offered at all. We have to have a network deal, Bob, to get sponsorship.'

'I heard,' I said, 'that unless it's prime time in America the Russians won't take it. Is that true?'

'Yes, oddly enough. Their TV values coincide exactly with ours. They reckon if it's safe enough for the American networks, it's safe enough for their comrades.'

'So what happens next?'

'I've given ABC until Friday noon to come up with a better offer. I'll ring you then.'

Next morning the phone rang. I had been trying for some time to track down Mick Jagger. I finally got him at home and he said he'd see me in the Savoy when he came to London. I bought a copy of *The Emperor*, a remarkable book about Ethiopia by a Polish journalist called Ryszard Kapuscinski, and took it to him. I had my little dog, Growler, with me at the time. The first thing he did when we entered the hotel suite was eat Jagger's breakfast. I had met Jagger only once before at a party after a Stones gig in Madrid one weekend when I had gone over to Spain with Paula to watch the World Cup Final. Today it was another friendly meeting. I told him about Ethiopia and asked him about the concert.

'Well, I don't know if the Stones would do it,' he said. 'Is David doing it?'
'Yes.'

'We're in the middle of this album and things aren't great at the moment. But yeah, I'm up for it, I'll do it even if the others won't.'

I was delighted. The more people like Jagger we got the more the American networks would buy. His involvement was vital. Besides, here was the man who had made my teenage years bearable, one of the greatest rock singers of all time having breakfast with me.

My main problem at the time was with the American acts, I explained. Michael Jackson just didn't seem to want to do it. I rang Quincy Jones to talk to him. I rang his manager, Frank de Leo, I rang Walter Yetnikoff, the Chairman of Columbia Records to talk to him. I was having real problems with all the American black acts, to be honest. 'Diana Ross's excuse is that she's in LA, whatever sort of an excuse that is. Kragen says Lionel Richie is "doing his album" and he can't do it. Prince had retired or something. Tina Turner is on tour, and Stevie Wonder's weird.'

'Why?' Mick asked.

'Well, I called Keith Harris, who's his big friend, and he rang Stevie, who said he didn't want to be the token black. So I told Keith he wasn't that. Billy Ocean, Ashford and Simpson, and Kendricks and Ruffin from the original Temptations were all doing it. Keith rang Stevie again and he said OK, he'd do it. Then a guy called Ewart Abner rang two days later and said he wasn't doing it, he didn't care what Stevie said . . . A fuck up. And most of the American bands just keep asking: "Is Bruce doing it . . . ?"'

'*Is* Bruce doing it?' Mick asked.

'Well, he's said he'll think about it, but I don't think he will. Landau says he's tired and he's just got married . . .'

'Fuck me, I would have thought that was a good reason *for* doing it.'

'Apparently he wants to spend some time with his missus.'

'Fuck me.'

'Anyway, I'll see him in Newcastle in a couple of days and ask him. Will you definitely do it?'

'Yeah, definitely, even if the rest won't, I'll put a band together and rehearse something.'

In Newcastle I met the head of the Wembley Caterers, ARA, who turned out to be a large American company.

'Either you forgo your profit or you give us a percentage,' I said.

'If you provide the staff for the aisles for the day, we'll give you ten per cent of what they sell.'

'Fuck off! We give you free staff and you give us ten per cent! How generous! That's less than the wages you'd have to pay anyway. You give us your profit or I'll ask everyone who buys a ticket to bring packed food with them and boycott your stalls.'

'I don't think you can do that.'

'I think I can do what I like, pal.'

The next day we went to a technical meeting at the BBC. 'OK. Who's doing the telephones for the fund-raising?' Silence. 'Who knows anything about telephones?'

A hand went up at the back. 'Well, me and my wife work in Support Services, it's part of the BBC. We'll try, but we don't have much time.'

Early on the Friday I phoned Mitchell in New York. 'How's it going?'

'The good news is that we've got a million-dollar sponsorship deal from Pepsi on the basis of our network TV deal. The bad news is that we haven't got a network TV deal yet.'

'ABC haven't called back?'

'ABC haven't called back.'

'Shit.'

'Shit.'

I had spoken to Pete Townshend over the years. I rang him now, and as usual he was refreshingly direct.

'Yes, of course I'll do it. But what you really want is for The Who to get together, isn't it?'

That was something I had not dared to ask. The final split in The Who was, I had heard, bitter and irrevocable. 'That would be unbelievable.'

'I'll see what I can do.'

The phone rang. It was Mitchell. 'ABC have come in for a million dollars.' Now I could really go for the Yanks.

Hal Uplinger had come up with the idea of putting a four-hour edited version in the diplomatic bag from the States to every country in the world which had a TV station, but which did not have the equipment to pick up from the satellites. We would reach an audience well in excess of a billion people. The idea of there being no representative of what had been the greatest band in pop music seemed unthinkable, so I wrote to Paul McCartney at home and asked if he would sing 'Let It Be': 'Beatles music for some reason evokes more emotional response than any other. "Let It Be" is like a hymn to faded dreams.' I asked him if he would do it at the end of the show. 'If you do, the world will cry,' I wrote. I knew he must get a hundred requests to do things, but I really felt that the programme would not be complete without him there. I was not writing to Paul McCartney, the man, I said, but to PAUL McCARTNEY the phenomenon. If he played, millions would watch who would not otherwise watch. That would mean money would come in which would not otherwise come in. If he felt he really couldn't do it, there would be no pressure. But if he did, it would be the crowning glory to the enterprise. As I sealed the letter, I knew I could do no more.

We had heard nothing positive from the head of British Airways. 'My partner, Ed, knows some guy in the press office there. I'll get him on the case,' said Harvey.

I decided to go to Paris where both the Stones and Duran Duran were recording albums. It was Ronnie Wood's birthday and there was a party in a little club. I cornered Bill Wyman and asked him to do Live Aid.

'Give us a break, Bob, we've done millions of those charity gigs.'

'Not this one you haven't. It's a one-off.'

'Look, even if we all agreed to do it, you'd never get Keith to agree.'

'Why not?'

'Cos Keith doesn't give a fuck.'

'That's the one argument there's no answer to,' I said. As it happened, Keith Richard did actually appear in Philadelphia with Bob Dylan, so maybe Bill was wrong.

I went on to see the Durans. Their reticence was bewildering. They are good friends of mine. They had been one of the bands who had initially been most keen. Now they were no longer a certainty. I could understand: the band was in a mess, going through one of those disruptive periods which all bands suffer from time to time. Two of the band had gone off and formed Power Station, a parallel band designed to give vent to their urge to do something more rock-orientated. The others were working on Arcadia, their own project. I went to the studio to see them. I decided the softly-softly approach was best. During a break in the recording one of them asked me how it was going. 'OK. We have Jagger, Bowie, Phil Collins, Elton, and Quo are reforming. The Who may be doing the same. We have Paul Young, Wham!, the Spans, Sting, Sade. We're doing all right.'

'Fucking hell, that's quite a line up.'

'Maybe we should do it after all.'

'Yeah, if you like. But we're doing all right. Still, I talked to John in New York and he said Power Station was doing it.'

'I didn't know that. Fuck me, we should do it.'

'Well look,' I suggested diplomatically, 'you and Nick and Roger could do

Arcadia in London, get on Concorde with Phil Collins, Power Station come on in America and then you join Andy and John for Duran. That'll stop all the rumour and be a bit of a vibe.'

'Brilliant,' said Simon, 'I'd love to play again.'

'Yeah,' said Nick, more cautiously.

Back in London I phoned Sir Kenneth Newman, the Commissioner of the Metropolitan Police, and asked if we could have free policing on the day. He rang back the next day and said yes. That was £15,000 saved, I reckoned.

The man from BBC Support Services rang. 'We've got twenty phones.'

'Twenty! That's no use. We need thousands.' There was no way British Telecom could provide that number so quickly. They said if I could put the concert off for a week, their new computerized system would be in use. But we couldn't change the date now, and set to work contacting companies with large switchboards dormant at weekends.

Harvey came back from Wembley. 'The Wembley people have offered to get their art department to design a Live Aid logo for us, but they say the merchandizing company who, like the catering company, have an exclusive franchise, want a percentage. They won't budge.'

'Well, I think we should ring the whole stadium with caravans selling Band Aid merchandise and advise people that anything else is a bootleg and the money is going straight into someone's pocket. It would be relatively easy to set up an alternative system.' 'I don't think it'll be necessary,' said Harvey. 'It's just Wembley acting the prick.' In fact, as the days went by and the head of the merchandising firm, Mick Worwood, became more and more involved, he became invaluable and took over the creating of the official Live Aid programme which, through advertising and production deals, was massively in profit, before a single copy was sold. He also helped to obtain sponsorship – crucial as the date drew nearer.

A letter arrived from the Stones' office. It said the band wished Live Aid well but felt unable to participate. I phoned Harvey. Harvey said he'd call Prince Rupert Lowenstein, the Stones' business manager. 'Does that mean all the Stones, Rupert?'

'Yes.'

I phoned Jagger. 'Mick, what the fuck . . .'

'Yes, it's OK. It's just hassle with the band; I have to say that at the moment. But I'll be there, I give you my word.'

We had got to the stage where everything was well underway in the UK, but in America, despite frequent phone calls to Bill Graham, nothing seemed to be happening. No venue had been decided upon and there were only a couple of weeks to go before the press conference at which everything was to be announced. The obvious venue was New York, both from a logistical and a symbolic point of view. In my mind it should be Shea Stadium, where the

Beatles had done their famous American concert. I decided I'd better go over and see for myself.

The trip was a disaster. I arranged to meet Ron Delsener, who was the big New York promoter. Delsener is a funny man in a brusque and rude New York way, but he could not seem to grasp the televisual nature of the event nor its global symbolism. He kept suggesting we should just do five nights at Forest Lawn which would make a lot more money than a one-off gig at Shea. I told him we had to try and get everything for free.

'Never happen,' said Ron.

'Yes, it can,' I said.

'Not with the unions.'

'Can we get Ed Koch in on this? He's a populist mayor.'

He took me off to a party to meet Ed Koch. 'Mayor, this is Bob Geldof,' said Ron to the Mayor who was a surprisingly tall man who moved about the room fast, talking very rapidly to groups of people in the beautifully re-decorated Mayoral residence.

'What can I do for you?' said the Mayor, looking over my shoulder to see if anyone more interesting was about to come in.

I explained briefly and speedily, and then I asked him for a free stadium.

'We'll look into that one, Bob.'

I asked him for a city subsidy.

'We'll look into that one, Bob.'

I asked him for free policing.

'We'll look into that one, Bob.'

'You do understand, Mr Mayor, that we expect half a billion people to watch this?'

Suddenly his gaze concentrated upon me. 'Half a billion?' He turned to his aide. 'We gotta do this. Ron, you got Bob's phone number. We'll be in touch, Bob.'

But Shea Stadium was a mess. It was being refurbished and a huge section of the seats was unsafe. The cost of the policing would be vast and Koch found that, as Ron had said, because of the unions he couldn't provide staff for nothing. Other unions were just as unco-operative. We considered Madison Square Garden, but it was too small and we'd have had to charge too much for the tickets. We looked at an alternative in nearby New Jersey. That meant bringing in another local promoter, John Sher. Giants' Stadium at the Meadow-lands would have been ideal, but we found that to get clearance from the football league, we would have had to buy ten thousand tickets at $25 each for the football game scheduled for the day after the concert. They demanded that their players announce the acts during the concert. It was a form of black-mail. The football league were scared that few people would come to their game. Bill Graham got them alternative practice sites. I also saw Mitchell again, who was proceeding well with the sponsorship deals, and flew back to London.

'Look, New York is out of the question so we are left with four options,' Harvey said. 'We can go with Graham in California, which is useless because of the time difference. We can go for Meadowlands and have all the problems with Delsener, Sher and the footballers. We can go for the RFK stadium in Washington which has no local promoter who I feel happy about, or we can go for Philadelphia which is only an hour from New York, is served by four airports and has one of the best promoters in the States, Larry Magid.'

'Washington would be good from a symbolic point of view . . . London, Washington, y'know.'

'But the stadium is in the middle of a freeway an hour from everywhere.'

'Philadelphia's crap. What symbolic significance does that have?'

'I don't fucking know. Who cares?' Harvey said in his pragmatic way. 'The stadium is free, no charge, whatever. Full co-operation of the mayor. Police, everything.'

'Why would they do all that for free?' I asked.

'Well, I suppose they need some good PR. They've just had that incident where the police bombed that house full of black anarchists, killed them all and set the whole block on fire.'

'Jesus, Harv, can we have Philadelphia with all that going on?'

Pete Townshend rang. 'Look, it's no good. I'll do it, but Roger will only do it if Kenny doesn't play. But John *won't* do it if Kenny doesn't play.'

'John won't do it. Why John?'

'He says it's because of what Roger has said about Kenny in the past. John says that Roger can never forgive Kenny for not being Keith.'

'Do you mind if I phone John? Will it do any good?'

'It won't do any harm.'

This was The Who, one of the greatest bands in the history of pop music. One of them, Keith Moon, the wild drummer, was dead. Kenny Jones had replaced him. The two protagonists, Roger Daltrey and Pete Townshend, lead singer and song-writing genius, were locked in a classic love-hate relationship. And John Entwistle stood with his bass, ever on the sidelines, ever dragged into the acrimony and bitter rows.

'John, what's wrong? I thought the problem was Townshend and Daltrey. Not you.'

'Roger won't play with Kenny, and anyway it's not just a question of Kenny. It goes far deeper than that. I just couldn't bear to get up on stage again and go through all that.'

'But John, I don't know, but I've heard none of you feel you said goodbye properly to your fans. Well, how better to do it than at Live Aid? Of course there are skeletons in the cupboard, but where better to lay them to rest than in front of the whole world? There will be a billion people watching. You'll never have the opportunity again.'

'Thanks, Bob, but you know, I just couldn't.'

'John, I hate to use this argument, but believe me I'm not doing this for personal interest, I'm not doing it because I want to see The Who together again. I'm doing it because there are children dying and if The Who perform it will be, of itself, a major event. More people will watch and more people will give. In the end, that's what it boils down to.'

'You know I will play with anyone on that day. But please don't ask me to get up on that stage again with the others after all these years. I don't think I could stand it. Anything else.'

I rang Pete. 'I don't know, I don't think he'll do it. Can I ring Roger?'

'If you like.'

I spoke with Daltrey at length. There were too many things that I couldn't understand going between those three. All the useless baggage and debris of twenty years of being together. They were always volatile. It was probably the source of their genius. In the end, though, I hated doing it. I gave him the only ultimate argument. If they played, they would be responsible for saving a few people's lives. It was true, but it sounded corny. It came in the end down to personal responsibility.

'That's a hard argument to answer, Bob.'

'It's the only argument there is, Roger.'

★   ★   ★

Harvey came back from Wembley. 'You know that artwork . . .'

'Yeah, it's good. Africa shaped like a guitar with Live Aid across the neck.'

'Well, they're charging us for it and insist that the designer gets a credit every time it's used.'

'You're joking.' I got on the phone. 'You agreed to do this for free, and now there's a bill. You realize that everybody involved in Live Aid is doing everything for free except you people. Well you can just fuck off . . . we're not paying for half an hour's doodle . . . Fuck off. Well, you can sue us . . . you can take your writ and shove it up your arse.'

Later Andy Zweck, who had worked on the Rock in Rio festival, said it was just a rip-off of their logo, anyway, with South America replaced by Africa. We wrote to the Rio people and they gave us permission to use it. But we still had to pay the guy. And he still rings up for a credit on things.

★   ★   ★

'It's got to be Philadelphia. It's a tried and tested option.'

'Fuck off, Harvey. It can't be Philadelphia for the same reason it couldn't be Milton Keynes or Stoke-on-Trent. It must be an international city.'

'Bob, it's got to be Philadelphia. It is 2 a.m. We have to announce Live Aid at press conferences in London and New York tomorrow. We do not have a venue. It has to be Philadelphia. Trust me.'

'OK, OK, Philadelphia. Jesus.'

The morning of the press conference Pete Townshend rang. 'We're doing it as The Who.'

★   ★   ★

The press conference brought a salutary restoration of perspective. Having to set forth the whole business to a group of people who knew little about it was a useful break from the mad blurring whirl of phone calls, flights, and meetings. Still the images of the African holocaust never left me during the endless round of requesting and demanding, cajoling and protesting, bargaining and bluffing, organizing and re-organizing. Coming when my exhaustion reached its most extreme, those memories were the whips which spurred me and which, in the last resort, I did not hesitate to use on others. But somehow the whole thing came together when we had to set out our stall for the media. We had the impressive line up of performers: David Bowie, Mick Jagger, Stevie Wonder, Sting, Phil Collins, Status Quo, Queen, Wham!, Spandau Ballet, Duran Duran, Paul Young, Sade, U2, the Cars . . . it was beginning to sound like a *Who's Who* of the pop industry. To cap it all we had the reformation of The Who and a man who, we were able to announce, was 'one of the biggest

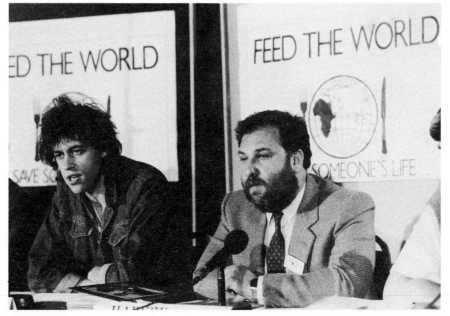

Harvey and I announcing Live Aid.

names in pop music'. We had, at the same time, two Band Aid ships already underway for Assab in Ethiopia loaded with grain, medical supplies and other relief goods. We had already delivered substantial quantities of emergency high-energy food and drugs by air to Addis Ababa and Khartoum. Kevin Jenden was beginning the negotiations in Sudan and Kuwait to buy two fleets of lorries which Band Aid would use to break the cartel of truck owners in the Sudan who had a stranglehold on the market which they had used to treble prices for the delivery of food to the famine-stricken areas in the west.

The press conferences were not without their problems, however, especially in New York where a certain section of the press attacked the line-up on the grounds that it contained few black acts. I was furious, as I had gone out of my way to ask all the big-name black acts in the States – Diana Ross, Lionel Richie, Michael Jackson, Prince – and had had no response. I had asked Quincy Jones to help and he had put two people from his office on to the problem. They had come up with very little, though not from want of trying. I said, 'I have asked them all. Perhaps you should address the question not to me, but to them.'

From this point the Live Aid carousel of chaos and confusion went into overdrive. Prince had just retired and it would be embarrassing to change his mind a month later. The fastest comeback in history. Could he do a video? OK.

Stevie says No, Yes, No, Yes. 'And we have Stevie Wonder,' we announced.

Next day I got an irate call. 'This is Ewart Abner. Who told you to announce Stevie Wonder?'

'Er, Stevie.'

'No, he didn't.'

'Who are you?'

'I'm involved in his management, how did you contact him?'

'Through Keith Harris, who spoke with him at 11 o'clock last night.'

'I'll call you back.'

I rang Keith. 'Keith, some guy called Ewart Abner says Stevie said no.'

'No, he said yes, he was going to do it. He'd decided.'

'Can you ring Abner?'

Ewart Abner rang me. 'Bob we're in sympathy with your position, but Stevie's finishing an album and he can't interrupt it. He really wants to do it, but I've insisted he continue on this project. We're about six months overdue and Motown are going crazy. I'm sure you understand so please issue a press statement to that effect, would you?'

'OK,' I said in tones of deep depression.

'This afternoon, Bob, or we'll have to issue our own.'

I didn't. They rang back and I still didn't. Maybe they did. I don't know, I didn't care.

Meanwhile, Kris Kristofferson had offered to play either by himself or with

Willie Nelson, who was still in at that point, and Waylon Jennings, and Neil
Young who Elliott Roberts managed.

'I'm not going to mention Tom, Bob,' said Elliott.

'Tom who, Elliott?' I sighed.

'Tom Petty, but forget I mentioned him.'

Tom Petty was a good addition, I don't know why I'd forgotten him.

But Kris Kristofferson kept getting messed around because Bill Graham
didn't want him on so he pulled out. Bryan Adams said he'd come down from
Canada which was great, because Bryan started Northern Lights, the Canadian
Band Aid. Then Cyndi Lauper whose boyfriend/manager had said she wouldn't
do it changed his mind and said she would. But then she had an operation and
went to hospital. She said she might do it in a wheelchair, but in the end she
didn't. Teddy Pendergrass *did*, which was fabulous, because it was his first gig
after an accident he'd had. There was a lot of stuff going down with the local
blacks and Teddy Pendergrass being at risk because he was a local black guy
himself and *maybe* shouldn't be doing the show. But then Patti LaBelle did it
and she is a local black. On the day Teddy cried and sang beautifully and said
something about being killed, and I thought 'Fuck me, what's happening
now?' Then Led Zeppelin said they were going to re-form and Phil Collins
was going to play drums and that would be like the second coming in the
U.S., and then Paul McCartney said 'yes' and someone from his office later
said, 'No one minds here if you want to call George and Ringo'. So I called
George who was in Maui, but he said, 'He didn't ask me to sing on it ten years
ago, so why does he want me now?' I said to Denis, his partner, 'It's friendly.
Can you make a gesture?' But no dice. But I didn't ever really think it was a
good idea, because one of the Beatles is dead. People in the papers said, 'Julian
could do it,' but Julian isn't his dad and it might have been distasteful. As Paul
said before his mike broke, 'Let It Be'.

I called Billy Joel. I liked him, he was a nice bloke. No problem, he'd do it.
I announced him. He had a problem getting his band together. Then his
manager rang. 'Hi, Bob. Billy can't get his sax player.'

'Can't he use another sax player?'

'No, Bob, he can't.'

'Oh. Can he just play piano by himself?'

'Bob, don't ask me to fuck with my artist's art. I would never ask my artist
to do that. This is his career.'

'It's only fifteen minutes.'

'Yes, but Billy isn't going to do a sloppy fifteen minutes, not in front of the
world. If he can't get his whole band together, he's out.'

In the States Bill Graham, who as a boy in Europe had narrowly escaped
death because of Hitler's anti-semitic policies, had recently organized a protest
against President Reagan's visit to the German cemetery where SS officers

were buried. In retaliation a pro-Nazi group had burned down his California offices and Bill was for weeks badly shaken. He also had similar problems at home. Live Aid was not the consideration uppermost in his mind.

I rang Paul Simon, whom I'd met and had an enjoyable argument with before. He said yes. Better than that, he said he'd try and persuade Dylan and maybe the two of them would do something together. I rang the Beach Boys. One of them was in Philadelphia when I rang. He was meditating, and he took it as a special sign that he had been in Philadelphia at the moment I asked them to do the Live Aid gig. They said yes.

Paula was interviewing Tina Turner for *The Tube*. I decided to go up and see her. 'Honestly, Bob, we can't do it. We're touring in Canada then. We have a date that night in Frederickstown,' said her manager, Roger Davies. He got out his diary to prove that it wasn't just an excuse.

In England tickets had been put on sale. They sold as fast as we could take in the money. That evening there were none left in London. We had sent some out to the provinces to be sold through coach firms. Within three days there were none left at all.

British Airways phoned. They offered us a package which included Concorde on the day with a radio link so that Phil Collins could broadcast from the plane, plus fifty-thousand pounds worth of free air tickets.

Roger Davies rang back. 'I've spoken to Tina. She wants to cancel the Frederickstown gig. Mick spoke to Tina as well, they're going to do something together.'

Bernard Doherty called. 'David and Mick want to do a transatlantic duet. Can we have a meeting to talk about it?' That evening we sat in Bernard's office: Mick Jagger, David Bowie and his PA, Coco, Harvey, Bernard and me. We rang Tony Verna, the technical director in New York.

'The problem is that if Mick is in the States and David is in London there will be a time-gap while the messages bounce back and forth between the satellites. We can get it down to half a second, but there'll be a gap.'

'Could we use the time delay as an echo, like in reggae?' I sang Bob Marley's 'One Love' as an example. Jagger and Bowie joined in. I sang, 'One love, one heart, let's get together and feel all right.' Then Bowie sang it. Then Jagger. Then together. Verna was somewhere in America listening to Bowie and Jagger crackling down the phone at him. He said later he was too shocked to run off and get a tape and record it for himself. It seemed unbelievable to me that I was sitting in a room with these two rock greats, working out a song, making suggestions to them, singing with them. SINGING with them. Fuck me! It was so odd hearing their two familiar voices together in that tiny room. Jagger was tilted back on his chair. Bowie sat beside me on a sofa. I started 'one love, one heart,' Jagger and Bowie harmonized on the last line, then David began in his low voice 'one love', and Jagger in a great blues shout repeated 'one love', then Bowie deep and sad 'one heart', Jagger like an old black woman 'one heart' and then joyously together 'let's get together and feel all right'.

'No, that won't work,' said Tony Verna. 'Because Mick in Philly won't be able to hear David in Wembley and vice versa. Only the TV audience will hear both.'

'That's worse than useless.'

'Well, the other option is to do a video of one of them singing and then synch them together so that it will look like it's live at each end, but one of them will be miming . . .'

The meeting ended on a down note. The miming would have been a cheat. 'Fucking hell,' said Harvey. 'That would've been amazing.' David and Mick went off to a nightclub together and spent the evening trying to outdo each other on the dance floor. It gave them an idea.

★   ★   ★

There were now weekly meetings, held at the BBC, of the European Broadcasting Union. It became increasingly clear that many of them did not understand the point of the exercise. Some of them were not organizing proper fund-raising facilities to go with the broadcast; they were simply treating it just as a massive pop concert. Others, who had understood that and had seen some hint of my irritation, were pretending to have telethons but had organ-

The original roster: spot the people who didn't play and which ones were missing.

Mick and David do their thing. Dancing in the make-up chair.

283

ized very little in reality. Others, like Danish TV, did not want to give any money to Live Aid. 'We always give it to the Lutheran Church.'

'Well, let the Lutheran Church organize their own concert. If you want ours, you give the money to Band Aid.'

The Germans had become suddenly reluctant because there had been a recent scandal in their country over the funds raised for some other telethon and they were having cold feet about the whole idea.

'Anyone who doesn't want to comply can just say so and I will take the programme away from them.'

'You can't do that. It's against the EBU rules. If it is available to one, it has to be available to all. You can't do that.'

'We'll see.'

Paul Simon rang. He was being messed about and he was upset. Every time he phoned anyone over there to get things organized he met a blank wall. He thought the whole thing was a mess. He felt that people were being deliberately obstructive to him and, as he and Bill don't get on, had decided to pull out. Willie Nelson, who is a very nice man, had already agreed to do it through his manager, and had been enthusiastic, but now had to withdraw. They offered an excuse, but I then heard it was because of Bill. The loss of both the acts was a serious blow to us. I made some calls to the States. It seemed that Bill Graham was still distracted. Whenever any of the people who had said they would play contacted his office, he was giving out the feeling that the whole situation was confused and that nothing was really going to happen. He and Mitchell had started to have rows, because Mitchell was contacting acts direct and not through Graham. Mitchell said he needed definite confirmation from individual bands in order to get television sponsors interested, and Graham's attitude wasn't helping. Harvey and I decided to go to the States. There were three weeks to go.

We met in New York with Bill Graham's people and with the staging crew. They had not yet put the tickets on sale, they didn't have a final bill of artists organized and they had even lost the plans for the circular stage which had been sent to them three weeks before. Graham had called in one of the best stage managers in the world, Michael O'Hearne. He knew what he was doing but he was being paid for it. We discovered that, unlike in Britain where everyone was working for nothing, in the States almost everyone expected to be paid. Only the bands and the promoters and Mitchell's crowd, Worldwide Sports and Entertainments, were working without payment; all the technical people, the PA and light companies, and everybody who was a member of a union had to be paid. We said no one was getting paid. They said there would be no show. It was too late to do anything about it. We cursed, but we realized that we just had to live with it. Philadelphia cost $3.5 million. Wembley cost $250,000. It was disappointing, because it was the spirit of the event that was important. It was everyone doing what they could for others.

It was someone's bright idea to drape the stage with the flags of every nation in the world. I hated the idea. It was cornball sentiment, I hate nationalism and, as Harvey said, 'All we fucking need is some cunt to hang Djibouti, or somewhere, upside down and we've got a civil war on our hands'. They had spent three weeks persuading the United Nations to let them have free copies of every flag of a member state, but they had lost the stage plans. O'Hearne had drawn up his own.

'But these are no good. You've divided the stage in two instead of three. That will never give you the time for these quick turn arounds when bands are doing just fifteen minutes each. In any case the stage ought to be identical in both places. This isn't two concerts, it's one.' In the event we were right. The turnarounds in Philadelphia were twice as long as Wembley and the stage looked constantly jammed. The Thompson Twins, for example, were given an impossible eleven minutes to set up their equipment.

We went to Philadelphia where Larry Magid's office turned out to be one island of sanity in a sea of blundering confusion. Harvey arranged to send two of his staff out from London to work from there duplicating with the American bands all the preparation we had done for Wembley. We met the deputy mayor and city officials, it was the first constructive meeting of the visit. 'Thank you for doing this,' I said to a senior official. 'We need it,' he said with appealing frankness.

Bill came alive at that meeting, making a brilliant speech to assembled city people. But relations between him and Mitchell had in effect broken down.

Mike now had several sponsors lined up and this took care of the cost of the event, thereby ensuring that the money donated by the public from the purchase of tickets or merchandise and from donations would all go to Live Aid. He had also put together an educational package to be distributed to schools and colleges, and newspapers and TV. There were also several public service messages taped. After the meeting we met executives from ABC. We had decided by this time that we were very pissed off with ABC. Mitchell had given them the earth in his attempt to get a network in on the deal. We were, for example, bearing the cost of all their outside broadcast technology, but they kept asking for more. Mitchell had managed to put together an 'ad hoc' network consisting of scores of independent TV stations who were going to take fifteen hours or more of the show. This alone covered eighty-five per cent of all TVs in the U.S. When ABC realized this they began to demand that all the biggest stars should perform within the three-hour prime time period that they were taking. They wanted exclusive acts from Britain – David Bowie, Elton John, Paul McCartney, The Who and Wham!

'We have to do it. We've given them our word,' said Mitchell.

'Have we fuck. They can shove off.'

'We have to network.'

'No, we don't. Mitchell's network represents 95 per cent of all the independent TV stations in America. We don't need them.'

Mitchell broke at that point. It was two in the morning in London. Harvey and I were on a conference line to him. There was a deep pause. I thought Mike was crying. He had been working the same as us, twenty hours a day with all the difficulties inherent in the U.S. production. He thought Graham was trying to screw him up. His team had put together and booked the biggest TV satellite link-up ever. There were sixteen satellites being used and countless ground stations. Now he was drained. He had no money and, like the rest of us, had put himself heavily into personal debt. Ananda Krishnan helped there, but this was the end. All his strategy had been based on ABC coming in. America's first ever network rock broadcast. Hours of it. 'Fine, I'll close everything down,' he said. 'I tried, but if you want me to . . .' and he broke off. I was exhausted. All day, all night, for months. I told Mike he was a genius, we needed him, there wasn't long to go, we needed ABC, but it had to be on our own terms.

I felt like crying myself. How many times did I have to say this and who would say it to me? Pulled apart by horses, I felt. Bands now constantly rang. People in every country had my phone number, every journalist had it. I thought it better to let them have it in case something came up and they needed me to check something before they printed it. Already I'd had problems.

I knew Huey Lewis from years ago. We had mutual friends in Mutt Lange, the Rats' original producer, and Phil Lynott of Thin Lizzy. I had met Huey again at the USA for Africa taping. Now he was a huge star, but he was still a laugh. I had rung him about Live Aid and he had said he didn't think it was a problem. He said his wife was expecting a baby and the only thing that would stop him was if the kid came before the gig. He didn't mind us using his name, however, if we wanted to.

I rang him again, nearer the date of press announcement and he said the others in the band felt they'd done their bit with the USA for Africa record and they'd also done a track for the composite album that followed it. I was getting suspicious. Why were all the West Coast bands so reluctant, what the hell was going on? Then I heard from another source, that someone was going around saying it wasn't going to happen, it was chaotic and unprofessional and that anyway they shouldn't do it, because it was essentially English and not American. This was confirmed when I called Huey's manager, Bob Brown. When I finished my conversation with Huey he said that he'd talk to the band and he'd still try and get there, depending on the baby's arrival.

After announcing we had Huey Lewis and the News, a story appeared more or less stating Huey couldn't appear because the band weren't sure about the distribution of funds. This was patent nonsense and, worse, it impugned our integrity, and, even worse, suggested we didn't know what we were doing when we had been working in Africa since January. I was incensed. I rang Bob Brown and told him that because of the public nature of the event, every meeting I had was minuted and every phone call was taped and I had in my hand two tapes of my conversation with Huey which said that the only reason he wouldn't do it was because of his wife's pregnancy and that if he wouldn't immediately withdraw his allegations, I would issue the tapes that afternoon to all three major networks.

'Is this conversation being taped?' Bob asked.

'Yes,' I replied. Of course I had no tape recording device. I was bluffing, but I had to get his suggestions withdrawn as they were untrue and extremely serious and would damage us severely. 'Look, if Huey doesn't want to do it, if *anyone* doesn't want to do it, it's not a problem. No one is forced to do it. It's only a bloody concert, for Chrissake.'

Bob then told me about people saying things and agreed to put out an amendment to their press release. He read me the text of his original press release which had been distorted, but still read badly. I was sad that Huey was out.

For every piece of good news something awful happened. It was the need to be able to encourage others, to always say, 'Of course it's possible,' that drained me. All day I would be on the telephone, and behind me would be a solid block of TV cameras. It was wearying. The French wouldn't participate. Every other country was not only taking the concert, they were also sending back a signal with one of their own bands, more or less exactly what the original idea had been. We had a man travelling between Moscow, Peking and Delhi fixing up their line and the Russian feed-back to us. I called the French Minister of Culture. He wouldn't talk to me. I called the head of the TV station. I told him it was a global cultural event. No, to them it was a pop concert and pop music was not French. They would show ten hours, late in the night and small hours. Wouldn't that be enough? 'I want children and old people and people who hate pop music to see it, so they can help,' I pleaded.

The Germans couldn't give us their money because we weren't a German organization. They were trying not to do an appeal at all. The Malays wanted to know if they could keep their money. Yes. No point in taking from the Third World to give to the Third World.

The cameras turned, their lights burning down my neck. I was scared at night in bed; quite literally, I lay in a bath of cold sweat. I would wake after being asleep for an hour, scared beyond reason. Imagine failing. Imagine failure on such a scale. The sheets were sopping wet. Paula wiped my back with a towel. For months she kept me sane. She and Anita, Fifi's nanny, answered the constantly ringing telephone. I had no answerphone and I couldn't take the phone off the hook in case it was important. It rang all day and all night. I often rose at six unable to sleep, my stomach in the knot you always read about, but never expect to experience. My head ached and buzzed most of the time. I didn't eat much. Steve and Mariella and Bernie and Linda at the press office slipped sandwiches over to me and I'd take them between phone calls. By now I was completely broke. Paula gave me money when I needed it. Our record contract had finished and I didn't know if I could get another one, nor did I have the time to think about it. I couldn't do Rats gigs to get money. I thought maybe I'd have to sell the house. But it didn't bother me too much, as I explained for the nth time to the nth journalist from the nth country what was going to happen and what we expected of their country. The days came and went. I was in a state of panic, but I couldn't show it. Everything had to be positive: 'Course you can do it.' 'Look, I'll ring him for you.' 'No we don't have any contracts with anyone, but they'll be there.' It had all been built on trust and a faith in some sort of decency. I was in Paris, New York, London, Newcastle, Philadelphia, New York, London. I'd come home numb, dreading the next day's papers where I'd read that someone else had pulled out and was blaming everyone but themselves in an attempt to alleviate the stigma of their own shame.

And now we'd finally come too far. I didn't care if ABC wanted to pull out, I couldn't care less. If the whole precarious, uncontracted thing unravelled, I didn't care. I'd tried. 'Mike we need you, and they're screwing you, so tell them they can go and fuck themselves.'

At the meeting with ABC we told them that they had what we wanted. 'You either take it or leave it. And if you take it the price goes up another half million bucks.' We delivered the ultimatum and then caught the plane back to London so that Harvey could brief and then despatch the two-man team he was sending over to Bill and Larry Magid.

ABC still had a good deal so when the three-hour ABC network special was confirmed, there was a lot of jockeying for position. Some people actually refused to play if they weren't on that. Some said they'd play, but only if I could guarantee network. It was no use me saying it would still be shown on 90% of the TV sets in America through the independents. Then ABC said the independents had to 'go down', i.e. not receive the transmission, while the network was on air. Eventually it was agreed MTV would 'stay up', but in the end I simply told people what they wanted to hear. If they asked whether they were 'network', I said 'yes'. It was easier that way.

The final acceptances were beginning to come in. I had called Dylan through everybody: personal friends, lawyers, record company. He had never said no, he'd also never said yes. Usually he spends the summer with his children on the West Coast, but we needed the person who articulated the conscience of an earlier generation. Elliott Roberts, his manager, had been brilliant, now he confirmed Dylan. This was excellent news for I still had no news from Ken Kragen about Lionel Richie. I therefore had to assume that we could not close the concert in Philly with 'We Are the World'. After that I originally thought we could end with Paul Simon's 'Bridge Over Troubled Water' and Dylan's 'The Times They Are a'Changin'' and then go onto 'Blowin' in the Wind'. Now Paul was out and Bob was in. Win some, lose some.

Eric Clapton was cancelling a gig at Caesar's Palace in Las Vegas. Black Sabbath were to reform too. Mick Jagger and David Bowie had produced their brilliant video of 'Dancing in the Street' to take the place of the abortive transatlantic duet. This was the result of Mick and David's night on the town. Mick was also to do a live duet with Tina Turner. Hall and Oates, who'd committed themselves early on, were to perform with Eddie Kendricks and David Ruffin of the original Temptations. This was the good stuff. Maybe this reconciliation of groups begun by The Who and these wonderful hybrids were unwittingly what Live Aid was about. I hadn't expected it, but people were using the opportunity of playing together the way a lot of them had always wanted to.

There is a general assumption that it was easy for bands to do it. It wasn't. Do you know how many times these people are asked to support things? Mick Jagger, for example, in the face of opposition from his own band, had to interrupt recording, come to England, rehearse and record a song with Bowie (who had to finish filming and put a band together and rehearse himself), choreograph and make a video, fly to America to rehearse with a new band, contact Tina Turner, rehearse a routine with her, then do the show. It meant weeks of work for free, and considerable inconvenience.

As well as Simple Minds and the Pretenders, Billy Ocean and Duran Duran flew to America with their equipment. They found rehearsal rooms, played for fifteen minutes, then flew home without charging a penny. Paul Young, Spandau Ballet and U2 flew in from everywhere. Bands paid for rehearsals and trucking, moving their stuff from coast to coast, cancelling lucrative concerts because this was where they wanted to be. They did a lot, those guys.

By this stage the American bands were at last starting to take the whole thing very seriously. Suddenly Bill Graham was fired with enthusiasm for the project and I began to understand his reputation. He got Madonna, Patti LaBelle, Joan Baez, Judas Priest, and many others. Then he started pushing people we didn't want. There were two acts in particular which he promoted on the West Coast. One of them threatened to pull out of their tour if they didn't get on the bill, the other said they would take their merchandising away from Bill's company. Ken Kragen, on location with Kenny Rogers, who I'd been calling, said Kenny could do it from London and maybe Lionel Richie would do it now, but it had to be secret, 'No,' I said. 'He's doing it or he's not. If he is then we'll announce it.' It would be awful if we couldn't end in America with 'We Are the World'. After all, every other country was doing their song.

Back in England The Who had had a rehearsal. It had been a shambles, there had been an almighty row and everyone had walked out after half an hour. 'It was a pretty standard Who rehearsal,' said Pete.

Mike Mitchell phoned late one night. 'We're having problems with Coke and Pepsi.'

'Why?' I yawned.

'Coke have bought up all the advertising time on ABC during the concert and they want permission to use the Live Aid logo.'

'But that'll make the whole thing look like a Coke event.'

'Exactly. Pepsi would be furious. They're sponsoring us for a million.'

Coke phoned. These days I seemed to be spending nineteen hours a day on the telephone. 'Can we have the logo?'

'No, Pepsi have got that.'

'But we're spending a million dollars on advertising.'

'But that money goes to ABC, not to Band Aid for Ethiopia.'

'We thought maybe we could do a separate deal, a T-shirt deal?'

'Well, we are calling it the Global Jukebox also, and we have a separate logo for that.' We didn't, but if it meant more money, they could have one.

'Could you freight it to us?'

I got a new logo made up next day and sent it over.

It was a curious feeling to be called a racist in the middle of all this. In January when I had been in Ethiopia, I was travelling with Jesse Jackson's wife in an old Hercules. One of her party was the director of Africare, a black American aid agency. He told me he could rarely get black sportsmen or black entertainment stars to do anything for them. He said they had 'little or no social responsibility or conscience'. They would mouth the rhetoric, but rarely understood or took interest in the issues. Now in England I had apparently offended the young black activist crowd by my lack of invitations to any black English or West Indian bands. This was seized on by the 'soul brothers' in the music press, who have done little or nothing for English black bands.

I explained that the purpose of Live Aid was to raise money. If a band sold a million records, it meant more people would watch than if they sold a thousand. If more people contributed, more people lived.

'Them black people dying, man,' said one screaming down the phone in broad Jamaican, a second earlier having sworn at me in pure Cockney.

'So what? I don't care if they're orange-skinned and live in Iceland, the fact they're black is irrelevant. What is relevant is they're dying needlessly. Who's the racist here?'

'We want representation.'

'Of what? There aren't any world famous million-selling reggae bands. If

Bob Marley were alive, I'd be on my knees begging him to play, but no one's heard of Aswad outside the universities. Put them on telly and people will switch if off. That's *here*. God knows what would happen in America, or India, or Africa for that matter. There's nothing wrong with Aswad or Steel Pulse, but you just have to face it, they don't sell many records. If I have a choice between Steel Pulse or Wham! on this show, I'll take Wham!'

'You're just putting your friends on. You just want to sell records. You racist Irish bastard.'

'If this was my personal choice of music, seventy-five per cent of the bands would not be on. As for selling records, these bands need to sell more records or get more publicity like a hole in the head. You're the ones that want that. And don't fucking call me a racist. I know plenty about that, you fascist. Don't talk to me about how oppressed you are, you whining shit, or how concerned you are for Africa. When did you do anything for the "motherland"?'

'If it's all these million-selling bands, why is your band on it then?' screamed my socially-conscience-stricken tormentor as a final parting shot. 'Because it's my ball and I'm going home with it if I can't play,' I answered.

Black Voice, a British black community newspaper mainly known to me for the excitable nature of its reporting and journalists, was calling Live Aid the racist event of the decade. The thing that bothered me was that these same people had never done a story on the famine, nor were they interested in doing anything to help those people. They were only interested in the very thing they accused others of. I was still as opposed to tokenism as I had been during the punk period. I wasn't interested in Uncle Tommery, having a black man there because he was black. Who cares? I wasn't interested in having an African on simply because he was African – he could have been Outer Mongolian for all I cared if he sold a million records. I was interested in pragmatics. I was interested in making money to prevent people dying. Several of those concerned citizens complained to the GLC, who were slightly embarrassed as they supported us, but also actively supported black rights. I had also just agreed to do something for their Equal Rights campaign so it seemed a bit odd for them to be calling me up and passing on a complaint of racism.

'Would you help if the black bands put on their own concert?' they asked.

'Absolutely.' I heard no more.

When David Bailey went to Africa to take pictures for his book – which has already raised £200,000 for Band Aid – he flew in the hold of a cargo plane, paid for all his living and travelling expenses, gave every moment of his time for free. At the launch of his book in London, a woman from the caring journal *Black Voice* attacked him for squandering money that could have gone to Ethiopia, assuming he'd travelled first class and, I suppose, swanked around the desert at Band Aid's expense. This attitude appalled, but did not surprise me.

From Australia Bill Gordon continued to phone at 4 a.m. The phone calls were coming continuously now. I'd begun taking it off the hook. One night I was awoken by a banging on the front door. It was a taxi driver. 'Sorry to wake you, guv, but your phone is off the hook and a guy called Bill Gordon keeps trying to ring you from Australia, but he can't get through so he phoned the BBC and they've sent me round to tell you to put your phone back on the hook.'

Originally the show had been going to Kerry Packer's TV station in Australia. They agreed to the whole thing, including a telethon. Then they lost a lot of money over a strike which had cost them thousands and they said they could no longer afford to show Live Aid or even to pay for the down line from the satellite. They asked me if we could find them $250,000 to run the show. I said I couldn't make the decision, I would go to the trustees. I argued that a quarter of a million dollars was small compared to a potential Australian revenue of $5 million for Band Aid and at that late stage it was almost impossible to go anywhere else. The trustees agreed and I told Australia's Channel 9 they could have the money out of our corporate sponsorship providing they guaranteed that should the Australian income not achieve $250,000 they would make good the shortfall. They agreed. The next day they dropped the whole show without any explanation to Gordon or myself. Hence the 4 a.m. wake-up.

'Get ABC,' I said, referring to the Australian national network.

'They won't run a telethon,' said Bill.

'Try,' I said.

He and I spoke to Grant Rule at ABC. He was very co-operative and asked us to wait so he could check things out. I couldn't believe this. I had never thought Australia would be a problem. And we had to have it as part of Live Aid. It would be laughable if the only country in the world not to show it was Australia. I called Molly Meldrum who hosted 'Countdown', Australia's pop show, and asked him to help. He is a powerful man there and we needed him desperately. Harvey had meanwhile gone to Channel 7, who had said they'd take it, but when I saw their telexes, I said to him, 'They're not agreeing to do the telethon.'

'Yes, they are, anyway it's more important to have the show on and anyway they're paying us.'

'Yes, but the point is active participation and the amount we'll get in the end will dwarf their fees.'

Harvey said, 'It's too late, I've already sent a confirming telex.'

Bill Gordon rang at 4 a.m. again. 'What's happening? Channel 7 say you've signed the deal and I've just confirmed it with Grant Rule.' I spoke to Harvey and we telexed Channel 7 and asked them to release us from our commitment. This they did in a very gentlemanly way and the show went ahead on ABC, including a massive concert from the Australians organized by Gordon and Molly Meldrum.

Tears For Fears were a big band. They were Number One in the States at the time of Live Aid. I had asked them to do the gig very early on and they had hoped to make it but in the event they couldn't. A few weeks before the event, they pulled out. Their manager had 'given me his word'. I spoke to him. 'Listen, I'm not pressuring you, it's your choice. But I think it's pathetic. After all the trouble I've been having with the Americans and now a fucking English band lets me down.'

'They've had a very hairy tour, Bob. There's a lot of internal dissent in the band. Maybe if they could use backing tracks?'

'They can hang by their bollocks from a gantry for all I care, so long as they sing live.'

Their manager went back to the band and told them, as they were sitting in the hotel room or on a beach in Hawaii, that every other band would be doing their best to keep some people alive. In the event two of the band left after a fight. The rest thought about using backing tracks but they were scared of not having a sound check which was only going to be possible for the first three bands, so they came out in the press and accused me of moral blackmail. I had never spoken to them. Boy George started doing something similar.

In the final couple of weeks I kept aside an hour and a half or so every day for interviews. The cameras would be set up in each one of the ten different rooms along the second floor corridor of Phonogram in London.

One interview stood out in the endless mind–numbing succession I was giving to TV, radio, newspapers, and magazines from all over the world. CBC TV came up to film me in the Phonogram offices. At the end they wanted to show me something.

'I haven't got time, lads, honest.'

'It'll only take a couple of minutes.'

'I really haven't time. I've another half dozen to do before I can go and I've got to leave in ten minutes.'

'Just watch the first minute. It's something we spliced together in the Hilton in Addis Ababa.'

They played a video. It was a short sequence of a child, weakened by hunger, trying and trying and trying again to stand up on his little matchstick legs. They had edited it over a record. It was the Cars' 'Drive'. The juxtaposition was bizarre. The child's pitiful courage turned the poignancy of the song into a profound sadness. *Who's gonna pick you up when you fall down? We can't go on saying nothing's wrong. Who's going to drive you home tonight?* My eyes filled with tears and my voice caught in my throat. 'We've got to have this, lads, for the day.'

'That's what we hoped you'd say.'

That video with its two incongruous components seemed another symbol of what Live Aid stood for. It is a beautiful song, ostensibly about love, but it is also a song about dependence. Something I hadn't realized, nor indeed had the writer of the song for when I showed him the video he was shocked. 'I never realized,' he said and broke off, too upset to continue. The artificial and at times indulgent world of pop was harnessed in an improbable marriage with the most basic human feelings of compassion.

Back at Harvey's office the room went silent as a church when I showed it. Phone calls ended prematurely. People stopped what they were doing and just watched. Bowie was in tears. He had been allocated five songs in the tight schedule. 'I want to give up one of my spots to show this. I'd like to introduce it,' he said.

In the States, Mike Mitchell was getting messages from world leaders to intersperse in the broadcasts. They had Julius Nyerere, Rajiv Gandhi, Coretta Scott King, and others. 'I can't see an awful lot of point unless you get the top people. Let's get Reagan and then we'll ask Gorbachev,' I said. Reagan was interested. The message came back from the White House that he would do it if Thatcher would. But although Downing Street was sympathetic, there seemed to be an unending variety of reasons why Mrs Thatcher could not find the time. I think they thought a message was too corny and would lay her open to criticism that she was belatedly capitalizing on a situation she or her government had done little to alleviate. I voiced their fears for them and said it was nonsense. Few governments had done anything beyond offering a standard response. Although this may have been a chance to do something else and to show their sympathy, especially in light of the Great VAT Battle over the Band Aid Christmas record, they politely declined.

'If we can get the Prince and Princess of Wales, that would be brilliant. Better than the politicians, in fact. Keep those tossers out of it and keep it non-political,' said Harvey.

'They might do it. He really owes pop music one after everything you have done for the Prince's Trust.'

'They're coming to a Dire Straits concert for the Prince's Trust at Wembley Arena. If you're going to be at Wembley Stadium to see Springsteen, why don't I get you in the line-up later to meet them and you can ask.'

The Princess of Wales came across. She was wearing a purple outfit.

'You look wonderful. I like the purple thing.'

'Do you? Thanks.'

I started to tell her about Live Aid.

'Will Phil Collins be there?'

'Yeah,' I told her about Phil playing both concerts.

'Oh good, I think he's great,' she said enthusiastically.

'What? Do you think he's sexy?'

'I'm not going to tell you who I think is sexy. Are you staying to see Dire Straits?'

'No, I have to go over to see Springsteen at the Stadium.'

'Oh, Bruce Springsteen,' she said more enthusiastically.

'What, you think *he's* sexy, too, do you?'

'I told you I'm not going to say who I think is sexy,' she laughed. Her head dropped and her huge eyes looked up. Prince Charles came across and we talked about Africa. Later that night the Prince's Trust let Harvey know that they would do it. They didn't wish to announce it yet, because they had to see if they could cancel something else.

The BBC Support Services people had now found five hundred phones around the country we could use for the telethon – essential for logging all the thousands of telephonic donations that we had always planned for. The American space agency NASA rang. They had agreed to allow a live television relay from the space shuttle which was due to be in orbit on the day. The captain would introduce an act, beginning as the spacecraft passed over Philadelphia and ending only seconds later as it passed over Wembley.

'Is Bruce doing it?' said the 950,000th person. 'Who fucking cares?' I thought through my fog. 'Think so,' I said. 'Great,' I heard through my fog. I stalked Bruce. It must have been terrible for him. His people were always too polite to tell me to go away. Barbara, in the office in New York, put up with my endless phone calls; 'He got married today.' 'He's making a video.' 'He's got the weekend off.' 'He's rehearsing.' And so did Jon Landau, his manager, who must get a million pricks a day on the phone. 'I don't know, Bob.'

'Jon, I changed the date for you.'

'I know, let's wait till England, and see how he feels.'

'Hi Bruce.'

'Hey, hi, Bob, how's it going?'

'OK. Congratulations.'

'Thanks man.'

I never asked him. I couldn't because I knew the answer and I didn't want to embarrass me or him. Three nights I went to Wembley and then I flew to Newcastle. 'Harvey, did you ask him?'

'No, I don't want to hassle him.'

'Well you gotta, man.'

'Did you?'

'No.'

'Well shut up.' In Newcastle we were with Paula and his wife, just talking. We talked about Truth or Consequences, that town in America I saw years ago, we talked of everything. Later at the hotel Springsteen and I talked again. We talked about everything except what it was necessary to talk about. Later

I said to Jon, 'Jon, it's in Philly. Twenty minutes from Jersey. Forget the band, just bring an acoustic, just be there.'

'Let's wait and see after Europe.'

'Jon, how was Europe?'

'He's tired, Bob. He wants some time with his wife. They've had no time. You understand. You don't need us. You've got everyone else. You've sold out. You got the stage there at Wembley. You can use that. That's our present, yeah? We'll pay for it.'

I was told by a mutual friend he thinks he wishes he had stuck the guitar in the back seat and come down. Pity.

Harvey came back from Wembley. 'Those bastards are giving the crew the run around over the stage, placing ludicrous and petty restrictions on everything. They can't do this, they can't do that. The Wembley management are apparently under pressure from ARA, who were pissed off at you announcing at the press conference that everyone should bring their own food and drink and boycott the catering.'

'Fuck 'em.'

'They are worried that ARA might withdraw from the catering franchise. It earns Wembley a lot of money. So they're giving our boys the run around. I'm going to see Jarvis Astair. He's the vice-chairman.'

PRICE OF A DREAM . . . Geldof shows the strain.
A photographer from the *Standard* finds me pulled apart by horses.

'I'll come with you.'

It was a very unpleasant meeting. Mick Worwood and Andy Zweck, the man who had put it all together, complained it was becoming impossible to work there. Harvey pointed out that he had worked with Wembley people for many years and had given the place over a quarter of a million pounds' worth of business every year. Yet people were being unreasonable with him, and he complained of one man in particular, Astair, who did not seem to want to take Harvey's points on board. I began to rage at him. 'Listen, you little shit,' he said to me, 'don't you come into my boardroom and tell me how to do business.'

It was the day before the concert. My back was beginning to hurt. Amid all the last minute arrangements was a discussion about whether we should get a horse in under the stage to pull it around if the power failed. Then I was asked to call the Norwegian Postmaster General to make sure that his 'locked box system' was in operation for collecting donations.

There were sound checks for the first three bands. The Rats were on third so that included us, but I never got to do it. There was so much else to occupy me that I only got to see the rest of the band doing it from a TV studio where I was doing the Terry Wogan Show as a bit of last minute build-up. For the last time I gave them the refrain which had become habitual. 'Don't go to the pubs tomorrow. Just for this one day, stay at home and stand by the phone from the moment we start.'

I intended to get an early night. At 2 a.m. the phone rang. It was the manager of an American band. 'My band need more time tomorrow. And if they don't get it we'll pull out.'

'Well, fucking pull out. I'm going to bed.'

CHAPTER XVI

Funny Ol' World Innit!

During the night the pain in my back grew worse. In the final days my main task, amid all the more mundane crises, had been to encourage those who became downhearted. Yet whenever I wavered myself there was nothing to turn to except my own rhetoric. Tiredness seeped through to the core and I understood the expression 'bone-weary'. I moved and thought solely on the impetus of the previous weeks. I put one mental step in front of the other simply because it was one less movement I had to make towards this fixed point – July 13. I was emotionally as well as physically exhausted and I was also in a state of suppressed panic. I lay awake until the small hours, my mind turning like an overheating engine, running through the endless permutations of the hundreds of things which could go wrong. Beside me Paula slept soundly. I dozed fitfully and woke about 7 a.m., my stomach sore with the tension. 'Fuck me, I'm nervous,' I said to Paula.

For all that I was about to appear before two billion people all over the world it did not cross my mind to wear anything other than the clothes I had automatically climbed into every morning that week. There had been a time when I would have carefully considered the night before what I would wear on stage and selected something from a wardrobe assembled with an eye to what fashion-conscious fans might expect. Now I just slung on my clothes from the day before. People had got used to seeing me dressed this way during the course of my many television interviews and appeals over the past few months, so that it might, anyway, have seemed rather tawdry to appear in stage glitter. As I climbed into the long flash limo to drive to Battersea Heliport that morning, I was overwhelmed with the paradox of the gesture, given the occasion. But the car had been provided free by a young girl who had gone to America, leased this mammoth, shipped it back to England and was looking for business. 'Good,' I said, 'you can drive me.'

The show was not due to start for four hours, but already, through the open windows on this hot summer's morning, I could hear television sets tuned in ready for the concert all along the street. '*And now there's four hours to go . . .*' I knew that at some time during the day, if our predictions proved correct, more than eighty-five per cent of the world's television sets would be tuned in to Live Aid. In this most dismal of English summers the sky was, for once, blue and there was not a cloud in sight as I looked up to see the Goodyear air blimp which was carrying the TV cameras over the stadium. People looked out of their windows and waved. One or two shouted, 'Good luck!'

'This is it,' I thought. 'Here we go.' I felt like a swimmer standing on the top board looking at the water below. It was a long way down.

At the heliport there were crowds of crew around the gate and live television cameras inside, 'Fuck me, this limo *is* too flash', I thought. Noel Edmonds had put his helicopter company at our disposal and we flew high across the roof-tops of London towards Wembley. It was only a couple of minutes before we could see the stadium and crowds of people pouring onto the pitch and running up towards the stage. The stage looked good from this height. We landed near the Wembley Conference Centre which we were using as a base for the performers so that there was plenty of room for everyone to park and then get ferried to the stadium by bus. People began to arrive in rapid succession. Spandau Ballet were the first I saw. I began to explain to people what the set-up was, though in the event very few people used the centre. Most of the performers stayed all day in the restaurant which the Hard Rock Café had built backstage at the stadium.

As we drove to the stadium, we were surrounded by thousands of kids all shouting to wish us good luck. It was the first big lift of the day. I made my way to Harvey's production office. A sign saying 'Kill Time and You Murder Success' was hung on the wall beside one of the dozens of clocks provided free to show the time all over the world. There was mayhem, but no more so than had become normal in recent days. Fifty phones and Fax machines in the office created a background hubbub over which everyone shouted. I gave Harvey a hug and we stood together for a few seconds, entering into a moment of quiet blankness which was as near as we could get at that point to embracing what it all meant. The key people had all been there a long time – Andy Zweck, the stage manager, Pete Smith and Jeremy Thoms, who designed and pieced the whole production together. The crew were rushing around with last minute requirements before the arrival of the Prince and Princess of Wales. Many of them had had no sleep for two days.

Paula and Fifi arrived with my father and Anita, Fifi's nanny. Since Canada my father and I had been friends. He hadn't thought it odd that his son, out of the blue, wanted to be a singer and had been full of encouragement and, I think, pride. 'Can you make money in a band?' he had asked. 'I think so,' I'd replied. 'Good luck then.' He was, I think, slightly bemused by it all, but he took it all in his stride. Now he wanted to be here to share the day with me. Our past was dead and buried.

Just before the performers lined up to meet Charles and Diana, Fifi, now barely two, was still practising her curtsey. She was supposed to present the Princess with a bouquet from which Paula was busy tearing the price tag with her teeth. The great fear was that Fifi would decide to hang on to the flowers, which she liked. To avoid this she had been given the bribe of a smoked salmon sandwich, which was the thing she loved most, with the promise that if she gave the flowers to the lady she could have another sandwich. Predictably enough as soon as Diana appeared she thrust the flowers at her with the cry, 'More fish, please'.

We made some small talk. 'I can't believe how small so-and-so is,' she said.

'Yeah, he's a dwarf all right.'

'Are you nervous?' asked Diana.

'A bit, yes.' We went off into another room to look at a map of Africa to give the TV cameras something to film. My back hurt as I pointed.

As we passed some kids, one said to the Princess, 'Your head's much bigger than it looks on telly.'

'Don't worry,' she responded, laughing, 'there's nothing in it.'

'You mustn't get to see anything when you go out to these places,' I said to Charles.

'Well, I get to see what they want me to see.'

'That's what I mean.'

We were talking about Africa when Harvey sidled up to me and whispered fiercely in my ear, 'For fuck's sake, you're supposed to be up in the box. It's time to start.'

'Do you mind, Harvey,' I said in a loud voice, placing my hand on my hip. 'Can't you see I'm talking to the Prince and Princess of Wales?'

We made our way up the little stairway to the Royal Box. In the little square of sky above us we could see the airship going over. The noise of the crowd was incredible. As we came out, it turned to a deafening roar. Half a dozen trumpeters and trombonists from a Guards regiment played the first few bars of 'God Save the Queen', then Status Quo came out and went straight into 'Rocking All Over the World'. It was a marvellous opening. Quo were like a cartoon encapsulation of everything rock and roll is supposed to be – ordinary blokes with long hair in denims playing a 12-bar loud.

I looked across at Chuck and Di. They seemed taken aback, but I think they felt glad that they had come. The wave of emotion coming from the audience was quite remarkable. They kept turning their backs on the stage and looking to us and waving. It was not like the atmosphere of a normal concert. It was more than excitement, it was more than enthusiasm, it was more than warmth. It was the feeling that this was the audience's day and they were happy to invite us all into it.

Everyone else in the box was gripped by it too. Bowie was grinning and waving. Elton John leaned over and grabbed my shoulder. Kevin Jenden began to cry. 'You did it, you bastard,' he said. I look around and said to Charles, 'It's wonderful. I don't believe it. It's imagination made real'.

Quo were well into it when Charles turned and shouted in my ear, 'We're having a concert at the Palace next week. I don't think it will be like this,

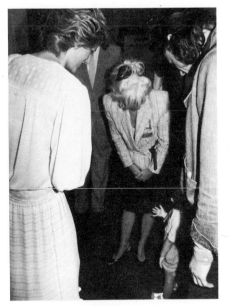

Fifi wonders where the fish is.

The family at Live Aid. Fifi and Dad with All Day Pass, Mum relegated to Special Enclosure.

unfortunately.'

'Who is it?'

'Bach and Handel.'

'I'm not very keen on classical, but I quite like Bach.'

'Would you like to come?'

'Yes I would. I'd love to see the palace.'

By Quo's second number he was tapping his brogues spasmodically. 'I think I've seen these chaps before.'

'Yes, they're Status Quo. They did a Prince's Trust for you.'

'That's right. Birmingham, wasn't it?'

'Did you ever like pop music when you were a kid?'

'Well, I did, actually. It's strange really, because when I was younger people say I had an almost natural sense of rhythm,' he said, clapping his hands hopelessly out of time.

Diana was enjoying herself and talking to Bowie and the others. When Quo finished Style Council came on.

'Right, I'm going to have to go soon now because we're on next. I don't want to blow it,' I said.

'Yes, we'll have to go soon. We're having lunch with my mother.'

'You'd better not miss that.'

'No, quite . . . but we'll stay for you.'

'OK. I hope you like it.'

I ran down through the audience. It was funny because it was so . . . 'matey' is the only word I can think of. Everyone was wishing you well or clapping you on the back and smiling. 'Go for it, Bob.' They were willing it on. Harvey was still uptight. He had been supposed to sit in the Royal Box, but couldn't. He told me, 'I just got the shits. If we run two minutes over on the first act, it's ten minutes over by the third and by the fifth we've blown it. I knew that nobody else would take the responsibility for turning the stage in the middle of someone's act if I didn't.'

The three-part stage system discussed in our first meeting had been adopted. Jeremy Thoms had designed it and with Andy Zweck built it. Springsteen's rectangular stage floor had been lifted off the stage and the circular rotating floor dropped in. The sound check the day before had been disastrous. It had taken three-quarters of an hour for the first group's changeover. No one believed it would work. 'Fuck me,' said Andy in pithy Australian tones. 'We shoulda got the horses to turn the thing after all.' Andy had worked non-stop with Jeremy and Pete Smith. Now on the day he held it all together. He was everywhere. He was calm and deliberate and in the end, after sixteen hours of music, we were just two minutes over time.

There was a system of lights on the stage. Green for OK, orange for one minute left and red for Get Off Now, finished or not. Despite the euphoria of the day every act, to a man, did as the lights told them. Everyone came off on time, even if it meant stopping in mid-song. Some even came off early.

I was looking for Pete Briquette, the Rats bass player, he was always late for everything, or else he would walk on stage without a lead for his bass and then have to walk off to get one. I wanted to make sure he was ready. We waited in the wings as Paul Weller's band finished dead on the minute. The stage turned so that our gear was up front and we walked out.

Before us was a mass of faces which moved like corn in the wind. They stretched across the floor of the stadium and up into the stands in all directions before me. It was the biggest crowd I had ever seen. And that was but the symbol of the vast audience we were addressing.

I turned to Fingers as he walked to his keyboard. 'Fuck me,' I mouthed slowly in awed terror at the noise and the size as I peeled off my jacket.

All through the organization of Live Aid I had reverted to speaking to my mother as I had as a terrified schoolboy. I could not explain some of the things that inexplicably came my way and helped me, and the coincidences. I'm aware as I'm writing this text, that this sounds like horseshit and almost too good to be true. That's too bad, because that's what happened and that's what it felt like. I looked out now at what I had wrought and thought, 'Well, this is it, Ma'. I lowered my head, desperately trying to collect my thoughts, scrambled by this shock and the months of preparation. Concentrate.

Fingers struck the opening notes of 'I Don't Like Mondays'. This was a day for unalloyed hits or classics, the Global Jukebox. Those first notes were like a sound heard faintly in the distance. I turned to look. Fingers seemed miles away across the huge stage. I gestured to the stage crew to turn up the monitors. I still could hardly hear, but I managed to catch the key and launched hopefully into the song. As soon as I had begun I felt completely in control of it. The pain in my spine vanished. After all these weeks, after all these divergences, here I was doing my job, doing what I was good at, doing what I enjoyed. As I began to sing, the preoccupations of the day disappeared. Everything else fell away, everything except the song, which, like so many others that day, revealed new layers of meaning. 'Mondays' had always been important to me, though there had been a time when I grew to despise the song because we had to sing it so often that it began to feel cheapened by the repetition. It was like an albatross around our necks and the more audiences wanted it the more heavy that weight became. But today there was none of that. It seemed absolutely correct. I sang it with renewed conviction and when I got to that line there was no doubting the power that it carried.

And the lesson today is how to die.

The song was brought to a halt by the massive roar of the crowd. I let them shout and then lifted my hand aloft with my fist clenched, and the audience fell into a massive breathing quietness. 'Please understand,' I willed that giant throng. I pushed my will through those wires. 'Please understand,' up to the satellites and down to the aerials and into the living rooms of the world. Quiet. I could hear the rustle of the quiet summer breeze. Quiet as I looked right to left, down the long stadium trying to see every face. And above me the sky was a clear cloudless blue.

The concentration of the moment was broken by the sudden banal, but very real, fear that the audience might begin to sing before me. If they did it might well be in the wrong key. And if so, I would probably pick up theirs rather than the one Fingers was playing.

Then the bullhorn crackles.

In the Royal Box Prince Charles turned to Paula and whispered, 'That is brilliant. Quite brilliant.'

At the end I grappled for words. It was so mundane, but it was true. The Greek chorus was quieted, the demons were silenced, peace had broken out in the civil war. 'I think this is the best day of my life,' I said.

Then in a fever of exuberance and excitement and real passion we steamed straight into the rock numbers 'Drag Me Down', the hit-that-never-was from our last album, and our other Number One, 'Rat Trap'. Fifi sang loudly in Charles's ear during 'Drag Me Down' because that was her favourite. It must have been odd for her seeing her father on these vast screens with the huge auditorium cheering. Or perhaps that is her childhood idea of normality.

In the middle of 'Rat Trap' the power failed for the first time that day. It

22721 HGENTS G

ATTN: MR. BOB GELDOF

THANK YOU FOR YOUR BEAUTIFUL WORK FOR HUMAN KIND

LOVE
YOKO ONO LENNON

KEA2573 LLX0039

WEMBLEY STADIUM

BAND AID
LIVE AID
SAT 13 JULY 1985

THE PRIME MINISTER

10 DOWNING STREET

15 July 1985

Dear Mr Geldof,

I am sorry that it did not prove to be possible for me to record a message for the tens of millions participating in and watching the Liveaid concert.

Your efforts have been an example to young people in this country and throughout the world, and I know that your lead has inspired the fund-raising activities of many others.

I share your concern about the tragic famine in Africa and its consequences; it is too easy to look at only by the short term problems while failing to be worried the longer term need to prevent a recurrence. I can assure you that, through the Overseas Development Administration and the European Community, I shall continue to do what I can to help.

Band Aid and all the other voluntary agencies have enabled ordinary citizens to help very directly in dealing with the famine crisis. Thank you and all those involved with you for your hard work - it has been quite invaluable.

Every good wish

Yours sincerely

Margaret Thatcher

Bob Geldof Esq

15 July 1985

TELENESSAGE
BOB GELDOF C/O
HARVEY GOLDSMITH ENTTERTAINMENTS
2ND FLOOR AVON HOUSE
360-362 OXFORD STREET
LONDON W1R 1FB

YOU DID IT. WE ALL DID IT. AND WE'RE BLOODY PROUD TO
SAY SO. LOTS OF LOVE TO PAULA AND FIFI.

PAUL AND LINDA MCCARTNEY

Mrs T, Mrs L and Mr and Mrs McC.

was off for about a minute and a half, in all probability, though at that moment it seemed to me ten times that long. But it did not matter. The crowd carried on singing for me. As we came off we were all overwhelmed by the experience. Gary, normally the most taciturn member of the band, turned to me, his guitar still in his hand, and said, 'Fucking fair play to you, mate'.

Elton John and George Michael were standing in the wings watching. 'Hey, you two, get off. You know no one's allowed here except people who are just about to go on,' said Harvey, as though he were addressing two star-struck kids who had sneaked backstage.

There was a circle of caravans backstage which functioned as dressing rooms. The band went off to get changed. We were allowed half an hour in the dressing room before we would be turfed out to make way for the next band. I was soaking wet, but I had nothing to change into and so went rushing off to the production box and spoke across the satellite link to Tony Verna.

'How does it look for TV?'

'Looks fabulous.'

But when the first American pictures came across, I was incensed that the cameras were acting true to the stereotype of rock concerts; long shots to naked girls dancing on boys' shoulders, with lingering close-ups of jiggling breasts.

'Don't you think, Tony, that aside from the fact it's irrelevant, this concert is about hunger and it may be considered offensive in a lot of African and Asian countries suffering from starvation to see a healthy American woman flaunting her well-being at them?'

'Bob, I have forty screens in front of me . . .'

'It may also be offensive to cultures who have a different morality and customs to us. They only need one excuse in the east to take us off the air and this could be it.'

'Message understood. No more tit-shots. Now go away.'

'Thanks, Tony.'

I did the rounds to check up on everything. David Bailey had already started work in his improvised studio by the dressing room caravans. He was individually photographing everybody who took part that day. I looked into the Hard Rock where everybody was waiting for their own spot. They sat around, drinking coffee and chatting. One or two gave me a thumbs-up. In Harvey's office everyone was on a high.

I went up to the Royal Box to see how Paula and my father were. My father had, as usual, met someone he knew and was collecting programmes from people for me to sign. 'Thanks a lot, Da, that's all I need.'

'Well done, lad,' he said, as if it had never crossed his mind that I would not pull it off.

The production caravans were so full of jostling technicians that it was impossible to get in. They were switching from channel to channel trying to discover the cause of the intermittent power failures.

I phoned Ireland. 'How's it going?'

'Great. The money is pouring in.'

I went off to find out how the Wembley fund-raising was developing. Suddenly a BBC newsman came up and complained to me that they weren't doing enough appeals on TV or radio. In the appeals box, I discovered that in donations Britain was behind the Irish who had a population only one-twentieth of the UK. I began to panic that not enough emphasis was being placed on the fund-raising, and felt sure that in the euphoria of the massive concert people were losing sight of the purpose of the whole event. 'Do the fucking appeals. What do you think this is all about? Give them the addresses. Give them the phone numbers.'

Elvis Costello was on the stage. Such was the sheer size of the bill that even a performer of his stature had time for only one song. 'This is an old Northern folk song,' he said. He sang 'All You Need Is Love'. He had the words written on his hand because he couldn't remember them. Sting sang alone too. It was stunning. Then Phil Collins joined him in 'Every Breath You Take', another song whose words took on a new dimension in the light of the occasion.

News had come through that morning that bad weather had postponed the launch of the space shuttle. So the captain couldn't announce the bands live from space as we'd intended, which was a great disappointment, but Concorde was still on. Phil finished his set at 15.46 London time and Noel Edmonds was waiting to whisk him off to Heathrow. It was the first time a helicopter had been allowed to land next to Concorde. Phil walked out of one and into the other. At the end of the supersonic flight he would have twenty-eight minutes to get from Kennedy airport to the stage of the JFK stadium in Philadelphia at 20.40 Eastern Standard Time. Concorde was re-routed to fly low over Wembley to an almighty cheer from the 80,000 crowd.

Paul Young was in the middle of a song at five o'clock when I walked onto the stage. He grinned as I took the microphone from him and said, 'Will you please welcome America to Live Aid'. Philadelphia flashed up on the big screens all around the stadium. It was an unreal feeling to watch Jack Nicholson come out on stage in Philadelphia and introduce the next act, U2, and then see Bono and Co walk out onto the stage in London. The Beach Boys, looking old but sounding ageless, waved and 3,000 miles away the audience waved back.

I rushed back into the production office and phoned Ireland. 'How's it going?'

'We've topped a million.'

I hurried across to the appeals room. My back was giving me real pain now. I was walking around with my spine bent like a vaudeville comedian. The doctor offered me a shot of painkiller but I did not want my senses blunted. There was too much to do. I was tired, tired, tired and I wanted to watch the show. But in the appeals room I raged again about how the Irish were beating us, still very afraid that people had lost the drift of the whole enterprise and had forgotten the fund-raising for the starving in Africa. The phones were not exactly jumping off the hook. Looking back on the videos of the event I can see that my fears were not justified. But at the time I was paranoid. I marched into the control room. 'Right, we're doing an appeal.'

'We can't. We got something just about to come in from America. It's . . .'

'Fuck America. We're doing an appeal.' I went up to the studio where Mel Smith and Griff Rhys Jones were about to do an appeal. I joined in just as the presenter said he was going to give the Band Aid address. 'Fuck the address. Who's going to *write in* with their money? They're going to go to the bank on Monday. Listen, there are phones there just lying dead. If you've given your money already, go to your neighbour and bang on their door and tell them to send some too.'

There were a few phone calls about my language but there were also a lot more calls pledging money. I was afraid people would give up when they couldn't get through. 'Keep trying,' I said. Some people in the South called the Scottish number and vice versa. I had hoped we would make a million from Britain. By the end of the day we had four million. By the end of the week we had thirty million. About twenty million people hadn't been able to get through during the day. I hobbled down to the production office. On the way I heard Queen begin their set.

Suddenly someone shouted at me. 'Quick, Bob. There's someone who wants to give a million pounds. They want to speak to you personally.' Bent double I rushed up the stairs again. 'It's Sheik Mani Al-Makhtoum from Kuwait. He owns the racehorses, he rules Kuwait.'

The voice on the line said that it wanted to make a donation on behalf of the people of Kuwait. It was a million pounds sterling. 'I'm here in London, but Live Aid is being shown in Kuwait. I'm watching it with my brother. We think it's a wonderful thing that you're doing this for the people of Africa. I would like to make a donation. One million pounds.'

I said 'thanks very much' and put the phone down. 'Fucking hell, someone's just given me a million quid.'

One system we had established was that people could make donations direct by phone, debiting their credit card. But because seventy-five per cent of all credit cards are owned by people in the south of England we had organized a nationwide scheme whereby people could pledge money by phone and then go into a Post Office on the Monday and pay it into a Giro account. A computer measured the level of response at any given time against the amount of calls coming in. My arm-twisting with various bands – that if they appeared, money would come in which would not otherwise have been given – proved to be entirely justified. But the telephone system broke down completely when the CBC video with the Cars' song on it was shown with its prolonged focus on the attempts of that single malnourished child to walk. Billy Connolly and Pamela Stephenson were supposed to be doing an appeal after that video. When the cameras came onto them, they were both in tears and couldn't speak. Later that night they showed it again on BBC 2 and when the camera came back to the presenter, he was devastated, tears pouring down his face. He began to shuffle his papers and look away. In the end he turned to the cameraman and said, 'I don't think we need to keep the camera on me.' The effect of the film was traumatic on everyone who saw it, but it also put the concert in perspective.

I phoned Ireland again. Ireland was becoming the yardstick by which we measured ourselves. 'It's amazing, Bob. We've got old ladies down here. More than a dozen of them. They say they have nothing to give except their wedding rings. They want us to pawn them for the money. They're standing here asking me for soap so they can pull them off their fingers and banging them on the counter because we won't take them. What should we do?'

I thought for a moment. 'Take them.'

The generosity that day was overwhelming. We heard of one young couple who sold their first home and gave us the money. People got carried away with the euphoria of it. Months later, one man was to write asking if he could have back some of the £3,000 he had given us. In Latin America, the money was pouring in in the same way. All over the world something quite unusual was happening. For whatever reason people were recognizing those hapless victims in Africa and registering their pity and disgust in whatever way they could.

Suddenly it occurred to me that though it grandly proclaimed 'Finale' at the end of the Wembley programme, we had not actually rehearsed anything. I called everyone together in the Hard Rock and dished out copies of the words of 'Do They Know It's Christmas'.

'We'll just run through it with an acoustic guitar. Who's got an acoustic?' The collected might of the British pop industry could not muster a single acoustic guitar between them. A stab of pain shot through my back as I bent to pick up a nearby electric guitar.

'OK, Gary, play this unamplified, will you?'

The lights went out. The power had gone again. 'Shit. Has anyone got a candle?' No one had. 'OK. We'll do it in the dark. David, are you there?'

'Yes,' said Bowie.

'Well, come here so you can hear the guitar. It's in C. You sing the first two lines, because Paul Young has had to leave. Right now, as far as possible, we'll stick to how we did it on the record. If you don't know the words, just do the tune and when the light comes back on, have a look at your bit of paper.' We ran through it. It was weird hearing all those famous voices sing in turn in the darkness. It was a shambles. 'OK. Let's do it again.'

Before we could, someone stumbled in and shouted, 'Bowie, Geldof, Townshend and Alison Moyet. On stage for "Let It Be" with McCartney.'

'OK. Can you run through it yourself while we're gone?'

My back was just one big ache. 'I think it's a trapped nerve,' said the doctor. 'Do you want a painkiller?'

'I'll have one after the finale, not yet.'

Before McCartney had gone on, there had been a short, intense rain shower. George Michael had been on stage at the time with Elton John to sing Elton's 'Don't Let the Sun Go Down on Me'. The irony of the rain only reinforced the poignancy. The shower lasted only ten minutes and was a welcome cooling for the crowds on such a hot day. But some of the rain got into the electrics. McCartney started to play 'Let It Be', but when he tried to sing he found the microphone was dead. He could not believe it. He had not played live for eight years and then that had happened. He was horrified. 'Be professional, Paul,' he said to himself, ferociously grinning and playing the song for the nth time, 'They'll fix it soon.' Then some of the audience realized the problem and started singing for him.

I did not realize this. I was round the other side of the revolving stage, lying down to rest before we went on. Bowie was rubbing my back and I fell asleep for a few seconds. Townshend and Bowie and Alison were all standing there waiting for the signal to go on. They didn't know Paul's power was down and couldn't understand why he kept playing verse after verse and never got to the chorus. 'I didn't know it was this long', muttered Townshend.

Spot the non-rock-legend. On the shoulders of the great, embarrassed but proud.

The biggest party ever held.

John Hurt, the actor, was on stage. He shook me. 'Come on Bob, wake up. Are you OK?'

'Do you know the words?' asked Bowie. It was a bit late if I didn't.

We walked on. Apparently as our figures appeared out of the shadows there was a huge roar in the Philadelphia stadium because the *New York Post* had been spreading the rumour that the Beatles were to reform long before I had even spoke to George. But for me there was legend enough in the reality. The line-up on stage was McCartney, Bowie, Townshend – and Geldof. It was like the fulfilment of some crazy schoolboy dream.

At the end Townshend and McCartney had decided they'd get behind me and grab hold of my legs and hoist me onto their shoulders. I nearly died of embarrassment. It was terrible. These people were pop greats. It wasn't false modesty. I already felt a fake singing with them. It was a moment of triumph but unlike the generals of imperial Rome no one needed to whisper in my ear, 'Remember you are but mortal'. My back was hurting something awful for a start.

'Fuck me, he's a heavy bastard,' said Townshend.

'Please put me down. I really don't want this.' I remember thinking, it may not mean much to someone not interested in pop, but looking back, I am still embarrassed but intensely proud that I was carried on Paul McCartney's and Pete Townshend's shoulders.

Everyone came on then for the finale. There was a tremendous feeling of oneness on that stage. There had been no rivalry, no bitching, no displays of temperament all day. Now everyone was singing. They had their arms around each other. I brought Harvey onto the stage and made him sing too. Elton was crying, everyone was crying. Not the easy tears of showbiz but genuine emotion. Down in the crowd the punters were crying. Even some of the photographers crowding round the stage were crying. The performance was still a shambles but perhaps the audience were prepared for that. 'This may be a bit of a cock-up,' I said. 'If you're going to cock it up, you may as well do it in front of the world.' Well, the world sang it. 'Feed the World' exploded out of that stadium and literally shot around the planet. 'All those satellites up there. All those years since sputnik. Well today they no longer said "Beep Beep".' It was a moment that let millions live. 'Remember this day,' I wrote later.

★   ★   ★

We were the twenty-ninth act on the Wembley stage that day, finishing one minute over time. I lay down on the stage and watched the people leave. The BBC continued to broadcast. Cliff Richard, who hadn't been able to do the show because he was already doing two charity gigs in Birmingham that evening, did a song with an acoustic guitar for the BBC cameras. I was content. We had got every major British pop artist of the last quarter of a century. Off stage the doctor gave me a painkiller and I went to look for Paula. She was

Back to the future.

doing some interviews for *The Tube*. She was supposed to be doing one with me.

'Well', I said, 'ask me a question.'

She just threw her arms around my neck and said, 'I'm so proud of you'.

'Come on. Let's go home.'

We tried to find a car to take us back into London, but they had all gone. We hitched a lift off some people we met in the car park. It took us hours to get back to Chelsea where I wanted to wash and change before going to Legends, the Bond Street night club, which had set up a large screen downstairs for us to watch the last third of the concert coming in from America. London was packed that night, as we crawled through the summer night's traffic jam.

I began to hum 'It's a Perfect Day' by Lou Reed. Overhead the fireworks from the Handel concert in Hyde Park exploded in the sky. People leant out of their windows and looked at them. People walked over to the car and hugged me. Some cried, 'Oh Bob, oh Bob,' not sneering, not uncontrollable, just something shared and understood. 'I know,' was all I could say. I did know. I wasn't sure what had happened in England, or everywhere else, but I 'knew'. Somehow something had gone right. Cynicism and greed and selfishness had been eliminated for a moment. It felt good. A lot of people had rediscovered something in themselves. This does sound pompous. Too bad.

I got home and switched on the telly. There it was. 'How weird!' I thought. I washed and changed. It was still there. I phoned a taxi and went to Legends. We watched the broadcast, drinking Scotch and soda, with plenty of orange juice on the side, for the evening was as hot as the day had been. Mick Jagger was wonderful. With Tina Turner he was sensational and hilarious. Hall and Oates were brilliant. Phil Collins appeared, to a cheer from the Legends crowd, with the words, 'I was in England this afternoon. Funny old world, innit?' He didn't like Philadelphia. He said to me later, 'If I could have, I'd have got Concorde straight back again'. It wasn't the crowd – he loved them. He said it was too heavy backstage; even pet dogs had security passes and some people were doing a big star thing. The stage was constantly crammed with people and the turnovers were too long. Still, people were enjoying themselves and dancing, and the donations rolled in, and other artists loved it.

For me the biggest disappointment of the evening was Dylan. He sang three of his classics, including 'Blowing in the Wind', which ought to have been one of the greatest moments of the concert. Unfortunately, the performance was catastrophic. He had met Keith Richard and Ronnie Wood in a night club in New York the night before and they had offered to back him. So, there they were – pop music's seminal songwriter and the world's greatest rhythm guitarist and his partner. But they were out of time, they couldn't stay in tune and they seemed to treat the song with disdain. (I later heard that the curtain had dropped between them and their monitors, so that they couldn't hear themselves perform.) Then he displayed a complete lack of understanding of the issues raised by Live Aid by saying unforgivably, 'It would be nice if some of this money went to the American farmers.' Something so simplistic and crowd-pleasing was beyond belief. Live Aid was about people losing their lives. There is a radical difference between losing you livelihood and losing your life. It did instigate Farm Aid, which was a good thing in itself, but it was a crass, stupid and nationalistic thing to say. It was to have been the finale, but thank God Ken Kragen had persuaded Lionel Richie to come and sing 'We Are the World'. Dylan left the stage and as he walked by his manager, he just looked up at him and said 'Sorry.'

There were a dozen people left in Legends, where we were presented with a Methuselah of champagne: a giant bottle containing the equivalent of four magnums. There were also two large cakes, one covered with black icing with the Live Aid logo on it in white. I gave it to Harvey. 'I see the confectioner has forgotten the credit for the artwork,' I said to him.

'I'm sure not. Maybe someone has already eaten it.'

It was 4 a.m. when we carried it out of the club and into the taxi to go home. It was dawn. Grey light was beginning to colour the night sky. A few birds had started to sing.

'Well,' said Harvey. 'That was a laugh, wasn't it?'

CHAPTER XVII

But Prime Minister....

I spent the day after Live Aid in bed. After that my personal priority was to get away for a break. The government of Mauritius contacted me and offered me a free fortnight's first class holiday there with no strings attached except a picture which could be captioned 'Bob Geldof on holiday in Mauritius'. I got out my atlas. Mauritius was dangerously near to Africa in my limited conception of geography. I could envisage the headline: 'Geldof Suns on Beach as Nearby Millions Starve'. With regret I turned it down and opted to visit a friend who had a farmhouse in a quiet part of Ibiza.

It had been a curious sight the Monday morning after Live Aid to see queues of people standing outside every bank and post office, waiting to give their money away. But that was not the half of it. We had raised $10 million in sponsorship even before the concert began; indeed by the time the concert took place we had already spent a million pounds of it buying a fleet of trucks in the Sudan. On the Monday after Live Aid we estimated that about £4 million had been collected in Britain. Then we got the news that Ireland alone had raised £5 million. After that the figures seemed to change hourly. Like Topsy, it just growed. At the last count Live Aid had raised $100 million, plus a significant amount in dollar contributions on specific projects from various western governments. And money is still coming in from merchandising, record sales, donations, and further donations.

But what was clear on my return from Ibiza was that once more we had raised more than money. We had raised a new constituency of feeling. Simply walking down the streets was evidence of it. People would come up to me and give me money. It got to the stage where I had to keep half of my jacket separate for these impromptu contributions. Sometimes it would be schoolboys with ten pence, other times it would be adults with a fiver or a tenner. Occasionally people would give me fifty or a hundred pounds. 'Put it into the Band Aid account at any bank or send it through the post,' I would tell them. They would wink or smile and tell me it was safer in my hands. Sometimes I would come home from a day round London with £500 in my pockets. Often people would add a comment: 'You tell them, Bob, you tell them like it is. About time somebody did, I wish I could get the chance'.

There was clearly an enormous amount of personal trust involved. People were very definitely giving the money to *me* and Band Aid in preference to one of the established aid organizations. At first, it was a burden; I did not want the responsibility of remembering which pocket contained my money and which Africa's. If a child gave me a halfpenny in the street I had to remember to make sure it found its way into the fund. Indeed, when people began actually shoving bags of coins from pub collections through my letter box in the middle of the night, I suspected that the whole thing was being set up by the press so that they could create a 'Geldof Pockets Cash' story.

But soon I came to see that what people were doing had a much greater symbolic than practical significance. I was becoming a kind of Everyman who went and did what they would have liked to do themselves, in the manner they would have chosen themselves. But this cult of personality was at worst infuriating and a burden and at best irritating. I wished to God I knew how to avoid it.

I had had some coaching in this role of Everyman after the Band Aid record when I had met Margaret Thatcher at the *Daily Star* awards. I knew I would only get a couple of seconds with her, so I had to be blunt. The editor, Lloyd Turner, had steered me towards her and the TV cameras were immediately on us for the confrontation between famine pop star and Prime Minister.

'Ah, Mr Geldof. I think it's wonderful what you've been doing with the Band Aid record.'

'Thank you, Prime Minister, but I was reading in *The Times* the other day that you were planning to spend ten million pounds to dispose of surplus EEC butter. Don't you think that is ridiculous?'

'There's nothing ridiculous about a healthy agriculture . . .'

'But we're producing a surplus when a part of the world is dying of starvation.'

'Mr Geldof, they can't eat butter.'

'They can eat butter oil. It's one of the things Band Aid has spent a lot of money on, and butter oil is a by-product of butter. In fact, it's absolutely essential in supplementary feeding, which is when people are at the last point of starvation.'

'Well we all, you know, have our own charities . . .'

'But Prime Minister, I don't think that the possible death of 120 million people is a matter for charity. It is a matter of moral imperative that we do something.'

All the time she tried to move away from me to end the conversation. But she could not stand to let me have the last word. Every time I said something, she came back. By now I was getting the icy stare. I had been pushed up close so that I towered above her. She was looking up with her death-ray glare.

'We're all trying.'

'It's not as simple as that,' she snapped.

'No, Prime Minister, nothing is as simple as dying.'

She did not allow me to end the exchange; more accurately she was dragged away by some dignitary before she could respond. Part of the conversation was broadcast on television. The response of the public was direct. 'You told her, Bob, you didn't bottle out when you got the chance. Good man!' It was as if I had said the unsayable. I felt like the boy who had pointed out the true nature of the Emperor's new clothes. The entire population, it seemed, knew that the EEC's Common Agricultural Policy was a nonsense. All the sophistry and technical jargon in Brussels and Strasbourg combined could not hide this. But anybody who said so publicly had seemed to fear that they would immediately be branded a fool who talked simplistic drivel. More importantly, they thought, 'He wasn't afraid. He told her. Wish the others did the same'. I *was* afraid of making a fool of myself, but I still had to seize my opportunity.

Thatcher seemed to me a strange woman. She was argumentative and combative but she hadn't patronized me. She had been compelled to put up a fight in our one brief exchange and seemed quite capable of staying there arguing all afternoon. I have heard from a very reliable source that at a meeting of senior ministers of the EEC in March 1984 she raised the issue of Ethiopia. She had apparently seen a report on the famine the previous evening and thought they should put aside the pre-arranged agenda for half an hour because 'shouldn't something be done about it?' The others disagreed and the meeting proceeded. But this was the exact opposite of her public utterances in December that year. A friend had said she is 'very emotional'. But her private thoughts and public actions are a world apart. He thinks it 'very strange'. I do too, if it is true. I was surprised when, as she left the lunch early, she came to my table, put her hand on my shoulder and whispered, 'Sorry I have to leave now. Please excuse me. I'll see you again, I hope'. She wrote me a letter the day before Live Aid wishing us luck. This again seems odd in the light of the row we had had over the Government's deduction of VAT from the eight million pounds raised by 'Do They Know It's Christmas'. For weeks, then, I had been going around telling people that one hundred per cent of their money, excluding VAT, would get to Ethiopia. Then people began to ask 'Why *excluding* VAT? Why not including it?' If, quite literally, everybody else was forgoing their profit, why not the government?

We had asked for the tax revenue, and the government said no.

'If charities are tax-exempted, why isn't a charity record?'

'Because all charity records will want exemption then.'

'No, just do it for us.'

'We can't do that.'

'Yes you can, you can say this is the sole exception.'

I worked through all the proper channels. I deliberately refrained from attacking the Government publicly. It seemed to me that the worst way to attack this Government was to hit it over the head with a brick or force it against a wall. It simply refused to budge. Intuitively I felt it was better to talk to Reginald who'd talk to John, who'd talk to Dick or whoever. That remained my policy throughout the entire period. If Live Aid was to work beyond one successful Saturday it had to remain above party politics. Its strategy had to be to ask the Government – or any government – for more, not attack it for what little it did at present.

I went to see Lord Gowrie, the nominal patron of the Band Aid Trust and at that time Minister of the Arts. Could he talk to some people? Had he seen a newspaper cartoon of rows of starving Africans with bowls in their hands marked VAT and a grotesquely fat and sweaty Chancellor of the Exchequer running along grabbing money from the bowls and stuffing it into a bulging sack? He would speak to people. The Irish government without prompting said they would release the VAT from the sales of the record in Ireland and spend it on famine aid. A nice diplomatic solution. No, the British government wouldn't buy it. Band Aid accountants were in touch with the tax authorities, but still had no luck.

The question of the refund of the VAT then degenerated into a party political issue. The leader of the Opposition, Neil Kinnock, wrote to Mrs Thatcher on the quiet and asked her to return the VAT. He stood to make no political capital out of it, so there was a good chance that she might concur. But she refused, so then the Labour Party unleashed the Parliamentary dogs of war and MPs like Skinner and Canavan reduced the whole thing to a political squabble, the very thing I had sought to avoid.

The next step was to respond to the political PR firm who offered to obtain a letter signed by all living ex-prime ministers asking Mrs Thatcher to return the VAT. But before this could be done a new opinion poll was released in *The Standard*, London's evening paper, showing that the Tories had fallen badly in popularity. Of those polled, apparently about a third of those who had changed their mind about voting Conservative did so specifically over the Government's action on VAT on the record. It had been Christmas time and this one single Scrooge-like act in a time of goodwill and massive support for Band Aid had resulted in a substantial loss of poll votes. One can only speculate whether this influenced the government announcement that the VAT on the Band Aid record would be spent on additional overseas aid specifically for Africa. The news was released purposely, I suppose, late on a Friday night; this was too late for most of the morning papers. The Sundays had already been printed, and by Monday it was stale news. It was a nice little piece of news management for no one likes to back down in public. I saw it on one front page, the *Daily Mail's*. Once more, without *me* doing anything except behind the scenes, the net effect was that the public began to see Band Aid as something which stood for common sense and common decency in a world marked by self-interest and double-dealing. Thus I became emblematic of Band Aid's aims without ever wishing to encourage a cult of personality.

Live Aid took this all a step further. Suddenly our constituency was global. Bishop Tutu and members of the Norwegian, British and Irish parliaments nominated me for the Nobel Prize for Peace. Invitations came from the U.S. Congress and the Australian people to visit them to receive awards. Even Russia felt the need to account to us. I had felt cheated by the Russians. We had been told the concert would go there live. It did, but only to a select 2,000 in some clubs in Moscow. It was cynical. They wanted the kudos of joining in this great global event, to be seen to be 'peace loving' and 'concerned'. But where was the Russian donation? Were the Soviet citizens allowed to contribute and had they even been told there was mass death in the country they supported with massive shipments of arms? 'They can't eat arms,' I exploded. They had wanted to involve one of their bands so they could reject criticisms of cultural isolation using one of their 'approved' artists. And then they cheated us.

I was not yet used to being taken so seriously. Who cared if this excitable pop star vented his spleen? 'Geldof Slams Ruskies' or something like that were the British headlines. 'The Russians are the only government to live up to their promises,' I said. 'They promised nothing and that's exactly what they've given.' No less a personage than one of Brezhnev's sons was hauled out to say I didn't know what I was talking about and that the Soviet government had poured fraternal aid into its revolutionary friend and ally. It had certainly poured planes, gunships and armaments in: I'd seen them. I had seen a lot of East European grain and cargo being unloaded, so where were the Ruskies? Funding a war, I imagined.

But it was a strange realization that out of this concert had come a constituency that had to be answered to by virtue of its very size if nothing else and, willy-nilly, I was the one at the head of it. Band Aid had raised the issue and spent the money that had accrued as a result. We then maintained the momentum. Once this had been done, it was necessary to deal with it on an educational level, providing schools and teachers with films and booklets on famine and its causes and results. The fourth and, I think, final responsibility is using this constituency to generate political change. All this now seems so logical, but all I had originally wanted to do was try and get £72,000. The rest followed and each new step seemed obvious.

I was taken aback by the fact that the Russians had found it necessary to answer our criticisms and was also aware of my own position. I represented nothing but myself and a few hundred million people who agreed with me on this issue. I represented no constituency, but a moral one, and I wasn't seeking anyone's vote so no one had a hold over me, and I could say and do as I liked, provided it was responsible. I had realized this before in Africa, when I could say things to ministers that no other agency could. The governments there had a hold over these agencies – they could throw them out as they had in the past if they didn't like what they were saying. They couldn't do that to us because we weren't actually there for them to throw out in the first place and they still had to listen to us if they wanted the money.

But as in England, where I didn't want to get involved in party politics, so too in Africa. 'I will shake hands with the devil on my left and the devil on the my right to get to the people who need help,' I would say, when I was first asked questions about the political complexion of some local government. This was crucial, for you could become bogged down in the myriad moral uncertainties of dealing with an imperfect political system. If one of these administrations prevented us getting help to area A, we would simply move to area B where there were equal numbers of people in need. We only had enough to help one lot. It is irrelevant in the end which one you choose. They are all dying, they all need help. In private we would twist arms. We would do deals allowing access to areas, air-lift material into war zones in the southern Sudan while the government in Khartoum, through intermediaries, asked us to contact the rebels in the south. There was a lot of that, but it is dangerous to elaborate as it jeopardizes Band Aid and others. These people are wary of us because of the press, our support and our financial power but they could also use us. This was not being big-headed, these were simply the realities I had to be aware of.

One of England's most respected political commentators was, in retrospect, to say that Band Aid was a subversive phenomenon in that it wrested the political initiative from the parliamentary process into the hands of ordinary people. We never thought about it like that at the time. But wherever I went I was accompanied by vast numbers of photographers, such was the interest among the general public in Band Aid's activities. Every camera became a symbol of popular authority. I had to use that. Not to, I felt, would be irresponsible. Here was an opportunity not only to extend the value of Band Aid's money through mutual projects with governments, but to try, as I'd seen Mother Teresa do, not just to get more money spent there, but also to force some political change in the West's way of thinking towards Africa that perpetuated the situation there. I wanted aid to be given without the financial and ideological conditions it comes with now, conditions that cannot be met by the beneficiary countries because they are imposed on the back of dying populations. It seems ridiculous to me that Africa received three billion dollars of aid in 1985, but paid out six billion in interest on loans to the world's banks.

Aid is given in direct proportion to how friendly a government is towards the donor. It is used as threat, blackmail, and a carrot. This is wrong. If you can help, do so and give graciously without conditions. This is not naive, it is humane. Aid by and large benefits the donor country as much as the recipient, more so in fact as it stimulates, by trade, the donor's economy, but leaves the recipient aid-dependent. In the end all aid is valueless if it doesn't encourage by investment in genuine development of a country. It is essential that Africans be allowed to develop themselves. It is no use us, through aid, imposing our values or morals or political systems on people who have completely different sets of principles and traditions. Attempts at democracy in most African countries are a waste of time. Autocracy often works better in developing societies where political choice, indeed any choice, is limited by the simple need to survive. If I am hungry, and I am offered bread or votes – I'll take the bread.

Political stability is also the main prerequisite of long-term development, therefore the wars that eat through these impoverished countries' budgets are murderous not only in the amount of bullets expended to take lives, but in the knock-on effect of the country not being able to afford to feed itself. Famine is aggravated by these conditions and famine is even more politically and economically destabilizing than war, so in a country burdened simultaneously by war and famine there can never be any development as the economy is exhausted by combating both. This leaves the country open to the blackmail of aid through the major powers. It becomes an aid junkie.

But imagine a healthy Africa. Imagine the trade with a continent at peace and developing. Europe would be the first to benefit, but our policies and those of the U.S. and the others are in direct opposition to this. Our current policies exacerbate the situation in Africa. They do not help stricken areas much in the long term and the immediate domino-effect is to destroy weaker communities. Aid may simply bail *us* out, by ridding us of surplus, by perpetuating our preposterous agricultural systems, by buying political allies and by keeping portions of our shipping, trading, manufacturing and agricultural industries afloat.

But I can't sit and watch people die on my TV. Aid is a perversion of an individual's instinct to help another suffering human. The simple compassionate act of giving a pound to help others is without condition and is pure. It is never so simple when there are billions at stake. Africa is in everybody's pocket but its own. Maybe all this is bullshit, but still maybe I could say all of it to those who count. This was the last thing I could do. What else was left?

★   ★   ★

The last time I'd been in Washington I'd seen Kissinger. I was pressed against the White House railings staring in at the candy-striped tents where Sadat and Begin would sign their treaty. Kissinger was on the lawn for a second before he disappeared. The Rats had been doing a concert that night but our hotel was raided the day before by the FBI, who believed that the West German newly-weds staying in the next room were Baader-Meinhof terrorists. After they had realized their mistake and talked into their shirt-sleeves, they asked us who we were and then went away disappointed. Perhaps they hoped they had stumbled upon some active service unit of the IRA, out to jeopardize the Middle East negotiations.

This time Harvey, Kevin Jenden and I were met and taken through customs by a political lobbyist and an assistant to Congressman Carr of Illinois, who was sponsoring our visit. Kevin, who was now spending most of his waking hours working as director of Band Aid, had begun as an enthusiastic amateur but was rapidly becoming quite expert in the nuts and bolts of relief and development issues. As we all discovered, it is really quite simple. Rank amateurs can grasp things quickly. In most trades or professions an ease with the jargon is the key, jargon being the 'mysterious' invented language which implies expertise. We had taken the advice of a professional political lobbyist on how best to pick our way through the quagmire of committees as it would have been so easy to become bogged down.

Two key men we needed to meet were Bob Carr of the Congressional committee on transport and Mickey Leland of the committee on hunger. It would be good, too, to see the Speaker, Tip O'Neill, and most importantly we needed to meet the senior officials of the U.S. Agency for International Development, USAID. Carr was also part of the Arts Council and on the House Appropriations Committee. I quickly recognized the system of power in Washington. It seemed that the more powerful the committee you were on, the more power accrued to you. Appointments to these committees seemed to be in the hands of the Speaker of the House, Tip O'Neill. Congressmen seemed perpetually worried, determined to maintain a high public profile for the folks back home to show them they were on top of things. With Bob Carr it was touch and go: he wasn't sure what would happen to him next time around.

When the American Government declared July 13th to be Live Aid day, the document which legalized this was the most signed bill ever to go through Congress. President Reagan didn't sign it until July 17th because he was on his sick bed after his operation. His signature was slightly wobbly. I was offered awards by Congress's arts caucus and, later, its black caucus.

The arts crowd had wanted this visit as star-studded as possible; the presentation of the award was intended to be a publicity stunt. Elton John was mentioned, Jagger, the usual crowd as well as Mitchell, Uplinger and Verna and his boys. Would we all go to all the parties? I said no. We were going to do business and we expected to walk away from Washington, DC with tangible results. U.S. Aid were the big boys, the greatest single donor in the world. It was important we talk and understand each other and do business. I was, as usual, scared I was going to cock things up. I was frightened that these men would have the better of me or have a better grasp of facts. But they didn't: we were *all* tap dancing. This was reassuring and confidence-boosting.

It was also odd. Here we were in the very seat of world power. We were awe-struck. Everything here affected every person on the planet. Famous deeds done by famous people were meant to be daily events here. I expected the very walls to throb with power – but they didn't.

I walked up the famous steps of the Capitol. It was a beautiful building, with its cupola in the centre and a web of little pillared circular rooms along the circumference. I'd seen this place so often in the news, it was terribly familiar. The movie wound on.

Everyone dropped behind me as we ascended, I had to be in front, I was the one who had to speak. What was going on here? What had led me to the motherlode of power? What was this scruffy pop singer doing on his way to meet those senators and congressmen. It was extraordinary. I *was* Mr Smith and I *had* come to Washington, and I was painfully aware of it. Like Mr Smith I could only speak plainly and bluntly, and if the issue became confused or clouded in the twists and turns of political thought processes, I would revert to the absolute morality of the argument. We strode across the exquisite marbled rooms and underneath the dome. We passed the pillared temple within a room where Lincoln, or someone, had lain in state. Now people came over to shake hands. 'Congressman so'n'so,' Bob Carr explained as we walked on. Visiting schoolkids asked for autographs, people turned to see who these important dignitaries were clattering across the marbled floor under the giant cupola. 'Live Aid' I could hear muttered from several voices rising up in respectful whispers around the vaulted dome. I had made an effort. I was very impressed to be here and I had put on my green and white flecked tweed type suit with my inevitable yellow-green baseball boots. I thought I was dressed to kill, they thought I looked outrageous. Afterwards kids would say I hadn't let them down by compromising the way I looked when I talked to the government. Even that seemed important to them. Young congressional assistants were lined up in the corridors asking for autographs. It seemed incredibly informal: imagine Downing Street or Home Office clerks thrusting autograph books at visiting delegations or dignitaries. On the doors behind were little brass plates with names that I would hear daily on TV engraved upon them. We turned the corner into a blinding wall of flashguns and TV lights. Microphones thrust at me from everywhere. Guards held the journalists back as we swept into a large room with a dais and perhaps thirty or forty microphones grouped around it. Inside the room were perhaps thirty members of Congress to whom I was introduced. They lined up in a neat queue. More arrived, presumably alerted by their aides that it might not be the worst thing in the world to have their photo taken with this 'Live Aid guy' for those voters back home. Congressman so'n'so grabbed my hand and the cameras popped. Few looked at me, they mainly turned sideways towards the cameras. Some had brought their children, which was OK because it was less formal. I met Mickey Leland from Houston, who was an important member of the Congressional committee on hunger.

I was then presented with my Arts Caucus Scroll. There were speeches, then more hand shaking. I was getting impatient. There is something seriously wrong when so many politicians pay court to a pop singer. Some were not just vote-catching, but genuinely impressed and excited at meeting me. 'I'm not bloody Brother Teresa,' I snapped at someone. 'Let's go,' I said to Bob Carr. I had stipulated the agenda before we arrived. They knew that we were not prepared to leave without firm undertakings from them that they should match us on a dollar-for-dollar basis on some of our mutually beneficial projects. We would double the spending power of the Band Aid donations that way.

Our first priority was USAID. We were shown into a large room with a horseshoe-shaped table and maps of the world everywhere. It was like a war-time operations room. The wall was studded with clocks showing the time in different parts of the world. The one which showed Zulu time had stopped at 6.35. We were received by members of the agency's permanent staff. They began to brief us about their individual roles. They had obviously been through all this before with the USA for Africa people.

I interrupted. 'Thank you. I don't mean to be rude, but we understand the function of USAID. USA for Africa has started only recently but we've actually been operating in Africa now for ten months. We have some matters we'd like to discuss in detail with you.'

Kevin produced a copy of the contract which ordained the distribution of American food aid in Sudan. 'This is a result of what U.S. Aid has been doing in Khartoum. The way your trucking operation has been set up, whether you know it or not, means you are maintaining a cartel which has trebled the price of distributing food in the past few months.'

'As a result, at the request of the agencies, we've had to embark on the purchase of a fleet of lorries in what is essentially a cartel-busting operation which has cost us a fortune, and it shouldn't really be our job,' I said. We passed across a copy of an article on the subject in *The Times*. 'The press are beginning to sniff at this thing, it's beginning to stink. You may not have realized it but your policy seems to be entirely wrong here.'

Suddenly they began to talk very differently. We embarked on a detailed discussion of the policy options in the areas where both Band Aid and USAID were involved, albeit with radically different levels of commitment. It was a good meeting and they were clearly concerned. Eventually they took us upstairs to see the boss, Peter Macpherson, who was a political appointee. 'We think you should talk to these guys. They have some points worth listening to,' one of the officials – a general – said to him. Macpherson listened.

Before launching into anything that could be construed as criticism, I wanted to establish a positive note. I was sincere in what I said although at the time I was speaking merely to give him room for manoeuvre. 'You cannot afford to lose the moral high ground here. Everyone knows that the Soviet policy is mainly to provide military hardware. The one ace America has to play is that it constantly responds more generously than any other country in the world. If people rarely mention it, that's only because it is taken for granted. If you lose that, you lose everything.'

Macpherson looked at the contract which Kevin had produced. 'You do understand the implication of this clause here,' said Kevin, beginning his detailed analysis . . . By the end Macpherson seemed genuinely concerned. 'I think we've got to look into this.'

USAID were happy to work with us. They are part of the State Department and thus political. They felt it was a good thing for them to ally themselves with us. They would be seen to support this populist cause their countrymen and voters had responded to so emphatically. More than that, they saw we were serious and could be effective, but maybe equally important was the fact that simply because they are political their efforts are constrained by the politics of any given country. Ethiopia, for example, is not delirious to have help from USAID. They suspected its workforce of being CIA people and no doubt some of them are, but as I said to the Minister in Addis, that's balanced out by the KGB's 'agricultural experts'. It works both ways however. Because Addis is 'unfriendly', USAID is less inclined to help in Ethiopia than in the Sudan, for example. We could bridge the gap. We could put together joint projects where they didn't have to be involved at all physically and where we could use our apolitical stance as a bargaining tool to gain concessions. We might be able to get USAID help if we could say we can have access to Area X. This has happened and has worked.

We were taken for lunch to the Speaker's dining room. Chandeliers winked and crystal sparkled on the horseshoe table. Various important people, some of whom I'd already met and most of whose names I'd forgotten sat there. I hadn't stopped talking and was looking forward to a quiet lunch but as I took my seat at the place of honour, the door crashed open and was quite literally jammed up with cameras, microphones and TV lights. Everyone turned to face them and smiled. Questions were shouted. Some tourists, extraordinarily (again: imagine this at a formal Downing Street lunch), shouted, 'That's the Aid guy'. 'Later guys, please,' said Bob Carr and Mickey Leland pleasantly, ensuring the all-powerful media were not offended. Two waiters pushed their weights against the door and forced it shut. To no avail. It immediately burst open with a new group of politicians who said Hello and talked and asked how they could help, and then left. 'Is Tip coming?' someone asked. 'Yes, he said he would.' The door burst open again, there was a great commotion, the cameras and lights were this time turned away from us, then Tip O'Neill and Senator Edward Kennedy pushed through. The waiters tried to hold back the reporters and everyone in the room stood up and adjusted their ties and jackets. 'Mr Speaker,' they all cried. Tip O'Neill is a powerful person. They were very respectful to Tip, their jobs depended on it. It surprised me. I thought it would be more like the English system where O'Neill would be a respected elder and not much more. By and large they ignored Edward Kennedy, who had come into the room with him.

Now they were standing beside me. It felt bizarre. I wish I could describe what all this was like. It wasn't just a shake hand and goodbye, I was here to talk to them as an equal, to achieve things. It didn't really bother me beforehand but, when I was there I thought, 'Oh Jesus, here we go . . .' and that distanced part of me that I've talked about before stood back and thought 'weird'. I was neither awkward nor awed. I exuded confidence and conviviality. But there I am at lunch in the Capitol, surrounded by powerful people under the lights of a hundred cameras and on each side of me is Tip O'Neill and Edward Kennedy. I had to stop myself staring and there was so much I wanted to ask them. Oh well, I thought, don't betray yourself, tell them what you think. You'll probably never see them again. Seize the time.

O'Neill was a huge, avuncular and amiable man with a red face, a bulbous nose, bushy white eyebrows and a shock of white hair. He looked like a man you might see in any Irish country bar, except that the native Irish have a pinched look which is entirely missing from the upright, well-fed faces of Irish Americans. Neither could join us for lunch but both wanted us to see them in their offices later in the day. We talked for a bit and as he was leaving Tip O'Neill asked me where I was from.

'I thought I heard the accent,' he said, when I told him it was Dublin, but he seemed genuinely surprised. It was evidence of the power of the Irish lobby there. He took my arm and turned me round to where the photographers stood snapping. The cameras were rolling. Putting his arms around me and with Teddy Kennedy on my other side, he addressed them. 'We very much admire this young man and any laws we have to pass to smooth his path and any red tape we have to cut to do likewise, we're going to do.' Whether he meant it or not was irrelevant, he'd said it and it was on camera. It was a propitious start to our dealings with the politicians which were to follow.

Over lunch I talked to members of the farming lobby about the way in which their interest coincided with those of the Africans in need. Agriculture in America is quite clearly caught up in a vicious circle. There are parallels with the follies of the EEC's agricultural policy. Basically there are too many farmers for America's needs. But because they represent a big voting lobby the government goes in for large-scale subsidies of agriculture. The problem arises from the fact that most of these subsidies are taken up and manipulated, not by individual farmers, but by the large agribusiness companies. Small farmers then need to go for greater subsidy and the end result is vast overproduction and massive amounts of money spent on storage or even on destroying the food. As many of the small farmers are squeezed out by agribusiness their debts increase and the bank forecloses on them. Eventually their banks collapse, which is what happened in 1984 with several of the major mid-Western financial houses. All this is aggravated by the huge $195.9 billion American trade deficit. Although I am ambivalent about food aid, it is the sole means of preventing starvation. Therefore, more food aid to Africa, I told the farming congressmen, would create genuine markets for these farmers. Eventually agricultural subsidies could be reduced. But the first step in the chain was that the U.S. government must increase its aid budget by a substantial percentage and decrease its all-embracing policy of subsidy that benefits nobody but agribusiness. 'So it is not just a moral requirement that you should give more aid to Africa,' I reiterated. 'It is also a sound economic one. Your leaders mouth platitudes about how Africa needs to stand on its own feet and then in the next breath announce a $50 million increase in internal agricultural subsidies. You need the African market as much as they need your food,' I concluded. I suggested that they create a separate caucus and become a power-block in order to help the small farmer by putting unified pressure on the administration.

I had talked so much that I hadn't finished my soup. Everything I said seemed to make sense to me. I was surprised how much I had learned since I'd started this and that I retained quantities of complex figures and could use them. When I needed to, I 'aw shucksed' and 'Mr Smithed' my way in best James Stewart tradition, but that was largely unnecessary. People listened and argued, but what they liked best, I think, was the lack of ambivalence.

Meeting Teddy Kennedy was unsettling. Harvey and I were shown into his office to wait for him. It was a small room in the Senate building. We were told as we waited that senior politicians tended to get larger offices. Kennedy is a senior senator, but he preferred this small one. All around Edward Kennedy's room were snapshots which have become icons of history: Mom and the boys, Dad and the boys, Robert running down the beach with his trouser legs rolled up and the football under his arm and the dog chasing him, John and the kids, John and Robert and Teddy. It was sad. The family photographs had taken on the air of being mere preludes to the great American tragedy.

I was familiar with every one of these mementoes, a personal past that was horrifically public. Kennedy came in. He smiled and was affable, but something of the atmosphere of those photographs clung to him. It was like someone's living room wall in Ireland come to life. That familiar Boston twang. He was getting jowly. The pores of his skin were large, the teeth still white, and the broken veins were visible through his florid complexion. I examined this man I already knew intimately. He cupped his forehead in his hand and rubbed his temple as he sat in his armchair. He seemed agitated. 'Aah,' he said, his jaws working and his mouth moving. I ran through a quick analysis of what we were doing and what I thought needed to be done. We talked about his visit to Ethiopia. He had been there just before I had. Some of the images of his trip had set themselves in my mind as examples of how I did not want to do it. Now he seemed to be coming round to Reagan's way of regarding the Ethiopians. 'So long as they are an unfriendly government the practicalities of the situation are that things will not substantially change.'

He was being pragmatic, but I said food aid should be considered differently to development aid, and that the principles of development itself needed to be re-examined. The bells rang for a vote in the Senate chamber and he asked us if we would like to see it. He led us down, chatting amiably once again, through the massed numbers of people milling about the corridors. This time the visitors were looking at Kennedy, as struck by seeing him in the flesh as I was. He took me onto the Senate floor, a surprisingly tiny but perfect room, and then returned with us to the galleries and explained the procedure while the vote was taken. I liked him, but I could not help feeling sad for him.

We did not scorn the tourist trail. It amazed me that unvetted visitors should be allowed to wander into the seat of government like this, unlike in the Kremlin or, indeed, Westminster. Wherever we went we would come across little crocodiles of rubber-neckers and their guides.

We went to the White House. The President was still ill, but there were moves to meet George Bush. I saw little point in this. The White House is very pretty. I'm interested in old furniture and carpets and I thought the stuff in that place was good. It is divided into small rooms that are easily livable in. The sitting rooms are plush but comfortable with a lot of French Empire seating and upholstery. There is a feeling of intimacy and I spent a long time looking at things. We crossed over to the Vice-President's office where Harvey demanded cuff-links. 'Yeah, I was told you give out cuff-links, where are they?' We were handed a box of vice-presidential cuff-links and a vice-presidential scarf-pin. Then we found a cupboard with vice-presidential stationery. 'From the office of the Vice-President' it said. We took lots of pens and 'Welcome Aboard Airforce I' cigarettes and then we left.

We went out to dinner that night with some politicians, one of whom seemed to have the sole ambition to meet Sade. 'Could you fix it up, Bob?' We heard all the dirt. Marriages there don't last. The pursuit of love has no place in this world dedicated to the pursuit of power. Marriages are often alliances between two families, like something from the Middle Ages in Europe. The Georgetown cocktail circuit is where most work is done and the congressmen miss these parties at their peril. They start work at 7 a.m. and they finish at 1 or 2 in the morning. Weekends are spent rushing back to constituencies thousands of miles away, but then there is the fear that you'll miss an all-important Sunday brunch which only those congressmen most assured of their voters' support could afford to attend. Being in Washington was like being in a Harold Robbins novel.

But while we were engaged in discussing the complexities of famine in back-room meetings, outside we carried on voicing the plain truths and certitudes for the consumption of the media. We developed a dual approach which was to stand me in good stead in my trips to Australia, to the European Parliament and around Africa. In public I asked the simple questions; in private I pressed for answers, commitments and financial packages on individual projects. Occasionally my reiterations of those simplistic, self-evident truths would lead people to underestimate us and think that they could take advantage.

I went to Australia to receive the prestigious Pater award. Receiving foreign awards meant I could get to the countries without paying, thank the people there for their contributions and see the governments. Leading politicians, of both major parties, were present at the award ceremony. I arrived at the same time as the Prince and Princess of Wales. The press there seemed to expect me to attack them. 'Don't you find it odd, Bob, to be here trying to raise money for the starving at the same time that Prince Charles arrives? He must be one of the richest men in the world. How do you cope with the contrast between his life and those of the people you saw in Africa?'

'I do not draw comparisons like that. The gap between the Third World and our world is so wide that it would be a nonsense to try to compare them. If I did the discrepancy between your own lifestyle and that of the average Ethiopian would be pretty sickening. Compared to them, even the poorest person in the West is wealthy beyond imagining.'

It was a cheap question. In fact the Prince of Wales had done a lot for Live Aid. In addition to a substantial personal donation, the amount of which I am not at liberty to disclose, he gave us a good deal of support. His mere presence at Live Aid added another dimension to the event, and it had been proved that the more dimensions there were, the more contributions came in.

Of all the people I have met since this began, Prince Charles is without doubt the one I have been most impressed by. I find myself more in agreement with him than anybody else. He is concerned, compassionate, highly intelligent and I think nervous about expressing himself. He is a maverick, and not just within the narrow parameters of the Royal family.

Harvey was in a panic the afternoon we went to the Palace for the concert of Bach and Handel. 'Should I order a Daimler?'

'If you want to.'

'It's not a bit much, is it?'

'I don't know.'

'What about a Merc?'

'Who cares, Harvey, we'll go in a taxi.'

'Nah. We gotta do the whole bit. I'll get a Daimler . . . What do you think?'

'Harvey, shut up, I don't care.'

'Nicole, order a Merc, will you?'

That night, as we pulled into the gates of Buckingham Palace, Harvey heaved a sigh of relief as he caught sight of all the Volvos and Rovers in the car park. 'Thank God I didn't get a Daimler.'

We were shown up the main stairway to the right by liveried staff. This was a palace in the grand style. Perhaps the private rooms are cosy, but the reception rooms seemed garish and too brightly lit. The gold leaf was too gold, the white paint too white, the Chinese vases were placed without an eye for proportion. I was disappointed. Paula and Harvey and myself drank in everything like shy schoolboys at a rich cousin's birthday party. The pictures were fabulous. Here were all the tangled web of royal relations painted throughout the centuries by the best. We followed the other concert-goers to the ballroom, a huge grand room with a massive organ at the back end and a canopied throne at the other. This was where the decorations and things are dished out. 'Very nice,' said Harvey. It is a tall room with superb acoustics. The orchestra appeared and set up in the arched area by the throne, then everyone stood up and the Prince and Princess came in. The show began.

I got bored quickly and wished I could use the excuse that I had to go to lunch with my mother, as Charles had done at Live Aid. At the half-time break we went through some pretty rooms to get our glass of wine and canapés. We stood in one circular room with a wonderfully ornate ceiling. It had a vast bay window which looked out on the palace lawns. It was difficult to believe you were in the centre of London, for no buildings rose above the levels of the trees on the edge of the grass.

Princess Diana came over. 'Hi,' she said. She wore a lacy, chiffony dress. 'Is that a Zandra Rhodes?' I said.

'Yes,' she replied, 'but it's meant to be off the shoulder, down here,' she said, indicating her upper arms. 'Every time I shake hands with someone, it shoots up around my neck so I've just left it there.' I like her, she's a laugh.

Prince Charles moved over with the Chairman of the Intermediate Technology group which specializes in producing appropriate low-tech inventions and equipment which can be easily manufactured on site in the Third World. He introduced us, then said, 'What do you think of the concert?' I shrugged. 'Oh, really, I thought you said you liked Handel?'

'I do, but it's just the odd bits I know. I prefer Bach so maybe the next half…'

'That's a pity,' he said, and we began talking of Africa. People tend to forget when they talk to Prince Charles that he has a wide frame of reference from which to draw his arguments. He has met most, if not all, of the African and other world leaders and, indeed, has probably known them in the different stages of their careers. It's interesting to hear him talk of them. Before he left to go back to the concert, Charles asked if I would visit one morning and have a chat with him. After I had returned from my trip to Africa, I was asked to Kensington Palace where the Prince has his office.

It is more of a house than a palace, and the rooms are of manageable size.

'Don't think much of the carpet,' I said, referring to the trellised lime green and grey thing with the Prince of Wales' crest I had tripped on coming up the wide stairs. 'Yes, it is rather garish, isn't it?' he said. His office was like a drawing room with a desk by a large window looking out on a courtyard. There were books everywhere and the desk-top was full of paper and pens and the ephemera of work.

Prince William came in and wanted his father to go and play with him. He said he couldn't, he had to talk to this man, indicating me.

'Why do you have to talk to that man?' said the young Prince.

'Because we have work to do,' said his father.

'He's all dirty,' said the boy.

'Shut up, you horrible boy,' I said. I was wearing my jeans and sneakers, as usual, and I had my normal five o'clock shadow.

'He's got scruffy hair and wet shoes,' said the boy, indicating my beloved and comfortable, but admittedly scuffed suede yellow-green sneakers.

'Don't be rude, run along and play,' said the now mortified father.

'Your hair's scruffy, too,' I retorted, to the boy who would be king.

'No it's not, my mummy brushed it,' answered my tormentor, before leaving the room.

'Sorry about that,' said the Prince.

'Out of the mouth of babes . . .' I answered magnanimously.

I told him of my trip. He wanted to know about the people I met and what Band Aid was up to. His sister was just about to leave for the Sudan and he asked about that. We talked about the endless conundrum of aid and Africa. We argued about appropriate technology and small schemes for development rather than the expensive, grandiose high-profile projects once favoured. Then the talk turned to architecture where I hold similar views to him. Bad architecture and design, perhaps more than any other single contributory factor, has altered our lifestyle and made our streets and lives more shabby and depressing. All modernist architecture is a denial of the spirit, ingenuity and aesthetic of man. I loathe it and am in agreement with Auberon Waugh, who suggests that upon meeting an architect at a party, you simply hit him.

Charles seems unsure about expressing his opinion in public. He always begins to fiddle with his cuffs or collar or tie when he's about to say something people might disagree with. When he talks of the inner cities, architecture, or medicine, or the quality of life, or the need to help others, millions agree with him, but he seems to be the only one saying it. Because of his position, he knows he will be attacked. 'It's all right for *him* to say that.' But precisely because of that he is in nobody's pocket, and therefore has nothing to gain or lose by saying what he thinks. He seems to be groping his way towards some new consensus that ideally expresses the wish of everyone. How ironic that royalty should become Everyman. In his avowal of the indeterminate spiritual aspect of man, of which all the things he talks about are a part, he is again, I believe, articulating something intuitively felt by people but not satisfied by the established Church. In his support of 'alternative' medicines, i.e. medicines practised here up to the turn of the century and still used in most parts of the world, he has given voice to something people feel about the Valium-based scientific rationalism of our current medical practice. Doctors, too, are not only out of touch, they have lost their touch. This isn't crankery, it is a commonly-held intuitive belief that things and institutions we have been led to believe in and are foisted upon us are no longer working. The holy grails of religion, medicine, social engineering, and others, have become tarnished. The only one of substance saying this in a low-key way is Prince Charles. We didn't talk of all this, but I did say he must continue to talk about these things. He will always be resisted, but a lot of people will agree.

Diana came into the room. I don't know them, but she seems to have relaxed him and given him confidence. She said hello, that she was going out; did he want anything, and maybe she'd see me in Australia. I said 'OK.' I left soon afterwards.

★   ★   ★

Money was pouring in to Band Aid. We had allocated twenty per cent of the money for immediate relief, twenty per cent for shipping and transport and the rest for long-term development projects which required careful vetting by our team of experts.

In a curious way, and one which I did not welcome, people didn't seem to think their money was being spent unless they saw me in Africa. I decided to go again in order to establish confidence and show people what was being done and also draw attention to the other affected Sahelian countries, some of which had rarely been heard of in Britain. It was a device to keep the famine in the news up to Christmas, to show another aspect of it and to seek advice on the best ways to spend the remaining money. British Aerospace offered us free use of an eight-man jet and we invited the BBC, *The Times* and the *Sunday Times* to accompany us, provided they paid for the fuel. The idea was to finance the project without spending any of the money donated by the public.

The trip was to begin in West Africa in Mali and then progress through the six countries which lay across the continent in the Sahelian belt which lies just below the Sahara. It was an instructive journey which showed that, although the weather had improved, the famine was far from over. It also gave us an understanding of the ordinary way of life for African peasants who were not caught in the apocalyptic crisis which afflicted the highlands of Ethiopia, but whose everyday life consisted of what we in the West would regard as abject destitution. The BBC pictures were sent all over the world and drew attention to the emergency which continues unremarked in so many parts of Africa.

Trucks and boats and rock 'n' roll.

Band Aid – The Magnificent Seven and me: (left to right) Kevin Jenden, Dee Flowers, Penny Jenden, Phil Rusted, Judy Anderson, Valerie Blondeau (standing), Ken Martin on Band Aid I.

The natural forces which created the context in which the famine existed were truly formidable; the sands of the Sahara were sweeping southwards at the rate of twenty miles a year and elsewhere land is degraded to desert through overgrazing and other bad land uses. In Burkina Faso we saw how efficient peasant co-operatives, albeit in the controlling hands of a nationalist Nasserite autocrat can, using no more than their native resources, reorganize agricultural practices to bring real hope for the future. In Niger we pushed north into the Sahara to examine the lot of a few of the millions of destitute nomads throughout the Sahel whose cattle and goats died long ago in a drought so severe that in many places even the camels had been wiped out. In Chad we flew carefully without navigation lights to avoid the missiles of any one of the four different armies who control different sections of this ravaged country which ought to be, given peace, fertile enough to produce enough grain to feed the entire Sahel. In the Sudan we became enmeshed in the intrigue and rivalry of the agencies there. This is Africa's largest country, and, although it is potentially one of the richest in the continent, is paralysed by unproductive mercantilism, political plotting and civil war. In Ethiopia we saw some of the success stories of earlier aid, but found once more how the internal politics of the Soviet-backed government and the anti-communist attitudes of the Western powers combined to limit the success of both the local and the international relief workers.

By now the style and the techniques of Band Aid were becoming well defined. Our aim was to find out what was needed by asking the local people and the aid workers on the ground. We were looking, in part, for needs which could be met by special appeals back home rather than by cash hand-outs. We wanted to use Band Aid as a conduit for other people's actions rather than set ourselves up as an operating agency. When it did come to projects which required the spending of money we looked for a government or inter-national body to approach to get dollar-for-dollar funding; we had found the American government happy to collaborate on this basis in the building of a million-pound bridge over the River Chari in Chad to enable the rapid transport of aid goods which at present come by canoe. We came to an arrangement with USAID and the U.N. whereby we bought a desperately needed truck fleet to get grain to the rebel provinces of Wollo, Tigre and Eritrea. In doing this cross-continental tour we were creating a device which enabled the media to report from places and air issues which might otherwise not have been covered. In my mobile press group I carried with me both the platform and the expertise to make best use of my policy of making bold statements in public and asking informed questions in private.

I was becoming less nervous about meeting these heads of government. Now I felt more confident about dealing with them.

The first of the African leaders whom I met on this trip was Captain Thomas Sankara, the revolutionary leader in Burkina Faso, the second country on our itinerary. Things had not got off to a promising start in Bamako, Mali's capital, which we visited first. There had been too much politeness and protocol for my liking, and I had asked the Red Cross, who were organizing the details of the trip, to try to cut it out in the next countries. In Bamako there had been too many courtesy meetings with civic dignitaries. They had wheeled out the Minister of Culture on the assumption that culture was the closest they could get to pop music. One of the journalists on the trip, David Blundy of the *Sunday Times* described the meeting in terms of the air conditioner which wheezed away in one corner of the minister's office. It flickered and grumbled, then faltered, then stopped. The conversation took a similar course. 'Why do they call Timbuctoo the mysterious city, minister?' I asked, in a desperate conversational gambit.

'If I knew, it would no longer be a mystery,' he replied. How we roared!!

'Is there somewhere I can go to hear some music?' I said, trying to inject a cultured tone.

'There will be a festival in two months,' he replied.

'I meant tonight,' I answered. In the uneasy silence the thought occurred to me that this was how Prince Charles had said things were for him, seeing only what they wanted you to see, making fatuous conversation with a man who had nothing to tell you.

In the days which followed I began to develop a horror of what I christened the Prince Charles Syndrome. It consisted of finding myself in a place of boundless interest and yet being hemmed in and frustrated by courtesy and etiquette. When we landed in Ouagadougou, the capital of Burkina, I took one look out of the aircraft window and shouted to the pilot to take off again. On the runway was a guard of honour of boy scouts, musicians and dancers.

'Welcome, Bob Gilduff,' they chanted, to the accompaniment of drums and clapping. One of the national radio stations dubbed me, seemingly without any sense of irony, 'Geldof d'Afrique'.

That night at Ouagadougou I walked, embarrassed, from the stage at a concert given in my honour after Burkina's version of Johnny Carson repeatedly invited me to sing with a band of revolutionary children called the Little Singers of the Raised Fist. He had been told emphatically in advance not to ask, but he insisted, so I walked off. They could not understand why I would not sing. I could not understand why they would want me to.

It was not in the best of moods that I approached the presidential palace for my private audience with Sankara. In the dark velvety African night the palace stood massive and ornate in imposing grounds which had obviously been laid out in the style of formal gardens in the French colonial days. An elaborate system of roadblocks, checkpoints and sentries stood between the people and their president. We waited in a high-ceilinged ante-room where hard-faced young men in army fatigues and machine guns lolled on Louis Quinze chairs. Sankara was not what I had been led to expect.

He sat in a chair in the corridor outside the presidential office, a svelte young man who looked uncomfortably like Eddie Murphy in a neatly fitted parachutist's jumpsuit. He seemed a little nervous about meeting me. He was an impressive character with a ready smile who expounded with large whirling movements of his arms the philosophy of populist revolution he had introduced. He seemed to equally despise the American and Soviet systems of economic imperialism which hold most African nations in thrall. He had set up a system of revolutionary committees to organize the peasants into co-operative efforts and make the most of the few resources the country had. He had also introduced a series of swingeing austerity measures which had greatly upset the powerful bourgeoisie in the capital who were now deprived of the French wines, perfumes and cheeses which they had previously imported while ninety-seven per cent of the nation went hungry. He drew little diagrams to explain the economy and the uneven distribution of wealth. 'When I was a boy I would see the president ride by in big cars. Now I'm president I have to get rid of the big cars to show people I'm serious.' He hitch-hikes to meetings of the Organization of African Unity. Other leaders reluctantly give him lifts. 'I will not spend money on useless things.' He was stranded in some country on the way home from the last OAU meeting. The President of that place wouldn't lend him his plane. When abroad he stays on the floors of his diplomats' bed-sitting rooms. They are not allowed hotels. All this seems childish, but it seemed to work. The people took example from this man and he made things difficult for his ministers who otherwise might be seduced by the little perquisites of power. This gave them a healthy dose of realism.

It was hot in the corridor. The humidity was high and a fog of insects surrounded all the lamps and swarmed irritatingly all over my skin. 'I do have an office with air conditioning but I do not use it,' he said. 'It costs a lot to run. Why should I have it when my people do not? It is a big office with a big desk.' He paused then added, 'Perhaps you would like to buy it from me?'

Sankara said his austerity measures were so harsh that they upset even himself. Perhaps I could send him some more tapes from England? He liked Bob Marley, and I had taken one of the journalists' cassettes of the Jamaican singer to give to him. 'I want to have a big concert in Ouagadougou. Do you think you could get people to play here? I play the guitar. I am thinking of forming a band.' I told him I was busy but that he could try the King of Thailand who was a fair sax player.

I liked Sankara. He had energy and a sense of humour. He was quite happy to discuss the potential shortcomings of his revolution which, though it seemed to be working well towards making the nation self-sufficient, had set up the machinery of an autocracy which could easily slip into fascism. Amnesty International had reported that he subjected his foes to barbaric forms of torture with blowtorches. Although it had nothing to do with aid, I felt I had a responsibility to ask him. It was the Everyman feeling again; this was the first subject anyone who knew anything about the place would have brought up in a pub conversation about the man. If I could put pressure on him, or if I could register my abhorrence perhaps it would do some good. I argued with him. He was quite open to that. He went on a rambling explanation about how in our countries people can still be put to death for treasonable acts like attempted coup d'etat. We don't actually have that problem, unlike him who has at least four attempts a year.

I interrupted and said, 'But do you torture people?'

'I'm coming to that, I'm coming to that,' he said smiling. He said he killed people who tried to overthrow him because he felt he was doing right for the country and if in the future other people plotted against him he would kill them too. He said Amnesty had made a mistake about him and they had written and apologized. But Amnesty say that they have not.

The odd thing was that he and the others did not refuse to answer such questions. Sometimes they were even keen to do so. Perhaps he had never been asked them before in such a direct manner; certainly his advisers would not do so, nor would any diplomat or resident aid worker intent on maintaining a long-term relationship with the man, nor would any journalist except as the final question in an interview which would be peremptorily terminated. I tried to make every conversation informal by lounging on the chairs, using a lot of physical contact, asking very blunt questions and making jokes. I argued with Sankara about justice, which I felt his People's Tribunals could not possibly dispense. 'What do you think you are, an African Robespierre?' I queried. 'No,' he laughed, 'but justice is above the law.' 'No,' I replied. 'Justice is a by-product of law and you cannot have a state if there is no law and the people are not qualified to interpret the law without prejudice.' We argued into the night. He is at a crossroads now which could lead him down the road to autocracy or he could become a genuine example for the future of Africa. On the other hand, he could be dead next year.

It was the same story with President Habré in Chad when I asked him if he felt the French had betrayed his country by abandoning it to Colonel Gadaffi, who now controlled almost a third of it. He shrugged and sighed and said somewhat sadly, 'As General De Gaulle said, states don't have friends, they only have interests'. Later, I repeated this to President Mitterrand who shrugged and said, 'Ask him who is paying for his army's wages'. These were the questions I wanted to ask for myself. It is intriguing to meet these people, and in case I never got the opportunity again I asked them about themselves rather than their policies. What makes them tick is the key to which way the country will go. I was going to ask Habré about the fact that he is said to have strangled his enemies with his bare hands, but he seemed so sad and statesman-like at the same time that it would have been crass and have interrupted the flow of constructive conversation.

It was almost midnight when we arrived in the Sudan. The streets of Khartoum were entirely deserted. We discovered that there was a curfew from early evening to dawn following an attempted coup against the government only a few weeks before. The restrictions only served to increase the sense of claustrophobia and reinforce the paranoia which the place has nurtured in the various relief agencies and charities there. Wherever the agencies operate, a certain amount of rivalry seems to spring up inevitably. It is not always as overt as the incident I had been told about in West Africa where a fist fight had developed between the representatives of two leading British agencies before a group of bewildered Africans whom they were supposedly there to help. But nearly always there is some element of tension. I had learned that on my first visit to Ethiopia where people from individual agencies would sidle up to me to lobby for cash for their own personal projects, despite the fact that I had made it quite clear that what Band Aid needed was a consensus view from *all* of them on what were the top priorities. Such inter-agency rivalry diverts people's energies from the real job in hand. In some cases it actually inhibits progress. It was in the hot-house atmosphere of Khartoum that we first came face to face with it. This time it took the form of direct criticism of Band Aid in Britain. Old-hand aid experts had contacted papers like the *Daily Express* to complain that they had offered their services to Band Aid and had not been taken up.

'Does Geldof know what he is doing?'

'How can a bunch of amateurs spend such a large sum properly?'

'Why are large amounts of Band Aid cash languishing in bank accounts instead of feeding the starving?'

The charges were predictable enough. Band Aid was run by volunteers but these volunteers, of course, included professional businessmen and women, lawyers, accountants, and a qualified anthropologist. But what made an aid worker professional, anyway? Was it the difference between being paid and unpaid? If so, then we were definitely all amateurs. Was the man I rang at Oxfam who had been working there three months a professional, and I, who'd been working in aid ten months, the amateur? Or was it just the standard knee-jerk self-protective response from all professionals who feel threatened by the fact that it's suddenly clear their job requires very little 'professionalism'? Working at the headquarters of most of the agencies is easy. Working in the field requires Trojan mental and physical strength and great expertise, but we were not in competition there. The decisions on funding the original emergency programmes had been taken in rapid response to requests from the field. Now that more complex long-term issues were being dealt with the board of trustees acted on the advice of a team of eminent academics all with regular working experience in the field. They came from specialist development departments in the universities of Sussex and Reading, from the School of Hygiene and Tropical Medicine and the School of Oriental and African Studies in London and from Georgetown University in Washington. The idea that they did not know what they were doing was risible.

But such allegations were given credence by the attitude which developed among certain individuals in other aid agencies. From the outset we had resisted approaches made to us by individual agencies. All decisions, we felt, could best be taken in the field by standing committees which included representatives of all the major agencies. They would give us a clear idea of the priorities for a given country or area. Individually the same people were likely simply to press for funding for their own pet project. People became cross when we refused to fund their particular scheme. Issues became personalized.

Back at home some of the backbiting continued with allegations that Live Aid had created no new money but had simply scooped the pool in one quick trawl of everything that would have been available to charities in general that year. It was, of course, impossible to refute such an argument because amounts raised in any given period vary according to the scale of any current disaster and the publicity it receives. Certainly it was not simply coincidence that Oxfam's income was up 200 per cent and Save the Children's 300 per cent in the same period, and that most other agencies dealing with famine had a large percentage increase also. We had helped, not subsumed them. The bitching did not concern me much. Our job was more in levelling the genuine criticism than in answering the carping kind, but it was harder trying to stay removed from inter-agency politics than party political ones.

I had arrived in the Sudan with an aching in-grown toenail. I had never experienced this before and it always seems such a ridiculous ailment, like gout or piles, but when it hits you it's bloody sore. I had spent all day in meetings and now I could barely walk. Kevin had been bitten by some insect in Chad and his thighs had swollen into balloons. The two of us, now exhausted as we came near to the end of our eighteen-hour-day, two-week trek across a continent, hobbled off to see an eminent surgeon in Khartoum. The patients at his surgery crowded round in the garden as he admitted them one by one. It seemed he was also a leading GP. He looked at our legs and said he'd see us an hour later at the hospital.

The hospital was lit garishly by fluorescent lights which buzzed and hopped with the usual insect life. It didn't look like the cleanest place in the world and I was thinking there were places I'd sooner be operated in. Kevin and I decided to literally hop it when a young intern walked in. He told us he would probably be doing both operations, overseen, of course, by Doctor So'n'so. Kevin and I rushed off again and were hobbling down the corridor deciding we could tolerate the pain when the good doctor arrived. Kevin went in first and came out all smiles. I was given three local anaesthetics but could feel the knife cutting and probing. Kevin took pictures, for Chrissakes. It was like being in some barbaric torture chamber. Water hissed and burbled against bleak tiled walls. I was sure I would contract gangrene. The anaesthetic wore off after an hour, and I still had two meetings to attend. I was in agony. I got to bed at two a.m. and rose early to catch a plane to western Sudan. My foot burned and ached. The more I walked the more it hurt. At one camp there was a little boy with a spastic arm inside his pullover; his sleeve hung limply beside him. 'What's wrong with your arm?' I asked him.

He showed it to me. 'I've got a bad spirit in it,' he said.

I pointed to my foot. 'What do you make of that?'

He stared at it. 'You've got an even worse one,' he said in tones of awe.

In Ethiopia, at an air-strip we saw Russian transporters carrying people from one of the camps to the southern re-settlement area. This was a contentious issue. Critics from agencies and western governments were saying it was a sinister government-inspired, political move to populate disputed areas and that the manner in which it was being carried out was brutal. On the other hand Brother Cesare, the Italian monk who ran Mekele camp, said to me, 'Where do these people go when they leave here? Do they return to their homes where there is no food or water, where the trees are gone and the soil eroded, only to return here in a month's time on the brink of starvation again? Where will I put these people? If there is somewhere else they can go, let them go there.'

Others said it was a logical decision, but the areas the people were being taken to had only relative fertility and that the ecological stability of the south would be threatened by a massive and sudden influx of refugees. They said too that the government had not prepared the areas for this influx and that there were no facilities for the immigrants.

Others said it was a way to speedily collectivize agriculture, a stated government aim. Others that because of the nature of the countryside it was difficult to control the population, so by bringing them together in easily accessible areas the government's power over them was increased.

We could see the straggling lines of people half a mile away quietly entering the holds of the *Antonovs*. The photographers snapped on their big lenses and surreptitiously began taking pictures. I imagined the end result, a long-distance shot implying a secret act being conducted and the long lines of 'victims' resembling, as indeed they did to me, the horror of the helpless victims of the concentration camps being loaded into the cattle trucks. 'Why are you using long lenses?' I said. 'Let's go over and look.'

We crossed the runways and approached the planes. No one stopped us. There were some guards slouching against walls, but I'd got used to them in the camps. The Russian crews were in civilian clothes. I talked to one young man from Kiev who had just graduated from Moscow University and spoke a few halting words of English. I gave him a Band Aid badge.

The people looked wretched. They had tiny bags on their backs and they held hands as they moved up the ramp of the plane. Few of them had seen aeroplanes before they moved to the camp, none of them had been in one. They were probably frightened, but they didn't show it. They were leaving their homeland forever. It could not sustain them. They and their families before them had lived there for thousands of years. The BBC was filming, nobody stopped them. I heard later the people were packed in so tight they were forced to stand holding their children above their heads. I didn't see that. The people were sitting on the floor of the military transporter. Later when the government stepped up resettlement and introduced quotas over-zealous officials apparently herded people together, threatening them if they didn't leave, and the abuses began. I certainly didn't see any of this and I was a completely unexpected visitor. The planes also were apparently not pressurized, so the people suffered cramp and sickness. It was a nightmare.

But Prime Minister....

The issue was clear: do we help in an area that is at best dubious or do we make a political judgement and refuse? Father Jack Finucane of Concern, the large Irish agency, said, while I was there in January, that they would never help in resettlement areas. But I myself being Irish knew that diaspora was a natural consequence of famine. Literally millions of people had left Ireland in the mid-nineteenth century to escape death by hunger. Still, in a chilling parallel with these planes crammed with humanity, hundreds of them had died below decks on the 'death ships' that took them to America.

Our policy was that we would help people whenever they were suffering and if they were suffering in the resettlement areas or the areas of civil war or any other politically affected area we would do our best to get to them.

I used the analogy of the concentration camps to someone who asked if I thought we were perpetuating an undesirable political policy by supporting the victims. The resettlement programme would continue whether or not we chose to help, just as Hitler's extermination of the Jews would have continued whether or not aid workers had contrived to help alleviate the suffering in the camps. Had I been alive during the War and had I been given the option of helping those people ease their pain for even one second I'd have done so, knowing full well the horror would continue. Our work employed the same argument. Concern, the agency which said it would never work in the resettlement areas, is now, twelve months later, the main agency working there.

I have heard all the reports on resettlement and I believe it to be partially an ideological programme that has resulted in brutality, misery and stupidity, but I also know the opposition to it is based round a conflicting ideology and is orchestrated, for outside forces' own ends. The EEC has now extracted a promise that resettlement will stop in exchange for aid. If you believe that you'll believe anything. If they stop it, it's because they no longer need it and if they don't want to stop it they won't.

* * *

The day after I returned from Africa I went to Strasbourg for a meeting of the European parliament. I had had an invitation from Lord Bethell, who is a Conservative MEP, and Catherine Crawley, a Labour MEP. I agreed on the understanding that it would be a non-party political gathering. I travelled with Nick Bethell as he lived in London. After two weeks of travelling in Africa I was not best pleased when the plane was diverted and we had a long overland drive with Bethell at the wheel. He would never get a job as a cab driver, let alone as a driver of a landrover in the far reaches of the deserts of Darfur. At the parliament building I was met by the large Irish contingent, including the Vice-President of the Commission, Paddy Lalor. They had been told not to make a big ceremony so they sort of slipped me an EEC gold medal. It was nice of them; it was like the time the old lady had slipped me the halfpenny at my first communion, or an affectionate uncle pushing some money discreetly into your hand. 'Ah sure, Bob, it's the least we could do for you,' said Paddy. A group of visiting Welsh women choristers burst into song for me in the main hall of the building. They were asked to be silent as the President of the German Republic was about to enter. The ladies kept going. As at the U.S. Congress, the MEPs and their aides and office workers asked for autographs to the disgust of the more protocol-minded officers. Kevin, myself and Ken Martin, our purchaser and shipper, met the German MEP Katherina Fock who is one of the main aid lobbyists. She explained to me the deficiencies in the system and the basis on which aid was given. This was a crucial meeting and I was to thank god for it later in the day.

On the way to the lunch Barbara Castle, the Labour ex-Cabinet Minister, asked me into a Labour group meeting. It turned out that they were refusing to attend the lunch because it was being organized by a Tory and wanted to meet me separately. I went in long enough to refuse.

'We're not going to a lunch paid for by the Tories,' said one MEP.

'They're paying for the grub. So what?'

'They can afford to pay for that, but they can't afford a proper foreign aid budget. They cut that like they cut everything else. Everything except their lunches.'

'Why don't you fuck off back to school?' I was incensed by the childishness. Was this the level on which people's lives were discussed – who paid for lunch?

'Well, if you're going to use language like that, lad . . .' interrupted another.

'You can fuck off as well.' Tempers were lost, I marched to the door.

'Bob, please stay, we've got something to say . . .'

'The place to say it is with everybody else. Now I'm going to have lunch with people from every other party – Communists, Social Democrats, Unionists, Liberals, Republicans, Tories – I don't care. The point about Band Aid is that famine is above politics, and you lot make the whole fucking thing a nonsense. It's not me or the Tories you're insulting. You're spitting in the faces of the dying.'

The exchange went on. They did put some points, but nothing startlingly new. What hope was there of concerted action from a united Europe when national self-interest and regionalized politics were still fought in the same pathetic manner?

It was a constructive lunch with questions from everyone, from an Italian Communist to the Ulster Unionist, John Taylor. I remembered this because later, when a furore blew up about me not getting an honour in the British New Year's Honours' List, he said that though it was extraordinary for a Unionist to say that a southern Irishman should get a medal, he thought I should get everything available. The Honours' List was a real storm in a teacup.

By that stage I'd got rows of honours, medals, awards and even honorary degrees from all over the world. One more was neither here nor there, though I didn't say so at the time because I thought it might seem impolite. But the incident did have the virtue of bringing me hundreds of letters from ordinary people and accolades like that one from Taylor, which I found touching.

After lunch I was taken to a massive auditorium. It was not the assembly room itself, but it felt almost as big. There were rows of tiered seats with all the paraphernalia for simultaneous translation and a lot of television cameras and journalists. I was horrified. I hadn't anticipated anything as grand as this, and I hadn't prepared a speech.

'Well, as you know, I've just come back from Africa. I haven't come here to give a formal address, but I'd just like to state some basic arguments and I'd like you to come back at me and interrupt if you think I've got it wrong.' They began to do that. The first was an Irish MEP. The thought suddenly struck me that it was rather like having an argument with a man in a pub in Grafton Street.

'You don't want the reform of the Common Agricultural Policy because half your constituents would go bust,' I said. 'The EEC agricultural subsidies are the only thing keeping Ireland afloat. You and I know that a lot of Irish farmers spend most of their time driving round in trucks filled with animals, crossing and recrossing the border so that they can keep picking up the subsidies.'

I began to talk about Chad and how the French government had abandoned Hissène Habré to the mercy of the Libyans. A furious French MEP got to his feet and began protesting. I matched him fact for fact. 'What is this secret agreement you've signed with Gadaffi? How come it's never been made public? How come the French army went in and then pulled out without checking on the Libyans?' He began shouting. I matched him shout for shout. 'What is in this secret deal for you? How come you're the only European country dealing in this way with Gadaffi?' He stormed out of the auditorium.

Suddenly politicians and journalists and people who had brought their children began clapping at the end of practically everything I said. 'The worst thing is that a lot of what the EEC does is excellent. You are the second biggest donor in the world. The airlift you have organized to the west of the Sudan has been an incalculable success. There is no disputing that. But the stupidity is that if you'd listened to the warnings you were given in the first place you could have built a road for what the airlift cost. And a road would have been there next year.'

I carried on at some length and suddenly found myself speaking fluently. All at once all the facts and figures, all the grumbles and frustrations accrued in weeks in the office in London and weeks in the field in Africa welled up from somewhere inside. I ended by saying that the EEC system had become constipated. 'For one day I don't mind acting as a laxative.'

There was applause at the end. The next day the press said that I had 'cut all before me with a brilliant grasp of the figures', or some such. I thought I had made rather a hash of it, and felt I'd let myself, Band Aid, and Joe Public down.

I went to Canberra to meet the Australian Prime Minister, Bob Hawke. Canberra is the compromise capital, chosen not to affront the civic pride of Sydney and Melbourne. Like any compromise it is not thoroughly satisfactory, having about it something of the dry bureaucratic atmosphere of Brussels or Strasbourg. Nothing much goes on except governmental affairs and I suspect Canberra probably resembles a ghost town at the weekends.

Bob Hawke is a populist and therefore careful of his image. He is very clever. We had an argument over the style of national government in Africa. He said, 'I agree with your analysis of Africa, but if Africa is to work, you must not presuppose the governments there are interested in the people's well-being.' He is quite right, a lot of power in Africa is concentrated in the hands of individuals who seek only their own aggrandisement.

I said, 'You must work and support the ones who do seek change, regardless of their ideologies and style of government. Providing they are genuinely helping their country, they must be encouraged. History and political dynamics will take care of the others.'

The conversation then turned to Australia's aid policy and what they had committed to the suffering countries in Africa. Australia's policy is essentially regional; most of its help is given to its less fortunate neighbours in South-East Asia and the Pacific. This, I claimed, had only limited validity. It might be good politically, but if the crises were in Africa or elsewhere, that's where they had to be dealt with. It's no use declaring you will only help if people are dying next door to you. That, he said, was a simplification. They had already sent massive aid under bilateral and multilateral agreements to Africa.

I pressed hard for the three requests which several agencies, including Australian ones, had asked me to put to the Prime Minister. I asked for 250,000 more tons of grain which was a direct request from those 'in the field in Africa'. I asked for the establishment of some African research stations into barren-land agriculture drawing on Australian experience, which was a recommendation from the Australian agencies. And I asked for the donation and refurbishment of ten Hercules planes which were standing moth-balled in Melbourne, a prospect already researched and requested by Action Aid Australia. I thought the Hercules the least attractive myself, but being wise to the vagaries of publicity, the most likely to be accepted as it was a strong media story. Planes are necessary for the transport of supplies in Ethiopia and the Sudan to inaccessible areas. To the agencies they are a mixed blessing as they cost a fortune to run and most agencies, including Band Aid, aim to spend their funds on long-term projects as opposed to the more immediate and desperately needed emergency relief which deals with short-term survival.

Band Aid did pay for a ten-day airlift of supplies to the people of the southern Sudan, who were cut off by war from any source of food. This was because the governments did not want to get politically involved.

I appealed to his sense of national pride by stating truthfully that Australia's unique expertise in arid-land agriculture would be of vital use in Africa, but the conversation returned to the planes and budgets. He said he'd see what he could do. I said we could help by trying to put together a coalition of governments or agencies to try and help fund part of the project if the cost to Australia of ten moth-balled planes was prohibitive.

On my return to Britain I was told the Prime Minister had gone on *Countdown*, the Australian top rock show, and announced that he was giving us two Hercules and 1.7 million Australian dollars to refit them. Weeks later we were told privately that the government expected us to pay a third of the costs, which were to be split between the Red Cross, the Australian Government and, supposedly, us. This surprised me as most governments pay the full costs of all planes working in the famine. The RAF, Luftwaffe, the Danes, the EEC, the Poles and Russians all paid their own costs. The Belgians had already supplied the Red Cross with a Hercules and were supplying crew and meeting costs. We called all the agencies and asked them if they wanted to join in a joint sponsorship. The answer was, inevitably, no; 'we've spent our money on long-term projects'. Band Aid's short-term emergency aid had been already spent, so we began calling governments. The U.S. and Britain said no, they'd already paid for their own planes. I raised the matter with Mitterrand, saying it would help France's recently tarnished image in the South Pacific, but it was the one request the French rejected. Band Aid had $250,000 left in Australia from funds donated by Australians during Live Aid. These were being held and monitored by the International Disasters Contingency Committee in Australia, but they said it was their money not ours, which was odd because it hadn't been given to them. We had reached an impasse. We talked to the New Zealand government. They said they might do something. Meanwhile the Australian High Commission called us. We explained our situation and said the government should pay all the planes' running costs. It was a tiny amount of money for a national government, but a major expenditure for an aid agency. The planes are working in Africa and we've heard nothing since. I wonder who paid.

My second official visit to the States was to receive an honour from the Congressional black caucus. I am not easily impressed, but I felt that this honour was one really worth having. In the past this award had gone to figures like Martin Luther King. I was the first white man to get it.

The presentation dinner was a sumptuous affair, attended by America's most prominent black leaders. Stunningly attractive women dripped with jewels and arrived in giant Cadillacs and limousines. What seemed peculiar, given the ostentatious circumstances, was the unthinking way in which blacks assumed there was a community of attitude and interest between them and the diverse peoples of Africa. I addressed the problem in my acceptance speech which followed a series of predictable denunciations of South Africa.

'I do not want anybody to fail to understand my total abhorrence of the mad evil, apartheid. This scar on the corner of my forehead is the mark of that. I gained it by being beaten by the Irish police during a march against apartheid when I was a schoolboy. It is a vile system whose days are thankfully numbered. But I want to draw a parallel. I am Irish and Irish Americans always irritate me. They pretend to be Irish when in fact they are Americans through and through. They have American attitudes and American values, which is right, and of which they can be justifiably proud. The problem comes when they begin to impose those values on a situation in Ireland which is totally alien to their understanding. It leads them into fund-raising which fuels the troubles over there and leads to more of my countrymen being killed. Make no mistake, black Americans are not Africans. They are Americans and they don't instinctively understand the problems of Africa any more than I do.'

I told them what a black cameraman with ABC TV sitting at my table had said to me. He had been appalled by the conditions in which people lived in South Africa. 'It's so bad down there that sometimes they don't even have toilet paper.' Was this the final concept of poverty? Was this the ultimate American fear? That one day the toilet paper would run out?

When I had been in Ethiopia I had heard of a visiting black American who had placed the headphones of his Sony Walkman on the ears of one of the starving children he had been filming. The child jerked in a spasm of fear. It had never heard western pop music before and now here was this fiendish noise invading its head like some evil spirit. The child continued to jerk with terror. 'Hey, look, the kid is really getting into the music,' the American had said. It was a metaphor for what was happening there on a political, economic and social front.

'What Africa has always suffered from, and continues to suffer from, is the imposition of alien values by outsiders. You have to go to Africa and find out what people want and then force your government to do something which is actually needed rather than continuing to impose through the World Bank and the IMF economic preconditions and requirements which, unwittingly or not, are more of a burden to the people of Africa than a help. And that is as true for the people who suffer in South Africa as it is for the famine-stricken regions. Inevitably the despicable regime of apartheid will fall but this is the African holocaust north to south, east to west, and it will take more than well-meaning platitudes of brotherhood to stop it and help these people.'

Any fear I had that they might misconstrue my intentions were dispelled by the applause which followed. Jesse Jackson detached himself from his entourage and approached me afterwards. 'I'll be in London soon. You give me your phone number and we'll get together, go out and knock some heads together.'

Back in Europe Live Aid was spawning a host of offshoots: Actor Aid, Air Aid, Art Aid, Asian Live Aid, Bear Aid, Bush Aid, Cardiff Valley Aid, Fashion Aid, Food Aid, the list went on longer than an alphabet. One of the most successful was School Aid, a project to raise simple equipment and foodstuffs like flour and sugar and have them shipped free of charge by British Rail to the Band Aid ships at Tilbury Docks. Its importance lay not so much in the goods themselves as in the consciousness-raising element of the exercise. We provided videos and information packs which tried to develop a new perspective on Third World issues and dispel some of the old unspoken clichés that Africans were lazy, feckless and ignorant people who brought much of their tragedy upon themselves. We showed that we had to change our own policies and that helping need not be guilt-motivated or based on misguided notions of 'charity'.

In France, School Aid had mushroomed on a massive scale, due in part to its brilliant organizer Lionel Rotcage and to the refusal of teachers to become involved with it, which had made it a symbol of rebellion for the schoolchildren who began organizing area conferences and electing School Aid ambassadors. The success of Action Ecole enabled me to meet President Mitterrand some months later and obtain major concessions from him.

I was totally bewildered by my reception in Ireland. For years people had either loathed or liked or ignored both the band and me. I had never lied or withheld my opinion in Ireland. Years ago I had finally nailed my colours to the mast and stated in public the things I thought wrong with the place. I had been vilified, denounced from the pulpit, and we had been banned from playing. People had been proud when we were Number One, as indeed was I, wearing a medal with the Irish colours for its ribbon on *Top of the Pops*. But I was now 'a credit to the nation'. Similarly, my ambivalent attitude towards Ireland altered. I saw the energy that could be tapped there, the huge generosity of the people, and I wondered what it could achieve with the shackles of history and morality removed. I returned to thank everyone for donating, in the final accounting, £7 million. That is £2 for every man, woman, child, and baby. It is the equivalent of the U.S. giving $500 million.

I was reassured when the 'official' Mercedes awaiting our arrival broke down after ten yards so Paula, myself and Fifi were jammed into the back of the VW minibus belonging to the TV crew covering our arrival. We were driven to Aras An Ūachtairan, the magnificent presidential house in Phoenix Park. We stumbled out of the van and into the fabulous Georgian building. The President showed us proudly around. There was refreshingly little pomp to either the house, the staff, or Dr Hillary, the President, who introduced me to the tea ladies, who asked for autographs. This was the old English Viceregal lodge with magnificent eighteenth-century plasterwork ceilings and equally fine Donegal carpets. I asked Dr Hillary if it wasn't a bit boring doing the job. This was a man who was President of the EEC Commission and has been in active politics all his life. The Presidency of Ireland is an elected post with a term of seven years, but no political power. Basically you make speeches, present things and open community gymnasiums. 'They're trying to get me to do another seven years' solitary, as I call it,' said the President ruefully.

I was presented with a cheque for £7 million. The President made a little speech and Fifi crawled on the carpet. I said, 'As the President represents Ireland, I can do this . . .' and I leant over to kiss the startled man on the cheek. He blushed. I said, probably for the first time, that I was proud to be Irish and that I would like to buy everyone in the country a drink with all this money, but as there were a few million other people who needed the drinks more than we did, the money would be going to them. The Lord Mayor of Dublin gave me a silver tankard and the City Manager gave me his Dublin City tie. They thought I was rude when in my speech I attacked the destruction of Dublin. I didn't mean to be rude, I just hate the wholesale devastation of what was once one of the prettiest small towns in Europe.

Garret Fitzgerald, the Prime Minister, is the sort of politician you would vote for every time if your instinct ruled your brains. He is singularly honest and strikes me as having an appealing lack of guile, sure doom for a politician. The problem is that he is an intellectual, something that has seldom helped politicians. They become plagued with doubt and equivocation. He is also burdened with a coalition government and falling ratings in the polls, but he is a genuinely good person.

We talked a long time. He promised to do whatever he could through the EEC. The conversation ranged through everything to do with Ireland. All my old frustrations reemerged and I asked him why, given the unity of purpose, energy and ability manifested during Live Aid, it was not possible for the Irish to turn that to use for themselves. He raised his shoulders and sighed, 'I don't know'.

★ ★ ★

The question was what to do next. There was a certain number of loose ends to tie. I went to the Indonesian Embassy to try to prevent the pirating of the Live Aid tape which was being done quite legally there because the Indonesian government has not signed any international copyright conventions. I wanted it stopped and any tax the government had gained to be repaid to us. I threatened to call in Australia for a tourist boycott of Bali and a boycott on imported Indonesian foodstuffs and if they didn't work, I'd take my sleeping bag and settle down outside the presidential palace in full view of most of the world's TV cameras until they gave in. The pirating stopped but by then they were probably finished manufacturing anyway. Once affairs like that had been seen to it was difficult to know if there was any further use for me or Band Aid.

I had set out to raise the issue. It has been raised. Part of the achievement of Band Aid was the memory it left of one day of decency in a tawdry world. We had shown that Edmund Burke was right when he said, 'Nobody made a greater mistake than he who did nothing because he could only do a little'. Live Aid had shown that whatever little you could do, there was a need for it and it was important that you do something.

One or two people talked about making Band Aid a permanent institution. I could not see the point. Why create another Oxfam when the original Oxfam already does such a good job? In any case it had never been our intention to compete with the established charities. Our role was to complement their work, and in the face of the holocaust which was sweeping Africa to create a new constituency; to help make people feel that we must take care of one another. We had made it exciting to help other people and we had created an educational basis of understanding. We had wielded our political strength and we had set up convoys of ships, hundreds of trucks, airlifts, clinics, tons of food and medicine, clothing, blankets, toys, endless projects had been funded and we had helped keep millions of people alive. It was a long way from £72,000. I decided to bring my activities with Band Aid to a close at the end of 1985 and leave Penny Jenden, who was to take over from her husband as the new director of Band Aid, to wind up the activities of the organization over the months that followed.

It was not quite as simple as that. At the end of December, as I was beginning to think of what 1986 might hold for me, I received a telex signed by all the major agencies in the Sudan. Nothing had changed, it said. All the lessons of the years before had gone unlearned. No preparations had been made since the last crisis for the transportation of food to the west of the Sudan where once more the harvest had failed, and there were millions of people at risk of starving during the rainy season of 1986. I began to talk in the press of the new crisis. The possibility of Sports Aid was in the air. It seemed there would be the need for it.

During a reconnaissance flight in the desert near Timbuktu, a helicopter crashed into a sand dune. It carried the organizer of the Paris–Dakar rally and the French pop singer Daniel Balavoine who had been prominent in School Aid in France. He was there to investigate the possibility of a link between the rally and Sports Aid. All five people on board were killed instantly. A message came that President Mitterrand would like me to join him at the Elysée Palace for lunch. I accepted, but before attending I gave an interview to the French TV station which had carried Live Aid and talked about the new crisis in the west of the Sudan. I also lambasted the station bosses for their handling of Live Aid which they had broadcast merely as a pop concert, minimizing the fund-raising element so that donations from France had been minuscule by com-parison with other European countries.

Mitterrand is a small, relaxed man so thoroughly at home in his palace he radiates and uses absolute authority with confidence. The Elysée Palace is a beautiful, large dolls' house upon which each president seems bent on leaving his mark. Each room in the honeycomb is decorated in a different style, marking the passing of period and president. It's rather like scrawling 'Kilroy was here' across the pages of French history.

We were brought into the Napoleon III sitting room with a blazing log fire. The Président de la République was announced by a formally attired major-domo in cutaway coat-tails and black tie. He sat on the sofa and beckoned a pretty blonde French chanteuse to sit beside him. I was led to the armchair be-side the sofa. M. Nucci, the Minister for Overseas Development, and the other government officials were scattered about the small room. Lionel Rotcage, the French Band Aid maestro, and two French pop stars who were active par-ticipants in Band Aid France sat on my right. It is difficult to make small talk through an interpreter, but when I got on to the subject of the Palace, he be-came houseproud. I remarked on the emerald green damask upholstery of the chairs and told him, 'You have the same taste as Nancy Reagan'. He threw his hands up either in horror or resignation and then blamed Napoleon III. He told a story of how when he had become President he had been very excited to receive a document marked 'Most Top Secret' with three seals indicating the highest level of priority. Inside the envelope was another 'For the eyes of the President only' and inside that was yet another envelope. Eventually he slit open the last seal and pulled out the menu for lunch at that day's cabinet meeting.

Mme Mitterrand came into the room. He introduced her and we moved to the dining room, left in the style of the seventies as a souvenir of Georges Pompidou. It looks like something the head of Smersh would sit in in a James Bond film.

Madame Mitterrand sat on my left and the President directly opposite across the wide, round table. We began talking about Africa. I explained that I had received telexes addressed to me personally from several agencies in Western Sudan about the populations there experiencing 100 per cent crop failure and thus starvation, despite the surpluses in the rest of the Sudan. Band Aid had spent three million dollars as had USAID on local purchase of food and transport, but this was meagre in the face of the problem. It needed immediate and dramatic action and no one seemed prepared to do it. I explained that there were still 100,000 tons of imported food in Port Sudan, that could be moved, but it took time to shift and again there wasn't much money to do it.

Mrs T says they cannot eat butter.

With President Mitterrand after an expensive lunch.

The reluctant general, leader of Sudan.

Pérez de Cuéllar, Secretary General of the UN, and I discuss fishing. 'It was this big.'

Bob Hawke recommends his barber.

Me and the Minister, Ouagadougou, Burkina Faso.

Tip O'Neill says 'How'. Ted Kennedy has his collar felt. Congressman Carr and I see the joke.

The Prime Minister advises the champion and the pop singer to keep it clean.

Suddenly Mme Mitterrand spoke, 'This is true, François,' she said. 'There is French food in Djibouti. I've seen it there stocked up and not moving.'

Nucci, the Minister, said, 'Yes, for some reason Addis has not sent the train back to load it and so it sits.'

'How much is there?' said the President.

'About 30,000 tons.'

'Move it,' said Mitterrand, 'get the Air Force. It seems to me the main problem is to move the food from Port Sudan to the west. We will do that.' M. Nucci made notes.

'I have also been asked by the agencies to ask you if we can have access to your Spot satellite,' I said. This satellite had not been launched yet, but it took detailed geographical and agricultural photos of the earth. If the agencies could have access to these pictures, they could be forewarned of any imminent disaster. They had asked both the Soviet and U.S. governments for access to this information, but had been refused or else charged so much money it became prohibitive. The primary purpose of the satellite was military, but both Nucci and the President said, why not? I had met Nucci before in Mali. He was a nice man and the best of the development ministers.

I had other requests, like paying L'Action Ecole, the French School Aid, their freight expenses. This they also agreed. By the time we had finished dessert we had been promised millions of dollars in vital emergency needs. It didn't solve the problems of the people in the west of the Sudan, but it had probably ensured their survival for a little while longer. I wondered why it always couldn't be so easy, but then you don't always have an ideologically sympathetic man in power with one eye on the upcoming elections and potential PR benefit. Mitterrand was one of those lucky people who can instigate action by the flick of his fingers and is not afraid or ashamed to use that power.

After lunch Mitterrand took me to a small ante-room. This was exactly as Napoleon had left it. The abdication papers he signed are there on a small table. The ink on his signature is smeared with tears. The President had brought me here after I had told him my daughter's name was Fifi. He indicated one of the lilac chaises longues and told me some nineteenth-century president had enjoyed some rather vigorous amorous activity there, and subsequently expired in the arms of the lady in question, a certain Madam Fifi. This, I told him, was what one expected of French palaces.

We went to the ballroom with its superb Gobelin and Aubusson tapestries. He showed me where he had knocked the wall through in eight places and put in arched French windows leading out to the garden which boasted his chosen modern sculptures. I said I thought they were awful. I told him of Mrs Thatcher and the Department of the Environment and how when she visits museums they always hide the best stuff in case she wants it for Downing

Street. He said he commissioned his specially. His office and its ante-room are in beautiful Louis XV style. He had two giant globes there which were presents for visiting heads of state. I asked if I could have one. 'When you're a head of state, which should be soon,' he said. Then he wrote the letter for my daughter that I'd asked for. He was in a good mood for a man whose lunch had cost him ten million dollars.

★ ★ ★

Back in London we again discussed how Band Aid should best be wound down. For the past year Band Aid had been the be-all and end-all of my life. Every hour of the waking day, seven days a week had been consumed by it. I knew that if I did not set a limit to it it would take over my entire life. 'It'll have to be all wound up by the end of 1986,' I said.

'But what about the projects? They need monitoring,' said Penny.

'Are you seriously suggesting that we hang around for fifteen years?' Some of our projects are that long-term.

'But the money is still coming in.'

'The money will carry on coming in for years. At the end of the year, we'll hand over to a standing committee made up of reps from all the agencies.'

That, when last I heard, was still the plan.

★ ★ ★

Band Aid must never become what I have always most detested – an institution. Its purpose, were it to continue, would get lost in the mine of professionalism and bureaucracy designed to nurture it, but only serving to obscure it. Band Aid would be more powerful in memory, where it will live as something that was wholly good and incorruptible and that worked.

Band Aid could easily continue without me. It is a big organization now, but it is only useful inasmuch as people support it. That support will drop away over the short term and with it Band Aid's access to those who can really effect change in the corridors of power. Then Band Aid simply becomes another fund-raising operation, the same as a dozen others. But it *was* different. It *was* extraordinary. I am too close to it now to stand back and see it in all its unlikely power and glory, but in future years I know I will wonder how the hell it was possible and what it was that enabled me to do it. I never once stopped to consider what happened next. I acted intuitively all the time. I played it by ear, as they say. I don't know why things fell into place as they did. The suggestion is not that this somehow was guided by a divine providence, but sometimes in the dead of night I seriously wondered, as I was swept along in a tide of events of my own doing and in my control, but somehow outside of myself.

When Band Aid closes down finally, I will heave a sigh of relief. We will

351

leave a legacy behind in Europe and America in the minds of young children and teenagers who may one day come to view Africa, not as a distant impoverished continent, but as a close neighbour being helped back to health. In Africa the legacy will be in lives. We never looked for monuments in the orphanages, hospitals or bridges built. They will fall down or be covered in sand and the trucks will rot. But it is not like Ozymandias, the king of kings, who advised us to 'look upon my works, ye Mighty, and despair! Nothing beside remains.' Something will remain, the legacy of Band Aid in Africa will be future generations allowed to live because of music and television and satellites and millions of people responding to the distant faint echo of their kinship with the rest of their species. Not humanitarianism – Humanity.

I am exhausted now, as I have been for the past seventeen months, but I am in no doubt that when famine occurs again, as it will – for we still will not alter the way we behave politically, not at least for years if ever – I will be asked questions by the media. But I am satisfied I have literally done as much as I am capable of doing, and I will always rail against those things I abhor. I will always try and avoid the cant and hypocrisy I loathe so much. I will continue being an 'awkward bugger'. But this can't be it, there's got to be other things I'm meant to do. What they are I don't know yet. I've got, on average, the same amount of time to live again and I'm looking forward to it. I'm sure it'll be interesting. But it's been pretty weird so far.

★ ★ ★

On the day of the Live Aid concert, the greatest assembly of rock musicians ever, at the end of seventeen hours of live music which had been watched by more people than any other event in history, Bill Graham stepped out onto the stage in Philadelphia. It was 11 p.m. In London I stepped out of the nightclub where I had watched the final section of the biggest concert the world had ever seen. It was 4 a.m.

For both of us there was a sense of triumph. 'I did it,' I thought.

'That was unbelievable,' thought Bill, 3,000 miles away.

In Philadelphia they were sweeping the stage. In London they were sweeping the streets. Around both of us were the last remnants of the mighty crowd.

As I climbed into my taxi, Bill walked down to look at the emptying stadium. Just in front of the stage were a group of kids, hanging around, still finishing what was left of their beer.

One of them turned to him and shouted. 'Hey you, Bill Graham'.

Bill looked down with an enquiring smile.

The kid shouted up. 'Is that it?'

It's something I keep asking myself.

INDEX

INDEX

"Dr. Raunikar has outlined biblical principles that are relevant and needed for today's singles. With the risks (physical, psychological, and spiritual) involved with dating in our culture, courtship could become a welcome practice in the Christian community."

PAUL MEIER, M.D.

NEW LIFE CLINICS, PLANO, TX

"As a single adult minister, I found that Chapter 5, 'Preparing to Be God's Choice for Someone Else,' was exactly what I needed to reaffirm the call and direction in my life. This is a must-read for every single."

DAVID EDWARDS

METRO BIBLE STUDY TEACHER, HOUSTON, TX

"Courting, not dating! What a revolutionary concept—it's only as old as the Bible itself. Parents, singles, and teenagers all need to learn how to keep friendships godly, how to hear God's voice in relationships, and how to make the right choice in a mate. Great material! *Choosing God's Best* is a must-read!"

DUANE MILLER

EXECUTIVE DIRECTOR, NUVOICE MINISTRIES, HOUSTON, TX

Choosing God's Best

WISDOM FOR LIFELONG ROMANCE

Dr. Don Raunikar

Multnomah Books *Sisters, Oregon*

CHOOSING GOD'S BEST
published by Multnomah Publishers, Inc.

© 1998 by Don Raunikar
International Standard Book Number: 1-57673-328-9

Cover photo by © TSM/Rob@Sas, 1998

Unless otherwise marked, Scripture quotations are from:
The Holy Bible, New International Version (NIV) © 1973, 1984 by International
Bible Society, used by permission of Zondervan Publishing House

Also quoted:
The Holy Bible, King James Version (KJV)

The Living Bible (TLB) © 1971. Used by permission of Tyndale House
Publishers, Inc. All rights reserved.

The Holy Bible, New Century Version (NCV) © 1991 by Word Publishing

The New Testament in Modern English, Revised Edition (Phillips)
© 1972 by J. B. Phillips

Printed in the United States of America

For information:
MULTNOMAH PUBLISHERS, INC.•POST OFFICE BOX 1720•SISTERS, OREGON 97759

Library of Congress Cataloging-in-Publication Data:
Raunikar, Don.
    Choosing God's best/by Don Raunikar.   p.cm.   Includes bibliographical
    references.   ISBN 1-57673-328-9 (paper)
    1. Single people—Religious life. 2. Courtship—Religious aspects—
Christianity 3. Dating (Social customs)—Religious aspects—Christianity.
I. Title.
BV4596.S5R38   1998   97-49264
241'.6765—dc21   CIP

99 00 01 02 03 04 — 10 9 8 7 6 5

To my heavenly Father for allowing me the privilege of being a conduit of Your love and wisdom to singles so that they might have a deeper, more intimate relationship with You. Thank You, Jesus, for guiding me in the writing of this book. I offer it for Your glory.

I want to express my deepest and sincerest gratitude to the following people:

To the countless people who have attended my singles seminars and sought my counsel. This book was inspired by your shared stories and intense pursuit for God.

To my friends and colleagues (too numerous to list, but you know who you are), who have prayed, provided feedback, encouragement and love throughout the whole process from idea to finished book.

To Matt Jacobson and the entire staff at Multnomah, who embraced the vision of biblical courtship and believed in this powerful message ministering to singles.

To Sue Jones for the countless hours of inspiration and godly wisdom in which you fine-tuned the concepts and ideas and made them into a manuscript.

To my parents, Fred and Eva, and my brother, Chuck, who exhibit God's intimate love relationship in our family.

To my wife, Kimberley: words could never fully express my heartfelt thanks. Many times my passion for God has caused you to endure many unexpected trials and tribulations. You are the wife of my youth whom God has chosen as His best for me.

May God bless each one of you for all that you have given to me.

CONTENTS

INTRODUCTION

*"For I know the plans I have for you," declares the Lord, "plans to pros-
per you and not to harm you, plans to give you hope and a future."*
JEREMIAH 29:11

If dating is so wonderful, why does it hurt so much?
Whether you're sixteen and single or seventy and single again, dating is much more likely to lead you to anxiety and disappointment
than to your marriage partner. If that's the case, why do so many
people keep at it? The ten most common answers are:

1. they're lonesome;
2. they're impatient;
3. they want to find a marriage partner;
4. they want to have fun and feel good;
5. they want to learn how to relate to the opposite sex;
6. their parents, peers, and the world tell them they should;
7. they're determined to live life according to their own
   schedule, not God's;
8. they want to develop social skills and emotional health;
9. they want to have certain needs met until a marriage
   partner is found;
10. they believe it will prepare them for marriage.

Even the secular world has started to admit there must be
something wrong with a dating system that creates so much pain
in people's lives. Some of the best evidence of this is the astounding success of a book entitled *The Rules: Time-tested Secrets for
Capturing the Heart of Mr. Right*. With some 900,000 copies in
print, *The Rules* soared to No. 1 on the *New York Times'* How-To
Bestseller List in 1996. This little paperback lists thirty-five old-
fashioned courting tips that essentially advise women to play hard

to get: don't call him, don't see him more than once or twice a week, don't open up too fast, don't live with him before marriage. Why is this book such a phenomenal success? "Because the rules work, and friends tell their friends," explains coauthor Ellen Fein, who has a *Rules* hotline, a monthly newsletter, twenty-five support groups nationwide, a movie deal, one or two seminars a week, and a personal consultation service.

But in fact, Fein and coauthor Sherrie Schneider were scooped by an even more popular book. God published His rules long before these two writers discovered "old-fashioned" courting tips. We might be even more surprised to learn that Fein and Schneider's motives for their rules are very similar to God's motives for His rules: protection and guidance. God isn't out to spoil our fun. (Remember, He created our desire for companionship in the first place.) His purpose is to keep us from the pain, heartbreak, and disappointment that come from trying to satisfy our needs out of selfishness instead of godliness.

Fein and Schneider developed their rules by trying to solve the relational hurts and dating problems of their single friends. "Ellen and I started telling our friends what we thought they were doing wrong," Schneider says. Eventually they put their advice in print. God did that thousands of years ago. We call it the Bible. We talk casually about "breaking" God's commandments, but the truth is that when we sin it's not the rules that are broken. It's us.

Singles looking for an alternative to dating have usually already experienced the pain of a broken relationship firsthand or know someone who has. Perhaps you've wanted to find your marriage partner according to God's way, but failed. Or you've never fully understood what God's way was. Or maybe you're a new Christian and this is one part of your life you've just recently decided to put in God's hands.

This book is for you. It will help you understand what plans God has for your life now. And it will help you see how your attitude toward today's relationships will affect your marriage and family in the future.

COUNTERFEIT ONENESS, GENUINE PAIN

But why talk about married oneness in a book intended for singles? Easy answer. The lasting consequences of your beginning will affect your ending. Many singles allow themselves to develop a counterfeit oneness with another person only to find their hearts ripped apart when the dating relationship ends. They feel as if they are losing part of themselves. Without a lasting commitment between two people, the rare and wonderful feeling of oneness with another person is artificial, counterfeit, and temporary.

As a young boy growing up in St. Louis, I watched as construction workers built the enormous stainless steel Gateway Arch on the western bank of the Mississippi River. With its massive arms stretching 630 feet above ground to meet in the middle, the arch was intended to be an impressive symbol of the city's reputation as the "Gateway to the West."

Construction started on the ground at two separate bases 630 feet apart. Like children playing with building blocks, the workers placed one stainless steel section on top of another. As the arms of the arch grew longer, everyone had the same thought: Will they meet in the middle?

Engineers calculated that if the two base sections were only 1/64 inch out of line, the center sections would completely miss each other at the top. In other words, the final result would depend on how they started. I never forgot the lesson.

In my practice as a psychotherapist, many of the couples I counsel just aren't meeting in the middle. Their marriages show the strain of not having spiritual, emotional, and physical oneness. Some marriage partners never experience the oneness God intended because their relationship was "out of line" with God's will from the beginning. Their marital problems actually began in their dating life and ended in divorce years later. Even in lasting marriages, the baggage left over from previous dating relationships can be frustrating and painful.

True oneness in a couple is like two sheets of plywood that are glued together: the bond is stronger than either of the pieces. If anyone or anything attempts to pull apart those two sheets, the result will be permanent damage to both pieces. Oneness in marriage was meant to be lasting, but counterfeit oneness will cause a dating couple to bond and break. Many singles are beginning to realize that the principles inherent in dating are not the same as God's principles. When we follow God's plan for relationships, we are healed and whole, not scarred and shattered.

THE COURTSHIP OPTION

Ned Ryun was a sixteen-year-old teenager who saw that the pain of dating was greater than the payoff. Ned's story appeared in a November 1995 *Focus on the Family* magazine article entitled "Courtship: The Comeback of the 90s."

In the article Ned's father, Jim Ryun—former Olympic champion and world record holder in the mile, and now a U.S. Congressman from Kansas—and his wife, Anne, describe how Ned made the decision not to date before the rest of the family embraced the concept of courtship. He and his twin brother, Drew, prayed to know God's will for their lives regarding friendships and dating. Ned was the first of the children to look at all the broken hearts and hurt feelings of the dating couples he knew and choose to practice biblically based courtship instead of play the dating game. His decision led the way for the rest of the family as each child in turn also chose to court rather than date.

That was six years ago. Since then, there have been no casual "tryouts" of dating partners as each of the four Ryun children waits for God to reveal His choice of a marriage partner. It has meant waiting for God to move, and believing that He will.

"That decision may seem hopelessly old-fashioned to you," says Anne in the article, "but our choice grew partly out of personal experience; as teenagers ourselves, we had encountered some of the drawbacks and dangers of dating. When I dated, my heart became emotionally tied to my steady, which created wounds of rejection that lasted for years. We wanted something better for our children."

"Dating waves good-bye at the door and says 'Be home by

midnight,'" notes Jim, "but courtship includes time spent with the entire family. In our home, a young man interested in Heather or Catherine is apt to find himself playing basketball with Ned and Drew or helping out in the kitchen after dinner."

For singles like Ned Ryun, courtship encourages group activities and ministry opportunities that allow couples practical and productive time together without spending lengthy periods of one-on-one time alone in isolated locations. Courtship enables a couple to look beyond physical attraction and focus on things that are truly important.

"GOOD" CHOICE OR "GOD'S" CHOICE?

"It sounds good," Jenny said, "but I don't understand how we are supposed to find this person—the one God has for us." I had been trying to explain the courtship concept to Jenny. She was thirty-six years old, single and worried. Her biological clock was ticking. She was certain there was something she should be doing to maximize her opportunities—places she should go, things she should do, people she should see.

"You don't have to *do* anything but concentrate on *being* the right person—the person God wants you to be—instead of *finding* the right person," I said. "Godly marriages are made by first living godly lives. It's God's responsibility to reveal whether you will marry and whom you will marry. The arrangement is up to Him."

How simple it sounded—God the matchmaker!

But what if God is "late"? Jenny was thirty-six. How much longer would she have to wait? She wants to have a family. For Jenny the "what ifs" were endless. Would it comfort her to know hard facts like those of a recent study indicating the most stable marriages of all occur at age twenty-eight and later? Would that make God any more on target or on time? God would not force Jenny to marry His choice, but He would not prevent her from marrying her choice.

If Jenny could see God as a matchmaker, she would discover a much deeper, more fundamental truth: God has a plan and purpose for our lives. But that plan is under constant attack, and the enemy isn't always dressed in black. As Oswald Chambers writes in *My Utmost for His Highest,* "It is the things that are right and noble and good from the natural standpoint that keep us back from God's best." The greatest enemy in choosing God's best is our own strong compulsion to choose what's good. But not every *good* choice is *God's* choice, and the difference can radically affect your future happiness.

NO MORE FAILURES

Dating creates more problems than it solves: broken hearts, illegitimate children, abortions, sexually transmitted diseases, and feelings of guilt or shame that can last a lifetime. As serious as these consequences are, the solution for them is simple: biblical courtship instead of dating. Courtship isn't just another form of Christian dating. It's radically different and proudly old-fashioned—as old as the Bible. Throughout this book we'll explore the differences between dating and courtship and look at some of the reasons why courtship will lead you to the right marriage partner when dating so often fails.

Although the process may seem difficult at first, it's been practiced successfully for thousands of years. Dating, by comparison, is less than a century old—on the timeline of history, little more than an experimental blip. As an experiment, though, it has been a total failure. With God's help, it's a failure you can avoid from now on.

The difference between a kingdom courtship and destructive dating in your life could mean the difference between reaping a harvest of broken hearts and the harvest of a loving relationship and lasting commitment. I have personally counseled both singles and courting couples through the courtship process, and have watched with thanksgiving and joy as they married and established their families. Some of them share their stories in the pages that follow. I wish it were true that singles turn to courtship out of love and obedience to God, but they rarely do. Pain seems to be what pushes most people toward obedience. When the pain of dating is greater than the payback, then and only then are people ready for an alternative. If you are one of those singles who has experienced the brokenness of a failed dating or marriage relationship, you will find healing in the courtship process this book describes. If you are single, you will find refreshing hope for your future.

If you desire real, eternal change in your relationships, take a moment and ask the Lord to speak to you through this book. Ask God to reveal His truths and embed His wisdom in your heart to develop relationships His way.

Chapter One

God's Antidote for Dating Disease

Therefore, everyone who hears these words of mine and puts them into practice is like a wise man who built his house on the rock. The rain came down, the streams rose, and the winds blew and beat against that house; yet it did not fall, because it had its foundation on the rock.

Matthew 7:24–25

CAUTION: The principles of dating are man-centered and culturally determined; courtship principles are God-centered and biblically based.

Each of us has a God-given urge to seek out an intimate relationship—physical, emotional, and spiritual—with the opposite sex. In biblically based courtship, a couple eventually satisfies that urge through a process that results in a lifetime commitment. In dating, however, a couple's immediate goal is not typically to work toward a selfless, lifelong relationship, but to satisfy a short-term physical or emotional need. The result is an endless series of temptations that often results in guilt, disappointment, frustration, and heartbreak.

Too often, dating leads to disaster rather than happily ever after. Here's a startling illustration that shows just how overrated dating is by people who use it to "shop around" for the right spouse. Write your name on a piece of paper, then write the names of your two closest friends. If all three of you marry, two of you probably won't stay married to your original partners. You'll either find another partner or join the ever-growing population of single-again adults.

Christian psychologist Dr. James Dobson began one of his recent *Focus on the Family* radio broadcasts by quoting researchers who predict that two out of three couples who marry this year will not remain together throughout their lifetimes. That means the majority of today's newlyweds won't be celebrating golden wedding anniversaries. Instead, they'll spend what should be the most relaxing, rewarding years of their lives picking up the pieces of failed marriages and trying to patch up broken homes. Without seeking and following God's plan, their marriages will falter.

The solution to the dating dilemma is so simple that people overlook it time after time, through one failed relationship after another. It reminds me of the little boy who was riding his bicycle down the street one day and noticed a big crowd up ahead under a railroad trestle. When he got to the scene he realized a big truck had tried to ease under the old, narrow trestle and had gotten stuck. The police were there but they couldn't do anything. Someone called a tow truck, but the big truck was stuck so tight the cable broke. Someone else called a construction company to see if they could raise the trestle with a hydraulic jack, but the trestle was too long. The fire department was there, along with the mayor, a man from the trucking company, a railroad supervisor, and the service manager from the local truck dealership.

While they were all standing around trying to figure out what to do, the boy rode up on his old Schwinn bicycle with multi-colored streamers dangling from the handlebars and playing cards fastened to the fenders so they made a flapping noise on the spokes. The boy jumped off his bike, walked behind the truck, and tried to talk to the puzzled men. But no one would listen.

After being ignored for a long time, the boy went home. For

six hours the truck stayed wedged beneath the trestle, and traffic was detoured to the other side of town. Later, the boy came back and saw that firemen were preparing to cut the top off the truck. Worming his way through the circle of men, the boy finally shouted above the noise of the crowd, "Wait! Why can't you just let the air out of the tires?"

The simple solutions are sometimes the hardest to see.

After nearly a century of substituting dating for God's principles of courtship, we may think we're stuck with the disastrous results, that there's no other way to find a marriage partner. Christian singles by the millions have wandered down the treacherous streets of dating and found themselves in destructive relationships that affect their lives forever. We've been like the crowd of adults around the stranded truck who could see the problem but overlooked the obvious solution.

The best answer has been the most elusive: Ditch dating and return to romance God's way.

DATING VS. COURTSHIP

Although the Bible never mentions the words "dating" or "courtship," it does give principles and guidelines for one-to-one, male/female relationships. The Bible says that after God created goodness all around, He looked at man and said, "It is not good for the man to be alone" (Genesis 2:18). Then He created woman as a helper suitable for man. At that moment, romance, marriage, and commitment became the very fabric of society.

But the fabric God wove is unraveling in today's culture.

We don't have to look very far to see a distorted picture of what was supposed to be a divine lifetime plan: one man and one woman committed to each other for life. *"For this reason a man will leave his father and mother and be united to his wife, and they will become one flesh"* (Genesis 2:24). God's intention for a husband and wife was monogamy. Together they were to form an inseparable union with "one flesh" being both a sign and an expression of that union.

God's solution for man's aloneness is marriage, not dating. Just as marriage became the first one-on-one, male/female relationship, the home became the foundational structure for the rest of society, and a committed relationship became the foundation of the home. In fact, God instituted the home before He created the church.

The principles of courtship are God-centered and biblically based. Courtship is a biblical process of finding and choosing a mate while glorifying God and honoring and respecting each other. Dating, on the other hand, is the world's alternative to courtship. Its principles are man-centered and culturally determined. The words "Christian" and "dating" don't go together because their principles are exact opposites. Christian dating is an oxymoron.

The primary distinction between dating and courtship lies in the intent of the relationship:

- When a couple begins a courting relationship, they both know the purpose of the relationship is to consider marriage. Conversely, casual dating is a romantic linking of a couple simply to enjoy each other's company for the present. In dating, both parties understand that while marriage may be possible in the future, neither person is seriously considering it at the moment. As a result, immediate pleasure is the whole purpose for dating, even for Christians who draw the line at sexual immorality.
- Courting has a long-term end in view. There are no casual "tryouts" in courtship, and it is reserved only for couples spiritually and emotionally ready for marriage.

Courtship is not merely a Christian way of dating. When we date, we often have a window-shopping attitude that has "self" as the base: How will we look "wearing" our prospective partner...having him...holding him...owning him? We try on another person for size and see whether their style suits us. In contrast, someone in a courtship relationship says, "I believe God has led me to you above all others and I will honor, cherish, and marry you." No broken hearts. No painful baggage. No walking out.

COURTSHIP IN THE REAL WORLD

Camille was a thirty-five-year-old mother who had been married thirteen years before her divorce. Even though her ex-husband had remarried and she was eager to be part of a two-parent home again, dating in midlife wasn't an appealing thought.

When men from her singles Sunday school class asked her for a date, she would go and then be sorry she went. The problems inherent in dating only multiplied the daily difficulties she faced as a new single mom. Eventually, she dated one person for several months, but the relationship didn't last. Camille's children had grown attached to the man, so when they broke up it hurt not only her but the kids as well.

"I started praying for God's protection because I just didn't want to live like that anymore," Camille said. "I prayed He would keep away anyone who wasn't the right one."

Camille had seen what prayer had done for a friend of hers who had recently married after trusting God to bring "the right one" into her life. She had watched God protect her friend from the pain of wrong relationships and knew God could help her the same way.

Camille's best friend had also sought God's help and protection. "She was very intelligent and attractive, but after that prayer she didn't get asked out very much," Camille said. "It was just God's protection of her. Eventually, a wonderful Christian man came into her life and they married."

Camille believed God honored her friend's prayers because she had a desire for purity above all else and a need to be a pure vessel in the presence of a holy God. She wanted that purity in her own life.

Camille prayed her own prayer of protection. Afterward, no one asked her for a date for three months. That had never happened before. She was attractive and popular. Men had always been attentive to her. To her own surprise, Camille wasn't bothered by the lack of social interaction. Even though she still had a desire to marry again, Camille was becoming content with being single and involving herself in church and community activities.

All of a sudden, God opened the floodgates. Three men asked her out at the same time. She told all three the same thing: "I don't date. I believe in courtship." Two of the three never stuck around to find out why. The third was an exception. Wade was familiar with the courtship concept and responded, "Any guy with his ear to God's mouth wouldn't be scared by it."

"Wade called a few times, and our friendship grew from acquaintance to casual friendship through interaction at church activities," Camille continued. "After our first conversation, I thought, 'Wow, what a godly man!' He had a desire for God that was what I wanted in a husband."

Wade understood her attitude toward dating and courtship. They spent that month praying about whether to enter into a relationship, particularly since Wade wasn't sure if he would ever marry.

"If he knew he was never going to get married, I didn't even want to start anything," Camille said.

Then Wade went away for a three-day weekend to pray and ask if Camille was God's choice for him. When he returned, their courtship began.

"I saw he was very interested in me and that I meant more to him than having to go through the obstacles," Camille said.

Obstacles? "Safeguards" may be a better word.

One of the most important safeguards was an accountability couple. Both sets of parents lived too far away to provide direction and guidance for the relationship, so Wade and Camille asked a godly couple from their church to serve in the major role of an accountability couple.

"We went to their home one evening, and Wade talked to the husband almost like he would have talked to my father," Camille said. Together they discussed the need for setting some boundaries to keep the relationship from moving too fast at the beginning and to allow both Camille and Wade to think clearly and hear God's voice.

"Our friends sent us to separate rooms in the house and told us to pray about how much time we should spend together at the beginning," Camille said. "After praying, I didn't have a sense of what our time together should be, but Wade came out saying we should see each other once a week for three hours and spend one hour a week on the phone. So with the blessings of our account-ability couple, we began our courtship."

During those early days of the relationship, Wade wrote to Camille and she began to know his heart more through his letters than their conversations. "When we started spending more time together, I dragged him around to all my older married friends and he did the same to me. We did this because we knew our friends would detect red flags that might not be obvious to us," she said. "We even went to pre-engagement counseling with my pastor, who likes to talk to couples *before* they get engaged." Their relationship had developed from an acquaintance and now was heading into an intimate friendship.

The two of them became involved with other couples in group activities and began attending a home cell group. In time, Wade also began joining in activities with her children. As their time alone became more limited by circumstances (work responsibilities and a long drive between houses), they no longer needed artificial limitations on their time. After a ten-week engagement, they were married.

How much time did the courtship process take? The time it took to develop a friendship, one month of prayer, one month of hardly seeing each other, two months of leading each other all over the city to visit friends, and a ten-week engagement. But it took a lifetime of learning to seek God's counsel.

"More and more I see how Wade is just the perfect person for me," Camille said. "The children were very excited and support-ive. If they had not been, I would have considered that as my counsel against the marriage.

"It's so important not to try to pick someone and make it happen but just to let God work in the situation. God is in control and desires what is best for us."

COURTSHIP CHARACTERISTICS

Courtship can be defined by eight basic assumptions a courting couple makes that embrace a lifestyle, values, and priorities completely different from dating:

Assumption One:

- **We view the marriage relationship not as a contract between two people but as a covenant between a couple and God.** His divine intention is an inseparable, monogamous union. Becoming "one flesh" is both a sign and expression of that union.

Assumption Two:

- **We decide not to date or "shop around" but to save ourselves physically, emotionally, and spiritually for the one person God would have us marry.** To exchange dating for courtship is to demonstrate faith in God's will and in His power to bring that will to pass in our lives. We wait on God's timing and God's revelation, believing that He will show us what to do and whom to marry.

Assumption Three:

- **While we wait for God to reveal His choice of a mate, we concentrate on being the right person instead of finding the right person.** We do this by involving ourselves in ministry, fellowship, and friendships that help us focus on our value and identity in Christ instead of our value to someone else. We learn to treat our friends in Christ as if they were brothers and sisters and to distinguish biblically appropriate behavior from behavior that compromises our physical and emotional integrity.

Assumption Four:

- **Once we have developed an intimate friendship with another person and believe they may be our intended partner, we enter a courtship with the understanding that marriage is the expected end result.** Unlike dating, we aren't casually "trying out" another person until we find a steady dating partner.

Assumption Five:

- **Because we enter a courtship relationship with a view toward marriage, we may have to delay considering courtship until we are in a position to marry and have laid a responsible foundation.** God expects us to spend our season of singleness preparing ourselves and laying the foundation for His blessing. For younger singles, this may mean no courtship during the high school years and perhaps not until after college.

Assumption Six:

- **We begin a courtship with the full knowledge and approval of both sets of parents or, if parental involvement is not possible, a spiritual accountability couple.** Accountability in the relationship is desired and created through the involvement of parents, another godly couple, or both. Courtship includes time spent with the entire family and allows an accountability couple to provide protection, correction, and direction.

Assumption Seven:

- **In the early stages of courtship, we begin by spending only limited amounts of time together and very little time one-on-one alone.** Often, couples who date become obsessive about being together. They spend most of their time alone in isolated locations. Unlike dating, courtship is designed to foster a relationship, not an addiction. The goal is to become one in spirit early in the relationship, progress to emotional oneness during the engagement period and then physical oneness after marriage. The early phase of courtship emphasizes getting acquainted with each other through family and group activities.

Assumption Eight:

- **We recognize that the engagement phase of courtship is usually shorter than most engagements in a dating relationship.** Courtship places the waiting period at the beginning, during a time of developing friendship, not at the end in an extended period of engagement. By taking more time to choose a mate and lay a good foundation for marriage, the engagement phase of courtship basically requires only enough time to prepare for the wedding and make final preparations for marriage.

PITFALLS AND BENEFITS

Does courtship always go as smoothly as it did for Camille and Wade? Even a biblically based approach to selecting a mate has its pitfalls when the people involved are imperfect beings in an imperfect world.

EVEN COURTSHIP CAN LEAD TO A FAILED RELATIONSHIP WHEN:

- Singles fail to establish an accountability couple, whether it's their parents or another godly couple.
- Singles fail to receive the blessing of the parents (or accountability couple).
- Parents (or accountability couple) and/or singles fail to listen to God and wait on His direction.
- Parents (or accountability couple) fail to take into consideration the desires and preferences of the singles.
- Singles fail to complete courtship preparation steps.
- Singles think courtship is just another form of dating.
- Each single expects the other to be "perfect."

- Parents (or accountability couple) expect the potential mate to be "perfect."

Even though we must be cautious to avoid the pitfalls, the benefits of courtship still greatly outweigh the destructiveness of dating.

COURTSHIP LEADS TO A LIFETIME WITH GOD'S CHOSEN PARTNER BY:

- Keeping the focus on Christ, not each other or the relationship.
- Bypassing the destructive dangers of physical, emotional, and spiritual counterfeit oneness involved in dating.
- Establishing and enhancing communication between parents and/or the accountability couple and the single persons.
- Establishing a chain of counsel for couples during their courtship, engagement and marriage to avoid the destructive pain of dating.
- Giving the parents and/or the accountability couple the opportunity to see the virtues and the faults in a future mate and encourage or correct them.
- Being based on accountability first, then completion of courtship preparation before courtship begins.
- Having commitment as its cornerstone, thus building a solid foundation for a lifelong marriage and preventing divorce from seeping through the cracks.

Courtship also leads toward a far more confident, contented life both before and after marriage, considering the fact that couples who are committed to each other in a monogamous relationship blessed by God:

- don't come home with sexually transmitted diseases,
- don't know the destructive pain of having an illegitimate child or trying to find an abortion doctor,
- don't spend their savings hiring divorce lawyers and their time hiding information about where they've been the night before, and

- don't carry lifelong pain from a destructive dating relationship.

Like everyone else, courtship couples will encounter trials, but thank God there are some problems they won't have and some pain they will never know.

DARE TO BE DIFFERENT

Starting in a new direction is usually frightening, particularly if everyone else isn't moving in the same direction you are. How many people do you know who have purposely chosen not to date because they are waiting for that one person God has chosen for them? Scary, isn't it? Yet God calls His people to a higher standard than the standard of the world. The basic demand on the Christian is the demand to be courageously different. And that's precisely where the problem lies—courtship makes you different.

The world likes a pattern and is suspicious of nonconformity. How distinct should the line be between the man and woman of the world and the follower of Christ? Jesus clearly states that when we come to Him by faith, God has chosen us out of the world (John 15:19). We can no longer be "part of the group" in the same way as before.

It takes faith and courage to wait on God. *"Wait for the LORD; be strong and take heart and wait for the LORD"* (Psalm 27:14). Waiting for the Lord means pausing for further instructions. We get in trouble when we make decisions impulsively, without waiting for God's timing and God's thinking. "But I'm thirty years old," you say. What does age have to do with it? Some people are forty years old and unmarried. While you're saying "poor them," they'll be saying "poor you" if you marry the wrong person. God has a reason for requiring your patience. Like the psalmist says, "Take heart." Let your heart take courage so you can resist following your own schedule and timing rather than God's, so you can resist the pressure of other people's attitudes and opinions, and so you can resist your own fear of failing to find a relationship.

SATISFYING THE HUNGER OF LONELINESS

Temptations come to us most often when our needs are unmet. Perhaps you're one of those singles who can deal with being different. Maybe you have the courage to stand alone. But can you deal with loneliness? Most singles falter when faced with the depression that comes from the pain of loneliness.

If you were Satan, how would you tempt a person to sin? You'd probably take a legitimate need and encourage them to meet it in an illegitimate way. When you are lonely and single, you are hungry for fellowship. And when you are hungry, you are more tempted to eat than when you are full. "The LORD God said, 'It is not good for man to be alone. I will make a helper suitable for him'" (Genesis 2:18). The need not to be alone is legitimate, but how we handle that need is important. God understands the need, and courtship offers us a way to meet our needs legitimately—

> without getting out of God's will,
> without missing God's planned blessing,
> without causing ourselves pain and grief,
> without causing hurt to other people, and
> without causing confusion in our lives.

Most of us know the story of Lot's wife and how she turned into a pillar of salt when an angel of God led the entire family out of a doomed city and warned them not to look back (Genesis 19:24–26). Lot's wife became paralyzed when she had difficulty turning her back on unhealthy and destructive relationships. The healthiest course of action would have been to follow the angel's lead.

When Camille prayed for God's help in choosing a mate, it wasn't just a prayer for a husband or a prayer for protection. It was a prayer for *purity*. Somewhere along the way, she understood what God was after. God always saves His best for those who are willing to wait for it. That's when the Holy Spirit comes and leads us out of the old life and into a new and better one.

Are you willing to wait for God's best?

COURTSHIP PROCESS

COURTSHIP PROCESS	PHASE 1: IDENTITY IN CHRIST	PHASE 2: MINISTRY INVOLVEMENT	PHASE 3: FOUNDATION BUILDING	PHASE 4: FRIENDSHIP LEVELS				PHASE 5: COURTSHIP AND ACCOUNTABILITY	PHASE 6: ENGAGEMENT	PHASE 7: MARRIAGE
				ACQUAINTANCE	CASUAL FRIENDSHIP	CLOSE FRIENDSHIP	INTIMATE FRIENDSHIP			
SPIRITUAL COMMITMENT	Commit yourself to being sold out to Christ. Be involved in activities that instill spiritual growth. Learn to be fully engaged to Christ before entertaining the idea of a relationship with another person. Be confident of who you are in Christ and gaining acceptance, worth and identity in Christ instead of in another person.	Be involved in ministry opportunities to utilize the talents and gifts God has given you. Learn what it means to serve, love, sacrifice, and yield your rights to others as Christ did for you.	Anticipate marriage and lay the foundation for a secure Christian home by completing practical preparations in the following areas: - Spiritual maturity - Godly character - Accountability - Emotional health - Financial stability - Vocational training - Parent training - Household training - Commitment	Focus on being totally content and feeling complete as a single engaged to Christ. Develop a life vision and direction about serving God through ministry opportunities. Avoid spiritual involvement with another individual at this point except for witnessing the Gospel of Jesus.	May be involved in a church activity with another individual. Discuss Christ and His kingdom in group settings or Bible studies, but avoid deep spiritual one-on-one talk.	Share with each other God's vision for your lives. Discover each other's spiritual gifts, maturity level, and desire to serve God. Experience deeper spiritual talk but limited intimate one-on-one talk.	Begin intimate spiritual talk related at the deepest level. Discuss possibility of marriage and the purpose and process of courtship as it relates to your love for God. Discuss need for spiritual covering and accountability.	Begin the process of becoming one spiritually. Spend one-on-one time together through shared prayer time and church attendance. Commit your courtship to glorifying Christ and helping each other grow in Christ.	Continue the process of becoming one spiritually through shared prayer, Bible study, and church attendance. Discuss which church and Sunday school to attend as well as activities and ministry opportunities. Develop a vision for the marriage reflecting Christ and His church.	Experience quality improvement by becoming one through prayer, Bible study, church involvement, and ministry opportunities. Relate at the deepest spiritual level. Make marriage and family decisions as one in Christ.
EMOTIONAL COMMITMENT			Before becoming emotionally intimate with someone else, rid yourself of emotional baggage left over from childhood and past dating relationships. Recognize that unresolved sin will influence your emotional health.	No emotional intimacy. Casual interaction. Limited shared feelings. No one-on-one activities.	No emotional intimacy, but share surface feelings. Share close friends or activities. No one-on-one activities.	Share deeper feelings but limit emotional involvement. Focus on external social activities instead of one-on-one intimate interaction.	Share each other's innermost thoughts, fears, failures, and hopes. Support each other in times of crisis and pain; share times of joy. Limit one-on-one emotional interaction.	Begin pre-engagement counseling. Seek your parents (or other godly counsel) to hold each other accountable. Discuss and write down boundaries and limits of relationship. Increase one-on-one emotional time together.	Begin becoming one emotionally. Spend one-on-one time sharing deep emotional feelings. Develop deep levels of communication. Understand male/female differences and roles within a biblical marriage.	Continue to become one emotionally. Commit and plan on one-on-one time every day by sharing feelings and reflecting Christ's love through grace, mercy, and forgiveness to one another.
PHYSICAL COMMITMENT					Side hugs (no full "body slam" hugs).	Side hugs plus holding hands.	Side hugs, holding hands, and short kisses. Only limited cuddling.	Increase holding hands, kissing and cuddling with caution. Hand-to-body touching but not intimate body areas.	Begin the process of becoming one physically. Share hugs, hold hands, kiss, touch sexual body areas (may experience a need to wait a number of days after the wedding for intercourse).
TIME ALONE PER PHASE				0 Hours		20 Hours	80 Hours	190 Hours	FOREVER

STUDY AND DISCUSSION QUESTIONS

1. If "self talk" is the message we tell ourselves, how did self talk affect Camille's life and decisions prior to marrying Wade? If God were listening to your self talk, what would He hear?

2. What can you learn about the character of God by looking at Him through the eyes of Camille and Wade? If people make decisions based on their views of God's nature and character, what do your decisions say about your view of God?

3. Read about the fruit of the Spirit in Galatians 5:22–23. Would these traits give you a greater potential for a successful marriage? Which traits do you have and which are you still having difficulty displaying? How could God's delaying your marriage have a divine purpose?

4. Describe in your own words the eight basic assumptions of courtship.

5. Describe in your own words the seven benefits of courtship.

6. Meditate and memorize: "'For I know the plans I have for you,' declares the LORD, 'plans to prosper you and not to harm you, plans to give you hope and a future'" (Jeremiah 29:11).

7. Pray: My Heavenly Father, I confess as sin believing the philosophies and traditions of dating which hindered my fellowship with You. I ask You to renew my mind with the mind of Christ and reveal to me a fresh new vision of a godly male/female relationship for my life. Strengthen my trust in You regarding my future relationships. Thank You for loving and forgiving me. In the name of Jesus. Amen.

CHAPTER TWO

A Prescription for Failure

But everyone who hears these words of mine and does not put them into practice is like a foolish man who built his house on sand. The rain came down, the streams rose, and the winds blew and beat against that house, and it fell with a great crash.

MATTHEW 7:26–27

CAUTION: Dating prepares a couple for divorce more than marriage.

When a building collapses or a bridge falls, the first thing engineers look at is the foundation. What was holding it up? What went wrong? Like an engineer inspecting fallen beams, I've spent a number of years examining the failed and flawed marriages of couples who file in and out of my office for counseling. Over and over I ask myself, "What should have been holding their marriage up? What went wrong?"

In the thirty years from 1960 to 1990, the number of divorces in the United States increased by more than 205 percent.[1] The biggest jump took place between the midsixties and midseventies, increasing at such a pace that by 1975, for the first time in history, more marriages in America were ended by divorce rather than by death.[2] Since the mideighties, a majority of all marriages have included at least one partner who has been divorced.[3]

And if the relationships between husbands and wives are so unstable, what about their children? A white child born in the early 1980s will have only a 30 percent chance of living to age seventeen with both biological parents at home. A black child has just a 6 percent chance.[4] As some children face family break-ups as many as two or three times in their childhood, we have to ask ourselves, "What's happening here? Where is the crack in the foundation?"

Almost all of these marriages are built on a foundation of dating experiences. Is it possible we're building our marriages on sand and reaping mudslides? Are we setting ourselves up to fail by relying on a flawed dating system for finding, selecting, and marrying a mate?

AN ALL-AMERICAN INVENTION

When we talk about dating, what exactly do we mean? In today's culture, *dating* usually describes a male/female, one-on-one relationship that goes beyond a close friendship. In other words, dating is often a code word that means a couple is intimate both physically and emotionally. That hasn't always been the case.

As social interactions go, dating is the new kid on the block. It has evolved differently for each generation and is far different now than it was thirty or sixty years ago. It may surprise you to know that dating is a somewhat recent American innovation and not a traditional or universal custom. It is actually less than a century old.

The rules of dating change with each new generation. The latest and most drastic change may be the fact that today's dating couples appear to have no rules at all!

Who pays? "Whoever asks for the date," says Megan Kraatz, a sixteen-year-old junior at Horton Watkins High School in the St. Louis suburb of Ladue.[5]

Who drives? "Whoever's sober," says senior Lisa Schiff, 17.

Who makes the first move? "Definitely girls," says seventeen-year-old Tasha Mahr, another Ladue senior.

How far do you go? "Depends," they say simultaneously.

Dating at the turn of the twenty-first century is somewhat similar to "going steady" in the 1950s, but not the same. Both words imply a special relationship beyond friendship. The exact meaning of the terms are a little vague even to today's youth culture, but basically a 1990s dating relationship is what one teenager terms "more serious, less casual, and higher maintenance" than going steady.

Although it's an unquestioned tradition in America today, "dating" didn't become a familiar part of the middle-class vocabulary until the mid-1910s. In 1914, *Ladies' Home Journal* used the term several times but safely enclosed it in quotation marks with no explanation of its meaning.[6] By the 1950s and 1960s, social scientists who studied American courtship found it necessary to remind the American public that dating was a "recent American innovation and not a traditional or universal custom."[7]

Here's how dating evolved while paralleling major changes in American culture and society.[8]

The Calling System (Nineteenth Century America)- By Invitation Only

Until the early 1900s, almost everything in America revolved around the home and family. Courtship then involved a "calling" system, which varied by region and social status. When a girl reached the proper age to receive male visitors, her mother or guardian invited young men to call.

The call itself was a complicated event governed by a myriad of rules covering appropriate topics of conversation, chaperonage, refreshments, length of visit, and length of time between visits. Each rule was a test of suitability, breeding, and background.

The Rating/Dating System (1910–1945)—The Men Take Charge

As the nation became urban and industrial, people came crowding into the cities. "Calling" was not viewed as practical for young people whose families were forced to live in the cramped spaces of only one or two rooms. For the poor and the working class, parlors and a piano for entertaining were unavailable.

Many young people fled the squalor and confinement of their urban homes for amusement elsewhere. A "good time" increasingly became identified with public places and commercial amusements rather than music and conversation in the girl's parlor. Young women whose wages would not even cover the necessities of life became dependent on men's "treats." Keeping company in the family parlor was replaced by dining, dancing, and movies. Courtship went public, left the chaperones behind, and became "dating."

At the same time, young women began taking advantage of new opportunities to enter the public world by going to college, taking jobs, and entering the new urban professions. In addition, widespread use of the automobile gave couples more mobility and privacy. It also led to a new phenomenon: "parking."

As American courtship began to change, the new dating system that emerged lessened parental control and gave young men and women more freedom. The dating system also shifted power from women to men. Courtship had always taken place in the girl's home—the women's sphere—or at functions largely devised and presided over by women. Dating moved courtship out of the home and into what had historically been the man's sphere—the world outside the home. While this eliminated some of the restrictive features of courtship, it also took away an element of protection for the woman.

From the mid-1920s until World War II, dating evolved into a system that sociologists described as "rating and dating." To rate, you had to date. To date, you had to rate. It wasn't about love, marriage, or families. It was about competition and popularity, with popularity clearly being the key. Popularity was not earned directly through talents, looks, personality or importance in organizations, but by the way all those traits translated into dates. Those dates had to be highly visible and with many different people or they didn't count.

Going Steady (1945–1965)—Shopping for Partners

After World War II, women outnumbered men in the United States for the first time in history. Statistically, there weren't enough men, popular or otherwise, to go around. The dating system that had valued popularity above all was unsettled by women's concerns about the new scarcity of men. In addition, both men and women began to grow weary of the demands of a competitive society and began to seek something stable in an unstable world. By 1950, "going steady" completely supplanted the rating/dating system among American youth. It meant a guaranteed date and greater sexual intimacy.

Just as the rating/dating system was making its exit, America experienced the highest marriage rate of any record-keeping country in the history of the twentieth century. At the same time, the average age at marriage fell dramatically. This meant that if girls were to marry at eighteen and boys at twenty, the preparation for marriage ("shopping around") had to begin in the midteens.

Misguided sociologists told parents to help their children become datable by putting the children in situations that would allow them to begin dating. After all, they stressed, dating was preparation for the important business of selecting a mate. The strategy was that, ideally, each boy and girl should date and know twenty-five to fifty eligible marriage partners before making a final decision.

This new dating philosophy meant many more partners, all of whom were potential partners for necking, petting, and sexual involvement. The dating system promoted sexual experimentation not only through the privacy it offered but also through the sense of obligation it fostered: The man paid for everything and the woman became indebted. The more money the man spent, the more physical involvement he felt he was owed.

The Sexual Revolution (1965 to the Present)—
Satisfaction Now, Questions Later

A significant percentage of young people had premarital intercourse during and before the Going Steady years, but sex before marriage did not become conventional behavior until the mid-1960s. By then, the nation was moving toward a sexual revolution that would create moral dilemmas unparalleled in U.S. history.

Before the "Make Love, Not War" philosophies of the Vietnam War era, society expected individuals *not* to be sexually involved before marriage. Today, as most singles will attest, sexual involvement is an unwritten expectation on the first date. By age nineteen, 86 percent of unmarried males are having sexual intercourse.[9]

Until the Sexual Revolution, the rules and rituals governing dating and marriage had been based on the concept of the man as provider. As more women entered the job market and achieved some degree of economic independence, the man-as-provider model began to clash with the realities of life. In a dramatic break with the past, today's women often make the first move, initiate phone conversations, and either pay the bill or share expenses. The rules of dating shifted when the roles of men and women shifted in society at large. To say that we now have *new* rules may not be as accurate as saying that today we have *no* rules.

As George Barna points out in his book *The Future of the American Family*, the breakdown in sexual morality that occurred in the 1960s was the consequence of a more serious breakdown in thinking about truth:

> The biblical view of truth posits that the ultimate authority in all matters of life, including family, is a matter of absolutes, not a matter of choices. Truth is not one of several alternatives one might or might not embrace according to one's personal preference. For many years this thinking about truth was reflected in the moral standards considered generally acceptable throughout the country and in legislation proposed and enacted. But over time, a pluralistic view took over. It posited that the ultimate authority was self, mediated by society and its laws. Whereas religious beliefs may inform some of the family-based decisions people make, neither the Bible nor any other religious-based teaching is considered inerrant.[10]

When traditional sexual and cultural attitudes came under fire in the 1960s, the traditional family found itself competing with strange ideas and practices that were passed off as acceptable alternatives to father/mother/child relationships, including homosexual families, multiple partner arrangements, and communes. The effects and consequences of these changes and others remain with us today and show no signs of weakening.

Alpha to Omega, God's Standards Never Change

A hundred years—the lifetime of dating in America—is a drop in the bucket to God. In the middle of such massive changes in our culture and relationships, one thing has not changed: God's standards. They are the same yesterday, today, and forever (Hebrews 13:8). God has sent us no revisions to His original requirements for sexual purity and no amendments to His principles. He hasn't changed His view on marriage, and He still believes in lifetime commitment.

Sexual sin is sin to God whether the person is fifteen or fifty-five. As He promises, we will reap what we sow (Galatians 6:7–8). And that's the rest of the story.

ROMANTIC RUSSIAN ROULETTE

When American singles gained their dating independence, they may have gotten more than they bargained for and lost more than they realized. Before today's emphasis on dating, singles based marriage considerations on many factors, including money, property, health, religion, or a combination of considerations—but always with parents overseeing the process. What worldly dating has done is cut out the counsel of parents and disproportionately exalt romantic attraction so that pairing on the basis of romance alone has become an American institution.

Like Russian roulette, the romantic emphasis of the dating game can gun down a person's life with only one relationship. Sexually transmitted diseases, illegitimate births, abortion, premature marriages, date rape, sexual promiscuity, and deep emotional pain have wreaked havoc on American families in ways unimagined a century ago. Even from a secular viewpoint excluding the biblical issue of sin, the following statistics are staggering.

Sex Before Marriage

In its 1994 survey on risky behavior among young people, the Centers for Disease Control and Prevention found that more than half the high schoolers in the United States have had sex. To many Christian singles (and parents) the following breakdown will be astonishing:[11]

Ninth grade	40 percent
Tenth grade	48 percent
Eleventh grade	57 percent
Twelfth grade	72 percent

Fifty percent of teenage girls between fifteen and nineteen years old have had sexual intercourse at least once, according to the 1995 National Survey of Family Growth, an in-depth government survey conducted every five years. In 1970, 29 percent of girls said they had sex.[12]

By age nineteen, 86 percent of today's unmarried males have had sexual intercourse, up from 78 percent in 1979.[13]

Forty percent of women become pregnant before they are twenty years old, giving the United States a higher teen pregnancy rate than any other industrialized nation. Half of teen pregnancies end in birth, one-third in abortion and the rest in miscarriage.[14]

Seventy-four percent of teenagers say they would live with someone before marriage or instead of getting married.[15]

More than 43 percent of women ages fifteen to twenty-four who gave birth in the early 1990s were not married, compared to only 14 percent in the early 1960s.[16]

Sexually Transmitted Disease (STD)

Five known venereal diseases existed in 1950; today more than fifty different organisms and syndromes are passed sexually.[17]

Every day, 33,000 new cases of a sexually transmitted disease are reported in America (12 million a year); one in four of the adult population has a permanent STD.[18]

At least 30 percent of single, sexually active Americans have herpes[19] and the herpes virus is spreading at the alarming rate of 500,000 new cases a year.[20]

A lethal disease can be transmitted by a single sexual contact with one infected partner.[21] Sexual contact includes French kissing.[22]

Divorce

If current divorce rates continue, two out of three marriages that begin this year will not survive as long as both spouses live.[23]

Before they reach the age of eighteen, two out of three children born this year will live in a single-parent household.[24]

For every one hundred marriages that took place in 1960, there were twenty-six divorces; in 1970, thirty-three divorces; 1980, fifty divorces; 1990, forty-eight divorces.[25]

Two out of three second or subsequent marriages eventually fail and last a shorter time than the first failed marriage.[26]

Among all marriages that take place this year, six out of ten will involve at least one divorced person.[27]

Of the more than fifteen million children growing up without a father in the house, more than half have never visited their father's home, 40 percent don't see their father at all in a typical year, and only one in six sees the father an average of once or more per week.[28]

Abortion

About 1.7 million abortions are performed annually, with nearly one-eighth during the second or third trimester. Ninety-three percent of the time, no "special cases" exist such as rape or incest, health problems, or a mother whose life is threatened.

Twenty-eight hundred teenage girls get pregnant every day; 40 percent will have abortions.

Fifty-four percent of mothers who chose abortion in a University of Minnesota study still had nightmares after five to ten years; 96 percent believed they had taken a human life.

Sad But True

Instances of sex per hour on daytime TV dramas: NBC, 4.6; ABC, 7.2; and CBS, 7.7.

Seventy percent of juveniles in state reform institutions grew up without one parent, usually without a father.

The chances of finishing high school drop 40 percent for a fatherless white child; 70 percent for a fatherless black child.

The divorce rate for women is highest among those fifteen to nineteen years old.

GOD'S STANDARDS SPARE THE PAIN WITHOUT SPOILING THE FUN

Did you ever take one of those biology classes where the teacher made you put a frog in a pan of warm water? The water feels good to the frog, so he doesn't move. Then you put the pan over a low heat and gradually increase the temperature. The frog still doesn't move. To him, the water feels warm and relaxing. As the water warms up, the frog's body temperature also rises. The inside becomes like the outside. At first it's not a problem. By the time the frog notices the change and tries to jump out, it's too late. He's been cooked.

When centuries of courtship evolved into a dating system, American families found themselves in a new pan of hot water. For a long time, parts of the new system felt very comfortable. It offered freedom from rituals and restrictions that were binding, but now the heat has been turned up and it's too late for some people to jump. Unlike the frog who adjusted to his environment and then found himself cooked, most singles can still save themselves and jump out of the dating scene pan if only they can feel the heat in time.

Because sexual sin is not just an act between two consenting adults but an act of disobedience to God, the dating struggle and the pressures it presents are particularly difficult for Christian singles. The result is inner turmoil. When God looked at Adam and said, "It's not good for man to be alone," His solution for man's aloneness was marital commitment, not dating. Positive examples of intimate male/female relationships in Scripture are not found apart from the perspective or framework of marriage.

Dating broadly deviates from the Judaic traditions and biblical principles of the Old Testament. In fact, nothing in the Bible mentions random or recreational dating, a concept that clashes with God's creation model of a male/female, one-on-one relationship that begins with the intent of marriage.

In recent years, America has seen a rise in couples trying out marriage without making the sacrifices and commitments God intended. As they experience the counterfeit oneness of a pseudo-marriage, many couples have begun living together as a sort of "trial marriage." Cohabitation jumped 740 percent between 1970 and 1989. Among adults ages eighteen to twenty-five, cohabitation skyrocketed by 1,892 percent from 1987 to 1989.[29]

Ironically, living together before marriage hasn't turned out to be as much of a protection against divorce as some may have envisioned. Studies show that cohabitors have an 80 percent greater likelihood of experiencing a marital breakup than couples who marry without a period of cooperative living.[30] One of the most enlightening statistics is that people who cohabit are more likely to be unfaithful to their spouses after getting married. This behavior reflects their casual regard for marriage. Cohabitors are less likely to see fidelity as important in marriage, are more likely to risk an affair if they have strong reason to believe their spouse will not find out, and are more likely to describe themselves as sexually attractive or erotic.[31]

In short, conventional wisdom isn't working!

A dating system that says "trial" marriages will increase your chances of a successful "real" marriage is out of tune not only with research statistics but also with God's plan. One of the reasons divorce is more likely among cohabitors who marry is that the act of "testing" the relationship amounts to a lack of commitment. When the dating attraction between two people disintegrates, which it usually does, one partner in the relationship is almost always still committed and left feeling rejected, abandoned, used, betrayed, and deeply wounded. That's what happens when dating takes on the characteristics of window shopping. We stand on the outside looking in, scan the merchandise with our eyes and focus on the most attractive object. We shop according to our wants, our wishes, and our lusts. And when we do, the other person begins to feel like used merchandise.

Dating has a self-centered focus. What can this person do for me? Instead of Christ's example of love through sacrifice, servant-hood, and commitment, many dating relationships are ruled by self-centeredness and emotions. When the good times are gone and self-gratification is a high priority, people move on to new relationships. In other words, when the going gets tough, the uncommitted get going.

God's standards are an umbrella of protection. When we—for whatever reasons—move out from under that umbrella, we no longer benefit from its protection. Instead, we become vulnerable to a shower of negative consequences. God's standards for courtship and marriage were intended to relieve the turmoil, not create it. When His standards are upheld between two mutually faithful partners, those individuals do not show up as divorce statistics. They don't fight over who gets the kids. They don't terminate pregnancies with abortion. They don't come home with herpes. They don't carry with them the pain of past dating relationships. God's standards were intended to spare our pain, not spoil our fun.

GOD'S WORD ON COURTSHIP AND DATING

Most books and articles about dating accept the premise that dating is a legitimate activity fully in accord with the word of God and the highest dictates of wisdom. Here are fourteen characteristics of dating that are specifically contrary to courtship based on biblical principles.

COURTSHIP

1. God-designed, one-on-one, male/female relationships with a view toward marriage.

2. Man takes the initiative in beginning the relationship by seeking the Lord and then the counsel of their parents.

3. Courtship begins at an age when the person is ready to get married.

4. Courtship can begin when a man is able to maintain a home; manage finances; and be a provider, protector, and leader of a family.

5. A woman prepares to be a helper to her husband, a mother, and a household manager.

6. Courtship takes place mostly in the home, at church, and in family activities.

7. The man's father gives counsel and final approval to whom his son is about to court; the woman's father screens and works with would-be suitors.

8. Courtship involves progressive levels of friendship: acquaintance, casual friendship, close friendship, and intimate friendship.

9. A parent (or a spiritual authority) to oversee the relational development and to provide accountability for spiritual, emotional, and physical involvement is encouraged and desired.

10. Spiritual oneness is prohibited before a courtship begins among Christian singles.

11. Emotional oneness is prohibited before the engagement period.

12. Physical involvement before marriage is prohibited.

13. Complete privacy is not encouraged.

14. Engagement is not viewed as a stopgap before marriage.

DATING

1. One-on-one, male/female relationships mostly seen apart from the prospect of marriage.

2. Man or woman can take the lead in initiating a relationship.

3. Dating usually begins in early teen years without concern for marriage.

4. The man is usually unable or has given little thought to meeting the criteria of being a husband or a father.

5. Women usually enter a relationship unprepared for a married life.

6. Dating takes place mostly away from the home and family environment.

7. If he is lucky, the father might meet the date. He finds out about his child's engagement after it occurs.

8. Dating quickly leads to emotional and physical involvement without development of a deep, lasting friendship.

9. A parent (or a spiritual authority) to oversee the relational development and to provide accountability for spiritual, emotional, and physical involvement is avoided.

10. Spiritual oneness is allowed, encouraged, and desired.

11. Emotional oneness is allowed, expected and encouraged during dating.

12. Physical involvement before marriage is allowed, expected, and even encouraged.

13. Complete privacy is permitted and encouraged.

14. Engagement is viewed as a stopgap measure for a couple that has made a mistake.

WHEN THE PAST INFECTS THE PRESENT

One morning, I received a desperate phone call from a prominent community businessman. Bill was a strong church leader and a dedicated family man. He and his family seemed like the perfect Christian family.

"Dr. Raunikar, I've got to see you today. I'm about to lose my wife and family!"

When Bill arrived in my office later that morning, his eyes were bloodshot, his hair was uncombed, and his clothes were wrinkled. He looked as if he had been awake all night.

As Bill and I prayed together, he cradled his head in his hands and wept.

"My wife screams that I've *never* been the godly man that other people think I am. She says I've *never* been able to meet her emotional needs and that I don't understand her. Our sex life is nonexistent; in fact, she won't even let me hug her! Yet she complains that I'm not affectionate with her. Ever since we were married, I've tried so hard to meet her needs, but it seems like I'm always making up for past mistakes."

In a loud cry, Bill added, "Pam wants a divorce!"

He paused for a long time, stared at the floor and then mumbled slowly, "What went wrong?"

With Bill's words ringing in my ears, I thought to myself, "What *did* go wrong?" What was the root of Pam's hurt and despair? Bill had not committed adultery. He spent a great deal of time with his family, was a successful accountant and a deacon in the church. He and his wife had attended numerous marriage enrichment conferences.

Bill placed God, his wife, and family as high priorities in his life. They had been married fourteen years and had three children: Michael, 10; Tracy, 8; and John, 5. No past or present major stresses seemed to exist in the relationship to point Pam hopelessly in the direction of divorce. Bill became a Christian when he was a child. He grew up in a Christian home and went to church on Sunday, but his walk with the Lord had been shallow in college.

"I knew I wanted to follow Christ, but I didn't know how to be different from all my friends," Bill said.

Unlike Bill, Pam did not grow up in a Christian home and did not live a straitlaced lifestyle in high school. However, when she was nineteen, Pam became a Christian and embraced a new lifestyle with great zeal, passion, and hunger for the Lord.

Bill and Pam met in a college class shortly after Pam became a Christian. Bill was impressed by her attractiveness and charming personality. Pam felt Bill was fun and hard working. She liked the fact that he went to church on Sunday. They eventually decided to get married and committed themselves to rearing their family in church and placing God first in their lives.

Now, fourteen years later, Bill and Pam were on the brink of divorce.

"I don't know what's wrong," Bill said. "Pam has been complaining about me ever since we started dating."

"Dating?" I said.

"Yes," Bill answered. "It began when we were dating."

There was that word again—"dating." How many times had I heard it from other people in pain? Thirty times? Fifty? One hundred? It had become a familiar word to me as I counseled couples with troubled marriages.

As I began to realize the root cause of Pam's desire for divorce, I asked Bill to be honest and intimate with me about his dating life before marriage. The more he talked, the more the scales seemed to fall from his eyes. For the first time, he saw that the destructive pain Pam was feeling had its roots in their dating life.

"When I met Pam, she was on fire for God," he said. "She had become a Christian only two months before we met. Even though I'd been a Christian for eleven years, she was more on fire for God than I was. I wasn't ready to be totally committed to God or to her, so I threw a little water on her flame.

"Do you think that's why she doesn't think I'm a spiritual leader?" Bill suddenly wondered aloud.

He paused for a moment, then continued, "Anyway, Pam fell for me right off the bat. I knew things between us were moving too fast, but I really liked her. The problem was that I wasn't ready to give up my independence, so sometimes I'd do things with other people just to keep control over my own life. I remember thinking, 'We're not married; we are only dating. I'm not obligated to her.' There were a few times I wasn't there when she really needed me. I'm not sure she's ever forgiven me for abandoning her when we dated."

Bill was right. The past had leaked into the present, and Pam's scars were fueling her desire for divorce.

"We went to church almost every Sunday," Bill said. "We would see a lot of young married couples worshiping together, and Pam would always say, 'Why can't we have a godly relationship like they have?'

"We dated each other for a while, but I broke it off because I wasn't ready to get married. The year before we started dating, Pam had dated someone else who had really hurt her because he didn't want to 'settle down.' Then I came along and did the same thing. It was bad timing. I remember making promises to her and then breaking them. I'd tell her one thing and then do something else—but that was before I realized I really did want to marry her. That was more than fourteen years ago!"

Bill stared into my eyes with a startled expression of self-discovery. "Do you think that's why she feels like she can't trust me?"

He was on the right track.

"There's something else I need to tell you," he continued. "Pam and I both had been sexually involved with other people before we met each other. Do you remember I said things moved pretty fast between us? I meant that it wasn't long before we were sleeping together. We both knew we shouldn't, but we just fell into it. After we started having sex, we stopped talking and started fighting. That's when I broke up with her and began dating an old girlfriend.

"We had a physical relationship before I ever started dating Pam, so it was easy to just pick up where we left off. It sounds terrible now, but it didn't seem so bad at the time. After all, Pam and I weren't engaged. Finally, I realized how much I cared about Pam and I went back to her. Even to this day, Pam is very jealous of other women I talk to. Do you think this might have something to do with why we're having trouble in our physical relationship and why Pam doesn't want sex anymore? She feels resentful and angry all the time."

"If your sex life is dead, Bill, what are you doing for yourself in the sexual area?"

"Well, to be honest with you, I watch pornographic movies on TV after Pam goes to bed, and a few months ago I started getting hooked on finding pornography on the Internet."

IF YOU CAN'T WIN THE DATING GAME, WHY PLAY?

Bill and Pam's problems are common among many Christian marriages today. Pain often drives people to act in ways that are comforting and anesthetizing in the short term, but negative and damaging in the long term. To medicate their pain and find pleasure, some people watch pornographic movies on late-night television. Others deaden the pain by fantasizing or yearning for a divorce that will allow them to escape.

When a marriage relationship is built on the unstable foundation of dating, the marriage will have difficulty during the storms of life. "But everyone who hears these words of mine and does not put them into practice is like a foolish man who built his house on sand" (Matthew 7:26). As a marriage and family counselor, I see it becoming increasingly common for couples to have marital problems caused by their involvement in the dating process before marriage. Bill's and Pam's marriage foundation was built on their dating experiences with others and with each other. Now their marriage was reaping the spoiled fruits planted in their dating experiences.

For years, Bill and Pam seemed to have a "good" marriage. At least it looked good to the rest of the world. But the problems that eventually surfaced in their relationship could be traced to the residual effects of their past dating lives. Singles who follow the world's principles for dating tend to experience a host of negative outcomes with their future mates, including a deep lack of trust, an inability to forgive, a tendency to withhold encouragement, an unsatisfactory sex life, and an inability to fully become one.

If dating has so many negative consequences on marriage, why do Christian singles date? I asked this question in a recent seminar. Here are some of the answers, a few of which were also listed at the beginning of this book. Which of them would you have given?

The reason I date is to:

- Find a marriage partner.
- Learn how to relate to the opposite sex.
- Develop social skills and emotional health.
- Have fun and feel good.
- Avoid loneliness and being alone.
- Have certain needs met until a marriage partner is found.
- Prepare myself for marriage.

Now comes the key question: Does dating truly produce results like those listed above? Have we been deceived in our own minds about the benefits of dating? Christian singles need to address these questions honestly.

Maybe dating isn't all it's cracked up to be. Consider the following truths about dating:

- Dating doesn't find you a marriage partner; God does.
- Dating doesn't teach you how to relate to the opposite sex; it teaches you how to have regrets through involvement with the opposite sex.
- Dating destroys rather than develops social skills and emotional health.
- Dating can quickly replace fun with pain and the "good" feelings can give way to hurt and resentment.
- Dating doesn't fill the void of loneliness inside you; only God does.

- Dating can't meet marital needs; only your mate can within the context of marriage.
- Dating doesn't prepare people for marriage; it prepares them for divorce.

BREAKING UP

If you do a lot of dating, you will do a lot of breaking up. The formula for dating is "breaking up minus one"—you break up with everyone you date, minus the one you marry, *if* you marry. Breaking up not only has a devastating effect on you as a single, but it also has residual effects on your marriage.

If the consequences are so severe, then why do dating couples break up? Here are twelve of the most common reasons:

- The excitement is gone and the relationship seems boring.
- The relationship is too demanding.
- Someone better comes along.
- The person you are dating is "not the one."
- One person is ready to marry and the other is not.
- Too much fighting and the relationship disintegrates.
- One person wants to "find someone better."
- "One person feels it isn't God's will for us to date or marry."
- There is something about the other person that you cannot live with.
- Your partner is not meeting your needs.
- Romantic feelings are gone and you don't care for them like you once did.
- You should never have been involved with the other person in the first place.

You may have noted that the excuses singles use to get out of a dating relationship are the same ones married couples use to seek a divorce. If you took Psychology 101 in college, you probably remember Pavlov's dogs. They were conditioned to salivate when they heard a bell. In the same way, dating relationships condition us to break up in times of adversity. When we hit tough times in marriage, we respond the way past experience has taught us— break up and start over. Is it easier for some people to leave a marriage because they have become conditioned to the "breaking up" part of a dating relationship? Could skyrocketing divorce rates be connected to a flawed dating system that encourages break-ups?

By following the world's principles of dating, we significantly increase the chances our marriage will fail. Like Bill and Pam, most Christian singles have embraced dating because they have never known an alternative and are unaware of the lasting, negative consequences. They are reaping the fallout from a destructive social convention. "Do not be deceived: God cannot be mocked. A man reaps what he sows" (Galatians 6:7). God says our past equals our present.

I agree that some breakdowns in marital relationships stem from childhood experiences. In fact, the greater the dysfunction in your family, the greater likelihood you have of being caught up in the dating game. But I see an increasing number of marriages being shattered by problems that have their roots in the couple's dating life before marriage. The pain from the past does leak into and infect the present—but it doesn't have to. When we follow God's plan, we are healed and made whole, not scarred and shattered.

GOD RESTORES WHAT DATING HAS DAMAGED

If you're involved in a destructive dating relationship or feel you have already blown the chance to have a biblically based marriage, God can and will restore you to a place where you feel whole, pure, and worthy of love from Him and a future mate. God will clean away the grime of past relationships so you can begin to see yourself the way He sees you. When you confess your relational sins, you are asking Him to wipe the mud from your soul and body.

Some will ask, "What wonderful Christian would want me for a spouse if they knew my past?" God's love covers a multitude of sins. If your future spouse has the love of Christ, they will see beyond your shameful past and into your blessed future. A godly spouse will keep their eyes on the Perfecter of the faith and not your past failures. They will be rejoicing about your future together and not dwelling on a forgiven past. God's love will freely flow through your spouse to you.

Others of you may be feeling guilt or shame from past dating experiences. But remember: Christ forgave your acts of sin when He died on the cross. If Jesus loved and forgave you, shouldn't you forgive and love yourself?

Hate your relational sins, but love yourself the way God loves you. And when the deceiver tries to remind you of your shameful past, you remind him how God has forgiven, loved, and blessed your future. The evil one will try to convince you that you are nothing more than a pauper, but in reality you are royalty, a child of the King.

God's plan for biblically based, healthy, healing relationships is courtship. You can avoid the lifelong heartache and disappointment of dating by focusing on Christ, making proper courtship preparations, and having a spiritual couple who can hold you accountable. If you are already in a dating relationship or think you have gone too far in the other direction, understanding the courtship process will teach you how to receive healing as God restores "the years the locusts have eaten" (Joel 2:25). Hang tightly and remember that the greater the devastation, the greater the restoration.

STUDY AND DISCUSSION QUESTIONS

1. Review these two scriptural references: (1) 2 Samuel 11:1–12:14 and (2) Ruth 2–4. Determine the following for each reference:

Where did the idea for the relationship originate?
What was the motive?
What were the goals?
What were the results?
Which of the two most resembles dating as we know it today?

2. Why would industrialization and urbanization have such a profound effect on changing an approach to marriage that had lasted for centuries? Can you think of other changes in society that may have contributed to the rise of the dating system?

3. Read Galatians 6:7. How does a marriage "reap" what was "sown" in dating?

4. How does dating trick us into continually comparing ourselves to others?

5. Why do you think Bill and Pam "stopped talking and started fighting" after they developed a physical relationship?

6. What do you think "dating idolatry" means and how can it happen?

7. When a relationship doesn't have commitment, what happens to trust? How important is trust to marriage? How important was it to Bill and Pam's relationship?

8. God says He will restore "the years the locusts have eaten" (Joel 2:25). If "locusts" refers to sin, what does this analogy mean in the context of relationships?

9. Meditate and memorize: "See to it that no one takes you captive through hollow and deceptive philosophy, which depends on human tradition and the basic principles of this world rather than on Christ" (Colossians 2:8).

10. Pray: My heavenly Father, I confess my relational sin with (other person) when I (state the act). I choose to crucify my flesh and follow Christ's example in my future relationships. I also give You all of my guilt and shame that I wrongly accepted and still carry from this dating relationship. Through submission I commit to honor and glorify You in my future relationships. Thank You for loving and forgiving me. I ask these things in the name of my Lord, Jesus. Amen.

CHAPTER THREE

Counterfeit Oneness

For this reason a man will leave his father and mother and be united to his wife, and they will become one flesh.
GENESIS 2:24

CAUTION: Dating couples often develop a counterfeit oneness that feels like marriage but lacks commitment and responsibility.

Rebecca constantly thought about Jim. She would sit at her desk and write his name on a notepad, then write her name next to his. They looked wonderful together. She would wait for his call and fantasize about their time in each other's company. If she wasn't with him in person, she was with him in her mind and heart. He had become part of who she was.

A wonderful, romantic picture except for one thing: Jim was married to someone else.

Why would anybody date another person who was already married? If dating is supposed to lead to a life partner, why begin a relationship that has all the earmarks of a disaster?

One of the biggest reasons people date is because they want

intimacy. They want to love and be loved, to accept and be accepted. Sometimes this need for intimacy is so intense that it takes people where they don't really want to go.

God designed the desire for intimacy to be met in Him and then in a marital relationship—the strongest, most intimate of all human relationships. In Genesis 2:18 (KJV), God made a "help meet" for Adam. The Hebrew translation of "help meet" is "completer." In other words, God's creative work in Adam was not complete until He made Eve. The goal was oneness. And so it is with marriage today. The goal is still oneness, yet many people are trying to find this fulfillment outside of marriage. When this happens, the oneness they create is counterfeit—something that looks like the real thing until you hold it up to God's light and see it for the weak, hollow, hopeless relationship it really is.

DISTORTING GOD'S PRINCIPLE OF ONENESS

When you glue two pieces of paper together then pull them apart, it's almost never a clean break. The fibers and fragments of one piece tear away and become part of the other. Our souls look the same way after we've glued ourselves to other people physically, emotionally, or spiritually outside of marriage. Because part of that person is still with us, "getting over" him or her is nearly impossible. Our thoughts and emotions are constantly being drawn back to the past so that sometimes we're not fully in the present.

The oneness principle of marriage was God's idea. "A man will leave his father and mother and be united to his wife, and they will become one flesh" (Genesis 2:24). God desires man to be one with Him and one with a mate, but the world perverts the oneness principle by tempting us with opportunities to be one with many people. Unfortunately, dating almost always means a temporary relationship. Except for the one person you marry, dating always ends by breaking up.

God didn't create human hearts to bond and break, bond and break, bond and break over and over again. We think we get over other people, but the method we use is often so dysfunctional that our lives are affected forever. Think of a breakup you've had in your life. Did it end in a way that would honor God, or did it end in one of the following ways:

- You "stuffed" or internalized your painful emotions.
- You ran to the next relationship to medicate the pain from the previous relationship.
- You got angry (and may still be angry). Anger is a sedative for pain.
- You withdrew or avoided the other person or perhaps all other people.
- You became a game player good at using others instead of being used.
- You made an inner vow: "I'll never let anyone hurt me like this again."
- You put up emotional walls that have kept you from becoming intimate with anyone.
- You manage the destruction and pain of the dating relationship through denial.

By the time most singles finally marry, they've already been through a series of shattered romances and broken hearts. God is not honored when we have scarred someone else or been scarred ourselves either physically, emotionally, or spiritually (Philippians 2:3). Such negative consequences are the result of a dysfunctional, destructive dating system that has no emphasis on commitment or responsibility.

Part of the problem is that people tell themselves they're looking for "love" in a relationship, yet the meaning of the word has been distorted to the point where it can mean anything we want it to. We say "God is love," but that's completely different from the Beatles telling us "Love is all you need" or Tina Turner asking "What's love got to do with it?" A fifteen-year-old boy declares that if his girlfriend "loves" him, she'll have sex with him. Once I heard a cowboy at a rodeo in Houston talking one minute about how he "loved" his wife, and the next minute about how he "loved" chili dogs.

True love is a decision that is consciously made. It is as much an act of the will as it is an emotion. It isn't sex, and it isn't a feeling. Love is a sacrificial commitment. "Greater love has no one than this, that one lay down his life for his friends" (John 15:13).

Christ showed ultimate love by His commitment to die on the cross. His choice to die was based on His love commitment, not a feeling. No feeling can be relied on to last in its full intensity or even to last at all. That's why love isn't just a feeling but a deep unity maintained by the will and deliberately strengthened by habit. When Christian couples ask for and receive God's grace (unmerited favor), they can have love for each other even at those moments when they do not like each other's behavior, just as we can love ourselves when we do not like our own behavior.

SIGNS OF TROUBLE

The unhealthy ties of counterfeit oneness can make a couple feel as though love is drawing them together and make it difficult to separate or be away from each other. That is the telltale sign of counterfeit oneness. Like a hunter who sets a snare for his prey, the enemy sets his trap for singles longing for intimacy and meaningful relationships only to capture them by the control of counterfeit oneness.

Many individuals don't understand why a certain person has such control over their lives and why they can't forget them. The bondage caused by counterfeit oneness can make individuals think they can't break up and escape—even when the dating relationship is abusive. If they are able to leave, counterfeit oneness sometimes acts like a powerful magnet drawing them back into a dysfunctional relationship.

How do you know if you have ever been infected by counterfeit oneness? You can gauge the degree to which you have become one with another person by the intensity of the pain you feel after a breakup. When the physical, emotional, or spiritual level of involvement is greater than the commitment level, you've experienced counterfeit oneness. It can happen on one level or on all three levels. When it does, most singles are unaware of its destructive consequences both to their relationship with God and to their oneness with their future mate.

Why is dating dangerous? Because it disproportionately exalts physical and romantic attraction and avoids commitment and responsibility. Dating emphasizes emotions, lust, and sensual desire—all of which demand a sexual response. Most couples "give in" to the physical desires created by romantic attraction. Even singles who don't want to become physically involved often do because they are fighting the very natures God gave them. Dating places Christian singles in compromising situations that require them to fight against their God-given innate desires to become one with another person.

Romance God's way starts with the commitment level first because the couple has the assurance that God is leading in the relationship. Their interest in each other may have started with some type of spiritual or emotional attraction, but no intimate friendship developed until they were certain of God's leadership with a view toward marriage. Once the couple discerns God's leading, then the male/female relationship God intended can progress naturally from commitment to spiritual oneness to emotional oneness to physical oneness. Any other plan or approach to marriage is out of the will of God for a child of God because it does not make allowances for the sovereignty of God.

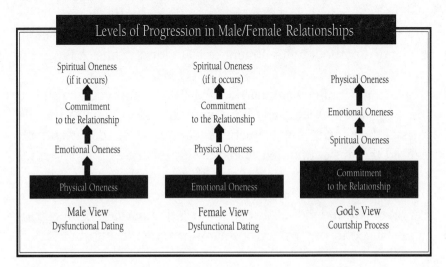

COUNTERFEIT PHYSICAL ONENESS

What happens to Christians who have been sexually involved before marriage? I can tell you the answer because I hear their stories almost daily. Like the two pieces of paper glued together and ripped apart, Christian singles who have not healed from broken relationships carry forever the memories and reminders of past sexual partners. In fact, those memories often become disruptive, destructive parts of their marriages to other people.

Back in the early 1980s there was a public service message about HIV on television with the slogan "Whoever you had sex with, you had sex with their partner, and their partner, and their partner..." When we become sexually involved with others we become one with them, and we become one with the one they became one with, and so on and so on. God explains these counterfeit body and soul ties in 1 Corinthians 6:16: "Do you not know that he who unites himself with a prostitute [sexual involvement] is one with her in body? For it is said, 'THE TWO WILL BECOME ONE FLESH.'" As you can see, the secular world is once again slow in catching up with God's Word in explaining the principles of relational failures.

Multiple sexual partners mean multiplied emotional baggage. Ben had been a Christian since childhood but had spent most of his life with little self-control over lust. He had carried on a sexual relationship with Vicki for many years, but eventually they broke up. He and Vicki had thought they were in love, but their relationship ended without commitment or even kind words. A few years later, he married Connie.

Ben and Connie were married less than a year when he started obsessing about Vicki. His head wouldn't stop playing the old tapes of their sexual involvement. After counseling, Ben eventually realized that his counterfeit oneness with Vicki was not only hurting his marriage to Connie but also his relationship with God.

God made sexual oneness in marriage to be the final consummation of two individuals becoming one. Premarital sexual experiences can bond one person to many partners, losing the original concept of bonding with one mate for a lifetime. Scripture warns that sexual involvement outside of the marriage relationship has consequences, and knowing God's will in this area is not complicated:

> *It is God's will* that you should be holy; that you should avoid sexual immorality; that each of you should learn to control his own body in a way that is holy and honorable, not in passionate lust like the heathen, who do not know God; and that in this matter no one should wrong his brother or take advantage of him. The Lord will punish men for all such sins, as we have already told you and warned you. For God did not call us to be impure, but to live a holy life. Therefore, he who rejects this instruction does not reject man but God, who gives you his Holy Spirit. (1 Thessalonians 4:3–8, italics added)

When we look for God's truths in the passage, here is what we find:[1]

1. Living a pure life pleases God.
2. God's will is that we avoid sexual immorality.
3. God wants us to learn how to control our bodies.
4. Our methods of controlling our desires must be holy and honorable.
5. The way we control our bodies will differ from the methods of unbelievers.
6. Gratifying our sexual desires outside of marriage always hurts someone.
7. We shouldn't take advantage of another person in order to satisfy our sexual desires.
8. These standards come from God, not from man.
9. If we disobey these instructions, we reject God.
10. Sexual sins have not only physical consequences but also spiritual consequences.

The dangers and complications of premarital sex intensify when each person thinks their situation is different—that somehow being in love has made everything okay. I have couples who come to me searching for God's will in their relationship and yet they are sexually involved. Scripture clearly says they are living outside the will of God. Their own unrepented sin will put a plug in their communication line with God (Isaiah 59:1–2).

In the story of Ben and Vicki, both of them thought they were in love at the time they were dating. Counterfeit physical oneness— a oneness outside the will of God—can cause two people to feel as though they are in love. Without the commitment of marriage, sexual relationships usually crumble when the new wears off—or when lust looks for another partner. Was it love or lust?

The Bible speaks of lust as deceitful, meaning that what many individuals assume to be love may actually be lust. Satan's counterfeit for God's physical oneness principle is called lust, and it lays the groundwork for counterfeit physical oneness.

At its core, lust actually becomes idolatry because looking for happiness in God's creation rather than in God Himself is idol worship. When something or someone becomes so important to you that you will give up God's values to have that thing or that person, you have created an idol. You may have shaped the idol in the beginning, but eventually the idol shapes you and even controls you.

Just as love is the fulfilling of God's law, lust is the violation of God's law. Lust says, "I have to have it, and I have to have it *now.*" In many ways, giving in to lust is no different than an addict giving in to a heroin habit. You start with a small amount and enjoy the "high" it gives you, and eventually you find yourself taking larger doses to reach the same high. Over time, even that high isn't enough and you want something more, so you increase the dosage. When your need for sex or physical intimacy is out of control and you're acting in ways you never thought possible, you are as much an addict as someone who shoots heroin. And the end result will probably be equally devastating.

Our flesh draws us to the pleasures of sin. Most singles are deceived into lusting for the pleasures of sin without seeing the painful consequences. We want to walk up to the edge of sin, look over the edge, then lean over—and many times step over—the line into sin, hoping not to reap the devastating consequences. But Hebrews 11:25 states that Moses preferred to share in the oppression of the people of God rather than "enjoy the pleasures of sin for a short time." The moral of the story: the pleasures of sin don't last, but the painful consequences can.

In some ways Ben was fortunate in the way his affair ended with Vicki. At least his memories weren't full of hate and bitterness, two emotions which often surface after sexual encounters. It's not uncommon for the man to lose interest or even begin to despise a woman after having sex with her. A good example is Amnon (2 Samuel 13:2), whose lust for Tamar was fanned by the knowledge that she was a virgin.

Amnon loved Tamar in her innocence, but after he had forced her to have sex, he hated her. She became an object to be used and discarded. "Then Amnon hated her with intense hatred. In fact, he hated her more than he had loved her" (2 Samuel 13:15). This Scripture passage speaks to us directly about our sexuality and lust:[2]

1. Inappropriate sexual desire can lead to sin.
2. Wrong friends encourage wrong behavior.
3. Sexual sin often involves deception.
4. We should avoid potentially compromising situations.
5. Intense sexual desires can cause irrational actions.
6. When lust is fulfilled and desires diminish, the ensuing guilt may result in hatred.
7. Alienation, hatred, and even violence can result from sexual sin.
8. Sexual sin can produce family conflict that will fracture the family for years.

One of the problems with lust is that so few people are willing to admit they have it. Eight out of ten people may be dealing with lust at this moment, but only one will admit it. That deception will cause them to fall. We must admit we have a problem before we can deal with it and keep it from controlling us.

Many people think lust will go away after marriage. They couldn't be more wrong. After marriage, lust that has been uncontrolled and unacknowledged acts like a tiger confined to a cage. It desires to get out even more. Think for a moment how many marriages, churches, and countries have been destroyed because of lust.

When all is said and done, the only real motive that will drive most people to purge the impurity of their hearts is their own desperate desire for intimacy with God.[3] The Bible says that the pure in heart are blessed and they will see God (Matthew 5:8). If purity is the condition for experiencing God's higher love, then lust is its satanic opposite with incredible power. By harboring lust, we limit our own intimacy with God.

> If your eye is pure, there will be sunshine in your soul. But if your eye is clouded with evil thoughts and desires, you are in deep spiritual darkness. And oh, how deep that darkness can be! (Matthew 6:22–23, TLB)

COUNTERFEIT EMOTIONAL ONENESS

Many Christians who have never been involved in a sexual affair have had *emotional* affairs. Counterfeit emotional oneness develops when you give your emotions to someone beyond what is required for friendship. Anyone who has felt the deep, gut-wrenching pain of a breakup or experienced an unhealthy relationship can relate to this type of counterfeit oneness.

In her book *Quest for Love,* Elisabeth Elliot tells the story of Holly and Scott, two marriageable singles who shared too much too soon.[4]

> What Holly thought would be an ordinary Sunday evening turned into an enchanted evening. She met Scott.
>
> "I'd seen him around church a few times, but it's a big

church and we had never spoken. During the social hour following the service, we got into conversation. He offered to drive me home, and—well, you know the story. He started calling me, we'd talk for hours on the phone. He decided to join the singles group, hung around afterward and we'd talk, and finally he actually asked me out. Sometimes he picked up the tab, but usually I paid my own way. I didn't want to feel obligated to him.

"Once when we had dinner together, he prayed," Holly confided to me, "thanking God for our friendship and for the fact that the singles group could witness a man and a woman who could be good friends without falling in love."

Without falling in love. Uh-huh. I've heard that story from both men and women, perhaps hundreds of times.

Who did Scott think he was kidding? Had it not crossed his mind that one of them might fall? One of the two always does. Poor Holly had fallen flat. She was in her early twenties and attractive, yet she told me she "had a problem." She did—her heart was on hold.

When your heart is on hold, you do what Holly did—a lot of praying and crying and hoping for the telephone to ring. Scott kept her hopes up. He invited her to a big family wedding, even to the reception meant only for family and close friends. Surely he must be getting serious. Would he put his feelings into words? Well, almost. He talked about marriage, telling Holly he often dreamed of having a wife and how he hoped to find one. He told her how much he wanted children, offering her his ideas on raising them. The time came when Holly could stand it no longer.

They were eating pizza by the fire in her living room. Scott always accepted her invitations. Once or twice he had brought flowers or a bottle of wine. Tonight he was enjoying the pizza, chattering away about a game he'd been to. But Holly's mind wasn't on the game.

"Scott," she said hesitantly, "we need to talk about something."

"Yeah?"

"I mean—like, we've been, you know, friends long enough."

The man was startled. He took a huge bite of pizza and said nothing.

"This is really hard for me to say, but, Scott, if you don't have any intentions of, well, a real relationship, I can't spend any more time alone with you. I've felt so comfortable with you. I can be myself—my real self, I mean. I've told you a lot of—well, of my heart. But if it doesn't—if you aren't, you know..." Her voice trailed off.

The silence was thunderous. Holly looked at Scott. Scott looked at the fire. After another bite and another gulp, he said he couldn't see himself married to her. The truth was, of course, that for months Holly had been seeing herself married to him. To her, a "real relationship" meant engagement, although she didn't use that word. In fact, she told me, she had never voiced any desire to be married to him. Hadn't she? Scott might be a little obtuse, but he knew what a "real relationship" had to mean. He thought he was forestalling any such complication by telling Holly about his hopes. Didn't she catch on that she wasn't what he was looking for?

In time, Holly did "catch on," but not before she was already wounded by counterfeit emotional oneness. Through the years I've counseled many couples like Holly and Scott. If we take a closer look at their story, we'll find some mistakes that are being repeated daily in the lives of many Christian singles:

- The greatest attraction between a man and a woman—even greater than apparel, makeup and hair styles—is shared conversation. The deeper the conversation, the deeper the attraction. Women are particularly good listeners and good conversationalists. This feeds the male ego and makes shared conversations especially seductive. Scott and Holly spent hours talking on the phone, and then he began to hang around after the singles group and they'd talk some more.

- Scott talked about his dreams and hopes, even how he felt about raising children. Sharing the wounds of the past and the dreams and visions of the future is the primary way couples create emotional intimacy, which is why deep one-on-one sharing should be saved for a committed relationship. Sharing the past makes you particularly vulnerable, and when you share the future, one of the partners almost always wants to be a part of the other person's dreams.

- Men tend not to be very giving. Consequently, the smallest sign of a man's interest can take on a significance to a woman that a man never intended. It did for Holly. Flowers and a bottle of wine. Dinner by the fire. She tried not to think anything about it, but she couldn't help herself.

- Holly was hesitant to bring up the subject of their relationship, always hoping Scott would mention it first. He never did, but he did manage to hint at the issue indirectly during a dinner prayer. Because women usually see the man as the initiator and want the man to lead, they're apprehensive about expressing their desire for a committed relationship. While they wait for the man to initiate the subject, they allow themselves to become more and more involved emotionally.

- Scott took Holly to meet his family and closest friends. Usually, such interactions are reserved for a "special" relationship beyond friendship, or so Holly thought.

- Holly spent a lot of time daydreaming about Scott and waiting for the telephone to ring. When longing to be with someone and thinking about them consumes your day, you know you're too involved emotionally. Women generally make themselves too available to men and tend to be too open and vulnerable. When your heart is on hold and the relationship isn't going anywhere (no commitment), pressing for explanations can be foolish. Quietly declining further invitations is probably better than letting your feelings build to a crescendo and ending in an emotional outburst. Preserving the friendship at this stage is usually impossible.

- Most of the time, counterfeit oneness comes into our lives in the form of a listening ear, a shoulder to cry on, or lips speaking words of encouragement. Women are particularly vulnerable to the need for emotional intimacy because God made them more "feelings" oriented. For a woman, two of the most appealing characteristics in a man are gentleness and compassion, and both have a lot to do with showing feelings. By limiting deep, personal conversations and the amount of one-on-one alone time they spend together, Christian singles can guard their hearts from becoming too involved until the commitment level of their relationship exceeds the emotional level.

For singles in a dating relationship, the by-product of counterfeit emotional oneness can be a great deal of bitterness, hatred, self-hatred, pain, and confusion, not to mention fear of rejection and abandonment. Singles who have experienced emotional oneness with others and lived to tell the tale may transfer their damaged emotions onto their mates and into their marriages. By the time they marry, their hurt could turn into subtle forms of anger directed at the wrong person.

Many marriages have faltered when partners have become emotionally entangled with someone else by allowing their conversation levels to go deeper than the commitment levels required for friendship. This is called emotional adultery. It can be as dangerous as physical adultery. Because most people aren't expecting to get involved emotionally, counterfeit emotional oneness starts out in a very subtle way. Most Christians, especially women, aren't likely to start an affair just out of physical lust. It's the emotional attachment that causes them to step over the physical line. As wonderful as it might be to discover someone who cares about you and supports you, fight the tendency to drift into emotional intimacy and then sexual intimacy. "Above all else, guard your heart, for it is the wellspring of life" (Proverbs 4:23).

Our need for emotional oneness is driven by the fulfillment we think we'll find with another person instead of the emptiness and abandonment we feel when we're alone. Like taking a pill for pain, being with someone may decrease the pain of being alone. This reduction in pain can feel so comforting that it actually makes us think we are in love. When that happens, the other person usually becomes the focal point for all our hopes and dreams. We feed on them. When they do not love us back in the way or to the degree we think they should, we feel hurt and angry.

Fear of loneliness and a desire for emotional intimacy can become just as controlling, damaging, and addictive as lust. And like lust, if they are left unacknowledged and uncontrolled, they can drive people to behavior they never thought possible. The true realization of an emotional addiction is when you recognize not how much you want someone, but how much you fear being without them. When that happens, you're only a step away from idolatry—making someone else your god. If you try to find relief for legitimate needs in unbiblical ways, counterfeit emotional oneness can produce a counterfeit god in your life.

Contrary to your feelings, loneliness is not a time of abandonment—it just feels that way. It actually can be a time of encounter at new levels with the only One who can fill that empty place in your heart. "So, humble yourselves under God's strong hand, and in His own good time He will lift you up. You can throw the whole weight of your anxieties upon Him, for you are His personal concern" (1 Peter 5:6–7, Phillips). Intimacy with God will fill the voids and pains in your heart that may have been created from childhood or past dating relationships.

COUNTERFEIT SPIRITUAL ONENESS

Although many single Christians have committed themselves to physical purity and some even realize the painful consequences of counterfeit emotional oneness, few recognize the dangers of becoming one spiritually with someone other than their future spouse. Because we are spiritual beings on a human journey, spiritual intimacy is the first and deepest level of a relationship. Our wholeness in this area must be reserved for the mate God selects. "Has not the LORD made them one? In flesh and spirit they are his. And why one? Because he was seeking godly offspring. So guard yourself in your spirit, and do not break faith with the wife of your youth" (Malachi 2:15).

Susan and Mike were "just friends"; they had never been physically or emotionally involved. They were in the same Sunday school class, choir, and Bible study when they decided to become prayer partners. Even though Susan truly believed they were just friends on a spiritual level with no intention of marriage, she wept in pain when Mike moved away to attend medical school.

"I feel like I'm being ripped at my spiritual core," she said. Susan was right. She had connected with Mike on the deepest of all levels—spiritual oneness. Her spiritual life had been so finely entwined with his that something of her left when he left. Mike's absence literally affected her relationship with God.

Susan's counterfeit spiritual oneness resulted from her deep desire to be more spiritual. This desire can cause problems when two people in a relationship aim their spiritual growth sideways instead of upward. We eventually will be disappointed and hurt when we depend on each other instead of God for our spiritual nourishment. If our spiritual life is wrapped up in other people, what happens when they walk out the door?

Today Susan is allowing God to break her counterfeit spiritual oneness with Mike so she can once again love her "first love," Jesus (Revelation 2:4). Now she will be free to experience all of the blessings intended for her in becoming spiritually one with God and later with her future mate.

Our deep desire to be more spiritual also opens us up for another type of deception that probably happens more than we would like to admit. Some people use prayer and spiritual talk as a form of manipulation. One prominent pastor in Houston tells about praying with his dates in college and not realizing until later that he had used religious talk and actions to manipulate girls into liking him. Women in particular are often more sensitive to a spirit life and have a God-given longing for a spiritual partner. Men who recognize this in women may have godly behaviors but ungodly motives.

UNMASKING COUNTERFEIT ONENESS

God did not intend for singles to become one with many individuals. He intended singles to become one with Himself, then—and only then—to become one with a mate.

"The Christian idea of marriage is based on Christ's words that a man and wife are to be regarded as a single organism," writes C. S. Lewis, one of the greatest Christian thinkers of the twentieth century. In regard to seeking sexual intercourse outside of marriage, Lewis warned Christians not to "isolate that pleasure and try to get it by itself, any more than you ought to try to get the pleasures of taste without swallowing and digesting."

The same can be said for the oneness of two people emotionally and spiritually outside the context of marriage. We shouldn't try to isolate those pleasures and get them by themselves any more than we should try to get the pleasure of taste without swallowing.

If you belong to God and are involved in a relationship of counterfeit oneness, you can't expect anything eventually other than grief. Rationalization is a monumental problem for many people but particularly for Christians. Under pressure we can make all kinds of excuses to rationalize immoral behavior.

Most Christians generally agree that sex outside of marriage is biblically wrong, so they have to rationalize their immoral behavior. They may justify sexual contact because they plan to marry the person. Or they may think they can become involved in a deeper physical relationship because they're in love.

Do any of these rationalizations make immoral behavior right in the sight of God?

Physical attraction has a way of shorting out the brain and sidetracking rational thought. One reason we get into immoral behavior is because we don't see immediate consequences. If we did, we might be more rational in our thinking. AIDS has been a good reminder that our behavior has consequences. Dating couples are more cautious and less casual about sex now than they were thirty years ago. The no-rules, free-love, free-sex philosophy of the 60s has given way to a whole new order of societal rules.

When we live by a list of rules—whether God's or man's—we can easily change or justify that list when temptations arise. If, on the other hand, we have an intimate fellowship with God and seek first to please Him, we will have more motivation to live a pure life. Obedience is how we show God we love Him, and the obedience must always come before understanding. Most singles, however, want to touch the stove before they'll believe it's hot.

If you had children, would you want them to obey you because they love you or because they are afraid of the consequences? Would you be able to sit down with your children and explain in detail all the physical and emotional consequences that could result from a one-night stand or a broken affair? No, not likely. Instead, you would want your children to obey you out of love and to trust you when you say that their own understanding will come later as they mature. So it is with God. He asks us to obey now and trust Him for the understanding that will come later.

Sexual sin is not just between two consenting adults; it's an act of disobedience to God. Partial obedience is total *dis*obedience. There is no "partial" way to obey God. More and more physical involvement is characteristic of today's dating relationships. If Christian singles stop short of intercourse but are physically intimate in every other way, their partial obedience is disobedience in God's eyes.

The result of this scriptural violation is that the relationship is directed away from God's path. His path leads to unity on the day of the wedding. A person does not have to know what the Scriptures say—or even care what they say—to experience the effects of violating them. God's law of sowing and reaping reveals itself in a person's life regardless of whether one is familiar with them.

Have you ever felt the effects of counterfeit oneness? Do you see how counterfeit oneness can harm your future marriage? If you are involved in a relationship that you know does not honor God, He desires that you break your counterfeit oneness with that person and be one with Him.

How do you do that? There isn't an easy way, but in the end the less painful way is the Band-Aid removal approach. If you had a Band-Aid on your arm, would it hurt more to rip it off in one quick pull or to slowly peel it off a little at a time? You know the answer.

Many people break up slowly in order not to hurt the other person or because they feel guilty or truly don't want to break up. This causes more pain and anger in the long run. If you want to position yourself for God's blessings in the future, you must disturb the present. Do it quickly. Time won't heal all your relationship wounds, but you can be restored to wholeness by breaking counterfeit ties with others both in the past and present and by becoming one with Christ until He gives you a mate.

If you've developed counterfeit oneness with someone you are currently dating and you know that they are "not the one," break up today! If you've developed counterfeit oneness with the person you believe God has chosen to be your mate, then confess your relational sin and begin following the courtship process. If you are suffering the residual effects from past counterfeit oneness, read on and be hopeful. God will restore your wounded soul.

STUDY AND DISCUSSION QUESTIONS

1. According to Genesis 2:23–24, what important place is a man's wife to have in his life?

2. Why is it significant that woman was created from Adam and not from the dust of the ground? If woman had been created from dust like Adam, would they have been two equal and separate identities?

3. Read 1 Corinthians 11:11–12. Does God's plan promote independence or interdependence? How does this relate to the differences between dating and courtship?

4. Have you ever experienced:

a) physical counterfeit oneness?

      b) emotional counterfeit oneness?

      c) spiritual counterfeit oneness?

      If so, what factors influenced this counterfeit oneness
and then influenced your breakup?

5. How will premarital sexual intercourse (1) affect your usefulness to God, (2) affect your relationship with Him and (3) affect His blessing on your dating relationship? What effect would it have on your spiritual relationship with your dating partner?

6. Meditate and memorize: "Above all else, guard your heart, for it is the wellspring of life" (Proverbs 4:23).

7. Pray: My heavenly Father, I humbly submit spirit, soul, and body to You. I renounce and confess my relational sins with (person). I no longer desire any ties with (person) and ask that You would destroy all counterfeit oneness with and memories of (person). Please break my sexual bonds, obsessive thoughts, emotional desires and dependencies with (person). Help me forget my illicit union with (person) so that I am free to give my body, soul, and spirit to You and my mate. Thank You for loving and forgiving me and setting me free. Amen.

CHAPTER FOUR

Making a "Good" Choice or a "God" Choice

Since we live by the Spirit, let us keep in step with the Spirit.
GALATIANS 5:25

PRINCIPLE ONE: Not every good choice is God's choice, and seeking God's will is the most important part of selecting your mate.

Deciding who you will marry is one of the most important decisions you will ever make. In a kingdom courtship, the primary reason for marriage should be the conviction that a particular match is God's choice for you—not just a good choice, but God's choice.

Most of the time, you won't have the luxury of choosing between people or circumstances that are totally bad or totally good. Nearly all your choices will appear good in some way, but only one will be part of God's perfect plan—His best for you. The chief enemy you will fight in choosing God's best will be your own strong inclination to make a good choice instead of a God choice.

WHEN GOD MAKES THE CHOICE

Randal Ross is a fourth-generation preacher pastoring a 13,000-member church in Lubbock, Texas. Thirty years ago he was a 1960s hippie with long hair, wire-rimmed glasses, and torn blue jeans. He had been offered college scholarships at many universities, including UCLA and Stanford, but he chose to major in biochemistry at a small, private college in Pennsylvania.

Randal was smart, athletic, and well liked. He also was stoned most of the time. Uppers, downers, LSD, he took them all. The more Randal partied at school, the more he got behind in his studies. The more he got behind, the more drugs he took to stay awake and study. Eventually Randal sold drugs so he could afford to buy drugs.

Although Randal had been captain of the wrestling team in high school, his college lifestyle took a toll on his body and he dropped to a gaunt 120 pounds. Then one day while he was sitting in the library, he couldn't remember his name or his dormitory. The room and the people in the room began to melt before his eyes. Colors spun in his head. He couldn't think clearly.

That week nineteen-year-old Randal Ross dropped out of college, and his father literally carried him to the car for the trip home. For the next few weeks, Randal stayed in his room during the day and walked the streets of Cleveland at night. Colors still spun in his head and confusion clouded his mind. Drugs and an abusive lifestyle had assaulted not only his body but also his mind.

Having grown up in church as the descendant of three generations of preachers, Randal felt humiliated and ashamed. Alone on Christmas Eve with a gun and enough drugs to take his life, Randal put a rock 'n roll album on the record player and prepared to commit suicide. But first he prayed.

"God," he said, "I sat in Your house all my life and never saw anything that interested me. If You are real, do something."

When Randal Ross tells that story today, he's usually standing behind a pulpit. That's part of the "something" God did. "God came into that room at 11:45 on Christmas Eve and healed my mind," he says. "The room quit melting, colors quit spinning, and my mind cleared."

But that's not all.

Three thousand miles away in California, Andrea Blegen was sitting in a Christmas Eve watchnight service when God spoke to her heart. "I want you to get up and go pray for the husband I will give you. At this very moment his life is hanging in the balance between life and death." She had never met Randal Ross and wouldn't for many years to come.

Andrea probably wouldn't have had a great deal of interest in the confused hippie she prayed for on Christmas Eve, but in God's time she eventually met God's man—the new and improved version. Sometimes there must be delays when God's plan includes not only our lives but also the lives of others. We may have to wait until they are ready (or until *we* are) before God can give us the go-ahead.

When we go to God and ask for His direction in choosing a mate, He has *three* answers: yes, no, or wait. "Wait" means we must pause in our search in order to get God's instructions. It's the most difficult of all the answers but sometimes the most necessary. God always saves His best for those who are willing to wait for it, but when we fail to wait, we are out of God's will. Even when we do the right thing out of God's timing, it's still disobedience and will bring frustration and confusion to what could have been a blessing. The right thing at the wrong time is the wrong thing.

GOD'S GIFT OF SINGLENESS

Before you can determine whom to marry, you must first answer a preliminary question: Does God want you to marry anyone, ever? Or is His plan for you to remain single? Scripture teaches that marriage, like salvation, is an unmerited gift from God (Genesis 2:18). When God wanted Adam to have a wife, He brought her to him. Their marriage was a gift from God. But Scripture also tells us that singleness is God's gift as well.

"I wish that all men were as I am. But each man has his own

gift from God," said the apostle Paul in 1 Corinthians 7:7. He wished all men were single like he was and free from the stresses of married life so they could devote themselves to God's work. "But each man has his own gift from God." In other words, God will either give to a person the gift of being married or the gift of being single.

People who are perpetually lonely as singles are usually the same people who are worried about what *isn't* happening to them instead of what they should be doing to minister to others. Their focus is inward, not upward. In 1 Corinthians 7, we are told to acknowledge singleness as good, allow it for our spiritual growth, and use it for God.

C. S. Lewis was single most of his life. He taught at Oxford and Cambridge Universities and used his free time as a single to write some of the best Christian literature available in the world today. As he grew older and was nearing retirement age, he met and married a woman he came to love intensely in their three short years together. What would the world have missed if Lewis had married earlier someone whom God had not chosen?

It happens. Singles become consumed with the idea of how wonderful life would be if they just had a marriage partner, and then they make concessions and compromises that lead to marriage out of God's timing and out of God's will. To feel accepted by another person and avoid the stigma of being single, they enter into unhealthy relationships and compromise values they once held dear.

The more consumed you become with the idea of marriage and/or sex, the more easily you can slip into a pattern of fantasizing. It might start as innocently as fantasizing about being with another person, perhaps someone at work or church. Then you might progress to fantasizing about the children you'd have together or where you would live. If they continue unchecked, your thoughts could become a full-blown X-rated video that stays stuck on replay in your mind until it replays in your life. The powerful feelings that accompany such thoughts can lead people into marriages God never ordained and intimate relationships He never approved.

The Bible declares that as a man "thinketh in his heart, so is he" (Proverbs 23:7, KJV). What a strange thought! How can you think with your heart? We normally associate thought with the brain and feelings with the heart. The phrase "to think in the heart" refers to thoughtful reflection. Many ideas are briefly entertained by the mind without ever penetrating the heart. But those ideas that do grasp us in our innermost parts are the ideas that shape our lives. When our thoughts are corrupted, our lives follow suit. We are what we think.

The great sixteenth-century theologian Martin Luther had an almost humorous view of mental fantasy that is relevant even today. "You can't keep a bird from flying over your head," he said, "but you can keep him from making a nest in your hair." The theology of thought is like nest-building. By the act of your will you cannot keep every thought pure and godly, but you can control what thoughts build a nest and take up residence in your mind. Scripture teaches that there's nothing wrong with being tempted. It's what we do with temptation that matters.

THE SINGLES CYCLE

The road to poor choices is so predictable among singles that we can define it and give it a name: The Singles Cycle. Here's how it works:

1. Blessing. Through God's goodness (literally translated "divine nature") you are provided everything you need for a godly life (2 Peter 1:3).

2. Ungratefulness. Something plants a seed of discontentment in your soul and you start to feel left out and irritated. As you focus on what you don't have, you become unhappy and ungrateful. What you do have no longer seems to be enough. These feelings may have been triggered by a friend who just got engaged or married. Or maybe you found yourself alone on a Saturday night with nothing more to think about than the ticking of your biological clock. Or maybe it was something small like a song lyric, a movie scene, or an answering machine with no messages. "God, what about me?" you say. Everybody but you seems to be having

fun and experiencing intimacy. In your mind, God hasn't provided what you need.

3. Depression. You may feel angry at yourself for passing up someone you were once interested in or for getting out of a relationship that had the potential for marriage. Singles often condemn themselves for being single and may even start believing something is wrong with who they are. It's inherent in our natures to assign blame when life isn't going well. Depression is part of self-blame. If you don't believe you're to blame, you won't get depressed. But if you blame yourself for being single, you'll suffer from depression. It's hard to keep from being depressed when you're focusing on what you don't have. What starts with self-pity or self-blame can progress to depression, resentfulness, anger, and bitterness. After you blame yourself for awhile, you may even start blaming God.

4. Poor Choices. Once you start to tell God (consciously or unconsciously) that you don't like the way He's running things, you may begin to take matters into your own hands. That's when the poor choices start, choices that are sometimes irrevocable. You may start believing that your standards are too high and anybody is better than nobody. You might return to a failed relationship or begin a sexual affair, perhaps even with a married person. You could find yourself dabbling in pornography or becoming engulfed in unhealthy coping mechanisms like addiction and eating disorders to medicate the pain of loneliness. You could even panic and marry a person who will keep your life confused and torn.

5. Discipline. In the midst of all the poor choices, you may feel guilt and condemnation, or conviction and godly sorrow. Satan aims to bog you down through the emotion of guilt and somehow convince you that your sin is too terrible to be forgiven and you'll never be of use to God. The Holy Spirit, on the other hand, uses conviction to bring your sin to the light of Jesus' love so the problem can be resolved. The result will be godly sorrow, not guilt. Instead of the feeling of failure, you'll experience deep spiritual growth in your life.

6. Deliverance. When you determine *by the act of your will* to

be grateful for whatever situation is yours, you will begin to be thankful. This trust in the Lord will lead to contentment and joy. God is in every circumstance—good or bad—that He allows to come to you. He will step into your life to change even unhappy or disastrous situations when you begin to thank Him for the situation itself. "Give thanks in all circumstances, for this is God's will for you in Christ Jesus" (1 Thessalonians 5:18). A spiritual inventory of your blessings will help you realize that although you may be lonely, God has blessed you and ministered to your needs in many ways.

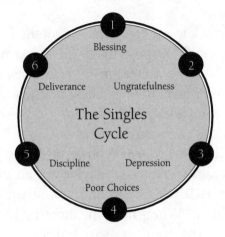

DON'T LIVE YOUR LIFE ON HOLD

If you've ever taken a raft trip down the Colorado River through the Grand Canyon, you've probably heard the head boatman give you a list of warnings and safety tips. "If you are thrown into the water," he says, "the currents will likely take you very deep into the river. You will lose your sense of up and down, and if you try to swim to the surface, you may well crash into the bottom of the river. Relax, hold your breath, remain calm, and your life vest will eventually raise you to the surface."

Have you ever found yourself deep in a confusing relationship or circumstances only to discover that all your frantic struggles just took you deeper and deeper? When you wait patiently for the still, gentle voice of the Lord, that's when you will discover which way is up. Nothing about your life as a believer is an accident, including your marital status. If you are living a godly, single life and still want to marry, the important thing is not to live "on hold" until you finally tie the knot. Let the Lord know your desire and then go on fully with your life as His man or woman. A seed must die before it can grow; so it must sometimes be with our hope for marriage. Many times we must die to the idea of marriage before God will bring it to life. Learn "to go to sleep" (Adam went to sleep and God made Eve) over the issue of marriage so that you're not constantly concentrating on the gift instead of the Giver by looking for a life partner.

If you let yourself live in the "what-ifs" of the future, you'll find yourself missing God's purpose in the here and now. It helps to remember that there are a great many circumstances worse than not being married. One of them is being married to someone who does not share your love and desire for God—someone whose commitment divides your commitment.

The life of Hudson Taylor is a powerful lesson in the value of God's wisdom regarding marriage. Taylor was an English missionary who died in 1910 after spending more than fifty years as a missionary in China. When he went there in 1854, nearly 380 million people in the country's vast interior had never seen a Westerner nor heard the name of Christ. With a heart for God, Taylor penetrated deep into Chinese culture. He dressed like the Chinese, learned their language, and lived among them. By the end of his life, 205 preaching stations, 849 missionaries, and 125,000 Chinese Christians were a testimony to a life surrendered to God.[1]

Hudson Taylor wielded a spiritual influence far beyond China. Even today, the ripple effect of his ministry is a part of our lives as Chinese Christians number in the hundreds of thousands worldwide. Taylor was single when he left England, but he eventually married another missionary in China. A small sentence in one history book has always intrigued me: "In England, Taylor had left behind his unfinished medical studies and the girl he had hoped to marry. She had refused to come with him."[2] What would the world have missed if Taylor had stayed home to marry someone God had not chosen?

God tested Taylor when He made him choose between God's will and his own desires. The day came in Taylor's life when he had to decide if it was more important to be in God's will or be married—the God choice over the good choice.

God still tests us today. We can't assume that the woman Taylor left behind was ugly, irritable, or contentious. He was a man of character who probably kept the company of a godly woman. Many people may have thought it was a good match, and perhaps the couple could have had a good marriage. But every good choice isn't God's choice.

If God gives you the gift of singleness, He may use that quality in a special way that would not be available to you as a married person—for a season or a lifetime. God's sovereign will is always meant for your good and His glory. If and when God decides you can best serve Him as a team member with a life partner, you won't need to change Sunday school classes, search the singles ads, or join a dating service. He will work out the circumstances. "He who finds a wife finds what is good and receives favor from the LORD" (Proverbs 18:22). This favor of the Lord is what God extends to His children in arranging the circumstances for them to meet their life partners.

God's favor was not lost on Hudson Taylor. In China, he eventually met and immediately fell in love with twenty-year-old Maria Dyer, the much-admired daughter of prestigious missionary parents. They had an uncommonly happy marriage because they shared a deep passion to evangelize China even at great personal sacrifice.

Seven years before his marriage to Maria and after his breakup with his fiancée, Taylor made a God choice that was painful and agonizing at the time. "What can I do?" he wrote to his sister. "I know I love her. To go to China without her would make the world a blank."[3] Instead of the "blank" life Taylor feared—the life we all fear—God brought purpose to his pain and honored his sacrifice. Even though it may have felt like a long wait, God was in the waiting. And so it is with us.

PERMISSIVE WILL OR PERFECT WILL

When we decide on our own that we are very compatible or totally in love with another person and therefore refuse to seek or wait for God's instruction, He will allow us to choose the good—His permissive will. But we will miss the best—His *perfect* will. The problem is that things don't work right when we are in only the permissive will of God (1 Corinthians 6:12).

I recently heard Christian author Elisabeth Elliot tell a story on her radio show that reminded me of the difference between God's permissive will and His perfect will. It was about a young girl named Katherine who was leaving for school.

> "Katherine," said the young girl's mother. "Don't leave without your galoshes."
>
> "Oh, Mother, please don't stop me now or I'll be late for school. Besides, I hate wearing those galoshes."
>
> "It snowed all night and you're going to need them," her mother said.
>
> "Please, just leave me alone and let me go. Can't I just have my way for once?"
>
> "This time you will," her mother said.

And so it is with us. We sometimes find that because of our own decisions we end up walking home in the slush without our galoshes.

When King Hezekiah became "mortally ill" (2 Kings 20), the prophet Isaiah came to him with the pronouncement that the king would not recover and needed to set his affairs in order and prepare to die. The Bible says that Hezekiah wept bitterly and pleaded with the Lord to spare his life. During a century-long period of Judah's history, Hezekiah had been the only king faithful to God. In response to the prayerful petition of a faithful servant, God gave Hezekiah his way and let him live fifteen more years.

Do you see the resemblance between Hezekiah's story and the story of the little girl and her mother? Both of them had their minds made up and pleaded to have their way. Out of love, both were permitted their choices. If we followed Katherine to school, we'd probably see that she did indeed walk home in the slush. As for Hezekiah, his actions after his recovery offended God and brought His anger down upon him and Judah. Even worse, he fathered a son who eventually became Judah's worst and longest reigning king. When Isaiah came with the pronouncement of Hezekiah's death, it truly would have been better for everyone if Hezekiah had unselfishly fit his life into God's perfect plan.

PUTTING GOD IN THE CENTER

In his popular workbook, *Experiencing God,* Henry Blackaby suggests we "find out where God is working and join Him there." We, on the other hand, are more likely to say, "God, here's the person I want to marry. Will You bless us?" The difference is the approach. One approach puts God at the center while the other puts ourselves at the center. When we make choices independent of God and then ask for His blessing, we're asking God to approve an idea that originated with us, not Him.

Throughout Scripture, God always takes the initiative. He sets the agenda. "We adjust our lives to God so He can do through us what He wants to do," says Blackaby. "God is not our servant to make adjustments to our plans. We are His servants and we adjust our lives to what He is about to do."

Once again we're back to the difference between a good idea and a God idea. How many times have we heard people say, "If God gave me a brain, He must expect me to use it"? Even though God gave us the ability to reason and make choices, what did He say about our thoughts compared to His?

"For my thoughts are not your thoughts, neither are your ways my ways," declares the LORD. "As the heavens are higher than the earth, so are my ways higher than your ways and my thoughts than your thoughts." (Isaiah 55:8–9)

God's knowledge and wisdom are far greater than ours. He can see the entire landscape while we concentrate on a single valley. We would be foolish to try to fit God into our mold and conform Him to our plans. Yes, He did give us a brain, and we should be smart enough to know that God's even smarter.

Once again, what's the difference between a good idea and a God idea? A good idea will work some of the time; a God idea will work all the time. Scripture warns us not to lean on our own understanding but to trust God wholeheartedly (Proverbs 3:5). When we are not willing to submit to God's leadership and authority in our lives, God will let us follow our own devices. In following them, we will never experience what God is waiting and wanting to do in us and through us.

ESCAPING THE TRAPS

Christians must realize that it is more important to be certain that a marriage is God's will than to judge our suitability for marriage by love, attraction, or compatibility. Our situations change and we grow through the years. We cannot predict future compatibility on our own. When we accept compatibility as the primary basis of marriage, we can be led into cultural traps such as living together before marriage to make sure we are compatible. Only God knows the end from the beginning. He is the one who creates love, not man.

It was Ruth's mother-in-law, Naomi, who made the choice of a husband for her (Ruth 3). It wasn't love at first sight, getting to know each other, or even a passionate kiss that brought Boaz and Ruth together. Romance wasn't the issue, although the story later became beautifully romantic as Ruth and Boaz developed an unselfish love and deep respect for each other. The issue was obedience, a "rightness" about the relationship. God was working in the situation, and He was using Naomi's kindness and moral integrity to guide Ruth. As a result, Ruth later became the great-grandmother of King David and a direct ancestor of Jesus.

Does the story of Boaz and Ruth interrupt your romantic vision of passionate love? Would you like the story more if the two had been lovers who glimpsed each other across the wheatfield and became passionately attracted? It happens to some people in some situations, but the qualities that are attractive in the beginning may prove difficult to live with in the long run. The man who falls in love with a woman's attentiveness may find it is the very quality that drives him crazy when he can't get enough space. The woman who falls in love with a man's drive to succeed may find that quality irritating and destructive when he spends more time at work than at home.

Dr. Neil Clark Warren, author of the popular book *Finding the Love of Your Life,* says your choice of whom to marry is more crucial than everything else combined that you will ever do to make your marriage succeed. "If you choose wisely," he says, "your life will be significantly easier and infinitely more satisfying. But if you make a serious mistake, your marriage may fail, causing you and perhaps your children immeasurable pain. Most of the failed marriages I have encountered were in trouble the day they began dating. The two people involved simply chose the wrong person to marry."

What might seem like a good choice at the time may not be a God choice for a lifetime. If you "lean on your own understanding," you may someday feel like the person who fell out of the raft into the Colorado River: The more you struggle, the deeper you go.

Just as Ruth was unaware of the larger purpose God had in mind for her life, you can't see the larger picture of your life. Because of Ruth's faithful obedience, her life and legacy carried great significance even though she couldn't see the end result. In a similar way, your faithfulness to God's leadership will bring a significance to your life that will extend beyond your lifetime. The question is not how to find a mate, but *who* will find the mate. God will direct you in choosing God's best.

COURTSHIP PROCESS	Phase 1: Identity in Christ
SPIRITUAL Commitment	Commit yourself to being sold out to Christ. Be involved in activities that instill spiritual growth. Learn to be fully engaged to Christ before entertaining the idea of a relationship with another person. Be confident of who you are in Christ and gain acceptance, worth and identity in Christ instead of in another person.
EMOTIONAL Commitment	
PHYSICAL Commitment	
Time Alone	

STUDY AND DISCUSSION QUESTIONS

1. Looking at 1 Corinthians 7:7–9, 25–40, list the reasons Paul gives for remaining single.

2. What activities and services are you involved in now that you would have to give up if you were married?

3. If God were to give you a "wait" answer to your prayer for a marriage partner, what character-building qualities or positive results might come from waiting?

4. Is there any area of your life where you have pushed God out and He has given you up to your own desires?

5. Why do you desire to be married? Be honest with yourself.

    a. To avoid the pain of loneliness
    b. The biological clock is ticking to have children
    c. To have legitimate sex without guilt
    d. To have someone take care of you
    e. (Fill in the blank)

6. Meditate and memorize: "Trust in the LORD with all your heart and lean not on your own understanding; in all your ways acknowledge him, and he will make your paths straight" (Proverbs 3:5–6).

7. Pray: My heavenly Father, I desire to follow Your perfect plan for my life. Help me discern my gift of singleness or of marriage. I commit to seeking Your perfect will for my life and my future mate. During my season of singleness I will place You in the center of my life and choose to be content in all things. I long for intimacy with You. Please fill the holes in my heart when I become lonely. I ask these things in the name of Jesus. Amen.

CHAPTER FIVE

Preparing to Be God's Choice

*Put on the new self, created to be like God
in true righteousness and holiness.*
EPHESIANS 4:24

PRINCIPLE TWO: Serving God is the best way to focus on your value and identity in Christ instead of your value to someone else.

A good juggler rarely looks at his hands. You'd think a juggler would look at the one spot where all the action is, but instead he focuses on the point where the objects stop ascending and begin their descent. He doesn't watch any one item, but keeps his focus on the highest point.

Like the juggler, we are constantly keeping multiple parts of our lives in motion—job, school, family, church, hobbies, and friends. When all these parts fly through the air with some sense of order, we feel in control. Then something unexpected happens. Everything that was moving in tandem suddenly falls around us in broken pieces and we wonder what went wrong. Sometimes we even blame God.

The juggler's secret of success is his focus. He doesn't concentrate on any one item to the neglect of others but keeps his attention on the highest point. In contrast, our tendency is to focus on one part of our lives to the exclusion of others. We think that success or happiness in one area will bring happiness overall. Isn't that what happens when we say, "I'll never be happy unless I'm married"?

Out-of-focus years are a waste because they're spent concentrating on ourselves—our wants, our likes, our wishes, our plans, our happiness. We sow a life of self, and then complain when we reap a harvest of depression, discouragement, and self-pity.

Like the juggler, we have to get hold of the secret before we can get control of the pieces. By focusing on our relationship with God (the highest point), we will find ourselves not only filled with God but also drawn to others who are filled with God. The irony here is that we actually become more appealing to the very type of person we desire to marry when we use our season of singleness to serve God and others.

KNOWING YOU'RE STILL GOOD
WHEN OTHERS SAY YOU'RE BAD

I was driving in the car recently, listening to a radio talk show targeted to parents of troubled teens. A psychologist was counseling the mother of a sixteen-year-old teenager. "How would your son fill in the blank at the end of this sentence?" he said. "'I only count when _____.'" The implication was that the answer would reveal the driving force behind the teenager's decisions, actions, and behaviors.

That question reminded me of a woman named Deb who thought she didn't count without her boyfriend. She gave in to his demands for sex ("say yes or I'm gone") because in her mind she felt as though she was nothing without him. She feared being rejected and abandoned. One demand led to another, and she gave in again when she felt forced by her boyfriend to have an abortion.

Years later, Deb went through a radical transformation after a faith conversion. When her view of God changed, so did her view of herself. "Self-esteem can't come from anywhere but Jesus," Deb now says. "He will love you in spite of your failings. If your self-worth is based on your looks, your parents' love, or the sense that you're great, it will fail. All that will pass."[1]

Like Deb or the troubled sixteen-year-old, we're all searching for what makes our lives count—for the person or the something that will keep us from feeling worthless. Far too many of us base our personal worth on what we believe the most important people in our lives think about us. We're constantly looking to someone else just to be told we are significant. We look around to see who's looking at us and spend far too much time wondering what they think. We may be making eye contact with someone, but will that someone bring us a lasting significance that won't walk out the door when they do?

The Bible makes an interesting statement about eye contact when it says in Psalms 32:8b, "I will guide thee with mine eye" (KJV). How can that be? How can God guide a person with His eye? If the eye is silent and makes no noise, the only way we could receive guidance from God's eye is to be looking directly at Him.

Somehow that sixteen-year-old and all the rest of us must come to the point of viewing ourselves as whole and complete people based on our relationship with Christ, not our value to someone else or even our marital status. The longer it takes to get to that point, the more opportunity we have for making damaging decisions that can affect our lives forever.

If the truest things about us are what God says and not what we've been told or what we sometimes feel, then it's important to know that God considers us a planned production. "We are God's workmanship, created in Christ Jesus to do good works, which God prepared in advance for us to do" (Ephesians 2:10).

The Greek word for "workmanship" sometimes has the connotation of a "work of art," and the words "prepared in advance" indicate God's sovereign purpose and planning. Our arrival on earth individually and collectively was no accident. God has prepared in advance a work for us to do—a good work. If we want to fulfill God's purpose for us, we have to look to God to show us where that good work is. The search for a mate is part of almost everyone's life at one time or another, but it isn't all there is to life or even the most important part. It's only one of the items we have to juggle every day—only part of the whole.

THE STRANGE THING ABOUT HAPPINESS

Frank Laubach once called himself "the happiest man in the world," which is a strange statement for a missionary who lost three children to malaria and dysentery. Laubach spent his life in remote parts of the world among the desperately poor. He organized a literacy program in the Philippines that became a global movement and literally changed millions—not thousands, but millions—of lives. He had the pleasure of watching men and women weep and jump for joy when they realized they could read. "I've never met anyone who has had as much fun as I have," Laubach said.

It's a strange thing about happiness. The people who look for it the most rarely find it. Why? Because happiness is the by-product of something else, and only a sovereign God who has planned a good work for us can guide us with His eye to that "something else." Without the eye contact, we will spend our lives pursuing what we don't have and can't find. No marriage, relationship, job, education, or hobby will ever be enough.

Not only do we have to look to God for His guidance in moving us toward circumstances that only He knows will give us joy and contentment, but we also have to realize that happiness is elusive. It's dependent on circumstances. Joy, on the other hand, is based on our relationship with the Lord. We can't have one without the other.

When we turn to the New Testament, we find that Paul and Silas were cruelly beaten at Philippi and put in jail under maximum security with their feet chained in stocks (Acts 16:19–40). No one could be happy under those circumstances, but the Bible says that they were praying and singing praise hymns to God while the other prisoners listened. We can understand prayer in such circumstances, but can we understand praise?

Throughout our lives, our circumstances will be both good

and bad. If they weren't, we'd already be in heaven. Because happiness depends on our circumstances, our happiness level will rise and fall according to what's happening to us. However, our joy can be consistent and abundant in the Lord no matter what the circumstances. Our fellowship with Him can transcend our worldly trials, just as it did for Paul and Silas.

Even more important, God can use our difficulties to build character in us. That is why we can "consider it pure joy" when we "face trials of many kinds" (James 1:2). Instead of trying to change our circumstances to be happy, we should concentrate on letting God work through our circumstances to change us and build godly character in our lives.

Although Frank Laubach had a doctorate, he never formally trained for literacy work or planned ahead to do it. He didn't graduate from college with a burning passion to teach the world to read. It was many years before God directed Laubach into literacy work, and both the work and the worth he found serving God grew out of painful circumstances that wouldn't make anyone happy. Nevertheless, God often uses our circumstances to build godly character and redirect our lives.

COMING TOGETHER OR COMING APART

Most marriages fall apart because the partners have not developed godly qualities that actually serve as foundational pillars in a marriage. The ability to love your mate, serve, and sacrifice is not a character quality God bestows on you the moment you say "I do." You can't learn to sacrifice, serve, or love by taking a course or reading a book. The only way you can develop those qualities is by being in such close fellowship with God that His love flows through you. Each time you apply His loving truths in a real-life circumstance, you take another step toward building godly character. It becomes more important to you to *be* an attentive, supportive spouse than to *have* one.

By focusing on your fellowship with God, you'll not only be fulfilling the work God has for you but you'll also be preparing yourself to be God's choice for someone else. You'll become the right person for another person. Your relationship with your future spouse will be only as strong as your fellowship with God.

As a Christian, your relationship to God will never change. Because of Jesus' death on the cross, you are and always will be a child of the King. What can and will change is your fellowship with God. To understand this, think about your relationship with your earthly father. He is and always will be your father. That will never change. What will change is your fellowship with him as you mature physically and emotionally and as a multitude of activities compete for your time. In a similar way, your spiritual growth and sin nature will affect your fellowship with God. You will either grow closer to Him or slip further away.

Just as your fellowship with your father never stays at the same level all the time, neither will your fellowship with God. You'll always be moving one way or the other. Your life will reflect the quality of your fellowship.

THE DISASTER OF MORAL COMPROMISE

In 1987, Donna Rice rose to notoriety after a secret affair with presidential hopeful Gary Hart. Her life in high school had revolved around church friends, choir, youth group, and missions trips. In college, she was a Phi Beta Kappa at the University of South Carolina and head cheerleader. What happened to plunge this "good Christian girl" into a national scandal?

After many years of self-imposed exile from public view, Donna recently emerged and talked candidly about the subtle compromises she made as a Christian and what she learned from the experience.

"The two Christian guys I'd dated since high school youth group graduated from college and drifted out of my life," Donna said, describing her senior year in college. "I began to compromise my Christian values—partying and dating guys who weren't Christians. I told myself, 'We won't get serious, so it won't hurt anybody.' Those decisions edged me toward a lifestyle that wasn't God-honoring."[2]

After college graduation, Donna gradually stopped attending

church and reading her Bible. She began to date a sexually experienced older man. Eventually she became a victim of date rape and was so ashamed that she didn't tell anyone.

"Because I felt like used goods and didn't understand that even though I'd lost my virginity I could still guard my virtue, I gradually and reluctantly became sexually active," she said. After winning the Miss South Carolina Pageant and relocating to New York City, she began to move in glitzy circles and strayed far from her Christian faith.

Over time, a succession of moral compromises led to a two-day pleasure cruise with former Colorado senator Gary Hart, a married man. As the news of their brief liaison leaked to the press, the media quickly characterized Donna as a home wrecker and "bimbo" party girl who hung out with rich men. No one talked about her being an honor graduate or Phi Beta Kappa.

The humiliation of a national scandal turned Donna's faith around. When she had no other place to go, she went to God. "I cried out, 'God, it took falling on my rear in front of the whole world to get my attention. Help me to live my life your way!' God answered my plea and flooded me with His presence and forgiveness and surrounded me with Christian fellowship."

For months after the scandal, Donna did nothing but rest, read her Bible, and be spiritually fed through Bible studies, prayer, and the counsel of godly Christians.

"In the process," she said, "I began to see how faithful and compassionate God is to bring ministry out of brokenness.... He's brought purpose to my pain."

Today Donna is married to a Christian husband and is director of marketing and communications for "Enough Is Enough!", a non-profit campaign to stop illegal pornography, assist sexual abuse victims, and make the Internet safe for children. She admits that the inner strength she now has comes "only as a result of drawing closer to God and following His will for my life rather than my own."

Most of the "slippage" we experience as singles comes just as it did for Donna Rice—a little at a time. Our relationship with God is never in jeopardy, but the quality of our fellowship with Him will determine what direction our lives take and where our focus will be.

Sexual immorality isn't the inevitable result of a breech in fellowship with God, but it would win the award for "Most Probable Occurrence" when our eye contact with God shifts to another human being. Let's return for a moment to the story of Camille and Wade in chapter 1. Other than the pain we all experience as a result of broken relationships, what would make a person say to God, "I will not date casually and I will wait for the one person you have for me"? Camille's decision was driven by her desire for purity and the need to be a pure vessel in the presence of a holy God. Like Camille, when we get a vision of the purity that God requires of us before He'll take us deeper into intimate fellowship, that vision can change everything—our relationships, our talk, our leisure time, our spending, our jokes, our vocations. It can even change the way we search for a lifetime partner.

WHO'S WAITING FOR A PERSON LIKE YOU?

Unlike Donna Rice, most of us don't appear in the *National Enquirer* when we lose our focus. When our self-serving nature takes us where we don't want to go, the trip is usually less publicized but may be just as devastating. Self-serving desires, interests, and goals can block our vision and keep us from seeing clearly what God wants us to do. Whenever that vision gets blurred, serving God is the best way to restore it. Involving ourselves in a ministry will take our minds off ourselves and even foster emotional healing.

Donna Rice's ministry to sexual abuse victims grew out of her pain. Her brokenness was the key to the deeper work of the Holy Spirit. That's what she meant when she said, "He's brought purpose to my pain." Chuck Colson's ministry grew out of his years in prison. Corrie ten Boom's ministry grew out of her painful experience in a Nazi concentration camp. Catherine Marshall's ministry grew out of her husband's death. Indeed, God can and does bring purpose to pain in the lives of His children, but He does not comfort us to make us comfortable. He comforts us to make us comforters.

Mother Teresa, a name almost synonymous with compassion and servanthood, tells a story about coming to the affluent West and visiting a beautifully decorated nursing home where she found many of the residents sitting in wheelchairs facing the door. "Why are all these people looking toward the door?" she asked. "Why aren't they smiling? I'm used to seeing smiles on all our people, even the dying ones."

"It's like this every day," the nurse replied. "They're always hoping someone will come and visit them. Their loneliness is eating them up."[3]

In your corner of the world, who do you think might be staring at the door waiting for a person like you? If God has comforted you in any way, how can you pass it on? "There are thousands of people dying for a piece of bread," says Mother Teresa, "but there are thousands more dying for a bit of love."

It's easy to think of Mother Teresa as a celebrity and see no link between her example and our everyday lives. After all, she won a Nobel Peace Prize. We forget she had no special prestige when she left her position as a high-school principal to begin serving the poorest of the poor. She was thirty-eight years old when she walked into a Calcutta slum and began to live with the dying, the forgotten, and the disfigured. No church asked her to do it; she chose it. On the first day of her life in the slum, she gathered five children to teach. Three days later there were twenty-five, and by the end of the year there were forty-one. Through the children, she began to penetrate the most squalid misery in Calcutta.

THE LESSONS OF SACRIFICE

To be like Christ is to be a servant. That's what the word "Christian" means: "Christlike." Although Christ lived as a sacrificial servant, most of us are not accustomed to sacrifices, even small ones. We expect a return for our efforts and know little of giving without receiving. Perhaps that's why it's hard to see a link between our everyday lives and the life of a person like Mother Teresa.

From birth to death, Jesus lived a flesh-and-blood life to give us a human example of what God meant man to be. To teach us servanthood, He washed the disciples' feet. Afterward, He told them, "I have set you an example that you should do as I have done for you" (John 13:15).

When Salome requested that her two sons, James and John, sit on each side of Jesus in His kingdom, Jesus used the opportunity to teach His disciples a different view of greatness—God's view. "You know that the rulers of the Gentiles lord it over them, and their high officials exercise authority over them. Not so with you. Instead, whoever wants to become great among you must be your servant, and whoever wants to be first must be your slave—just as the Son of Man did not come to be served, but to serve, and to give his life as a ransom for many" (Matthew 20:25–28).

In 1 Peter 2:16b, the apostle who once denied Jesus does a 180-degree turnaround and urges us to "live as servants of God." For the word "servants," Peter uses the Greek word *doulos*. It means "a slave, one who is in permanent relation of servitude to another, his will being altogether consumed in the will of the other." The word "permanent" describes the kind of service God desires us to offer. How many of us can say without a doubt that we will be serving God twenty years from now regardless of where we live, whom we live with (or without), our health, our job, our finances, our friends, and our feelings?

If the life of Christ is to be our pattern, then it's time to give God something sacrificial—something that will cost us effort, time, or money. We don't have to start with big, noble sacrifices. We can start in small ways by finding one of God's causes that interests us or by aiding in a mission effort or a church effort. At first it may take only an hour or a small amount of money, but God will bless it. As we continue to give, we will discover a desire to broaden our giving. In time, our sacrificial giving will become such a joy that it will be part of who we are. By making small sacrifices initially, we may grow to the point of making the grand ones.

Although most singles have a deep desire to be married, they don't usually realize the amount of sacrifice required to have a Christ-centered marriage. Many married people become frustrated after marriage because they have not developed the character quality of sacrifice. Learning to sacrifice *before* marriage helps people sacrifice *after* marriage.

Many times God uses ministry as a practical means to bring two singles together. After He has placed a future mate in your heart during prayer, ministry can be an excellent way to confirm God's direction in your mate selection. If you want to know whether a man will be a good father, watch him work in a nursery of two-year-olds. You may get a glimpse of the future. If you want a wife who will be flexible and adaptable, join her on a mission trip and see how she copes with no electrical outlets and no toilet paper in the outhouse. Watching how other singles minister is one of the best ways to evaluate their character before pursuing them (or being pursued) in courtship.

Beginning a courtship from the starting point of a ministry helps cement a solid focus on God and others. Although the list of ministry opportunities is long and varied, it can include the following:

- Sunday school leader
- Missions trip sponsor
- Nursing home visitation
- Church office volunteer
- Children's leader
- Library volunteer
- Tape ministry
- Hospital visitation
- Music and worship team member
- Choir participant
- Nursery worker
- Bus ministry
- Crisis pregnancy center volunteer
- Youth worker
- Recreation team leader
- Bible study leader
- Newsletter ministry
- Homeless shelter volunteer

In the midst of your giving and serving, it is important to remember that your role is not so much to do good deeds as to stay connected to God and give away what He gives you. Your focus should be on your relationship with God, not your performance.

Mother Teresa liked to use the analogy of electricity: "The wire is you and me; the current is God. We have the power to let the current pass through us, use us, and produce the light of the world—Jesus."[4] The emphasis is on *being,* not *doing.* We're only the wire; He's the current.

Because God does use us to touch other lives, every follower

COURTSHIP PROCESS	Phase 1: Identity in Christ	Phase 2: Ministry Involvement
SPIRITUAL Commitment	Commit yourself to being sold out to Christ. Be involved in activities that instill spiritual growth. Learn to be fully engaged to Christ before entertaining the idea of a relationship with another person. Be confident of who you are in Christ and of gaining acceptance, worth and identity in Christ instead of in another person.	Be involved in ministry opportunities to utilize the talents and gifts God has given you. Learn what it means to serve, love, sacrifice and yield your rights to others as Christ did for you.
EMOTIONAL Commitment		
PHYSICAL Commitment		
Time Alone		

of Jesus is given one or more spiritual gifts. These gifts are God-given abilities to serve in a way that exceeds natural talent (1 Corinthians 12:7). We become effective and fulfilled when we are doing exactly what God has wired us to do and what He has enabled us to do by activating our gifts through the power of the Holy Spirit.

It doesn't take long to figure out that God had given Mother Teresa the gift of mercy, but it may take longer to recognize God's gift to you. When you realize that your spiritual gift(s) is connected to His calling on your life, you may begin to see your season of singleness a little differently. What you might view as loneliness or aloneness, God may view as an opportunity for you to mature spiritually as you fulfill His calling on your life. It's the old "horse before the cart" story. First things first.

Billy Graham is probably the best-known preacher and minister in the world today. Can you imagine him married to anyone but Ruth Bell Graham, the daughter of Presbyterian missionaries to China? What she learned growing up in a missionary home prepared her to be the wife of one of the world's most famous men. Self-sacrifice. Dependence on God. Love for God's Word. Concern for others. "The Lord certainly knew what He was doing when He chose her for my wife and number-one adviser," Graham says.[5]

In spite of these good words, Graham wasn't always so sure about God's plan. In college, he had a disappointing romance with a girl who chose someone else. Struggling to get over the pain of a broken relationship, he wrote to his roommate and confidant: "I have settled it once and for all with the Lord. No girl or friend or anything shall ever come first in my life. I have resolved that the Lord Jesus Christ shall have all of me. I care not what the future holds. I have determined to follow Him at any cost."[6] First things first.

Ruth, on the other hand, was rising early every morning and praying for her husband's future ministry—the husband she still hadn't met. At that point in time, she didn't even know Billy Graham but she knew enough to put first things first.

WHAT IF GOD SAYS NO?

As you involve yourself in ministry and service, God may bring you a partner with whom you can share your ministry and your life. He did for Donna Rice. He did for Billy Graham. He may for you. But what if He doesn't? What will your response be if God doesn't say yes to the prayer that is closest to your heart—the prayer for a partner?

"There are times," writes Christian author Max Lucado, "when the one thing you want is the one thing you never get. You're not being picky or demanding; you're only obeying His command to 'ask God for everything you need' (Philippians 4:6, NCV). All you want is an open door or an extra day or an answered prayer, for which you will be thankful."[7]

Lucado tells about the time his two-year-old daughter fell into a swimming pool and almost drowned. Fortunately, a friend saw her and pulled her to safety.

"The next morning in my prayer time," he says, "I made a special effort to record my gratitude in my journal. I told God how wonderful He was for saving her. As clearly as if God Himself were speaking, this question came to mind: *Would I be less wonderful had I let her drown? Would I be any less a good God for calling her home? Would I still be receiving your praise this morning had I not saved her?*"

Let me ask you the same thing. Will God still be a good God if He says no to your prayer for a partner? If your request is delayed or even denied, will you still serve Him and praise Him? The number-one concern for most women is getting married while they still can have children. If you are forty-five and single, is God any less good?

The greatest test some of us face is trusting God's goodness in every area of our lives. Insisting that we have to be married before we can be happy demonstrates that we don't trust God. It shows we don't understand that He is a God of love, planning and allowing only what is good for us, with or without a spouse. "'For I know the plans I have for you,' declares the LORD, 'plans to prosper you and not to harm you, plans to give you hope and a future'" (Jeremiah 29:11).

If you're constantly looking at every member of the opposite sex as a potential mate and letting "the hunt" occupy all your thinking, it's a sign you're not really trusting God. If you make marriage the focus of your life, you will waste months or even years waiting for an imaginary companion. Even worse, your constant desire to be in a dating relationship will hinder your spiritual growth.

To focus your mind on "the highest point," pray that God will work His good will in you as He conforms you to the image of Christ. If marriage is in His plan for you, pray that God will give you the wisdom and discernment to make the right decision and that He will begin now preparing both of you for each other. Then put aside the looking, hoping, and hunting and concentrate on serving God.

STUDY AND DISCUSSION QUESTIONS

1. In 1 Timothy 6:6, Paul says "godliness with contentment is great gain." Paul is referring to our being content to let God fill the voids in our lives. What are some ways people search for happiness and try to fill the voids?

2. Remembering the analogy of the juggler, pick any item you mentioned in your answer to the first question and explain how a singular focus on it might affect a person's life.

3. Explain how immorality might be considered a process. In contrast, how is the struggle for purity a process?

4. People sometimes look for relief from pain in unbiblical ways. What are some of these ways? How do they relate to question number one?

5. 1 Peter 4:10–11 tells us that each person should use "whatever gift he has received to serve others...so that in all things God may be praised through Jesus Christ." What gift has God given you and how can you use it to serve others?

6. If God were to provide you a lifetime partner this month or even this year, would you be a better spouse now than if you had

met that person three years ago? In what ways are you different today than you were three years ago?

7. Meditate and memorize: "Just as the Son of Man did not come to be served, but to serve, and to give his life as a ransom for many" (Matthew 20:28).

Meditate and memorize: "Greater love has no one than this, that one lay down his life for his friends" (John 15:13).

8. Pray: My heavenly Father, teach me to be a sacrificial servant to glorify You and spread the love of Christ. Please direct me into the areas of ministry where You desire me to serve You and Your kingdom. Help me not to focus on my happiness, but to gain an eternal perspective on my life. Jesus, thank You for loving and serving through Your sacrifice on the cross. Amen.

CHAPTER SIX

Crumble Proofing Your Foundation

Unless the LORD builds the house, its builders labor in vain.
PSALM 127:1

PRINCIPLE THREE: Anticipate marriage by completing practical preparations that will lay the foundation for a secure Christian home.

I can still see my college professor standing at the front of the room drawing a horizontal line across the blackboard. "This," he said, "is your timeline. It represents your life." Then he began to divide the line into sections. One chalk mark for early childhood, another for grade school, then teen years, college, marriage, work, childrearing, retirement.

"As long as everything is in its place and at its proper time, life will be less complicated," he said. "But if the events of your life get out of order, you'll make life harder for yourself."

Then he drew a circle around marriage and moved it ahead of college. And he took childrearing and put it ahead of marriage. "I'm not saying you won't succeed, but I'm saying that success will be harder and your chance of failure will be greater when you get things out of order."

Our daily lives are a testimony to the importance of timing and order (Ecclesiastes 3:1–8). Why do children crawl before they walk? Why don't ten-year-olds drive cars? Why does winter come before spring?

Suppose you had a cake baking in the oven, and you were sitting in the kitchen enjoying the aroma of things to come. Then, suddenly, twenty minutes before the timer rings, you decide you want to take the cake out of the oven. But it's only partially baked. Gooey spots are everywhere, and it's not fit to eat.

Such a decision would obviously be ridiculous. Yet that scenario parallels what we do as believers when we try to outrun God's timing and take ourselves out of His preparation time too soon. We do not give God time to reveal His purposes in the way He knows is best.

It's been said that there's no such thing as coincidence, just God's plan unfolding in unexpected ways. If you've ever experienced the miracle of God's timing, you know how true that statement is. You can't anticipate how or when God will unfold His plan for your marriage, but the Bible teaches that there is always a preparation time—a time to plant and sow before you reap and harvest (Galatians 6:7–9).

While you wait for God's timing, you must anticipate the unfolding of His will by completing practical preparations that will lay a solid foundation for your home. This foundation will take time to build, because the building material is *you*:

> ...your spiritual maturity
> ...your godly character
> ...your accountability
> ...your emotional health
> ...your financial stability
> ...your vocational training
> ...your parent training
> ...your household training
> ...your commitment

COURTSHIP PROCESS	Phase 3: Foundation Building
SPIRITUAL Commitment	Anticipate marriage and lay the foundation for a secure Christian home by completing practical preparations in the following areas: - Spiritual maturity - Godly character - Accountability - Emotional health - Financial stability - Vocational training - Parent training - Household training - Commitment
EMOTIONAL Commitment	Before becoming emotionally intimate with someone else, rid yourself of emotional baggage left over from childhood and past dating relationships. Recognize that unresolved sin will influence your emotional health.
PHYSICAL Commitment	
Time Alone	

God's job is finding you a mate and then revealing to you His choice in His time. Your job is to prepare yourself to be someone else's mate while you wait for God's revelation. Most singles usually get it backwards. We find a mate without consulting God, get married and then discover we weren't prepared for the problems and responsibilities inherent in marriage.

Just as cutting the preparation time for the cake ruined the final product, failing to prepare for marriage *before* courtship can create such a weak foundation for your future home that you'll be like the foolish man who built his house on sand. When the rains came, he lost everything to a mudslide (Matthew 7:26–27).

One-fourth of all adults who marry eventually become divorced.[1] As divorce becomes more prevalent, the figure inches upward. But divorce isn't what's killing marriages. Divorces don't kill and marriages don't fail; people do. Conversely, it isn't marriages that succeed; people succeed who work at marriage and are willing to be obedient to following the roles God intended. Marriage doesn't necessarily make you any better or worse. It simply tests and reveals what you brought into the marriage internally (spiritual maturity, godly character, emotional health, commitment) and externally (accountability, finances, vocational, household and parent training).

The word "wedding" actually means the "wed or bride price" and refers to the biblical dower or dowry.[2] In biblical times, both the husband and wife brought a dowry to their marriage. The groom brought a dowry as demonstration of his love, but more importantly, he brought it to protect his wife and children if he died.

The woman's dowry was usually given to her by her father, who had both a voice and a financial responsibility in the marriage of his daughter. Receiving a dowry from both her husband-to-be and her father helped protect the wife and laid a solid economic foundation for the new home.

While we no longer have to provide a dowry in the biblical sense of the word, we do still bring our internal character and external possessions to the marriage as a dowry. We lay the foundations of our new home spiritually, economically, and morally by how we prepare while we wait for God's timing. Like a dowry, what we bring to the marriage will protect the home from discord leading to divorce. And like the principles established in biblical times, our courtship and marriage should occur only when the man can support a family, when the parents approve, and when the preparation process that follows has been completed.

YOUR SPIRITUAL MATURITY

Research has consistently shown that religious commitment and marital success are closely related.[3] But spiritual maturity doesn't necessarily have a lot to do with religion, which refers more to a person's denomination and church affiliation. Spiritual maturity is deeper. It's the inner faith and deep beliefs you have. It's intimacy with God.

Intimate companionship with God will affect your marriage in at least three important ways:

- **It will affect how you hear God's voice.**

If selecting a mate and beginning a courtship are dependent on God's timing, how will you know God's timing? How will you know when God is revealing the partner He has for you? In Henry Blackaby's book *Experiencing God*, he says the moment God speaks to you is God's timing, and God will speak when He has a purpose in mind for your life. Your ability to know His voice will come as a result of the intimate love relationship you share with Him. Like the mature sheep in a flock, the voice of the shepherd is more recognizable after you've spent time together in the field.

- **It will affect your intimacy with your spouse.**

If you deeply desire intimacy with someone else, you first must have deep intimacy with God. God won't allow you to be more intimate with another person than you are with Him. Because of this, your intimacy with your spouse will be no greater than your intimacy with God. A breakdown in your intimacy with God will short-circuit intimacy with your spouse.

- **It will affect the success of your marriage.**

Contrary to what you might think, choosing the right partner is not the most important part of a successful marriage. Even the right partner eventually will irritate you, hurt your feelings, disappoint you, and make you mad. Your desire to be obedient regardless of your feelings or the actions of another person is the most important part of making your marriage a success. That desire will flow out of your intimate love relationship with God.

When you were born again spiritually, you didn't just come into a new understanding of God; you entered into a new relationship with God. The New Testament repeatedly describes the Christian faith in relational terms: God's family (Ephesians 2:19), brothers and sisters in Christ (James 2:15), God the Father (Matthew 6:9), the firstborn among many brothers (Romans 8:29). Christianity is relational by nature, and relational Christianity is about living in intimate companionship with God the Father.

The Bible says that even the demons believe in one God (James 2:19). If knowing what the Bible teaches about God were enough, Satan and all his demons would be righteous. But they aren't. Having knowledge about God is totally different from having fellowship with God, and being informed is not the same as being transformed.

The number-one requirement for coming into intimate companionship with God is passion for God. That is the solitary key to living in His presence and experiencing His rest. The journey into knowing God intimately must begin with passion for God Himself. "As the deer pants for streams of water, so my soul pants for you, O God. My soul thirsts for God, for the living God" (Psalm 42:1–2). Intimacy with God is the greatest predictor of marital success.

YOUR GODLY CHARACTER

At six o'clock one cold morning, a young man rang the doorbell at the address of the parents of a young woman with whom he had decided to begin a courtship. Her father had asked for the meeting and scheduled the time and place. When the young woman's mother opened the door, she ushered the young man into the living room and left him there. Forty-five minutes later, the father entered the room.

Without an apology, he began to ask simple, almost nonsensical questions.

"Can you spell?" he said.

Puzzled but calm, the boy answered, "Yes, sir."

"All right. Spell *table*."

"T-a-b-l-e."

"Good. How are you at numbers?"

"Not bad," the young man said.

"Add three and three."

"Six," replied the young man.

"That's good," replied the father. "I've got to go now, but if you'll come back tonight, my daughter will be here."

Later in the day, the father had lunch with his daughter and gave her an explanation. "The young man has the qualities of a good husband. I tested him on self-denial and made him arrive at the house at 6 A.M. He had to get up early, get out in the cold, and do it without complaining.

"Next, I tested him on promptness. He arrived on time.

"Then, I examined his patience. I made him wait forty-five minutes to see me.

"Next, I tested his temper. He never showed signs of irritation or anger.

"Finally, I tried his humility by asking him questions that a seven-year-old child could answer, and he never showed signs of indignation."

Mystified by her father's strange behavior, the young woman asked why he would conduct such an unusual test. "Because the value of all we *do* depends on the kind of people we *are*," her father said. "I simply wanted to know who he is before he becomes part of who you are."

Although the young woman's father was either very wise or very strange, his point is important. All we *do* depends on the kind of people we *are*. Being comes before doing. God is far more interested in our character than our circumstances. Because of this, He will take us through whatever experiences are necessary to develop His character in us.

"But the fruit of the Spirit is love, joy, peace, patience, kindness, goodness, faithfulness, gentleness and self-control" (Galatians 5:22–23). These words describe the kind of person Christ is and Christians should be: loving, joyful, patient, self-controlled, kind, gentle. Christians cannot produce these character qualities on their own, but they can bear the fruit of God's Spirit working through them. Jesus described Himself as the vine, God the Father as the gardener, and Christians as the branches (John 15:1–8). No branch, He said, can bear fruit by itself. Producing the fruit isn't the work of the branch; it can only bear the fruit. The vine is what sends its life-giving sap *through* the branches. A godly character is the fruit of the Spirit.

	Spiritual Gifts		Fruit of the Spirit
Romans 12	Ephesians 4	1 Corinthians 12–14	Galatians 5:22–23
Prophecy	Apostleship	Apostleship	Love
Service	Prophecy	Prophecy	Joy
Teaching	Evangelism	Teaching	Peace
Encouraging	Pastoring	Service	Patience
Giving	Teaching	Administration	Kindness
Administration		Wisdom	Goodness
Mercy		Knowledge	Faithfulness
		Faith	Gentleness
		Healing	Self-control
		Miracles	
		Discernment	
		Tongues	
		Interpretation	

SPIRITUAL GIFTS	FRUIT OF THE SPIRIT
- Have to do with service—given *to* us *for* others	- Have to do with character, not specific actions
- The means to an end	- Is the end (Romans 1:11–13)
- What a person has	- What a person is
- Given from without	- Produced from within
- Plural	- Singular
- All gifts not possessed by every believer	- Each variety of fruit should be in all believers
- Will cease	- Permanent (1 Corinthians 13:8–10)

Have you ever wondered why the above passage from Galatians refers to fruit as a singular noun but then lists nine character traits? Why isn't it plural? When God's Spirit produces Christ's character in us, we bear all varieties of the fruit at once, not a fragment of one without the other. In street terms we'd call it a package deal. We can't be gentle and at the same time unkind. We can't be loving and at the same time impatient. In other words, we aren't going to be fragmented when God's character is developed in us.

When you allow the character of Christ to be formed *in* you, something very important happens *to* you. You become a person of integrity, and integrity isn't just another virtue or character trait. It is the *result* of a godly or Christ-like character.

In his book *What Would Jesus Say,* Lee Strobel explains the word *integrity* by defining the word *integer,* which comes from the same root word.[4]

An integer is a math term meaning a whole number, like 5 or 20 or 100. The opposite of an integer is a fraction like one-half or one-third. Strobel says integrity means wholeness, completeness, or entirety. Another related word is *integrated,* which is when all aspects of your life are working together in harmony.

You can stop looking to another person—the "right" person—to make you feel whole because another person can't do that for you. Marriage won't make you whole; the right partner won't make you whole; the right group won't make you whole; the right job won't make you whole. Only a love relationship with God will produce the godly character that will make you a person of integrity—a whole person. When a Christ-like character results in your becoming a person of integrity, your life will be made whole and all aspects of your life will work together in harmony even in the midst of turmoil.

If the value of all you do truly does depend on the kind of person you are, then let the life-giving sap of the Vine run through you while you wait for God to show you someone else who is abiding in the Vine. "If a man remains in me and I in him, he will bear much fruit" (John 15:5).

YOUR ACCOUNTABILITY

Southern Baptist pastor Don Davidson of Danville, Virginia, has an interesting story to tell about a plane flight that ended in a twenty-minute conversation with a famous fellow passenger, Jim Bakker.[5] The rise and fall of Bakker as founder of the now-defunct PTL television ministry was national news for years both before and during his five-year imprisonment.

Davidson said he found himself genuinely liking this scarred and broken evangelist, partially because the Virginia minister realized how easy it would be for him or any other minister to fall. Davidson explained that all ministers are vulnerable to the right mixture of sex, power, money, and lack of accountability. Lack of accountability? Yes. Davidson placed it right up there with sex, power, and money.

Lifestyle slippage problems (a fancy way of saying "sin") begin when our own perceived needs take priority over our commitment to Jesus Christ. A key element to keeping ourselves from rationalizing unbiblical behavior is to develop accountability for ourselves. Because keeping ourselves accountable doesn't come naturally, we have to put accountability structures in place through a friend, pastor, small group, married couple, or family member.

Accountability is answerability, an effort to have others hold us answerable for our actions. Recounting his own accountability experience, Colorado Christian University professor Mark Dorn describes his twice-a-month meetings with a friend:

> We are not holding each other accountable in any particular area, yet we are significantly accountable to each other. I ask him important questions about his life, marriage, relationships, and growth. We're committed to a vulnerable honesty with one another. We're not afraid to speak hard truth, but neither do we see ourselves as each other's counselor. We are both stubbornly committed to calling forth the best in each other as well as serving as roadblocks to the poor directions we see each other moving in.[6]

We are never too old nor do we outgrow the need to be under authority. Even as single adults, it is still important to listen to our parents and their counsel and/or the counsel of other godly people. "Listen to your father, who gave you life, and do not despise your mother when she is old" (Proverbs 23:22).

YOUR EMOTIONAL HEALTH

Some of us carry wounds from the past, some carry scars. Some of us have buried our painful memories, and some relive them over and over.

Buried memories surface anew when we encounter problems in marriage, and the past may determine how we deal with those problems. Some people marry hoping that the marriage will serve as a blotter to eradicate past pain. They soon learn that God allows marriage to serve as a suction that draws the pain to the surface to be healed.

Marriage does not change our past. It works in just the opposite way. It tends to reveal past hurts, and all our efforts to keep those memories hidden may eventually result in a crumbling marriage.

What happens after marriage if you experienced a great deal of rejection as a child or adolescent? Many people grow up from childhood believing that acceptance and affection have a price tag and must be earned by accomplishing something, attaining some goal, or refraining from doing something.

Once people who have experienced rejection are in a marriage relationship, their need for attention, acceptance, and affection is perpetual and consuming. This puts a great burden on the partner and on the marriage.

Past rejection may not be your problem. Maybe for you it is the residual effects of having a perfectionist mother or a verbally abusive father. Or maybe you grew up in a dysfunctional home or have past unresolved sins that keep you torn up inside.

You may know with your head that you have unconditional acceptance from God, but that knowledge may not have gotten down into your heart. Perhaps intellectually you know you are forgiven, but you may not know it emotionally. Therefore you never feel worthy.

During the preparation time for marriage, it's important to become fully aware of any issues from the past that might interfere with your marriage relationship. In a similar way, if you have unrepented sin that hasn't been dealt with or reconciled, don't carry it with you into marriage and assume it will go away. The memory of that sin will surface in ways you haven't even considered.

Much of the suffering in marriages today is caused by memories. As you grow older, your storehouse of memories increases, and your personality and general makeup are the results of those memories. Past pain and bad memories not only can affect your marriage but they also can haunt your courtship. They can hinder your ability to hear the voice of God and affect the way you interact with other people. They can interfere with your ability to develop a oneness relationship with another person either spiritually, emotionally, or physically.

There is one more ironic fact about emotional health. A direct correlation exists between emotionally unhealthy singles and singles who resist courtship, embracing and defending dating instead. Emotionally unhealthy singles tend to be byproducts of the dysfunctional homes in which they were raised. These homes tend to be poor examples of godly male/female, husband/wife relationships and full of the characteristics of dating.

Because your emotional health is so important, it's imperative that you find a good Christian counselor *before* you consider courtship and let God be the Lord of your past as well as your present and future. Let Him heal your emotional wounds and free you from the crippling experience of a painful past.

YOUR FINANCIAL STABILITY

A 1992 "Family in America" survey conducted by the Barna Research Group revealed that the most common source of marital stress is financial hardship.[7] In a separate study exploring people's beliefs about divorce, 57 percent of the married people contacted believe that financial problems are the most probable cause of divorce.[8]

Why would finances be so high on the list of problems affecting marriage? One of the responses from a participant in the Barna study may help answer that question:

> It has been so difficult to focus on the relational needs of my wife and kids when I can't figure out how to make ends meet financially. Sometimes I hate going home because the problems are just compounded. I already have two jobs, and we live a fairly simple life, but I'm about ready to crack under this pressure. School loans, car loans, braces for Katie, health insurance premiums, and on and on. This has really driven a wedge between my wife and me. It's just not much fun, and more and more I wonder if this is all worth the effort.[9]

Those words came from a man who hates going home at night because he feels so overwhelmed by the financial needs of his family. If we were to talk to his wife, we might find that she also works full-time *outside* and full-time *inside* the home. Here are two people who got married so they could have the consistent companionship of each other, yet they probably spend very little time together. Financial hardship has become a wedge separating them.

Although it is true that we live in a new day of women working outside the home, most women still have what seems to be a natural desire to be provided for by their husbands. While women may enjoy volunteering for church or charity activities or even getting a job to make extra money, the majority like such opportunities on a voluntary, extracurricular basis. They don't appreciate being forced to make money or lead the household. In fact, they feel insecure when they are not being taken care of properly. Security is close to the top on a woman's list of needs.

A nationwide survey conducted by *USA Today* revealed that among households with two parents present, 73 percent of the respondents would prefer one of the parents stay at home with the children if money were not an issue.[10] Because money is an issue for most families, it's important to lay a financial foundation for your family in the following ways:

- A single man should have a vocation before he considers courtship, and if possible he should be debt free when he marries. In a similar way, the woman also should be debt free before marriage. Working to pay off bills can be a valuable way to learn financial responsibility. Very few couples who begin marriage "in the hole" can dig their way out; instead, they just dig a deeper hole. Those who would like to know more about financial management from a Christian perspective can write Larry Burkett, c/o Money Matters, P.O. Box 100, Gainesville, GA 30503.

- The man in a marriage should assume the leadership role in financial responsibility and decision making (1 Peter 3:1–7). God created man to be the initiator and Eve to be his helpmate and companion. While the final responsibility for finances rests on the man, God may speak to the woman and minister to the husband through her. The virtuous wife described in Proverbs 31—the one "worth far more than rubies"—was not only a good wife and mother, but she also knew a great deal about money. The Bible says she was a manufacturer, importer, manager, realtor, farmer, seamstress, upholsterer, and merchant. (It's interesting to note that Scripture never mentions her appearance.)

- Christian women feel a great need to be righteously led by their husbands, but they don't want their marriage to be the man's first experiment with budgeting and employment. In the same way, a man needs a wife who can manage the household on available resources, not credit. If a woman's lifestyle before marriage doesn't reflect this ability, she is unlikely to learn it easily after marriage. Knowing about savings plans, budgeting, life insurance, employment benefits, and retirement funds should be just as much a part of your single life as your married life. Financial responsibility begins before marriage, not after.

- When you tithe the first tenth of your income to God (Malachi 3:8–12), you affirm that He owns everything and that you are being obedient to His command to give Him the first and best of what He has given you. If you haven't done this as a Christian single, tithing won't be any easier after you're married. God says if you will test Him in the area of tithing, He will "open the floodgates of heaven and pour out so much blessing that you will not have room enough for it" (Malachi 3:10). What more could you want for your marriage than an outpouring of God's blessings?

YOUR VOCATIONAL TRAINING

At the beginning of this chapter, we talked about the importance of order and timing. We said you make life harder when you don't do things in the proper order. Using the word "house" to symbolize the life of an individual or family, Scripture talks about the farmer who built his house in the spring: "Finish your outdoor work and get your fields ready; after that, build your house" (Proverbs 24:27). If the farmer builds his house when he should be planting his fields, he'll go a year without food. He'll make life harder for himself and his family.

Now read the same proverb one more time with added emphasis: "Finish your outdoor work (vocational training) and get your fields ready (employment); after that, build your house (career, marriage, and family)." One, two, three. It's a progression. For a man to get married when he is in a season of preparing for work is both dangerous and disruptive because he can't devote himself fully to either pursuit. One or both will suffer from lack of attention and probably produce long-term consequences.

Very few married couples in today's world seem able to make it financially without both partners being employed for some part of their marriage. The job is the prime concern in many families. More men than ever before have been reared by mothers who worked outside the home, and these men generally have come to expect their wives to have jobs and share responsibility for financial burdens.

On the other hand, many women in today's world have finished college and invested $30,000 to $40,000 in career training. They're ready for a job. They want the role of wife and mother, but they also want to take advantage of career opportunities. Trying to develop themselves in both work and marriage simultaneously can produce inner tension in a woman because the role expectations are opposite in these two areas of life.

What would happen in the career world if a woman were warm, emotional, expressive, noncompetitive, and supportive? Conversely, what would happen in her marriage if she were controlling, pushing, self-assertive, competitive, and dominant? Do you see the problem? It's difficult to switch roles. The woman has to create two different lives at once. Many women decide to remove themselves from one of these roles just to decrease the tension in their lives. They either quit their job or their marriage. Men do not encounter these problems because they are expected to exhibit the same characteristics in both marriage and occupation, so their tension and ambivalence are less.[11]

After nearly two decades of being the first women in American history to juggle the responsibilities of both a career and family on a massive scale, many of today's women indicate they are ready to opt for a more traditional role. In 1991, a Roper poll of women nationwide found that for the first time in ten years, women's top lifestyle preference was no longer a career along with a family.[12]

This reversal in attitudes is made even more curious by reports that show American men, who once resisted the woman's entrance into the workplace, now overwhelmingly approve of women working outside the home. Nine out of ten men under thirty believe that women should be allowed to work, regardless of their family circumstances.[13]

In the 1950s and 1960s, America had relatively few mothers who worked outside the home. The children who came out of those homes grew up with unprecedented career opportunities. Young women were encouraged to be all they could be. As a result, more than nineteen million U.S. families in the 1980s had two breadwinners.[14]

Forty years ago we had no widespread test cases to tell us how family life might change as a result of changes in the workplace. Today's mothers *are* the test cases. What we may have learned from their experience is that women really can't have it all, even when the opportunities are abundant. The role expectations of a career are opposite to those of family life, and the resulting tension may be a larger contributor to divorce than we know. Research by Andrew Greeley and the National Opinion Research Center found that, when lifestyle conditions are statistically accounted for, working mothers are more likely than homemakers to get divorced.[15]

During this time of preparing for your marriage, it's important to consider the trade-offs that must come if you have a two-income family or if you marry before your season of job preparation is finished. You cannot have it all. Some choices will exclude others. Now is the time to count the cost and seek the mind of Christ regarding the family He will someday give you.

YOUR PARENT TRAINING

Many family study experts say the birth of the first child is a major crisis for many couples. Why? Because they probably spent more time preparing to get their driver's license than they did preparing for parenthood.[16] Most couples are only vaguely aware of all that is entailed in the task of parenthood, especially since our culture excels at painting a picture of sex apart from the possibility of becoming a parent.

Because most families today have only two or three children, very few people grow up caring for a younger sibling. For many couples, the first diaper they ever change belongs to their first child. At least when you learn to drive a car, someone sits in the seat next to you and gives commands until you get it right. When you're a parent, no instructor is around at 2 A.M. when the baby wakes up and cries for an hour. You're on your own.

So how do you learn to be a parent? You start by realizing that you're not ready for courtship and marriage unless you're ready to think of yourself as a parent. A couple that gets married with the understanding that "we won't have children for a few years" is not ready to get married. Even for those willing to use birth control, children may come along due to God's sovereignty despite the couple's best efforts to the contrary. Whenever two people have a child before one or both is ready to accept the responsibility, some area of that child's life probably will be neglected.

For most people, marriage and children are complementary; they go together. The Bible says that children are a reward from the Lord (Psalm 127:3). The emphasis in Scripture is on children as a gift rather than as a possession. You can anticipate this gift in your life—a holy gift—by finding ways to develop parenting skills that will give you driving experience before you go for the learner's permit. Volunteer in your church nursery. Babysit for your friends. Coach a Little League team. Teach a Sunday school class. Help in vacation Bible school. Be there for someone else's child. All that you learn will help you be there for your own children. Having your first child doesn't have to be a major crisis in your marriage. Instead, that child should be the gift you expected and wanted the day you began your courtship with the mate God gave you.

YOUR HOUSEHOLD TRAINING

Men and women are not ready for marriage until they're ready to maintain a home. Faucets need fixing, lawns need mowing, floors need vacuuming, bathrooms need cleaning, and dishes need washing. The "to do" list is endless.

Do you know where the air filter is on the air conditioner? What about the lint catcher on the dryer? Or the vacuum bag? Or the oil in the car? Would you believe that couples actually fight over who changes what when?

Traditional roles for men and women might appear to have changed in recent decades, but a new study from British psychologists at Birmingham University tells us that even the most "progressive" couples, who share responsibility for earning a living and for the household, regress to "old-fashioned" roles once a baby is born. Psychologist Gill Cappuccini told a British Psychology Society conference that the wife ends up spending the most time with the baby and doing most of the housework, while the husband's career becomes more important.

Some people might resist the idea that women should know more than men about baking, sewing, home decorating, and child care, but the truth is that most couples do revert to traditional roles once the children arrive. The man probably is going to be mowing the lawn while the woman is fixing supper and the baby is in the playpen. Preparing for your role ahead of time will help smooth the way not only for a well-managed home but for less tension between partners.

Burned toast and clogged drains can become disproportionately important when it's your drain, your toast, and your frustrated spouse. Perhaps you've heard the old saying that the fleas come with the dog. In other words, you shouldn't buy the dog if you don't want to deal with the fleas. Marriage is much the same. If you're not prepared to deal with the inconvenience of household chores and home maintenance, you're not ready for marriage.

YOUR COMMITMENT

Marriage is an unconditional commitment to an imperfect person. That commitment begins in courtship when you determine that God is leading you to a particular person—an imperfect person—as a lifetime partner. You should never consider a courtship until you are ready and able to make a lifelong commitment to someone who cannot be and never was designed to be all you wanted.

If God directs you to a courtship relationship leading to marriage, what are you really saying when you make a commitment to the other person? According to the traditional wedding vow we've all heard many times, you're saying the following:

1. I will love you until one of us dies.
2. I will honor you until one of us dies.
3. I will cherish you until one of us dies.
4. I will not be involved with any other "substitute mate."
5. I will perform all the duties of a spouse until one of us dies.
6. I will be loving and faithful through every kind of circumstance for as long as the two of us live.

Unless you are prepared to make that kind of commitment to another person, you're not prepared to begin a courtship. Courtship isn't "trying out" another person. Courtship should be the result of God's definite direction and of your commitment not only to another person but also to God's leadership. Commitment is what makes trust possible, and not even love will hold some marriages together when trust is broken. How can you share the deepest parts of who you are with someone you don't trust, and how can children grow healthy and strong in a home environment without intimacy?

True commitment does not depend on the other person's behavior or the degree of their commitment. Instead, you're saying you are committed to love and loyalty for a lifetime no matter what. That is exactly what Jesus says to you. In your relationship with Him, He is committed to you for eternity no matter what.

"We've asked God about our relationship but God hasn't told us to get married." If that's what you think and how you feel, then why are you in a relationship that God has not directed and ordained? When you are unable to commit to marriage but are intimate with another person emotionally, physically, or spiritually, one of you will be defrauded in the relationship. Someone will be wounded through counterfeit oneness. One person will care more than the other. Write it down. Carve it in stone. Commit it to memory. An uncommitted relationship will end in pain. As a safeguard, the commitment level in a relationship should always be one step ahead of the physical, emotional, and spiritual level.

If you have completed the preparation steps for marriage but are still unable to make a commitment, the problem usually can be traced to a deficiency in one of the areas discussed in this chapter. Perhaps you feel reluctant to take on the financial responsibilities of marriage or maybe the scars of a failed relationship have made you afraid of failing again. When your lack of commitment becomes a *fear* of commitment, it might be time to consider that fear is from Satan, not God. God doesn't give you a spirit of fear (2 Timothy 1:7, KJV). You can't live in fear and trust God at the same time.

Fear is really the natural by-product of an anxious spirit, and an anxious spirit is living under the false assumption that you can manage life yourself. Believing that with your own effort, you can maneuver circumstances into a satisfying outcome is a sure prescription for experiencing feelings of failure down the road. The longer fear is allowed to continue, the longer you will miss the good things God has for you.

BUILDING ON CRUMBLE-PROOF CONCRETE

Being together feels so good and satisfying that couples don't always feel a need to work at building a foundation for a lasting relationship. But the time will come when just being together won't be enough. Togetherness will lose its magic when routine and restlessness replace romance. How you handle such changes in your relationship will be largely determined by the foundation you build and bring into your marriage as a dowry. Routine and restlessness can be the wind and rain that will beat on the walls of your home. Or it might be finances, health problems, troubled teens, or a long list of other problems that can wreak havoc on marriages.

Regardless of what brings the storm, your foundation will be the concrete slab that supports you through the storm. You can't wait until the day you move into the house to pour the slab. Instead, you must lay the foundation long before the house is built. Part of laying that foundation is delaying everything else. You don't build walls before you pour concrete. In a similar way, you shouldn't begin a courtship until you have completed the preparation process that lays the foundation for marriage.

STUDY AND DISCUSSION QUESTIONS

1. Can you describe an instance when less may be more in regard to money and marriage?

2. In your personal hierarchy of needs, what are your top three needs in a relationship?

3. Intimacy with God affects whether you view life from God's perspective or man's. Explain how both perspectives might affect each of the following:
  • Your paycheck

- Your sexual relationship
- Your elderly mother-in-law
- Your weekend
- Your house
- Your dyslexic son

4. Choose any topic discussed in this chapter and explain how ignoring that issue before marriage might adversely affect a couple's relationship after marriage.

5. How would you answer the following?

    a. Am I ready to be a parent?

    b. Have I completed my vocational training?

    c. Am I ready to make a lifelong commitment to my mate?

    d. How do I feel about dumping my monetary debt on my future spouse?

    e. Am I emotionally healthy?

    f. Am I refining my godly character and maturing spiritually?

6. Meditate and memorize: "Finish your outdoor work and get your fields ready; after that, build your house" (Proverbs 24:27).

7. Pray: My heavenly Father, I desire to build a foundation in my life that will have an eternal, righteous effect. I commit not to begin a courtship until You have built a solid foundation in my life. Please build my foundation for marriage based on commitment, spiritual maturity, godly character, accountability, emotional health, financial stability, and vocational, parental, and household training. Thank You for the many blessings You have given me. In the name of Jesus. Amen.

CHAPTER SEVEN

Relating without Dating

It is God's will that you should be holy...for God did not call us to be impure, but to live a holy life.
1 THESSALONIANS 4:3,7

PRINCIPLE FOUR: Be "set apart" (sanctified) in your friendships by committing yourself to biblically appropriate behavior that won't compromise your integrity or defraud another person.

"If I don't date, how will I ever get to know anyone? "Whether that is the right question or not, it certainly is the most frequently asked question regarding biblical courtship. Singles tend to view dating as a legitimate search for a marriage partner. In fact, most singles have a hard time trying not to see a potential mate in every person they meet. A dating perspective keeps you focused on how to meet and get to know other available singles.

From a courtship perspective, however, God does the seeking and searching. He brings the right person into your life and has the responsibility of revealing that choice to you. If you have a willing heart, He will supply the wisdom you need to discern His choice when the time is right (Isaiah 55:9). You can't speed up the process or fix the problem by your own efforts; you can only miss His plan. It's an issue of time versus intensity. Dating focuses on intensity at the beginning of the relationship, whereas courtship uses time for the development of the relationship.

"Missing the mark" is a biblical term for missing God's perfect plan. Translated into English, the Greek word *hamartia* means "sin." It carries with it a mental image of an archer aiming his arrow at a specific target and missing. The implication is clear. We sin when we miss God's perfect plan.

BEHIND THE MASK

Learning to build solid friendships is an important aspect of preparing for the marriage relationship. One of the major cries I hear in marriage counseling is "my spouse is not my best friend." A vast collection of research studies proves that you tend to be happiest with someone who is much like you. That seems to suggest that most people will find their spouses from within their own pool of friends, a pool usually comprised of people with similar interests and ideas.

When God does begin directing you to a possible marriage partner, it is very appropriate to ask how you get to know each other without dating. The issue is not that you can't spend time together, but *how* can you be together in ways that will avoid counterfeit oneness? The aim is not to curse dating but to avoid the shortcomings of dating. You do this by avoiding activities that encourage intimacy without commitment or accountability.

In a dating relationship, it's easy to put up a facade for three to eight hours and never reveal who you really are. How many times have you or one of your friends been involved in a relationship and found that after the first three months the scales fell off your eyes? You met the other person—the real person—for the first time. "I didn't know he/she was like that," you say to yourself. Bad temper, selfish attitude, controlling spirit, manipulative nature, moody disposition. The list of possibilities is endless. The discovery process also can work in the reverse—but rarely does. You can discover good qualities as well as bad, but most people's good qualities are already on display.

If you're one of the people who was able to break through a dating partner's facade in the first three months, you're fortunate. Many of the couples I counsel complain that the other person was never "like that" before they married. The facade didn't come down until after the wedding. Over and over they say that the person they married isn't the person they dated. How can that be?

Masking our unpleasant qualities is easy to do in today's dating world. Most couples are alone and completely absorbed in each other much of the time they are together. They rarely see the other person interacting within a family or group setting. What people are like within their own families before marriage can be a reliable indicator of how they will act in a new family after marriage and after the new grows old.

Courtship stresses time spent with each other's family and in ministry and group activities. How people treat others is a good barometer of how they will treat you when the honeymoon is over. How they serve others indicates how they will serve you. Spending every minute alone while the bloom is still on the rose won't give you a clear picture of what the garden will look like in another season.

Although the intimate friendship you develop with your future mate will last for a lifetime, that won't be the best part of following a courtship process designed to guard your heart and your integrity. You will be positioning yourself and your children for the generational blessings that will come from the hand of a loving God who will bless you for your obedience. Bringing God's spiritual power into your future marriage will require your commitment to being "set apart," holy and sanctified, in your personal relationships.

IT ALL BEGINS WITH FRIENDSHIP

Friendships or nonromantic relationships usually begin when outside circumstances throw two people together in the midst of a group. As acquaintances within the group, the two discover they have mutual interests. After that discovery, the relationship grows and they begin to build trust and understanding. Then they become friends. A solid friendship will be the springboard for beginning a healthy courtship.

Building this friendship in the context of a group will free you from many of the pressures that develop in one-on-one dating situations. For instance, the two of you don't have to worry about keeping the conversation going all by yourselves. Neither of you has to worry if the other person is boring or unpleasant. If you are on a one-on-one date and you don't hit it off just right, you could be in for a very long night. What if the other person has interests totally different from yours? What if their sense of humor is totally different? What if they seemed nice enough at the office but revealed themselves to be all passion and self-centeredness on a date? Until you know and trust each other thoroughly as close friends, you should avoid one-on-one, time-alone situations.

Ladies, how many times have you had to come up with the excuse that you're busy when a guy asks you out and you really don't want to hurt his feelings? Or guys, how many times have you ended a date knowing you would never ask her out again but you still say, "I'll give you a call"? Both behaviors are deceptions, and today's dating system is full of them. It's not what we say, it's what they hear that matters. We are responsible for the other person's perception of the relationship. Allowing them to believe a partial truth is the same as telling them a whole lie.

Obviously, it is important to have friends, but the problem comes with the level and intensity of your friendships. The courtship process includes four basic levels of friendship involvement, each level leading to the next: *acquaintance, casual friendship, close friendship,* and *intimate friendship.* The following figure describes these four levels and the spiritual, emotional and physical commitments that are a part of each level.

COURTSHIP PROCESS	Phase 4: Friendship Levels			
	Acquaintance	Casual Friendship	Close Friendship	Intimate Friendship
SPIRITUAL Commitment	Focus on being totally content and feeling complete as a single engaged to Christ. Develop a life vision and direction about serving God through ministry opportunities. Avoid spiritual involvement with another individual at this point except for witnessing the gospel of Jesus.	May be involved in a church activity with another individual. Discuss Christ and His kingdom in group settings or Bible studies, but avoid deep spiritual one-on-one talk.	Share with each other God's vision for your lives. Discover each other's spiritual gifts, maturity level, and desire to serve God. Experience deeper spiritual talk but limited intimate one-on-one talk.	Begin intimate spiritual talk related at the deepest level. Discuss possibility of marriage and the purpose and process of courtship as it relates to your love for God. Discuss need for spiritual covering and account-ability.
EMOTIONAL Commitment	No emotional intimacy. Casual interaction. Limited shared feelings. No one-on-one activities.	No emotional intimacy, but share surface feelings. Share close friends or activities. No one-on-one activities.	Share deeper feelings but limit emotional involvement. Focus on external social activities instead of one-on-one intimate interaction.	Share each other's innermost thoughts, fears, failures, and hopes. Support each other in times of crisis and pain; share times of joy. Limit one-on-one emotional interaction.
PHYSICAL Commitment			Side hugs (no full "body slam" hugs).	Side hugs plus holding hands.
Time Alone			10 Hours	20 Hours

If you've dated very much at all, you've probably had the experience of sitting down with another person and having "the talk." That's the conversation a couple has when at least one of them may say, "God just wants us to be friends." Yet that person's behavior sent out an entirely different message for weeks and months prior to "the talk." Instead of taking responsibility for inappropriate behavior and poor choices, the person who is uncommitted to the relationship essentially puts the blame on God.

You could and should have a number of friendships with the opposite sex on an acquaintance level and sometimes a casual level. A few times in your life you may experience a male/female relationship that develops to a close friendship, but this should be the exception, not the rule. When you enter into friendships on close and intimate levels, you walk on fertile ground for the nurture of counterfeit oneness (see chapter 3). When one person ends a relationship, leaving the other feeling defrauded, it's not God's fault. God doesn't direct two people into an intimate friendship and then change His mind in midstream.

Think about your relationships. What friendship levels do you have in your life? Do you think the other person involved would view the friendship on the same level? When two people are clear and in agreement with each other and God, they will feel blessed and encouraged, not defrauded. If God wants you to be "just friends," He'll tell you on the front end. No Christian with his ear to God's mouth should move to a closer friendship level than God's guidance allows. Two people involved in a godly relationship won't need to have the talk that ends in pain.

SEXUAL OR EMOTIONAL FRAUD

We've talked a lot about relationships that deceive others and cause pain, but we still may not see it the way God sees it. Scripture specifically warns against defrauding other people and underscores its seriousness by saying, "He who rejects this instruction does not reject man but God" (1 Thessalonians 4:8). In other words, this is no small problem or light teaching. God means business.

When Paul talks about defrauding other people, he uses the Greek word *pleonekte* (1 Thessalonians 4:6), which means stimulating sexual desires that cannot be righteously fulfilled. This is a sin committed by unmarried persons or by married people in relationships outside their marriage. It is one person manipulating another person either sexually or emotionally for one's own advantage. Because the other person is being cheated, the English translation becomes "defraud."

Manipulating another person sexually or emotionally is done daily in a thousand different settings from the office to the classroom, to the counseling office, to the church staff, to the Sunday school, to the parked car, the motel, the private home, and the factory workplace. Most of the time it's done with our awareness but sometimes we defraud another person unconsciously because we don't understand a basic truth: Men and women don't think alike.

The famous poet Robert Browning probably said it best when he wrote, "Love's so different for us men." What did he mean? Psychologist and highly acclaimed author Dr. Archibald Hart understands the difference. After confidentially surveying more than 600 men representative of what he calls "mainstream, middle-of-the-road, normal, heterosexual men," Hart asserts what even the poets know: men give love for sex, and women give sex for love.

"This is such a fundamental difference from the way women see sex that you really wonder how men and women ever get together on this issue," Hart says. In his book *The Sexual Man,* Hart discusses this basic difference between the sexes:

> Love and sex are inextricably linked in most women's thinking. Not so for men. This is why platonic love or friendship can be so easily misread by males. A woman, for instance, might think that only a friendship is developing with a male acquaintance at work. She enjoys doing things with him. She knows the boundaries. They laugh, share stories, and have lunch. For her it is all platonic, pure friendship. There's no love, so there can't possibly be anything sexual, assuming she's not trying to seduce him in the hope that the relationship will go further.
>
> The man, oblivious to his deeper feelings, only thinks

with his hormones. "She's interested in sex," he thinks. "She's got to be. Why else would she be so friendly?" Is he right? Not at all. And if he tries to take it further, he could be in serious trouble.

Men and women view the link between love and sex differently. But instead of making sex simpler for men, this difference makes it more complex. Men don't have an innate defense against sexual arousal, so they have to construct it for themselves. Not many men are effective in creating this protection, so ladies beware. *Men don't always do a good job of being "just friends" with a woman* (italics added).[1]

Hart's illustration of the friendship between two acquaintances at work also points up another basic difference between men and women: Men respond to visual and touch stimulation whereas women react to touch and verbal stimulation. A man's sexual hormones are aroused quickly by sight. All he needs to see in many cases is a suggestive picture and his hormones kick into gear. Women are stimulated by intimate conversations that express feelings and emotion, especially in a romantic environment or atmosphere. They want to talk about how they feel and hear the man talk about his feelings. In a conversational environment, they're usually good listeners, and a good listener will feed a male ego.

DIFFERENCES THAT MAKE A DIFFERENCE

Man	Woman
• Does not link sex with love	• Sees love and sex inextricably linked
• Stimulated by sight and touch	• Stimulated verbally and by touch
• Logical	• Intuitive
• Objective	• Subjective
• Impersonal	• Personal
• Steady (sometimes inflexible)	• Changeable (usually adaptable)

- Thing-centered
- Straight to the point
- Looks for essentials
- Future-minded (long-range goals)
- Needs significance in life
- Tendency to egotism
- Soul modest and body free
- Desires sex
- Neglects tasks

- People-centered
- Sensitive to other's responses
- Looks for aesthetics
- Present-minded (short-term goals)
- Needs security
- Tendency to jealousy
- Body modest and soul free
- Dreams of love
- Nags partner (often about neglecting tasks)

- Defeated by discouragement
- Defeated by loneliness

When we look at the differences between the sexes, we have to acknowledge that the differences *do* make a difference. As an outgrowth of the frustration and desperation sometimes experienced when we want to be married, many singles overreact to any attention from someone of the opposite sex, especially if that someone is attractive. If a man looks at a woman twice, a woman might begin to imagine all kinds of possibilities. If a woman happens to sit by a man at a social function, he may think she's sending him come-ons. What one person thinks is light conversation between two people, another might interpret as an invitation to deeper involvement.

Him: "But you didn't see how she looked at me. A woman doesn't look at you like that if she's not sending a signal. I'm sure she wants to see me."

Her: "But we talked for twenty minutes. He didn't have to talk to me that long. I'm sure he likes me."

With the God-given attraction that we have for the opposite sex, many problems will stalk Christian singles who don't want to defraud another person and do want to deepen their fellowship with Christ. Many of these problems can be solved by keeping brotherly love brotherly, which is a biblical concept expressed in 1 Thessalonians 4:9: "Now about brotherly love we do not need to write to you, for you yourselves have been taught by God to love each other."

"Brotherly love" in Greek translates to *philadelphia,* a word that outside the New Testament almost without exception denotes the mutual love of children of the same father. In the New Testament, it always means love of fellow believers in Christ, all of whom have the same heavenly Father ("taught by God"). Paul was admonishing us to love each other with the love of spiritual brothers and sisters who have the same heavenly Father.

If you took Paul's words to heart and put them to action in your life, how would brotherly love change your friendships? To begin with, you'd have to treat others as though they were your natural-born brothers or sisters. Whatever you would be willing to do with, to, or for a natural-born brother or sister, you'd have to be willing to do with, to, or for another person. In a similar fashion, what you wouldn't do in the case of a sibling, you shouldn't do in the case of a friend (1 Timothy 5:1–2).

The activities you would do with a sibling should also be all right to do with the opposite sex, except for these cautions: avoid long activities together; avoid deep, intimate one-on-one time together; and allow a long period of time to pass before you plan another activity with that person.

When you make the commitment to treat everyone like a natural-born brother or sister, you will be amazed how easily you can distinguish between biblically appropriate behavior and behavior that is inappropriate. You will know the difference between friendly, uplifting behavior and those actions that stifle and destroy friendships or stimulate wrong thoughts.

With a brother or sister, you don't spend time playing romantic, emotional games or sending nonverbal messages through sensual looks and sexy moves. You don't have clandestine meetings or touch each other in ways that leave the other person wondering what you meant. You don't make suggestive comments with sexual overtones.

WHERE DO YOU DRAW THE LINE?

When the good parts of a friendship turn sour—or even sordid— what's really happening? The Bible says that everything God created and designed for man's use was good, but Satan is a perverter (Acts 13:10). He takes the good and distorts it. Then it becomes sin. Satan's unclean spirits do this by influencing us to go beyond the boundary of the will of God.

Our own appetite for food is a good example of this distortion process. Certainly God intended us to have an appetite, but appetite taken to an extreme becomes gluttony. Physical rest taken to an extreme becomes laziness. Carefulness becomes fear. Self-respect becomes conceit. Love becomes lust.

To be responsible stewards over all that God has created, we need to develop boundaries like God's. When Satan tempted Eve to question God's boundaries and His truth in the Garden of Eden, the consequences were disastrous. If Satan's evil spirits can distort reality for us so that we become confused about the truth, we will begin to move outside God's boundaries in very subtle ways. Confusion may be the key word here. It means knowing the truth but believing a lie. Satan is the author of confusion.

When we watch television programs that show unmarried people enjoying sexual relationships with no negative consequences, it's easy to become confused. "What's the big deal?" we say. When we watch movies that portray the bad guy as the misunderstood good guy, it's easy to be confused. Is he good or bad? Who makes the rules and who sets the standards?

Defining and Defending Your Boundaries

Knowing the truth about God and His boundary lines puts limits on us. When we see where God draws His lines, we will know where to draw ours. Those boundaries will define and guard our hearts and keep us from defrauding others (Proverbs 4:23).

The time you spend with someone else, particularly if the friendship has no boundaries, has a direct correlation with the progression of counterfeit oneness. The more time you spend with someone, even in a group, the more likely that friendship will kick up a level or two to that of a close friend or an intimate friend.

An intimate friendship with a person of the opposite sex should only occur when you believe God is directing you to that person as a potential marriage partner. You tread on dangerous ground when you allow a male/female friendship to develop into an intimate friendship that doesn't have accountability or commitment. Failing to put limits on your relationship—limited time, limited communication, limited intimacy—will make you vulnerable to counterfeit oneness.

When no boundaries control your closeness, your relationship can become susceptible to Satan's perversion. He'll take the good in your friendship and turn it into something distorted. In the end, you'll pay the price in pain. Counterfeit oneness outside of marriage *always* has painful consequences even though it may take years for the consequences to surface.

In the popular book *Boundaries,* by Dr. Henry Cloud and Dr. John Townsend, the authors compare personal boundaries to physical boundaries. In the physical world, boundaries are easy to see: fences, signs, walls, moats with alligators, manicured lawns, or hedges. They all indicate where property begins. The owner of the property is legally responsible for what happens on that property, and nonowners are not.[2]

In a similar way, personal boundaries are anything that helps to differentiate us from someone else or show where we begin and end. Have you ever had a breakup in a relationship and come away feeling like you don't know who you are? Sometimes counterfeit oneness in intimate friendships can so blur the boundary lines between us and another person that we lose sight of who we are in Christ and begin to assume the identity of the other person. When that happens, we've lost control of our lives and values. God calls us to *love* others, but He doesn't want us to *be* others.

One sure sign of boundary problems is when we've given another person so much power in our lives that our relationship with that person affects our relationships with others. If that special someone isn't with us or around us or a part of what we're doing, we can't enjoy who we're with and where we are. Sometimes we almost seem to "catch" something from them and pass it on. If they're not happy, we're not happy. If they're not having a good day, we're not having a good day. If they have a cold, we sneeze.

Let's imagine, for example, that you have a farm and Joe Bob has a farm. You're neighbors and you both have cattle, but there's no fence separating your property. You enjoy Joe Bob's friendship and like having a close neighbor. When a few of his cows wander over and eat your grass, it's a little irritating but you ignore it. Why? Because you want a close friend. Then one day half of his cattle cross over onto your farm and eat the grass your cattle need. Even then, you don't say anything because you want Joe Bob to like you and accept you. You don't want him to be mad at you. Eventually the cattle wander up to your house and eat the roses in your flower garden. That's when you explode. Then you wind up building a twelve-foot brick wall around your property, and your good friend Joe Bob doesn't know why.

Boundaries have to be set *before* a situation occurs, not after. A late fence won't save the grass and roses already eaten or the angry words already said. If you wait until you are in the middle of the situation, you've waited too long. When you're on the couch at midnight in an intimate embrace, it's probably too late to decide how you feel about premarital sex. Trying to draw a boundary in the middle of a hormonal attack won't be very well received.

Once our boundaries have been established, they must be maintained. The firmer the boundary, the easier it is to preserve. If our boundaries are not clearly and firmly set, we may be tempted to let down our guard. We drop our boundaries and let other people trespass on our property for a number of reasons:

- We drop them for a payoff. Many times that payoff is nothing more than the fulfilling of a deep need to have someone be our friend and like us in order to avoid loneliness.
- Some people don't grow up with boundaries and don't know what boundaries are. They can't drop what they've never known.
- Some people are victims of physical, sexual, or emotional abuse that has left them with a poor sense of boundaries. Their experiences have taught them that their property can be invaded by others even if they say no.

According to Cloud and Townsend, individuals with mature boundaries are the least angry people in the world. The more biblical our boundaries, the less anger we will experience. Boundaries are what keep us from feeling violated and victimized.

Many singles believe there is no harm in "boundary-less" friendships. In fact, they encourage deep and bonding relationships. The result is that they open up their whole hearts and souls within two or three dates and then wonder why they're struggling so hard with lust. The extent to which we involve our emotions is the extent to which we will struggle with physical temptations. It's a reliable formula: the greater our emotional involvement, the more difficult our physical struggle.

Boundary setting at its best occurs when both parties understand appropriate behavior, and agree on boundaries and the consequences of violating them. Unfortunately, agreement doesn't always happen. God clearly set boundaries when He gave us the Ten Commandments, but most of humanity has been disagreeing with His boundaries since the days of Moses. The Ten Commandments are not arbitrary boundaries but expressions of truth deriving from the nature of God. He even spelled out the results of breaking those boundaries. We can't control how someone else will react to our efforts to line up our boundaries with God's, but we can do as God did for Israel: draw the boundaries, announce them, and share the results. God did not control the behavior of Israel, but He did control His own behavior. We are not God but we do have the principles of God and can live by them.[3]

Like the old adage says, "Good fences make good neighbors." In a similar way, good boundaries make good friendships. When a friendship leads to marriage, you will still need to remember how to build and maintain boundaries. Even in marriage, which is the most intimate of all human relationships, preserving individuality within the context of oneness is an important part of a healthy relationship.

The Myth of "Christian Dating"

Although the concept of dating is not supported by God's Word, a few of God's Old Testament followers entered into dating-type relationships that had severe consequences.

- King David developed an interest in a woman based on physical beauty (2 Samuel 11:2–4). He watched her from a rooftop and then sent his messengers to bring her to him. In essence, he had a one-night stand. The resulting guilt brought David to his knees before God, but the lies and the tragic consequences could not be reversed.
- Solomon was the wisest man who ever lived, but because he selected wives based on his own ideas, his heart was gradually drawn away from the Lord (1 Kings 11:4). Ultimately, he found that relationships don't create happiness; only joy from the Lord produces contentment.
- Samson was the strongest man on earth, but his low standards and refusal to listen to his parents' counsel led him to a woman who captured his interest, clouded his judgment, and put him in bondage (Judges 16).

Examples of dating-type relationships do exist in the Bible, but they are negative examples. God uses these examples to warn us not to follow our natural inclinations but to receive His guidelines for finding and choosing a godly partner.

Dating clashes with God's creation model. From Adam and Eve throughout Bible history, godly male/female relationships were always in the context of marriage. The first one-on-one relationship between opposite sexes was with a view toward marriage. When God, Eve's Father, brought Eve to Adam, this was the first biblically recorded "date." What was the purpose of the "date"? Marriage and oneness. "This is now bone of my bones and flesh of my flesh;…and they will become one flesh." (Genesis 2:23a, 24b).

The major problem with casual, recreational dating is that it encourages a one-on-one relationship outside of marriage and without commitment. Singles should not be surprised when they discover they have fallen into sexual intimacy that has no commitment. One-on-one dating is designed specifically for sexuality and physical attraction.

Often dating couples break up after being physically involved. Some even try to remain friends. But once you've been sexually involved with someone, it is very difficult to scale the relationship back to a friendship level. More often than not, the physical counterfeit oneness that develops during the dating relationship will draw you back into a physical relationship, even though you are now "just friends."

Because dating focuses inherently on self and away from God, it is even more devastating to Christians than to nonbelievers. Anything that violates God's principles is detrimental to the person involved, regardless of how well it is accepted by the rest of the world. Christian dating is nothing more than Christians following worldly traditions (Matthew 15:9). In fact, the term itself is a misnomer. It implies that dating is Christian when, in fact, its principles are man-centered and culturally determined. The principles of courtship, on the other hand, are God-centered and biblically based.

The dating experiences of most Christians fit into thirteen categories, all of which can lead to someone feeling defrauded and angry:

1. Friendship dating
2. Discipleship dating
3. Missionary dating
4. Video dating
5. Pharisee dating
6. Messiah dating
7. Honeymoon dating
8. Commit-a-phobic dating
9. Perfectionist dating
10. Good-time Charlie dating
11. Love bucket dating
12. Classified dating
13. Desperation dating

Friendship Dating

Two people are dating but they say they're "just friends." Their commitment and understanding is on a friendship level but their behavior is on a dating level, including the following:

- Long phone conversations
- Giving gifts for birthdays, Christmas, and other occasions
- Sharing deep, intimate conversations
- Eating lunch or dinner together regularly
- Going to movies together or to other one-on-one activities on an exclusive basis

All relationships start out as friendships, but in friendship dating one person is likely to become committed to the relationship and begin hoping that the other person will get committed too. When that doesn't happen, the one who is the most committed may begin to feel used and angry.

Discipleship Dating

Christians date other Christians who are not on the same level spiritually. They start thinking they can help the other person grow as a Christian. Women often want a man who will surpass them spiritually and be the spiritual leader in the home, so they disciple the man. What does it say about a woman spiritually if she wants to be surpassed? Even if the other person does begin to grow as a Christian, a difference in spiritual maturity will still exist between the dating partners. Some maturity comes only with time, and if you have been a Christian for a while, your dating partner will have some catching up to do before there is mutual respect and support in the faith you share. Another caution involves the interaction of men and women spiritually (1 Timothy 2:12). Do not disciple members of the opposite sex. The late-night Bible study with the man and woman falling asleep side by side on the couch is not a wholly righteous scene. In male/female discipleship, one partner may appear to be growing spiritually when in fact that person is making choices to please another person, not God. Such a shallow commitment will rarely stand the test of time. In marriage counseling situations, we often hear the words, "I only went to church so she'd marry me."

Missionary Dating

Christians date non-Christians and expect to witness to them. ("I'm dating the neatest guy and he'd be so awesome if he'd just become a Christian.") It is true that you may witness to your non-Christian date, but be aware that you are playing with fire. A non-believer might show an interest in God in order to date you. If the relationship fails, that person's faith is likely to falter. And what if you think you've fallen in love? Where will your loyalty be then? To be "in love" is not necessarily to be in the will of God. You will surely love the person God wants you to marry, but He does not necessarily want you to marry someone just because you think you're in love. You must come to grips with what you will do if your boyfriend or girlfriend does not become a Christian. Do not ask God if it is His will for you to marry a non-Christian. He has already told you it is not (2 Corinthians 6:14–18). If you say you are a follower of Christ and then willfully disobey Him, your verbal commitment is a lie. Although this type of dating has the same pitfalls as discipleship dating, its lasting consequences are far more devastating if the couple marry and the other person has not become a Christian. In such a circumstance, you cannot, in the will of God, be married.

Video Dating

This is a copycat of secular video dating. Some major metropolitan areas actually have Christian dating services that allow a person to choose a Christian dating partner from videotaped interviews. This is supposedly for the person who doesn't have enough time to find someone special or doesn't have a large enough pool of prospective partners. (If you don't have time to find someone special, you don't have time to be married!) This brings us back to our central question. Who is doing the finding? You or God? If

God wills you to marry, He doesn't need a video or a dating service to bring that person into your life, and you don't need to be interviewing applicants and making trial runs!

Pharisee Dating

Pharisees will date you and talk about religion in order to appear godly and get you to like them. They are wolves in sheep's clothing, and they often can be found in church singles departments. They talk the talk but they don't walk their talk. Their motives aren't always as pure as their conversation and eventually their behavior will show it. Men are particularly aware that most Christian women are eager to find a spiritual mate who might someday be the spiritual head of their household. Just as a Venus flytrap plant uses a scent to attract its victim, the pharisee dater uses spiritual talk to trap an unsuspecting partner.

Messiah Dating

Messiah daters are always trying to save someone. This doesn't mean "save" in the sense of a spiritual conversion (although it can include this experience), but it means a willingness to be there for other people, fix their problems, or rescue them from a crisis. The messiah dater is often a strong Christian with a commitment to service. They're only too happy to help, and they usually find the person who is only too happy to be helped. Today we call anyone who continually rescues another person a codependent. In effect, codependent, boundary-less people "cosign the note" of life for the irresponsible person they are trying to help. Just as we can interfere with the law of gravity by catching a glass tumbling off the table, people can interfere with the law of sowing and reaping by stepping in and rescuing a person from the natural consequences of irresponsible behavior. The helper is the one who winds up paying the bills physically, emotionally, and spiritually. While the giver suffers the consequences, the taker continues to be loved, pampered, and treated nicely. Establishing boundaries forces the person who is doing the sowing to also do the reaping.

Honeymoon Dating

Many people want to have a dating relationship like a honey-moon. In other words, they want the benefits of marriage without the hard work and headaches of marriage. They want to spend their single life having their physical and emotional needs met as if they were on a perpetual honeymoon of weekends spent eating out, sleeping over, and getting someone else to do their laundry. These people want the security of being with someone, but they are quick to dodge the commitment and responsibility of mar-riage. These individuals tend to have dating relationships that last for years and never make a marital commitment.

Commit-a-phobic Dating

At first you might not even be interested in him. He comes on like gangbusters, setting his sights to capture his prey. He calls every day, then several times a day to the point of being controlling. You interpret his pursuit as someone who truly cares, but for him, it's the hunt that gives him a thrill. He sends flowers and cards, and within a short time says he loves you. He smothers you with com-pliments and attention while his sincerity clouds your thinking. You look at engagement rings, talk about kids and where you might live. Then all of a sudden, after you've committed your warm heart to him, he goes cold. The calls begin to wane while he stops saying he loves you.

Like a deer stunned in the headlights of a car, you're frozen in con-fusion and fright. You begin to pursue him to gain some sense of secu-rity and stability. As your desire increases for him, he pulls away from you. He eludes all your questions and stops returning your calls. You finally talk, and he says he's "not ready for a serious relationship." The main cause of a commit-a-phobic's behavior is a fear of commitment along with an unwillingness to grow up and become responsible. The commit-a-phobic is drawn like a magnet to a desperation dater.

Perfectionist Dating

Once he finds some imperfection he believes he can't live with, he moves on to greener pastures. He may start off with the intention of being honorable, but after finding something wrong, he says you're "not the one." He has either met someone else or hopes to meet someone else. He is looking for the Christian "Barbie Doll." He medicates his pain of singleness by fantasizing about the perfect woman. Any person he meets will never be able to live up to his fantasy.

A perfectionist may seem charming, confident, and a "good catch," but he is actually insecure. He tends to base his self-worth and value on his possessions rather than on Christ. He may believe that if he is going to marry, he will settle for nothing less than his vision of a perfect wife. He has a never-ending search for the perfect bride. The only problem is that his distorted vision of a perfect wife may not be God's choice for him as his wife. He is drawn to the classified dating personality.

Good-time Charlie Dating

This is typically a charismatic man whose dating focuses on himself, pleasure, and immediate gratification. He medicates his pain with pleasure and he hides his insecurity by being easy-going. His irresponsible actions, uncommitted words, and irrational behaviors are followed by a deep sense of gratitude and sincerity. His inability or unwillingness to develop intimate relationships is rooted in self-centeredness. He is shallow and wants to keep a relationship at a superficial level because he is truly afraid of intimacy. With total disregard toward meeting others' needs, his self-centered focus is on meeting his own needs and whatever makes him feel good.

A single with the good-time Charlie personality is extremely lonely because he never gets past the superficial level in a relationship. He shows signs of emotional immaturity in his interpersonal, professional, and spiritual life. Because he is unable to develop mature, intimate relationships, he seeks worldly alternatives to fill the relational void in his heart. Due to the familiarity of unstable relationships in childhood, he feels most comfortable in a world of unstable relationships. He tends to be attracted to the love bucket dating personality.

Love Bucket Dating

Primarily women fall under the love bucket dating personality. A hole in her love bucket has developed over the years from a lack of affirmation and attention from men, in most cases, her father. No matter how much love she feels from God and others, it is never enough. The love she receives runs out the rusted hole of her heart as fast as it is poured in. In turn, she has a never-ending search for someone to love her. She always enters into a relationship with the expectation that *this* relationship will fill her love bucket. Generally, she mistakes sex and attention for love.

She cannot feel love from and toward God because she is always seeking love from men. Decisions and behaviors are based on the need for love, rather than on following the Lord's direction. Even if a love bucket finds a relationship, the relationship can't fill the hole. Only Christ can. She needs to spend time allowing God to heal her soul. Empty love bucket personalities tend to find good-time Charlies.

Classified Dating

This type is usually a single woman who makes an unrealistic list of whom she will or will not date. This list has little to do with intrinsic or eternal value and has everything to do with external material things. Like a classified ad, she lists items such as a man with an annual income over $75,000, who drives a BMW; is great looking; loves God; and enjoys the outdoors, travel, and intimate conversation. If any man does not meet the criteria, she will not even consider friendship with him. The outcast who doesn't meet the grade is snubbed and brushed aside.

Because she follows the list instead of God, she tends to pass up wonderful Christian friendships that could possibly reveal the one God intends for her to marry. This list generally causes the single to become frustrated because she can't find anyone who matches her criteria. In the end, she is still single into her thirties and forties. At that time, she may become so desperate that she drops all criteria, disregards God, and marries anyone who will marry her. A single person who follows the classified dating pattern tends to be attracted to the perfectionist.

Desperation Dating

Desperation can alter a person's thinking. What causes this desperation? Sometimes it's the ticking of the biological clock. Other times it's the single parent who feels overwhelmed with the financial pressures of life. Or it could be the unbearable pain of loneliness. The desperate single takes the situation out of God's hands and into her own hands.

She focuses on her looks to attract the opposite sex. She tends to compare herself to others. She makes herself too available and will accept unacceptable behavior from her companion. The despair she felt before the relationship began is much greater now that the relationship has failed. A single person who dates out of desperation is attracted to the commit-a-phobic personality.

KEEPING FRIENDSHIPS GODLY

Keeping our friendships godly may not be easy, but we can do it by setting boundaries ahead of time. Seven guidelines for biblically appropriate behavior will help keep our relationships pure at every level of friendship:

1. Keep your friendships inclusive, not exclusive. It's better to go out in a group. If you want to be alone, you're not "just friends" or you want to be something more than friends. "Let us not give up meeting together, as some are in the habit of doing, but let us encourage one another—and all the more as you see the Day approaching" (Hebrews 10:25).

2. Keep your friendships open, not closed. You don't need privacy. If you need to discuss confidential or sensitive subject material, do it in an open place during the day or away from a group of people, but never alone. You can still talk in private within a large group setting. "Woe to those who go to great depths to hide their plans from the LORD, who do their work in darkness and think, 'Who sees us? Who will know?'" (Isaiah 29:15).

3. Keep your friendships shoulder-to-shoulder, not face-to-face. Don't be absorbed in each other; share interests beyond your friendship. "So whether you eat or drink or whatever you do, do it all for the glory of God" (1 Corinthians 10:31).

4. Keep your friendships nonsexual. You don't need to hold hands, put arms around each other, or kiss. Physically treat the other person as you would a same-sex friend or a brother or sister. "Do not rebuke an older man harshly, but exhort him as if he were your father. Treat younger men as brothers, older women as mothers, and younger women as sisters, with absolute purity" (1 Timothy 5:1–2).

5. Keep your talk honoring to God. Flirtatious talk can lead people to think there is something more in the relationship than really exists. "Do not let any unwholesome talk come out of your mouths, but only what is helpful for building others up according to their needs, that it may benefit those who listen" (Ephesians 4:29).

6. Keep track of where you are on the friendship chart. What is the level of your friendship (acquaintance, casual, close, intimate)? If the need arises, discuss your friendship level with the other person in the relationship. "A righteous man is cautious in friendship, but the way of the wicked leads them astray" (Proverbs 12:26).

7. Keep track of how much time you spend together. The time and intensity of the relationship is the best indicator of the level of your friendship. "Whoever obeys his command will come to no harm, and the wise heart will know the proper time and procedure" (Ecclesiastes 8:5).

WHAT DO YOU NEED?

Perhaps you should start now evaluating your friendships in regard to each of the following questions:

- What is the friendship level of this relationship?
- What does the other person in the relationship believe about the friendship level?

- Is there any inappropriate behavior in this relationship?
- What boundaries need to be established?
- What behavior needs to be changed?

If you discover the need for new boundaries in any of your relationships, it may be wise to get another person's point of view and discuss your evaluations with an accountability partner. If there are any red flags or warning signs that will head you off before you career over a cliff in your relationship, this is when they should show up. How well you read the road signs now may dictate the size and significance of any detour that lies ahead.

STUDY AND DISCUSSION QUESTIONS

1. Our overall attitude is more important than any single factor of our behavior. What kind of statement do you make when you walk into a room? What do you think a person observing you would conclude without even speaking to you?

2. The way we talk says a great deal about our values. Coarse talk is common in the world but has no place in the vocabulary of a Christian. How does Ephesians 5:4 describe coarse talk?

3. God made us obviously different as males and females. At the risk of second-guessing God, why do you think He did that? How has it affected your relationships?

4. Have you or has someone close to you had a broken friendship that might have turned out differently if each person had treated the other as a brother or sister? How would you conduct your friendship differently today?

5. Describe a situation in which Person #1 might misinterpret Person #2's intent based on the actions of Person #2.

6. Meditate and memorize: "So whether you eat or drink or whatever you do, do it all for the glory of God" (1 Corinthians 10:31).

Meditate and memorize: "Treat younger men as brothers and older women as mothers, and younger women as sisters, with absolute purity." (1 Timothy 5:1b–2).

7. Pray: My heavenly Father, I desire to live a pure and holy

life which honors You. Help me set appropriate boundaries so that I treat the opposite sex as I would my own siblings. Teach me the differences between men and women so that I might avoid defrauding anyone. Jesus, please bring the friendships into my life that You desire. Thank You for setting the example of friendship by being my Friend, that I might be Your example to others. Amen.

CHAPTER EIGHT

Recognizing God's Voice

Do not be anxious about anything, but in everything, by
prayer and petition, with thanksgiving, present your requests to God.
PHILIPPIANS 4:6

PRINCIPLE FIVE: Submit your will to God in making decisions and ask for nothing more, nothing less, and nothing else but His perfect will.

Scripture is filled with stories of people who heard God calling and, through that calling, followed the Good Shepherd and found the will of God. Jacob met an angel. Joseph had a dream. Paul saw a blinding light. Samuel heard a voice. John had a vision. God spoke to men thousands of years ago and is still doing so today. He has not changed. At every point of history, He waits to show us the way.

The voice of God came to Jesus at all the great moments of His life. It came at His baptism, when He first began the work that God gave Him to do (Mark 1:11). It came on the Mount of Transfiguration, as He again affirmed taking the way that led to Jerusalem and the cross (Mark 9:7); and it came again when the human part of Him needed the strength of the Father to face the ordeal of the cross (John 12:27–34).

"What God did for Jesus, He does for every man," says William Barclay, a profound scholar and world-renowned Scottish interpreter of the New Testament. "When He sends us out upon a road, He does not send us without directions and without guidance.... Our trouble is not that God does not speak, but that we do not listen." The ability of the sheep to know the shepherd is as true today as it was in biblical times.

Somewhere on the road between Carlsbad and Cloudcroft, New Mexico, is a small fruit stand that sells cherry cider and homemade bread. The stand sits in front of a fenced home guarded by an Australian sheep dog. Behind the home are more than 4000 sheep grazing in lush green valleys—the valleys of Rebecca, Jacob, and Joseph.

"We don't use the sheep dog to herd sheep," said the woman working in the fruit stand. "The dog scares the sheep. My daughter's a veterinarian and she's the shepherd. It's just like in the Bible. When she goes to the valley and calls the sheep, they know her voice and they follow her."

The woman was right; it's in the Bible. "My sheep listen to my voice; I know them, and they follow me" (John 10:27). Scripture provides us with a verbal picture of a good shepherd whose sheep hear His voice and who constantly cares for the flock. In fact, we are told that the sheep know and understand the shepherd's voice and will never answer to the voice of a stranger.

In biblical times—and sometimes even today in Palestine—sheep were kept in sheepfolds similar to the corrals where we keep horses today. Many flocks with numerous shepherds often were kept overnight in one sheepfold. How would you separate them the next morning? It was simple. Each shepherd walked to the gate of the sheepfold and called for his own sheep. Only those who were his would walk out the gate with him.

The relationship between sheep and shepherd is and always has been quite different in Palestine than in some other countries. In Britain, sheep are largely kept for butchering; in Palestine they are kept for their wool. As a result, sheep in Palestine are often with the shepherd for years and may even have affectionate names.

In Palestine, the shepherd walks in front of the sheep because the shepherd's job is to make sure the path is safe. And so it is with Jesus. Once we've been called out to follow the Good Shepherd, He does not keep the path a secret or desert us at crucial times. He may not map out the whole journey, but He will always give us knowledge of the next safe step.

ATTUNING YOUR EAR TO GOD'S VOICE

If you have a hard time hearing God's voice, you may be in trouble at the very heart of your Christian experience. Remember, the problem is not that He doesn't speak but that we, for whatever reason, have trouble listening. In other words, there may be a plug in the line. None of us should expect to hear from God until we are fulfilling essential conditions for knowing His will. Check your life against these issues as you ask for God's guidance.

1. Quick Fix vs. Intimacy with God

Your relationship with God is the key to hearing when God speaks to you. There's not a method to follow. The sheep know the shepherd's voice because they spend time with him. A newborn lamb is not nearly as in tune with the shepherd's voice as a sheep who has been with the shepherd for many years. That's why it is so important to develop a oneness with Jesus before trying to determine God's direction for a mate. The object of prayer is intimacy with God, not quick answers. Instead of seeking the God who gives the answers, we often approach Him with an attitude that says, "I've gotta know who to marry and I've gotta know *now!*" The minute the emphasis is on God answering your prayer when and how you want Him to, instead of on your intimacy with God, you've already missed the point! *"I am the vine; you are the branches.* If a man remains in me and I in him, he will bear much fruit; apart from me you can do nothing" (John 15:5, italics added).

2. Don't Ask Unless You're Willing to Accept God's Answer

Don't ask for guidance unless you are prepared to act on it and have a desire to know and do *all* the will of God. God is always willing to make His purpose known, but He will not show you His will if you are merely *considering* doing it. Your heart has to give up any will of its own in regard to the matter. If you can't find an answer, perhaps you have some secret reservation or predetermined choice. As the Lord of your life, God knows how He wants to bless you, what He desires to develop in you, and what He plans to do through your life. It's up to you to come to the place where your own desires are neutral, and you sincerely want only His perfect will. Submit the situation to the Lordship of Jesus and ask for nothing more, nothing less, nothing else than the perfect will of God. You can be stubborn and insist that God give you what you want, but in the end you may not want what you get. "As the heavens are higher than the earth, so are my ways higher than your ways and my thoughts than your thoughts" (Isaiah 55:9).

3. You Can't Expect God to Shout

Quiet is essential to effective listening. You can't jam your mind with carnal influences twelve hours a day and expect God to reveal His plans to you during a commercial. If you're doing all the talking or you're too busy to listen, you probably won't hear what the still, small voice of the Spirit is saying. "Be still, and know that I am God" (Psalm 46:10).

4. Watch Out for a Plug in the Line

If you are passively or openly rebelling against God in some area of your life, you are grieving and quenching the Holy Spirit and putting a plug in the very pipeline God uses to deliver His messages. Two people who are physically involved with each other will have a difficult time discerning God's will when they're disregarding His rules for godly relationships. Guidance always will be hindered or misunderstood if there are still sinful areas in your life that God has urged you to get right. How can He show you more if you have not obeyed the things He has already shown you? (Luke 16:10). Whenever you pray, God's Spirit will point back to that thing He wants you to get right. Unconfessed sin is a prime reason why many do not know God's will. "But your iniquities have separated you from your God; your sins have hidden his face from you, so that he will not hear" (Isaiah 59:2).

5. Be Willing to Be God's Fool

God gave us common sense, and He expects us to use it. Most of the time, His will makes sense to our reason and intelligence, but not always. Sometimes His direction cuts across all human reason, and even goes totally contrary to it. When the inner voice of God speaks clearly, obedience may be counted as madness in the eyes of the world. But if you are willing to be God's fool, then you will see His power. "The man without the Spirit does not accept the things that come from the Spirit of God, for they are foolishness to him, and he cannot understand them" (1 Corinthians 2:14).

6. Feel the Balance between God and the Bible

God's guidance will never go against scriptural principle. The Bible is a record of God's revelation of Himself to man. His will is expressly revealed in His Word. If you look to the Spirit alone for guidance without the Word, you can open yourself up for possible deception. If you look to circumstances alone without the Word, you can be deceived. In seeking God's direction, check to see that prayer, Scripture, circumstances, and the counsel of other believers agree in the direction you sense God leading you. You can't see the agreement if you have no time for prayer and Bible study and the only advice you're getting is from nonbelievers. "Come, let us go up to the mountain of the LORD…He will teach us his ways, so that we may walk in his paths" (Micah 4:2).

WHAT DOES GOD SOUND LIKE?

God speaks in all sorts of ways. Sometimes He reveals His will to us by an impression. Sometimes He speaks by an inner voice. Sometimes we can hear Him speaking through the voice of a stranger, a friend, the words of a song, a thought from a book, a verse of Scripture. God has no special formula or method for communicating with His people, but His guidance can be broken down into three general categories: personal, corporeal and supernatural.

Personal Guidance (Individual and Direct)

God Communicates through His Word. God sometimes communicates to us when we meditate on His Word. The original Hebrew rendering of "meditate" carries the word picture of a cow chewing its cud, just as the modern word implies gradually breaking a thought down, working it over and over in your mind. When we meditate on Scripture—consider it, reconsider it, digest it, and apply it to our lives—God's Word permeates our very beings and we begin to see our situation from God's viewpoint. Once we glimpse our lives from God's viewpoint, we begin to desire the things that God desires. Then it is easy for Him to give us the desires of our hearts (Psalm 37:4).

God's Word has basic principles we can follow for guidance and direction in determining His will for us in selecting a mate. For example, Scripture specifically warns against marrying a nonbeliever. "Do not be yoked together with unbelievers. For what do righteousness and wickedness have in common? Or what fellowship can light have with darkness?" (2 Corinthians 6:14). That is God's direction, and He will never reveal something contrary to His Word. If you receive a message that does not agree perfectly with the Word of God, disregard it because God never contradicts His Word (Psalm 119:4–5, 24).

Sometimes during prayer or a time of temptation and difficulty, God will bring to mind a verse of Scripture that gives you clear instruction (2 Timothy 3:14–17). In your spirit you know the verse is God's communication to you. You know that you know. And at other times you might find a verse that "fits" like the missing piece to a puzzle—the piece that reveals the whole picture.

Unfortunately, some sincere believers have concluded that when the Bible was completed, God's communication to us also was completed. They believe we should receive every message from God *only* through the Scriptures. This view underestimates how strongly God desires to be involved in our lives, and it certainly fails to take into account centuries of Christians who have experienced God speaking in many different ways.

God Communicates through the Witness of the Holy Spirit.
The Holy Spirit will tell you whatever He hears from the Father,
and He will glorify Jesus (John 16:13–14). "The Spirit himself tes-
tifies with our spirit" (Romans 8:16). In the Old Testament, the
presence of the Holy Spirit was selective and temporary. The
anointing was given as a temporary gift to provide God's power
and direction in some area of service. The Spirit never indwelt a
person permanently and could be withdrawn (1 Samuel 16:14).
After Pentecost, however, the Holy Spirit became universal and
permanent among believers.

Before the turn of the twentieth century, Amy Carmichael traveled to India as a missionary. She stayed there until her death in
1951. Amy was a single woman in her twenties when God began
to use her to save thousands of young girls from cult prostitution
in Hindu temples. In her book *Chance to Die,* Elisabeth Elliot
recounts the story of a time on the mission field when Amy heard
the inaudible inner voice of God.

> Amy described for one of her "children" a transaction that
> had taken place when she was alone in a cave in Arima.
> Having gone there to spend a day in solitude, she faced
> with God feelings of fear about the future. Loneliness hov-
> ered like a specter on the horizon. Things were all right at
> the moment, but could she endure years of being alone?
> The devil painted pictures of loneliness which were vivid
> to her many years later, and she turned to the Lord in des-
> peration. What can I do, Lord? How can I go on to the
> end? His answer: "None of them that trust in Me shall be
> desolate."[1]

The voice of the Good Shepherd is gentle, familiar sounding,
and loving. It leaves you with a sense of spiritual uplift and rejoicing, never fright (John 10:3–5, 14–16, 27–28). It doesn't make
you feel worried or afraid. The still, small voice of the Holy
Spirit—an inner voice—is able to "check" you inside as to
whether something is of God. As you are praying along a certain

line and contemplating what to do, if there is a check in your spirit—a "something on the inside" that tells you not to do a certain thing—that is the inward witness of the Holy Spirit. You must never act on a doubtful impression, especially if it is accompanied by haste. God leads, but Satan pushes. Rushed urgings are usually of the enemy. God's Spirit may "hound" you ("the Hound of Heaven") in terms of softly and repeatedly bringing something to mind, but be suspicious of anything that makes you feel driven or in any way obsessed.

God's Voice...	Satan's Voice...
• Stills you	• Rushes you
• Leads you	• Pushes you
• Reassures you	• Frightens you
• Enlightens you	• Confuses you
• Encourages you	• Discourages you
• Comforts you	• Worries you
• Calms you	• Obsesses you
• Convicts you	• Condemns you

God Communicates by "Engineering Our Circumstances."
God often speaks to us in the language of our circumstances, but it takes discernment and wisdom to determine if these circumstances are intended to give godly direction. Something will happen and we'll say, "I wonder if that's the voice of God." Oswald Chambers says that a Christian must always remember "that nothing touches our lives except that God allows it and speaks through it." He calls it "God engineering our circumstances." We must constantly be trying to discern God's voice in the circumstances of our daily lives and asking ourselves, "What really is happening here and what does this circumstance mean?" But remember, Satan also tries to use circumstances to give his direction and tempt us away from God's path.

Have you ever prayed, "God, if You want me to do this, then You open the door. If You don't, then You shut it"? Putting all the responsibility on God is a lot easier than waiting on God to let us know the answer through His Holy Spirit. Sometimes it takes periods of waiting to hear the inward witness of the Holy Spirit. Circumstances cannot always be a clear indication of God's leadership, and "opened" and "closed" doors are not always God directing us. Prayer, Scripture, circumstances, and the counsel of other believers must agree in the direction we sense God leading us. If we are too impatient and self-willed to wait on God, we may find ourselves running dangerously ahead of God's guidance.

Corporeal Communication (Other Christians)

God Communicates through Godly Men and Women. Counsel from those you know to have a pure and trustworthy walk with God is invaluable when you're moving toward a major decision (Proverbs 12:15; 15:22; 1 Thessalonians 2:13). Advice from mature Christians should confirm a message God has already given you, not send you off in a new direction. You can hear a confirming voice through another person. Still, if God has something important to tell you, He will speak to you directly.

A fundamental premise of courtship is the need for the guiding counsel of a parent or some other godly person. This counsel should affirm what the voice of God is telling you, not dictate whom you should marry. Counsel from others should be more in the area of principles, not pronouncements. Concerned and loving suggestions aren't necessarily final or direct statements from the Lord. But true godly counsel will always line up with the Word of God and scriptural principles. If it brings confusion, condemnation, or discouragement, disregard the word because it didn't come from God (1 Corinthians 14:33; James 3:17–18).

Some believe that parents, regardless of whether they are Christians, have a chain of command or authority to decree God's will for their child's marriage partner. "Children, obey your parents in the Lord, for this is right" (Ephesians 6:1). The Greek word for "children," *ta tena,* denotes a young child, not an adult son or daughter. Therefore, seek the counsel and direction of your parents but have faith in the Lord. If you have non-Christian parents, they may not know the will of God, but God has the power to work through them in your behalf.

God Communicates through His Servants in the Ministry. Just as the prophets of the Old Testament once heard "the voice of the Lord" and spoke "the word of the Lord" to the people, God has called certain people today to speak for Him. Sometimes God will use a message or sermon anointed by the Holy Spirit to bring needed light when you are facing a difficult decision (Isaiah 6:8–10; 1 Corinthians 2:1–5). The same cautions that were mentioned above in seeking advice from mature Christians also must be used in confirming counsel from servants in the ministry. Scripture does not indicate that a pastor, church elders, or spiritual leaders have prerogative to dictate to those under them in personal decisions, especially in regard to marriage. Seek the counsel of those whom God has placed in authority over you, but seek the Lord first. Once again, counsel from servants in the ministry should confirm the direction God has given you, not necessarily give you an entirely new direction.

God Communicates through the Gifts of the Holy Spirit. Scripture records incidents when God confirmed direction through such gifts in His body as prophecy, words of knowledge, and words of wisdom. Study their functions in Scripture. Such words are simply spiritual parallels to individual, godly counsel and preached messages. They should not be looked on with more authority than any of the other means the Lord chooses to use. Never act solely on a "word" given to you by another. (Romans 12:6–8; 1 Corinthians 12:1–12). Someone with a special gift of prophecy or a word of knowledge for you may believe they are able to tell you whom God wants you to marry, even though they may not be related to you, be in any special position of spiritual authority, or be a previous acquaintance. Be cautious with any individual who prophesies over you. In Scripture, counsel or guidance is never indicated as one of the uses of prophecy. Prophecy should not be used to give you direction but only to confirm what you have come to believe is God's direction for your life.

Supernatural Communication

Cases of "supernatural" guidance or special divine intervention are rare, but they do happen. They are rare not because only a few people ever reach the "exalted height" of such direct contact. Instead, God may sometimes choose to act in this way because those on the receiving end may be so spiritually insensitive and dull at the time that they might never hear or understand without God's direct intervention.

The Audible Voice of God. God has spoken to people audibly. Just as He spoke to Saul on the road to Damascus (Acts 9:1–7) and to Jesus in front of a crowd of witnesses (John 12:27–30), God's voice can come as an audible sound, not just a mental impression.

Peter Marshall, a Scottish preacher who eventually became chaplain of the U.S. Senate, heard God's audible voice one black, moonless night when he took a shortcut home across a desolate moor. Marshall heard someone call his name, not once but twice. He stopped dead still, stumbled, and fell to his knees. Feeling around in a semicircle in the darkness, he found himself on the brink of an abandoned stone quarry. One more step would have sent him plummeting to certain death. Marshall never doubted the source of that voice and always felt that God must have had a great purpose for his life to have intervened so specifically. Many years later, Marshall's significant accomplishments were depicted in the popular Hollywood movie *A Man Called Peter.*

Visions and Dreams. A dream is like a spiritual TV commercial— short and presented at a time when our whole attention can focus on it (in our sleep). Visions, on the other hand, are superimposed over the normal visual reality around us and do not happen when we are asleep. If you believe that God may be trying to speak to you in one of these ways, prayerfully consider the details of your dream or vision and remember they may represent symbols or principles, not necessarily absolutes. Once again, remember that the voice of the Good Shepherd doesn't make you feel worried or afraid. If you experience a vision or dream that brings confusion, condemnation, or discouragement, disregard it as not coming from God. As you read earlier, God's communication will leave you with a sense of spiritual uplift, not a feeling of fright (Isaiah 6:1–8; Matthew 1:19–21; Acts 10:9–16).

A word of warning: It's easy to become fascinated with the "special cases" and exalt these above the simple and ordinary ways God speaks to us. On the other hand, it's also easy to be skeptical of supernatural guidance and deny its existence because of our own lack of experience with the supernatural. That would be similar to someone saying love doesn't exist simply because they've never been in love.

To deliberately seek or glorify any form of guidance is an outright invitation to spiritual deception. The minute you start to specify how you want to hear from God—such as "putting out a fleece"—you open yourself up to being deceived by the Enemy, who also speaks in the same spiritual sphere and dimension as the voice of the Holy Spirit.

We are not to seek or specify *how* God should speak, but only seek Him in any way that He wishes to make Himself known. The *relationship* is the key to knowing God's voice and hearing when He speaks. Asking God for a sign is often an indication of unbelief. Sometimes in Scripture God did give a miraculous sign to assure people that the word they heard was from Him. One example is in Judges 6, where by setting out a fleece of wool, Gideon sees a sign that God will protect him in battle against the Midianites. At other times, Jesus condemned the scribes and Pharisees as a "wicked and adulterous generation" when they asked for a miraculous sign. It may be important to remember that Mary was the only example in the New Testament of a marriage decision based on a supernatural occurrence.

Identifying God's Voice

There's a very fine line between the real and the false, between reality and fanaticism. It's easy to step across that line and cause damage. While some people have rejected the miraculous ways of God and become dry and dead in their spiritual lives, other Christians have gone to the opposite extreme and accepted anything. They have followed what they call "the Spirit" and left the Word.

By learning how to identify God's voice, we can increase our degree of certainty and sift through all the conflicting voices that often keep us confused and frustrated. The following points are briefly summarized from a more lengthy discussion in Charles Stanley's book *How to Listen to God*.

•God's voice often conflicts with the world's reasoning. Although there are exceptions, when God requires something of us, it usually clashes with what the world considers to be the natural, reasonable course of action. Jesus said that when a man strikes you on one cheek, you should turn the other (Matthew 5:39). If someone wants you to go one mile, you should go two. Jesus usually did the opposite of what people expected, and on occasion He may ask us to do something that seems illogical to our rational minds.

•God's voice will clash with our fleshly nature. God will never tell us to do anything that gratifies the flesh. If what we hear urges us to gratify the flesh, forget what anyone else says, and do as we please, it isn't God. He doesn't speak in those terms. God calls us to listen to a voice that always seeks the benefit of others as well as ourselves.

•God's voice considers the effects on other people. If there is a harshness or crudeness toward others in what we hear, it is not from God. Satan's evil spirits tell us that we can do what we want and shouldn't worry about the rippling effects of our lives on other people. In contrast, God has not only our best interests in mind but also the good of all concerned.

•God's voice is patient, not rushed. Nowhere in Scripture does God tell us to rush into a decision. Though there may be times when we need to hear from God quickly, He will never tell us to rush in blindly. In contrast, Satan's deceiving spirits always encourage us to act immediately because he knows if we back off to think and pray long enough, we'll reconsider.

•**God's voice always considers the consequences.** Satan's deceiving spirits tell us to "move on, go ahead, make the decision, don't worry about the consequences." God, however, is always interested in the ramifications of our actions. Whenever God speaks, He has our future in mind and He will cause each of us to ask, "If I make this decision, what will happen to my family, my job, and my walk with God?"

•**God's voice is not discerned by nonbelievers.** When God leads us to seek counsel from another person, He wants us to check out the lifestyle of that person. Why should a believer go to a nonbeliever to get advice that will affect his life? If the Holy Spirit is the phone line to God, seeking advice from nonbelievers would be like cutting the phone line before you tried to call home.

•**God's voice will bring peace to our spirits.** When God speaks, one of the most prevalent signs is a sense of calmness in the spirit. It may not be tranquil at first. In fact, it may be full of conflict and strife, but the longer we listen, the quieter and more peaceful our spirits become. We will never have God's peace about disobedience. We may be able to believe with our minds, but we will never be able to believe with our spirit and exercise faith.[2]

THE ACID TEST

Read the last paragraph of the previous section one more time— the part about having peace in your spirit. It's the most important way you can identify God's guiding voice. If a word seems right and agrees with the Word of God but you have no inner peace, wait for God's further guidance. "Let the peace of Christ rule in your hearts" (Colossians 3:15).

The New Testament use of the word "rule" literally means "to function like an umpire." The attitude of peace that only Christ gives is to rule in your relationships. Learn to let the presence or absence of the peace of God in your heart be the umpire of your human relationships. Satan's evil spirits and your flesh can speak to you and even quote Scripture, but neither one can counterfeit

God's deep, settled peace. "And the peace of God, which transcends all understanding, will guard your hearts and your minds in Christ Jesus" (Philippians 4:7).

What Happens When Nothing Happens

If God speaks and you hear but do not respond, a time could come when you will not hear His voice. Disobedience can lead to a "famine of hearing the words of the LORD" (Amos 8:11). But God could have other reasons for His silence in a person's life.

One of the reasons God doesn't tell us some things instantaneously is that we're not always ready. He may be withholding information until we are prepared to listen. In the process of waiting, He changes us and prepares us to hear His message. Oswald Chambers calls this "the discipline of darkness." The nation of Israel knew they were headed for the Promised Land, but they did not know where they were going from day to day. "By day the LORD went ahead of them in a pillar of cloud to guide them on their way and by night in a pillar of fire to give them light, so that they could travel by day or night" (Exodus 13:21).

God is not compelled to tell us everything we want to know the moment we desire the information. Revelation is a progressive process, and God reveals only as much as a person can understand. We do not start with advanced theorems when we want to teach a child simple arithmetic. God teaches people what they are able and fit to learn at the moment.

God's timing, especially His delays, may make us think He is not answering—or at least not answering the way we want. But God is always on time. Even though He doesn't hurry, He's never a minute too late. When Lazarus's sisters sent a message to Jesus telling Him their brother was sick, they expected Him to come immediately. Instead, He waited two days. By the time He got there, Lazarus was dead and in the tomb. Jesus raised Lazarus from the dead, but His delay had a specific purpose. And so it is with us. We must wait patiently for God's timing and know that He will meet all our needs according to His perfect schedule and purpose. We must accept by faith that "wait" *is* an answer from

God and that He has a reason for requiring our patience. Like the sisters of Lazarus, sometimes we must experience a death to our own vision before we can catch a glimpse of God's perfect plan.

THE BOTTOM LINE

There is a bottom line to hearing God speak. *The ability to hear God's voice comes from an intimate love relationship with God.* The key to recognizing His voice doesn't come neatly packaged in a twelve-step plan. That's why those who do not have the relationship do not hear what God is saying.

Remember the 4000 sheep from the beginning of the chapter, the ones in the valleys of Rebecca, Jacob, and Joseph? Those three valleys have those names because in each valley there is a mature sheep with that name. God can make Himself available to every person, but the New Mexico veterinarian who cares for those sheep doesn't have time to have a personal relationship with every lamb in the field. Instead, she has cultivated a relationship with the lead sheep, and their names are Rebecca, Jacob, and Joseph. The young lambs will follow the mature sheep, and the mature sheep will follow the shepherd. The stragglers who wander off are the ones most likely to be caught by coyotes and mountain lions.

You have the opportunity to know the Good Shepherd in such an intimate way that eventually you will learn to know and recognize His voice. While that love relationship is developing, you may need the wise counsel of "mature sheep"—those who have walked with God over a long period of time. Then one day when you least expect it, you may find that you've become the one with the enduring relationship that has stood the test of time. You will be the mature sheep in someone else's life, and those lambs may very well be your own children.

The ability to know and discern the Shepherd's voice can only occur if Jesus Christ lives in your heart. If you believe Jesus Christ is not Lord of your life, take a moment to ask God through prayer to forgive you of your sins and give Him control of your heart and life. Then you will be able to truly hear, understand, and receive God's direction for your life and direction toward a future mate.

STUDY AND DISCUSSION QUESTIONS

1. What does John 8:47 say about a person who does not hear what God says?

2. Explain how your lifestyle can affect your spiritual hearing. What "hearing aid" changes can you make in your life to hear God's voice more clearly?

3. If Satan can counterfeit almost any good thing, what can he not do that will help you identify his interference in your life? How can knowing this affect your decisions?

4. In what specific ways would marriage between two believers be different from marriage between a believer and a nonbeliever?

5. If you are dating a non-Christian now, answer the following questions honestly from your own heart:

- Is this relationship causing you to disobey God's commands?
- Are you closer to God today than you were before the relationship?
- Are there changes God wants you to make in this relationship?

6. Meditate and memorize: "My sheep listen to my voice; I know them, and they follow me" (John 10:27).

7. Pray: My heavenly Father, I desire to follow Your perfect will in every aspect of my life. Reveal to me anything in my life that hinders me from hearing Your voice. Deepen my desire to spend time with You in prayer that I might pray without ceasing. Develop in me patience when I don't hear an answer, or when Your answer is "Wait." Jesus, increase my longing for an intimate love relationship with You. Amen.

CHAPTER NINE

Becoming Accountable

The way of a fool seems right to him, but a wise man listens to advice.
PROVERBS 12:15

PRINCIPLE SIX: Have an accountability couple (parents, another godly couple, or both) oversee your courtship to provide protection, correction, and direction.

Picture yourself driving around a bend in the road when you see men frantically waving red flags and yelling, "The bridge is out! Go back!" You'd never keep going in such a hazardous circumstance. Yet many people essentially drive on in their dating relationships when they disregard the warnings of family and friends who see trouble ahead. Ignoring their warnings is not only arrogant but also dangerous. You could soon find yourself careening over a cliff into an abyss of pain and wondering how you got there.

One of the major differences between dating and courtship is the accountability factor. Accountability means being willing to have others hold you answerable and accountable for your actions. It means being open to direction and counsel. While dating avoids accountability like the plague, courtship embraces it like a vaccine. The result is protection from the epidemic of divorce and pain that plague our nation.

Listening to advice from people who care about you shouldn't be difficult, but for some people it's a huge stumbling block. They're usually the same ones who won't stop at service stations and ask for directions. In her bestselling book *You Just Don't Understand,* Deborah Tannen proposes that men hate to ask for directions because it humiliates their egos.

"When you offer information," she writes, "the information itself is the message.... If relations are inherently hierarchical, then the one who has more information is framed as higher up on the ladder by virtue of being more knowledgeable and competent."[1]

Tannen says the person who gives the information "sends out a metamessage of superiority." Does seeking and receiving advice from others, especially our own parents, somehow make us feel inferior and less capable? Do pride and ego block our ability to accept counsel and direction?

Accountability doesn't mean being dominated by authority but rather receiving the protection of authority. "Plans fail for lack of counsel, but with many advisers they succeed" (Proverbs 15:22). "Listen to your father, who gave you life, and do not despise your mother when she is old" (Proverbs 23:22). Even if you are a thirty-five-year-old single adult, it's still important to listen to your parents and their counsel. Your loved ones want your happiness as much or more than you do.

Usually it's best if the accountability comes from your own parents, particularly your father, but if that's not possible, then church leaders or a godly couple should fill the gap. The major roles of the person or couple holding you accountable should be threefold:

1. Express affirmation or concern about your choice of a partner in a courtship.
2. Oversee the courtship process in your life.

3. Become accountable for the spiritual, emotional, and physical progress of your courtship.

Although you ultimately are responsible for your own marriage and must be totally free to make the final choice, much of the wisdom of your decision is dependent on the accuracy of your information. Because there is so much to know and learn about yourself and another person, you need help in the awareness process. We all have blind spots in regard to ourselves or another person that are invisible to us. We need other people to point out the problem areas that we might otherwise overlook or minimize.

When the Bible says "a wise man listens to advice" (Proverbs 12:15), notice that the writer says "listens" instead of a variety of other word choices such as "takes," "heeds," or "follows." In other words, you are accumulating information, not receiving marching orders. You are to make a wise decision based on the best, most accurate information available. But the decision is yours.

When your own pride and ego keep you from seeking advice ("this is my decision, not theirs"), then the problem actually is much larger than you think. Too much pride also will keep you from hearing the counsel of God because "God opposes the proud" (James 4:6). The Bible says that God dwells with the humble (Isaiah 57:15) and they are in constant contact with Him. The humble know when He speaks and are quick to obey. If God chooses to delay, waiting is not difficult for the humble.

Proud people work on their own initiative. They want to obey only their own self-exalting impulses. Humility, on the other hand, sees the value of the larger group, the church, or the family unit. Pride sees only the individual. If you truly want God's direction, favor, and blessing in the selection of a lifetime partner, you cannot seek Him at the same time you pridefully ignore the counsel of those He put in authority over you.

COURTSHIP PROCESS	Phase 5: Courtship and Accountability
SPIRITUAL Commitment	Begin the process of becoming one spiritually. Spend one-on-one time together through shared prayer time and church attendance. Commit your courtship to glorifying Christ and helping each other grow in Christ.
EMOTIONAL Commitment	Begin pre-engagement counseling. Seek your parents (or other godly counsel) to hold each other accountable. Discuss and write down boundaries and limits of relationship. Increase one-on-one emotional time together.
PHYSICAL Commitment	Side hugs, holding hands, and short kisses. Only limited cuddling.
Time Alone	80 Hours

Blind Spots and Red Flags

In my private practice as a psychotherapist, I met this week with three couples who are engaged or want to be engaged, but whose parents won't bless their marriages. This isn't uncommon for couples who date. A tragic split often exists between parents and singles over marriage plans because the couple did not receive the parents' blessings at the beginning of the dating relationship. Courtship avoids this painful situation by obtaining a blessing from both sets of parents *before* the courtship begins.

Have you ever wondered why parents of the bride and groom are given special seating at the wedding? It's not because they're paying for the celebration but because they are part of the marriage covenant. The commitments they make during the ceremony are just as binding as the vows of the couple. The final responsibility of parents for their sons and daughters is to determine with them God's will for a life partner. Afterwards, the parents serve in a chain of counsel for their children and grandchildren. As a result, the parents enter a wedding ceremony in the line of authority, but they leave in the line of counsel.

Why does the father walk the bride down the aisle? Because the father is saying to his daughter, "I am endorsing this man as God's very best choice of a husband for you, and I am now bringing you to him." And why does the minister look into the crowd and say, "Who gives this woman to be married to this man?" Because that question and its response symbolizes not only the full blessing of the parents but also the transfer of responsibility to the groom by the father. A daughter is under the authority, protection, and responsibility of her father until she is married (Numbers 30:3–5). It is, therefore, the father who transfers this responsibility to the groom.

We make a mistake when we start thinking that we're the only ones involved in a marriage decision. We forget that a new partner affects everyone's life in both families. And so does a divorce. Sometimes we may find ourselves thinking, "Why shouldn't I do as I please, as long as it doesn't hurt anyone else." The truth is that whether we are young or old, we cannot do as we please and not hurt other people in the process. Scripture continually insists on the principle of our connectedness as a fact of human life: "So in Christ we who are many form one body, and each member belongs to all the others" (Romans 12:5).

When Isaac took Rebekah for his wife (Genesis 24), he wasn't the only one involved in the selection process. A trusted servant and a devoted father also played a vital part in bringing Rebekah and Isaac together. The father, Abraham, had a lot at stake in terms of whom his son would marry. His grandchildren would be the next link in a long chain of descendants that God had promised would be a blessing to all nations of the earth. Just as it was for Abraham and all the generations that would follow him, each of us is linked to previous generations behind us. Our ancestors are in our genes, in our bones, in our marrow, in our physiological and emotional makeup. We, in turn, will be written into the children who come after us.

In biblical times, a son's wife was usually chosen by the parents. Abraham followed the custom of the day when he sent his oldest, most trusted servant to look for a wife for Isaac. When Eliezer arrived in Abraham's homeland, he went straight to a spring to wait for the women of the town to come draw water. While he prayed for guidance, the Bible says Rebekah appeared before Eliezer had even finished praying.

During Eliezer's prayer, he submitted a plan to God. Instead of asking God to send a woman with beauty or wealth, he asked for a woman who would offer water to his camels. Was it a strange request? No, it was a wise strategy. Eliezer was looking for a woman with an attitude of true service, someone who would go beyond the expected. An offer to water his ten camels would indicate that kind of service attitude. It takes thirty gallons of water to satisfy a single camel, and the pots used for carrying water were large and heavy. Scripture says he even watched to see if she would finish the job (Genesis 24:21). Eliezer was looking for someone with a heart for doing more than was expected. God provided that person and so much more.

Unlike in the time of Abraham, most of you won't have your parents choose your mate. But some things don't change with time. Your parents and others who care about you will be watching to see the heart attitude of the person you bring home. You may be caught up in the romance of the relationship, but those around you will be watching at the spring to see signs of godly character and spiritual maturity. Their red flags will be your protection against your own blind spots.

THE QUESTIONS MOST ASKED

Answers to these frequently asked questions will explain some of the most important guidelines for the role of an accountability couple:

Question: When does accountability start?
Answer: Today wouldn't be too soon. That's why you'll find accountability listed in chapter 6 as one of the nine practical preparations you should make *before* marriage. In fact, accountability is so important that it should become a part of your life *regardless* of marriage. It's a crucial factor in keeping you from leading a double life—the one you live on Sunday and the one you're tempted to live the rest of the time.

A key element that keeps you from rationalizing unbiblical behavior is to develop accountability for yourself. Because keeping yourself accountable doesn't come naturally, you have to put an accountability structure in place through a friend, pastor, small group, married couple, or family member. By being open and honest with this person or group of people, you willingly allow them to serve as a roadblock to you if they see you moving in a dangerous or destructive direction. The enemy's evil spirits always attack from the back, unexpectedly and unseen. An accountability partner serves as the wing man who watches your backside.

Question: Why do you keep referring to an accountability *couple*? Does it have to be two people?

Answer: You don't have to have a couple to hold you accountable, but it's especially advisable when you are searching for a mate and approaching a courtship period in your life. As we said earlier, if at all possible the accountability should come through your own parents, and in particular your father as the spiritual head of the home. Because your courtship partner should be spending almost as much time with your accountability couple as with you, it would be complicated and ill advised if your accountability partner is the same sex as your courtship partner. It's also better if the accountability couple is older and spiritually more mature.

If you're a single man, for instance, it's not enough just to have another single man from your Bible study be your accountability partner. Would you want another man your own age spending a large amount of time alone with the girl you want to marry? Many potential relationship problems are eliminated when an older man and woman serve as your accountability couple.

If you grew up in a dysfunctional home, choosing a godly couple as accountability partners will provide a good opportunity to see a godly family and observe how a healthy Christian home functions before you establish your own home.

Question: How do I approach someone with this accountability idea?

Answer: Start with your parents first. If you have Christian parents but they're unfamiliar with courtship, give them this book to read and ask them if they will accept the parental role in courtship. If they accept, pray together and begin to discuss the courtship process. If your Christian parents are already familiar with and trained in courtship principles, stop and thank God for His grace in your life.

For singles whose parents are not believers, you still should honor them by explaining the courtship process and asking if they will accept the parental role in courtship. If they accept, pray that God will speak through them. God can and will use even unbelieving parents to provide guidance in the courtship process. Try to see this as a great opportunity to minister to your unbelieving parents. Not only are you honoring God by honoring your parents, but your nonbelieving parents also will have a front-row seat to see God's will unfolding in your life.

It's a sign of maturity when a person sincerely seeks advice, counsel, and direction. Most parents and in-laws will be pleased to see you do this. Because your parents do have caretaking responsibilities toward you, it should set their minds and hearts at ease that you want them to know what you are doing and that you are interested in their input and blessing.

Depending on how well you listen to and follow their advice, you will be establishing with your parents and in-laws a base for open communication in the future. More than that, by discussing these issues with both sets of parents, you and your future spouse will be strengthening your commitment to each other and your intention to fulfill your responsibilities to one another.

If your parents won't accept the parental role in courtship or if an extreme case of parent/child abuse makes their involvement impossible, ask God to give you direction in finding a godly married couple to perform the parental role. The church should fill the void when a father or mother is not available. Look for a godly couple to serve as "surrogate" parents, a couple that has a successful marriage and is gifted in wisdom and discernment.

Question: What if a person's parents are dead or they live too far away to spend time with the single couple?

Answer: If your father is deceased, go to your mother and ask her to fill your father's accountability role. If both are deceased, seek the Lord about finding a godly man and his wife to assume an accountability role during the courtship process.

If your father is in a different geographical location, discuss the issue with him and ask him what he would like you to do. If at all possible, your father and mother should stay involved in your courtship process regardless of the miles that separate you. But it is still wise to have an accountability couple in the same town. In fact, you should encourage your parents and your "surrogate" parents (accountability couple) to discuss their roles with each other by phone. When your parents live far away, it's important that your potential mate meet your parents before the courtship begins or at least talk to them on the phone.

Ruth is an excellent example of a single who did not have her parents for counsel in a courtship. So she sought counsel in a godly older woman, her mother-in-law, Naomi. Naomi said, "My daughter, should I not try to find a home for you, where you will be well provided for?" Ruth said, "I will do whatever you say" (Ruth 3:1–5). After she endured tragedy in her life, the Lord provided Ruth (through the counsel of Naomi) a godly husband, Boaz.

A family or families in the church should "adopt" singles as their own, just as Naomi did when she took Ruth with her from Moab. Married couples in the church should look upon this as their responsibility—a calling from God. If widows may be cared for by the church (1 Timothy 5), single women in particular should be cared for by the church. These principles need to be adopted not only by individuals, but by individual churches.

Question: If singles have been out of the house and living on their own for many years, is it still necessary to seek the advice and blessing of their parents?
Answer: The principle we mentioned earlier of having someone watch your backside for evil attacks applies regardless of whether a person lives with his parents or alone. Everyone has blind spots and everyone needs help to see problem areas that we tend to overlook or minimize. In most cases, no one knows you better or wants what is best for you more than your own parents, regardless of how long you've been gone from home.

Question: What specifically does an accountability couple do?
Answer: If the whole point of accountability is to be open and honest with another person and be receptive to their advice and insights, then this will require you to initiate opportunities for your accountability couple to spend time with the person you hope to marry. You must include your potential mate in many of

the normal activities of home life with your parents or accountability couple (for example, eating meals together, family time, ministry involvement, entertain together, attending church, working in the yard, washing dishes). In a similar fashion, your parents or "surrogate" parents would commit themselves to initiating opportunities to be with you and your potential mate.

In addition, the single man should ask the parents and/or "surrogate" parents to hold him accountable in the following areas:

- Commitment level at each stage of the courtship.
- Time limits at each stage of the courtship.
- Spiritual involvement at each stage of the courtship.
- Emotional involvement at each stage of the courtship.
- Physical involvement at each stage of the courtship.

The single man and woman should discuss each of these areas and determine what boundaries they want on their relationship in each category. When they have agreed on the boundaries and limits, they should write them down and make a commitment to live within the agreement. Then they should pray with their accountability couple to confirm their commitment to follow these areas before God. The accountability couple has the permission of both singles to hold them accountable to these commitments.

Before you plunge into courtship accountability, let me give one last word of caution. The parents or "surrogate" parents holding you accountable are not to tell you whom you must marry, but rather affirm what God has already told you. God will speak to you about the purpose and direction of the courtship before He speaks to anyone else.

Question: When should accountability end?
Answer: Never. Accountability should start today and continue throughout your life. Every couple needs guidance, even after the honeymoon. Within the first ninety days after their wedding, most marriages begin to plant their dysfunctional roots. An accountability couple must be right by your side for encouragement, support,

and direction. Through the counsel and guidance of the accountability couple, the roots of marital disharmony can be pulled up without taking hold and causing future damage in your marriage.

An accountability couple can be a wonderful resource for things to come. They can give you invaluable guidance in child rearing, finances, career, ministry choices, and interpersonal relationships, just to name a few. For some young couples whose parents are deceased, the accountability couple can become the parents they no longer have. If your parents are not Christian, the accountability couple can be an example of a godly home and a source of godly parental counsel.

SOLVING THE IN-LAW PROBLEM

Every week I meet with parents who are not happy with the mate their child has chosen. Many of these dating couples did not try to receive their parents' blessing for their selection of a mate until after the engagement. In fact, many times the parents first hear about their child's engagement "through the grapevine." Could this be the cause of many of our in-law problems?

The dating process naturally excludes parents from any type of involvement in the shaping of the relationship. Most of the time the parents don't get involved because they are afraid they might offend their child, or even worse, be seen as being old-fashioned or nosy. But dating couples who do not receive the blessing from their parents risk permanent relational damage in their families. Families can be divided for years to come, not to mention extreme tension during special family get-togethers.

Courtship, on the other hand, places the blessing at the initial steps of the courtship process. As soon as possible, the couple should ask for a blessing and, if appropriate, a blessing should be given to the couple. This process develops strong in-law relationships and avoids parents threatening not to come to a wedding because they do not like whom you have chosen for a mate. Countless numbers of in-law problems could be avoided if the blessing had been received at the beginning of the courtship, not at the end of the dating relationship.

THE PARENTS' PERSPECTIVE

What should the parents do if the couple does not seek a blessing or, even worse, goes against their counsel and marries? Before the marriage, share with a loving heart how you honestly feel. Be bold, firm, straightforward, and sincere. On one hand, remember that this is a very emotional time for the couple who are thinking from their feelings. Lovingly guide them to seek the Lord in their decision and seek other counsel if they will not listen to you.

After the marriage, you must support this couple 100 percent even if the couple married against your wishes. This may be difficult for parents who affectionately poured their life into their child only to see rebellion, disrespect, and dishonor. If this is the case, parents may first need to confess any anger or hatred they may have toward the individuals or the couple. Then the parents need to spend time with the Lord asking for His healing and love for this couple.

The last step is the most important. God reconciled with us through Jesus' death on the cross. Reconciliation between the parents and the couple is not only imperative for the blessing of future generations, but it is also essential in our walk with the Lord. It is difficult to feel the love, peace, and joy of the Lord when there is division in your family. Receive and give the blessing at the beginning of the courtship and avoid the pain of division and separation from your loved ones.

STAYING OUT OF TROUBLE

Other than your own intimate love relationship with God, nothing will keep you out of relational trouble better than having someone hold you accountable for your words, actions, and intentions. Most singles, especially men, don't like accountability in relationships because it means the secret sins they have committed in the relationship will be brought into God's light and someone else will know (Psalm 90:8). It will be almost impossible to be defrauded or to defraud another person if you are submitting to the wisdom and counsel of an older, godly couple. That fact alone will save you immense pain and make the whole process worthwhile beyond measure.

STUDY AND DISCUSSION QUESTIONS

1. As you've watched your friends date, marry, or break up, what "blind spots" have you noticed in their relationships? What do they tend to ignore, minimize, or never see in the other person? Why do you think this happens?

2. If singles defy parental advice and marry without the blessing of their parents, how would this affect their marriage in years to come?

3. If you were serving as someone else's accountability partner and this person thought he/she had found a lifetime mate, how could you be helpful in your accountability role? How would it affect you in terms of a time commitment? What character qualities would you look for in the potential mate?

4. List the five areas in which a couple should be held accountable.

5. Through prayer, ask the Lord to reveal to you an accountability couple.

6. Meditate and memorize: "The way of a fool seems right to him, but a wise man listens to advice" (Proverbs 12:15).

7. Pray: My heavenly Father, I ask that You would reveal my accountability couple to me, and me to them. Thank You in advance for bringing an accountability couple into my life. Reveal to me any hidden pride which hinders me from listening to the counsel of others. Teach me to be open and honest about my secret sins. Jesus, thank You for Your love and protection in my life. Amen.

CHAPTER TEN

Two Becoming One for a Lifetime

So they are no longer two, but one. Therefore
what God has joined together, let man not separate.
MATTHEW 19:6

PRINCIPLE SEVEN: Develop your spiritual oneness as a couple during your courtship period, your emotional oneness during engagement, and your physical oneness during marriage.

On September 1, 1983, a Korean airliner carrying 269 passengers unknowingly penetrated Soviet airspace and was literally blown out of the sky by a Soviet fighter jet. The innocent passengers of Korean Airlines Flight 007 plunged into the icy ocean below.

In the tense days that followed, investigators searched for clues to help unravel the mystery of the airliner's strange flight. How could the plane have wandered so far off course? Was it a spy mission? No, according to investigative reports; it was simply a navigational error. The Korean pilots accidentally punched in the wrong set of navigational coordinates after a refueling stop in Alaska. From that point on, every new set of coordinates they entered sent them farther off track and ultimately into Soviet air-space.[1]

When an initial wrong decision points you in the wrong direction, subsequent decisions will only take you farther off course. When this happens, you can unknowingly find yourself in enemy territory. Whom you marry will be a decision so profound that it will be like punching in navigational coordinates that will affect the rest of your decisions as long as you live. Depending on whether you marry in or outside the will of God, every subsequent decision will either move you closer to God or carry you farther off course until you become dangerously vulnerable to the enemy's attack.

When you consider the enormous importance of choosing the "right" marriage partner, it's no wonder that dating creates such anxiety. An anxious spirit is the by-product of living under the false assumption that we can manage life ourselves.

Courtship starts by seeking God's leadership in the selection process rather than thinking we can maneuver circumstances (and people) on our own to obtain a satisfying outcome. By choosing to follow the courtship process, we admit to God and ourselves how easily we can punch in the wrong set of coordinates if we're left to follow our own inclinations.

If you are a child of God, He will never allow you to become more intimate with another person than you are with Him. Your desire for intimacy with your mate will not be fulfilled until you first develop an intimate love relationship with God.

Forty-seven times in the Gospel of John, Jesus said He was under God's orders, and that He never *did* anything or *said* anything until His Father gave the command. This perfect obedience was what made Him one with His Father and what gave the Father confidence in the Son. When anyone opens the windows of his mind and heart toward God, then God will tell him what to do and help him do it. That obedience, resulting from a love relationship, is what makes you one with the Father, but first you have to be willing to open the windows of your mind and heart toward God.

COURTSHIP PROCESS	Phase 5: Courtship and Accountability	Phase 6: Engagement	Phase 7: Marriage
SPIRITUAL Commitment	Begin the process of becoming one spiritually. Spend one-on-one time together through shared prayer time and church attendance. Commit your courtship to glorifying Christ and helping each other grow in Christ.	Continue the process of becoming one spiritually through shared prayer, Bible study, and church attendance. Discuss which church and Sunday school to attend as well as activities and ministry opportunities. Develop a vision for the marriage reflecting Christ and His church.	Experience quality improvement by becoming one through prayer, Bible study, church involvement, and ministry opportunities. Relate at the deepest spiritual level. Make marriage and family decisions as one in Christ.
EMOTIONAL Commitment	Begin pre-engagement counseling. Seek your parents (or other godly counsel) to hold each other accountable. Discuss and write down boundaries and limits of relationship. Increase one-on-one emotional time together.	Begin becoming one emotionally. Spend one-on-one time sharing deep emotional feelings. Develop deep levels of communication. Understand male/female differences and roles within a biblical marriage.	Continue to become one emotionally. Commit and plan on one-on-one time every day sharing feelings and reflecting Christ's love through grace, mercy and forgiveness to one another.
PHYSICAL Commitment	Side hugs, holding hands, and short kisses. Only limited cuddling.	Increase holding hands, kissing and cuddling with caution. Hand-to-body touching but not intimate body areas.	Begin the process of becoming one physically. Share hugs, hold hands, kiss, touch sexual body areas (may experience a need to wait a number of days after the wedding for intercourse).
Time Alone	80 Hours	190 Hours	FOREVER

GOD REVEALS, MAN INITIATES, WOMAN RESPONDS

When Atlanta hosted the 1996 Olympics, the organizers produced a variety of musical presentations around the theme "Follow the Dream." Sounds good, doesn't it? In fact, it sounds so good that many people build their lives on a philosophy of following their dreams. But is it a biblical concept?

Some singles medicate the pain of loneliness by fantasizing and dreaming about having the perfect Christian marriage. This fantasy has all the earmarks of disaster, because it brings two imperfect people together who are looking for a perfect marriage. It places unreasonable expectations on the partners that can never be satisfied.

Through the years, I have counseled many Christian men who have walked the straight line and kept themselves pure. Because they have walked the high road, they want to find—and believe they deserve to find—the perfect Christian Barbie doll. They're always complaining that they can't find anyone to marry, and I tell them they are looking too intently at outward appearances (1 Samuel 16:7). They're dreaming with their eyes open.

Christians don't follow a dream; they follow God's revelation. They look toward the Revealer. As God reveals His will, our obedience is the only outward expression we have of demonstrating our faith in His ability to direct our lives.

Many times in Scripture God calls Himself Israel's Bridegroom and calls Israel His Bride; He calls Christ the Head and refers to the church as the Body and the Bride. It would be foolish to think this symbolism doesn't mean anything to God. He is the same God who instituted the blood sacrifice and water baptism, the same God whose earthly presence was represented by the Ark of the Covenant, and the same God Who sent His Spirit in the likeness of a dove at the baptism of His Son. Symbolism is not lost on the God we serve.

Scripture compares the marriage relationship to Christ's relationship to the church (Ephesians 5:23–33):

- The husband is the head of the wife as Christ is the head of the church.

- As the church submits to the leadership of Christ in every-thing, so wives should submit to their husbands.
- As Christ loved the church and gave Himself for her, hus-bands should love and give themselves for their wives (devote themselves to the good of their spouse).
- Husbands ought to love their wives as their own bodies.

The scriptural idea is that when a husband and wife become one flesh, a man should love his wife as if he were loving one who was part of himself (Genesis 2:24). In spite of how we often hear these verses misquoted, the word "obey" does not appear in Scripture with respect to wives, though it does with respect to children. "Submit," on the other hand, emphasizes mutual sub-mission, especially when compared to Ephesians 5:21: "Submit to one another out of reverence for Christ." The idea is one of will-ingly yielding your own rights. When the husband is giving him-self sacrificially for his wife, it's not a one-sided submission. God's design for marriage is a sacrificial male leading an honoring female.

Males, as their physical design alone shows, are made to be initiators. Females are made to be receptors or responders. The further we move from the original order God ordained, the more confused our lives will become.

God's Design: He is the Revealer

In his book *The Road Most Traveled,* pastor Robert Jeffress talks about a cartoon that many of us saw years ago. In the cartoon, Daffy Duck has an argument with his real-life animator about the direction of the story line. The argument grows so intense that the artist gets disgusted and erases Daffy from the picture! The moral: whoever is drawing the picture has total control.[2] God is sover-eign.

Jeffress compares the argument between Daffy and the cartoon illustrator with the argument between Job and God. After losing all his assets, children, and health, Job had serious questions he wanted answered. But God remained silent...for a while. Then He spent four chapters lecturing Job and reminding him of His sovereign control over the universe:

> "Where were you when I laid the earth's foundation? Tell me, if you understand. Who marked off its dimensions? Surely you know!" (Job 38:4–5)

> "Do you send the lightning bolts on their way? Do they report to you, 'Here we are'? Who endowed the heart with wisdom or gave understanding to the mind?" (Job 38:35–36)

> "Does the hawk take flight by your wisdom and spread his wings toward the south? Does the eagle soar at your command and build his nest on high?" (Job 39:26–27).

> "Will the one who contends with the Almighty correct him? Let him who accuses God answer him!" (Job 40:2)

In His extended monologue, God never once answered the question "Why?" Instead, He answered the question "Who?" God revealed Himself, not His grand design.[3] In essence He said, "Trust Me."

How will you know whether God wants you to marry or stay single? "Trust Me," God says.

How will you know whom to marry when the time is right? "Trust Me," God says.

How will you meet this person if you don't date? "Trust Me," God says.

A spiritual God created this physical universe, and the physical always will be controlled by the spiritual. That's a hard concept for the human mind to grasp.

You may have heard the story about a man walking up a steep hill in Greece. As he followed a narrow trail around the side of the hill, he slipped and fell. Grasping a branch protruding from the hillside, the man began to yell for help.

"Help me! Someone help me," he screamed.

Then he heard a voice. "I'll help you."

"Who are you?" the man said.

"It's the Lord."

"Save me, Lord!" said the man.

"First, let go of the branch."

For a long moment the man was silent. Then he yelled, "Is there anybody else up there who can help me?"

Even for those who have been believers for a long time, trusting God is hard to do when all the circumstances point to a different conclusion. God's revelation of Himself won't be much help to us if we refuse to believe what He says. Job did finally voice his trust in God's plan (Job 42:2–3), and to his credit, Job did it *before* God rewarded him. He did it without knowing if life would ever get better. In the midst of tremendous loss, Job trusted God's sovereignty regardless of the circumstances. More important, he trusted God's love. There will never be a contradiction between God's sovereignty over our lives and His love for us.

Do you remember what Adam was doing when God brought Eve to him (Genesis 2:22)? He was asleep. In fact, the Bible doesn't tell us that Adam even complained about being lonely or asked for a companion. Instead, we're left with the impression that God anticipated Adam's need before Adam even knew he had a need. Everything about my own experience with God assures me that He still operates the same way today. God is working on your behalf even before you know what to ask for or before you know there's a need. Real contentment is realizing that a sovereign God is already at work on your behalf regardless of how the circumstances look.

God's Design: Man Initiates, Woman Responds

Men are the ones on whom God originally laid the burden of responsibility as head, initiator, and leader. They are responsible for seeking and pursuing a mate. As the responder, the woman must wait for the man to initiate the relationship. That doesn't mean that God may not reveal His will to the woman first, but it does mean that she can't take that information and be the initiator.

When God gets ready to move in a man's life, He'll have His own conversation with the bridegroom. If the woman initiates the relationship, it often sets a precedent that never changes. She'll still be leading the man years later.

In her book *Quest for Love,* Elisabeth Elliot lists eight steps that are appropriate for a man in determining whether marriage is a part of God's plan for him:

1. Stop everything—intimacy, dating, any "special relationship."

2. Be silent before God. Lay your life before Him, willing to accept the path He reveals. If there's no answer, do nothing in that direction now. Wait.

3. If it seems the answer is yes, go to a spiritual mother or father (someone older in the faith, someone with wisdom and common sense who knows how to pray) and ask them to pray with you and for you about a wife. Listen to their counsel. If they know somebody they think suitable, take them seriously.

4. Study the story of Abraham's servant who was sent to find a wife for Isaac (Genesis 24). He went to the logical place where he might find women. He prayed silently, watched quietly. The story is rich in lessons. Find them.

5. Keep your eyes open in your own "garden." You don't have to survey all the roses before you pick the one for your bud vase. When you spot the sort of woman you think you're looking for, watch her from a respectful distance. Much can be learned without conversation, let alone "relationship." You should learn about her from others who know her and from those you can trust to keep their mouths shut. Does she give evidence of being a godly woman? A womanly one? Expect God to lead (Genesis 24:14).

6. Proceed with extreme caution, praying over every move. By this I do not mean mumbling prayers while you're charging across the church parking lot to ask her for a date. I mean giving yourself whatever it takes, whether weeks or years, to take His yoke and learn of Him. It is "good for a man that he bear the yoke in his youth."

7. Talk to her in a casual setting. You will be able to discover if she is a woman of serious purpose. Do not mention "relationships," marriage, feelings.

8. Give yourself time to think. Go back to your spiritual mother or father.

Elliot follows up these suggestions with this advice: "If you find yourself falling for a girl who offers you only casual friendship, or worse, the cold shoulder, first get it settled with God that she is the one to pursue. Even if a woman tells a man to 'get lost' but he knows in his heart she's the right one, he can still wait and pray for God's timing. I know of many married couples whose courtship began this way."[4]

In recent months I have met in counseling sessions with two women who have been dating the same men for six years. Neither of their boyfriends is willing to make a marriage commitment. The women wanted me to talk to these men so I could "help" each one see why he had been unwilling to make a commitment.

One of the men had the Christian Barbie doll mentality I referred to earlier. The woman he was dating was attractive, but he was waiting for the perfect beauty queen—the one with no flaws. The other man was waiting for "romantic feelings" or something mystical to happen. In the meantime, they both were spending their lives uncommitted to women who were committed to them. I told each man the same thing: You have to focus on what God wants you to do rather than some mystical meeting of the hearts.

Sometimes people are more concerned about finding a "soul" mate than they are a "sole" mate. The two aren't always the same. If you're an extrovert, for instance, can you imagine your soul mate being an introvert? If you prefer quiet nights in front of the fire, would a soul mate want to go dining and dancing with three other couples? Would your soul mate be a spender if you're a saver? Would a soul mate leave dirty clothes on the floor and dirty dishes in the sink?

People trying to make other people like themselves is often at the heart of the conflicts we have with those we love, both before and during marriage. Opposites do seem to attract—and then they attack. If a man approaches everything methodically and logically, he can't understand why his wife can't be more practical and less frivolous and spontaneous. If one spouse is frugal and keeps a close watch on the checkbook, why can't the other be more reasonable and less of a spendthrift?

If we look at Genesis 2:18, we'll see that God intended for spouses to *complement* each other, not *duplicate* one another.[5] The New International Version of the Bible translates the Genesis passage in the following way: "I will make a helper suitable for him." God looked at Adam, saw he needed another human with whom to share his life, and then made a helper suitable for him. The Hebrew word translated "suitable" literally means "opposite." God's plan is to bring us a mate who can support us where we are weak and fill in the gaps where our own lives have holes. Extroverts need time to be introspective. Savers need to buy a few gifts, and spur-of-the-moment doers need to sit down for some serious planning.

The mystical soul mate doesn't often appear in marriages. Instead, God is more likely to give you someone who will complement your weak areas. Together you make a whole person. You become one. These differences that can divide you are the differences of two unique personalities rather than a betrayal of all your hopes and dreams. The type of love you need is the same type God displays to you—an unconditional commitment to an imperfect person.

Your focus cannot be on attractiveness or mystical romantic feelings. You must focus on what God wants. If your supreme goal is to follow Christ, you will be directing your energies far more toward the will of God and the service of others than toward your own heart's longing. When you do that, you'll have the best training you can get for marriage.

LEAVE AND CLEAVE

Leave and cleave are God's definitive words setting the foundational laws of marriage into effect. "Therefore shall a man leave his father and his mother, and shall cleave unto his wife: and they shall be one flesh" (Genesis 2:24, KJV). The word "leave" in this passage means "to loosen or relinquish." When God said that a man should leave his father and mother when he married, He meant that a man was to relinquish the highest position of commitment and devotion previously given to his parents in order to give that position to his wife.

God did not say that a man is to stop honoring his parents, which is a commandment that is to last throughout a person's lifetime (Exodus 20:12). And He didn't say leave home when you're eighteen or when you have a job or when your parents irritate you. He established leaving for the purpose of marriage.

Whether you are physically in your parents' home or 300 miles away, spiritually you are still under their protection if you're single. You are still admonished to honor them. I get calls from parents who are very worried and angry because their single adult children have gotten engaged to people the parents hardly know or may not even have met. The fact that these singles didn't seek the counsel of their parents sometimes causes such a breech in relations that the parents don't attend the wedding or Christmas visits become a nightmare.

Leaving is not possible emotionally if there are unresolved conflicts between the parents and a son or daughter. As a result, it's important to have harmony surround the decisions of marriage, including whom and when to marry. The pre-engagement period (courtship) is a time of building in-law relationships and receiving blessing from the parents.

It's significant that God does not state that a woman should leave her parents and cleave to her husband, but rather that the man must do the leaving. Once parents give their approval for a marriage, it is no longer the son's duty to give priority to their counsel, although he should always seek their counsel. The wife must know that her husband has transferred his ties from his parents to her and together they are establishing a new household.

In addition to leaving their parents, men also have to be willing to leave the single life. For some men that's hard to do. They grow accustomed to being single, and after marriage they still want to act in single ways. Leaving singleness to live with a new lifetime partner will require a new lifestyle, new friendships, and even a different thought process that constantly and consistently takes into account the good of their family.

After God commanded man to leave his parents, He told him to "cleave" unto his wife. "Cleave" means "to pursue with great energy and to cling to something zealously." Sounds like work, doesn't it? Pursue and cling zealously. From the beginning, God knew that marriage would take work and commitment. He designed marriage to operate as the second most important priority in your life, second only to your personal relationship with God. We must first love God above all others, have the spiritual calling to leave and then the commitment to cleave before we can become one flesh with one another. Outside of this, we break God's laws and boundaries and will suffer the consequences.

SPIRITUAL ONENESS: THE COURTSHIP PERIOD

The intimacy involved in cleaving includes far more than the physical relationship. It begins by achieving oneness of spirit. In fact, the most important goal of the courtship period is to build spiritual oneness.

This is a spiritual bonding time between the couple and both sets of parents. It's a time when everyone involved tries to work through doubts to determine if the relationship is of God. Spiritual oneness is vital to a marriage and it's best to have it before other aspects of marriage command the couple's attention. Discussing spiritual matters through prayer, Bible studies, church attendance, ministry, missions work, and service opportunities is an excellent way to build the marriage on a solid foundation. As you seek God's will together in decision making and share how and what God is teaching you as an individual, your spiritual oneness with each other will become more and more complete. As you face trials and challenges, remember that relying on God's faithfulness during these times is one of the primary ways strong spiritual bonds are formed.

Spiritual oneness begins during the courtship stage and should grow throughout the marriage. Spiritual oneness can stop growing if the couple stops being involved in spiritual activities together. One of the major complaints I hear in marriage counseling is that there is not spiritual oneness. This can occur even when each individual is growing in the Lord, but they are not growing *together* in the Lord. Make it a priority to plan spiritual activities together beginning in your courtship and carry them throughout your marriage. That will ensure a continual growth toward becoming spiritually one.

Unlike dating, courtship is designed to foster a relationship, not an addiction. Often, couples who date become obsessive about being together. They spend most of their time alone in isolated locations. As a result, one or both partners tend to lose interest, miss the excitement of the early adrenaline flow, and leave the relationship to search for a new "high" with someone else.

Courtship, on the other hand, begins by spending limited amounts of time together and very little one-on-one time alone. The goal is to become one in spirit early in the relationship, progress to emotional oneness during the engagement period and then physical oneness after marriage. The early phase of courtship emphasizes getting acquainted with each other through family and group activities to learn what the other person is genuinely like. No one knows a person better than parents and siblings, and the way people act with their families is an indication of what they will be like in a new home setting after marriage.

Instead of the usual "premarital" counseling, couples must seek pre-engagement counseling during the courtship period. If they wait until they are engaged and almost married, they may find themselves going ahead with the marriage despite the results of counseling. They may feel pressured to marry because they've already bought the wedding dress, told their friends, and ordered invitations. They may rationalize that they can "make it work," but they rarely do.

How long should a courtship last? A typical courtship can last from three to twelve months before the engagement. If the couple is older and more mature, the need for a lengthy courtship may be unnecessary, assuming their spiritual life is strong. Developing physical temptations is a major concern during lengthy courtship periods, particularly if the couple is together frequently (once or twice a week or more). Accountability in the physical area is a must if the courtship becomes lengthy.

That being the case, how far can you go physically during a courtship period? "Do not arouse or awaken love until it so desires" (Song of Songs 2:7). When we reach a point of physical involvement in which we begin to become aroused, we have crossed into the threshold of sin. Waiting until we've become aroused is a dangerous indicator to let us know we've gone too far. We are like little children who refuse to believe the flame is hot until we get burned! We must set physical boundaries in advance and limit physical involvement during a courtship.

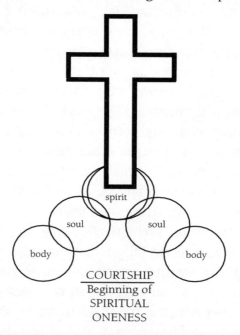

spirit

soul   soul

body   body

COURTSHIP
Beginning of
SPIRITUAL
ONENESS

EMOTIONAL ONENESS: THE ENGAGEMENT PERIOD

During the engagement period, a couple begins to become one emotionally as they spend one-on-one time together sharing deep emotional feelings.

In the later months of courtship or perhaps into the early days of the engagement period, the couple has greater freedom to be alone. This time together will help build the heart-to-heart communication that is so important to the foundation of a marriage.

For the foundational structure of your emotional oneness, Dr. David Ferguson and Dr. Don McMinn have identified ten intimacy needs that should begin during your engagement period:[6]

- Acceptance
- Affection
- Appreciation
- Approval
- Attention
- Comfort (empathy)
- Encouragement
- Respect
- Security
- Support

Emotional oneness begins in the engagement stage and should grow throughout your marriage. However, its growth may be stunted or completely arrested if the couple no longer shares deep, heartfelt feelings and begins to avoid honesty and vulnerability with each other. One of the major complaints I hear in marriage counseling is the lack of intimacy in the marriage. This almost invariably results from too slow a growth rate in emotional oneness. Make it a priority to build trust in one another, and plan time alone to ensure the development of emotional oneness beginning during the engagement and continuing throughout the marriage.

The engagement phase for courtship is usually shorter than engagements in a dating relationship. Because of society's high divorce rates, dating couples sometimes distrust their choices and prefer long engagements to test the relationship. In contrast, the courtship process places the waiting period at the beginning, during friendship, not at the end, during the engagement. For singles who believe in sex within the context of marriage, lengthy engagements can weaken their resolve and strain their relationships. By taking more time to choose a mate and lay a good foundation for marriage, the engagement phase of courtship basically requires only enough time to prepare for the wedding and make final preparations for marriage.

In view of the impending marriage, sexual involvement at this point can be easily rationalized. For the Christian, however, there is one rule and one rule only: total abstention from sexual activity outside of marriage and total faithfulness inside marriage. That's it. Hands off and clothes on. If you violate God's revealed will and purpose in your life, you also will block the ministry of the Holy Spirit as He seeks to instruct and bless you as a couple. The enemy tries to entangle you through counterfeit emotional oneness early in the relationship (see chapter 3), but God desires to bless you through emotional oneness during the engagement period.

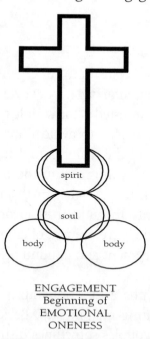

ENGAGEMENT
Beginning of
EMOTIONAL
ONENESS

PHYSICAL ONENESS: BECOMING ONE IN MARRIAGE

In marriage, the couple begins the process of becoming one physically.

It is a process, not a single act. Preparation for your physical oneness actually starts much earlier through the development of your emotional and spiritual oneness. Affection, tenderness, admiration, and devotion all play an increasing role in your physical oneness, but they don't just suddenly appear the first ten minutes you're in a honeymoon suite. As you've spent time together, ministered together, and shared your feelings, those emotions should have grown in you as you grew toward one another. So many marriages start by becoming one physically and don't develop emotional and spiritual oneness. Later when the physical activity drops off, the couple finds there's nothing left of their relationship because they never developed a deeper oneness.

God symbolizes the covenant between Himself and man with Christ's shed blood on the cross. In fact, every time a covenant is made, bloodletting occurs to seal the covenant. This blood covenant even occurs between a virgin woman and man the first time they have sexual intercourse. This is a symbol of the importance of the covenant of marriage.

With limited or no physical involvement in your relationship prior to marriage, special caution should be taken during your wedding night and honeymoon. Trauma can occur when a couple goes from no physical involvement to intercourse within twenty-four hours of the marriage ceremony. Just as it takes time for spiritual and emotional oneness to develop, so it is with physical oneness. Seek counsel, read Christian books on physical intimacy, and most important of all, discuss these sexual issues with each other and other couples.

One of today's popular marriage counseling books lists *affection* as the top need for wives in a marriage. It also lists sexual fulfillment as the top need for husbands.[7] The typical wife doesn't understand her husband's deep need for sex any more than he understands her deep need for affection. Without the environment of affection, however, the sexual event is unpleasant and unsatisfying for women. Most men don't understand that. If enough affection exists in the environment of a marriage, sex can come naturally and often.

MARRIAGE
Beginning of
PHYSICAL
ONENESS

DARE TO BE DIFFERENT

The only real malady that ultimately will cause your marriage to fail is that the life of Christ is not being formed in you. If your supreme goal is to follow Christ, the rule of your life will be "my life for your life, my needs for your needs." When each person *works* to do that, God is honored. His original design for marriage—a sacrificial male leading an honoring wife—will work when we work.

From the moment of conversion, believers are governed by a whole different set of laws. One way to understand this is to watch the odd behavior of a helium balloon in an automobile. When the car accelerates, the balloon moves forward. When the car stops, the balloon flies to the rear. This is exactly opposite the behavior of all other bodies in the car, including the driver.

The balloon acts differently because it contains a lighter-than-air gas. The car's forward motion pushes all the air to the back; the air then shoves the lighter helium forward. Braking forces the air forward, which drives the helium backward. In other words, the balloon acts differently because a different vapor indwells it. A different internal content produces a different external behavior.

Courtship is like the helium balloon. It responds to a whole different set of laws. It's a plan made in heaven for marriages made in heaven. If you choose it, you will move differently than those around you.

- You'll avoid the pain of destructive dating.
- You'll avoid the pitfalls of counterfeit oneness.
- You'll establish an accountability couple.
- You'll complete the courtship preparation steps.
- You'll focus on your identity in Christ.
- You'll be "set apart" in your friendships.
- You'll seek God's will in the selection of your mate.
- You'll listen for God's voice and instruction.
- You'll receive marital blessings in your marital oneness for generations to come.

Others may not understand, and those others may even be your own family. But in the end, like the man who built his house on the rock, your marriage will still be standing when the rain comes, the streams rise, and the winds blow. When you trust God to be the rock of your romance, you'll receive the blessings that come when you commit yourself to romance God's way.

That doesn't mean this book is only for single men and women beginning a courtship. This book is to provide guidance and direction during all the seasons in your life. As you pass through one phase of the courtship process into another, refer again to the suggestions here, always remembering to look for the will of the Creator who made man and woman. Always choosing God's best.

STUDY AND DISCUSSION QUESTIONS

1. This chapter talks a great deal about trusting God. Trust is also one of the most important factors in a marriage. Explain the

roles of predictability and dependability in building trust first with God and then with your spouse.

2. Look at the following verses from the Word of God and explain what they tell you about how God listens: Psalm 16:1–2; 34:15–18; Jeremiah 33:3. How do you listen when God has something He wants to say to you?

3. Before you marry, you may be drawn to your partner because of a specific character trait that you see as a strength. Later you may begin to view that strength as a weakness. Can you explain how a person's greatest strength also might be that person's greatest weakness?

4. Compare and contrast the difference between becoming one and counterfeit oneness.

5. What does it mean to "leave and cleave"?

6. Meditate and memorize: "So they are no longer two, but one. Therefore what God has joined together, let man not separate" (Matthew 19:6).

7. Pray: My heavenly Father, I commit to developing spiritual oneness during my courtship, emotional oneness during my engagement, and to wait for physical oneness until marriage. Jesus, I believe You are the Revealer, the man is the initiator, and the woman is the responder. At the appropriate time, help me to leave my parents and cleave to my spouse. Thank You, Jesus, for being the example of a loving husband to Your bride the church. Amen.

Notes

Chapter Two
A Prescription for Failure

1. Marriage and divorce statistics are accumulated and reported by the National Center for Health Statistics in Washington, D.C. The percentage of increase was computed from their data as reported in *Statistical Abstract of the United States,* 1990 (Washington, D.C.: U.S. Department of Commerce, Bureau of the Census, 1990).

2. George Barna, *The Future of the American Family* (Chicago, Ill.: Moody Press, 1993), 67.

3. Ibid., 70.

4. Jessica Gress-Wright, "Liberals, Conservatives and the Family," *Commentary* (April 1992), 43–46.

5. Chris Holmes, "Whatever Happened to High School Sweethearts," *St. Louis Post-Dispatch* (14 February 1996), E1.

6. Beth L. Bailey, *From Front Porch to Back Seat: Courtship in Twentieth-Century America* (Baltimore, Md.: Johns Hopkins University Press, 1988), 16.

7. Quoted from Professor Ruth Shonle Cavan. "Some Expert Opinions on Dating," *McCall's* (August 1961), 125.

8. Bailey, *From Front Porch to Back Seat.* Historical data tracing development of dating in America was summarized from more than 140 pages of information.

9. Nadine Joseph, Pamela G. Krupke, Bonnie Fischer, and Regina Elam, "The New Rules of Courtship," *Newsweek* special issue: "The New Teens" (summer/fall 1990), 27.

10. Barna, *The Future of the American Family,* 33–34.

11. Stephen Arterburn and Jim Burns, *Steering Them Straight* (Colorado Springs, Colo.: Focus on the Family Publishing, 1995), 57–58.

12. Associated Press news report (May 1, 1997). Newly released statistics compiled by the U.S. Department of Health and Human

Service's 1995 National Survey of Family Growth, May 1, 1997.

13. Joseph, et al., "The New Rules of Courtship," 27.

14. Associated Press news report (May 1, 1997). See above.

15. Dave Rice, *This Side Up*, "Understanding Your Teenager in 50 Minutes or Less," seminar audio tape for National Institute of Youth Ministry, San Clemente, Calif., 1994.

16. Barna, *The Future of the American Family*, 135.

17. U.S. Department of Health and Human Services, Public Health Service, Centers for Disease Control, Divison of STD/HIV Prevention, *1991 Annual Report*, 3.

18. Robert G. DeMoss Jr., *Sex & the Single Person* (Grand Rapids, Mich.: Zondervan Publishing House, 1995), 145.

19. Joe McIlhaney Jr., *Sexuality and Sexually Transmitted Diseases* (Grand Rapids, Mich.: Baker Books, 1990), 14.

20. U.S. Department of Health and Human Services, *1991 Annual Report*, 13.

21. Paul C. Reisser, *Sex and Singles, Reasons to Wait* (Colorado Springs, Colo.: Focus on the Family Publishing, 1993), 7.

22. McIlhaney, *Sexuality and Sexually Transmitted Diseases*, 142.

23. Norval Glenn, "What Does Family Mean?" *American Demographics* (June 1992).

24. Barna, *The Future of the American Family*, 23.

25. Ibid., 67.

26. Ibid., 71.

27. Ibid., 70.

28. Arterburn and Burns, *Steering Them Straight*, 47.

29. Barna, *The Future of the American Family*, 131.

30. Ibid., 133.

31. Ibid., 135.

CHAPTER THREE
COUNTERFEIT ONENESS

1. Extracted in part from Arterburn and Burns, *Steering Them Straight*, 60.

2. Ibid., 59.

3. Ideas condensed from a larger discussion by Philip Yancey, *The Jesus I Never Knew* (Grand Rapids, Mich.: Zondervan Publishing House, 1995), 118–119.

4. Elisabeth Elliot, *Quest for Love* (Grand Rapids, Mich.: Fleming H. Revell, 1996).

CHAPTER FOUR
MAKING A "GOOD" CHOICE OR A "GOD" CHOICE

1. Information compiled from "Hudson Taylor & Missions to China," a special issue of *Christian History* 15, no. 4.

2. John Woodbridge, ed., "China's Millions," *More Than Conquerors* (Chicago, Ill.: Moody Press, 1992), 51.

3. Elliot, *Quest for Love*, 114.

CHAPTER FIVE
PREPARING TO BE GOD'S CHOICE

1. Frederica Mathewes-Green, "Postabortion Interviews Reveal What Would Have Changed Their Minds," *Christianity Today* (9 November 1995), 22.

2. Donna Rice's story summarized and quoted from "Enough Is Enough," an interview by Ramona Cramer Tucker appearing in *Today's Christian Woman* (September/October 1996).

3. Lee Strobel, *What Would Jesus Say* (Grand Rapids, Mich.: Zondervan Publishing House, 1994), 71.

4. Strobel, *What Would Jesus Say*, 65.

5. "Billy Graham," *Pathfinder in Evangelism* (Chicago, Ill.: Moody Press, 1992), 177–178.

6. Ibid., 177.

7. Quote and subsequent illustration excerpted from "Parachutes, Thorns, and Grace," *Discipleship Journal* (November/ December 1996), 22–27.

CHAPTER SIX
CRUMBLE PROOFING YOUR FOUNDATION

1. Barna, *The Future of the American Family,* 68.

2. Paul Jehle, *Dating vs. Courtship* (Plymouth, Mass.: The Plymouth Rock Foundation, 1993), 91.

3. As quoted by Neil Clark Warren, *Finding the Love of Your Life* (Colorado Springs, Colo.: Focus on the Family Publishing, 1992), 40.

4. Strobel, *What Would Jesus Say,* 91.

5. Baptist Press news release (December 1996).

6. Mark S. Dorn, "Accountability: Checklist or Relationship?" *Discipleship Journal* (July/August 1996), 82.

7. Barna, *The Future of the American Family,* 58.

8. Ibid., 59. Based upon results of a nationwide telephone survey conducted in 1990 by Patricia Tanaka & Company. Sample size was 1,000 respondents.

9. Ibid., 59.

10. Ibid., 172.

11. H. Norman Wright, *So You're Getting Married* (Ventura, Calif.: Regal Books, 1985), 94.

12. Roper data cited in Debra Goldman, "Death in the Family," *Adweek* (October 7, 1991), 10.

13. Frances Goldscheider and Linda Waite, *New Families, No Families?* (Berkeley, Calif.: University of California Press, 1991), 11.

14. Wright, *So You're Getting Married,* 94.

15. The National Opinion Research Center study cited here is described completely in Andrew Greeley's book, *Faithful Attraction* (New York: Tor, 1991).

16. Wright, *So You're Getting Married,* 91.

CHAPTER SEVEN
RELATING WITHOUT DATING

1. Dr. Archibald D. Hart, *The Sexual Man* (Dallas, Tex.: Word Publishing, 1994), 38–39.

2. This section briefly summarizes concepts by Dr. Henry Cloud and Dr. John Townsend, *Boundaries* (Grand Rapids, Mich.: Zondervan Publishing House, 1992).

3. Gary Chapman, "Good Fences Make Good Neighbors," *Home Life* (September 1966), 38.

CHAPTER EIGHT
RECOGNIZING GOD'S VOICE

1. Elisabeth Elliot, *Chance to Die: The Life & Legacy of Amy Carmichael* (Grand Rapids, Mich.: Fleming H. Revell, 1987).

2. Charles Stanley, *How to Listen to God* (Nashville, Tenn.: Thomas Nelson, 1985).

CHAPTER NINE
BECOMING ACCOUNTABLE

1. Deborah Tannen, *You Just Don't Understand* (New York: Ballantine Books, 1986), 62.

CHAPTER TEN
TWO BECOMING ONE FOR A LIFETIME

1. Robert Jeffress, *The Road Most Traveled* (Nashville, Tenn.: Broadman and Holman Publishers, 1996), 26.

2. Ibid., 171.

3. Ibid., 173.

4. Elliot, *Quest for Love*

5. Jeffress, *The Road Most Traveled*, 86–87.

6. Dr. David Ferguson and Dr. Don McMinn, *The Top Ten Intimacy Needs* (Intimacy Plus, 1994).

7. Willard F. Harley Jr., *His Needs, Her Needs* (Old Tappan, N.J.: Fleming H. Revell, 1986).

For more information regarding seminars
and speaking engagements, please contact:

Dr. Don Raunikar
New Life Clinics
6200 Savoy, Suite 650
Houston, Texas 77036

Phone: (713) 974–6965
Fax: (713) 974–6891
www.wise-words.com